CAMBRIDGE
UNIVERSITY PRESS

Shaftesbury Road, Cambridge CB2 8EA, United Kingdom

One Liberty Plaza, 20th Floor, New York, NY 10006, USA

477 Williamstown Road, Port Melbourne, VIC 3207, Australia

314–321, 3rd Floor, Plot 3, Splendor Forum, Jasola District Centre, New Delhi – 110025, India

103 Penang Road, #05–06/07, Visioncrest Commercial, Singapore 238467

Cambridge University Press is part of Cambridge University Press & Assessment, a department of the University of Cambridge.

We share the University's mission to contribute to society through the pursuit of education, learning and research at the highest international levels of excellence.

www.cambridge.org
Information on this title: www.cambridge.org/9780521885478

First published 2007

A catalogue record for this publication is available from the British Library

ISBN 978-0-521-88547-8 Hardback

WORLD TRADE ORGANIZATION

Dispute Settlement Reports

2005
Volume V

Pages 1797-2292

CAMBRI
UNIVERSITY

THE WTO DISPUTE SETTLEMENT REPORTS

The *Dispute Settlement Reports* of the World Trade Organization (the "WTO") include panel and Appellate Body reports, as well as arbitration awards, in disputes concerning the rights and obligations of WTO Members under the provisions of the *Marrakesh Agreement Establishing the World Trade Organization*. The *Dispute Settlement Reports* are available in English. Volumes comprising one or more complete cases contain a cumulative list of published disputes. The cumulative list for cases that cover more than one volume is to be found in the first volume for that case.

This volume may be cited as DSR 2005:V

TABLE OF CONTENTS

ANNEX I

ANSWERS OF PARTIES TO THE PANEL'S QUESTIONS AND OTHER COMMENTS AND DOCUMENTS RECEIVED FROM PARTIES

ANNEX I-12

BRAZIL'S COMMENTS ON THE 22 DECEMBER US COMMENTS CONCERNING BRAZIL'S ECONOMETRIC MODEL

20 January 2004

TABLE OF CONTENTS

Page

I. BRAZIL'S INTRODUCTORY COMMENTS 1801

II. PROFESSOR SUMNER'S COMMENTS CONCERNING THE US CRITIQUE OF HIS MODEL 1808

List of Exhibits

Agricultural Outlook Tables, USDA, November 2003, Table 19	Exhibit Bra- 394
"Trade Issues Facing the US Cotton Industry," Speech by Dr. Mark Lange, President and CEO, National Cotton Council, 6 January 2004.	Exhibit Bra- 395
"Farm Groups Shocked at UC Economist's Testimony in WTO Dispute," Western Farm Press, 2 September 2003.	Exhibit Bra- 396
"Report of the Commission on the Application of Payment Limitations for Agriculture," August 2003.	Exhibit Bra- 397
Western Farm Press, 7 January 2003	Exhibit Bra- 398
Acreage Discrepancies.xls	Exhibit Bra- 399
List of Publications of Professors Babcock and Beghin	Exhibit Bra- 400

I. BRAZIL'S INTRODUCTORY COMMENTS

1. Brazil's response to the US 22 December 2003 Comments Concerning Brazil's Econometric Model ("US Critique") is divided into two parts. First, Brazil provides some introductory comments setting the US Critique into perspective. And, second, Brazil offers Professor Sumner's detailed response to the US critique.

2. The United States Critique initially focuses on proving a point that has never been contested by Brazil, i.e., that the Sumner model is not exactly like the FAPRI model. As Professor Sumner points out, he never claimed that his model was identical to the FAPRI model. The United States points to no contradictions between what Professor Babcock has stated and what Professor Sumner stated in Annex I or his other statements concerning the links between his model and the FAPRI model. Nevertheless, while there are differences between the Sumner

model and the FAPRI model, the record is undisputed that the core elements of the FAPRI model – the hundreds of demand and supply equations – are identical. The differences in Professor Sumner's model are primarily the result of his use of the CARD international cotton model and additions to the FAPRI model made by Professor Sumner. The additions were necessary to enable the FAPRI/CARD modelling framework to respond to the questions before this Panel.

3. The United States Critique asserts that Professor Sumner's choice of baselines has prejudiced the outcome to such an extent that his results are not usable.[1] But the record shows that the significant acreage, production, export and price effects found in Professor Sumner's Annex I results using the CARD international cotton model and the amended FAPRI US crops model based off the (recalibrated) FAPRI preliminary November 2002 baseline are essentially the same even when used against other baselines.[2] The United States first argued that Professor Sumner should have used the FAPRI 2003 baseline.[3] Professor Sumner responded by running his model on that later baseline.[4] There were no significant changes between Annex I and those results for either the period from MY 1999-2002 or in the period from MY 2003-2007.[5] The United States Critique raises a new argument that Professor Sumner manipulated the FAPRI preliminary November 2002 baseline.[6] This allegation is wrong. Any differences are the result of a necessary recalibration of the model following the use of the CARD international cotton model rather than the FAPRI international crops models and some update incorporating more recent macroeconomic data.[7] As Professor Sumner demonstrates below, there are no significant differences with his Annex I result by using this slightly modified baseline.[8] Indeed, the fact that Professor Sumner's simulation model generates nearly identical results regardless of the baselines used demonstrates the robustness of the Sumner model.

4. In criticizing Professor Sumner's modelling of the four different types of contract payments, the United States repeats its baseless arguments that the contract payments have absolutely no effect on production decisions for upland cotton. The notion that an estimated[9] $4.7 billion[10] of amber box (presumptively

---

1 US 22 December 2003 Comments on Brazil's Econometric Model, paras. 35-38, especially para. 38.

2 These other baselines include the original FAPRI preliminary November 2002 baseline and the official FAPRI January 2003 baseline.

3 US 7 October 2003 Oral Statement, paras. 36-39.

4 Exhibit Bra-325 (Results of Professor Sumner's Modified Model Based on the January 2003 FAPRI baseline); Exhibit Bra-326 (Results of Professor Sumner's Modified Model) and Exhibit Bra-331 (Description of Methodology Comparing the Analysis of US Upland Cotton Subsidies Under the January 2003 Baseline to Analysis under the November 2002 Baseline, Daniel A. Sumner, November 2003).

5 *See* Exhibit Bra-326 (Results of Professor Sumner's Modified Model).

6 US 22 December 2003 Comments on Brazil's Econometric Model, para. 36.

7 *See* Professor Sumner's discussions below, Response to Section III.

8 *Ibid.*

9 Brazil is still waiting the United States to provide the data that would permit the calculation of the exact amount of support to upland cotton from the contract payments. Brazil hopes that the United States will produce the data on 20 January 2004.

trade- and production-distorting) subsidies paid to current producers of upland cotton and allocated as support to upland cotton had no effect on upland cotton production has been, and remains today, incredible. The United States has never explained why upland cotton base acreage payments are so much higher than other programme crops (except rice). The obvious reason is that Congress and the NCC expected the bulk of acreage historically planted to upland cotton to continue to be planted to upland cotton, a high-cost crop. Nor has the United States been able to explain how there could be no production effects when US upland cotton producers would have lost $332.79 per acre over a six-year period if they had received no contract payments.[11] NCC representatives stated that these payments were "critically needed"[12] to "make ends meet"[13], i.e., to cover their cost of production.

5. In fact, Professor Sumner has been, in the view of Brazil, probably overly conservative in his estimation of the effects of these contract payments on US upland cotton production. Brazil notes that the nature of Professor Sumner's modelling does not permit an assessment of the cumulative losses such as the $332.79 per acre over a six-year period. Even Professor Sumner acknowledges that his use of only $0.25 of each direct payment dollar as having production effects is probably low in light of the obvious impact of this subsidy in supporting the continued survival of many US producers.[14] Similarly, Professor Sumner's use of only $0.40 of each counter-cyclical payment dollar as having production effects[15] is also low in light of the fact that $1 billion in payments in MY 2002 were crucial to the economic survival of many upland cotton producers. In light of the evidence produced by Brazil, the US Critique that Professor Sumner's analysis is fundamentally wrong for not concluding that these huge subsidies, filling almost half of the cost-revenue gap, have no effects is completely unjustified.

6. The United States Critique also expresses amazement that Professor Sumner could attempt to model the effects of export credit guarantees. The fact that FAPRI has not yet modelled this subsidy is completely irrelevant. Nor is Professor Sumner blazing new economic ground by modelling export credit guarantees. The NCC has a team of economists working with the United States on this dispute, headed by Gary Adams, a former FAPRI economist who worked on the FAPRI upland cotton model.[16] NCC economists concluded in 2001 that major changes to the GSM 102 programme would result in 500,000 fewer bales being exported from the United States and result in a 3 cent per pound increase

---

[10] This figure is based on Brazil's estimates at paragraph 8 of its 9 September 2003 Further Submission as updated by the table at paragraph 8 of its 22 December 2003 Answers to Questions.

[11] Brazil's 2 December 2003 Oral Statement, para. 27.

[12] Brazil's 22 July 2003 Oral Statement, paras. 52-54 and 58-60 and exhibits cited therein.

[13] Exhibit Bra-324 (NCC Chairman's Report by Kenneth Hood, 24 July 2002, p. 2).

[14] Brazil's 9 September 2003 Further Submission, Annex I (paras 48-51 setting out high and low estimates of production effects for the four contract payments).

[15] *Ibid.*

[16] *See* Exhibit Bra-395 ("Trade Issues Facing the US Cotton Industry," Speech by Dr. Mark Lange, President and CEO, National Cotton Council, San Antonio, 6 January 2004), Lange noted that Gary Adams had spent "countless hours" working with USTR on the Brazil upland cotton dispute.

in prices.[17] It is curious that the United States, assisted by NCC economists, now seeks to contradict the conclusions of the beneficiaries of this GSM 102 programme by asserting that there were no production, export or price effects from this subsidy. The NCC's 2001 findings, which Professor Sumner used conservatively to estimate the production, export and price effects of the export credit guarantee programmes, was supported by the fact that $1.6 billion in US upland cotton exports between MY 1998-2002 were covered by GSM 102 export credit guarantees.[18] Further support for the NCC's 2001 estimate comes from the US Congressional Research Service that concluded that guarantees have "mainly benefited exports of wheat, wheat flour, oilseeds, feed grains and cotton".[19] Andrew Macdonald has also testified to the export-enhancing effects of the US GSM 102 programme.[20] In its evaluation of the US Critique's claim that Professor Sumner – and the 2001 NCC economists – incorrectly estimated the effects of removing the GSM 102 subsidies, the Panel must consider this uncontested evidence.

7. The United States Critique also challenges Professor Sumner's modelling of the effects of removing crop insurance subsidies. The US Critique focuses primarily on the fact that FAPRI has not yet modelled these subsidies.[21] But this is irrelevant. What is relevant are the facts which show that $788 million in crop insurance subsidies were provided to upland cotton producers between MY 1999-2002.[22] And it is relevant that USDA's own economists found that lower pre-2000 ARP Act crop insurance subsidies had significant production and price effects for upland cotton (as opposed to other programme crops).[23] Current higher crop insurance benefits under the 2000 ARP Act would certainly have higher effects. Professor Sumner's crop insurance modelling is also consistent with USDA's own economists' conclusion that the "availability of subsidized crop insurance affects farmers' current crop production decisions by creating a direct incentive to expand production".[24] It is uncontested that the amount of crop insurance subsidies received by upland cotton producers is directly related to the amount of upland cotton they plant.[25] Given this evidence, it was reasonable for Professor Sumner to conclude that each dollar of crop insurance subsidies had direct effects on US production.

---

[17] Exhibit Bra-41 ("The Future of Federal Farm Commodity Programmes (Cotton)," Hearings before the House of Representatives Committee on Agriculture, 15 February 2001, p. 12).

[18] Brazil's 9 September 2003 Further Submission, para. 188.

[19] Brazil's 9 September 2003 Further Submission, para. 189.

[20] Brazil's 9 September 2003 Further Submission, Annex II (Statement of Andrew Macdonald, paras 49-50).

[21] US 22 December 2003 Comments on Brazil's Econometric Model, paras 25-30.

[22] Brazil's 9 September 2003 Further Submission, Table 1, para. 8.

[23] Brazil's 22 August 2003 Rebuttal Submission, paras. 62-66.

[24] Exhibit Bra-63 (C.Edwin Young, Randall D. Schnepf, Jerry R. Skees and William W. Lin: "Production and Price Impacts of US Crop Insurance Subsidies: Some Preliminary Results, p. 4).

[25] Brazil's 22 August 2003 Rebuttal Submission, para. 53.

8. With respect to Professor Sumner's modelling of marketing loan payments, the US Critique is essentially silent.[26] This silence is no doubt due to the fact that Professor Sumner's model uses exactly the same elasticities and estimates of effects as the FAPRI model, for which the United States has indicated it has no objection.[27] Further, Professor Sumner's findings regarding the effects of marketing loan payments between MY 1999-2002 are very much consistent with those of Westcott/Price who found that in MY 2001 that marketing loan payments caused 3 million additional acres to be planted to upland cotton with an implied price decline of 10 cents per pound (or 33 percent of the MY 2001 price).[28] Brazil has already addressed the various US critiques of the use of so-called "lagged prices" by noting that USDA, FAPRI, Professor Sumner and a host of other economists have used these prices in countless models and that any use of futures market prices in large-scale simulation models is impossible.[29] Further, the faulty and primitive US futures methodology for estimating the production effects of marketing loan programmes is no substitute for the comprehensive models used by USDA, FAPRI and Professor Sumner.[30] Most pointedly, the US futures methodology suffers from the fatal flaw that it does not even focus on the price that does get the attention of US producers who depend on marketing loan payments – the adjusted world price (AWP).[31]

9. Nor does the US Critique find any fault with Professor Sumner's analysis of the Step 2 subsidies.[32] Brazil notes that Professor Sumner models the effects of Step 2 domestic and export subsidies in exactly the same manner as FAPRI. Professor Sumner's Step 2 analysis is also completely consistent with the overwhelming evidence that Step 2 export and domestic subsidies have significant production, export, and world price effects. As with the GSM 102 subsidies, the NCC has been quite vocal in praising the production and export effects of the Step 2 subsidies.[33] There would simply be no basis for the United States to contradict these testimonies from the users and beneficiaries of the Step 2 programme.

10. The Panel must also assess the validity of the US critique in view of the overwhelming non-econometric evidence that the US subsidies had significant

---

[26] The United States points out a typo (US 22 December 2003 Comments on Brazil's Econometric Model, paras. 73-74) that did not affect the actual analysis undertaken by Professor Sumner (*see* below, Comments on Section VI).

[27] *See* below, Comments on Section VI.

[28] Brazil's 7 October 2003 Oral Statement, paras. 31-33 and the references contained therein.

[29] *See* Professor Sumner's 9 October 2003 Closing Statement attached as Annex II to Brazil's 9 October 2003 Closing Statement, his 2 December 2003 Oral Statement (Exhibit Bra-342, paras. 24-28), Exhibit Bra-345 (paras. 6-14) as well as Brazil's 22 December 2003 Answers to Questions, paras. 37-42).

[30] *See* Brazil's 2 December 2003 Oral Statement, paras. 42-55.

[31] *Ibid.*

[32] The United States points out a typo (US 22 December 2003 Comments on Brazil's Econometric Model, paras. 76) that did not affect the actual analysis undertaken by Professor Sumner (*see* below, Comments on Section VI).

[33] For an example of the extensive evidence supporting this fact, *see* Brazil's Further Submission, paras. 141, 178-180.

production, export and price effects.[34] For example, the Panel must ask whether it is reasonable to conclude, as the United States argues, that $12.9 billion dollars in amber box, presumed trade-distorting subsidies had no effect on US production, US exports, and world prices. It is further uncontested that USDA's own data shows that the average US upland cotton farm would have lost $872 per acre during MY 1997-2002 – but had a "profit" of $106 per acre when subsidies are included in their revenue.

11. Further, the Panel must also examine the US Critique of Professor Sumner's analysis in light of the evidence of other econometric studies examining the effects of removing US upland cotton subsidies. The United States has argued that all these studies – including USDA's studies – were wrong in finding significant production, export, and price effects. Would the United States also argue that all of these other economists analyzed the US upland cotton subsidies and their effects on the (world) upland cotton market "for the express purpose of achieving pre-conceived results"? [35]Brazil submits that a common sense analysis of these other studies, including USDA's own studies, shows that Professor Sumner's results are both valid as well as conservative. They are certainly within the ranges of the other econometric studies in the record and consistent with what would be expected given the non-econometric evidence in the record.

12. Finally, Brazil notes US suggestions that Professor Sumner made modelling choices "for the express purpose of achieving pre-conceived results"[36] and "in order to exaggerate acreage and ultimately price impacts".[37] These are offensive and inappropriate charges directed at one of the world's leading agricultural economists. Members of the NCC admitted that "Dr. Sumner is a brilliant economist" who is "well-respected" and a "widely recognized UC [University of California] economist" who is a "confidant to the administration on trade and other issues".[38] Personal attacks by the United States against Professor Sumner's integrity are ironic given the fact that only seven months ago he was one of only two private US economists to be asked by the Chairman of the US Commission on the Application of Payment Limitations for Agriculture, Chief USDA Economist Keith Collins, to testify before that Commission. In evaluating the effects of additional payment limitations, the Report of the Commission relies, inter alia, on the testimony and advice provided by Professor Sumner.[39]

13. While the US Government has attacked Professor Sumner's professional integrity, the leaders and members of the US National Cotton Council have gone

---

[34] *See inter alia* Brazil's 9 September 2003 Further Submission, Sections 3.3.4.1-3.3.4.6; Brazil's 7 October 2003 Oral Statement, Section 2; Brazil's 18 November 2003 Further Rebuttal Submission, Sections 3.1-3.4, 3.7; Brazil's 2 December 2003 Oral Statement, Section 5.

[35] US 22 December 2003 Comments on Brazil's Econometric Model, para. 9.

[36] *Ibid.*

[37] US 22 December 2003 Comments on Brazil's Econometric Model, para. 1. *See* also para. 38.

[38] Exhibit Bra-396 ("Farm Groups Shocked at UC Economist's Testimony in WTO Dispute," Western Farm Press, September 2, 2003)(quoting Earl Williams, President of California Cotton Ginners and Growers Association).

[39] Exhibit Bra-397 ("Report of the Commission on the Application of Payment Limitations for Agriculture," August 2003).

further during this long dispute. They have met with and pressured Professor Sumner to discontinue his work before the Panel.[40] Moreover, NCC members have and continue to seek to cut off research and scholarship funds for the University of California at Davis, in protest of Professor's Sumner's work in this dispute.[41] One NCC member representative even went so far as to be quoted as saying that "if this had been a military issue, what Dr. Sumner did would be called treason".[42] Recently, the President of the NCC threatened both Professors Sumner and Babcock with unspecified action following the end of the WTO proceedings, stating "*[i]n another time and venue there will be a full examination of the actions taken by these 2 economists*".[43] This threat was elaborated in a recent analysis in a leading Agricultural Newspaper, the Western Farm Press:

> In the trade issue with Brazil, NCC President and CEO Mark Lange remains incensed at [Brazil's] WTO action. *More specifically, he is angry because two US economists hired on to Brazil's payroll and prepared testimony against the United States in the WTO action.* University of California economist Dan Sumner, former assistant secretary of agriculture, was hired to assist in the case. Lange added that Sumner 'appears to have hired' Professor Bruce Babcock, an agricultural economist at Iowa State University and director of the Center for Agricultural and Rural Development to attempt to modify the Food and Agricultural Policy Research Institute baseline projections for use by the Brazilians." This action was taken without the knowledge of FAPRI," said Lange of the University of Missouri-based facility. Lange said Babcock receives federal funds for the CARD programme and *he pledged "a full examination of the actions of these two guys" once the WTO issue is settled.* California cotton industry leaders and others have protested Sumner's actions to the dean of U.C. Davis school of agriculture and have lobbied for private research and scholarship funds to be withdrawn from the University in protest of Sumner's actions.[44]

14. Over the past six months, NCC members have been instrumental in coordinating efforts to attempt to force officials of the University of California at

---

40 Exhibit Bra-396 ("Farm Groups Shocked at UC Economist's Testimony in WTO Dispute", Western Farm Press, 2 September 2003)("group of representatives from cotton, wheat and rice met with Professor Sumner in mid-August to express their displeasure over his testimony before the Panel").

41 Exhibit Bra-396 ("Farm Groups Shocked at UC Economist's Testimony in WTO Dispute", Western Farm Press, 2 September 2003)(Earl Williams, President of the California Cotton Ginners and Growers Associations was quoted as stating "And we are going to bring pressure to bear on the university that would allow someone from a public, taxpayer supported institution to have such latitude that can reap such harm on the supporters of the University".).

42 Exhibit Bra-396 ("Farm Groups Shocked at UC Economist's Testimony in WTO Dispute", Western Farm Press, 2 September 2003) quoting Earl Williams.

43 Exhibit Bra-395 ("Trade Issues Facing the US Cotton Industry," Speech by Dr. Mark Lange, President and CEO, National Cotton Council, San Antonio, January 6)(underlining added); *See* also Exhibit Bra- 398 (Western Farm Press, 7 January 2004 , p. 3).

44 Exhibit Bra-398 (Western Farm Press, 7 January 2004, p. 2).

Davis to require Professor Sumner to stop his work in this dispute.[45] To their credit, these U.C. Davis officials have refused to bend to the pressure.

15. As Dr. Lange's statements quoted above indicates, the NCC now has focused on Professor Babcock for his very limited role in working with Professor Sumner in the application of parts of the FAPRI and CARD models. Professor Babcock's letter[46] is addressed to leading House and Senate staff members who have "relied on FAPRI and CARD to provide objective and high quality quantitative and qualitative assessment of US farm policy alternatives". Professor Babcock's letter states he is "prepared to do whatever it takes to mend this relationship, including disassociating myself from future official FAPRI analyses if so desired". The letter provides the Panel with insights into the type of pressure imposed by the NCC on the economists providing the Panel with assistance in this dispute.

16. These efforts by the representatives of the US upland cotton producers who are heavily dependent upon US subsidies and US Congressional support for their economic survival is perhaps understandable, but nonetheless deplorable. Professor Sumner has demonstrated considerable courage and fortitude in continuing his work to assist the Panel and ultimately all WTO Members in this dispute. Brazil has no doubts that the United States is also appalled at the prospect that either of these two distinguished economists would suffer any adverse professional consequences from their assistance to the Panel and the Parties in this dispute. Given the obligation of all WTO Members to cooperate and assist the Panel in making an objective assessment of the facts of a dispute, Brazil is certain the United States will unequivocally condemn any such threats, including those now being made by the US National Cotton Council.

17. With these introductory remarks in mind, Brazil presents below Professor Sumner's response to the US 22 December 2003 Comments Concerning Brazil's Econometric Model.

II. PROFESSOR SUMNER'S COMMENTS CONCERNING THE US CRITIQUE OF HIS MODEL

Response to "Comments from the United States of America Concerning Brazil's Econometric Model" dated December 22, 2003
Daniel A. Sumner
20 January 2004

18. This response to the US critique of the modelling work on US cotton subsidies conducted by myself and my colleagues addresses each of the US comments in the order in which they appear in the US critique submitted on 22 De-

[45] Exhibit Bra-396 ("Farm Groups Shocked at UC Economist's Testimony in WTO Dispute," Western Farm Press, 2 September 2003).
[46] Exhibit US-114.

cember 2003. However, let me start with some general comments I feel are in order.

19. Much of the US critique repeats the description of my adaptations to the FAPRI model, as provided in Annex I and subsequent documents.[47] The model I developed was based on the core domestic crops model of FAPRI with several additions and modifications to fit the questions before this Panel. I stated in detail where my model made those additions and modifications.[48] Thus, these US comments add nothing by reasserting that my model was not identical to the FAPRI model. Since I never claimed that my model was the FAPRI model, I frankly do not understand the point of these repeated assertions that are written as though they were exposing some revelation.

20. Second, the United States at least three times asserts claims about my motivations for modelling choices. Twice in the very first paragraph the United States asserts that my modelling choices were made "in order to exaggerate" acreage and price impacts. Then in paragraph 9, the United States asserts that my modelling choices were made, "for the express purpose of achieving preconceived results". I am puzzled how the United States would claim to have any evidence about my motivation. But more important, these statements suggest seriously immoral and unprofessional behaviour on my part. This is a very serious charge that I do not take lightly. I submit that besides being simply wrong, such attacks have no place in these proceedings.[49]

21. Most of the substantive issues raised in the US critique are simply restatements of assertions that the United States disagrees with the modelling choices made in Annex I.[50] My arguments for why I modelled the policies as I did have been provided to the Panel on several previous occasions and there is no reason to repeat those arguments in this document. I will refer to those arguments as necessary in footnotes.

Section II

22. Paragraphs 5 to 11 of the US critique are devoted to reasserting what I stressed in Annex I that was submitted many months ago, namely that I made adaptations to the FAPRI modelling framework. As I have explained, the FAPRI framework alone was not appropriate for the analysis of the questions before this

---

[47] *See* my Closing Statement on 9 October 2003, attached as Annex II to Brazil's 9 October 2003 Closing Statement, and my statements in Exhibits Bra-313 to 315, my 2 December 2003 Statement to the Panel in Exhibit Bra-342, as well as the detailed reactions to US criticism of my model in Exhibits Bra-343-345.

[48] *See* Annex I to Brazil's 9 September 2003 Further Submission and Exhibit Bra-313.

[49] Some of the economic material presented by the United States in this case has been authored directly by Dr. Glauber. I note that the 22 December 2003 "Comments" are not attributed to anyone by name, therefore I am unable to respond directly to any individual person with respect to these personal charges.

[50] However, the United States does not propose other methods for modelling the subsidy programmes in case they disagree with my model choices. They simply state that these programmes should not cause any effects – a position that is clearly untenable given the other economic evidence about the effects of the programs, including statements by the users and beneficiaries of the programmes.

Panel and therefore I modified and supplemented the framework. However, let us put these modifications and additions in perspective. Of the hundreds of equations used to compute the results, almost all are directly taken from the FAPRI domestic crops model. The basic behavioural supply and demand equations are taken directly from the FAPRI model as are the elasticities used to quantify those equations. In Annex I, and in subsequent documentation[51], I tried to avoid taking credit for work that was not mine. At the same time, I tried to be clear about the distinctions between my work and that of FAPRI and CARD.

23. Professor Bruce Babcock from CARD – with whom I worked together in his private capacity – provided a letter to Congressional staff economists[52] who are familiar with "official" FAPRI analysis of US policy questions, but who have not followed these proceeding closely. In that letter, Professor Babcock explained to them what he and I have always been clear about and had already stated to this Panel. My analysis used part of the FAPRI modelling system, but was not conducted by the full FAPRI team and was not "official" FAPRI analysis. These Congressional staff members had not had access to Annex I or other material submitted to this Panel and Professor Babcock felt a need to clarify these facts. There was no new information in the letter that he sent these staff members that was not already included in Annex I and in the subsequent material provided to the Panel.

24. For example, Professor Babcock points out that the baseline was the November 2002 preliminary FAPRI baseline not the official 2003 FAPRI baseline that became available after I undertook my analysis. He also points out that I used the CARD international cotton model rather than the FAPRI full international model in my analysis.[53] This is not new to those of us who have participated in this Panel proceeding, but Professor Babcock decided to make these clarifications to the Congressional staff members.[54]

25. One point made in the Babcock letter – and emphasized in the US critique – is the obvious fact that if a different team of analysts with a different model had conducted the analysis the results would have been different. That is always true. Different analysts to whom the same question is posed would come up with at least a somewhat different model. Obviously a FAPRI team conducting an official "FAPRI" analysis would have developed a model that is at least somewhat different from my adaptations. In part this occurs because, with complex issues involved, the questions themselves may be interpreted slightly differently, and because, in many cases, there are a range of equally acceptable approaches to an economic modelling choice. It is much less clear how the direction of the results would have changed if different teams with different models conducted

---

[51] *See* in particular Exhibit Bra-313.

[52] Exhibit US-114.

[53] I will discuss the latter issue in greater detail in my comment on Section VII.

[54] The letter responds a perception of concern among some in the United States about the participation of US economists and US based models providing evidence on behalf of Brazil. In particular, Professor Babcock clarified that his FAPRI colleagues at the University of Missouri had not participated in the analysis and that this work was done in a private capacity not at a part of an "official" FAPRI project.

analyses. As the review of the independent literature and the independent models in this case suggests, most analyses of US cotton subsidies have found larger impacts than I found in my research.[55] It is not clear whether an "official" FAPRI analysis would have found larger or smaller impacts if FAPRI would have been posed the same questions as those posed in Annex I, and if the FAPRI team analyzing these questions had considered all the evidence presented to this Panel.

Section II. A.

26. The heading of this section is oddly contradicted by its content. The heading says the "Brazil Model Not Comparable to the FAPRI System", yet the next three paragraphs proceed to compare these two models. Several incorrect assertions are included here, but these are repeated in more detail in later sections and so are dealt with below. However, one clarification is important to make both here and below. Whereas the FAPRI system does not include separate explicit provisions for crop insurance and export credit guarantee programmes, this does not imply that the FAPRI system assumes that there are zero supply impacts of these programmes. Rather, effects of these programmes are imbedded in the baseline of the FAPRI framework.

27. If the FAPRI system had been posed questions about the impacts of crop insurance or export credit guarantee programmes, the natural approach would be to proceed as described in Annex I and in subsequent submissions: to ask how a new scenario with these programmes removed would differ from the baseline that includes these programmes. This procedure was precisely what FAPRI analysts did when they analyzed payment limit rules for the Commission on Payment Limitation in analysis presented in June 2003.[56] The FAPRI framework also does not contain any explicit provisions on payment limitations. These were added to the system for the analysis of the effect of payment limitations, much as I added equations on crop insurance and export credit guarantees for purposes of my Annex I analysis.

28. It is simply wrong to assert that, because a programme is not identified separately in the FAPRI framework, its effects must be assumed to be zero. Furthermore, as discussed further below, in some cases the best evidence on the impact of a programme is from the users of that programme. This was my judgment about the impacts of the export credit guarantee programmes. It certainly makes no sense whatsoever to assume that a programme has zero effect, simply because its impacts, which are known to be positive, are difficult to quantify precisely.

Section II. B.1

29. I explained in great detail the basis for my approach to PFC, DP, MLA and CCP payment programmes.[57] Clearly I disagree with the assertion made in

---

55 *See* for example the review of independent studies in Exhibit Bra-344.

56 *See* for example, FAPRI analysis FAPRI-UMC Report #05-03 and #06-03 to be found at http://www.fapri.missouri.edu/FAPRI_Publications.htm and partly reproduced in Exhibit Bra-228.

57 Annex I, paras. 37-51; and my oral statements on 22 July (Exhibit Bra-105, paras 20-33), 2 December (Exhibit Bra-342, paras 31-37) and my closing statement on 9 October (Part 4); Exhibits Bra-

paragraph 16 and 17. There is no new content here and there is no reason to repeat my argument and evidence. I note, however, that no "official" FAPRI analysis of these payment programmes has asked the question how acreage would respond if cotton programmes were removed while the payments for the other programme crops remained in place. The FAPRI analysis is concerned with the very different question of what would be the impact for all crops if the payment programmes were removed for all crops simultaneously. Therefore, I had to make some adjustments to the treatment of these programmes, as the question that faces this Panel could not be answered by the traditional FAPRI framework. In addition, as footnote 57 highlights, my judgment is that the programmes all have some commodity-specific acreage impact for cotton.

30. The table referred to in paragraphs 21 through 24 simply shows that when the planting impact of these payment programmes for cotton are assumed to have no specific impact on cotton acreage, but only a broad and diffuse effect on all programme crops,then the resulting acreage impact will indeed be nearly zero.

Section II. B.2

31. Annex I as well as subsequent submissions and oral discussions with the Panel have explained in detail my approach to the production impacts of crop insurance and why my approach, for example by leaving out risk reduction impacts, is conservative.[58] The approach is straightforward. The crop insurance subsidy lowers costs to cotton growers and the acreage impact of lower costs in percentage terms may be calculated by multiplying the lower per acre costs by the elasticity of supply. The FAPRI framework has not been used to assess the production impacts of crop insurance. But the impacts of crop insurance subsidies are implicit in the FAPRI baseline.[59] My approach made the impacts explicit so that I could assess the acreage effects of removing the subsidy. This is discussed in somewhat more detail below.

32. Paragraphs 25 through 30 and the table referred to there simply repeat the US claim that hundreds of millions of dollars of crop insurance subsidies for cotton producers has had zero effect on farmers' choices to grow cotton. I dis-

---

280, Bra-313, and Bra-345 (paras 18-34). Some of the key arguments I made can be summarized as follows:

- none of the studies in the literature analyzes the amount of payments made in connection with a specific crop that are received by current producers of that crop,
- none of the studies in the literature focuses on the specific effects of these payments for cotton due to
  - the high per-acre payments for cotton reflecting higher costs of production,
  - the restrictions on planting fruits and vegetables affect particularly cotton production,
- direct and counter-cyclical payments give farmers an incentive to produce the crop for which they have base acreage,
- future updates of base induce farmers to plant their base acreage to the programme crop or even expand the area planted to the programme crop.

[58] *See* also Exhibit Bra-313.

[59] While there is no specific equation modelling the effects of crop insurance, its effects are part of the baseline that projects a level of planted acreage against the background of the continuation of the crop insurance programme.

agree and my model has quantified these impacts using FAPRI elasticities and other features of the FAPRI US crops model.

33. Not withstanding the "intuition" of the United States, the analysis that underlies paragraph 29 of the US critique is evidence of faulty economic reasoning. Furthermore, the US claim about how the FAPRI model treats crop insurance subsidies is misleading at best.[60] As noted above, the FAPRI framework includes the value of crop insurance subsidies implicitly and has not previously been used to analyze the impact of eliminating crop insurance for cotton. Crop insurance for cotton is a service purchased by farmers on a per-acre basis in their business of producing cotton. The subsidy provided by the US government lowers the cost of this service. It is a principle of basic economics that a subsidy that lowers marginal costs results in the same impact as a direct price subsidy on output. Following this principle, I first calculate the regional cotton crop insurance subsidy rate per acre of cotton as a percentage of net revenue and then multiply those subsidy ratios times the elasticity of cotton acreage response applicable to that region. The United States is right that there are more complex ways to model the impact of crop insurance, for example, by noting that crop insurance has an additional acreage impact due to risk reduction. But, the methodology I apply is straightforward, conservative and based on intuitive economic logic and basic principles.

Section II. B.3

34. Paragraphs 31 through 34 and the table to which they refer again simply repeat the US assertion that billions of dollars of subsidized export credit guarantees for cotton exports have zero effect on US production and exports. I find this implausible on its face and based my quantification of the impact on estimates provided by representative of users of the programme. This seems to me to be a reasonable approximation. My use of that estimate was conservative relative to the National Cotton Councils estimates, as explained in detail in response to questions from the Panel[61], and as the US acknowledges in footnote 17 to paragraph 32 of its critique. The National Cotton Council testified that the impact on export was 500,000 bales and the impact that I estimate is considerably smaller. I use my model, based significantly on FAPRI elasticities and other parameters to calculate the price, acreage and other impacts of the initial shift of 500,000 bales. This resulted in much lower net impacts on price and export quantities than estimated by the National Cotton Council.[62]

Section III

35. In paragraphs 35 through 38 of the US critique, the United States points out that the baseline prices reported in Annex I are not the same as baseline

---

60 Paragraph 29 of the US Critique.

61 Brazil's 27 October Answers to Questions, paras. 104-107.

62 In table 5.Ig of Annex I, I report an average export effect of 300,000 bales and an average US price effect of about 0.5 cents per pound, as opposed to the NCC estimate of 500,000 bales and 3 cents per pound.

prices provided to the United States by Professor Babcock on November 26 as part of the model documentation.[63] The United States implies that I have manipulated the baseline to generate higher effects.[64] This allegation has no basis whatsoever.

36. The documentation delivered by Professor Babcock[65] was the FAPRI US crops model that was calibrated with the system of FAPRI international crops models to reproduce the FAPRI November 2002 preliminary baseline projections. The Annex I analysis began with these FAPRI November 2002 preliminary baseline projections. However, the Annex I results were developed by linking the FAPRI US crops model with the CARD international cotton model that was developed by researchers at Iowa State University. Unfortunately, the description of the baseline in Annex I and subsequent submissions was imprecise by not making this distinction explicit. Instead, I labelled the baseline as an (unpublished) FAPRI November 2002 preliminary baseline rather than a slight modification thereof. This slight modification was required for internal consistency reasons, as explained below.

37. The table below provides a full comparison of the differences in the baseline reported in Annex I and the FAPRI November of 2002 preliminary baseline. As can be seen, they are different but those differences are very small overall.

38. There are two reasons for the small differences between the baseline projections used in the Annex I analysis and reported in Annex I and the November 2002 FAPRI preliminary baseline projections. The first was caused by the need to calibrate the CARD cotton model rather than the FAPRI international model with the US crops model. Consistency with the CARD international cotton model implied very small changes in the baseline. The second source of difference was that new macroeconomic projections became available in late November, 2002. These new macroeconomic projections were incorporated into the CARD international cotton model. I stress that the equations of the FAPRI US crops model were not changed in any way. Again, the slight changes between the baseline projections are solely a result of the calibration of the model, once with the FAPRI international crops models (FAPRI preliminary November 2002 baseline) and once with the CARD international cotton model (Annex I model), as well as the updated macroeconomic data used.

39. To put this baseline issue in perspective, Brazil has provided the Panel with several sets of results from similar models on several alternative baselines, including the official FAPRI 2003 baseline.[66] The bottom line is that these results are extremely robust to those alternative baselines and slight modifications to modelling specifics.

---

63 *See* Exhibit Bra-346.

64 Paragraph 38 of the US critique.

65 Exhibit Bra-343, para. 11 and Exhibit Bra-346.

66 This includes my Annex I model based off the FAPRI preliminary November 2002 baseline, my cotton-focussed model based off the FAPRI preliminary November 2002 baseline and the FAPRI January 2003 baseline, as well as a number of independent third party studies (Exhibit Bra-344).

40. The same robustness applies to the results using the FAPRI November 2002 preliminary baseline and the modification applied. The United States assertion that the Annex I baseline meaningfully affects ("exaggerate[s]"[67]) the effects of removing US cotton subsidies is, therefore, unfounded.

41. To analyze the validity of the US assertion, we have recalibrated the CARD international cotton model (used to generate the Annex I results) to replicate exactly the FAPRI November 2002 preliminary baseline. We also used the macroeconomic projections used by FAPRI in November 2002.[68] Rerunning the model of Annex I yields results that are nearly identical to those reported in Annex I. Removal of US cotton subsidies would decrease US production by an average of 24.9 per cent from 2003 to 2007.[69] Mill use would decrease by 6.4 per cent.[70] US exports would decrease by 41.5 per cent.[71] The US Season average price would increase by 15.1 per cent.[72] Importantly, the A index price would increase by 10.6 per cent. In Annex I, I reported a change in the A index price of 10.8 per cent relative to the baseline.[73] This difference of less than 0.2 percentage points is simply not material.

42. In sum, it is unfortunate that this confusion occurred in the labeling of the baseline used in Annex I. The important point, however, is that it has not affected the results of my analysis. Indeed, having run the Annex I model off the non-modified version of the FAPRI November 2002 preliminary baseline projections provides one more indication of the robustness of those results.

Comparison between baseline projections

	2003	2004	2005	2006	2008
	Planted Area (million acres)				
Annex I baseline	13.7802	14.8798	14.7722	14.6525	14.2744
FAPRI baseline	13.7820	14.7205	14.7716	14.6584	14.2519
	Harvested Area (million acres)				
Annex I baseline	12.0444	13.0666	12.9761	12.8739	12.5282
FAPRI baseline	12.0462	12.9164	12.9751	12.8791	12.5068
	Yield (bales per acre)				
Annex I baseline	1.3325	1.3328	1.3410	1.3494	1.3579
FAPRI baseline	1.3325	1.3328	1.3408	1.3492	1.3578
	Production (million bales)				

[67] Paragraph 38 of the US critique.
[68] Both of these modifications result in an Annex I modelling system that is calibrated to exactly generate the FAPRI preliminary November 2002 baseline. It no longer contains any modifications that the United States criticizes as generating overstated resulting effects (paragraphs 36-37 of the US critique).
[69] The Annex I result was 26.3 percent (para. 65).
[70] The Annex I result was equally 6.4 percent (Table I.5a).
[71] The Annex I result was 44 percent (para. 68).
[72] The Annex I result was 15.3 percent (para. 69).
[73] The Annex I result was 10.8 percent (para. 70).

	2003	2004	2005	2006	2008
Annex I baseline	16.0497	17.4157	17.4010	17.3715	17.0121
FAPRI baseline	16.0519	17.2152	17.3974	17.3769	16.9818
	Free Stocks (million bales)				
Annex I baseline	4.9155	4.6527	4.3863	4.3458	4.0330
FAPRI baseline	4.8188	4.4349	4.2145	4.1920	3.8837
	Imports (millions bales)				
Annex I baseline	0.0050	0.0050	0.0050	0.0050	0.0050
FAPRI baseline	0.0050	0.0050	0.0050	0.0050	0.0050
	Mill Use (million bales)				
Annex I baseline	7.7825	7.7018	7.6339	7.5896	7.5245
FAPRI baseline	7.7429	7.6547	7.5968	7.5532	7.4927
	Exports (Million bales)				
Annex I baseline	9.7667	9.9817	10.0384	9.8275	9.8054
FAPRI baseline	9.9042	9.9495	10.0260	9.8513	9.8024
	Season Average Price ($/lb)				
Annex I baseline	0.450	0.477	0.503	0.512	0.539
FAPRI baseline	0.457	0.488	0.512	0.520	0.547
	A Index Price ($/lb)				
Annex I baseline	0.507	0.534	0.558	0.576	0.596
FAPRI baseline	0.524	0.547	0.568	0.587	0.605
	Adjusted World Price ($/lb)				
Annex I baseline	0.372	0.398	0.419	0.436	0.455
FAPRI baseline	0.387	0.410	0.428	0.446	0.463
	Step 2 Payments ($/lb)				
Annex I baseline	0.057	0.060	0.063	0.047	0.052
FAPRI baseline	0.054	0.060	0.063	0.047	0.052

Section IV

43. In section IV of the US critique, the United States claims that my model does not forecast future or explain historical outcomes of cotton plantings and that variables, such as the ratio of soybean to cotton futures prices, are more highly correlated to acreage variations in the seven years from 1996 to 2002.[74] The United States claims that this has some relevance for the validity of my model and its simulation results. These claims are seriously flawed.

44. Section IV of the US critique demonstrates a complete lack of understanding of the role of policy simulation models. A policy simulation model is not designed to and does not have the capability of forecasting. Policy simulation models are designed to ask "but for" counterfactual questions not to attempt to replicate a specific history or forecast the future. Specific statistical tools apply to forecasting economic time series – generally based on some variant of regres-

[74] *See inter alia* paras. 39-42 of the US critique. This is the entire theme of section IV.

sion analysis – to forecast/predict future or explain historic outcomes of, for instance, cotton plantings. Contrary to the assertion of paragraph 39 of the US critique, no professional economist would ever propose a simulation model designed to consider the impacts of policy alternatives as the appropriate tool for forecasting the future or for explaining historical data for an industry. I certainly would never propose the use of a policy simulation model for forecasting purposes.[75]

45. I begin my response to the US critique in section IV by noting that – as I understand it – the questions before the Panel relate to the analysis of the effects of the US cotton subsidies, not to predict cotton plantings for future marketing years.[76] The simulation model that I have presented in Annex I and in later submissions to the Panel addresses exactly that first question before the Panel. Given the baseline that covers historical data for marketing years 1999-2001 and projections for marketing years 2002-2007, my simulation model asks what would have been or what would be the effects of removing the US subsidies on US acreage, use and exports of cotton as well as on cotton prices and other variables.

46. The United States is wrong when it implicitly claims that the ability of a policy simulation model to forecast or account for variations in a time series provides any useful guide to its reliability in terms of the simulation results that it generates – for example in assessing what may happen if policy variables were to change.

47. Forecasting models are typically based on multivariate time series regression analysis that accounts for short-run and long-run trends, serial correlation of times series and exogenous factors. In agriculture, projecting acreage choices would likely involve projecting climate variations, pest trends, and many other variables.(Any standard econometrics textbook provides the basics for forecasting economic time series.[77])

48. Neither my Annex I model nor the FAPRI policy model (nor the USDA policy models) provides an appropriate framework for statistical analysis explaining historical variations in acreage or for forecasting future acreage.[78] The purpose of simulation models is to isolate the effects of, for instance, subsidy

---

[75] I note that the claims made by the United States about the "Sumner model" apply with equal (lack of) force to the FAPRI models themselves. No one uses these models to forecast, nor should they. The models are used and useful to ask "but for" questions, which forecasting models are not in a position to do.

[76] Thus, any assertions of the United States that my model cannot predict future or explain past outcomes of cotton planting is not a relevant factual statement that helps this Panel determine the effects of the US cotton subsidies.

[77] See for example, William H. Greene, *Econometric Analysis* Prentice Hall; 5th edition (2002) (cited in Brazil's 22 December Answers to Questions, para. 42) A classic and still useful reference is Charles R. Nelson, *Applied Time Series Analysis for Managerial Forecasting,* Holden Day, San Francisco. (1973).

[78] Running the same correlation calculations that the United States applied to my model off the FAPRI or USDA's FAPSIM model would very likely not reveal significantly higher correlations as these simulations models are – like my adaptation of the FAPRI model – not designed for that purpose.

programmes as they occur against the baseline results. Policy simulation models do not claim to be useful for forecasting purposes and they are not. But this is irrelevant to their stated purpose as "but for" (counterfactual) policy analysis tools.

49. My simulation model assumes "average" trends for many variables that change in real world situations, but are set at averages in the baseline (or at historical outcomes). For example, my model assumed average weather conditions for marketing years 2002-2007. However, no doubt, there will be years with weather better than the average and years with weather worse than the average. The model cannot predict this, and, therefore, any deviations in the real world that impact on, for instance, planting decisions, would result in "projections" by the model to be necessarily wrong – to the extent that important outcomes of variables, such as weather, deviate from the baseline.

50. A simple illustration may clarify the point that statistical regression models and policy simulation models serve different purposes. Consider a period in which a large direct production subsidy was in force, but the parameters of the programme did not change. Given changes in climate, agronomic factors or other economic incentives, planted acreage would change over the period, but none of the changes in acreage would be due to changes in the subsidy, because there were none. The result of any time-series regression analysis of a limited number of data points is incapable of isolating the effects of variables, such as subsidy programmes, that do not change considerably during the period under analysis. Other variables would explain the variation in acreage over the period and would be better predictors of future acreage shifts so long as the large subsidy programme remained unchanged.

51. But does this mean that the large direct production subsidy is irrelevant to planted acreage? No, of course not. Does this mean that a model to consider the amount of acreage that would be planted, but for the subsidy, should assume the subsidy was irrelevant? No, of course not. Therefore, a statistical regression (or correlation) model applied to analyze the effects of such "constant variables" would fail to capture their importance. In sum, only a policy simulation model, of the general sort that I have provided in Annex I will adequately isolate the effects from the cotton subsidy programme hidden in the regression analysis.

52. Similarly, policy simulation models are not usually very good at forecasting future or explaining past events, as explained above. Does this mean that the simulation analyzed the effects of the subsidy programmes incorrect? [79]No, of course not, if they are properly designed.

53. The United States further claims that there are small positive or negative correlations between the expected net revenue and planting decisions, as a result of my model.[80] The table referred to in paragraphs 43 though 52 of the US critique and the discussion in those paragraphs also illustrate the misunderstanding that the United States evidently has about model evaluation and the meaning of

[79] The United States implies this in paragraphs 40-50 of its critique.

[80] Paragraphs 43-46 and table at paragraph 49 of the US critique

the statistics they produce. The table at paragraph 49 reports simple correlations coefficients based on seven observations for a few variables. First, I note that the sample size for these variables is simply too small for any meaningful statistical analysis. Second, simple (univariate) correlation coefficients are not measures of explanatory power as the United States implies, for example, in paragraph 42 of its critique.[81] Simple correlation coefficients tell us nothing of interest when many variables affect an outcome.[82] This again highlights the difference between forecasting or explanatory models and policy simulations models that ask "but for" counterfactual questions. Nothing in this section of the US critique relates in any way to the usefulness of models for policy analysis.

54. Correlation coefficients measure linear statistical relationships between two variables in isolation from all other influences. They do not indicate causation and they do not even indicate a statistical relationship between variables that takes place in the real-world situation when there are many simultaneous statistical and causal relationships in place. It follows that the figures presented in the table at paragraph 49 are not indicative of causation or even of the contribution to statistical explanatory power in the current case where many variable are interrelated. Whether the figures are positive or negative, large or small, they have no statistical significance and provide no meaningful information.

55. In sum, the US statement at paragraph 50 of its critique has no basis whatsoever. As with all policy simulation models, including the FAPRI and USDA simulation models, any single factors or set of variables in my model are not necessarily expected to "explain" the time series data. The model was not designed to explain historic events or predict future outcomes. Instead my model is designed to simulate what would be expected to happen if US subsidies were removed. A test of the model would be to observe responses if subsidies were removed and other factors were held constant. Presenting a set of simple correlation coefficients on seven years of historical data over which subsidies remained in place provides no evidence of any relevance.

56. Finally, I refer the Panel to the many instances in which I have addressed the question of lagged prices used to model farmers' price expectations at planting time.[83] I will not repeat these arguments here to respond to the US criticism that I should have used futures market prices.[84] I would note that Brazil's sub-

81 Paragraphs 41-42 and 45-49.

82 The case of cotton plantings is a good example. Planting decisions are a function of expected revenue itself determined by expected market revenue and expected government payments. It is further a function of expected revenue for other crops, of weather conditions at planting time, of expected demand for the crop, expected weather during the growing season and so forth. Simple univariate correlation measures linear statistical relationships, not causation or even statistical relationships if there are many factors that potentially affect the outcome of a variable. This explains that there may be a negative correlation where one intuitively expects a positive correlation as a result of ignoring the effects of all other factors on the variable to be explained.

83 *See* my 9 October Closing Statement attached as Annex II to Brazil's 9 October Closing Statement, my 2 December Oral Statement (Exhibit Bra-342, paras. 24-28), Exhibit Bra-345 (paras.6-14) as well as Brazil's answers to question 213 from the Panel on which I have provided input (Brazil's 22 December Answers to Questions, paras. 37-42).

84 *See* paragraphs 51-52 of the US critique.

missions have thoroughly addressed the US arguments that US farmers planting decisions are made in accordance with futures market prices.[85]

Section V

57. This section of the US critique repeats again that my model differs from the FAPRI US crops model. It also asserts that the United States had difficulties in replicating results of my analysis from the electronic files. This section also reveals that the United States made several mistaken "assumptions" about how certain variables entered the model. As indicated before, given the complexities of working with these models, both Professor Babcock and I have repeatedly offered to work with the United States to replicate my results.[86] US government or other economists working on the US critique of my model could have contacted either Professor Babcock or myself requesting any needed information or assistance with any problems they have had. If they would have done so, we could have clarified any ambiguities and the United States could have avoided the evident errors made in applying my model. However, they did not contact either of us. As a result they made inappropriate assumptions and have failed to apply the model correctly.

58. Let me begin by addressing the US statements about the differences between the Annex I model and the FAPRI model.[87] The essence of those differences was explained in Annex I while the operational details were specified more precisely in Exhibit Bra-313. Annex I attempted to provide a relatively simple heuristic discussion of the modelling approach. Exhibit Bra-313 provided the operational equations. These operational specification are made explicit in equations (4), (5) and (6) in Exhibit Bra-313. As explained in Exhibit Bra-313, my approach to the PFC, MLA, DP and CCP payment programmes and for crop insurance was to use a constant regional acreage elasticity (taken from the FAPRI crops model publications).[88] These elasticities were the averages of the time-varying elasticities used over previous periods, as reported by the FAPRI US crops model that I adapted. I then apply this constant elasticity to the percentage effects of the subsidy on net revenue. This constant elasticity modelling is well established in the literature.[89] Paragraphs 53-56 of the US critique misstate the operational model I used and ignore the information in Exhibit Bra-313 that explains how the heuristic explanation in Annex I was operationalized.

---

85 Brazil's 2 December Oral Statement, Section 5.2 and the accompanying exhibits, as well as my oral explanations on 3 December, including Exhibit Bra-371.

86 *See* my oral statement on 2 December (Exhibit Bra-342, para. 5 and 8), Exhibit Bra-331 (para. 10), letter of Professor Bruce Babcock attached to Brazil's 5 November letter to the Panel

87 *See* section V

88 The regional supply elasticities used for the constant elasticity calculations to determine the PFC, DP, MLA and CCP effects and the crop insurance effects are as follows: Corn Belt, 0.219; Central Plains, 0.942; Delta, 0.544; Far West, 0.041; South East, 0.615; and Southern Plains, 0.362.

89 *See* Sumner, Daniel A., and Michael Wohlgenant, "Effects of an Increase in the Federal Excise Tax on Cigarettes," American Journal of Agricultural Economics, 1985, vol. 67, 235-242.

Sections V. A to V. C

59. In sections V. A and V. B, the Unites States fails to acknowledge that, because the level of net returns vary from year to year, the constant elasticity specification explained in Exhibit Bra-313 means that the impacts of the PFC, MLA, DP, CCP and crop insurance programmes will vary as well. When one recognizes this commonly applied feature of my specification, there is no inconsistency whatsoever between the acreage impacts in the periods 1999 through 2002 and 2003 through 2007.

60. In fact, the United States acknowledges its understanding of the operational specifications explained in Exhibit Bra-313 in paragraphs 63 through 66 of section V. C. And they acknowledge that with constant percentage effect, the number of acres shifted will depend on the percentage impacts of the subsidies on net revenue, not the absolute dollar impacts. The US observations about the programme effects in section V. A (paragraphs 57-60), section V. B (paragraphs 61-62) and in the table that follows paragraph 62 of the US critique are explained by my explicit description of the operational specifications of the Annex I model in equations (4) through (6) in Exhibit Bra-313. It is therefore puzzling why the United States included Section V. A and V. B in the document at all, since they provide no new information. The United States first simply mischaracterizes my approach as linear, and then states that the results are not in line with that linear characterization. As I explained in Exhibit Bra-313 (equations (4) through (6)) and as repeated by the United States in section V. C, my model uses a constant elasticity, constant percentage effect for these impacts.[90]

61. Let me clarify this a little further. The FAPRI US crops model applies a constant linear response to any added revenue. My Annex I model takes the same approach for all variables that are included from the standard FAPRI US crops model. This refers to all variables for which no modifications are reported in Exhibit Bra-313. The FAPRI linear system means that a $100 increase in subsidy has the same effect on acreage whether the base revenue is $200 or $1,000. My alternative approach is used for PFC, MLA, DP and CCP payments as well as crop insurance. It implies that a subsidy that is a constant 10 percent of net revenue has a constant percentage effect on acreage. Hence, a $100 increase in subsidy has a bigger percentage effect on acreage if base revenue were $200 (a 50 per cent increase) than if base revenue were $1,000 (a 10 per cent increase). Constant percentage impacts and constant elasticity models are far more common in the economics literature than are strictly linear models. Constant percentage effects do not imply larger impacts in general. In effect, a constant percentage effect says that subsidies have a bigger acreage effect when they are a bigger share of net revenue than when they are a smaller share of net revenue.

62. Section V. B on crop insurance contains some additional US mistakes in applying my model. The United States seems to apply a constant per-acre crop insurance benefit for all regions. This is inconsistent with my approach and with

---

[90] I note that contrary to the US assertion in paragraph 66, my methodology has not changed between Annex I and Exhibit Bra-313.

reality. As explained in paragraphs 54 and 55 of Annex I, crop insurance subsidy rates differ substantially by region and my model incorporates those differences. When the constant percentage effects are incorporated and when one applies the different regional subsidy rates, there is absolutely no inconsistency between the results in the period from 1999 through 2002 and the period 2003 through 2007.[91]

Section V.D.

63. The point of paragraphs 67 and 68 and the table to which they refer, which follows paragraph 70 ("Example of Southern Plains Acreage Impact"), are not at all clear. Most importantly, the United States is simply incorrect that I used only market revenue plus marketing loan gains as the basis for the percentage calculation.[92] The full net revenue including all programme payments are included in the model specification. It is not clear why the United States made this mistaken assumption.

64. In addition, the labelling of the table itself is not clear. For example, neither Annex I nor my other submissions include regional acreage effects of subsidy programmes. This is because the focus of this case is on national and international impacts. It appears that it was the United States which calculated the figures reported in the table following paragraph 70 ("Example of Southern Plains Acreage Impact"). I note that the marketing year 2005 planting effect of crop insurance in the Southern Plains that the United States labels "Sumner Impact" exceeds the effect I report in Annex I for the entire United States.[93] This reason for this seems to be that the United States presents first round effects, i.e., effects before any feedback effects (second-round effects) from both the US crops model itself as well as before any feedback from the CARD international cotton model. To be clear, these US figures are not the equilibrium figures that I reported in Annex I. They are also not the first-round effects that were intermediate for the results reported in Annex I because of mistaken US assumptions, as discussed below.

65. Further, the column (2) of the US table at paragraph 70 ("Example of Southern Plains Acreage Impact") is labelled "Programme Revenue," yet includes crop insurance. I assume this refers to the total subsidy per acre, not programme revenue. Also, the "programme revenue" only includes revenue from DP and CCP payments as well as crop insurance. No revenue from the marketing

---

[91] The United States claims in paragraph 62 that the existence of crop insurance had a negative impact in the acreage in the Corn Belt and that this would be an implausible result (paragraph 62 of the US Critique and the accompanying table). This is, however, not true. Net crop insurance subsidies in the Corn Belt were negative over time, with indemnity payments being below premium payments. Therefore, the program provided farmers with a net negative return causing negative acreage impacts. This is an entirely plausible result. *See* below the discussion on the amount of crop insurance subsidy payments (at paragraph 66, note 96 below). I also note that cotton is not an important crop in the Corn Belt and that crop insurance benefits in the more important regions in the Southern Plains and in the Southeast are much higher.

[92] *See* paragraph 68 of the US Critique.

[93] *Compare* the 0.446 million acres reported by the United States without offering any source with the results I have reported in Annex I, Table I.5d, which is 0.420 million acres.

loan programme (10.06 cents per pound in MY 2005 pursuant to an AWP of 41.94 cents per pound reported in the baseline)[94] is included in the calculations. By not including marketing loan payments in its calculations, the United States does not follow its own proposition of what the right approach is.[95] Rather, it has excluded marketing loan revenue entirely from its calculations in the table at paragraph 70 of its critique ("Example of Southern Plains Acreage Impact"), leading to distorted elasticity calculations.

66. There are a number of further problems in the examples the United States provides in the tables at paragraph 70 of the US critique ("Example of Southern Plains Acreage Impact") that seem to account for the differences they have created by misapplying my model. Let us use the crop insurance calculations as an example. I calculate that the Southern Plains crop insurance subsidy is $26.14 per acre, not $24.67 per acre[96], as the United States enters into its table in the "programme revenue" column. Furthermore the acreage elasticity that I use is not 0.28, but rather 0.362. These two further obvious errors in the US application of my model account for the bulk of the differences that the United States seems to imply (incorrectly) were errors on my part.

67. Besides this, the table following paragraph 70 of the US critique ("Example of Southern Plains Acreage Impact") not only contain numbers that are not my reported impacts, they also make the serious conceptual error of simply adding the impact of each programme across the columns to get a "total" effect. This is an error because the effects of the programmes are not independent. In order to estimate the impacts of removing these three sets of programmes together, one must simulate that scenario explicitly. The resulting impacts will be smaller than the sum of the impacts of removing each programme one at a time. For example, if one removed the crop insurance programme for cotton, supply would fall and the market price of cotton in the United States would rise. This would imply that the CCP programme would have a smaller subsidy element and its effect would be smaller. The fact that the United States reported the simple sum of impacts across programmes and represented that as the impact due to the three sets of programmes together seems to demonstrate either an inadvertent error or a basic lack of understanding of how the programme and the model operates.

Section V. E

68. There are several problems and inconsistencies in the discussion and tables included in this section. These problems also apply to the calculations in section V. D.[97] The United States improperly applied my model and, therefore, it is not surprising that they found different results. I note that the United States in paragraphs 71 of its critique states that "reasonable assumptions were made to

94 *See* Annex I, Table I.5a.

95 *See* paragraph 68 of the US Critique.

96 The regional crop insurance subsidy rates that I use are as follows: Corn Belt: -$0.70; Central Plains: $28.24; Delta: $7.37; Far West: $13.62; Southeast: 15.71; Southern Plains: 26.14.

97 I have combined the discussion of these points to avoid any repetition in an already lengthy and technical document.

facilitate the calculations". I repeat again that Professor Babcock and myself offered the United States our assistance in replicating the results. Any request for assistance would have avoided these problems and the need for the United States to make "reasonable assumptions ... to facilitate the calculations".

69. One important problem that vitiates any claims in this section is that the numbers that are labeled "Sumner's Reported Impacts" in the three charts that follow paragraph 72 are not what I reported in Annex I Tables I.5.b, I.5.c and I.5.d.98 The United States compares two sets of numbers that were evidently generated by the United States, neither of which is the result that I actually reported to this Panel.

70. As noted above, it seems that the United States provides direct acreage effects (so-called first-round effects) that do not take into account feedback effects from either the US crops model or the CARD international cotton model. These feedback adjustments are very large and the US figures do not represent the new, much smaller, equilibrium effects.

71. With this in mind, I will address the US arguments in section V. E. The UnitedStates claims that my approach to estimating the acreage impacts of removing PFC/DP, CCP/MLA, and crop insurance subsidies is deeply flawed because theirattempted replication of the my methodology showed sharply lower impacts in 2002 – 2007 than what they claim were my estimated impacts.[99] As I will demonstrate, the difference between the two sets of estimates of the United States is primarily due to differences in the magnitude of elasticities of supply the United States used, as compared to the elasticities that I actually used. The United States applied time-varying, linear elasticities[100] because this is what is suggested by the FAPRI linear modelling framework. My Annex I results of the effects of these listed programmes are, however, based on a constant elasticity structure. As I will show, the US implementation of the United States' method using time-varying, linear elasticities is deeply flawed and leads to a dramatic underestimation of the effects. To clarify this step by step, I take as a starting point the US implementation of my Annex I methodology.[101]

72. The United States calculates time-varying, linear elasticities by multiplying the slope coefficient in the FAPRI US crops model by real net revenue (net revenue divided by a GNP deflator) and dividing the result by base acreage.[102] Net revenue used in this calculation is expected market revenue plus marketing loan gains. Contrary to the US approach and as discussed above, I use a set of elasticities that does not vary with time. The first chart below shows how the

---

98 Nor are these the figures that I have reported using the FAPRI January 2003 baseline (Exhibit Bra-325)

99 Paragraph 69 of the US Critique and second set of tables following paragraph 70 of the US Critique, as well as the three charts following paragraph 72 of the US Critique.

100 I have explained that in my comments on section V.A-V.C.

101 All calculations are presented in Exhibit Bra-399 ('AcreageDiscrepancies.xls') attached to the electronic version of this document.

102 Base acres are the acreage planted under the baseline scenario.

different elasticity estimates change the estimated acreage effects of removing PFC/DP, CCP/MLA, and crop insurance subsidies.[103]

Chart 1

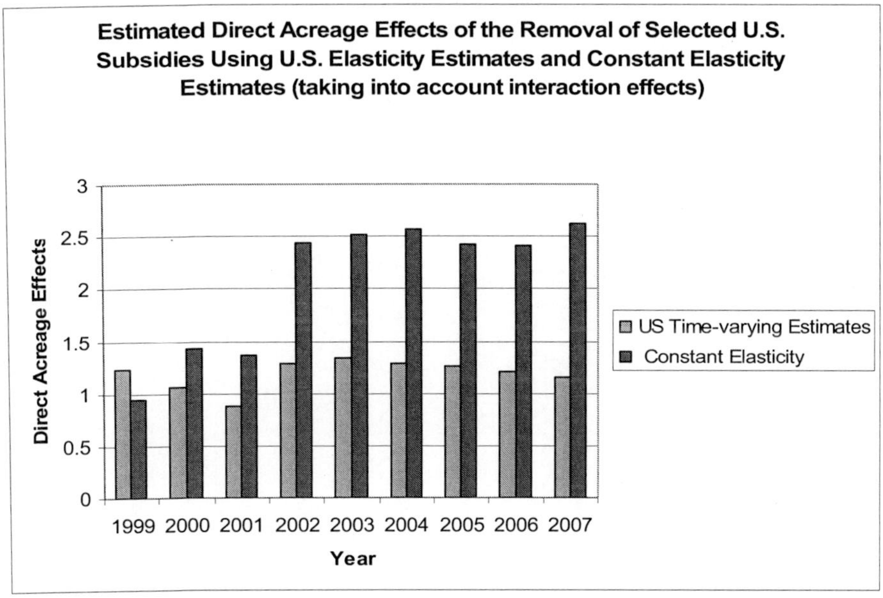

73. I note again that these acreage effects are "first-round" effects that represent an intermediate calculation step towards estimating the new equilibrium results. Therefore, these figures are conceptually different from the equilibrium acreage effects reported in Annex I.[104]

74. These effects are also not the same as the first-round acreage effects that I have estimated using the Annex I model because of differing subsidy levels, as explained below.

75. I note that the effects reported in chart 1 are quite similar to the pattern of effects presented by the United States, as reported in the charts following paragraph 72 of the US critique.[105] I have included the aggregate effects from these three programmes, controlling for interaction effects between them, which accounts for the differences between my figures and the sum of the figures presented by the United States.

---

[103] The chart presents total effects from all three subsidy programs (PFC/DP, MLA/CCP and crop insurance) and controls for interaction effects.

[104] The Annex I effects take into account second round effects on price and quantities resulting from the first round effects and also the feedback from the CARD international cotton model leading to an equilibrium effect.

[105] They are not identical, as the United States used the FAPRI January 2003 baseline provided with my cotton-focused model for these calculations. The similarity of the figures demonstrates again the robustness of the model if different baselines are used.

76. I also note that, in chart 2, the pattern of acreage effects estimated by my use of a constant elasticity model specification[106] is consistent with the pattern of the importance of these subsidies, i.e., the share of the total net revenue presented by these subsidies.

Chart 2

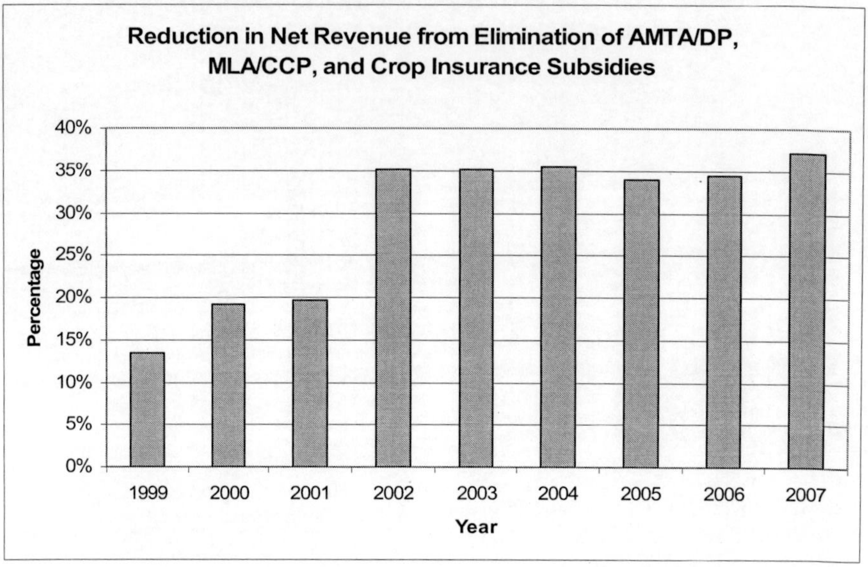

77. The results in chart 1 would suggest that most of the discrepancy between the first-round effects that lead to my Annex I results and those first-round effects calculated by the United States is due to different assumptions regarding elasticities.

78. However, it is not true that the difference in the assumptions regarding the elasticities does primarily account for the difference. First, there is much less difference between the results from the two assumptions regarding the elasticities once an error in the United States' method for calculating its time-varying, linear elasticities is corrected.[107] As documented in the Final USCROPS2003.xls file[108], the United States calculates the supply elasticity by multiplying the slope parameter by real net revenue and then dividing it by base acreage. Net revenue in this calculation includes marketing loan gains and expected market revenue, but it does not include crop insurance subsidies and the other government subsidies that are to be removed in this simulation.[109] As the United States correctly points out when they question whether I included these subsidies for the calcula-

[106] I have discussed this feature of a constant elasticity model in my comments on section V.A-V.C above.

[107] As discussed below, the United States also uses compares results from two different baselines.

[108] Exhibit US-115.

[109] I note that I also made this point in my comments on section V.D above.

tion of the percentage change in net revenue from subsidy removal[110], these subsidies should also be counted towards net revenue when calculating the elasticity of supply.[111] The mistaken assumption by the United States that I have not done so seems to have let the United States to also leave these revenue components out of their calculation, thereby generating misleading results.

79. The following chart 3 shows that when the time-varying, linear elasticities are correctly calculated, then the choice of time-varying, linear elasticities or constant elasticities makes much less difference to the estimated impacts of subsidy removal than suggested by the United States in the three charts following paragraph 72 of the US critique.

Chart 3

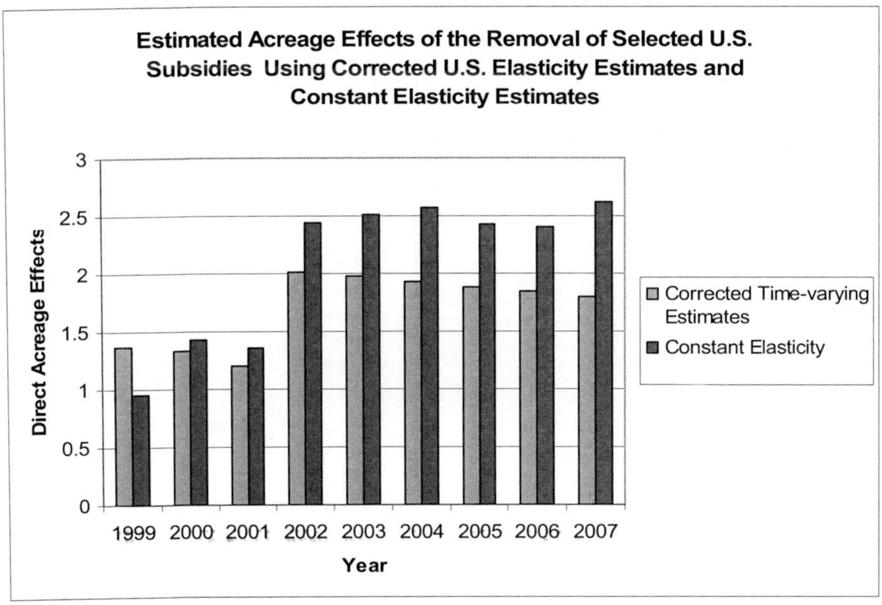

80. Finally, one last source of difference is that the United States uses the model calibrated to the FAPRI 2003 baseline[112] rather than the baseline used to estimate the effects reported in Annex I. The next chart (4) compares the actual direct acreage effects (first round effects) from removal of PFC/DP, CCP/MLA, and crop insurance subsidies based off the baseline used to generate the Annex I results to those that would have resulted from using the correct US time-varying, linear elasticity approach, the correct net revenue estimates and the same baseline. As shown below, adopting the corrected United States procedure compared to my constant elasticities approach would have resulted in a dramatic increase in

110 *See* paragraph 68 of the US Critique.

111 I note that I correctly included these subsidies.

112 Provided by Brazil as an attachment to its 18 November 2003 Further Rebuttal Submission.

the estimated impacts of removing these subsidies in 1999, somewhat higher estimates in 2000 and 2001, and a bit lower estimates in 2003 to 2007.

Chart 4

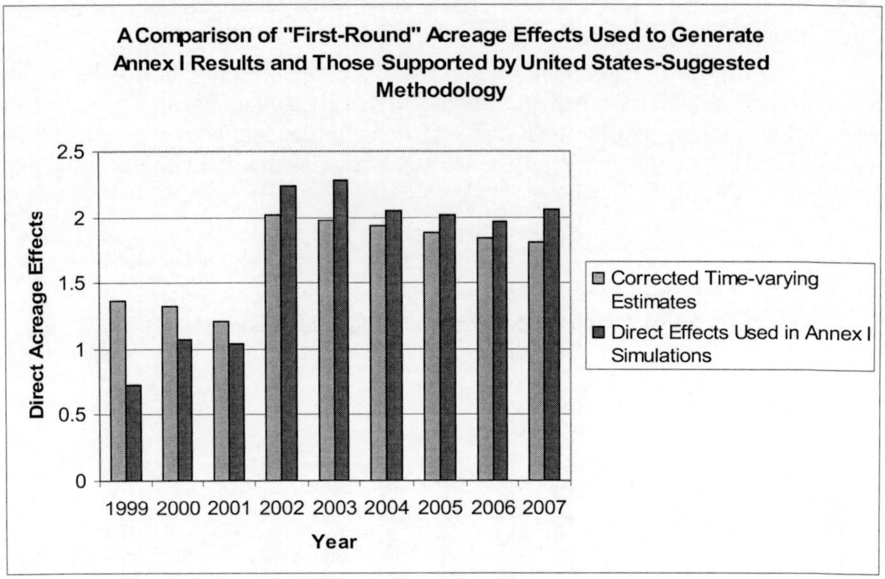

81. In sum, the bottom line of these calculations is that, if the United States had followed the approach that they and I agree would be correct for calculating total net revenue and resulting time-varying, linear elasticities, the resulting effects would not be significantly different whether simulated using constant elasticities or time-varying, linear elasticities. I used the constant elasticity method because it makes the common sense assumption that equal percentage changes in net revenue should give rise to similar changes in acreage.[113] As noted above, this is also a standard approach in economic literature.

82. Finally, I would like to stress that any remaining differences from using different elasticity approaches are still on the level of "first round" effects, not equilibrium effects. The resulting equilibrium effects would show results that are even less different based on the choice of time-varying, linear versus constant elasticities. In short, this choice does not meaningfully affect my Annex I results.

Section VI.

83. In paragraphs 73-74 of the US critique, the United States calls into questions my modelling approach for the marketing loan programme by describing it as revealing a "lack of knowledge of the programme, a broader deficiency in economics or some previously unknown modification of the FAPRI or CARD models". These allegations are baseless. Indeed, the United States simply identi-

---

[113] I have discussed this above providing the example of a $100 payments and base revenues of $200 and $1000.

fied a typo in the transcription of equation 2 in Exhibit Bra-313. This transcription typo was not made in the electronic model and, therefore, does not affect the results of my Annex I model. In the Annex I model, as in the FAPRI US crops model, the acreage in year 't' is affected by the loan rate in year 't' (not the loan rate in 't-1' as erroneously reported in Exhibit Bra-313). I regret the inconvenience if this typo caused some confusion.

84. It turns out that, contrary to what the United States implies in paragraph 74 of its critique, this typo introduced no ambiguity at all and would not have affected the results in any significant way. The fact is that the loan rate for cotton is essentially constant over the full period of analysis and, thus, the loan rate in period 't' is equal to the loan rate in period 't-1'.[114] Despite the tone of the paragraph, the model was clear, and the subscript 't' or 't-1' make no difference at all in this case. Yet, I stress again that this typo only occurred in the transcript of equation (2) in Exhibit Bra-313, and not in the electronic versions of the Annex I model itself.

85. In paragraph 74 the United States makes a major issue of what amounts to their own semantic confusion. The model that I use for the marketing loan benefits for cotton is as specified in equation (2) (noting the typo discussed above). As noted by the United States, the electronic versions of the models show that the marketing loan effect is based on the difference between the loan rate and what is labeled as the loan repayment rate. For crops other than rice and cotton the loan repayment rate is the US market price of the crop (a local market price). For cotton and rice the loan repayment rate is an international price and, for cotton specifically, it is the adjusted world price (AWP). Thus, there is no discrepancy between Exhibit Bra-313 and the electronic documentation provided. The formulation that I use for the marketing loan impacts is the same as the FAPRI US crops model.

86. Paragraph 75 of the US critique simply repeats their discussion from the section V. C., which I have addressed above.

87. Finally, in paragraph 76 of its critique, the United States alleges that I have taken an "illogical" approach on specifying the export effect of Step 2 payments that constitutes "a departure from the specifications in the FAPRI framework." Similar to my response to the US critique at paragraph 73, I regret that I made another typo in the subscript in Exhibit Bra-313 that was not included in the electronic version of the model and, therefore, does not affect my results. Of course exports in period 't' market the crop produced in that period. The US marketing years are calibrated so that this is generally true. The United States is correct that, with the typo, equation (7) obviously makes no sense. The subscript should have referred to production in period 't' rather than 't-1', which, of course, is the equation contained in my model as well as in the FAPRI US crops model. Despite the US tone in paragraph 76, I expect the United States is aware that the specification of equations (7) and (8) follow the FAPRI model, as provided in

[114] I note that the loan rate was 51.92 cents per pound in marketing years 1999-2001 and 52 cents per pound in all later marketing years, so there is a tiny difference between 2001 and 2002.

the electronic verification of both the FAPRI US crops model as well as my cotton-focused model. Removal of the export step-2 and domestic step-2 subsidies increase effective demand for US cotton by lowering the effective net price paid by buyers.

Section VII

88. In paragraphs 77 through 80 of the US critique, the United States notes that the CARD international cotton model used different supply and demand elasticities than found in a paper by FAPRI-Missouri economist Seth D. Meyer. In fact there are several sets of such elasticities in the literature.

89. I relied on the CARD model and the CARD elasticities for four simple reasons. First, the authors of the published studies that underlie the CARD international cotton model include Professors Babcock and Beghin, who are two of the most widely-published and respected agricultural economists in the field. The scholarly credibility of their work and that of their CARD colleagues has been reinforced by scores of professionally-refereed academic articles to their credit as well as awards and other accolades.[115] In terms of quality objective research in agricultural commodity market economics and related areas, the CARD team has a long distinguished track record and a top notch professional reputation. By contrast, I do not know the professional work of Seth D. Meyer, and have not been able to locate any of his work in professionally-refereed publications.

90. Second, the CARD international cotton model was the model that had been used by CARD in its respected work on other international commodity analysis. I would note that the various CARD international commodity models developed by Professors Babcock and Beghin and their colleagues have been used and relied upon in a number of different studies and been published in professionally referred publications.[116]

---

115 Exhibit Bra-400 (List of Publications of Professors Babcock and Beghin).

116 Refereed articles using CARD international models:

Fuller F., J. Beghin, J. Fabiosa, C. Fang, H. Matthey, and S. De Cara. "China's Accession to the WTO. What Is at Stakes for Agricultural Markets?" *Review of Agricultural Economics* 25(2) (2003): 399-414.

Beghin J., B. El Osta, J. Cherlow, and S. Mohanty. "The Cost of the US Sugar Program Revisited," *Contemporary Economic Policy* 21 (1) (2003): 106-116. Reprinted in *International Sugar Journal* 105 (2003): 293-303.

Fuller F., J. Beghin, S. Mohanty, J. Fabiosa, C. Fang, and P. Kaus. " Accession of the Czech Republic, Hungary, and Poland to the European Union: Impacts on Agricultural Markets," *The World Economy* 25(3) (2002): 407-428.

Fang C., and J. Beghin. "Urban Demand for Edible Oils and Fats in China. Evidence from Household Survey Data," *Journal of Comparative Economics*, 30 (4) (2002): 732-753.

Fabiosa, J.F., D.J. Hayes and H.H. Jensen. 2002. "Technology Choices and the Economic Effect of a Ban in the Use of Over-the-Counter antibiotics in US Swine Rations." *Food Control* 13(2), 97-101.

Hayes, D.J., H.H. Jensen, L. Backstrom, and J.F. Fabiosa. 2001. "Economic Impact of a Ban on the Use of Over-the-Counter Antibiotics in US Swine Rations." *International Food and Agribusiness Management Review* Vol 4., p 81-97.

91. Third, the elasticity parameters incorporated in the CARD model are well within the range of estimates found and applied for many agricultural commodities. Finally, the United States provides no evidence to support a suggestion that the Meyer estimates are in any way more appropriate for the questions posed by this Panel than the estimates imbedded in the CARD model. Therefore, United States assertion that use of the CARD model somehow "exaggerates" impacts is simply unfounded.[117]

Conclusion

92. The Annex I model adapted from the FAPRI US crops model and the CARD international cotton model is an appropriate tool for both forward- and backward-looking "but for" counterfactual US agricultural policy analysis questions, such as those facing this Panel. The conservative results from my Annex I model are well within any plausible range and supported by other economic and econometric evidence.

93. Over the past months of this lengthy proceeding, I have responded to each criticism raised by the United States at various occasions[118] and have explained why none affects the validity of my model or its results.

94. Professor Babcock and I have been fully transparent about the manner in which the effects of the US subsidies have been simulated and I have rebutted any US allegations that I made my modelling choices to achieve pre-conceived results. To that end, I have explained each of my modelling steps and offered my assistance to the Panel and the United States to facilitate the understanding of this complicated econometric model and its results.

95. The United States has criticized my choice of baseline and I have provided analysis under various other baselines, demonstrating the robustness of my results. The United States has also criticized my modelling choices for PFC, MLA, DP and CCP payments, crop insurance and export credit guarantees. I have provided evidence that these choices were reasonable and, in fact, conservative. Concerning the largest US subsidy, the marketing loan programme, I note that the United States has not criticized its modelling. I have explained that the use of lagged prices for a large-scale policy simulation analysis is standard and does not generate biased or exaggerated results – in fact, no futures prices could or have been used in such models.

96. In sum, I stand by my conclusions in Annex I "that very large subsidies provided to US producers and users of upland cotton have had and will continue to have large impacts on quantities of US cotton produced, used and traded and on both US and world prices of cotton".

Fuller F., J. Beghin, S. Mohanty, J. Fabiosa, C. Fang, and P. Kaus. " The Impact of the Berlin Accord and European Enlargement on Dairy Markets," *Canadian Journal of Agricultural Economics,* 47 (5) (1999 –appeared in 2000): 117-130.

[117] It is also useful to remind ourselves that larger elasticies may mean smaller price impact, but also imply larger impacts on quantities and in particular larger acreage elasticities mean more acreage in the non-subsidized countries that is driven out of cotton by the US cotton subsidy programmes.

[118] *See inter alia* US 7 October 2003 Oral Statement, paras. 26-50 and US 22 December 2003 Comments on Brazil's Econometric Model.

ANNEX I-13

COMMENTS ON US ANSWERS TO QUESTIONS POSED BY THE PANEL FOLLOWING THE SECOND SUBSTANTIVE MEETING OF THE PANEL

28 January 2004

TABLE OF CONTENTS

Table of Cases Cited

Short Title	Full Case and Citation
EC – Sugar Exports I (Australia)	GATT Panel Report, *European Communities – Refunds on Exports of Sugar Complaint by Australia,* L/4833 – 26S/290, adopted 6 November, 1979.
EC – Sugar Exports II (Brazil)	GATT Panel Report, *European Communities – Refunds on Exports of Sugar Complaint by Brazil,* L/5011 – 27S/69, adopted 10 November, 1980.
US – Gasoline	Appellate Body Report, *United States – Standards for Reformulated and Conventional Gasoline*, WT/DS2/AB/R, adopted 20 May 1996.
EC – Hormones	Appellate Body Report, *European Communities - Measures Concerning Meat and Meat Products (Hormones),* WT/DS26/AB/R, adopted 13 February 1998.
Australia – Salmon	Panel Report, *Australia – Measures Affecting Importation of Salmon,* WT/DS18/R, adopted 6 November 1998.
EC – Bananas	Panel Report, *European Communities – Regime for the Importation, Sale and Distribution of Bananas – Recourse to Arbitration by the European Communities under Article 22.6 of the DSU*, WT/DS27/ARB, adopted 9 April 1999.
Brazil – Aircraft	Panel Report, *Brazil – Export Financing Programme for Aircraft,* WT/DS46/RW, adopted 28 August 2000.
Indonesia – Automobiles	Panel Report, *Indonesia – Certain Measures Affecting the Automobile Industry,* WT/DS54/R, adopted 23 July 1998.-

Argentina – Textiles and Apparel	Panel Report, *Argentina – Measures affecting Imports of Footwear, Textiles, Apparel and Other Items*, WT/DS56/R, adopted 22 April 1998.
Canada – Aircraft	Panel Report, *Canada – Measures affecting the Exports of Civilian Aircraft,* WT/DS70/R, adopted 20 August 1999.
Canada – Aircraft	Appellate Body Report, *Canada – Measures affecting the Exports of Civilian Aircraft,* WT/DS70/R, adopted 20 August 1999.
Japan – Agricultural Products	Appellate Body Report, *Japan – Measures Affecting Agricultural Products,* WT/DS76/AB/R, adopted 19 March 1999.
Korea – Dairy Safeguards	Appellate Body Report, *Korea – Definitive Safeguard Measure on Imports of Certain Dairy Products*, WT/DS98/AB/R, adopted 12 January 2000.
Canada – Dairy	Appellate Body Report, *Canada – Measures Affecting the Importation of Milk and the Exportation of Dairy Products,* WT/DS103/AB/R, adopted 27 October 1999.
Canada – Dairy (21.5) (II)	Appellate Body Report, *Canada – Measures Affecting the Importation of Milk and the Exportation of Dairy Products,* WT/DS103/AB/RW, adopted 17 January 2003.
US – FSC	Appellate Body Report, *United States – Tax Treatment for "Foreign Sales Corporation",* WT/DS108/AB/R, adopted 20 March 2000.
Australia – Leather	Panel Report, *Australia – Subsidies Provided to Producers and Exporters of Automotive Leather,* WT/DS126/R, adopted 16 June 1999.
Australia – Leather (21.5)	Panel Report, *Australia – Subsidies Provided to Producers and Exporters of Automotive Leather,* WT/DS126/RW, adopted 11 February 2000.
US – 1916 Act	Appellate Body Report, *United States – Anti-Dumping Act of 1916,* WT/DS136/AB/R, adopted 26 September 2000.
US – Wheat Gluten	Panel Report, *United States – Definitive Safeguard Measures on Imports of Wheat Gluten from the European Communities,* WT/DS166/R, adopted 19 January 2001.
US – Wheat Gluten	Panel Report, *United States – Definitive Safeguard Measures on Imports of Wheat Gluten from the European Communities,* WT/DS166/R, adopted 19 January 2001.
Chile – Agricultural Products (Price Band)	Appellate Body Report, *Chile- Price Band System and Safeguard Measures Relating to Certain Agricultural Products,* WT/DS207/AB/R, adopted 23 October 2002.
US – CVD's on EC Products	Appellate Body Report, *United States – Countervailing Duties on EC Products,* WT/DS212/AB/R, adopted 8 January 2003.
Canada – Aircraft II	Panel Report, *Canada – Measures Affecting the Export of Civilian Aircraft,* WT/DS222/R, adopted 19 February 2002.
EC – Sardines	Appellate Body Report, *European Communities – Trade Description of Sardines,* WT/DS231/AB/R, adopted 23 October 2002.
EC – Sardines	Panel Report, *European Communities – Trade Description of Sardines,* WT/DS231/R, adopted 23 October 2002.
Japan – Apples	Appellate Body Report, *Japan – Measures affecting the Importation of Apples,* WT/DS245/AB/R, adopted 10 December 2003.

List of Exhibits

Second Declaration of Andrew Macdonald, 27 January 2004.	Exhibit Bra- 401
"Genetically Engineered Cotton Suffering from Production Problems", Organic Consumers Organization, 11 January 2002.	Exhibit Bra- 402
"NCC will Intensify Emphasis for Quality, Yield Answers", Western Farm Press, 3 March 2001.	Exhibit Bra- 403
"Benefits - BT Cotton", Monsanto Imagine.	Exhibit Bra- 404
"Sample Costs to Produce Cotton Transgenic Herbicide- Resistant Acala Variety", San Joaquin Valley, University of California Cooperative Extension, 2003.	Exhibit Bra- 405
"Cotton Cost-Return Budget in Southwest Kansas", Kansas State University Agricultural Experiment Station and Cooperative Extensive Service, October 2003.	Exhibit Bra- 406
Documents on Cost of Production Insurance Plan for Cotton.	Exhibit Bra- 407
Export – Import Bank of the United States, Standard Repayment Terms.	Exhibit Bra- 408
Ex-Im Bank Fee Schedule.	Exhibit Bra- 409
Export Insurance Services.	Exhibit Bra- 410
"The Federal Scoop: US Government Financing for Service Exports", Export America, May 2003.	Exhibit Bra- 411
Cotton and Wool Situation Outlook and Outlook Yearbook, USDA, November 2003, Table 16.	Exhibit Bra- 412
"Agricultural Cash Rents", USDA, NASS, July 1999.	Exhibit Bra- 413
"Agricultural Land Values and Cash Rents," USDA, NASS, August 2003.	Exhibit Bra- 414
"Agricultural Land Values", USDA, NASS, April 1999.	Exhibit Bra- 415
"What is a Farm Bill?", Congressional Research Service, Report for Congress, 5 May 2001.	Exhibit Bra- 416
"Commodity Program Entitlements: Deficiency Payments", USDA, May 1993.	Exhibit Bra- 417
Washington Post v. United States Department of Agriculture, 943 F. Supp. 31 (D.D.C. 1996).	Exhibit Bra- 418
Allocation Calculations Based on Brazil's Methodology and US Summary Data.	Exhibit Bra- 419
Agricultural Outlook Tables, November 2003, Table 17.	Exhibit Bra- 420
ERS Briefing Room: Farm Income and Costs: US Farm Sector Cash Receipts from Sales of Agricultural Commodities, USDA.	Exhibit Bra- 421
Fruits and Tree Nuts Yearbook, USDA, October 2003, Table A-2.	Exhibit Bra- 422
Vegetables and Melons Yearbook, USDA, July 2003, Table 3.	Exhibit Bra- 423
Allocation Calculations Based on US Methodology and US Summary Data.	Exhibit Bra- 424

Questions from the Panel to the parties –
second substantive Panel meeting

I. TERMS OF REFERENCE

192. Regarding the interest subsidies and storage payments listed by the United States in its response to the Panel's Question No. 67:

(a) Please provide a copy of the regulations under which they are currently provided and under which they were provided during the marketing years 1996-2002;

(b) Please indicate whether there are any such payments which are not provided to implement the repayment rate for upland cotton within the marketing loan programme. USA

Brazil's Comment:

1. The United States finally confirms that the "other payments" (*i.e.,* interest and storage payments) are not separate subsidies but rather a component of the marketing loan programme.[1] The US acknowledgement eliminates any question whether such payments are within the Panel's terms of reference.[2] Brazil's request for the establishment of a panel clearly includes "subsidies and domestic support ... relating to marketing loans ... providing direct or indirect support to the US upland cotton industry".[3] Based on the US answer, Brazil amends the table at paragraph 8 of its 22 December 2003 Answers to Question 196 to add $65 million "other payments" to the $832.8 million for marketing loans, for a grand total of $887.8 million in marketing loans for MY 2002. Brazil also makes similar changes for MY 1999-2001 that combine "other payments" and marketing loan payments in Table 1 of Brazil's 9 September 2003 Further Rebuttal Submission.

193. Are interest subsidies and storage payments already included in the amounts shown in your submissions to date for payments under the marketing loan programme? Has there been any double-counting? BRA

194. Does the United States maintain its position stated in response to the Panel's Question No. 67 that "it would not be appropriate for the Panel to examine payments made after the date of panel establishment"? If so, please explain why. Can Brazil comment on this statement? BRA, USA

Brazil's Comment:

2. Brazil's 22 December 2003 response to this question, particularly its reference to the request for the establishment of the panel and existing jurispru-

---

1 US 22 December 2003 Answers to Questions, para. 2.

2 US 30 September 2003 Further Submission, paras. 6-7; US 7 October 2003 Oral Statement, para.2.

3 WT/DS267/7, p. 2 (paragraphs relating to both the 2002 FSRI and the 1996 FAIR Act).

dence, provides a comprehensive response to the points raised by the United States.[4] Brazil would offer the following additional comments to the US Answer.

3. Contrary to the suggestion at paragraphs 3-4 of the US 22 December 2003 response, Brazil's 11 August 2003 response to Question 19 did not change in any way the scope of Brazil's request for the establishment of a panel ("Panel Request"). Question 19 asked Brazil to clarify the measures in respect of which Brazil sought relief. Brazil's answer referred to one set of measures relating to Brazil's serious prejudice claims as those involving domestic support and export subsidy payments that had been made and were required to be made by the terms of the various statutory instruments identified in the Panel Request from MY 1999 through MY 2007. Some of these payments are relevant to Brazil's present serious prejudice claims for the period MY 1999-2002, and some of the payments are relevant to Brazil's threat of serious prejudice claims for the period MY 2002-2007. But as Brazil indicated in its 22 December 2003 Answer to Question 195, the text of the Panel Request (as well as Brazil's 11 August 2003 Answer to Question 19) in no way limits the type or scope of the payments made under those statutory and regulatory instruments up to 18 March 2003.

4. It is curious that the United States in its 22 December 2003 response takes an opposite position in this dispute than the one it took as the complaining party in the only other WTO serious prejudice dispute.[5] In *Indonesia – Automobiles*,,[6] the measures at issue provided for past, present, and future subsidy payments. Indonesia argued, similar to the US arguments here, that the effects of expired measures could no longer be examined for the purposes of current serious prejudice under Articles 5 and 6 of the SCM Agreement. Rejecting such a restrictive interpretation of Articles 5 and 6, the panel noted that:

> If we were to consider that past subsidies were not relevant to our serious prejudice analysis as they were "expired measures" while future measures could not yet have caused actual serious prejudice, it is hard to imagine any situation where a panel would be able to determine the existence of actual serious prejudice. Thus, we decline to proceed on the course suggested by Indonesia.[7]

At no time did the panel find, as Indonesia argued, that only non-expired subsidies paid under the measures at issue up until the date of establishment of the panel should have been considered for the purposes of assessing serious prejudice. Indeed, the US position in this dispute is practically the same as what Indonesia argued – and the US argued against[8] – in *Indonesia – Automobiles*. Brazil recalls the consistent US positions that (a) so-called "recurring" subsidies for MY 1999-2001 cannot be the basis for any serious prejudice claims[9], combined

---

4 Brazil's 22 December 2003 Answers to Questions, paras. 3-5.
5 US 22 December 2003 Answers to Questions, paras. 3-5.
6 Panel Report, *Indonesia – Automobiles*, WT/DS54/R.
7 Panel Report, *Indonesia – Automobiles*, WT/DS54/R, para. 14.206.
8 Panel Report, *Indonesia – Automobiles*, WT/DS54/R, paras. 4.44-4.50.
9 US 30 September 2003 Further Submission, para. 94.

with (b) its claim that only *current* 2002 subsidies up to 18 March 2003 (*i.e.*, eight months of subsidies for MY 2002) can be the basis for any serious prejudice claims.[10] Given these two arguments, in the words of the *Indonesia – Automobiles* panel, "it is hard to imagine any situation where a panel would be able to determine the existence of actual serious prejudice".

5. As in *Indonesia – Automobiles*, the legal statutes and regulations set out in the Panel Request that mandate the payment of subsidies did not change between 18 March 2003 and 20 January 2004. Indeed, the 2002 FSRI Act and its implementing regulations will remain identical (unless amended by the US Congress) until the end of MY 2007. Nor has the 2000 ARP changed since 18 March 2003. The mandated subsidies from these statutes and regulations were flowing before 18 March 2003 and they will continue to flow thereafter. This case does not present the situation where a new legal instrument providing subsidies is enacted after the panel request was established. Nor is it even a situation as in *Chile – Agricultural Products (Price Band,*[11], in which a significant amendment to the legal instrument covered in the panel request was made long after the panel was established. The rationale of the Appellate Body in *Chile – Agricultural Products (Price Band)* and of the panel in *Indonesia – Automobiles* is to allow the Panel to conduct the required objective assessment under DSU Article 11 based on all the relevant facts. These decisions are also grounded in the need for the "prompt settlement" of disputes under DSU Article 3.4 – and are structures to avoid the endless filing of precision-timed annual disputes and the litigation gaming strategy envisioned by the US argument.

II. ECONOMIC DATA

195. Does the United States wish to revise its response to the Panel's Question No. 67*bis*, in particular, its statement that "the United States ... does not maintain information on the amount of expenditures made under the cited programmes to US upland cotton producers"? Did the United States make enquiries of the FSA in the course of preparing its original answer? USA

Brazil's Comment:

6. Brazil notes that the US answer is largely unresponsive to the Panel's question.

7. The Panel's question whether the United States "maintains information" is straight-forward. A correct answer would have been "yes". The ordinary meaning of the word "maintain" is "practice habitually", "observe", "cause to continue (a state of affairs, a condition, an activity)".[12] The United States consistently misled Brazil and the Panel by stating that USDA never collected, organized and

---

[10] US 11 August 2003 Answers to Questions, para. 134; US 22 December 2003 Answers to Questions, paras. 3-5.

[11] Panel Report, *Chile – Agricultural Products (Price Band)*, WT/DS207/R, paras. 7.3-7.8.

[12] New Shorter Oxford Dictionary, 1993 edition, p. 1669.

maintained information regarding the amount of contract payments paid to current producers of upland cotton.[13] There is no doubt that these statements were false and misleading. It is significant that the United States has made no attempt to refute the evidence produced by Brazil in its 18 November 2003 Further Rebuttal Submission regarding the FSA forms completed by practically every US farm receiving contract or marketing loan payments.[14] Nor can the United States dispute that all of the information collected from the contract and acreage forms is (and was) maintained in a centralized database in USDA's Kansas City facility. The rapid response of USDA's Kansas City office to the rice FOIA request provides compelling evidence of the habitual practice of the US government in "maintaining" both contract and planted acreage information.[15] Indeed, the strongest proof of the United States' misleading conduct is the fact that USDA produced within three weeks the rice data in response to a FOIA request, and that the United States effectively admitted in its 18 and 19 December 2003 and 20 January 2004 Letters to the Panel that it maintains this information.

8. In fact, the United States continues to mislead the Panel in its 22 December 2003 Answer to Question 195. It states that "because those payments are decoupled from current production, expenditures under such programmes are not tracked by whether the recipient produces upland cotton".[16] Neither Brazil nor the Panel ever asked the United States how the programmes are "tracked". Rather, the Panel asked whether the United States "maintains information" that would permit the calculation of the amount of such payments. As Brazil has demonstrated in using the rice FOIA request[17], in discussing its proposed methodology, and in using the incomplete summary data provided by the United States on 18/19 December 2003, this is a simple exercise.[18]

9. The United States also asserts that "Brazil has also not asserted that the United States maintains information on the receipt of decoupled payments for upland cotton base acres by upland cotton producers".[19] Once again, the United States misleads and misrepresents. What Brazil asserted was that the United States maintains information in a centralized database on the amount of contract acreage, contract yields, and upland cotton plantings on contract acreage that would permit the ready calculation of the exact amount of contract payments received by current producers of upland cotton.[20] The fact that the United States

---

[13] US 27 August 2003 Comments on Brazil's Rebuttal Submission and Answers to Additional Question, paras. 20, 21, 27; US 11 August 2003 Answer to Question 60; The United States made similar statements during the consultations held between November 2002 and January 2003.

[14] Brazil's 18 November 2003 Further Rebuttal Submission, Section 2.2.

[15] Exhibit Bra-368 (Second Statement of Christopher Campbell – Environmental Working Group, 1 December 2003).

[16] US 22 December 2003 Answers to Questions, para. 6.

[17] Exhibit Bra-368 (Second Statement of Christopher Campbell – Environmental Working Group, 1 December 2003).

[18] Brazil's 20 January 2004 Answers to Additional Questions, paras. 43-55; Brazil's 28 January Comments and Requests Regarding US Data, Section 9.

[19] US 22 December 2003 Answers to Questions, para. 7.

[20] Brazil's 18 November 2003 Further Rebuttal Submission, Section 2.2.

claims not to have performed the simple calculation from this data does not mean the United States does not maintain the information requested by Brazil and the Panel.

196. Please provide the latest data for the 2002 marketing year on payments under the marketing loan, direct payments, counter-cyclical payments, user marketing certificate (step 2) programmes and export credit guarantee programmes. BRA, USA

Brazil's Comment:

10. Brazil notes the new and increased figures ($415 million) that the US 22 December response presented for Step 2 payments during MY 2002. This figure should replace Brazil's figure presented at paragraph 8 of its 22 December 2003 Answers to Questions.[21]

197. Please provide actual data for 2002/2003 for US exports, US consumption and per cent of world consumption to replace the projected data in Exhibit US-47. If available, please provide projected data for 2003/2004 to replace the forecast data. USA

Brazil's Comment:

11. The US 22 December 2003 response admits at note 24 to the table at paragraph 15 that the US "consumption" standard for "world market share", within the meaning of Article 6.3(d) of the SCM Agreement, includes tabulating US exports and US imports and US domestic consumption of US origin upland cotton.[22] This acknowledgement that imports are also included highlights the fact that the United States is double counting exports as part of the world market share of the exporting country and part of the world market share of the *importing* country.[23] Since internationally-traded upland cotton is not similarly included twice in the total "world consumption," summing up the individual world market shares of all countries generates a total world market share vastly exceeding 100 per cent – a manifestly absurd result.[24] As Brazil has stated before, the Panel should not rely on the US interpretation of world market share as share of world consumption – the proper interpretation of the term refers to the share of world exports.[25]

12. Further, Brazil notes the new information presented by the United States concerning US upland cotton exports in MY 2002 and 2003. These figures (11.9 million bales and 13.2 million bales respectively) would replace Brazil's latest

---

21 *See* Brazil's comment on US 22 December 2003 Answer to Question 192(b) above concerning the treatment of "other payments." US 22 December 2003 Answers to Questions, para. 2. This US statement eliminates any doubt that "other payments" are within the Panel's terms of reference.

22 US 22 December 2003 Answers to Questions, para. 15 (note 24).

23 *See* Brazil's 2 December 2003 Oral Statement, para. 66. *See* also Brazil's comment on Question 136, below.

24 *See* Brazil's comment on Question 136, below.

25 *See* Brazil's 7 October 2003, Oral Statement, paras. 38-41; Brazil's 18 November 2003 Further Rebuttal Submission, paras. 170-173; Brazil's 2 December 2003 Oral Statement, para. 66.

information, as contained in Exhibit Bra-302 (11.3 million bales and 11.2 million bales respectively). These new facts support Brazil's threat of serious prejudice claim under Article 6.3(d) and footnote 13 of the SCM Agreement. For both marketing years, the US world market share, *i.e.,* the US share of world exports, is or will be even above its previous three-year average, strengthening the consistent trend of increasing world market shares since MY 1996 (as well as since MY 1986).[26]

198. Please comment on the respective merits of the price-gap calculations of MY1992 deficiency payments in US comments of 27 August, footnote 14 ($867 million), and Brazil's response to the Panel's Question No. 67 ($812 million). BRA, USA

Brazil's Comment:

13. As indicated in Brazil's 22 Decembers Answers to Questions, Brazil agrees with the US methodology of calculating MY 1992 deficiency payments[27] for purposes of an AMS approach, as developed by the United States in its 27 August 2003 Comments on Brazil's 22 August 2003 Rebuttal Submission.[28]

14. However, Brazil strongly disagrees with the US proposition that the US AMS calculation of deficiency payments is "conservative".[29] The US calculation is the only appropriate one under paragraphs 10 and 11 of Annex 3 of the Agreement on Agriculture. The United States suggests that it should have used "eligible" acreage rather than "actual" acreage for the calculation.[30] However, paragraph 10 of Annex 3 does not refer to eligible acreage; it refers to "the quantity of *production* eligible to receive the applied administered price".[31] Production eligible to receive the applied administered price under the deficiency payment programme is calculated based on the eligible, participating acreage and the applicable programme yield (not the actual yield). Any production exceeding the programme yields and any production on acreage that did not participate in the deficiency payment programme necessarily was not eligible production. Thus, the fact that theoretically more acreage could have participated in the upland cotton deficiency payment programme (*i.e.,* those farms opted to not participate) cannot artificially inflate the upland cotton AMS figure resulting from this programme. Thus, any production that takes place on a farm not participating in the deficiency payment programme is not, in fact, eligible to receive the applied administered price and, therefore, cannot be part of the AMS calculation under paragraphs 10 and 11 of Annex 3.

---

26 *See* Brazil's 27 October 2003 Answers to Questions, paras. 123-129. *See* also Brazil's 22 December 2003 Answers to Questions, paras. 133-139, concerning Brazil's arguments regarding a "consistent trend."

27 Brazil emphasizes that it does not agree with to applying any price-gap calculation method for the calculation of marketing loan payments for AMS purposes. *See inter alia* Brazil's 27 August 2003 Comments on US Rebuttal Submission, paras. 10-16.

28 Brazil's 22 December 2003 Answers to Questions, para. 10.

29 US 22 December 2003 Answers to Questions, para. 19.

30 *Ibid.*

31 Emphasis added.

199. What is the composition of the A-Index? We do note footnote 19 and, for example, Exhibit BRA-11, but please explain more in detail how this index is calculated. BRA

200. Concerning the chart on page 37 of Brazil's further rebuttal submission, why did Brazil use a futures price at planting time? Is this a relevant measure for assessing acreage response? BRA

201. Is data available to show the proportion of US upland cotton production sold under futures contracts, and the prices under those contracts, at different times during the marketing year? If so, please provide summarized versions to the Panel. How does a futures sale impact the producer's entitlement to marketing loan programme payments? BRA, USA

Brazil's Comment:

15. Brazil notes that the study cited by the United States[32] on upland cotton farmers' use of hedging instruments is relatively dated (from 1996) and analyzes a time period during which prices were high. Therefore, it may not reflect farmers' use of hedging instruments during the period of investigation.

16. In addition, Brazil notes that the futures market is not only used as a hedging instrument by US farmers, but also by farmers in other parts of the world, including Brazilian farmers.[33] It is also used by speculators.[34] It follows that the number of open contracts does not bear any relationship to the amount of the US upland cotton crop hedged by futures contracts at the New York futures market.[35]

202. Concerning paragraph 7 of the US oral statement, are the expected cash prices shown for February only? Can the US provide the prices for January and March of each year as well? USA

Brazil's Comment:

17. Brazil notes that the expected cash price is not the relevant price for purposes of analyzing the effects of the marketing loan programme. Since any marketing loan benefits are calculated as the difference between the loan rate and the adjusted world price, it would be necessary to look at the expected adjusted world price to draw any conclusions.[36] This point is admitted by the United States in paragraph 75 of its 22 December 2003 Answers to Questions:"... because farmers will receive a government payment for the difference between the loan rate and the adjusted world price".[37]

---

32 US 22 December 2003 Answers to Questions, para. 20.

33 Exhibit Bra-281 (Statement of Andrew Macdonald – 7 October 2003, para. 13).

34 *Ibid.*

35 The United States appears to suggest this relationship in paragraph 21 of its 22 December 2003 Answers to Questions.

36 *See* Brazil's 2 December 2003 Oral Statement, Section 5.2 for further details on this point.

37 Brazil addresses this point in greater detail in its comment on Question 212 and 213 below.

18. Brazil also notes that the figures presented by the United States differ to a minor degree from the ones presented by Brazil.[38] Brazil does not know the reason for these minor differences and does not consider them to be material.

203. Please provide information concerning the organization, mandate, credentials and standing of FAPRI. BRA

204. Which support to upland cotton is not captured in the EWG data referred to in Brazil's 18 November further rebuttal submission? BRA

205. Does the United States accept or agree with the EWG data submitted by Brazil? If not, please explain your reasons. USA

Brazil's Comment:

19. As a preliminary comment, the United States answer does not rebut evidence from EWG's expert analyst that the EWG data undercounts the amount of contract payment and marketing loan payment subsidies.[39] While it undercounts the data, the EWG data and the estimates generated by Brazil's 14/16th methodology for MY 2002 are very close. Brazil estimates the MY 2002 direct payments to current cotton producers at $454.5 million[40], while the EWG data shows MY 2002 direct payments to current cotton producers of $451.4 million.[41] Similarly, Brazil's estimates that the MY 2002 CCP payments to current cotton producers were $935.6 million[42], while the EWG data shows $893 million.[43] Thus, as Brazil has argued, the EWG data could certainly be used by the Panel as evidence *supporting* Brazil's 14/16th methodology, as explained previously and elaborated further below.

20. The US 22 December 2003 response asserts, at paragraph 25, that Brazil has overestimated the support to upland cotton from contract payments. However, the summary US data produced on 18 and 19 December 2003 seems to show that only between 10-20 per cent of US upland cotton producers planted upland cotton on non-cotton base acreage.[44] The EWG data showed that, in MY 2002, 15 per cent of the contract payments received by current producers of

---

38 *Compare* US figures at paragraph 22 of the US 22 December 2003 Answers to Questions with Brazil's figures as reported in Exhibit Bra-356 (January – March Quotes of the December Futures Contract, Expected and Actual AWP and Cash Price) and at paragraph 44 of Brazil's 2 December 2003 Oral Statement.

39 Brazil's 18 November 2003 Further Rebuttal Submission, paras. 29-30; Exhibit Bra-316 (Statement of Christopher Campbell, paras. 12-15); Brazil's 22 December 2003 Answer to Question 204, paras. 25-26.

40 Brazil's 18 November 2003 Further Rebuttal Submission, para. 8.

41 Exhibit Bra-317 (Environmental Working Group Database: Table of Results, Table 2).

42 Brazil's 18 November 2003 Further Rebuttal Submission, para. 8.

43 Exhibit Bra-317 (Environmental Working Group Database: Table of Results, Table 2).

44 *See* Electronic PFC and DCP Summary Files provided by the United States on 18 and 19 December 2003 respectively, data for upland cotton production on farms without upland cotton base. Brazil notes that this does not mean that these farms have no contract base acreage whatsoever. Instead, the United States has withheld that data (Brazil's 28 January 2004 Comments and Requests Regarding US Data, Section 2).

upland cotton were from other contract acreage crops.[45] The United States refused to produce any information regarding current upland cotton production on non-upland cotton base acreage.[46] However, the EWG database – although understating the amounts – supports a finding that farms producing upland cotton received a significant amount of non-upland cotton contract payments. The EWG database therefore also supports an adverse inference by the Panel that the actual data withheld by the United States would show even higher payments to current upland cotton producers than the EWG data or the Brazilian estimates. It also demonstrates that the EWG data is not a comparable substitute for the information requested by the Panel on 8 December 2003 and 12 January 2004.[47] The EWG data contains no information about acreage planted and, thus, does not allow for any farm-specific allocation. It is also incomplete in terms of actual payments made.

21. The US statement in paragraph 24 of its 22 December 2003 response focuses on the large number of farms not receiving direct payments. What the United States largely ignores is the predominance of very small non-cotton producing farms that receive very small upland cotton base payments. In fact, according to the US summary data, the 45 per cent of farms that received upland cotton contract payments (but did not produce upland cotton) received only between 15 and 25 per cent of the upland cotton contract payments.[48] It is undisputed that the bulk of upland cotton is produced in very large operations[49], and the EWG data confirms this.[50] The EWG data shows that 5 per cent of farms receiving the highest amounts of upland cotton payments account for 41-45 per cent of marketing loan payments, *i.e.,* 41-45 per cent of production. The top 10 per cent of farms account for 55-58 per cent of production, and the top 20 per cent of farms account for 70-72 per cent of production.[51]

22. The United States makes the assertion in paragraph 25 of its 22 December 2003 response that in MY 2000-2002, "*only* 71, 77, and 74 per cent respectively of upland cotton base acreage payments went to farms that planted upland cotton". The United States claims this EWG data shows that Brazil's 14/16th methodology overestimates the amount of contract payments to upland cotton. This is incorrect. First, even the incomplete EWG data shows a very high percentage of

---

45 Exhibit Bra-317 (Environmental Working Group Database: Table of Results, Table 5 (MY 2002)).

46 US 18 and 19 December 2003 Letters to the Panel and US 20 January 2004 Letter to the Panel. *See* also Brazil's 28 January 2004 Comments and Requests Regarding US Data, Sections 2-3.

47 *See* Brazil's 28 January 2004 Comments and Requests Regarding US Data which details the information that could have been adduced with the information withheld by the United States.

48 *See* Electronic PFC and DCP Summary Files provided by the United States on 18 and 19 December 2003 respectively. The upland cotton contract acreage on farms not producing upland cotton represents between 15 and 25 per cent of total upland cotton contract acreage. Brazil has used contract acreage as a proxy for payments, which is a conservative proxy, as presumably the less productive farms (*i.e.* those with lower yields and thus fewer payment units per payments acre and fewer payments per acre) stopped producing upland cotton.

49 Brazil's 27 October 2003 Answer to Questions, paras 7-8.

50 Exhibit Bra-317 (Environmental Working Group Database: Table of Results, Table 3).

51 *Ibid.*

upland cotton contract payments directly connected with the current production of upland cotton. Second, the EWG data cannot be used to calculate the amount of non-upland cotton base payments attributable to current producers of upland cotton.[52] Because the EWG data cannot match contract acreage and planted acreage of the same farm – it is payment data, not acreage data. Given the fact that 10-20 per cent of US upland cotton is planted on farms without upland cotton base (but some other base acreage)[53], non-upland cotton contract payments would make up for the shortfall alleged by the United States.[54] This further highlights the need for the withheld US data. The United States obviously knows what the data shows and can easily calculate the amount of non-cotton base payments allocable to upland cotton production. The US decision not to release even "non-confidential" data that would show the amount of allocated payments is strong evidence that it knows that the actual data is larger than the EWG and Brazilian estimates.

23. Finally, the United States in paragraph 26 argues that summary data it produced on 18/19 December 2003 shows that in MY 2002, 29.4 per cent of total cropland on farms receiving upland cotton contract acreage payments was planted to upland cotton. This figure is highly misleading, because it includes all of the acreage from farms with upland cotton base acreage that do not plant upland cotton. When only farms that currently produce upland cotton are included, then about 50 per cent of the cropland acreage on these farms that actually produce upland cotton was planted to upland cotton. Indeed, the United States acknowledges this fact in paragraph 186 of its 22 December 2003 Answers to Questions.

24. Further, because of the US refusal to provide the information requested by the Panel on 8 December 2003 and 12 January 2004, it is impossible to determine from the US incomplete summary data the diversity of the cropland for upland cotton producers accounting for the majority of upland cotton production. Indeed, strong evidence that upland cotton producers concentrate in upland cotton production is found in the EWG data, which shows that 85 per cent of the contract payments received by upland cotton producers were *upland cotton* payments.[55] This supports USDA's own reports on cotton specialization, which indicate that the considerable bulk of cotton is produced in farms that specialize largely in upland cotton production.[56]

---

[52] Without the farm-specific data the United States has refused to produce, it is impossible to know for certain what non-upland cotton contract payments received by current upland cotton producers are properly allocated to upland cotton production.

[53] Even for those farms that mainly plant on upland cotton base, additional non-upland cotton contract payments would need to be allocated. *See* Electronic PFC and DCP Summary Files provided by the United States on 18 and 19 December 2003 respectively. *See* also Brazil's 20 January 2004 Answers to Additional Questions, paras. 43-55 and Brazil's 28 January 2004 Comments and Requests Regarding US Data, Section 9.

[54] *See* Brazil's 28 January 2004 Comments and Requests Regarding US Data, Section 9.

[55] Exhibit Bra-317 (EWG Database: Table of Results, Table 5, MY 2002, top line, far right side under "percentage of total contract payments", 85.07 per cent).

[56] Brazil's 27 October 2003 Answer to Question 125(a), paras. 7-10.

206. Please explain how the graph in paragraph 40 of the US further rebuttal submission was derived. In so doing, please clarify whether the figures are on a cents per pound basis or some other basis. What averaging method was used? Can you prepare individual charts showing average US and Brazilian cotton prices for each of those third country markets? USA

Brazil's Comment:

25. The United States asserts in paragraph 28 of its 22 December 2003 response that "FOB is greater than FAS except where the vessel is not changed at the port of export, in which case the values are equal". As set forth in the Second Declaration of Andrew Macdonald, "in practice there is in fact no difference in cost between FAS and FOB, since the ship loads and unloads the cargo, and thus, the difference in selling price between cotton which is sold FAS and cotton which is sold FOB is negligible".[57] Further, Mr. Macdonald agreed with the US statement quoted above, but noted that "vessels are rarely 'changed' in the port," and even if they were, "there would be an insignificant interest loss and thus, no difference between FAS and FOB values".[58] Brazil directs the Panel to Mr. Macdonald's Second Declaration, in which he provides additional details supporting his expert opinion.[59]

26. Brazil notes that the United States does not appear to have any difficulty with comparing Brazilian FOB prices with US FAS prices since it makes this comparison in the graph in paragraph 30 of its 22 December 2003 Answers to Questions. Because of the negligible difference between these two types of prices based on export value, Brazil agrees that there is no difficulty in comparing such FOB and FAS prices. This would include the various pricing comparisons between US and Brazilian prices set out in Brazil's 22 December 2003 Answers to Questions 233 and 235.

27. Finally, Brazil notes the US acknowledgement that the United States used only a "simple average unit price" comparison between US and Brazilian prices in paragraph 30 of its 22 December 2003 response. As Brazil has indicated, from a statistical point of view this is a totally inappropriate way to compare prices because of the enormous distortions it creates.[60] The United States should have used "weighted average" unit value pricing comparisons.

207. Please indicate whether any of the measures challenged in this dispute *obliges* cotton farmers to harvest their crop in order to receive the benefit of the programme (subsidy). USA

---

[57] Exhibit Bra-401 (Second Declaration of Andrew Macdonald, 27 January 2004, p. 2).

[58] *Ibid.*

[59] Exhibit Bra-401 (Second Declaration of Andrew Macdonald, 27 January 2004).

[60] *See* following webpages which discuss, in a variety of contexts, the significant distortions that can occur with statistics by using simple averages as opposed to weighted averages: http://www.statcan.ca/english/edu/power/ch13/estimation/estimation.htm; http://www.grantedc.com/publications/Grant%20Co%20Washington%20W&FB%20Report%202003.pdf

Brazil's Comment:

28. The United States confirms that the marketing loan programme requires farmers to harvest their upland cotton to receive marketing loan payments.[61] In addition, the Step 2 programme requires the use or export of upland cotton to trigger payments.[62] Brazil notes that the crop insurance programme requires farmers to *plant* upland cotton to receive premium subsidies. No harvest is required from farmers to receive indemnity payments, which in turn may trigger additional reinsurance payments to the private insurance companies running the crop insurance programme.[63]

208. Please provide data for the marketing years 1992 and 1999-2002 of the "quantity of production to receive the applied administered price" (*Agreement on Agriculture*, Annex 3, paragraph 8) for purposes of a price-gap calculation of support through the marketing loan programme. USA

Brazil's Comment:

29. Brazil notes that this question directly implicates earlier evidence and arguments demonstrating that the United States has never used a "price-gap" methodology for calculating its marketing loan portion of AMS, *inter alia*, for upland cotton.[64] Rather, the United States has always used and notified a *budgetary* methodology in accounting for marketing loan payments (marketing loans, loan deficiency, certificate payments, and interest & storage payments).[65] In particular, when it agreed with other WTO Members on what the US "base level" would be for purposes of Total AMS, the United States chose to calculate marketing loan payments using a budgetary approach.

30. This is easily seen by first examining Exhibit Bra-191[66], which is a document in which the United States notified "supporting material related to commitments on agricultural products contained in Schedule XX - United States". Marketing loan payments for upland cotton are listed on page 20 of the document. The document lists the US loan deficiency payments for upland cotton for MY 1986 as $126.860 million, for MY 1987 as $0.364 million, and for MY 1998 as $42.038 million. Comparing these figures with the actual budgetary outlays for loan deficiency payments in MY 1986-88, as set out in Exhibit Bra-4, show the same figures (rounded out). Similar *budgetary* outlays are used for marketing loan gains and interest and storage payments that are also related to "marketing loan payments". In addition, Exhibit Bra-191[67] contains an Annex which is the "Supporting Table for Cotton:Deficiency Payment Calculation for GATT AMS." This table is there because the United States used the "price-gap"

61 US 22 December 2003 Answers to Questions, para. 31.

62 *Ibid.*

63 Brazil's 24 June 2003 First Submission, paras. 80-83.

64 *See* Brazil's 27 August 2003 Comments on US Rebuttal Submission, paras. 10-16.

65 *See, e.g.,* Exhibit Bra-191 (G/AG/AGST/USA, p. 20); Exhibit Bra-47 (G/AG/N/USA/43, p. 20); Exhibit Bra-150 (G/AG/N/USA/10, p. 18).

66 G/AG/AGST/USA, p. 20.

67 G/AG/AGST/USA, p. 21-22.

formula of Annex 3, paragraph 10 of the Agreement on Agriculture to calculate the AMS for deficiency payments. But no such supporting table exists for marketing loan payments, because a *budgetary* approach was used. In short, there is no doubt that the United States Total AMS Commitments were based, *inter alia*, on the US decision to use *budgetary* outlays for calculating its marketing loan payments for upland cotton.

31. The US decision under Annex 3, paragraph 10 to use budgetary outlays instead of the price-gap formula in calculating upland cotton AMS for marketing loan payments is legally binding on the United States. Annex 3, paragraph 5 states that "[t]he AMS calculated as outlined *below* [*i.e.,* paragraphs 6-13 of Annex 3] shall constitute the *base level* for the implementation of the reduction commitments on domestic support." The marketing loan budgetary decision reflected in G/AG/AGST/USA was incorporated into the US schedules and set the US "base level" of total AMS. The title of the G/AG/AGST/USA suggests its legally binding character – "Supporting Tables Relating to Commitments on Agricultural Products in Part IV of the Schedules." These "supporting tables" were the basis upon which the "final bound commitment level specified in Part IV" of the US schedule was determined.

32. Annex 3, paragraph 5 of the Agreement on Agriculture indicates that the United States is bound by its initial decision to calculate AMS using a budgetary approach (as permitted in Annex 3, paragraph 10 of the Agreement on Agriculture). This conclusion follows from the text of Article 6.3 of the Agreement on Agriculture:

> A Member shall be considered to be in compliance with its domestic support reduction commitments in any year in which its domestic support in favour of agricultural producers expressed in terms of Current Total AMS *does not exceed the corresponding annual or final bound commitment level specified in Part IV of the Member's Schedule.*

33. Further, Article 3.2 provides that "[s]ubject to the provisions of Article 6, a Member shall not provide support in favour of domestic producers in excess of commitment levels specified in Section I of Part IV of its Schedule". The United States' "final bound commitment level specified in Section I of Part IV" of the US Schedule is currently $19.1 billion. Nothing in Article 6 or any other provision of the Agreement on Agriculture permits a Member such as the United States to change its Annex 3, paragraph 10 choice of budgetary or price gap calculations for the purposes of calculating *current* AMS.

34. Brazil has previously detailed the reasons why permitting Members to reverse the Annex 3, paragraph 10 choice to calculate *current* AMS for a product would make the disciplines of Article 3.2 and 6.3 of the Agreement on Agriculture inutile.[68] The United States never denied it has always notified marketing loan payments using a budgetary approach, and has never rebutted Brazil's ar-

[68] Brazil's 27 August 2003 Comments on US 22 August 2003 Rebuttal Submission, paras. 10-16.

guments that permitting a Member to change its election under Annex 3, paragraph 10 to calculate *current* AMS would lead to the nullification of a Member's obligations under Articles 3.2 and 6.3. Indeed, the US Answer to Question 208 provides the best example of such a nullification, when the United States admits that "if the applied administered price for marketing years 1999-2002 were compared to the 1992 applied administered price, the resulting negative numbers ... show the decrease in the level of support from MY 1992."[69] Translated, this means that the huge increase in marketing loan payments to $2.5 billion in marketing loan payments in MY 2001 would not be counted towards US total AMS for MY 2001.

35. Brazil emphasizes again that while the United States makes what are theoretical arguments in this dispute, its WTO partners properly rely on the past and most recent US notifications.[70] And these notifications consistently demonstrate that the United States properly treats the *budgetary outlays* for marketing loan payments for cotton as well as other programme crops as part of its total current AMS. These notifications further demonstrate that US budgeted outlays for marketing loans have significantly increased in MY 1999-2002 over the level of such loans in MY 1992.[71]

36. In light of the arguments and evidence set out above, there is little need for Brazil to comment on the calculations provided by the US 22 December 2003 response. Brazil notes that the US applies a contradictory approach to the quantity of eligible production for MY 1992 and MY 1999-2002. For example, the United States uses actual production figures calculated from *harvested* acreage for MY 1999-2002, while it calculates eligible production for MY 1992 as *planted* eligible acreage multiplied by the *yield on harvested* acreage.[72] This grossly overstates the eligible production. In fact, the US "eligible production" figures even overstate *actual* production in MY 1992 by 432,333 bales.[73] The actual eligible production for MY 1992 was 6.485 billion pounds[74], not the 7.748 billion calculated by the United States.[75] When compared to the actual production eligible for marketing loans in MY 1999-2002, the Panel can see that significantly greater US upland cotton production was provided marketing loan benefits in each of those later years compared to MY 1992.

---

69 US 22 December 2003 Answer to Question 208, para. 37.

70 *See, e.g.,* Exhibit Bra-191 (G/AG/AGST/USA, p. 20); Exhibit Bra-47 (G/AG/N/USA/43, p. 20); Exhibit Bra-150 (G/AG/N/USA/10, p. 18).

71 Brazil's 9 September 2003 Further Submission, Table 1.

72 US 22 December 2003 Answer to Question 208, paras 33-35.

73 *Compare* US figure at paragraph 33 of its 22 December 2003 Answers to Questions (16,142,333 bales) with the actual production in MY 1992 of 15,710,000 bales, as reported in Exhibit Bra-4 ("Fact Sheet: Upland Cotton", USDA, January 2003, p. 4).

74 11,164,726 planted eligible acres times 0.837 (share of planted acres that was harvested (Exhibit Bra-4 ("Fact Sheet: Upland Cotton," USDA, January 2003, p. 4 (Abandonment Rate))) times 694 pounds per harvested acre (Exhibit Bra-4 ("Fact Sheet: Upland Cotton," USDA, January 2003, p. 4 (Yield))).

75 US 22 December 2003 Answers to Questions, para. 33.

209. It is understood that the data in the graph in paragraph 5 of the US oral statement are as at harvest time, while the data in the graph in paragraph 39 of Brazil's oral statement are as at planting time. Please explain why the trend of US acreage increase/decrease differs between these two graphs. BRA, USA

Brazil's Comment:

37. Brazil reemphasizes its position that only planted acres constitute a reliable measure for planting decisions in a single country, such as the United States.[76] This is highlighted by the fact that changes in planted and harvested acreage for the United States during MY 1996-2003 do not move in parallel. Contrary to the US assertion that the "movements in acreage figures are *fairly similar*"[77], in fact, the US planted and harvested acreage changes are in entirely opposite directions in 3 out of 8 marketing years[78], vary by great magnitudes in a further 3 out of 8 marketing years[79], and are "fairly similar" only in 2 out of 8 marketing years.[80] This overall picture can hardly be called "fairly similar" movements. Brazil refers the Panel to its 22 December 2003 Answer to Question 210[81], demonstrating that in fact US planted acreage and a proxy for worldwide planted acreage move in quite opposite directions, demonstrating that US producers of upland cotton do not take their planting decisions based on the same market-based price factors as other producers worldwide.[82]

210. Are worldwide planted acreage figures available? BRA, USA

Brazil's Comment:

38. Brazil agrees that no data on harvested acres is available on a worldwide basis. However, Brazil strongly disagrees that the only possible comparison between US and worldwide upland cotton acreage needs to be done on the basis of harvested acreage.[83] As discussed before, the only valid measure of farmers planting decisions is planted acres, as harvested acres figures are distorted by variations over time in the abandonment rate.[84] Therefore, it is critical to use planted acreage for the United States in any analysis of congruence in planting decisions between the United States and the rest of the world. However, harvested acres may serve as a proxy for planted acreage on a worldwide basis.[85]

---

[76] Brazil's 27 October 2003 Answers to Questions, paras. 27-28; Brazil's 18 November 2003 Further Rebuttal Submission, para. 87; Brazil's 22 December 2003 Answers to Questions, paras. 30-32.

[77] US 22 December 2003 Answers to Questions, para. 39.

[78] MY 1997, 1999, 2000.

[79] MY 1996, 1998, 2001.

[80] MY 2002, 2003.

[81] Brazil's 22 December 2003 Answers to Questions, para. 31-36.

[82] Brazil's 18 November 2003 Further Rebuttal Submission, Section 3.4 (containing further references).

[83] US 22 December 2003 Answers to Questions, para. 40.

[84] Brazil's 27 October 2003 Answers to Questions, paras. 27-28; Brazil's 18 November 2003 Further Rebuttal Submission, para. 87; Brazil's 22 December 2003 Answers to Questions, paras. 30-32.

[85] Brazil's 22 December 2003 Answers to Questions, para. 32.

On this basis, no congruence exists between the planting decisions of US upland cotton farmers and upland cotton farmers worldwide.[86] But, even if one were to look at harvested acres for both US and worldwide planting decisions, there is no congruence in the movements.[87]

211. Brazil presents a graph in paragraph 59 of its further rebuttal submission indicating the increasing cumulative loss incurred by cotton producers. Please comment on the argument that US cotton producers could not continue operating without subsidies. In particular:

(a) to what extent does the use of 1997 survey technological coefficients with annually updated values affect the results?

Brazil's Comment:

39. Brazil reads the Panel's question as requesting the United States to provide an estimate of how much the updated 2003 USDA ARMS 1997 survey overstates the $872 per acre deficit between total costs and market revenue for the period MY 1997-2002. The United States' 22 December 2003 response declines to provide any dollar per acre estimate. Indeed, the US response appears to raise more questions than it provides answers.

40. The United States has claimed that the 2003 USDA cost data used by Brazil in calculating the $872 per acre deficit[88] cannot be relied on by the Panel.[89] Because this is a fact asserted by the United States, it has the burden of establishing it.[90] The Panel should expect the United States, which employees the USDA personnel who created the 2003 cotton update of the 1997 ARMS study, to have provided statements or other evidence from these cost experts explaining why the 2003 update is unreliable and cannot be used by the Panel. No such statements were provided. Brazil has examined the websites of USDA and the US National Cotton Council carefully and cannot find any warnings that the 2003 upland cotton costs and revenue are unreliable. Indeed, the current NCC website provides a direct link to the ERS-USDA costs and returns website for each major US region.[91] Presumably, the NCC intended its Members to rely on such data or they would not have included the link. Further, the United States neglected to inform the Panel that the 2003 upland cotton cost and revenue data has benefited from a "new costs of production estimation methodology" implementing the American Agricultural Economics Association (AAEA) Recommendations.[92] It is reasonable for the Panel to find that the 2003 cotton updates

[86] Brazil's 22 December 2003 Answers to Questions, para. 33.

[87] Brazil's 22 December 2003 Answers to Questions, para. 34.

[88] Brazil's 18 November 2003 Further Rebuttal Submission, Section 3.1.

[89] *See e.g.* US 22 December 2003 Answers to Questions, para. 43.

[90] *See e.g.* Appellate Body Report, *Japan – Apples*, WT/DS245/AB/R, para. 157 ("It is important to distinguish, on the one hand, the principle that the complainant must establish a *prima facie* case of inconsistency with a provision of a covered agreement from, on the other hand, the principle that the party that asserts a fact is responsible for providing proof thereof.").

[91] http://risk.cotton.org/CotBudgets/cotbudget.htm, visited 20 January 2004.

[92] *See* www.ers.usda.gov/briefing/FarmIncome/Glossary/compare.htm visited 28 January 2004. A link to this ERS page is provided on the NCC Webpage.

to the 1997 ARMS study using this new AAEA-recommended methodology results in a more accurate estimate of cotton costs and revenues – not a less accurate estimate.

41. What the United States attempts to prove in its 22 December 2003 Answer to Question 211(a) is that the use of biotechnology cotton ("BT cotton") has lowered costs, and that somehow these lower costs were not reflected in the annual updated USDA costs and returns surveys. It is noteworthy that the United States now admits that the USDA personnel updating the 1997 ARMS study *properly* updated the cost of production data to show increased upland cotton seed costs.[93] But, without citing any proof, the United States asserts that these same personnel that *properly* updated the cotton cost data (to reflect *increased* (BT-cotton and overall) seed costs) improperly failed to "capture the *cost savings* from technological changes that alter the mix of production activities and inputs."[94]

42. The credibility of this assertion is difficult to accept given the fact that the US government during the period of investigation touted the productivity benefits of using, *inter alia*, BT-cotton.[95] Indeed, an Economic Research Service-USDA Report updated through 27 October 1999 analyzed ARMS data concerning the use of BT cotton.[96] The ERS report identified increased yields and lower use (and hence costs) of pesticides as indicated below:

> Comparison of mean yields shows that in most cases (4 of 7 region/year cases for which data were sufficient) adopters of Bt cotton appear to obtain statistically significant higher yields than nonadopters. Although less prevalent, similar results (2 of 5 cases) were observed for Bt corn. For the case of herbicide-tolerant crops, the results are mixed: only for a few regions and in some years are yields higher for adopters. Most of the time (4 of 5 for corn, 9 of 13 for soybeans, 3 of 5 for cotton), differences in yields are statistically insignificant.
>
> Comparison of mean pesticide acre-treatments for 1997 shows that in most cases (2 of 3) the adoption of Bt cotton reduces treatments of insecticides normally used on the pests targeted by Bt. In 1 of 3 cases, total treatments for all other cotton pests are higher for adopters than nonadopters. Insecticide treatments for Bt-targeted pests on corn are significantly lower for Bt users than for nonusers. Adoption of herbicide-tolerant varieties accompanied statistically significant reductions in herbicide treatments in 4 of 8 cases across all crops, mostly for soybeans.

---

93 US 22 December 2003 Answer to Question 211(a), para. 45.

94 *Ibid.*

95 See http://www.ers.usda.gov/publications/tb1906/tb1906b.pdf visited 28 January 2004; US 22 December 2003 Answers to Questions, para. 44 (note 44).

96 http://www.pestlaw.com/x/guide/1999/USDA-19990625A.html visited 28 January 2004.

It is difficult to imagine how USDA ERS personnel working with ARMS survey data could arrive at the conclusions of (a) higher yields for BT cotton and (b) lower use of pesticides and chemicals in 1999 as detailed above, but the USDA personnel updating the cotton cost data in 1999-2002 could *not.* This evidence suggests that because information on the cost savings for using BT cotton were widely available for farmers and the ERS, then they would also be known to those updating the cotton cost survey. Thus, the Panel can conclude that the published USDA cost survey properly identified both cost increases and cost savings.

43. Finally, to attempt to answer the Panel's question concerning the graph at paragraph 59 of Brazil's 18 November 2003 Further Rebuttal Submission, Brazil analyzed the extent to which any alleged overstating of costs could impact on the huge $872 per acre cost-revenue gap. The answer, as outlined below, is very little.

44. To conduct this analysis, Brazil first assumed, contrary to the evidence outlined above, that the USDA employees updating the cost savings data[97] "got it wrong". Brazil then determined that the largest published estimate of the possible cost savings for using BT-cotton was $20 per acre.[98] The next step was to determine that between 1997-2002 an average of 58 per cent of cotton acreage was planted to BT-cotton between MY 1998-2002. This is reflected in the graph below:[99]

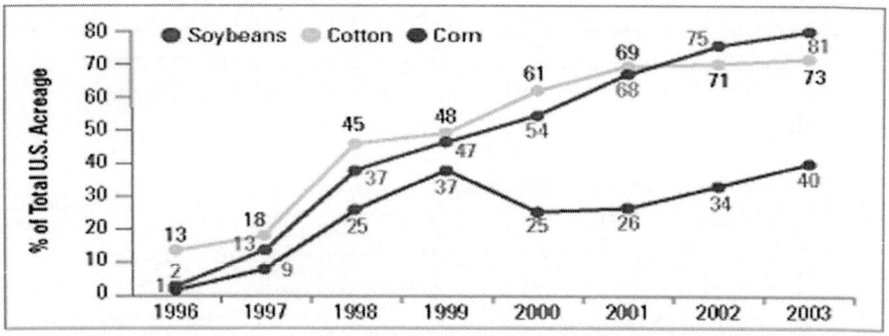

45. With 58 per cent of US acreage between 1998-2002 was planted to BT-cotton, this meant that the average per acre national cotton cost savings was $12 between 1997-2002 (0.58 x $20). But recall that the United States answer claims that the USDA 1998-2002 cost data reflects the cost increases for BT-cotton seed, but not the cost savings from use of fewer chemicals. Therefore, to reflect

97 Brazil's 27 October 2003 Answers to Questions, p. 56 (setting out USDA data).

98 Exhibit Bra-404 (Monsanto Imagine, "Benefits – BT Cotton" downloaded from www.monsanto.co/monsanto/layout/our_pledge/bnefits/bt_cotton.asp visited 28 January 2004). The document concludes that the average US cotton farmer using BT –cotton has "average net incomes ... increased by $50 per hectare in the United States" The Monsanto assertion of $50 per hectare translates into $20.2 per acre because one hectare constitutes 2.47 acres.

99 http://www.whybiotech.com/index.asp? id= visited 28 January 2004.

the *net* cost savings, Brazil further deducted the difference in between increased cotton-seed in 1997 and between 1998-2002 ($12.8 per acre).[100] Thus, in the best-case US scenario, the total amount of average cost savings allegedly *not* reflected in published USDA data was $24.8 per acre.

46. Brazil recalls that the total six-year *deficit* between total costs and total revenue from USDA's 2003 revenue and costs estimates (*i.e.,* the updated 1997 ARMS Study) is $872 per acre.[101] Brazil then assumed (1) the accuracy of the $12 per acre net cost reduction from using BT-cotton, (2) that the $12 per acre net cost savings existed for the entire 1998-2002 period, and (3) that USDA cost experts updating the 1997 ARMS Study in 1998-2002 were not aware of such cost reductions or improperly failed to include them in the latest USDA update of cotton revenue and costs, then the 1997-2002 deficit between USDA's total reported costs and total market revenue would still be $748 per acre.[102]

47. In sum, while Brazil believes that at least some of the assumptions listed above are highly questionable, the "best case" that the United States could have put forward (but did not) shows continued huge long-term deficits of $748 per acre between US producers' total costs and their market revenue. In short, the United States has not met its burden of proving that its own USDA data was hopelessly flawed. Brazil and the Panel can properly rely on the 2003 cotton cost and revenue data showing either $872 or $748 average per acre deficits between costs and market revenue during MY 1997-2002. Both figures reflect huge gaps between market revenue and total costs of production. As Brazil has argued, this evidence strongly supports the significant impact of the US subsidies on US production, exports and on world prices.

(ii) Comment on US Argument concerning Canada Dairy

48. Finally, Brazil notes the US attempt to distinguish the Appellate Body's decision in *Canada – Dairy* in paragraph 42 of the US 22 December 2003 Answer to Question 211. In assessing the credibility of these new US arguments, it is instructive to review what the United States argued before the Appellate Body in *Canada – Dairy*. First, on the issue of whether average cost of production data should be used, the United States made the following arguments in *Canada – Dairy*:

> [T]he Panel correctly recognized that an individual producer cost of production benchmark was unworkable. The Panel noted that governments rarely have the sort of detailed, producer-specific information that such a test would require. Indeed, as discussed be-

---

[100] This was done by subtracting the amount of increased seed costs in Exhibit Bra-323 (Costs and Returns of US Upland Cotton Farmers, MY 1997-2002) from MY 1997 – this was 0 in 1998, $1 in 1999, $13 in 2000, $20 in 2001, and $30 in 2002.

[101] Brazil's 18 November 2003 Further Rebuttal Submission, paras. 59-62.

[102] This figure has been calculated by applying the $12 per acre time five years (which is conservative, because in earlier years less Bt-cotton was planted) and also deducting the yearly increases in seed costs (compared to the 1997 basis), since the $12 represented a net cost saving, *i.e.,* net of cost increases to due higher seed costs.

> low, Canada itself was unable to supply the necessary data regarding individual producer participation in the CEM market to support its claim that no payments were being made.…In sum, the Panel's reliance on the CDC's average total cost of production data as a 'sufficient, albeit conservative, approximation of the average total cost of production of the Canadian dairy industry' is consistent with the Appellate Body's instruction to sue an average total cost of production benchmark in this case.

49. The Panel will recall that the United States in this dispute has argued that using an average total cost of production was not appropriate.[103] Yet, as in *Canada – Dairy*, the issue in this dispute is not whether there are *certain* producers that may sell cotton (or milk) below their total cost of production. Of course, there will be some efficient producers who will be able to do so, even with few or no subsidies. Rather, the issue generally in both cases is whether, on *average*, the producers' total costs of production are above the prices received by the producers in the relevant markets. Thus, as in *Canada – Dairy,* the average total cost of production generated by USDA and used by Brazil is more than a "useful approximation".

50. The United States' arguments in this dispute that fixed costs should *not* be considered by the Panel mirrored arguments made by Canada in *Canada – Dairy*. Consider the following arguments made by the United States (which were accepted by the Appellate Body) in *Canada – Dairy* and which are practically identical to arguments made by Brazil in this dispute:

> With respect to imputed costs, the Panel correctly recognized that these are "real costs" that a producer must recoup in order to stay in business over time. In economic terms, these costs represent opportunity costs or the costs associated with opportunities that are foregone by not putting the producers' resources to their best use. The producers' resources include family labour, its managerial services, and its capital. There is a cost associated with using all of these resources. For example, if a farmer foregoes the opportunity to earn cash wages off the farm in order to contribute his labour to the farm's production, the value of his labour is properly counted as an economic cost to the farm even though the farmer does not pay cash wages to himself. Likewise, it makes no sense to suggest, as Canada does, that the farm which hires labour and management services is incurring a cost, while the farm that uses family labour and management is making a profit.[104]
>
> Likewise, the Panel correctly concluded that there was no basis to exclude the marketing, transportation, and administrative costs included in the CDC cost of production data. …[T]he panel properly

---

[103] US 18 November 2003 Further Rebuttal Submission, Section IV.F.3(1) – (4).

[104] Appellee Submission of the United States, *Canada – Dairy (21.5)(II),* para. 40 (*see* http://www.ustr.gov/enforcement/briefs.shtml).

> concluded that these are also 'real costs' that producers must recoup if they are to remain in business over time. ...The costs incurred by the farmer that must be recouped to avoid going out of business do not stop at the 'farm gate'.[105]

Brazil agrees with the United States that all of the costs identified above (which the Appellate Body accepted in its decision) are "real costs" that a producer must recoup "in order to stay in business over time". This is precisely Brazil's point in this case.

51. The United States argues that *Canada – Dairy* is inapposite because "the issue for which Brazil seeks to use total costs is not whether a subsidy exists but to evaluate the effect of the subsidy, an altogether different analysis".[106] First, this is incorrect as a factual matter. One use of the total cost of production data by Brazil has been as circumstantial evidence to demonstrate that contract payments are support to upland cotton and that such payments provide a benefit to US upland cotton producers.[107] This is directly analogous to the issue of whether the subsidy existed in Article 9.1(c) of the Agreement on Agriculture in *Canada – Dairy*.

52. Second, the evidence of the total cost of production was used in both cases to demonstrate that both dairy and cotton producers were selling their products into a market well below their total costs of production. In *Canada – Dairy*, Canadian producers were selling C-milk into the export market well below their total cost of production. In cotton, the US producers were selling into all identifiable markets at well below their total costs of production.[108] And in both cases, the subsidies provided by the Canadian and US governments permitted these producers to continue to produce without regard for the gap between market revenue and total costs of production. In sum, without both the *Canada – Dairy* panel and this Panel examining *total* costs of production, it would be difficult to determine whether all the alleged subsidies existed, and second, to determine the role that subsidies played in maintaining production.

(a) to what extent do producers base planting decisions on their ability to cover operating costs but not whole farm costs? USA

Brazil's Comment:

53. Brazil generally agrees that covering operating costs are important to producers who are making planting decisions "in the short term – that is, the market

---

[105] Appellee Submission of the United States, *Canada – Dairy (21.5)(II)*, para. 42 (*see* http://www.ustr.gov/enforcement/briefs.shtml).

[106] US 22 December 2003 Answer to Question 211, para. 42.

[107] Brazil's 22 August 2003 Rebuttal Submission, paras. 30-41; Brazil's 18 November 2003 Further Rebuttal Submission, paras. 59-72; Brazil's 2 December 2003 Oral Statement, paras. 25-33.

[108] *Compare* the prices set out in Brazil's 22 December 2003 Answers to Questions 233 and 235, and in Exhibits Bra-383 – Bra-388, *with* US total cost of production data in Exhibit Bra-323 (Costs and Returns of US upland cotton Farmers MY 1997-2002).

price for one year".[109] And it is true that during a one-year "short term" period, a producer may be able to afford to receive revenue that only meets its operating costs and at least some of the fixed costs.[110] But the US 22 December 2003 Answer to Question 211(b) appears to suggest[111] that even over a long-term period of time – between 5-10 years – producers can continue to plant upland cotton oblivious to whether they meet their total costs of production. This is, of course, economic nonsense for agriculture or any other economic sector.

54. Basic economics holds that no business can continue to operate unless its total costs of production are met over the long term. The United States recognizes this when it states, in its 18 November 2003 Further Rebuttal Submission, that "in the long run, producers will have to cover these asset and overhead (i.e., economic) costs".[112] USDA's ERS suggests that the long term is a period between 5-10 years[113], and Christopher Ward testified that the normal recovery period for cotton equipment investments is 5-7 years.[114] In light of this evidence, Brazil focused on *total costs* for a six-year period of time between MY 1997-2002 in analyzing the long-term cost/revenue gap.[115] By contrast, the US graph at paragraph 47 of its 22 December 2003 Answer to Question 211(b) improperly focuses on only operating costs. Neither the US graph nor the US response provides any hint as to how US cotton producers could survive for six years without market revenue covering their fixed costs, *i.e.,* covering lease or mortgage payments, paying labor, recovering equipment costs, and paying taxes and insurance.[116] In fact, the land-specific costs must be paid every year simply to be able to continue farming on leased land or to avoid foreclosure in the case of owner-operators.[117]

55. The US arguments that economists are only concerned with examining operating costs, and not total costs, are simply not correct. For example, the University of California Cooperative Extension economists conduct a large number of studies regarding costs of production for different types of, *inter alia*, upland cotton farms in California. Every one of these studies, which are relied on throughout the agricultural industry in California and other states, contains a

---

109 US 9 October 2003 Closing Statement, para. 12 (The full context of the quote is as follows: "Total costs are relevant over the long-term, but Brazil uses this (inaccurate) number to compare to revenue in the short term – that is, the market price for one year.").

110 *See* Exhibit Bra-283 (Statement of Christopher Ward – 7 October 2003, paras. 7-10).

111 *See* in particular the graph at paragraph 47 of the US 22 December 2003 Answer to Question 211(b).

112 US 18 November 2003 Further Rebuttal Submission, para. 122.

113 Exhibit US-84 (Production Costs Critical To Farming Decisions, William D. McBride, ERS, p. 40 (quoted in US 18 November 2003 Further Rebuttal Submission, para. 118).

114 Exhibit Bra-283 (Statement of Christopher Ward – 7 October 2003, para. 10).

115 This was not, therefore, a "randomly selected period," as the United States alleges in paragraph 41 of its 22 December 2003 Answer to Question 211(a).

116 *See* Brazil's 18 November 2003 Further Rebuttal Submission, paras. 64-69 (setting forth composition of fixed costs. This evidence has never been rebutted by the United States).

117 *Ibid.*

detailed examination of all types of costs.[118] Other economic studies of the cost of production similarly provide for total costs, including the land charge and rents.[119]

56. Additional evidence that total costs are relevant to planting decisions even in the short term of one year is found in several documents on an intended but not introduced "Cost of Production Insurance Plan for Cotton". The entire intent of this project to develop new a insurance programme was to provide comprehensive insurance covering *total costs* – not just operating costs.[120] If upland cotton producers were solely concerned with covering only their operating costs each year, then the project would not also have sought to provide cotton producers with protection from increased fixed costs such as leasing land, employing workers, and annual financing costs for replacement equipment. Yet, the "Cost of Production Insurance Plan for Cotton" programme focused on *annual* protection that would include all types of costs, because that is what the sponsors perceived farmers needed.

57. Finally, the Panel should recognize that the most efficient low-cost US producers will be able to withstand lower market prices without the need for significant subsidies for a year or two. But higher-cost producers will not. The ERS study on production costs cited by the United States highlighted the ability of higher-cost producers to survive in the shorter term only through government payments:

> Low-cost producers are generally better able to survive periods of low prices and thrive when prices improve, while high-cost producers are often the first to exit farming when prices are low.[121]

** ** ** **

[118] Exhibit Bra-405 (Sample Cost to Produce Cotton – Transgenic Herbicide-Resistant Alacla Variety, San Joaquin Valley, University of California Cooperative Extension, 2003). A large number of cost of production studies by the University of California Cooperative Extension for cotton, as well as for many other crops, can be found at www.ucanr.org/CES.CEA.shtml.

[119] Exhibit Bra-406 (Cotton Cost-Return Budget in Southwest Kansas, Kansas State University Agricultural Experiment Station and Cooperative Extensive Service, October 2003).

[120] Exhibit Bra-407 (Documents on Cost of Production Insurance Plan for Cotton)("Review of the FCIC Cost of Production Insurance Plan for Cotton," Sparks Companies, Inc., 15 September 2003, p. 11, 12 and 16. (COP insurance policy is based on the *farmer's total cost*.")); "Underwriting Review of FCIC Cost of Production Insurance Plan for Cotton," Jeffrey T. LaFrance, Ph.D, 13 September 2003, p. 5 ("… the basis for the guarantee is not a farmer-chosen percentage of expected or predicted revenue; rather it is a percentage of an estimate of the *total cost of production*.); "Review of Poposed 'Cost of Production Insurance Plan for Cotton,' Jerry R. Skees, Dr. Barry J. Barnett, Dr. J. Roy Black, and James Long, 15 September 2003, p.32 ("Purchasers will be required to provide estimates of variable expenses per acre, *fixed expenses per acre, and land expenses per acre* in addition to the acreage and historical yield information required for existing cotton insurance products.") emphasis added

[121] Exhibit US-84 (Production Costs Critical To Farming Decisions, William D. McBride, ERS, p. 40). This study includes a graph regarding wheat farmers on page 41 which illustrates that low-cost producers can survive much lower prices while higher-cost wheat farmers require much higher prices even to meet their operating costs. The same dynamic exists for US cotton farmers.

> Also, this cost-price squeeze has put an emphasis on enhancing revenues through a variety of sources, such as government programmes, and on controlling or cutting costs. Government programme support has likely helped many producers remain in business and may explain why structural adjustments in these industries have been gradual.[122]

Many US upland cotton producers are "high-cost" producers, according to USDA's latest comprehensive cost of production survey.[123] Brazil notes that Professor Sumner found that roughly 70 per cent of US planted acreage would continue to be planted to upland cotton even without the US subsidies.[124] This finding that 30 per cent of the US cotton acreage would not remain planted to cotton is consistent with the conclusion that it is the category of high-cost cotton producers that would not be able to survive without US subsidies – even in the short term.

212. Brazil states in paragraph 37 of its oral statement that studies of Westcott and Price found that the effect of the programme on cotton is to add an additional 1 to 1.5 million acres during marketing years 1999-2001 and to suppress US prices by 5 cents per pound. Does the US reject these findings? Why or why not? USA

Brazil's Comment:

58. At the outset, Brazil notes that USDA economists Westcott and Price are among the most experienced and well-respected USDA analysts, who both have long records of publication of US government reports and other research studies. They have an in-depth knowledge of the marketing loan programme. Further, they received comments and suggestions for their study from leading US agricultural economists such as Professor Bruce Gardner.[125] Westcott and Price's study was their best estimate of the effects of the marketing loan programme. It bears repeating that they developed their study independently of this dispute in 2000.

59. The Westcott/Price study is an approved USDA paper published by USDA's Economic Research Service.[126] It is only during this dispute that the United States' government began to characterize this study as an "interesting 'academic' exercise"[127], whereas, outside this dispute, its results represent USDA's official view on the effects of the marketing loan programme.

---

[122] Exhibit US-84 (Production Costs Critical To Farming Decisions, William D. McBride, ERS, p. 41).

[123] Exhibit Bra-16 ("Characteristics and Production Costs of US Cotton Farms", USDA, October 2001).

[124] Brazil's 9 September 2003 Further Submission, Annex I, Table 5a.

[125] Exhibit Bra-222 ("Analysis of the US Commodity Loan Program with Marketing Loan Provisions," USDA, AER 801, cover page).

[126] Exhibit Bra-222 ("Analysis of the US Commodity Loan Programme with Marketing Loan Provisions", USDA, AER 801).

[127] US 22 December 2003 Answers to Questions, para. 48.

60. Brazil recalls that the US Payment Limitations Commission, chaired by USDA's Chief Economist, requested Westcott and Price to update their study and analyze the effects of the marketing loan programme in MY 2001.[128] This official US Commission never criticized the approach chosen by Westcott and Price; rather, the Payment Limitations Commission relied on it. It is not clear to Brazil why the United States considers this study to be appropriate for analyzing effects of current agricultural policies and for considering policy reform proposals such as more effective payment limitations in a domestic political context, but, when US upland cotton subsidy programmes undergo multilateral scrutiny in a WTO context, the United States considers the very same study to be fatally flawed and unreliable.

61. Indeed, the United States goes so far as to characterize the Westcott/Price study as irrelevant for the analysis of this Panel.[129] The United States claims that using baseline projections for the period MY 1999-2001 will not suffice for the Panel's analysis, as the Panel needs to assess "actual conditions".[130] Brazil notes that the 2000 USDA baseline actually projected much higher prices than occurred during the period MY 1999-2001, thus the 5-cent per pound price suppression found by Westcott and Price understate the effects of "actual conditions".[131] This is confirmed by the fact that, when Westcott and Price used actual data to update their study for the Payment Limitations Commission, their results showed much stronger effects of the marketing loan programme.[132] Brazil notes that Professor Sumner has analyzed the effects of the marketing loan programme using actual MY 1999-2001 data.[133] Not surprisingly, the overall results of both Westcott/Price studies are in line with Professor Sumner's results.[134]

62. The United States also rejects the Westcott/Price study because its lagged price analysis based on the 2000 USDA baseline allegedly would not reflect farmers' actual price expectations.[135] Brazil and Professor Sumner have addressed the issues of the inappropriateness of using futures prices in complex modeling systems before.[136] The undisputed evidence is that – as the United States itself admits[137] – futures market prices cannot be used for such modeling systems.[138]

---

128 Brazil's 7 October 2003 Oral Statement, paras. 31-34.

129 US 22 December 2003 Answers to Questions, para. 48.

130 US 22 December 2003 Answers to Questions, para. 49. Brazil notes that the United States understands "actual conditions" to refer to actual price expectations held by US upland cotton producers. These are, however, as Brazil and the United States agree, "fundamentally unobservable".

131 Brazil also notes that the 2000 USDA baseline contained actual data for MY 1998, *i.e.,* the Westcott/Price study used USDA's FAPSIM model for retrospective analysis.

132 *See* Brazil's 7 October 2003 Oral Statement, paras. 31-34.

133 *See* Annex I of Brazil's 9 September 2003 Further Submission, para. 4, Table I.5e (regarding the data used, baseline and resulting effects of the marketing loan programme).

134 *See inter alia* Brazil's 7 October 2003 Oral Statement, paras. 9, 34.

135 US 22 December 2003 Answers to Questions, paras. 50-51.

136 *See* Brazil's 20 January 2004 Comments on US Model Critique, para. 56 (for further references).

137 US7 October 2003 Oral Statement, para. 34.

138 Brazil offers additional rebuttal arguments in its comment on the US 22 December 2003 Answer to Question 213, below.

63. Brazil also notes that Westcott and Price in their updated MY 2001 analysis used actual MY 2001 prices as farmers' price expectations. This credits farmers with accurate information about upcoming prices and represents a third approach to modeling price expectations – the others being of course lagged prices and futures market prices.

64. In the context of its critique of the Westcott/Price study, the United States repeats its contention that futures market prices are the appropriate indicator for upland cotton farmers' price expectations, and that the effect of the marketing loan programme can be judged by looking at farmers' expectations about the US seasonal average cash price in the upcoming marketing year.[139] *This approach is simply factually wrong. There is no question that marketing loan payments are based offthe adjusted world price – not a cash price.* Both Brazil and Professor Sumner explained this fact in detail on 2 and 3 December 2003.[140] Indeed, the United States acknowledges this fact elsewhere in its 22 December 2003 Answers to Questions.[141] Thus, the effects of the marketing loan programme would depend on upland cotton farmers' expectations about the adjusted world price. All of the repeated US arguments that there are no effects of the marketing loan programme for upland cotton in MY 1999-2001 because the expected US cash price was above the loan rate are simply meaningless.[142]

65. The US argument that the marketing loan programme has no effects if the expected US cash price is above the loan rate is, however, also wrong on its merits.(The same would be true had the United States relied on the correct price – the adjusted world price.)Brazil demonstrated that the spread between the January to March quotes of the December futures contract and the adjusted world price is (i) 18.5 cents[143] (if measured against the average AWP for the following marketing year) or (ii) 12.22 cents[144] (if measured against the December

[139] US 22 December 2003 Answers to Questions, para. 51. *See* also US 18 November 2003 Further Rebuttal Submission, Section IV.G (for earlier US arguments using this fatally flawed approach).

[140] *See* Brazil's 2 December 2003 Oral Statement, Section 5.2 and Exhibits Bra-370 – Bra-371. *See* also Brazil's 22 December 2003 Answers to Questions, para. 155; Brazil's 20 January 2004 Answers to Additional Questions, para. 21.

[141] US 22 December 2003 Answers to Questions, para. 75. Also Exhibit US-126 calculates the marketing loan benefit correctly as the difference between the loan rate and the adjusted world price, rather than – as implied by the United States in its other arguments – as the difference between the loan rate and the cash price.

[142] US 22 December 2003 Answers to Questions, para. 51. Brazil is puzzled to learn that the United States continues to ignore these basic facts about the operation of the marketing loan program for upland cotton and continues to rely on this seriously flawed argument. Brazil recalls again that the United States is fully aware of its error, as demonstrated by its statements in paragraph 75 of its 22 December 2003 Answers to Questions and by Exhibit US-126, both of which rely on the adjusted world price as the basis for calculating marketing loan benefits.

[143] Exhibit Bra-356 (January – March Quotes of the December Futures Contract, Expected and Actual AWP and Cash Price).

[144] Exhibit Bra-370 (The Difference Between the Adjusted World Price and the December Futures Contract), presented by Professor Sumner on 3 December 2003.

AWPs).[145] Subtracting this spread from the average of the January to March quotes of the December futures contract provides the expected adjusted world price (i) for the upcoming marketing year and (ii) for the upcoming December. As Professor Sumner has explained, it is also not at all clear which futures prices to use for any such calculations.[146] Taking the quotes of just one month for a single futures contract, as the United States does, is an overly simplistic approach.[147] But whether one assumes that farmers look at the average AWP for the upcoming marking year or at some particular AWP for a specific month such as December, the fact is that the expected world price has always been well below the loan rate during MY 1999-2002.[148]

66. Moreover, even if the expected adjusted world price would not have been below the loan rate, that does not mean that there are no effects from the marketing loan programme. As Professor Sumner explained on 3 December 2003, this is because farmers have a probability distribution for the expected adjusted world price. That means they will expect with a certain likelihood that the adjusted world price will be below (or above) the mean of the expectation.[149] It follows that even if farmers expect the mean of the probability distribution for the AWP to be above the loan rate, they will nevertheless expect some marketing loan payments to be made.[150]

67. In sum, Brazil emphasizes that the Westcott/Price studies are important evidence of the effects of the upland cotton marketing loan programme that corroborate the effects found by Professor Sumner and the effects that are implied by all the non-econometric evidence for the effects of the US upland cotton subsidies presented by Brazil.

68. Finally, Brazil notes a new US argument that undercuts the US arguments regarding the peace clause. The United States argues for the first time in its 22 December 2003 Answers to Questions that the marketing loan programme *does not guarantee* US upland cotton producers 52 cents per pound in income.[151]

---

[145] Concerning the problems inherent in the choice of the exact spread, *see* Exhibit Bra-345 (Response to Further US Criticism of the Annex I Model of the Effect of US Cotton Subsidies – Daniel Sumner, 2 December 2003, para. 13).

[146] Bra-345 (Response to Further US Criticism of the Annex I Model of the Effect of US Cotton Subsidies – Daniel Sumner, 2 December 2003, paras. 11-12).

[147] Bra-345 (Response to Further US Criticism of the Annex I Model of the Effect of US Cotton Subsidies – Daniel Sumner, 2 December 2003, para. 12).

[148] *See* Brazil's 2 December 2003 Oral Statement, paras. 43-47, and Professor Sumner's oral explanation on 3 December 2003.

[149] *See* Exhibit Bra-371 (Simple Example of the Calculation of Expected Marketing Loan Benefit).

[150] Professor Sumner's oral explanations on 3 December 2003; Brazil's 2 December 2003 Oral Statement, para. 48; Brazil's 22 December 2003 Answers to Questions, para. 155.

[151] In passing, Brazil notes that the use of 14 cents as marketing loan facilitated revenue was taken from the assumptions in USDA's own FAPSIM policy simulation model (Exhibit Bra-222 ("Analysis of the US Commodity Loan Program with Marketing Loan Provisions," USDA, AER 801, p. 11)). In addition, Westcott and Price demonstrate that the additional marketing loan facilitated revenue for MY 1999 is 12.7 cents – very close to the authors' assumption (Exhibit Bra-222 ("Analysis of the US Commodity Loan Programme with Marketing Loan Provisions," USDA, AER 801, p. 8)). Finally, Exhibit US-126 does not contradict the appropriateness of using 14 cents, as Exhibit US-126 does not

Rather, there is additional revenue generated by the marketing loan programme that increases the effective support level – so-called "marketing loan facilitated revenue".[152] This revenue results from several sources. First, US farmers receive a domestic farm price when selling their crop. This price is consistently above the adjusted world price, off which the marketing loan payments are based.[153] It follows that US farmers receive additional revenue, as the US farm price plus the difference between the loan rate (52 cents) and the adjusted world price (below the US farm price) will exceed 52 cents.[154] Second, by cleverly marketing their upland cotton crop, US farmers can maximize this additional marketing loan facilitated revenue, which Westcott and Price assumed to be *14 cents*.[155]

69. In Exhibit US-126, the United States provides monthly data on the amount of additional marketing loan facilitated revenue. This actual data demonstrates considerable additional positive revenue "facilitated" by the marketing loan programme. Thus, using an adjusted world price as the loan repayment rate for upland cotton (as opposed to a local posted county price used for other crops except rice) increases the revenue guarantee beyond the official loan rate, as shown by the data in Exhibit US-126. This data, however, understates the real effect for two basic reasons. First, it calculates the additional revenue based on an average national cash price that may be quite different from the price an actual upland cotton farmer receives for its crop. Second, and more importantly, it omits the second source of "marketing loan facilitated revenue" – the timing decisions of farmers in marketing their crop and taking out marketing loan benefits.

70. The existence of additional marketing loan programme facilitates revenue further highlights the importance of the upland cotton marketing loan programme in assisting upland cotton producers to close the gap between costs and market returns. It also invalidates further the US argument during the peace clause phase of this dispute that a rate of support should be used for purposes of the "peace clause" analysis, as the rate of support is the only measure that the United States controls.[156] The United States now admits that it does not control the rate of support either, as the rate of support may be above (or even below) 52 cents, depending on market conditions[157], and farmers' timing decisions for the marketing of their crop. Nor does the United States control the flow of marketing

provide the entire marketing loan facilitated revenue received by farmers (*see* Brazil's arguments in the main body of its comment).

[152] US 22 December 2003 Answers to Questions, paras. 50-52. Brazil notes that this additional revenue in rare circumstances can also turn out to be negative.

[153] *See* Brazil's 27 October 2003 Answers to Questions, chart at paragraph 172 and Exhibit Bra-311 (Side by Side Chart of the Weekly US Adjusted World Price, the A-Index, the nearby New York Futures Price, the Average US Spot Market Price and Prices Received by US Producers from 1996 to the present).

[154] US 22 December 2003 Answers to Questions, paras. 50-52. Brazil notes that this additional revenue may also turn out to be negative, as shown by Exhibit US-126.

[155] US 22 December 2003 Answers to Questions, para. 52.

[156] *See inter alia* US 11 July 2003 First Submission, para. 94; US 22 July 2003 Oral Statement, paras. 12-13.

[157] These market conditions are in particular reflected in the spread between the adjusted world price and the cash price received by US upland cotton producers.

loan payments, as there is no mechanism in the upland cotton marketing loan programme to stem or control the flow of upland cotton marketing loan payments. This is precisely one of the reasons that Brazil has challenged this mandatory programme as causing a threat of serious prejudice.

213. What differences, if any, can be observed in the results of econometric models in the literature which use lagged prices and those which use futures prices to analyse the effect of prices on planting decisions? BRA, USA

Brazil's Comment:

71. The United States focuses its response entirely on Professor Sumner's model. In fact, it does not provide an answer to the question posed by the Panel. Brazil recalls that this question asks for differences in results that can be observed from models *in the literature* that use lagged prices and futures prices. In its 22 December 2003 response to this question, Brazil detailed that there are no comparable models that use futures prices, but that all models discussed in the context of this proceeding – as well as all other large-scale multi-commodity models – use some variant of lagged prices.[158]

72. At the outset, Brazil notes that the United States *has presented no econometric model* in this dispute. The United States has not taken advantage of the economic and econometric expertise of USDA's Economic Research Service to substantiate econometrically its argument that $12.9 billion in upland cotton subsidies have had no effect on production and exports of US upland cotton and have had no effects on US or world prices.

73. Instead, the United States has criticized various aspects of Professor Sumner's model.[159] In particular, it has focused its critique on Professor Sumner's approach to modeling farmers' price expectations. However, Professor Sumner and Brazil have effectively rebutted all of these criticisms.[160]

74. The United States cites Andrew Macdonald in support of its propositions that futures prices are the better price indicators.[161] However, once again, the United States takes a quote out of context. What Mr. Macdonald actually said in the cited paragraph is that New York futures prices are an indicator of the direction in which prices will move in the future, *i.e.,* price trends, not an indicator of actual price in the future.[162]

75. The United States further cites a US government study that allegedly demonstrates that a certain percentage of US upland cotton producers rely on the

---

158 Brazil's 22 December 2003 Answers to Questions, paras. 37-42.

159 US 7 October 2003 Oral Statement, paras. 26-50; US 22 December 2003 Comments on Brazil's Econometric Model.

160 *See* Exhibit Bra-345 (Response to Further US Criticism of the Annex I Model of the Effects of US Cotton Subsidies – Professor Daniel Sumner, 2 December 2003, paras. 6-14, with further references).

161 US 22 December 2003 Answers to Questions, para. 57

162 Exhibit Bra-281 (Statement by Andrew Macdonald – 7 October 2003, para. 13, even clearer paras. 17, 28, 31).

New York futures market to *price* their crop for actual sales.[163] While Brazil cautions against the use of the specific results of the study (as it is somewhat dated)[164], Brazil agrees that at least some farmers *price* their crop with reference to the New York futures price. However, what this study *does not demonstrate* is that US upland cotton producers rely on the futures market in *making their planting decisions* many months before marketing.

76. The basic question that arises from the US criticism is the following:is Professor Sumner's approach to model farmers' price expectations biased towards generating stronger effects? The United States correctly notes that "[t]he lagged prices used by Brazil and [Professor Sumner] can[,] at best, be an approximation of farmers' price expectations".[165] This is an obvious fact; the actual price expectations of thousands of farmers are "fundamentally unobservable".[166]

77. There are three basic approaches to modeling farmers' price expectations:(1) using lagged prices, (2) using futures market prices if available, and (3) using rational expectations in various forms, including crediting farmers with complete information (*i.e.,* using the actual price as the expected price[167]).

78. It is not clear that any of these approaches lead to *a priori* biased results. However, it is standard practice among economists to use lagged prices in a large-scale, multi-commodity econometric policy simulation framework. FAPRI, USDA and the US Congressional Budget Office ("CBO") use lagged prices in their models. Indeed the United States admits that using futures prices for these models is not feasible and has never been done.[168] Had Brazil attempted to use this unconventional and untested approach for its model, the United States could have raised legitimate concerns as to the reliability of the model results. Any such results would have been purely speculative.[169]

79. Indeed, Brazil would have had to develop equations to predict futures prices for those commodities for which a functioning futures market exists. It also would have had to use an altogether different modeling approach for price expectations for crops for which there is no futures market. Again, this would have been purely speculative.[170]

80. The approach favoured by the United States is not itself free of problems.[171] So far, futures market prices have only been used in statistical estimation using aggregate time-series data and not in econometric policy simula-

---

[163] US 22 December 2003 Answers to Questions, para. 58.

[164] *See* Brazil's comment on Question 201, above.

[165] US 22 December 2003 Answers to Questions, para. 56, *see* also para. 64.

[166] Brazil's 9 September 2003 Further Submission, Annex I, para. 18.

[167] Westcott/Price have chosen this approach for the update of their study for purposes of the Payment Limitations Commission.

[168] US 7 October 2003 Oral Statement, para. 34.

[169] Exhibit Bra-345 (Response to Further US Criticism of the Annex I Model of the Effect of US Cotton Subsidies – Daniel Sumner, 2 December 2003, paras. 9-14).

[170] *Ibid.*

[171] *Ibid.*.

tions.[172] Using it for modeling purposes raises further questions about the choice of futures contracts, the time period over which quotations are used, and calculations of appropriate spreads, among others.[173]

81. In sum, there are good reasons that FAPRI, USDA and the CBO use lagged prices in their policy simulation models. The Panel will recall that the FAPRI model (using lagged prices) was influential in the policy-making process leading to the 2002 FSRI Act, and that FAPRI, USDA and CBO models (all of which are based on lagged prices) are used regularly in US policy evaluation and formulation. Professor Sumner's approach uses a simple and commonly used proxy for the fundamentally unobservable price expectations of farmers.[174] Brazil is puzzled that the United States now views the very approach that every credible econometric policy simulation model takes as a significant error once this approach is used by Brazil in this dispute.

82. The United States further argues that in years with strong exogenous shocks lagged price models are poor proxies for price expectations.[175] The United States criticizes Professor Sumner's MY 2002 results as grossly overstated.[176] Brazil notes that it is has never relied on Professor Sumner's results of individual years. Instead, Brazil has used averages of the effects of the US programmes in MY 1999-2002 and MY 2003-2007. Using these averages mitigates any problems that may have existed from the use of lagged prices in any individual year.

83. Finally, Brazil notes that the United States relies on elasticities supplied by Professor Sumner in Annex I to calculate acreage responses from the expected lower cash prices in MY 2002.[177] However, these US calculations the United States are meaningless for several reasons. First, the futures prices used by the United States are problematic. Using only a single month's quotes for a single contract does not appropriately model the complexities of farmers' planting and marketing timings.[178] Second, it is unclear from the US response whether the United States used an appropriate spread for the calculation of price expectations held by farmers.[179] Third, it is therefore unclear whether the United States has calculated the appropriate change in price expectations between MY 2001 and 2002. Finally, even assuming that all of these problems did not exist, the

---

[172] Exhibit Bra-345 (Response to Further US Criticism of the Annex I Model of the Effect of US Cotton Subsidies – Daniel Sumner, 2 December 2003, para. 9).

[173] Exhibit Bra-345 (Response to Further US Criticism of the Annex I Model of the Effect of US Cotton Subsidies – Daniel Sumner, 2 December 2003, paras. 11-13).

[174] Exhibit Bra-345 (Response to Further US Criticism of the Annex I Model of the Effect of US Cotton Subsidies – Daniel Sumner, 2 December 2003, para. 14).

[175] US 22 December 2003 Answers to Questions, para. 61.

[176] US 22 December 2003 Answers to Questions, para. 63.

[177] *Ibid.*

[178] Exhibit Bra-345 (Response to Further US Criticism of the Annex I Model of the Effect of US Cotton Subsidies – Daniel Sumner, 2 December 2003, para. 12).

[179] Brazil's 2 December 2003 Oral Statement, para. 44; Exhibit Bra-345 (Response to Further US Criticism of the Annex I Model of the Effect of US Cotton Subsidies – Daniel Sumner, 2 December 2003, para. 13).

results calculated by the United States using Professor Sumner's elasticities fail to provide meaningful results. These elasticities were applied in Professor Sumner's model to obtain direct effects, *i.e.,* effects before any feedback from the FAPRI US crops model and the CARD international cotton model.[180] Thus, the results are nowhere near the results that one would have obtained using Professor Sumner's full Annex I model. For all these reasons, Brazil strongly disagrees with the conclusion that the marketing loan programme did not have any effect in MY 2002. Brazil also recalls its arguments and evidence regarding the serious flaws in the US application of its futures price methodology using expected cash prices rather than expected adjusted world prices.[181]

III. DOMESTIC SUPPORT

214. Please provide a copy of regulations regarding the marketing loan programme and loan deficiency payments published at 58 Federal Register 15755, dated 24 March 1993. What does this regulation indicate about the target price? USA

215. Please expand or comment on the statement at paragraph 91 of the US further rebuttal submission that the counter-cyclical target price ceases to be paid when the farm price rises above 65.73 cents per pound. In this scenario, should the Panel disregard Direct Payments? BRA, USA

216. How many times have upland cotton producers been able to update their base acres since 1984? How do upland cotton producers come to note the possibility of future updating? Please provide examples of relevant material. BRA, USA

Brazil's Comment:

84. In addition to its own answer[182], Brazil offers two comments to the US response to this question. First, the United States makes a factual mistake in describing the calculation of base acreage under the deficiency payment programme.[183] While the United States' description of the calculation of deficiency payment crop base as the rolling five-year average minus the high and low year would be correct for other deficiency payment crops, upland cotton (and rice) had a special provision.[184]7 CFR 1413.7(c) mandates the calculation of upland cotton base as "the average of the acreages planted and considered planted to such crop for harvest on the farm in each of the 3 crop years preceding such crop year.[185] For farms participating in the programme, all current base acreage was

---

[180] *See* Brazil's 20 January 2004 Comments on US Model Critique, paras. 64, 70.

[181] *See* Brazil's comment on Question 212, above.

[182] Brazil's 22 December 2003 Answers to Questions, paras. 47-50.

[183] US 22 December 2003 Answers to Questions, paras. 67-68.

[184] Exhibit Bra-26 (7 CFR 1413, Deficiency Payment Program, 1993 edition).

[185] Exhibit Bra-26 (7 CFR 1413.7(c)).

"considered planted".[186] Therefore, for the base to change, farmers had to opt out of the programme.[187]

85. Second, Brazil does not consider credible or relevant a statement by the United States that "[g]iven the current US fiscal situation,"[188] any further base update four years from now seems "unlikely". The Panel must determine whether the 2002 FSRI Act update of the direct and counter-cyclical payment base is a violation of paragraphs 6(a) and (b) of Annex 2 of the Agreement on Agriculture.

217. What is the reason for reducing payments under the PFC and direct payments programmes for planting and harvesting fruit, vegetables and wild rice on certain base acreage? Please comment on the statements by the European Communities that "the reduction in payment for fruit and vegetables, if the EC understands correctly, is in fact designed to avoid unfair competition within the subsidising Member." (EC oral statement at first session, first substantive meeting, paragraph 29) and "To find otherwise would not permit a WTO Member wishing to introduce decoupled payments to take account of important elements of internal competition (...)" (EC response to Panel third party Question No. 5). USA

Brazil's Comment:

86. The United States does not answer the Panel's first question as to "what is the reason" that PFC and direct payments are reduced for planting and harvesting fruits, vegetables, and wild rice. No reason is provided in the US 22 December 2003 response.

87. Nor does the United States take advantage of the Panel's second question to comment on the statement made by the European Communities that "the reduction in payment for fruit and vegetables, is in fact designed to avoid unfair competition within the subsidizing Member".[189] No US comment is provided. The EC argument involves considerable speculation about the "design" of the US measures. With the United States deciding not to provide any such reasons, the Panel is left without a factual basis to know whether the US reduction of payment based on growing fruits and vegetables is intended to "minimize any distortion which may be caused by any decoupled payments in markets which were historically undistorted by subsidies".[190]

88. The EC argument appears to attempt to impose a "trade distortion" test to the criteria of Annex 2, paragraph 6. However, Brazil notes that the EC argued that a decoupled domestic support measure need *not* be tested with regard to the "fundamental requirement" in Annex 2, paragraph 1 to determine whether it has

[186] Exhibit Bra-26 (7 CFR 1413.3, "Considered planted acreage").
[187] Brazil's 22 December 2003 Answers to Questions, para. 47.
[188] US 22 December 2003 Answers to Questions, para. 70.
[189] EC 23 July 2003 Oral Statement, para. 29.
[190] EC 11 August 2003 Answer to Third Party Question 11, para. 30.

"trade distorting effects".[191] Nor do any of the specific criteria in paragraph 6(b) of Annex 2 refer to "trade distorting effects".[192] Annex 2, paragraph 5 requires the specific criteria of Annex 2, paragraph 6 to be met for a direct payment measure to be included within the green box.

89. But even if Annex 2, paragraph 6(b) included a "trade distorting effects" test, the EC is simply wrong that the elimination or reduction of PFC and direct payments when fruits and vegetables and wild rice are grown does not "distort" trade. The EC argument ignores the distortion in trade in the products on which payments are focused, *i.e.,* upland cotton and the other programme crops rather than fruits, vegetables, and wild rice. Limiting or prohibiting payments for types of products representing 60 per cent of the value of production in a region such as California, Florida, or Arizona has the effect of maintaining production in the 40 per cent of the value of crops for which programme payments are received.[193] This "distorts" the trade in the agricultural crops receiving the payment by *maintaining or increasing their production.* The practical effect of the PFC and direct payment restriction is that the resources are targeted towards certain "types" of crops only. Negotiators intended that measures that were so linked to current production were not properly part of the green box.

90. In light of this evidence, the EC's argument boils down to asserting that trade distortions for products that traditionally have been subsidized should be permitted in order to prevent trade distortion in markets for non-subsidized products. Thus, the EC's argument is not one that would avoid distortions; it is one of *maintaining* existing distortions, contrary to the object and purpose of the Agreement on Agriculture.[194]

91. The only thing the US 22 December 2003 response does is to repeat earlier faulty arguments attempting to defend the fruits, vegetables, and wild rice payment limitation.[195] The US response is useful because it finally clarifies that the US argument boils down to the assertion that if a direct payment measure does not *require* production, then it cannot violate Annex 2, paragraph 6. The US 22 December 2003 response states, at paragraph 73, that "paragraph 6 [no subsection listed] prohibits basing payments on production requirements ... ".[196] It further states that the reduced PFC and direct payments "are not 'related to, or based on, the type or volume of production' *since the recipient need not produce anything at all*".[197] But there has never been an issue whether PFC and direct

[191] EC 11 August 2003 Answer to Third Party Questions 6 and 9, paras. 17, 23-25.

[192] Indeed, the United States has acknowledged that such effects can be presumed if the specific criteria in paragraph 6 of Annex 2 are not complied with. *See* US 11 August Answer to Question 31, para. 65 ("if a new measure does not conform to the basic and applicable policy-specific criteria in Annex 2, it will not have the benefit of the presumption that it meets the fundamental requirement of the first sentence.").

[193] Exhibit Bra-105 ("Statement of Professor Daniel Sumner at the First Meeting," para. 24); Oral Statement of Brazil, paras. 65-66.

[194] *See* Brazil's 22 August 2003 Rebuttal Submission, paras. 8-9, note 15.

[195] US 22 December 2003 Answers to Questions, para. 73.

[196] *Ibid.*

[197] *Ibid.*

payments require production. All this means is that they comply with Annex 2, paragraph 6(e), in that "no production shall be required in order to receive such payments". But what about Annex 2, paragraph 6(b), which must be interpreted to have a separate meaning apart from paragraph 6(e)?

92. Paragraph 6(b) focuses on the *amount* of payments related to the *type* of production. In other words, if a farmer decides to produce something (recognizing that he or she need not under Annex 2, paragraph 6(e)), does the direct payment provision condition the *amount* of payment on the *type* of production undertaken? The answer with respect to the 1996 FAIR and the 2002 FSRI Act for PFC and direct payments is a clear "yes". The amount of the PFC or direct payments falls when prohibited crops are grown – and increases when the prohibited crops cease to be grown. These legal provisions send a fairly compelling message to the farmer – channel your current production into *certain* crops to continue receiving the full amount of direct payments today. This re-couples payments to current production.

93. The United States claims, at paragraph 73 of its 22 December 2003 response, that all a producer need do to receive the full payment is to "*merely* refrain from producing fruit, vegetables, or wild rice".[198] This is an interesting dismissal given that the practical effect of this provision is to direct production away from crops that represent up to 60 per cent of the value of available options for cotton farmers in states such as Florida, California, and Arizona.

94. Moreover, the logic of the US argument leads to an evisceration of any disciplines in Annex 2, paragraph 6, and is therefore contrary to the object and purpose of that provision. Consider the following hypothetical:a measure provides for a direct payment that was reduced by 75 per cent if a farmer produced any of 99 per cent of the available crop options; as a practical matter, farmers could only plant one or two crops (or no crops) and still receive the full payment. Under the US argument, because the farmer had no obligation to grow any crops, it could "merely refrain" from producing 99 per cent of available crops. Like the fruits, vegetables and wild rice exception, this argument would emasculate the green box requirement of Annex 2, paragraph 6(b).

218. Please comment on the testimony of USDA Chief Economist Keith Collins cited in paragraph 36 of Brazil's oral statement regarding the trade-distorting and production-distorting nature of the marketing loan payments. USA

Brazil's Comment:

95. The United States states in its response to this question "that marketing loan payments are *potentially* production- and trade-distorting".[199] Yet, Keith Collins' statement did not say "potentially" production- and trade-distorting. Dr. Collins stated that marketing loan payments "are *unambiguously* trade-distorting

---

198 Emphasis added.

199 US 22 December 2003, Answers to Questions, para. 74 (emphasis added).

and production-distorting".[200] This is quite a different statement than the one the United States appears to "agree" to. Coming from the Chief Economist of the USDA, who is one of the most-widely respected agricultural economists, it is positive evidence that marketing loan payments are not only "potentially" production- and trade-distorting, but that these payments have, in fact, "unambiguously" distorted US production and exports of upland cotton. But Dr. Collin's statement also confirms what other evidence in the record already demonstrates:the effect of the marketing loan programme is to sustain economically unviable US production of upland cotton, that in turn increases US exports and suppresses world prices.[201]

96. In a further response to this question, the United States itself provides the reason why its arguments about the expected cash price as a meaningful measure of the effects of the marketing loan programme are seriously flawed. The United States confirms that marketing loan benefits are not paid off the cash price (so that any expectations about future cash prices would matter), but that "farmers will receive a government payment for the difference between the loan rate and *the adjusted world price*".[202] Thus, what potentially matters in evaluating the effects of the marketing loan programme is the expected adjusted world price, and not the expected cash price.[203] Looking at the expected adjusted world price, it is below the loan rate in all marketing years during the period of investigation and, therefore, the marketing loan programme is expected to have a significant effect on US farmers' upland cotton planting decisions.[204] This fact confirms all the other evidence presented by Brazil to demonstrate the trade- and production-distorting effects of the marketing loan programme.[205]

IV. EXPORT CREDIT GUARANTEES

219. Under the *Agreement on Agriculture* the general position is that the use of export subsidies, both those listed in Article 9.1 as well as those within the scope of Article 1(e) which are not so listed, may only be used within the

---

[200] Brazil's 2 December 2003 Oral Statement, para. 36 and Exhibit Bra-211 ("The Current State of the Farm Economy and the Economic Impact of Federal Policy," Hearings before the Committee on Agriculture, US House of Representatives, p. 43)(emphasis added).

[201] Brazil's 9 September 2003 Further Submission, Section 3.3.4.7.1; Brazil 7 October 2003 Oral Statement, paras. 31-33; Brazil's 18 November 2003 Further Rebuttal Submission, Sections 3.1, 3.2, 3.4 and 3.7.1; Brazil's 2 December 2003 Oral Statement, Section 5.2.

[202] US 22 December 2003 Answers to Questions, para. 75 (emphasis added).

[203] Brazil's 2 December 2003 Oral Statement, Section 5.2. Brazil notes that the United States, in Exhibit US-126, appears to acknowledge this fact, as it calculates the marketing loan benefit as the difference between the loan rate and the adjusted world price, rather than the cash price, as the United States implies in its other arguments.

[204] Brazil's 2 December 2003 Oral Statement, Section 5.2, in particular paras. 44-50 (including Exhibits Bra-356-359) and Professor Sumner's oral explanations on 3 December 2003 (including Exhibit Bra-370-371).

[205] Brazil's 9 September 2003 Further Submission, Section 3.3.4.7.1; Brazil 7 October 2003 Oral Statement, paras. 31-33; Brazil's 18 November 2003 Further Rebuttal Submission, Sections 3.1, 3.2, 3.4 and 3.7.1; Brazil's 2 December 2003 Oral Statement, Section 5.2.

limits of the product specific reduction commitments specified in Part IV of Members' Schedules. One might therefore have expected that Article 3.3 of the *Agreement on Agriculture* would have prohibited the use of both listed and non-listed export subsidies in excess of reduction commitment levels in the case of scheduled products and, in the case of non-scheduled products, would have simply prohibited the use of any export subsidy. Instead, the Article 3.3 prohibition is limited in both cases to export subsidies listed in Article 9.1. What significance, if any, does this contextual aspect have for how Article 10.2 might be interpreted having regard, *inter alia*, to:

(a) the fact that export performance-related tax incentives, which like subsidized export credit facilities were consideredas a possible candidate for listing as an Article 9.1 export subsidy in the pre-December 1991 Draft Final Act negotiations, have been held (for example, in *United States – Tax Treatment for Foreign Sales Corporations*, WT/DS108) to be subject to the anti-circumvention provisions ofArticle 10.1;and

(b) the treatment of international food aid and non-commercial transactions under Article 10? USA

Brazil's Comment:

97. Brazil agrees with the United States that Article 8 of the Agreement on Agriculture assumes the role the Panel suggests one might have expected Article 3.3 to play.[206] Article 8 prohibits the use of both those export subsidies listed in Article 9.1 and those not listed in Article 9.1 other than in conformity with the Agreement on Agriculture and the commitments specified by a Member in its Schedule.

98. However, Brazil does not consider that this fact provides illuminating context for the interpretation of Article 10, including Articles 10.1 and 10.2. The question is whether Article 10.2 of the Agreement on Agriculture exempts or carves-out export credits from the disciplines included in Article 10.1. The Appellate Body has concluded that to exempt or carve-out particular categories of measures from general obligations such as the export subsidy obligations in the Agreement on Agriculture, the exemption or carve-out must be *explicit* in the text of an agreement.[207] Article 10.2 includes no such explicit exemption or carve-out.[208] The negotiators knew how to make such an exemption or carve-out explicit, as evidenced by, for example, Article 13 of the Agreement on Agriculture, footnote 15 to Article 6.1(a) of the SCM Agreement, and the second para-

---

[206] *See* US 22 December 2003 Answers to Questions, para. 79.

[207] Appellate Body Report, *EC – Sardines*, WT/DS231/AB/R, para. 201-208; Appellate Body Report, *EC – Hormones*, WT/DS26/AB/R, para. 128.

[208] *See* Brazil's 22 July 2003 Oral Statement, paras. 100-115; Brazil's 22 August 2003 Rebuttal Submission, paras. 99-100; Brazil's 27 August 2003 Comments on US Rebuttal Submission, paras. 33-52; Brazil's 18 November 2003 Further Rebuttal Submission, paras. 219-220; Brazil's 2 December 2003 Oral Statement, paras. 73-76; Brazil's 22 December 2003 Answers to Questions, paras. 51-57.

graph of item (k) of the Illustrative List of Export Subsidies.[209] The United States has not rebutted these arguments.

99. Instead, the United States appeals to what it considers to be "similarity" between the treatment of export credit instruments and international food aid in Articles 10.2 and 10.4.[210] These two provisions are fundamentally different, however. Article 10.2 announces Members' intent to work toward negotiations on specific disciplines for export credits, and calls on Members to adhere to those disciplines once they are adopted. As Brazil noted in its 22 December 2003 Answers to Questions, the nature of the disciplines negotiated and the way in which they are transposed into the WTO will dictate the effect they will have on claims against export credits under Article 10.1.[211] At least for the time being, however, Article 10.2 does not meet the standard for carve-outs or exemptions set by the Appellate Body in *EC – Sardines* and *EC – Hormones*, and export credits are subject to the disciplines of Article 10.1.[212]

100. Article 10.4 similarly does not meet the standard for exemptions or carve-outs set by the Appellate Body in *EC – Sardines* and *EC – Hormones*. However, it does provide specific disciplines for international food aid through reference to FAO and Food Aid Convention provisions. In Brazil's view, Article 10.4 could be considered an example of the situation envisioned in paragraph 56 of Brazil's 22 December 2003 Answers to Questions.[213] Article 10.4 sets out a benchmark against which to determine whether particular international food aid measures constitute "export subsidies", within the meaning of Article 10.1. Thus far, the Appellate Body's decisions (in *US – FSC*[214] and *Canada – Dairy*[215]) have directed panels to contextual guidance included in the SCM Agreement for this determination. In a case against international food aid measures, however, a panel could look to the alternative benchmarks set out in Article 10.4 as context for its determination whether those measures constitute "export subsidies" for the purposes of Article 10.1.(A panel could also look to a Member's notifications to the Committee on Agriculture. The United States, for example, notifies international food aid – or some portion of the international food aid provided by it – as export subsidies to be counted towards its reduction commitments.[216])

220. What will be the relevance of Articles 9 and 10.1 of the *Agreement of Agriculture* to export credit guarantees when disciplines are internationally agreed? BRA

---

209 *See, e.g,.* Brazil's 2 December 2003 Oral Statement, para. 75.

210 US 22 December 2003 Answers to Questions, paras. 80-82.

211 Brazil's 22 December 2003 Answers to Questions, paras. 51-57.

212 *See* Brazil's 22 July 2003 Oral Statement, paras. 100-115; Brazil's 22 August 2003 Rebuttal Submission, paras. 99-100; Brazil's 27 August 2003 Comments on US Rebuttal Submission, paras. 33-52; Brazil's 18 November 2003 Further Rebuttal Submission, paras. 219-220; Brazil's 2 December 2003 Oral Statement, paras. 73-76; Brazil's 22 December 2003 Answers to Questions, paras. 51-57.

213 Brazil's 22 December 2003 Answers to Questions, para. 56.

214 Appellate Body Report, *US – FSC*, WT/DS108/AB/R, para. 136-140.

215 Appellate Body Report, *Canada – Dairy*, WT/DS103/AB/R and WT/DS113/AB/R, paras. 87-90.

216 *See, e.g.,* Exhibit Bra-99 (G/AG/N/USA/39, p. 2).

221. In respect of the table in paragraph 161 of the US August 22 rebuttal submission (concerning the cohort specific treatment of export credit guarantees), the Panel notes the subsequent US agreement (footnotes 82 and 96 in US further submission of 30 September 2003; footnote 160 in US 18 November further rebuttal submission) to Brazil's assertion (footnote 67 in Brazil's 27 August 2003 comments on US rebuttal submission) that the total figure net of re-estimates should be $230,127,023 instead of the figure which originally appeared ($381,345,059).

(a) Please submit a corrected table reflecting all of the necessary information to produce this result, to the extent this is possible for the reasons indicated in footnote 96 in US further submission of 30 September 2003.

Brazil's Comment:

101. The data provided by the United States in the chart accompanying its response demonstrates that using the net present value methodology imposed by the US Federal Credit Reform Act ("FCRA"), premiums for the CCC guarantee programmes over the period 1992-2002 were inadequate to cover the operating costs and losses of the programmes, in the amount of $230 million.[217] For a complete assessment under item (j), administrative expenses in the amount of approximately $39 million should be added.[218]

102. Brazil addresses further the US chart in its comments on other US answers, below.

(b) Please clarify whether and how the Panel should treat the figures in Exhibit BRA-182 for the net lifetime re-estimates for each respective cohort.

Brazil's Comment:

103. The United States' response is inaccurate. In stating that "all of the first five cohorts (1992-1996), including 1994, are profitable",[219] the United States oddly neglects to account for the most recent reestimate data, which it has included in its own chart, provided with its response to question 221(a). That chart shows massive upward reestimates in 2003 for the 1992, 1993, 1994, 1996, 1997 and 2001 cohorts. Accounting for those reestimates, the 1994 cohort, which the United States asserts is nearly closed[220], does *not* show profitability. Nor do the 1997, 1998, 2000, 2001 or 2002 cohorts.

104. The United States is implying that over time, cohorts will turn out to be positive. The data does not support this implication. Upward reestimates con-

[217] US 22 December 2003 Answers to Questions, chart included in response to Question 221(a).

[218] Exhibit Bra-133 (Guaranteed Loan Subsidy and Administrative Expenses of US Export Credit Guarantee Programmes GSM 102, GSM 103 and SCGP).

[219] US 22 December 2003 Answers to Questions, para. 86.

[220] US 22 December 2003 Answers to Questions, para. 93.

tinue, even on "older" cohorts, and net results do not suggest profitability with anywhere near the uniformity suggested by the United States.

105. Finally, Brazil emphasizes that showing gains or losses for particular *cohorts* is not relevant for the purposes of item (j), which calls for the assessment of a "*programme*" across its entire portfolio.[221]

(c) The Panel notes that the CCC 2002 financial statement in Exhibit BRA-158 refers to annual "administrative" expenses of $4 million, and that the US has also referred to this figure in its submissions (e.g. US first written submission, paragraph 175). Please confirm whether the figures in the table in paragraph 161 of the US August 22 rebuttal submission (or a corrected version thereof) includes "administrative expenses", of approximately $4 million per year over the period 1992-2002, and explain why (or why not) this affects the substantive result.

Brazil's Comment:

106. Brazil agrees that for a complete assessment under item (j), administrative expenses in the amount of approximately $39 million[222] should be added to the $230 million of losses recorded in the chart accompanying the US response to question 221(a), or to $211 million of losses recorded in the Brazilian chart included as Exhibit Bra-193.

(d) Please identify what is considered an "administrative expense" for this purpose.

(e) The Panel notes the US statement in paragraph 160 of its answers to Panel questions following the first meeting that all cohorts are still open although the 1994 and 1995 cohorts will close this year. Is this still an accurate statement? If not, please indicate whether any cohorts have since "closed" for the period 1992-2002.

Brazil's Comment:

107. The United States' response is inaccurate. Using the most recent data available, provided by the United States with its response to question 221(a), the subsidy figure net of reestimates for the 1994 cohort will in fact be positive, indicating losses. Based on this same data, the same thing can be said for other "older" cohorts, such as 1997 and 1998. Moreover, the United States' data demonstrates that 2002 and 2003 reestimates for "older" cohorts 1992, 1993, 1994, 1996 and 1997 are all *upward*, indicating adjustments for even greater losses than previously anticipated.

---

221 *See* Brazil's 2 December 2003 Oral Statement, para. 81; Brazil's 18 November 2003 Further Rebuttal Submission, para. 248; Brazil's 27 August 2003 Comments on US Rebuttal Submission, para. 61.

222 Exhibit Bra-133 (Guaranteed Loan Subsidy and Administrative Expenses of US Export Credit Guarantee Programmes GSM 102, GSM 103 and SCGP).

108. Brazil emphasizes, however, that showing gains or losses for particular *cohorts* is not relevant for the purposes of item (j), which calls for the assessment of a "*programme*" across its entire portfolio.

(f) **The Panel notes the current "high" figures for 1997 and 1998 indicated in the original US chart. Pending their confirmation and/or updating by the US, why does the US assert that a cohort will *necessarily* reach a "profitable" result (for example, the 1994 cohort, which has almost closed still indicates an outstanding amount)? Do "re-estimates" reflect also expectations about a cohort's future performance?**

Brazil's Comment:

109. Once again, the United States' response is inaccurate. The United States asserts that data for the 1994 cohort indicate profitability.[223] Using the most recent data available, however, provided by the United States with its 22 December 2003 response to question 221(a), the subsidy figure net of reestimates for the 1994 cohort will in fact be positive, indicating losses. Based on this same data, the same thing can be said for other "older" cohorts, such as 1997 and 1998. Moreover, the United States' data demonstrates that 2002 and 2003 reestimates for "older" cohorts 1992, 1993, 1994, 1996, 1997 are all *upward*, indicating adjustments for even greater losses than previously anticipated.

110. The United States shows *no evidence* to support its assertion that Pakistani and Ecuadorean defaults account for an important part of the poor performance of the 1997 cohort.[224] Nor does it offer any evidence to show that those defaults were rescheduled, or that they are performing. Additionally, the United States' assertion that it expects the 1998 cohort to show profitability is not supported by the data included with its response to question 221(a).[225] As recently as 2002, upward reestimates were made to the 1998 cohort, indicating that there is no discernible trend of profitability.

111. In any event, Brazil notes that showing gains or losses for a particular *cohort* is not relevant for the purposes of item (j), which calls for the assessment of a "*programme*" across its entire portfolio.[226]

(g) **Why should the Panel "eliminate" the 2001 and 2002 cohorts from its examination, as suggested in paragraph 198 of the US further rebuttal submission?**

---

223 US 22 December 2003 Answers to Questions, para. 93.

224 US 22 December 2003 Answers to Questions, para. 94.

225 *Ibid.*

226 *See* Brazil's 2 December 2003 Oral Statement, para. 81; Brazil's 18 November 2003 Further Rebuttal Submission, para. 248; Brazil's 27 August 2003 Comments on US Rebuttal Submission, para. 61.

Brazil's Comment:

112. The United States confuses two issues in paragraphs 96-97 of its response.[227] First, it notes that reestimates need to be applied to the subsidy estimate included in the prior, actual year column of the US budget, since the original subsidy estimate included in the budget year column of the US budget includes subsidy figures for some guarantees that are budgeted but not in fact granted. In other words, fewer guarantees are granted than were budgeted to be granted. Brazil recognized this in Exhibit Bra-193, as does the United States in the chart included with the US response to question 221(a). Nonetheless, both Brazil and the United States reach the same conclusion – over the 10-year period, operating costs and losses outpace premiums collected for the CCC programmes (even before administrative expenses are included in the calculation). The United States tracks losses of $230 million in the chart accompanying its response to Question 221(a), and Brazil tracks losses of $211 million in Exhibit Bra-193.

113. The second point the United States makes is that the data it has presented in its response to question 221(a) includes no "operating experience" with the 2001 and 2002 cohorts.[228] This is wholly inaccurate. Estimates of costs and losses are based, first and foremost, on historical experience with borrowers.[229] Moreover, the chart included in the US response to question 221(a) shows that reestimates – which are in part made to reflect operating results – have already been made for both the 2001 and 2002 cohorts.

114. Finally, the United States' assertion that there is a "trend of negative reestimates"[230] is not borne out by the data provided by the United States itself, in its response to question 221(a). In 2002, upward reestimates were made for the 1992, 1993, 1994, 1995, 1996, 1997 and 1999 cohorts. Similarly, in 2003, upward reestimates were made for the 1992, 1993, 1994, 1996, 1997, 2001 and 2002 cohorts. It is not at all "reasonable to expect that in the fullness of time the data will … reflect further negative reestimates for cohorts 2001 and 2002",[231] as the United States asserts, for the simple reason that recent data provided by the United States shows significant upward reestimates *across all cohorts*, including "older" cohorts that are presumably closer to closing.

115. For all of these reasons, the US suggestion that the 2001 and 2002 cohorts should be disregarded by the Panel in its item (j) analysis should be rejected.

---

[227] US 22 December 2003 Answers to Questions, paras. 96-97.

[228] US 22 December 2003 Answers to Questions, paras. 96, 99.

[229] *See e.g.* Brazil's 22 August Rebuttal Submission, para. 113 (including notes 234-235), Exhibit Bra-118 (Federal Accounting Standards Advisory Board, STATEMENT OF FEDERAL FINANCIAL ACCOUNTING STANDARDS NO. 19, *Technical Amendments to Accounting Standards for Direct Loans and Loan Guarantees in Statement of Federal Financial Accounting Standards No. 2* (March 2001), p. 16 (para. 36) ("Actual historical experience of the performance of a risk category is a *primary factor* upon which an estimation of default cost is based.")).

[230] US 22 December 2003 Answers to Questions, para. 98.

[231] *Ibid.*

(h) Why should the Panel "eliminate", in addition, the 2000 cohort, as also suggested in paragraph 198 of the US further rebuttal submission for which information is presumably more "complete"?

Brazil's Comment:

116. The United States notes that the original subsidy estimate for the 2000 cohort was reduced to reflect the fact that fewer guarantees were granted than were budgeted to be granted.[232] This is wholly irrelevant, and does not even remotely imply *profitability* for those guarantees that were actually issued in fiscal year 2000. As the data provided by the United States in its response to question 221(a) demonstrates, there is still a large positive subsidy estimate, indicating losses, for the 2000 cohort.

117. Moreover, the data provided by the United States in its response to question 221(a) shows that, as cohorts age, downward reestimates can not be assumed. In 2002, upward reestimates were made for the 1992, 1993, 1994, 1995, 1996, 1997 and 1999 cohorts. Similarly, in 2003, upward reestimates were made for the 1992, 1993, 1994, 1996, 1997, 2001 and 2002 cohorts. Brazil also notes that cohorts that are "older" than the 2000 cohort – such as the 1994, 1997 and 1998 cohorts, continue to show positive subsidy estimates, or losses.

118. For these reasons, the US suggestion that the 2000 cohort should be disregarded by the Panel in its item (j) analysis should be rejected.

(i) Under the US approach, at what point in time could a Panel ever make an assessment of the programme, if it had to wait for each cohort to be completed before it could be "properly" assessed? Why is it inappropriate for the Panel to include these "most recent years" in its evaluation, as the US suggests in paragraph 199 of its 18 November further rebuttal submission? USA

Brazil's Comment:

119. Brazil notes that the United States has not answered the Panel's question. In the United States' view, it is only appropriate to make an assessment of a programme under item (j) using a net present value accounting methodology once all cohorts in a period are closed. The United States specifically argues as follows:

> Not until the cohort is closed can one make an assessment as to whether or not that particular cohort represents a cost to the Federal Government.[233]

120. According to the United States, no cohort in the period 1992-2002 has yet closed. Therefore, in the United States' view, were the Panel to undertake a 10-year assessment of the CCC programmes under item (j) using a net present value accounting methodology, it could only do so for the period 1982-1991. Of

232 US 22 December 2003 Answers to Questions, para. 101.

233 *See e.g.* US 11 August 2003 Answers to Questions, para. 159.

course, since net present value accounting for the CCC programmes only began in 1992, following passage of the FCRA in 1990, subsidy estimate and reestimate figures would be unavailable for this period.

121. In insisting that it is necessary to wait until cohorts are closed to be used for the purposes of item (j), the United States is effectively saying that net present value accounting is not an appropriate way to assess a programme under item (j). As the United States is well aware, the whole point of net present value accounting, endorsed by the US Congress and the President of the United States in the FCRA, is to assess the costs of contingent liabilities, like guarantees, when they are issued, rather than when they are paid (on a default of the underlying loan). Brazil notes that there are important retrospective elements to the net present value accounting methodology imposed by the FCRA – initial estimates of costs and losses are based, first and foremost, on historical experience with borrowers[234], and reestimates are calculated annually to adjust initial estimates as dictated by actual results. In any 10-year period, of course, the most recent years will have been subject to fewer reestimates than the earlier years. This is not, as the United States suggests, a *flaw* in the methodology. It *is* the methodology. The methodology records what the US Congress, the US President and US government accountants agree is a more actuarially appropriate means of assessing the costs and losses of contingent liabilities like guarantees.[235]

122. The United States' rejection of net present value accounting as an accurate way to make an assessment under item (j) is particularly odd given the United States' conclusion that it would be inappropriate "to subject the [CCC programmes] to the analytical yoke of the unique circumstances of the Polish and Iraqi defaults over 10 years ago . . ".[236]

123. The United States had previously made this assertion, albeit only with respect to Iraq.[237] The United States has offered no support whatsoever for this assertion[238], which is inaccurate in at least two respects. As Brazil has noted, these defaults were *not* "over 10 years ago". The US General Accounting Office reports that the losses in Iraq occurred over the period 1990-1997.[239] Nor are these defaults "unique," as the United States argues. As discussed below in Brazil's comments on the US response to question 225, the evidence regarding *write-*

[234] *See e.g.* Brazil's 22 August 2003 Rebuttal Submission, para. 113 (including notes 234-235), Exhibit Bra-118 (Federal Accounting Standards Advisory Board, STATEMENT OF FEDERAL FINANCIAL ACCOUNTING STANDARDS NO. 19, *Technical Amendments to Accounting Standards for Direct Loans and Loan Guarantees in Statement of Federal Financial Accounting Standards No. 2* (March 2001), p. 16 (para. 36) ("Actual historical experience of the performance of a risk category is a *primary factor* upon which an estimation of default cost is based.")).

[235] Brazil's 22 July 2003 Oral Statement, para. 128.

[236] US 22 December 2003 Answers to Questions, para. 102.

[237] US 22 August 2003 Rebuttal Submission, para. 172.

[238] As the party asserting this fact, the United States bears the burden of proving it. *See e.g.* Appellate Body Report, *Japan – Apples*, WT/DS245/AB/R, para. 157 ("It is important to distinguish, on the one hand, the principle that the complainant must establish a *prima facie* case of inconsistency with a provision of a covered agreement from, on the other hand, the principle that the party that asserts a fact is responsible for providing proof thereof.").

[239] Brazil's 27 August 2003 Comments, para. 65 (and document cited at note 81).

offs by the CCC (not even mentioning defaults that are *not* written off) demonstrates that the Iraqi and Polish defaults are not at all "unique".

124. Setting factual inaccuracies aside, if the United States wants to put post-1991 defaults on pre-1992 guarantees behind it, it should *embrace*, rather than *reject*, the net present value accounting methodology adopted in the FCRA. Using net present value accounting and the FCRA formula to make an assessment of the CCC programmes under item (j), the United States is not held accountable (in these proceedings, at least) for post-1991 defaults on pre-1992 cohorts. Post-1991 activity on pre-1992 CCC guarantees is treated separately[240], and is not in any way included in the data provided by the United States in its response to question 221(a), or by Brazil in Exhibit Bra-193. Even without the effect of the Iraqi and Polish defaults, both the United States and Brazil conclude that the CCC programmes have lost money over the period 1992-2002 (the United States puts those losses at over $230 million; Brazil at $211 million). (For a complete assessment under item (j), administrative expenses in the amount of approximately $39 million should be added.[241])

125. Rejecting the use of net present value accounting to assess the CCC programmes under item (j) does not keep the United States from cherry picking the results of the FCRA formula to make its case. According to the United States, using data for *some* cohorts that have not yet closed is acceptable, but using data for other cohorts that have not yet closed is not acceptable. Several points are clear regarding the United States' approach.

126. First, it is factually inaccurate for the United States to assert, in paragraph 103 of its response, that "trends" suggest that annual downward reestimates on older cohorts will continue and will grow. The chart included with the US response to question 221(a) indicates *upward* reestimates in 2002 *for every cohort* during the period 1992-1999. Similarly, that same chart shows *upward* reestimates in 2003 for the 1992, 1993, 1994, 1996, 1997 and 2001 cohorts. Moreover, that same chart shows "trends" of positive net subsidy estimates after adjusting for cumulative reestimates, even for cohorts that the United States considers are close to closing – 1994, 1997 and 1998. In other words, *these aging cohorts are losing money*. Thus, it is not at all factually accurate to conclude that reestimates are generally downward as a cohort ages and approaches closure, or that as a cohort approaches closure, the data suggests that it will have made money.

127. Second, even if one accepts the US argument that the 2001 and 2002 cohorts should be left out of the calculation because there are not yet any "operating results" for those years (a point that is itself factually inaccurate, as addressed

[240] *See e.g.* Exhibit Bra-116 (Office of Management and Budget, Circular No. A-11, Section 185, p. 185-4); Notes to Financial Statements contained in Exhibit US-129 (US Department of Agriculture, Office of Inspector General, Financial and IT Operations, Audit Report, Commodity Credit Corporation's Financial Statements for Fiscal Years 2003 and 2002, Audit Report N° 06401-16-FM (November 2003) p. 15).

[241] Exhibit Bra-133 (Guaranteed Loan Subsidy and Administrative Expenses of US Export Credit Guarantee Programmes GSM 102, GSM 103 and SCGP).

by Brazil above)[242], this does not explain the United States' decision to eliminate the 2000 cohort – for which it acknowledges there are "operating results" – when it concludes that "cohorts 1992-1999, taken as a whole, currently reflect a net negative reestimate (i.e., profitable performance)".[243] When the 2000 cohort is included, the data provided by the United States in the chart accompanying its response to question 221(a) show losses. This is a gross example of the cherry-picking exercise in which the United States would have the Panel engage to gerrymander a result in the United States' favour. Consistent with the Panel's duty to make an objective assessment of the facts, it should not accept this approach.

128. Third, the US approach does not tell the Panel anything about how the CCC *programmes* fare when assessed under item (j). Item (j) calls for an assessment of the entire portfolios of the *programmes* themselves.[244] In contrast, the US approach only offers some indication of how particular, carefully-selected *cohorts* are performing (and as discussed in the previous two paragraphs, the results do not even reflect profitability for those cohorts). The data provided by the United States itself demonstrates that using the net present value methodology imposed by the FCRA, premiums for the CCC guarantee *programmes* over the period 1992-2002 were inadequate to cover the operating costs and losses of the programmes, in the amount of $230 million.[245] For a complete assessment under item (j), administrative expenses in the amount of approximately $39 million should be added.[246]

129. If the Panel does not consider that net present value accounting is an appropriate way of assessing the CCC programmes under item (j), Brazil has also demonstrated that the long-term operating costs and losses of the programmes outpace premiums collected, using a *cash-basis accounting* methodology. The chart included at paragraph 165 of Brazil's 11 August 2003 Answers, reproduced below, tracks this result:

242 US 22 December 2003 Answers to Questions, para. 99.

243 US 22 December 2003 Answers to Questions, para. 103.

244 *See* Brazil's 2 December 2003 Oral Statement, para. 81; Brazil's 18 November 2003 Further Rebuttal Submission, para. 248; Brazil's 27 August 2003 Comments on US Rebuttal Submission, para. 61.

245 US 22 December 2003 Answers to Questions, chart included in response to Question 221(a). *See also* Exhibit Bra-193.

246 Exhibit Bra-133 (Guaranteed Loan Subsidy and Administrative Expenses of US Export Credit Guarantee Programmes GSM 102, GSM 103 and SCGP).

Fiscal year	Premiums collected (88.40) + Recovered principal and interest (88.40) + Interest revenue (88.25)	Admin. expenses (00.09) + Default claims (00.01) + Interest expense (00.02)
1993	$27,608,000 + $12,793,000 + $15,672,000[247] = $56,073,000	$3.320,000[248] + $570,000,000[249]+ $0[250] = $573,320,000
1994	$20,893,000 + $458,954,000 + $0[251] = $479,847,000	$3,381,000[252] + $422,363,000[253] + $0[254] = $425,744,000
1995	$18,000,000 + $62,000,000 + $0[255] = $80,000,000	$3,000,000 + $551,000,000 + $10,000,000[256] = $564,000,000
1996	$20,000,000 + $68,000,000 + $26,000,000[257] = $114,000,000	$3,000,000[258] + $202,000,000[259] + $61,000,000[260] – $266,000,000
1997	$14,000,000 + $104,000,000 + $26,000,000[261] = $144,000,000	$4,000,000[262] + $11,000,000[263] + $62,000,000[264] = $77,000,000
1998	$17,000,000 + $81,000,000 + $54,000,000[265] = $152,000,000	$4,000,000[266] + $72,000,000[267] + $62,000,000[268] = $138,000,000
1999	$14,000,000 + $58,000,000 + $0[269] = $72,000,000	$4,000,000[270] + $244,000,000 + $62,000,000[271] = $310,000,000
2000	$16,000,000 + $100,000,000 + $99,000,000[272] = $215,000,000	$4,000,000[273] + $208,000,000[274] + $62,000,000[275] = $274,000,000
2001	$18,000,000 + $149,000,000 + $125,000,000[276] = $292,000,000	$4,000,000[277] + $52,000,000[278] + $104,000,000[279] = $160,000,000

247 Exhibit Bra-126 (US budget for FY 1995, p. 156).
248 *Ibid.*
249 *Ibid.*
250 No budget line, Exhibit Bra-126 (US budget for FY 1995, p. 156).
251 Exhibit Bra-95 (US budget for FY 1996, p. 162).
252 Exhibit Bra-95 (US budget for FY 1996, p. 161).
253 Exhibit Bra-95 (US budget for FY 1996, p. 162).
254 *Ibid.*
255 Exhibit Bra-94 (US budget for FY 1997, p. 176).
256 Exhibit Bra-94 (US budget for FY 1997, p. 175).
257 Exhibit Bra-93 (US budget for FY 1998, p. 175).
258 Exhibit Bra-93 (US budget for FY 1998, p. 174).
259 Exhibit Bra-93 (US budget for FY 1998, p. 175).
260 *Ibid.*
261 Exhibit Bra-92 (US budget for FY 1999, p. 106).
262 Exhibit Bra-92 (US budget for FY 1999, p. 105).
263 Exhibit Bra-92 (US budget for FY 1999, p. 106).
264 *Ibid.*
265 Exhibit Bra-91 (US budget for FY 2000, p. 112).
266 Exhibit Bra-91 (US budget for FY 2000, p. 111).
267 Exhibit Bra-91 (US budget for FY 2000, p. 112).
268 *Ibid.*
269 Exhibit Bra-90 (US budget for FY 2001, p. 112).
270 Exhibit Bra-90 (US budget for FY 2001, p. 110).
271 Exhibit Bra-90 (US budget for FY 2001, p. 111).
272 Exhibit Bra-89 (US budget for FY 2002, p. 118).
273 Exhibit Bra-89 (US budget for FY 2002, p. 116).
274 Exhibit Bra-89 (US budget for FY 2002, p. 117).
275 *Ibid.*
276 Exhibit Bra-88 (US budget for FY 2003, p. 120).
277 Exhibit Bra-88 (US budget for FY 2003, p. 118).
278 Exhibit Bra-88 (US budget for FY 2003, p. 119).
279 Exhibit Bra-88 (US budget for FY 2003, p. 120).

Fiscal year	Premiums collected (88.40) + Recovered principal and interest (88.40) + Interest revenue (88.25)	Admin. expenses (00.09) + Default claims (00.01) + Interest expense (00.02)
2002	$21,000,000 + $155,000,000 + $61,000,000[280] = $237,000,000	$4,000,000[281] + $40,000,000[282] + $93,000,000[283] = $137,000,000
Total	$1,841,920,000	$2,925,064,000
Long-term Net Cos0	**$1,083,144,000**	**$1,083,144,000**

130. In Exhibit US-128, the United States has also provided data to be used for an assessment of the CCC programmes under item (j) using cash-basis accounting. As discussed further in Brazil's comment to the US response to question 222, the data offered by the United States in Exhibit US-128 leads to the same conclusion, when adjusted to account properly for the impact of rescheduling on defaults.[284]

131. Finally, an even more fundamental approach demonstrates the incredibility of the United States' assertion that "trends" suggest that the CCC programmes are making and will continue to make profits. Congressional testimony by USDA officials and reports by the US General Accounting Office demonstrate that 1990-1997 defaults on Iraqi and Polish CCC guarantees amounted to approximately $4 billion.[285] The US General Accounting Office also noted in 1995 that defaults on Russian and Former Soviet Union GSM 102 guarantees similarly reached $2 billion by the end of 1993, and that despite repeated rescheduling agreements, those debts were not being repaid.[286] These defaults were not, there-

---

280 Exhibit Bra-127 (US budget for FY 2004, p. 109).

281 Exhibit Bra-127 (US budget for FY 2004, p. 107).

282 Exhibit Bra-127 (US budget for FY 2004, p. 108).

283 *Ibid.*

284 At paragraph 103 of its 22 December 2003 response, the United States refers to "the uniform performance of reschedulings". The United States has offered no proof that its reschedulings are performing. Yet as the party asserting this fact, the United States bears the burden of proving it. *See, e.g.,* Appellate Body Report, *Japan – Apples*, para. 157 ("It is important to distinguish, on the one hand, the principle that the complainant must establish a *prima facie* case of inconsistency with a provision of a covered agreement from, on the other hand, the principle that the party that asserts a fact is responsible for providing proof thereof."). In fact, according to the US General Accounting Office, rescheduling of GSM defaults has not historically been "performing," and has rather been in arrears. *See* Brazil's 22 August 2003 Comments, para. 99 (and note 94).

285 *See* Brazil's 11 August 2003 Answers to Questions, para. 167 (second bullet point), *citing* Exhibit Bra-87 ("Testimony of August Schumacher Jr., Under Secretary, Farm and Foreign Agricultural Service, USDA, before the Subcommittee on General Farm Commodities, Hearing on the Asian Financial Crisis, 4 February 1998," p. 10-11) and Exhibit Bra-157 (US General Accounting Office, REPORT TO THE CHAIRMAN, TASK FORCE ON URGENT FISCAL ISSUES, COMMITTEE ON THE BUDGET, HOUSE OF REPRESENTATIVES, *International Trade: Iraq's Participation in US Agricultural Export Programs*, GAO/NSIAD-91-76 (November 1990), p. 27 (Table IV.2)). *See also* Brazil's 18 November 2003 Further Submission, para. 251.

286 *See* Brazil's 22 August 2003 Rebuttal Submission, para. 109 (note 226), *citing* Exhibit Bra-181 (US General Accounting Office, Report to the Ranking Minority Member, Committee on Agriculture, Nutrition, and Forestry, US Senate, *Former Soviet Union: Creditworthiness of Successor States and US Export Credit Guarantees*, GAO/GGD-95-60 (February 1995), p. 50-52 and Table 2.6). *See also* Brazil's 18 November 2003 Further Submission, para. 251.

fore, all "over 10 years ago", as the United States suggests at paragraph 102 of its 22 December 2003 response. Nor are they "unique", as the United States also suggests at paragraph 102. In addition to this $6 billion in defaults, the United States' response to question 225 cites to further "written-off" or "forgiven" defaults of $20 million. This does not, of course, account for other defaults that have not yet been written-off or forgiven.

132. *Even if premiums collected over the entire lifetime of the CCC guarantee programmes are considered, these defaults, in the amount of over $6 billion, would mean net losses in the amount of over $5.5 billion.*[287] Brazil emphasizes that this is just taking account of the defaults about which Brazil is aware. Brazil also notes that while the United States emphasizes the role of rescheduling in the recovery of defaults (which Brazil disputes in its comments on the US answer to question 222 below), the more than $6 billion in defaults discussed here *have not been rescheduled*, or at least where they have been (in the case of Russian and Former Soviet Union), they are in arrears.[288] This demonstrates that long-term operating un-recovered and non-recoverable costs and losses for the CCC programmes have outpaced premiums collected by a considerable amount.

133. Item (j) does not require the Panel to adopt or to reject any particular methodology to assess the CCC guarantee programmes.[289] Nor do the *facts* require the Panel to endorse any one methodology to determine that the CCC guarantee programmes constitute export subsidies under item (j). Brazil has demonstrated that under *any* methodology, properly applied, premiums for the CCC guarantee programmes over the period 1992-2002 were inadequate to cover the operating costs and losses of the programmes.

222. For GSM 102, 103 and SCGP, please provide year-by-year amounts from 1992 to 2003 with respect to: (i) cumulative outstanding guarantees; (ii) claims paid; (iii) recoveries made; (iv) revenue from premiums; (v) other current revenue, including interest earned; (vi) interest charges paid; and (vii) administrative costs of running the programmes. Please indicate any allocation methodologies used to calculate administrative costs. USA

---

[287] Brazil has calculated that the highest amount of premiums that could have been generated would amount to approximately $450 million. *See* Brazil's 11 August 2003 Answers to Questions, para. 167 (second bullet point). Data included in Exhibit US-128 suggests that Brazil is over-estimating the amounts of premia collected.

[288] The US General Accounting Office noted that defaults on Russian and Former Soviet Union guarantees reached $2 billion by the end of 1993, and that despite repeated rescheduling agreements, those debts were not being repaid. Exhibit Bra-181 (US General Accounting Office, Report to the Ranking Minority Member, Committee on Agriculture, Nutrition, and Forestry, US Senate, *Former Soviet Union: Creditworthiness of Successor States and US Export Credit Guarantees*, GAO/GGD-95-60 (February 1995), p. 50-52 and Table 2.6). Brazil raised this point in its 22 August 2003 Rebuttal Submission (at para. 109, note 226) and its 18 November 2003 Further Submission (para. 251). It remains unrebutted by the United States.

[289] *See* Brazil's 22 December 2003 Answers to Questions, paras. 68-75.

Brazil's Comment:

134. Exhibit US-128, provided by the United States in response to this question, allegedly demonstrates that using a cash basis accounting methodology, the CCC export credit guarantee programmes generate money. In fact, the United States claims that revenue collected outpaces total expenses for the three programmes by $666 million. Brazil has offered a similar chart at paragraph 165 of its 11 August 2003 Answers. Brazil's chart demonstrates that the CCC programmes lost $1.048 billion over the period of FY 1993-2002. The total difference between the US result and Brazil's result is $1.75 billion.

135. This figure closely corresponds to the total "Claims Rescheduled" figure reported by the United States in Exhibit US-128.[290] Indeed, the difference between the chart provided by the United States in Exhibit US-128 and Brazil's chart in paragraph 165 of its 11 August 2003 Answers lies in the treatment of rescheduled debt.[291] The United States treats defaulted guarantees that have been rescheduled as 100 per cent recovered on the day the terms of the rescheduling are agreed.[292] Brazil, on the other hand, has treated rescheduled claims as receivables, until they have been actually recovered.[293] Only once CCC actually collects incremental amounts on a rescheduled claim is the corresponding incremental amount of the default considered "recovered" and no longer a loss to CCC.[294] Under Brazil's approach, whatever portion of rescheduled claims is collected in a particular year is treated as a recovery, whereas under the United States' approach, the *entirety* of the rescheduled claims is treated as a recovery at the moment the terms of the rescheduling are agreed.

136. Brazil's approach is the more actuarially appropriate of the two, and is consistent with the cash-basis accounting preferred by the United States in this dispute. Under cash-basis accounting, when financial commitments are rescheduled, they would normally be re-amortized on a new, longer payment schedule that reduces the amount of each periodic payment due from the borrower. Re-

---

[290] The fact that both figures do not match exactly is explained by the fact that the United States analyses data covering FY 1992-2003 on a cohort-specific basis, while the data available to Brazil covers FY 1993-2002 and represents actual performance of the CCC programs during a given fiscal year.

[291] If the Panel were to compare all other totals, it would readily see that the totals correspond, taking into account that the US data covers FY 1992-2003 and is on the basis of cohorts, while Brazil's data covers only FY 1993-2002 and represents the actual performance of the programs in a fiscal year. Brazil does not have access to FY 2003 data, as the actual figures for that year will only be published in connection with the FY 2005 budget.

[292] *See* Exhibit US-128. The United States defines "Claims Outstanding" (G) as "Claim Payments" (D) minus "Claims Recovered" (E) minus "Claims Rescheduled" (F). It follows that a rescheduled claim no longer constitutes an outstanding claim at the moment the terms of the rescheduling are agreed. Instead, for accounting purposes, the rescheduling is simply treated as 100 percent recovered.

[293] This is the reason that Brazil treats recovered principle as a revenue inflow for accounting purposes. The principle recovered is netted against the claims paid by CCC (*see* Brazil's 11 August 2003 Answers to Questions, para. 163).

[294] Contrary to this approach, the United States nets defaults paid against the sum of recovered and rescheduled defaults (*see* Exhibit US-128). However, it only *hopes* to eventually recover rescheduled debt; the rescheduling alone does not mean it will do so.

scheduling does not mean that a creditor *collects* on an outstanding claim – it just means that the creditor *hopes* to do so in the future by reducing the amount the borrower has to pay each month.[295] CCC, in fact, acknowledges that all it possesses following a rescheduling is a receivable, and that not all receivables are collectable.[296] (And in fact, CCC rescheduling has historically been in arrears.[297]) The US approach, therefore, overstates the effect rescheduled guarantees have on claims paid, by automatically treating rescheduled guarantees, in every instance, as actual recoveries of claims paid, at the moment the terms of the rescheduling are agreed.(Indeed, the CCC's Financial Statement for FY 2002 and 2003 confirm that rescheduling of export credit guarantee receivables covered both principle and interest, thereby confirming that not all of the rescheduled debt performs and that additional interest charges were also rescheduled.)[298]

137. Brazil maintains its position that it is not appropriate to treat as "recovered" those losses (resulting from defaults) that were actually incurred by the CCC export credit guarantee programmes and that are rescheduled, until such a point in time when the money *actually has been recovered.* Therefore, Brazil maintains that its cash-basis formula is the appropriate one. It follows that the CCC export credit guarantee programmes suffered losses of $1.1 billion between fiscal years 1993-2002, resulting in a finding that the CCC programmes operate at premium rates inadequate to cover the long-term operating costs and losses of the programmes, within the meaning of item (j).

223. Are the premium rates applicable to GSM 102, 103 and SCGP subject to regular review as to their adequacy in enabling the operating costs and losses associated with these programmes? If so, what criteria or benchmarks are taken into consideration for this purpose? Secondly, how do the premium rates applied compare with the implicit cost of forfaiting transactions and with premiums for export credit insurance? USA

---

295 *See* Exhibit Bra-115 (US General Accounting Office ("GAO"), Report to the Chairman, Subcommittee on Criminal Justice, US House of Representatives Committee on the Judiciary, "Loan Guarantees: Export Credit Guarantee Programs' Long-Run Costs Are High," GAO/NSIAD-91-180, 19 April 1991, p. 3 (Table 1, Note *a*) ("GAO/NSIAD-91-180") (accounts receivable for the GSM programmes "[i]ncludes delinquent payments and *rescheduled debt not yet due*.") (emphasis added).

296 Brazil's 27 August 2003 Comments on US Rebuttal Submission, para. 64.

297 Brazil's 22 August 2003 Comments, para. 99. *See also* Exhibit Bra-181 (US General Accounting Office, Report to the Ranking Minority Member, Committee on Agriculture, Nutrition, and Forestry, US Senate, *Former Soviet Union: Creditworthiness of Successor States and US Export Credit Guarantees*, GAO/GGD-95-60 (February 1995), p. 50-52 and Table 2.6 (noting that in 1995 defaults on Russian and Former Soviet Union guarantees reached $2 billion by the end of 1993, and that despite repeated rescheduling agreements, those debts were not being repaid.); Exhibit Bra-152 (GAO, Statement of Allan I. Mendelowitz, Director, Trade, Energy and Finance Issues, National Security and International Affairs Division, before the Task Force on Urgent Fiscal Issues of the Committee on Budget of the US House of Representatives, *Status Report on GAO's Reviews of the Targeted Export Assistance Programme, the Export Enhancement Programme, and the GSM-102/103 Export Credit Guarantee Programmes*, GAO/T-NSIAD-90-53, 28 June 1990, p. 14 (noting that historically, the majority of GSM support that is rescheduled is "in arrears.").

298 Exhibit US-129 (CCC Financial Statements for FY 2002 and 2003 – Audit Report, USDA, Office of the Inspector General, Report No. 06401-16-FM, November 2003, Note 5, p. 22).

Brazil's Comment:

138. Although the United States asserts that premium rates for the GSM-102, GSM-103 and SCGP programmes are "reviewed annually"[299], it offers no evidence to support this assertion.[300] As Brazil has already noted, both USDA's Inspector General and the US General Accounting Office have noted the CCC's failure to change its premium rates or to reflect credit risk in those rates – and its inability to do so given the one-per cent fee cap included in US law – as evidence of a failure to cover costs and losses.[301]

139. The CCC guarantee programmes are unique financing instruments that are not available on the market.[302] Brazil has demonstrated that forfaits and CCC export credit guarantees are not similar financial instruments, and therefore that the terms for forfaits cannot serve as benchmarks against which to determine whether CCC export credit guarantees confer "benefits".[303] The United States has offered *no* evidence that the two instruments "compete as a method for trade financing over comparable tenors in similar markets ...."[304] Further, the regulations for the CCC programmes belie the United States' assertion that "an importer does not necessarily realize any benefit from a CCC export credit guarantee".[305] The regulations state that the programmes operate in cases where banks "would be unwilling to provide financing without CCC's guarantee".[306] To summarize the differences between the two instruments, the essential function of a CCC guarantee is to make possible an export sale that would otherwise be impossible. A forfait, by contrast, does not make an impossible sale possible, but instead merely allows an exporter to collect its receivable without waiting for that receivable to come due.[307] This opportunity, offered by the forfait, only arises if the CCC guarantee has made the sale happen in the first place.

140. Even if the two instruments were similar, the United States has not met its burden to establish (under either Article 10.3 of the Agreement of Agriculture, or as the party asserting the fact) that CCC guarantees are provided on terms no better than those offered for forfaiting instruments on the market. Although the

---

[299] US 22 December 2003 Answers to Questions, para. 107.

[300] As the party asserting this fact, the United States bears the burden of proving it. *See* Appellate Body Report, *Japan – Apples*, para. 157 ("It is important to distinguish, on the one hand, the principle that the complainant must establish a *prima facie* case of inconsistency with a provision of a covered agreement from, on the other hand, the principle that the party that asserts a fact is responsible for providing proof thereof.").

[301] Brazil's 22 December 2003 Answers to Questions, paras. 63-64.

[302] *See* Exhibit Bra-190 (Affidavit of Marcelo Franco, Seguradora Brasileira de Crédito à Exportação).

[303] Brazil's 22 August 2003 Rebuttal Submission, paras. 103-105; Brazil's 27 August 2003 Comments on US Rebuttal Submission, paras. 68-70; Brazil's 7 October 2003 Oral Statement, para. 72; Brazil's 18 November 2003 Further Rebuttal Submission, paras. 233-241; Brazil's 2 December 2003 Oral Statement, para. 79; Brazil's 22 December 2003 Answers to Questions, paras. 65-66.

[304] US 22 December 2003 Answers to Questions, para. 109.

[305] *Ibid.*

[306] Exhibit Bra-38 (7 CFR 1493.10(a)(2) (GSM 102 and GSM 103 regulations)). *See also* Exhibit Bra-38 ((7 CFR 1493.400(a)(2) (SCGP regulations)).

[307] *See, e.g.,* Brazil's 18 November 2003 Further Rebuttal Submission, para. 237.

United States curiously repeats its argument that it "does not have access to specific implicit rates available in the marketplace"[308], Brazil presented evidence regarding forfaiting fees five months ago, with its 27 August 2003 submission. That evidence demonstrates that forfaiting fees are well above fees for CCC export credit guarantees.[309] It also demonstrates that unlike CCC guarantee fees, which vary on the basis of only one factor – the length of the underlying credit – forfaiting fees additionally vary according to the risks involved in the transaction[310], as one would expect of any market-based financial instrument.

141. Similarly, export credit insurance and CCC export credit guarantees are not similar financial instruments, and therefore the terms for export credit insurance cannot serve as benchmarks against which to determine whether CCC export credit guarantees confer "benefits". The United States has acknowledged the differences between CCC guarantees and export credit insurance.[311] One critical difference, noted by the WTO Secretariat in the WTO document quoted by the United States in paragraph 108 of its 22 December 2003 response, is that premia for insurance vary according to the credit rating or risk status of both the importer and the importing country.[312] In contrast, neither importer risk nor country risk have *any* impact on the premiums payable for GSM 102, GSM 103 or SCGP guarantees.[313] Moreover, Brazil notes that while export credit insurance is indeed available for agricultural commodities, export credit insurance for agricultural commodities is limited to 360 days, or the expected/useful life of the commodity in question.[314] In contrast, CCC guarantees are available for terms of up to 10 years.[315]

142. Even if the two instruments were similar, the United States has not met its burden to establish (under either Article 10.3 of the Agreement of Agriculture, or as the party asserting the fact) that CCC guarantees are provided on terms no better than those offered for export credit insurance obtained on the market. The United States argues that "[p]rivate commercial quotes for export credit insurance are simply not available to the United States".[316] Brazil attaches two premium fee schedules:first, a fee schedule published by Export Insurance Services, Inc., a private broker for export credit insurance for small businesses offered by

---

308 US 22 December 2003 Answers to Questions, para. 109.

309 Brazil's 27 August 2003 Comments on US Rebuttal Submission, paras. 76-77 and Exhibit Bra-199 (Trade and Forfaiting Review, Volume 6, Issue 9 July/August 2003).

310 Brazil's 27 August 2003 Comments on US Rebuttal Submission, paras. 75-76.

311 US 11 August 2003 Answers to Questions, para. 179. The United States has correctly observed that "[i]f the commercial market does not offer a particular borrower the exact terms offered by a government, then the government is providing a benefit to the recipient ..." Panel Report, *Canada – Aircraft II*, WT/DS222/R, Annex C-2 (para. 7) (emphasis added).

312 G/AG/NG/S/13, para. 9.

313 *See* US 11 August 2003 Answers to Questions, para. 184; Brazil's 11 August 2003 Answers to Questions, paras. 192, 195.

314 Exhibit Bra-408 (Export-Import Bank, Standard Repayment Terms), p. 3 (Chart II, no. 2), 4 (second bullet point). Brazil made a similar point with respect to forfaits. *See* Brazil's 27 August 2003 Comments, para. 78.

315 Brazil's 24 June 2003 First Submission, para. 101.

316 US 22 December 2003 Answers to Questions, para. 109.

the US Export-Import Bank ("Ex-Im Bank") (Exhibit Bra-410); and second, a fee schedule published by Ex-Im Bank itself for export credit insurance for small businesses (Exhibit Bra-409).

143. The Panel will note that the rates in Ex-Im Bank's own fee schedule, which do not even include administrative fees that would be added by a private broker such as Export Insurance Services, exceed those offered for CCC guarantees by considerable margins.[317] When administrative fees levied by a market-based institution are accounted for, the differences become even more pronounced.[318]

144. This comparison likely understates the extent to which CCC rates are below-market, for two reasons. First, government support from Ex-Im Bank does not constitute a market benchmark for the purposes of Article 1.1(b) of the SCM Agreement.[319] Nonetheless, this comparison demonstrates that the CCC guarantee programmes do not even meet *non-market* benchmarks.[320] Second, the comparison involves export credit insurance for small businesses. As noted by the US International Trade Administration's Foreign Commercial Service, export credit insurance for small businesses is offered at reduced premium rates.[321]

145. Finally, because the provisions address somewhat different disciplines and could require different means of implementation, Brazil reiterates its earlier request that the Panel find that the CCC programmes constitute export subsidies by virtue of *both* Articles 1 and 3.1(a) of the SCM Agreement *and* item (j).[322]

224. Please indicate how the CCC's cost of borrowing was treated in the 2002 financial statement of the CCC, in Exhibit BRA 158. USA

---

[317] *Compare* Ex-Im Bank schedule in Exhibit Bra-409 *with* CCC fee schedule in Exhibit Bra-155.

[318] *Compare* Export Insurance Services, Inc. fee schedule in Exhibit Bra-410 (p. 6-7) *with* CCC fee schedule in Exhibit Bra-155.

[319] *See* Appellate Body Report, *United States – Countervailing Duties on EC Products*, WT/DS212/AB/R, para. 124 (Appellate Body questions whether a "fair market price" is reached when a government "shapes" the market, stating that "[t]he Panel's absolute rule of 'no benefit' may be defensible in the context of transactions between two private parties taking place in reasonably competitive markets; however, it overlooks the ability of governments to obtain certain results from markets by shaping the circumstances and conditions in which markets operate."). *See also* Arbitrator's Decision, *Brazil Aircraft*, WT/DS46/RW, para. 6.95 (One reason the Panel offered for rejecting a proposed benchmark was that the benchmark was "the direct result of a *government* guarantee," rather than an indication of the "commercial or market rate of interest."). *See also id.*, paras. 6.90-6.92, 6.104.

[320] The Panel will recall that Brazil made a similar comparison between Ex-Im Bank export guarantee fees and CCC export guarantee fees, and reached the same result. *See* Brazil's 22 August 2003 Comments, para. 110.

[321] Exhibit Bra-411 (*The Federal Scoop: US Government Financing for Service Exports*, EXPORT AMERICA (May 2000), p. 33).

[322] Brazil's 18 November 2003 Further Rebuttal Submission, para. 228.

Brazil's Comment:

146. Brazil notes that it has accounted for CCC's interest expense and revenue figures (lines 00.02 and 88.25 of the US budget) in its cash-basis accounting methodology.[323]

225. Please indicate whether there was any instance where the CCC "wrote off" debt and, if so,please indicate the accounting regulation or principle used. If a "written off" debt is subsequently recovered, do the CCC's accounts reflect both the interest cost and interest received in relation to the debt during the time it was "written off"? USA

Brazil's Comment:

147. As noted in Brazil's comment on the US response to question 221(i), if the Panel uses a net present value accounting methodology to assess the CCC programmes under item (j), the United States would not be held accountable (in these proceedings, at least) for write-offs on pre-1992 cohorts. Activity on CCC guarantees issued before 1992 is not in any way included in the net present value data provided by the United States in its response to question 221(a), or by Brazil in Exhibit Bra-193.[324] Even without the effect of the write-offs detailed in paragraph 114 of the US 22 December 2003 response – all of which relate to pre-1992 cohorts – both the United States and Brazil conclude that the CCC programmes have lost money over the period 1992-2002 (the United States puts those losses at over $230 million; Brazil at $211 million).[325] (For a complete assessment under item (j), administrative expenses in the amount of approximately $39 million should be added.[326])

148. Under a cash-basis accounting methodology of assessing the CCC programmes under item (j), the United States should be held accountable for write-offs and "debt forgiveness" (as defined in paragraph 113 of the US response) that occurred during the period 1992-2002, even if it relates to guarantees that were issued before 1992. Although this is not clear from the US 22 December 2003 response, to the extent that the write-offs catalogued in paragraph 114 of the US 22 December 2003 response are related to *defaults* that occurred in the period 1992-2002, Brazil presumes that the defaults themselves would be included in the line item (00.01) for default claims, which are tracked in the chart included at paragraph 165 of Brazil's 11 August 2003 Answers to Questions, and reproduced in Brazil's comments on the US response to question 221(i), *supra*. Applying a cash-basis accounting methodology, Brazil demonstrated that long-term operat-

---

[323] *See* Brazil's 11 August 2003 Answers to Questions, para. 165. *See also* Brazil's comments on Question 221(i), above.

[324] As Brazil notes in its comment on Question 221(g), however, estimates of costs and losses made in the context of the FCRA formula are based, first and foremost, on historical experience with borrowers. Thus, prior defaults would tend to lead to positive subsidy estimates on new guarantees.

[325] *See* US 22 December 2003 Answers to Questions, response to Question 221(a); Brazil's Exhibit Bra-193.

[326] Exhibit Bra-133 (Guaranteed Loan Subsidy and Administrative Expenses of US Export Credit Guarantee Programmes GSM 102, GSM 103 and SCGP).

ing costs and losses outpace premiums collected over the period 1992-2002 for the CCC programmes, by $1.083 billion.

226. If a debt was "written off" more than ten years ago, does it still create a cost to the programme? If so, how is this reflected in the 2002 financial statement of the CCC, in Exhibit BRA 158 (or any other material)? USA

Brazil's Comment:

149. As discussed in Brazil's comment on the US response to question 225, if the Panel uses a net present value accounting methodology to assess the CCC programmes under item (j), the United States would not be held accountable (in these proceedings, at least) for write-offs that occurred more than 10 years ago. The reason is that those write-offs would relate to guarantees issued prior to 1992. Activity on CCC guarantees issued before 1992 is not in any way included in the net present value data provided by the United States in its response to question 221(a), or by Brazil in Exhibit Bra-193.[327]

150. Under a cash-basis accounting methodology of assessing the CCC programmes under item (j), the United States would not be held accountable for write-offs and "debt forgiveness" that occurred more than 10 years ago (at least in this proceeding), assuming that the period of review is 1993-2002. This is because the underlying defaults would also have occurred more than 10 years ago, even before the write-offs or forgiveness.

151. However, Brazil would like to correct the United States' mischaracterization of Brazil's position about the 10-year period of review for an assessment under item (j). Brazil does not agree, as the United States asserts, that an examination beyond 10 years is "inappropriate".[328] Rather, Brazil considers that a 10-year period is *adequate* in this case to get a picture of the performance of the CCC programmes' portfolio. If the Panel wishes to look beyond that 10-year period, Brazil does not believe that doing so would be "inappropriate". Brazil has noted that should the Panel wish to corroborate evidence showing that over the period 1992-2002, the long-term operating costs and losses for the CCC programmes outpace premiums collected, it could look to CCC's 2003 financial statements, which state that uncollectible amounts on pre-1992 CCC guarantees outpace premiums collected during the period 1981-1991 by nearly $2 billion.[329]

---

[327] As Brazil notes in its comment on the US response to Question 221(g), however, estimates of costs and losses made in the context of the FCRA formula are based, first and foremost, on historical experience with borrowers. Thus, prior defaults would tend to lead to positive subsidy estimates on new guarantees.

[328] US 22 December 2003 Answers to Questions, para. 102.

[329] Notes to Financial Statements contained in Exhibit US-129 (US Department of Agriculture, Office of Inspector General, Financial and IT Operations, Audit Report, Commodity Credit Corporation's Financial Statements for Fiscal Years 2003 and 2002, Audit Report N° 06401-16-FM (November 2003) p. 15). Brazil notes that unlike the CCC 2002 financial statements included in Exhibit Bra-158, the CCC 2003 financial statements included in Exhibit US-129 are not publicly available on the USDA website. *See* http://www.usda.gov/oig/rptsauditsccc.htm.

227. The United States has indicated that Brazil continues to "mischaracterize" the amount of $411 million in the 2002 financial statement of the CCC, in Exhibit BRA 158, pp. 18 & 19. Can the United States please indicate how it believes this amount – referred to on p. 19 of the Exhibit as "Credit Guarantee Liability-End of Fiscal Year" - should be properly characterized? How, if at all, does it represent CCC operating costs or losses? USA

Brazil's Comment:

152. In paragraphs 117-118 of its 22 December 2003 response, the United States again rejects use of the FCRA formula as an appropriate methodology to make an assessment of the CCC programmes under item (j), since it is based on "estimates". As noted above, the United States' view is that it is only appropriate to use a net present value accounting methodology once all cohorts in a period are closed.[330] In paragraphs 117 and 121 of its 22 December 2003 response, the United States argues that the "credit guarantee liability" figure included in the CCC financial statements, which is calculated using a net present value accounting methodology, does not reflect "losses", within the meaning of item (j), but instead only estimated losses.

153. This does not stop the United States from appealing to the FCRA formula when it believes it suits its purposes to do so. In paragraph 119, the United States cites with approval the $22 million credit guarantee liability figure used in CCC's 2003 financial statements as evidence of "good performance" by the CCC guarantee programmes. Brazil notes, however, that at page 4 of the notes to its 2003 financial statements, CCC defines the term "credit guarantee liability" as "the estimated net cash outflows (loss) of the guarantees on a net present value basis".[331] Thus, the $22 million figure still represents a "loss", as does the $230 million cumulative figure listed in the chart included with the US response to question 221(a). For a complete assessment under item (j), administrative expenses in the amount of approximately $39 million should be added.[332]

154. Finally, Brazil directs the Panel's attention to the massive increase from 2002 to 2003 in the losses CCC considers it will incur at the time all post-1991 guarantee cohorts are closed. At page 15 of the notes to its 2003 financial statements, CCC estimates that when all post-1991 cohorts close, it will have lost

[330] *See e.g.* US 11 August 2003 Answers to Questions, para. 159 ("Not until the cohort is closed can one make an assessment as to whether or not that particular cohort represents a cost to the Federal Government.").

[331] Notes to Financial Statements contained in Exhibit US-129 (US Department of Agriculture, Office of Inspector General, Financial and IT Operations, Audit Report, Commodity Credit Corporation's Financial Statements for Fiscal Years 2003 and 2002, Audit Report N° 06401-16-FM (November 2003) p. 4).

[332] Exhibit Bra-133 (Guaranteed Loan Subsidy and Administrative Expenses of US Export Credit Guarantee Programmes GSM 102, GSM 103 and SCGP).

$1.16 billion (as opposed to the $770 million it reported in its 2002 financial statements).[333]

228. What accounting principles should the Panel use in assessing the long-term operating costs and losses of these three programmes? For example, if internal US Government regulations require costs to be treated differently to generally accepted accounting principles, is it incumbent on the Panel to conduct its analysis in accordance with that treatment? BRA, USA

V. SERIOUS PREJUDICE

229. What is the meaning of the words "may arise in any case where *one or several* of the following apply" (emphasis added) in Article 6.3 of the *SCM Agreement*? Please comment on the possibility that these words indicate that one of the Article 6 subparagraphs may not be sufficient to establish serious prejudice and that serious prejudice should be considered an additional or overriding criterion to the factors specified in the subparagraphs. BRA

230. Please comment on Brazil's views on Article 6.3 of the *SCM Agreement* as stated in paragraphs 92-94 of its further submission. USA

231. Do you believe that the now-expired Article 6.1 and/or Annex IV of the *SCM Agreement* are relevant context for the Panel's interpretation of Article 6.3? USA

Brazil's Comment:

155. For the reasons Brazil has previously articulated, Brazil disagrees that Article 6.1 and Annex IV of the SCM Agreement are relevant context for interpreting the present text of Part III of the SCM Agreement.[334]

156. The US 22 December 2003 response to Question 243 confirms the fundamental role that Annex IV plays in its analysis of actionable subsidies in Part III of the SCM Agreement. The United States treats Annex IV as if the title of the Annex were "Calculation of the Total Ad Valorem Subsidization for Subsidies Subject to Part III of the Agreement". But all participants know and agree that Annex IV is dead. If it were not, then Brazil's submissions would certainly have been far more concise, as the total *ad valorem* subsidization for the US subsidies is 95 per cent over the four-year period of investigation.

157. The US reference in paragraph 131 of its 22 December 2003 Answer to Question 231 to the Appellate Body report in *US – CVD's on EC Products* is

---

[333] Notes to Financial Statements contained in Exhibit US-129 (US Department of Agriculture, Office of Inspector General, Financial and IT Operations, Audit Report, Commodity Credit Corporation's Financial Statements for Fiscal Years 2003 and 2002, Audit Report N° 06401-16-FM (November 2003) p. 15). The United States reports that premiums of $246 million were collected on CCC guarantees over the period 1992-2003. *See* Exhibit US-128.

[334] Brazil's 18 November 2003 Further Rebuttal Submission, paras. 96-107; Brazil's 2 December 2003 Oral Statement, paras. 4-6.

inapposite. That case involved countervailing duty measures, not actionable subsidy measures and claims under Part III of the SCM Agreement. The Appellate Body's citation to Annex IV was in the context of citing to a long list of SCM provisions that refer to the "recipient" of a "benefit" in the SCM Agreement. The Appellate Body did not, as the United States seeks to do in this case, use Article IV as the sole legal basis for the wholesale inclusion of countervailing duty methodologies into Part III of the SCM Agreement.

158. In paragraph 132 of its 22 December 2003 Answer, the United States continues to make the assumption that contract payments are "not tied to the production of upland cotton". As a factual matter, Brazil has demonstrated that contract payments *are* tied to the production of upland cotton.[335] The evidence of much higher upland cotton per-acre payments, among many other facts, demonstrates that the *de jure* "flexibility" is, in practice, not exercised by upland cotton producers[336], and that the bulk of the upland cotton contract payments are paid to current upland cotton producers.[337]

159. More importantly, while the United States repeats its calls for Brazil to implement various allocation methodologies in paragraph 132 of its 22 December 2003 Answers to Questions, it refuses to provide the information that would allow Brazil or the Panel to even perform a calculation using the flawed US methodology based on Annex IV. And the United States is just plain wrong to suggest in paragraph 132 of its 22 December 2003 response that Brazil has "refus[ed] to countenance any allocation of the decoupled payments it has challenged ... ". Brazil's 20 January 2004 Answer to Question 258 explained in greater detail in Brazil's methodology for allocating the payments.[338] Brazil even demonstrated that applying the US allocation methodology with the flawed and incomplete US 18/19 December 2003 data resulted in levels of support to upland cotton that were consistent with Brazil's 14/16th Methodology.[339]

232. How, if at all, should the Panel take into account the effects of other factors in its analysis of the effects of US subsidies under Article 6.3? If the Panel should compare the effects of other factors to establish the relative significance of one compared to others, how would this be done? What would be relevant "factors" for this purpose? BRA

233. In Brazil's view, what is or are the "same market(s)" for the purposes of Article 6.3(c)? Does Brazil's view of "world market" imply that regardless of which domestic (or other) "market" is examined, price suppression will be identifiable? BRA

---

335 *See* Brazil's 22 August 2003 Rebuttal Submission, Section 2.2 and references included therein. *See* also Brazil's 18 November 2003 Further Rebuttal Submission, Section 3.7.5.

336 *See* Brazil's 22 August 2003 Rebuttal Submission, Section 2.2 and references included therein. *See* also Brazil's 18 November 2003 Further Rebuttal Submission, Section 3.7.5.

337 Brazil's 18 November 2003 Further Rebuttal Submission, Section 2.1; Brazil's 28 January 2004 Comments and Request Regarding US Data, Section 9. *See* also Brazil's comment on Question 205, above.

338 Brazil's 20 January 2004 Answers to Additional Questions, paras. 43-55.

339 Brazil's 28 January 2004 Comments and Requests Regarding US Data, Section 10.

234. Does "significant" price suppression under Article 6.3(c) necessarily amount to "serious" prejudice within the meaning of Article 5(c)? Could the level of "significance" of any price suppression under Article 6.3(c) determine whether any prejudice under Article 5(c) rises to the level of "serious prejudice"? USA, BRA

Brazil's Comment:

160. The US 22 December 2003 response again ignores the determination of the panel in *Indonesia – Automobiles*, which found that the term "significant" in Article 6.3(c) required examination of a link between the size of the margins of undercutting and whether those margins could "meaningfully affect suppliers of the imported product".[340] Under this "meaningfully affect" standard, the focus, at least for the purposes of Article 6.3(c)[341], is on producers of the non-subsidized like product. Have their revenue, investments, or crop choices been "meaningfully affected" by the level of price suppression experienced? These are the types of questions that provide guidance as to whether a particular level of price suppression is significant or not. The notion of "meaningfully affect" and "serious prejudice" are, in essence, equivalent for the purpose of Article 6.3(c).

161. The US 22 December 2003 response to Question 234, at paragraph 136, states that "[t]he use of the term 'significant' however, would seem to be intended to prevent insignificant price effects from rising to the level of serious prejudice." But this statement presumes some sort of an objective standard exists by which to judge what are "insignificant price effects". The United States provides no suggestions how this Panel or future panels are to make such an abstract determination. The United States' position implies that the "Panel will know them when they see them". But the Article 6.3(c) test, at least, requires the Panel to make an assessment of the relationship between the price effects and serious prejudice. And this link is to be judged by whether the price effects are "significant".

162. The Panel should firmly reject the two-step process suggested by the US interpretation. The first step would require a finding, using some unknown, non-textual standard, of whether a particular price level of suppression is "significant". Evidence that Brazilian producers would have lost $71.5 million during MY 1999-2002 from only one cent per pound of price suppression[342] would be totally irrelevant for the first step.[343] Only if a panel makes this "significant"

340 "Although the term "significant" is not defined, the inclusion of this qualifier in Article 6.3(c) presumably was intended to ensure that *margins of undercutting so small that they could not meaningfully affect suppliers of the imported product* whose price was being undercut are not considered to give rise to serious prejudice..." (emphasis added). Panel Report, *Indonesia – Automobiles*, WT/DS54/R, para. 14.254.

341 Brazil notes that Articles 6.3(a), (b) and (d) do not contain similar qualitative or quantitative qualifiers.

342 Brazil's 9 September 2003 Further Submission, para. 258 (citing a $143 million loss from a 2 cents per pound level of price suppression).

343 A good example of evidence that would be irrelevant under the first part of the US test is found in the testimony of Christopher Ward. He indicated that a 10 percent increase in prices for Mato

finding, divorced from any impact on producers, would it move to the second step, *i.e.,* whether that level of now-significant price effects caused serious prejudice. But such an interpretation, like many proposed by the United States in this dispute, would leave Members who lost millions of dollars due to the effects of subsidies without a remedy. There is no textual basis for such a result, which would be contrary to the object and purpose of the SCM Agreement. In sum, the Panel should adopt the *Indonesia – Automobiles* standard of judging significance in light of whether the particular level of price suppression "meaningfully affects" non-subsidized suppliers of the like product.[344]

163. But even if the Panel decides to adopt some sort of numerical standard not reflected in the text of Article 6.3(c), Brazil has also set forth evidence showing that the levels of price suppression found by a number of different economists are "significant".[345] In assessing whether the various levels of price suppression found by USDA and other economists are "significant," the Panel should take into account the fact that upland cotton is a primary commodity traded in huge volumes and produced and consumed in a large number of countries. Under these circumstances, any measurable and identifiable effect on the *world* price from the subsidies provided by a single Member is important. In this case, the Panel is faced with particularly compelling facts – during MY 1999-2002 (and even during MY 1997-1998) the record shows that the absolute numerical levels of price suppression caused by some or all of the US subsidies were significant, ranging from 4 to 26.3 per cent of the world price, and 10 to 33.6 per cent of the US price.[346]

164. Finally, the United States argues in paragraph 136 that the effect of Brazil's interpretation is that any production subsidy would run afoul of Part III of the SCM Agreement, thus turning it into a prohibited subsidies provision. There is no basis for this argument. First, it is difficult to see how extremely low levels of production subsidies (0.0001 cents per pound price effects in the US example) could "materially affect" any competing producers of the non-subsidized Member. Only production subsidies that generate price suppression significant enough to "materially affect" competitors would be subject to the disciplines of Part III. This is far from an insignificant threshold, and gives meaning to the word "significant".

Grosso producers in MY 2000 and MY 2001 would have permitted them to cover their variable costs for MY 2001 and come close to covering variable costs in MY 2000. However, because of the losses they suffered without such revenue increases, many Mato Grosso producers reduced production or were forced out of cotton production. Mato Grosso production fell by 34 per cent between MY 2000 -2001. Exhibit Bra-283 (Statement of Christopher Ward – 7 October 2003, paras. 8-10 and accompanying graph).

[344] The US example of a per-unit payment of 0.0001 cents per pound in paragraph 136 is irrelevant, because under its hypothetical, this particular level of price suppression could never "meaningfully affect" any suppliers of the like product.

[345] Brazil's 9 September 2003 Further Submission, Table 22; Brazil's 7 October Oral Statement, paras. 30-34.

[346] See Brazil's 9 September 2003 Further Submission, paras. 148-161, 190, 200-232, 254, 379-384 and Table 23.

165. Second, this US argument is similar to other arguments it has made to the effect that any limitations on the amount of subsidies would change "actionable" subsidies to "prohibited" subsidies.[347] The United States loses sight of the basic fact that an actionable subsidy that creates adverse effects is a violation of WTO rules. No Member has the right to provide unlimited production subsidies *if* they cause serious prejudice. Members deciding to impose discretionary or mandatory limits on the amount of production subsidies may significantly diminish the possibility that such subsidies create significant price suppression or an ongoing threat of serious prejudice. But it is wrong for the United States to argue that because the only practical way to impose limitations on production subsidies may be some sort of a cap on such subsidies necessarily an actionable subsidy is turned into a "prohibited subsidy".[348]

235. Please comment on paragraphs 8, 9 and 10 of the US 2 December oral statement, in particular, why the average Brazilian price is shown as lower than the average US price. BRA

236. The Panel notes Exhibit US-47 (and the chart in paragraph 13 of the US 2 December oral statement). Please provide a conceptually analogous chart to Exhibit US-63 with respect to data relating to the US interpretation of "world market share". USA

Brazil's Comment:

166. Brazil considers it telling that the United States does not provide the percentage figures underlying the chart at paragraph 138 of its 22 December 2003 response. This is because the percentage figures reveal that the US methodology suffers from a fatal flaw. The sum of the US world market share, as defined by the United States[349], and the "rest of the world" market share, as defined by the United States[350], far exceeds 100 per cent. To clarify this point, Brazil presents the following table, based on the data provided by the United States in Exhibit US-47 and in response to question 197.[351]

---

[347] US 2 December 2003 Oral Statement, paras 83-84.

[348] *Ibid.*

[349] "(Domestic Mill Use + Exports)" / Total World Consumption; *see* US 22 December 2003 Answers to Questions, para. 137.

[350] "(Non-US Domestic Mill Use (*i.e.* consumption) + Non-US Exports) / Total World Consumption.

[351] US 22 December 2003 Answers to Question, para. 15 and Exhibit US-120. Since the United States did not provide any data on "Non-US Exports," Brazil has used USDA published figures on "Foreign Cotton Exports" from USDA's Cotton and Wool Yearbook (Exhibit Bra-412 (Cotton and Wool Situation and Outlook Yearbook, USDA, November 2003, Table 16).

	US Domestic Consumption	US Exports	World Consumption	Non-US[352] Domestic Consumption	Non-US Exports	US Share[353]	Non-US Share	Total Share
	million bales					per cent		
1995	10.647	7.675	86.040	75.393	19.900	**21.29**	**110.75**	**132.05**
1996	11.126	6.865	88.031	76.905	20.100	**20.44**	**110.19**	**130.63**
1997	11.349	7.500	87.138	75.789	19.300	**21.63**	**109.12**	**130.76**
1998	10.401	4.298	84.640	74.239	19.400	**17.37**	**110.63**	**128.00**
1999	10.194	6.750	90.957	80.763	20.600	**18.63**	**111.44**	**130.07**
2000	8.862	6.740	92.172	83.310	19.800	**16.93**	**111.87**	**128.79**
2001	7.696	11.000	94.381	86.685	18.100	**19.81**	**111.02**	**130.83**
2002	7.270	11.900	97.930	90.660	18.700	**19.58**	**111.67**	**131.25**
2003	6.200	13.200	97.690	91.490	19.100	**19.86**	**113.20**	**133.06**

167. Indeed, as the Panel can readily see, the "rest of the world" "world market share", as defined by the United States, exceeds 100 per cent – a result that defies any logic.

168. For the ease of the Panel's reference, Brazil presents an excerpt from its own figures originally presented in Exhibit Bra-302,[354] showing that, under Brazil's and USDA's definition of the "world market share," the total world market share equals 100 per cent.

	US upland cotton exports	Non-US upland cotton exports	World upland cotton exports	US Share	Non-US Share	Total Share
	million bales				per cent	
1995	7.375	19.394	26.769	27.55	72.45	100.00
1996	6.399	19.384	25.783	24.82	75.18	100.00
1997	7.060	18.534	25.594	27.58	72.42	100.00
1998	4.056	18.559	22.615	17.94	82.06	100.00
1999	6.303	19.805	26.108	24.14	75.86	100.00
2000	6.303	19.170	25.473	24.74	75.26	100.00
2001	10.603	17.072	27.675	38.31	61.69	100.00
2002	11.266	15.796	27.062	41.63	58.37	100.00
2003	11.225	17.690	28.915	38.82	61.18	100.00

169. Brazil will address the US arguments that the world market share means share of world consumption in detail in its comments on the following questions.

237. Could a phenomenon that remains at approximately the same level over a given period of time be considered a "consistent trend" within the

352 "World Consumption minus US Domestic Consumption."

353 The 2003 figure differs a little from what would seem to be the 2003 figure in the US table at paragraph 138 of the US 22 December 2003 Answers to Questions. It appears that the reason is the United States use of its non-updated figures from Exhibit US-47, rather than the updated MY 2002 and 2003 figures from its 22 December 2003 response to Question 197, para. 15.

354 *See* also Brazil's 27 October 2003 Answers to Questions, paras. 123-129.

meaning of Article 6.3(d)? Do parties have any suggestions as to how to determine a "consistent trend", statistically or otherwise? BRA, USA

Brazil's Comment:

170. As noted in its 22 December 2003 response to this question, Brazil agrees that a phenomenon that remains at approximately the same level over a given period cannot be considered a consistent trend.[355] However, as detailed in that answer, this is not the situation facing this Panel. The data clearly establishes that, in MY 2001, 2002 and 2003, there is an increase in the US world market share over the previous three-year average, and that this increase follows a consistent trend since MY 1996 (and MY 1986).[356] In response to this question, the United States again relies on an utterly wrong interpretation of the term "world market share" in Article 6.3(d) of the SCM Agreement. The term does not mean "world consumption share", but world market share of exports, as detailed by Brazil many times, including in these comments.

238. According to the US interpretation of the term "world market share":

(a) should the domestic consumption of closed markets be added into the denominator?

Brazil's Comment:

171. Brazil understands that the Panel's question referred to the distinction between "competitive markets," where world upland cotton producers/exporters compete for available share of world exports, and "closed markets", where no competition for export market share can take place because of subsidies like the domestic Step 2 programme, tariffs, or non-tariff barriers.[357] The US 22 December 2003 response, at paragraph 140, affirms that the United States would greatly increase and distort the Article 6.3(d) denominator by including, *inter alia*, all sales of US upland cotton in the US market. Yet, there is little "international trade" in the US domestic upland cotton market, because there were only marginal imports during MY 1999-2002.[358] The effect of the US argument is to obscure and hide the huge volume and market share increase in US exports in "competitive" markets during MY 1998-2003. As Brazil has argued, the US

---

[355] Brazil's 22 December 2003 Answers to Questions, para. 134.

[356] Brazil's 22 December 2003 Answers to Questions, paras. 133-139; Brazil's 27 October 2003 Answers to Questions, paras 123-129. Brazil further notes the new information presented by the United States concerning US upland cotton exports in MY 2002 and 2003. These figures (11.9 million bales and 13.2 million bales respectively) would replace Brazil's latest information, as contained in Exhibit Bra-302 (11.3 million bales and 11.2 million bales respectively). These new facts strengthen Brazil's threat of serious prejudice claim under Article 6.3(d) and footnote 13 of the SCM Agreement. *See* US 22 December 2003 Answers to Questions, para. 15 and Brazil's comment to US 22 December 2003 Answer to Question 197, above.

[357] Brazil detailed its arguments concerning the focus of Article 6.3(d) on competitive markets and where "trade" takes place in its 7 October 2003 Oral Statement, paras. 38-41.

[358] For example, between MY 1999-2001, US imports represented only 0.2 percent of total US mill use of upland cotton. *See* Exhibit Bra-4 ("Fact Sheet: Upland Cotton," USDA, January 2003, p. 4-5).

focus on "consumption" as opposed to "trade" is contrary to the text, context, and object and purpose of Article 6.3(d).[359] Article 6.3(d) focuses on "trade", not domestic consumption, and thus involves competitive world markets where exports and trade take place.[360]

172. It is noteworthy that the US answer ignores un-rebutted evidence that USDA's top economists and analysts repeatedly use the phrase "world market share" to describe and analyze how US agricultural exporters are performing in competitive world markets for exports.[361] The United States never provided a single instance in which USDA economists – or any other Member's economists – included domestic US consumption in their analysis of the US "world market share". This is because the unique US notion of "consumption" (which combines exports, domestic use, and imports as part of "consumption") simply does not exist (in the literature or trade statistics) outside of the US arguments in this case.

(b) if US production and consumption increased by the same percentage, whilst the rest of the world's production and consumption remained steady, would this imply an increase in the US "world market share" by a different percentage?

Brazil's Comment:

173. The US 22 December 2003 response in effect acknowledges, at paragraph 142, that the US subsidies could be subject to a challenge under Article 6.3(d) even though those subsidies did not cause any increase in US exports. Under the US theory, even though none of the non-subsidized producer/exporters of upland cotton would have lost any world export market share, these producers could initiate a claim against the United States under Article 6.3(d), in addition to Article 6.3(a), because the US domestic production and domestic consumption increased. This US response highlights the disconnect between its theory and the reality of what Article 6.3(d) really is about – the impact of subsidies on trade in the product in question in competitive international markets.

174. Of course, the Part III of the SCM Agreement discipline addressing the Panel's hypothetical factual situation is Article 6.3(a). The United States argues in paragraph 143 that "Brazil's approach … would allow a larger or even dominant upland cotton consumer to provide huge per-unit production subsidies that increased the share of its own domestic consumption that its production supplied *without any disciplines under Article 6.3(d)*, regardless of the impact on other Members who could potentially supply that increasing domestic consumption" (emphasis added). But what the US-posited hypothetical outlines is a classic "displacement or impedence" case under Article 6.3(a)." But for" the "huge per-unit production subsidies", the non-subsidized Member exporters would have

[359] Brazil's 7 October 2003 Oral Statement, paras 38-41; Brazil's 27 October 2003 Answers to Question, paraa. 202-206; Brazil's 18 November 2003 Further Rebuttal Submission, paras. 170-172; Brazil's 2 December 2003 Oral Statement, paras. 62-65.

[360] Brazil's 7 October 2003 Oral Statement, para. 39.

[361] Brazil's 7 October 2003 Oral Statement, note 78.

increased or maintained their export market share in the market of the subsidizing Member. Thus, interpreting Article 6.3(d) to mean the "world market share of exports" does not leave non-subsidized Member producers who are squeezed out of the subsidizing Member's market without a remedy. And the fact that Article 6.3(d) does not *also* discipline the situation covered by Article 6.3(a) is hardly surprising, since negotiators presumably intended different provisions to cover different situations.

175. Indeed, the US argument in paragraph 143 highlights the fallacy of its interpretation. It argues that "the ordinary meaning of 'world market share' in Article 6.3(d) … would capture impacts both on the market of the subsidizing Member (as in Article 6.3(a)) and in third-country markets (Articles 6.3(b) and 6.3(c))".[362] But if that were true, then there would be no need for Articles 6.3(a) and 6.3(b).[363] The US interpretation would render one of the sets of disciplines a nullity, in violation of the customary rules of treaty interpretation as codified in the *Vienna Convention.*

176. Finally, rather than capturing all the possible instances where subsidies can cause serious prejudice in world markets, the US "consumption" interpretation of "world market share" leaves a gaping hole in the serious prejudice remedies. The facts of this case show how the US interpretation would completely hide the huge US increase in world market share of exports – from 25 per cent in MY 1999 to 41.6 per cent in MY 2002. Where a Member uses subsidies to capture export market share in the competitive world market, it causes serious prejudice by limiting the opportunities for non-subsidized Members to increase their exports.[364] The record shows that African upland cotton producers, with among the lowest world production costs, actually *lost* world market share to the United States between MY 1998-2002.[365] Yet, the US interpretation of Article 6.3(d) would deny them, as well as Brazil, any remedy to challenge such an increase in the US world market share of exports.

(c) does Saudi Arabia have a small world market share for oil? USA

Brazil's Comment:

177. Contrary to the US 22 December 2003 response, Brazil has no difficulty appreciating the relevance of the Panel's question. Even accepting the US fig-

---

[362] US 22 December 2003 Answers to Questions, para. 143.

[363] Article 6.3(a) disciplines the situation described in the Panel's question: a Member using subsidies to increase the share of domestic consumption satisfied by domestic supply (*i.e.,* displacing or impeding imports into the market of the subsidizing Member). Article 6.3(b) disciplines such effects of a Member's subsidies (displacing or impeding exports) in a third country market. Article 6.3(c) disciplines significant price effects of a Member's subsidies in all markets. Brazil's 2 December 2003 Oral Statement, para. 63.

[364] *See* Brazil's 9 September Further Submission, paras. 451-456; paras 444-453 (facts supporting the interconnected relationship between the serious prejudiced due to price suppression and the serious prejudice due to increased world market share); Annex III Statements by Brazilian producers Christopher Ward, Jaime Naito, Aloysio Lerner and Ronaldo Spirlandelli de Oliveria, among others.

[365] Brazil's 9 September 2003 Further Rebuttal Submission, Section 7.1 and Figure 26 following para. 282.

ures, which include Saudi Arabian consumption of crude oil to produce refined products that are then exported, the US response highlights the significant (25 per cent) difference between their "consumption" methodology and a world market share of exports methodology.[366]

239. How does the US respond to Brazil's assertions that, under the US interpretation of the term "world market share":

(a) there would be no WTO disciplines on production-enhancing subsidies that increase a Member's world market share of exports? (see paragraph 64 of Brazil's 2 December oral statement);

Brazil's Comment:

178. The US 22 December 2003 response confirms Brazil's arguments that the US interpretation leaves no direct remedy for a Member who either loses or is not able to increase its world market share of exports as a result of another Member's subsidies.[367] The United States asserts in paragraph 147 of its answer, that Article 6.3(b) provides such a remedy. But that provision only addresses a non-subsidizing Member's right to contest the effects of subsidies in, *inter alia*, increasing a subsidizing Member's export market share in an *individual* third country market. The *EC – Sugar Exports I (Australia)* and *EC- Sugar Exports II (Brazil)*[368] disputes demonstrated how difficult it can be for a non-subsidizing Member to demonstrate displacement or impedence in an individual third country market. Article 6.3(d) helped to address this legal vacuum by providing clear, objective guidelines for subsidizing Members to know when their increase in world market share of exports would be subject to disciplines, and to provide an objective basis for the injured non-subsidized exporting Member to evaluate and protect its rights.

179. The United States further argues, in paragraph 147 of its response, that Article 5(a) of the SCM Agreement would provide a remedy for a non-subsidized Member who lost world market share in exports. But while that provision relates to "injury to the domestic industry of another Member", footnote 11 of the SCM Agreement qualifies that the "injury" "is used in the same sense as it is used in Part V"." Injury" is defined in Article 15.1 *et seq.* of the SCM Agreement as that caused by (a) the volume of the subsidized *imports* and the effect of the subsidized imports on prices in the domestic market for like products, and (b) the consequent impact of these imports on the domestic producers of such products. In the context of this dispute, this remedy would appear to apply only to US subsidized exports to the Brazilian market (*i.e.,* the "domestic" market). Contrary to the US argument, Article 5(a) would not address the situation covered by Article 6.3(d), where Brazilian exporters suffer serious prejudice by an increase in the US world market share of exports.

---

[366] US 22 December 2003 Answers to Questions, para. 145.

[367] *See e.g.* Brazil's 2 December 2003 Oral Statement, para. 64.

[368] GATT Panel Report, *EC – Sugar Exports I (Australia)*, L/4833 – 26S/290, para. 4.26-4.27; GATT Panel Report, *EC – Sugar Exports II (Brazil)*, L/5011-27S/69, para. 414.

180. Finally, the United States claims, at paragraph 147 of its response, that Article XVI:1 of GATT 1994 would provide Brazil with the right to challenge the US world market share for exports. Brazil agrees that GATT Article XVI:1, as read in conjunction with GATT Article XVI:3, provides for a very analogous recourse as that provided for in Article 6.3(d), *i.e.,* any subsidies that increase exports and lead to an inequitable share of world export trade. But the United States contradicts itself in offering up an Article XVI:1 remedy (which is inexorably linked to Article XVI:3, second sentence) in paragraph 147, while arguing elsewhere that this provision is no longer applicable and has been replaced by Article 6.3.[369]

181. In sum, the Panel is left with the US interpretations that (a) there is no longer any disciplines for a Member suffering from a decrease in its world market share for exports under Article XVI:3, second sentence on the one hand[370], and (b) Article XVI:3's presumed successor, Article 6.3(d), does not apply to the world market share of exports. In effect, Members are left without any explicit protection for their loss of world market share of exports due to massive subsidization. Such a result defies the text, context, and object and purpose of Article 6.3(d), as Brazil has repeatedly argued.

182. In any event, whether there may be – outside Article 6.3(d) of the SCM Agreement – indirect disciplines that may provide some relief to non-subsidizing Members whose rights have been nullified and impaired by a subsidizing Member's increase in world market share of exports does not free the Panel from its obligation to interpret the term "world market share" in Article 6.3(d) in accordance with its "ordinary meaning, in their context and in light of the treaty's object and purpose". Brazil demonstrated that under a *Vienna Convention* analysis, the term "world market share" means world market share of exports – not consumption.[371]

(b) a Member's exports would have to be disregarded in calculating their "world market share" in terms of "world consumption"? (see e.g. paragraph 65 of Brazil's 2 December oral statement)USA

Brazil's Comment:

183. In paragraph 148 of its 22 December 2003 response, the United States does not address the substance of the Panel's question or Brazil's earlier arguments. That is, the United States does not respond to the fact that its methodology double counts exports as part of the world market share of the exporting country *and* the importing country.[372] In effect, the United States requires this Panel to ignore this illogical conceptual error in its interpretation of the term

---

[369] US 22 December 2003 Answers to Questions, para. 149.

[370] US 22 December 2003 Answers to Questions, para. 146.

[371] Brazil's 7 October 2003 Oral Statement, paras. 38-41; Brazil's 27 October 2003 Answers to Question, para. 202-206; Brazil's 18 November 2003 Further Rebuttal Submission, paras. 170-172; Brazil's 2 December 2003 Oral Statement, parass 62-65.

[372] The United States admits that its methodology counts imports as part of domestic consumption. *See* US 22 December 2003 Answers to Questions, Table at para. 15 and note 24.

"world market share". Instead, the United States insists that it is not incumbent upon the Panel "to interpret the term 'domestic consumption'".[373] Brazil agrees, but that is because the term "domestic consumption" is nowhere to be found in the text or context of Article 6.3(d) of the SCM Agreement. Nor is it consistent with the object and purpose of Article 6.3(d). But since the United States would read "consumption" into that text, then the Panel must closely examine its meaning, using appropriate context to do so. And it should reject the use of that term if it leads to an interpretation that is illogical, leads to absurd results, and otherwise fails to live up to the standards on the interpretation of international treaties, as set out in the *Vienna Convention*.

240. Does Article XVI:3 of GATT 1994 provide context in interpreting Article 6.3(d) of the *SCM Agreement*? Do these provisions apply separately? If not, could it indicate that "world market share" is intended to mean the same as "share of world export trade"? USA

Brazil's Comment:

184. Regarding the first question, Brazil has previously detailed the basis for its arguments that Article XVI:3, second sentence of GATT 1994 provides very important context for interpreting Article 6.3(d).[374] In response to the Panel's second question, Brazil has demonstrated that these provisions do apply separately, for the reasons Brazil has earlier stated.[375] With respect to the third question, the phrase "world market share" in the text of Article 6.3(d) is intended to mean the same thing as "share of world export trade".[376]

185. The United States points out several differences between Article XVI:3 and Article 6.3(d), one of which is its faulty interpretation that Article XVI:3, second sentence only deals with "export" subsidies. Brazil has earlier demonstrated that the pool of subsidies that could cause serious prejudice is the same for Article 6.3(d) and Article XVI:3, second sentence.[377]

186. The United States further argues that Brazil agreed in the Tokyo Round Subsidies Code that GATT 1994 Article XVI:3 is limited to export subsidies.[378] This is not correct, as demonstrated by the text of the Tokyo Round Code.[379] It

---

373 US 22 December 2003 Answers to Questions, para. 148.

374 Brazil's 18 November 2003 Further Rebuttal Submission, para. 172.

375 Brazil's 27 October 2003 Answer to Question 161, para. 130 and Question 196(b), paras. 202-206.

376 Brazil's 18 November 2003 Further Rebuttal Submission, paras 170-172; Brazil's 7 October Oral Statement, paras. 38-41.

377 Brazil's 27 October 2003 Answer to Question 185, paras. 194-201; Brazil's 18 November 2003 Further Rebuttal Submission, paras 178-179.

378 US 22 December 2003 Answers to Questions, para. 149.

379 US 27 October 2003 Answers to Questions, para. 130. For purposes of Article XVI:3 of the General Agreement and paragraph 1 above:

(a) "more than an equitable share of world export trade" shall include any case in which the effect of an export subsidy granted by a signatory is to displace the exports of another signatory bearing in mind the developments on world markets;

uses the language "shall include" and "export subsidy" in connection with the notion of a more than equitable share of world trade.[380] Thus, an inequitable share of world trade may result from export subsidies, but it is not limited to that source. Moreover, whatever the interpretation of these terms may have been in the now extinct plurilateral Tokyo Round Subsidies Code, the only text that continues to exist is the ordinary meaning of the words used in Article XVI:3, second sentence, which must be interpreted according to its ordinary meaning in its context, and in light of the object and purpose of the GATT. Yet, the United States argues that even that provision is "incapable of definition or application".[381]

187. The United States argues in paragraph 151 that the use of the term "market" provides the fundamental key to its interpretation. The US argument would include *all* markets where upland cotton is produced, consumed, or used when it states that Article 6.3(d) is *not* limited to "markets in international trade". But this argument ignores the fundamental focus of Article 6.3 (as well as Part III of the SCM Agreement itself) on *international* trade and the impact of subsidies on *competition* between subsidized and non-subsidized producers and their products. For example, Article 6.3(a) involves situation, in which exporters are impeded or displaced from the market of the subsidizing Member. Articles 6.3(b) and 6.4 involve the situation, in which the export share of a subsidizing Member squeezes out or limits the export share of the non-subsidizing Member in a third country market. And the United States has argued that Article 6.3(c) only involves situations, in which prices are suppressed in markets where competition between the subsidized products and the non-subsidized like products take place.[382] In essence, the key to initiating a claim under all three of these provisions is demonstrating that "trade" and "competition" have been affected through the use of subsidies.

188. The Panel must ask how is it possible that Articles 6.3(a) – (c) only apply to situations where international trade and competition actually take place (or are impeded from taking place), while Article 6.3(d) is totally different – it is to be read without any reference to competition and trade *at all*? The United States asserts that the "world" in "world market share" means the "entire world," without regard to whether there is trade or competition between subsidizing Member products and those of non-subsidizing Members.[383] But this slavishly literal reading goes too far. Brazil submits that read in this context, along with the other contextual provisions such as "trade" in footnote 17 of the SCM Agreement, and Article XVI:3, second sentence, that the US interpretation is simply wrong.

(b) with regard to new markets traditional patterns of supply of the product concerned to the world market, region or country, in which the new market is situated shall be taken into account in determining 'equitable share of world export trade'[.]

[380] *See* US 27 October 2003 Answers to Questions, para. 130.

[381] US 22 December 2003 Answers to Questions, para. 149; US 27 October 2003 Answers to Questions, paras. 131-132.

[382] US 18 November 2003 Further Rebuttal Submission, paras. 37-40.

[383] US 22 December 2003 Answer to Questions, para. 151.

189. The United States further argues, at paragraph 149 of its response, that "Brazil has not offered any objective definition" of "equitable share". This is incorrect.[384] Further, the fact that certain GATT and WTO provisions express disciplines in broad terms, such as "equitable" or "reasonable" or "serious" or "significant," does not mean that a treaty interpreter can simply throw up his or her hands and find, as the United States urges, that a provision is incapable of interpretation. Article 31 of the *Vienna Convention* provides that "the words of a treaty are to be given their ordinary meaning, in their context and in light of the treaty's object and purpose".[385] Further, the Appellate Body held in *US – Gasoline* that "an interpreter is not free to adopt a reading that would result in reducing whole clauses or paragraphs of a treaty to redundancy or inutility".[386] Thus, the Panel should reject this US attempt to condemn Article XVI:3.

190. However, should the Panel decide that GATT Article XVI:3, second sentence is, indeed, inapplicable, then this certainly strengthens the basis for the Panel to interpret the phrase "world market share" in Article 6.3(d) as meaning the "share of world export trade". It is inconceivable that negotiators – who certainly did not expressly terminate the application of Article XVI:3, second sentence – would also intend, without making it explicit, that there would be no disciplines for subsidies that allowed Members to seize world market share of exports in competitive markets.

241. How does the US reconcile its data on consumption for 2002 in US Exhibit 40, Table 1 with the "consumption" data it refers to in its 30 September submission, paragraph 34, Exhibit US-47 or US-71? USA

Brazil's Comment:

191. The US 22 December 2003 response appears to have clarified that the graph in paragraph 34 of its 30 September 2003 Further Submission relates to US finished cotton fibre consumption, while the "consumption" referred to in Exhibits US-40, US-47 and US-71 relates to upland cotton lint consumption by US textile mills. Brazil has demonstrated the irrationality of the US world market share of upland cotton consumption data in terms of Article 6.3(d). Brazil has also demonstrated the irrelevance of the US arguments concerning the US consumption of finished textile products.[387]

242. How much of the benefits of PFC, MLA, CCP and Direct Payments go to land owners? If not all of the benefits go to land owners, what proportion goes to producers? USA

---

[384] Brazil refers the Panel and the United States to its oral answers to the Chairman's questions during the October 2003 meeting of the Panel, paras. 17-18 of Brazil's 9 October 2003 Closing Statement, and paras. 189-193 of Brazil's 27 October 2003 Answers to Questions.

[385] Appellate Body Report, *US. – Gasoline,* WT/DS2/AB/R, p. 17.

[386] Appellate Body Report, *US – Gasoline,* WT/DS2/AB/R, p. 23.

[387] Brazil's 7 October 2003 Oral Statement, para.25.

Brazil's Comment:

192. The Panel's question is set out in a section entitled "Serious Prejudice" and uses the word "benefit" relating to contract payments. Brazil will address its comments to the US 22 December 2003 response in two senses of the word "benefit". First, Brazil will address its comment with respect to the definition of the term "benefit" as it is used in Article 1.1(b) of the SCM Agreement. Second, the question also appears to address "benefit" in a more generic sense, as it relates to the effects of contract payments on US production, exports, and the world price of upland cotton. Brazil believes it is this second sense of the term "benefit" to which the Panel's question was directed. However, the United States' answer concludes by asserting that "35 per cent of the value of decoupled payments would benefit upland cotton producers"[388], suggesting that it interpreted the Panel's question as directed at the term "benefit" in the sense of Article 1.1(b) of the SCM Agreement. The United States also suggests that the remaining 65 per cent of the US contract payments do not constitute a benefit within the meaning of Article 1.1(b) of the SCM Agreement.

"Benefit" under Article 1.1(b) of the SCM Agreement

193. As set forth below, for the purposes of Article 1 of the SCM Agreement, the record shows that 100 per cent of contract payments are paid to the bank accounts of current upland cotton producers on terms that constitute "benefits".

194. Under the 2002 FSRI Act, direct and counter-cyclical payments are *only* paid to "producers on farms for which payment yields and base acres are established".[389] "Producers" are defined in the Act as "an owner, operator, landlord, tenant, or sharecropper that shares in the risk of producing a crop and is entitled to share in the crop availability for marketing from the farm, or would have shared had the crop been produced". A similar definition of "producer" existed for the 1996 FAIR Act.[390] As implemented, USDA acknowledges that contract payments "are paid only to farm operators rather than farmland owners, with payment benefits split between the operator and owners in the case of crop-share rental arrangements".[391] Thus, the only "landlords" or "owners" who directly receive contract payments are those who are producers of upland cotton, *i.e.,* those that share in the risk of producing an upland cotton crop.[392] The USDA study further states that "[t]he operators' receipt of the PFC payments compensates for higher land costs that may result from the effects of the PFC programme".[393]

---

[388] US 22 December 2003 Answers to Questions, para. 158.

[389] Exhibit Bra-29 (Sections 1103 and 1104 of the 2002 FSRI Act).

[390] Exhibit Bra-28 (Section 111(b) of the 1996 FAIR Act).

[391] Exhibit US–78, p. 44.

[392] *See* Brazil's 22 July 2003 Oral Statement, para. 57; Brazil's 22 August 2003 Rebuttal Submission, paras. 19, 24.

[393] Exhibit US–78, p. 44.

195. Brazil has proved that without the receipt of the PFC, market loss assistance, direct and counter-cyclical payments in their bank accounts, US upland cotton producers could not meet their costs – including their lease and land-related costs. Even if these current producers may subsequently write checks to their landlords who do not share in the risk of producing a crop, that does not mean that the subsidies that the producers are legally entitled to receive from USDA do not provide them with a "benefit", within the meaning of Article 1.1(b) of the SCM Agreement, as the United States appears to argue. Rather, the full amount of the payment is made to the current producers.

196. The Appellate Body has held that a "benefit" exists if a financial contribution is received by a "recipient" or a "producer" of the subsidized good on terms more favourable than those available to the recipient in the market.[394] Producers of US crops who have contract base acreage receive these payments from USDA. In *Canada – Aircraft*, the Appellate Body established that "a benefit does not exist in the abstract, but must be received and enjoyed by a beneficiary or a recipient", noting that "the term benefit, therefore, implies that there must be a recipient".[395] The Appellate Body in *US – CVD's on EC Products* held that "the focus of any analysis of whether a 'benefit' exists should be on 'legal or natural persons' instead of on productive operations".[396] Contrary to the US arguments, it is legally irrelevant for purposes of determining the existence of a "benefit" under the SCM Agreement whether a benefit received by a "recipient" is subsequently transferred to other non-recipients.

197. The United States' 22 December 2003 response continues its efforts to transform this dispute into a countervailing duty investigation based on now-defunct Annex IV of the SCM Agreement. The United States alleges in paragraph 158 of its 22 December 2003 response that only 35 per cent of PFC, market loss, CCP and direct payments "would benefit upland cotton producers". If the United States is using the word "benefit" in the sense of Article 1.1(b) of the SCM Agreement, then the statement is legally as well as factually wrong. As Brazil has demonstrated above, 100 per cent of the four types of contract payments are paid to the bank accounts of current upland cotton producers. Thus, there is no doubt that each of the four contract payment subsidies confers a "benefit" to upland cotton producers.

---

[394] In *Canada – Aircraft*, the Appellate Body found that:

> ...the word "benefit", as used in Article 1.1(b), implies some kind of comparison. This must be so, for there can be no "benefit" to the recipient unless the "financial contribution" makes the recipient "better off" than it would otherwise have been, absent that contribution. In our view, *the marketplace provides an appropriate basis for comparison* in determining whether a "benefit" has been "conferred" because the trade distorting potential of a "financial contribution" can be identified <u>by determining whether the recipient has received a "financial contribution" on terms more favourable than those available to the recipient in the market.</u>" (emphasis in original and underlining added)

Appellate Body Report, *Canada – Aircraft*, WT/DS70/AB/R, para. 157; The same language is included in Appellate Body Report, *US – CVD's on EC Products*, WT/DS212/AB/R, para. 106.

[395] Appellate Body Report, *Canada – Aircraft*, WT/DS70/AB/R, para. 154.

[396] Appellate Body Report, *US – CVD's on EC Products*, WT/DS212/AB/R, para. 110.

198. Finally, even if this case was a countervailing duty investigation, under existing CVD procedures, 100 per cent of the contract payments – not 35 per cent – would be allocated across the production value of the producers. This is, again, because, first, the total amount of benefits to the company producing the subsidized goods would be calculated. No deductions are made depending on how the subsidy is used by the recipients (*i.e.,* to pay rents).100 per cent of the subsidy is countervailable. Only in case the subsidy is not *de facto* tied to the production of the subsidized product, is there in a second step an allocation of the benefit (100 per cent) over the total value of the company's production.

Use of "benefit" to assess the amount of subsidies that could cause serious prejudice

199. The more likely use of the term "benefit" in the Panel's question is the extent to which contract payments contributed to and will contribute to the serious prejudice suffered by Brazil. In other words, to what extent do contract payments enhance and support the production and exports of US upland cotton, and to what extent do they suppress world prices? Brazil has produced evidence, *inter alia*, through Professor Sumner's analysis, that the contract payments have various effects on production, exports and world prices. The isolated effects of these contract payments are less than those created by the marketing loan programme. Brazil acknowledged that one reason why the serious prejudice effects of PFC payments are relatively small is because a certain percentage of the payments were capitalized into land values and subsequently into land rents.[397] Brazil noted that this evidence is supported by Professor Sumner's conclusions because significant amounts of the PFC payments (approximately two thirds) were available to generate production effects.[398] Finally, Brazil also demonstrated that the total USDA-estimated increase in land values from PFC payments translated into less than one per cent of an upland cotton producers' total costs.[399]

200. The United States 22 December 2003 response now claims for the first time that only 35 per cent of the value of decoupled payments benefited upland cotton production during the period of investigation.[400] Having asserted this fact, the United States bears the burden of proving it.[401] But even a cursory look at the evidence proffered by the United States shows that this assertion is simply not true.

201. The US assumption is that every dollar of every contract payment placed into the bank accounts of producers *leasing* land (approximately 65 per cent of

[397] Brazil's 27 October 2003 Answer to Question 179, paras. 164-167.

[398] Brazil's 27 October 2003 Answer to Question 179, para. 167.

[399] *Ibid.*

[400] US 22 December 2003 Answers to Questions, para. 157.

[401] As the party asserting this fact, the United States bears the burden of proving it. *See e.g.* Appellate Body Report, *Japan – Apples*, para. 157 ("It is important to distinguish, on the one hand, the principle that the complainant must establish a *prima facie* case of inconsistency with a provision of a covered agreement from, on the other hand, the principle that the party that asserts a fact is responsible for providing proof thereof.").

upland cotton land is "leased" or "rented") is immediately required to be paid to non-producer landlords.[402] The United States produced no evidence that 100 per cent of even PFC payments (let alone market loss assistance, direct or counter-cyclical payments) to cash rent cotton producers were consumed by increased rents during the period of investigation or since contract payments began in 1996.[403] Further, the United States produces no evidence that 65 per cent of the upland cotton land is cash-rented. In fact, only 25 per cent of the US upland cotton land is cash-rented, whereas 40 per cent is share-rented.[404] As established above, share-rent lease agreements mean that the landlord is considered a producer of upland cotton. Therefore, even under the flawed US theory, much more than just 35 per cent, in fact at least 75 per cent, should be considered benefits to upland cotton producers.

202. But do the facts even support the US allegation that rents increased because of the contract payments? Indeed, the most recent USDA cotton cost of production data shows that the opportunity cost of land decreased from $58.33 per acre in MY 1997 to $46.76 per acre in MY 2002.[405] This data was reinforced by testimony in 2001 by the NCC President, who disagreed with the suggestion that "the payments that we are receiving are increasing land values or holding them up".[406] Instead of PFC payments, the NCC President stated his belief that the "strong economy outside of agriculture ... has supported land values ... ".[407] This cotton-specific cost data and testimony by the recipients of PFC payments contradicts the US "35 per cent" assumption.

203. It is also possible to test the US "35 per cent" assumption by examining non-cotton-specific cash rent and land value data. If the US assumption were correct, then cash land rents for cropland in states where upland cotton is produced should have increased significantly since the guaranteed PFC payments started in MY 1996. Further, it would be presumed, if the United States is correct, that 65 per cent of all the PFC upland cotton-related payments (as well as the other three contract payments) were captured by increased cash rents for

402 US 22 December 2003 Answers to Questions, para. 158.

403 Furthermore, even cash-rent landlords also make decisions that affect production such as land levelling, irrigation installation and related investments. Therefore benefits to landlord have significant effects on yields and acreage planted to cotton.

404 Exhibit Bra-16 (Characteristics and Production Costs of US Cotton Farms, USDA, October 2001, p. 23).

405 Exhibit Bra-323 (Costs and Returns of US Upland Cotton Farmers, MY 1997-2002, USDA).

406 Exhibit Bra-41 (Congressional Hearing, "The Future of the Federal Farm Commodity Programmes (Cotton)," House of Representatives, 15 February 2001, Testimony of Robert McLendon, p. 21). Mr. McLendon responded to a question by Congressman Dooley who stated: "I am concerned that a significant portion of that is going to be capitalized in rents, land values – and, you know, I hope we find ways in which we can structure our program so ... we can actually see asset valuations that are more commensurate with actual market conditions ... ."

407 Mr. McLendon was accompanied at the Congressional Hearing by now-President of the NCC, Mark Lange (then Chief NCC Economist), who said nothing to contradict Mr. McLendon's sworn testimony. *See* Exhibit Bra-41 (Congressional Hearing, "The Future of the Federal Farm Commodity Programs (Cotton)," House of Representatives, 15 February 2001, p. 6).

cropland during MY 1996-2002. But this is simply not the case, as demonstrated below.

204. USDA carefully tracks cropland cash rents in all US states. In almost all of the 16 states where cotton is produced, land rents for cropland increased only slightly between MY 1996 and MY 2003.[408] This is in contrast to the value of cropland which increased to a far greater extent.[409] The United States seeks to have the Panel assume that both cropland values and cash rents increased significantly by stating, in paragraph 156 of its 22 December 2003 response, that "land rent data ... follows the same trend" as land values. This is a misleading statement because, while cash rents increased, they did so at a much lower rate. For example, in Texas, cash rents for land increased 13.5 per cent ($18.50 to $21.00 per acre) during 1996-2003 while the value of an acre of cropland increased 28 per cent, from $674 in 1997 to $937 in 2003.[410] The increase in cash rents in Texas is less than the inflation rate (17 per cent) for the seven-year period.[411]

205. Cash rents in other US states producing upland cotton increased by similar amounts:[412]

US State[413]	Cash Rent 1996	Cash Rent 2002	Difference	Percentage Change
Texas	$18.50	$21.00	$2.50	13.5 per cent
Oklahoma	$25.60	$27.00	$1.40	5.5 per cent
Arkansas	$48.80	$53.00	$4.20	8.6 per cent
Louisiana	$53.00	$57.00	$4.00	7.5 per cent
Mississippi	$45.00	$54.00	$9.00	20.0 per cent
Alabama	$39.00	$36.00	- $3.00	-7.7 per cent
Florida	$30.00	$32.00	$2.00	6.7 per cent
Georgia	$36.40	$39.00	$2.60	7.1 per cent
South Carolina	$23.80	$28.50	$4.70	19.7 per cent

206. As the figures demonstrate, the increase in cash rents is below the inflation rate of 17 per cent in most of the states. The highest numerical increase between 1996 and 2002 is $9 in Mississippi. Being extremely conservative, Brazil has assumed that this Mississippi increase represents the increase in cash rents for all US upland cotton cropland. It follows that for MY 2002 (with 13.8 million acres planted to upland cotton) and with about 25 per cent of upland cotton land

408 Exhibit Bra-413 (USDA, NASS "Agricultural Cash Rents, July 1999, p. 2-3); Exhibit Bra-414 (USDA, NASS "Agricultural Land Values and Cash Rents," August 2003, p. 12-13.)(examining cropland cash rent values).

409 Exhibit Bra-415 (USDA, NASS, "Agricultural Land Values", April 1999, p. 4); Exhibit Bra-414 (USDA, NASS, "Agricultural Land Values and Cash Rents," August 2003, p. 12-13).

410 Exhibit Bra-413 (USDA, NASS "Agricultural Cash Rents, July 1999, p. 2-3); Exhibit Bra-414 (USDA, NASS "Agricultural Land Values and Cash Rents", August 2003, p. 12-13.)(examining cropland cash rent values).

411 http://woodrow.mpls.frb.fed.us/research/data/us/calc/ ($1.00 in 1996 is worth $1.17 in 2003).

412 Exhibit Bra-413 (USDA, NASS "Agricultural Cash Rents, July 1999, p. 2-3); Exhibit Bra-414 (USDA, NASS "Agricultural Land Values and Cash Rents", August 2003, p. 12-13.)(examining cropland cash rent values).

413 Data for several other states is distorted by the fact that cash rents for irrigated land, which is not used for upland cotton production, are shown.

cash-rented, these $9 mean that $31 million of the total of $454.5 million[414] in direct payments found their way into increased cash rents for upland cotton land.[415] Thus, USDA's own data shows that only 6.8 per cent of the MY 2002 direct payments could have been attributable to increased cash rents – not 65 per cent as the United States asserts.

207. It should be noted that none of this analysis includes CCP payments. If CCP payments were included with direct payments, the percentage share would be even lower. Generally, the United States agrees that cash rents also reflect long-term expectations about crop prices and programme benefits. While direct payments are paid regardless of prices, CCP payments vary with prices. Therefore, one can expect that the payments will be discounted by a margin reflecting the uncertainty about the availability of CCP payments in future years for which cash rents are fixed.

208. The United States claims that cash rents are "sticky" and do not respond quickly to the increased net revenue from the use of the land.[416] The United States further suggests that the estimated 34-41 per cent of PFC payments captured for MY 1997 as set out in an August 2003 ERS study will be higher for later years.[417] But the evidence outlined above suggests that cash rents for cropland did not increase significantly between MY 1996-2002, and thus do appear to reflect to any considerable extent the effects of PFC or other contract acreage payments. The US assertion amounts to speculation, as the authors of the August 2003 study properly acknowledge.[418] Cash rents may be just as easily, if not more, affected by expected low prices for upland cotton, as suggested by the NCC President[419], or other factors such as interest rates. The absence of evidence of significant cash rent increases more than seven years after enactment of the 1996 FAIR Act suggests that whatever production effects from direct payments and CCP payments exist presently will continue to exist in the future – supporting Brazil's threat of serious prejudice claims.

209. The above discussion has focused on PFC payments, since that is the only type of contract payment for which the United States presented evidence. However, the United States "35 per cent" assumption also was made regarding CCP payments and market loss assistance payments.[420] The Panel will look in vain for

---

[414] Brazil's 22 December 2003 Answer to Question 196, para. 8.

[415] 13.8 million acres times 0.25 times $9 equals $31,050,000.

[416] US 22 December 2003 Answer to Question 242, para. 157.

[417] *Ibid.*

[418] Exhibit Bra-310 ("The Incidence of Government Program Payments on Agricultural land Rents: The Challenges of Identification," Roberts, Kirwan, Hopkins, p. 769) ("It could be ... [and] [m]ore research is needed to verify these incidence estimates to ascertain the time it takes for rents to reflect changes in associated government payments and to measure how incidence is ultimately capitalized into land values.").

[419] Exhibit Bra-41 (Testimony of Roberto McLendon, p. 7)("I think people that are professional farm managers have been concerned for the last 2 or 3 years that we are going to have a decrease in land values because they saw it in the 1980's. We had low prices and a bad situation. Again, in my opinion, we have had such a strong economy outside of agriculture it has supported land values, but that support won't last forever ... .")

[420] US 22 December 2003Answer to Question 242, para. 158.

any evidence produced by the United States that only 35 per cent of MY 2002 CCP payments benefited upland cotton producers who cash rent upland cotton cropland. Because CCP payments are triggered on a year-by-year basis depending on low prices for upland cotton, a non-producing landlord cannot know in what amount CCP payments will be made. Further, as Brazil has demonstrated repeatedly, given the high non-land-related production costs involved in producing cotton, most US producers simply could not profitably produce cotton without CCP payments. Therefore, there is little, if any, basis for a non-producing landlord to demand increased rents to capture CCP payments.

210. The evidence that is before the Panel indicates that every eligible upland cotton producer planting on upland cotton base acreage (approximately 75 per cent of such producers), received a CCP check in MY 2002.[421] The record shows that the high costs of these producers meant that they had to use this money to cover their production costs, including the costs related to the cash rents they were required to pay. Thus, in an immediate "cover your annual costs" sense, 100 per cent of the payments each year of the period of investigation "benefited" the producers of upland cotton.[422]

211. Similarly, the United States provides no evidence concerning how much of the market loss assistance payments during MY 1998-2001 did not benefit upland cotton farmers. Brazil demonstrated that all producers (not non-producing landlords) planting on upland cotton or other base acreage were entitled to receive market loss assistance payments. The producers had the legal right to receive these payments. Thus, the United States did not meet its burden of showing that only 35 per cent of the market loss payments "benefited" upland cotton production.

212. Finally, the United States provides no evidence to support its argument that only "35 per cent" of the amount of direct payments under the 2002 FSRI Act "benefit" producers of upland cotton. As Brazil demonstrated, in MY 2002, US cotton producers needed all of the direct payment subsidies to cover their production costs and to re-coup losses from MY 2001.

213. Brazil recalls its showing that even under the US approach, the percentage should be 75 per cent rather than 35 per cent, *i.e.,* including land that is owned or share rented by producers. However, also for producers that cash rent their upland cotton land, not all of their contract payments are capitalized in land values and translated into higher cash rents. Thus, by far the greatest portion of contract payments is available to cause production effects along the lines discussed in the literature and by Professor Sumner[423], as well as by Brazil.[424]

---

[421] Brazil's 18 November 2003 Further Rebuttal Submission, Section 2.1, para. 23; Brazil's 9 September 2003 Further Submission, paras. 59-331; Brazil's 22 August 2003 Rebuttal Submission, para. 50 *citing* Exhibit Bra-173 (Revised Estimate of Support Granted by Commodity via Counter-Cyclical Payments).

[422] Brazil's 27 October 2003 Answers to Question 125(c), paras. 15-25.

[423] Brazil's 9 September 2003 Further Submission, Annex I, paras. 37-42 and Exhibits Bra-280 and Bra-345 (paras. 18-34).

[424] Brazil's 18 November 2003 Further Rebuttal Submission, Section 3.7.5.

214. In conclusion, 100 per cent of the contract payments paid to, received, and deposited in the accounts of current "producers" of upland cotton (applying Brazil's allocation methodology) in MY 1999-2002 constituted a "benefit" within the meaning of Article 1.1(b) of the SCM Agreement.[425] The relevant issue regarding "benefit" to production is not, as the United States argues, the amount of the funds paid; this dispute does not involve a countervailing duty investigation. Rather, the focus of any generic "benefit" analysis is on the *effects* of the subsidies. The record shows that the various types of contract payments stimulated US production of upland cotton to different extents, ranging from 15 per cent for PFC payments to 40 per cent for CCP payments, as estimated by Professor Sumner.[426]

243. Can the Panel assume that any support at all, even marketing loan programme payments, benefits upland cotton if an upland cotton producer has other agricultural production besides upland cotton? USA

Brazil's Comment:

215. Contrary to the assumption permeating the US 22 December 2003 response, Brazil reiterates that there is no legal requirement for a claimant under Part III of the SCM Agreement to quantify on an *ad valorem* basis the amount of the challenged US subsidies.[427] Annex IV – which the US response shows is the *only* legal basis for its arguments – is dead. Even when alive, it only applied to Article 6.1(a), not Article 6.3 of the SCM Agreement. The Panel's obligation under Part III of the SCM Agreement is to conduct an objective assessment of the evidence regarding the "effects" of the challenged subsidies. This means it must first examine the evidence regarding whether each of the supports is a "financial contribution," confers a "benefit," and is "specific".

216. Detailing the precise amount of the financial contribution ending up in the bank accounts of US upland cotton producers is not a legal pre-requisite to Brazil's actionable subsidy claims. If the Panel finds that Brazil is legally required to examine the exact *amount* of the subsidies in order to assess their "effects," then it need only ask why the United States has refused to produce the evidence to determine such an amount.[428] In the absence of the most accurate evidence, withheld by the United States, Brazil refers the Panel to evidence and the allocation of the amount of "support to upland cotton" it has presented in the peace clause portion of its various submissions.[429] This evidence is part of the record

---

[425] Similarly, 100 per cent of the contract payments, as allocated by Brazil, were "support to" upland cotton, within the meaning of Article 13(b)(ii) of the Agreement on Agriculture.

[426] Brazil's 9 September 2003 Further Submission, Annex I, paras. 43-51.

[427] Brazil's 18 November 2003 Further Rebuttal Submission, paras. 96-107; Brazil's 2 December 2003 Oral Statement, paras. 4-6. *See* also Brazil's comment on Question 231, above.

[428] US 18 and 19 2003 December Letters to the Panel; US 20 January 2004 Letter to the Panel; *See* also Brazil's 28 January 2004 Comments and Requests Regarding US Data.

[429] These facts are summarized in Annex 1 to Brazil's 9 October 2003 Closing Statement, but are also contained in a number of Brazil's earlier submissions to the Panel beginning with its 24 June 2003 First Submission; S*ee* also Brazil's 18 November 2003 Further Rebuttal Submission, Sections 2.1 and 2.4; Brazil's 2 December 2003 Oral Statement, Sections 5.1 and 5.3.

pursuant to Brazil's alternative arguments and is offered as evidence of the amount of such subsidy payments.

217. With the above-referenced qualifications, Brazil would answer the Panel's question with a qualified "yes". First, Brazil agrees with the United States' assumption, in paragraph 159 of its 22 December 2003 response, that the full amount of marketing loan payments for upland cotton production "benefits" US producers even if they also produce other crops. The logic of the US assumption means that the full amount of crop insurance and Step 2 payments, which are also *de jure* linked to production, sale or export of upland cotton, would "benefit" upland cotton production. With respect to contract payments, Brazil's allocation methodology first considers every acre of upland cotton grown on an acre of upland cotton contract base to "benefit" (or constitute "support to") upland cotton.[430] In other words, Brazil's allocation methodology does assume that all such cotton to cotton matches do "benefit" upland cotton, regardless of the other agricultural production of the farm.[431] Brazil notes that the cotton to cotton matches accounts for most of the contract payments to current upland cotton producers.[432] However, for those cotton producers growing cotton on non-upland cotton base acres, Brazil does *not* ignore other agricultural production of the particular farm. Rather, it allocates the payments attributable to upland cotton based on the overall composition of programme crops for that particular farm.[433] Of course, Brazil's methodology could not be fully applied because of the refusal of the United States to produce the necessary farm-specific information.[434]

218. The US 22 December 2003 response highlights the differences between the parties on how to allocate the "benefit" for payments made under the four types of contract payments. Further, the US response reflects the parties' differences over whether the quantification exercise is relevant for the peace clause "support to cotton," or whether it is instead relevant for assessing Brazil's claims under Part III of the SCM Agreement.

219. Brazil's position is that the allocation[435] of contract payments is required in the peace clause portion of the proceeding. Brazil has set forth in considerable detail the factual evidence supporting the *de facto* link between the contract

---

[430] Brazil's 20 January 2004 Answers to Additional Questions, para. 47.

[431] Brazil's 20 January 2004 Answers to Additional Questions, paras. 44-48.

[432] *See* Electronic PFC and DCP Summary Files provided on 18 and 19 December 2003 respectively. *See* also Brazil's 18 November 2003 Further Rebuttal Submission, paras. 22-24.

[433] Brazil's 20 January 2004 Answers to Additional Questions, paras. 48-55. Thus, contrary to the US assertions in the last sentence of paragraph 163, Brazil does not advocate allocating a non-tied payment across the total value of the recipients production.

[434] Brazil's 28 January 2004 Comments and Requests Regarding US Data, Sections 4, 8 and 9.

[435] Brazil's 11 August 2003 Answer to Question 40 provided detailed analysis regarding the application of its 14/16th methodology. Brazil explained in its Rebuttal Submission that: "Necessarily, this process requires allocation of support that may be provided to producers of more than one type of agricultural product, but which is not provided to producers *in general*." *See* Brazil's 11 August Answer to Question 40. An allocation process is also required with respect to Annex 3 para. 7 support to processors of agricultural products," 'to the extent that such measures benefit the producers of the basic agricultural product." Brazil's 22 August 2003 Rebuttal Submission, note 33.

payments and the production of upland cotton.[436] Brazil further provided considerable detail concerning its allocation methodology and the application of that methodology.[437] Brazil even attempted to apply the US "across the value of the farm" methodology, based on the incomplete and scrambled US data.[438] Brazil presented extensive legal arguments supporting the requirement under Article 13(b)(ii) to collect and tabulate any and all support for a specific commodity such as upland cotton.[439] For example, Brazil's 22 August 2003 Rebuttal Submission stated:

> [T]he phrase "support to a specific commodity" ... read in its context, requires the Panel to tabulate any non-green box domestic support payments that are linked in some manner to the production of upland cotton. Contrary to the US arguments,[440] there is nothing in the text of Article 13(b)(ii) limiting the support to only that provided to a single commodity. Nor does the text limit support to only that *requiring* a recipient to produce or to produce a specific commodity as the United States alleges.[441] Rather, it requires examining whether a specific commodity receives support from a domestic support measure identified in the chapeau of Article 13(b) and whether there is some sort of link between the support at issue and the specific commodity.[442] Thus, the question of "support to a specific commodity" is fundamentally a factual question requiring an examination of different types of support set out in the *chapeau* of Article 13(b).[443]

220. The US 22 December 2003 response reiterates, in paragraphs 161-163, the US peace clause arguments that the absence of any *requirement* to produce upland cotton in the statutory provisions of the 1996 and 2002 Farm Acts for direct and counter-cyclical payments (as well as PFC and market loss assistance payments) completely insulates these subsidies from any actionable subsidy challenge during the implementation period. Brazil demonstrated how this ex-

[436] The United States has refused to produce the most relevant information – the precise amount of contract payments received by current US upland cotton producers. Brazil summarized much of the available evidence, demonstrating that the contract payments are, *de facto*, tied to the production of upland cotton, in its 9 October 2003 Closing Statement, Annex I.

[437] Brazil's 11 August 2003 Answer to Question 40. Brazil's 22 December 2003 Answer to Question 258, paras. 43-55; Brazil's 28 January 2004 Comments and Requests Regarding US Data, Sections 9 and 10. *See* also Brazil's 11 August 2003 Answer to Question 40. An allocation process is also required with respect to Annex 3 para. 7 support to processors of agricultural products," 'to the extent that such measures benefit the producers of the basic agricultural product." Brazil's 22 August 2003 Rebuttal Submission, note 33.

[438] Brazil's 28 January 2004 Comments on Data Provided by United States, Section 10.

[439] *See* Brazil's 22 August Rebuttal Submission, paras. 13-22; Brazil's 22 August 2003 Comments on US Answers, paras. 48-53, 58, 61; Brazil's 11 August 2003 Answers to Questions, paras. 54-55, 57-58, 61-64, 66-72, 129-132; Brazil's 24 July 2003 Closing Statement, para. 8; Brazil's 22 July 2003 Oral Statement, paras. 13-26; Brazil's 24 June 2003 First Submission, paras 130-134.

[440] US 11 August Answer 2003 to Question 38, para. 81.

[441] *Ibid.*

[442] *Compare* Brazil's 11 August 2003 Answer to Question 41, paras. 57-58.

[443] Brazil's 22 August 2003 Rebuttal Submission, para. 14.

tremely narrow US "production requirement" test is contrary to the *chapeau* of Article 13(b)(ii), contrary to the context of Annex 2, paragraph 6(e), contrary to the context of Annex 3, paragraphs 10, 12, and 13, and contrary to the context of the AMS definition in Article 1(a) (referring to "in general"). [444]Brazil also demonstrated that the US "production requirement" test is contrary to the object and purpose of the Agreement on Agriculture, because it carves out huge amounts of amber box subsides from any discipline of the SCM Agreement during the implementation period.[445]

221. The United States argues, at paragraph 163 of its 22 December 2003 response, that Brazil's allocation methodology "eliminates the concept of non-product specific support for purposes of the peace clause since a non-tied payment may always be allocated according to the recipient's production". Brazil notes again its fundamental disagreement with the US assumption that $935.6 million in CCP payments and $454.5 million in direct payments paid in MY 2002 to current producers of upland cotton are "untied" subsidies.[446] The overwhelming evidence in the record shows they are *de facto* "tied" to upland cotton production.[447] Further, the United States incorrectly assumes that "non-product specific support" is the language set out in Article 13(b)(ii). The actual text is "support to a specific commodity", which requires the tabulation – and allocation if necessary – of any and all support provided to producers, users, or exporters of a particular product. The test is not whether the domestic support *requires* production, but rather whether the domestic support provides support for the production of a particular commodity.[448]

222. Further, as Brazil noted in its 11 August 2003 response, all of the domestic support measures challenged by Brazil have an "upland cotton specific link in terms of historic, updated, or present upland cotton acreage, present upland cotton production or prices, or upland cotton groups of insurance policies or other specific upland cotton provisions"[449]The ordinary meaning of the terms "non-product specific" support that is provided "in general" is support to producers of all or almost all commodities or agricultural products, such as irrigation, state credit programmes, and other infrastructure subsidies such as farm roads. Thus, even if the peace clause test were "product-specific support," Brazil's interpretation does not read out any meaning to "non-product specific support".

---

[444] *See,* in particular, Brazil's 22 August 2003 Rebuttal Submission, paras. 15-22 (legal arguments), as well as factual evidence regarding each direct payment subsidy, in paras. 24-52. Since August, Brazil has presented considerable additional evidence establishing the *de facto* link between each type of contract payment and the production of US upland cotton. *See* Annex 1 of Brazil's 9 October 2003 Closing Statement; Brazil's 27 October 2003 Answers to Questions, paras. 7-26, 37-40; Brazil's 18 November 2003 Further Rebuttal Submission, Section 3.7.5; Brazil's 2 December 2003 Oral Statement, Section 5.3.

[445] Brazil's 22 July 2003 Oral Statement, paras. 21-25.

[446] Brazil's 22 December 2003 Answers to Question 196, para 8.

[447] *See e.g.* Brazil's 9 October 2003 Closing Statement, Annex I; Brazil's 27 October 2003 Answers to Question 125(2)(a), paras. 7-25; Brazil's 18 November 2003 Further Rebuttal Submission, Section 3.7.5.

[448] Brazil's 22 August 2003 Rebuttal Submission, paras. 15-22.

[449] Brazil's 11 August 2003 Answer to Question 41, paras. 57-58.

223. In sum, Brazil's methodology for allocating the various subsidy payments that "benefit" or "support" upland cotton is reasonable and based on an extensive factual record demonstrating the link between such payments and current upland cotton production. If the United States disagreed, it was required to do more than simply assert the *de jure* form of the legal instruments of the contract payments. Rather, it must produce the farm-specific evidence that would permit a detailed assessment of the "other agricultural production" (and the value) of each producer of upland cotton. It has refused to do so. Therefore, the US 22 December 2003 response to Question 243, besides being largely legally and factually wrong, is an astounding display of hubris in light of the US refusal to produce the very evidence that would permit the application of the methodology it advocates.

244. What proportion of the 2000 cottonseed payments benefited *producers of upland cotton*, given that payments were made to *first handlers*, who were only obliged to share them with the producer to the extent that the revenue from sale of the cottonseed was shared with the producer? (see 7 CFR §1427.1104(c) in Exhibit US-15). BRA

245. Can a panel take Green Box subsidies into account in considering the effects of non-Green Box subsidies in an action based on Articles 5 and 6 of the *SCM Agreement*? BRA, USA

246. Can a panel take prohibited subsidies into account in considering the effects of subsidies in an action based on Articles 5 and 6 of the *SCM Agreement*? BRA, USA

Brazil's Comment:

224. The Panel is well aware that Brazil considers Article 5 and its reference to "any" subsidy to require the Panel to take prohibited subsidies into account for a serious prejudice claim.[450] There is no contradiction between the implementing obligations of a Member under Articles 4.7 and 7.8 of the SCM Agreement. Thus, the Panel must take prohibited subsidies into account in considering the effects of subsidies in an action based on Articles 5 and 6 of the SCM Agreement.

247. Can the Panel take into account trends and volatility in market and futures prices of upland cotton after the date of establishment of the Panel? If so, how do they affect the analysis of Brazil's claim of a threat of serious prejudice? BRA, USA

Brazil's Comment:

225. Brazil's 22 December 2003 response to this question covers most of the points raised in the US 22 December 2003 response. In response to the US argument at paragraph 149 that the Panel's terms of reference as well as Brazil's

[450] Brazil's 22 December 2003 Answers to Questions, para. 147; Brazil's 27 October 2003 Answers to Questions, paras. 108-110.

threat claims are limited to subsidy payments up to, but not after, 18 March 2003, Brazil refers the Panel to its Comments to Question 194 above, and to its 20 January 2004 Answer to Questions 257(ii), at paragraphs 17-22. Brazil has, further, responded to improper use of futures prices at the time of planting, instead of the adjusted world price, in its Comments to Questions 212 and 213, above.

VI. STEP 2

248. In respect of the level of Step 2 payments in certain time periods, the Panel notes, *inter alia*, footnote 129 in the US first written submission; footnote 33 in the US 18 November further rebuttal submission; and Exhibit BRA-350. Have Step 2 payments ever been zero since the elimination of the 1.25 cent per pound threshold in the FSRI Act of 2002? In what circumstances could a Step 2 payment be zero? How does the elimination of the 1.25 cent per pound threshold in the FSRI Act of 2002 affect your response? BRA, USA

Brazil's Comment:

226. Brazil notes the US admission that one of the reasons for the elimination of the 1.25 cent threshold is to "correct for some long term changes in the valuation of currencies".[451] Thus, the United States effectively admits that Step 2 payments cause US exports to increase despite the appreciation of the US dollar. In fact, the United States has never rebutted the considerable evidence that one of the main effects of the US upland cotton subsidies is to cause US exports of upland cotton to increase even when the US dollar is appreciating rapidly.[452]

249. The Panel notes that the definition of eligible "exporter" in 7 CFR 1427.104(a)(2) includes "a producer":

(a) How does this reconcile with Brazil's argument that Step 2 "export payments" do not directly benefit the producer?[453] How, if at all, would this be relevant for an analysis of the issue of export contingency under the *Agreement on Agriculture* or the *SCM Agreement*? BRA

(b) How does this reconcile with Dr. Glauber's statement in Exhibit US-24, p. 3 (referring to "the 1990 Farm Bill and subsequent legislation") that Step 2 payments do *not* go directly to the producer? USA

(c) What proportion of Step 2 "export payments" go to producers? Please supply supporting evidence. USA

---

[451] US 22 December 2003 Answers to Questions, para. 171.

[452] Brazil's 9 September 2003 Further Submission, paras. 124-128 and the Exhibits cited therein; Brazil's 18 November 2003 Further Rebuttal Submission, paras. 78-80.

[453] For example, Brazil's response to Panel Question 125, para. 14.

VII. REMEDIES

250. Does Brazil seek relief under Article XVI of *GATT 1994* in respect of expired measures? What type of recommendation would the Panel be authorized to make? (Brazil further submission, paragraph 471 (iii))BRA

251. In light, *inter alia*, of Article 7.8 of the *SCM Agreement*, if the Panel were to find that any subsidies have resulted in adverse effects to the interests of another Member within the meaning of Article 5 of the *SCM Agreement*, should it make any recommendation other than the one set out in the first sentence of Article 19.1 of the DSU? BRA

252. Without prejudice to any findings by the Panel, if the Panel were to find that any of the challenged measures constitute prohibited subsidies within the meaning of Article 3 of the *SCM Agreement*, what are the considerations that should guide the Panel in making a recommendation under Article 4.7 of the *SCM Agreement* relating to the time period "within which the measure must be withdrawn"? What should that time period be? BRA

VIII. MISCELLANEOUS

253. Regarding the adjustment authority related to Uruguay Round compliance in s.1601(e) of the FSRI Act of 2002 (the so-called "circuit-breaker provision"):

(a) Does it relate to export credit guarantees, crop insurance and cottonseed payments?

(b) Does it relate only to compliance with AMS commitments?

(c) Is the authority discretionary? If so, can its exercise be limited by the legislative branch of government?

(d) How would the Secretary exercise her authority to prevent serious prejudice to the interests of another Member? How would she exercise her authority to prevent a threat of serious prejudice to the interests of another Member? At what time and on the basis of what type of information would she exercise her authority?

(e) What does "to the maximum extent practicable" mean? In what circumstances would it not be practicable for the Secretary to exercise her adjustment authority? USA

Brazil's Comment:

227. In its arguments at paragraphs 176, 178 and 180 of its 22 December 2003 response, the United States speculates about the "thoughts," "anticipations," "contemplations," "understandings", and "belief" of the US Congress. Yet it provides no citation to the extensive Congressional debates on the 2002 FSRI Act. Speculation about legislative (or negotiators') intentions not backed up by reference to the record of the debates is not positive evidence. Further, if any Member

could successfully plead compliance with WTO rules by simply inserting language asserting the provision "provides assistance to producers in a way that is consistent with [its] obligations under the Uruguay Round Agreement on Agriculture"[454], then there would be little role for any WTO panel. The only "evidence" of US legislators' intent before the Panel is the text of the 2002 FSRI Act.

228. In sum, the record now shows that both Brazil and the United States agree that (1) Section 1601(e) applies only to Total AMS[455], (2) Section 1601(e) does not apply to serious prejudice caused to US trading partners by US subsidies to upland cotton covered by the 2002 FSRI Act[456], and, (3) the 2002 FSRI Act does not provide any discretion for the USDA Secretary specifically to limit the amount of *upland cotton* marketing loan, Step 2, direct or counter-cyclical payments.[457]

254. Would payments made after the date of panel establishment be *mandatory* under the marketing loan, direct payments, counter-cyclical payments and user marketing certificate (step 2) programmes, but for the circuit-breaker provision? USA

Brazil's Comment:

229. Brazil established that marketing loan, Step 2, direct and counter-cyclical payments are mandatory, within the traditional mandatory/discretionary distinction under GATT/WTO law.[458] In its 20 January 2004 Answers to Additional Questions, Brazil has responded to US arguments that conditions attached to the payment of subsidies would make these subsidies non-mandatory.[459]

230. Brazil notes further that the listed programmes are not only mandatory within the meaning of WTO law, but are also mandatory under US budget law. They create a legal entitlement to the payment.[460] While the United States now

---

[454] US 22 December 2003 Answer to Question 253(a), para. 176.

[455] US 22 December 2003 Answer to Question 253(b), para. 178.

[456] US 22 December 2003 Answer to Question 253(d), para. 180.

[457] US 27 October 2003 Answer to Question 162, para 95 ("The statutory authority for marketing loan payments, step 2 payments, and counter-cyclical payments does not provide the Secretary with the authority to arbitrarily decline to make these payments to qualified recipients."), para. 97 ("there is no present limit on the total amount of payments that can be made under each of these programs although for counter-cyclical payments a maximum total outlay can be calculated using the base acres, base yields, and maximum payment rate for each commodity produced during the historical base period.").

[458] *See* Brazil's 20 January 2004 Answers to Additional Questions, paras. 17 (with further references), 24-30.

[459] Brazil's 20 January 2004 Answers to Additional Questions, paras. 27-30.

[460] Exhibit Bra-416 ("What Is A Farm Bill," Congressional Research Service, Report for Congress, 5 May 2001) ("Commodity programmes are entitlements. Expenditures are based upon programme rules and commodity market conditions. Eligible farmers are guaranteed legislatively-specified support based on these rules and conditions."). USDA noted with respect to an earlier commodity program – the deficiency payment program – that "[d]eficiency payments are entitlements; that is, spending is determined by rules that define eligibility and govern benefit levels rather than by the annual appropriations process. USDA and Congress have no control over deficiency payment outlays." (Exhibit Bra-417 ("Commodity Program Entitlements: Deficiency Payments", USDA, May 1993).

argues that payments depend on the availability of funds[461], the legal entitlement nature of these programmes means that payments must be made – if necessary after CCC funds have been replenished.

231. Finally, Brazil recalls that the United States argued in the peace clause portion of this dispute that is has no control over the flow of the upland cotton subsidies.[462] In fact, there is no legal mechanism to stem, or otherwise control, the flow of these upland cotton subsidies, which cause a permanent source of uncertainty in the world upland cotton market.[463] Thus, the US subsidies cause a threat of serious prejudice, in violation of Articles 5(c), 6.3(c) and 6.3(d) as well as footnote 13 of the SCM Agreement, and GATT Articles XVI:1 and 3.

255. How does Brazil respond to US assertions concerning the circuit-breaker provision? (see US 2 December oral statement, paragraph 82). Does this mean that US subsidies cannot be "mandatory" for the purposes of WTO dispute settlement? BRA

256. The United States submits that the Panel cannot make rulings without allocating precise amounts of payments to upland cotton production. However, to the extent that such precise data is not on the Panel record, to what extent can the Panel rely on less precise data, and on reasonable assumptions, in fulfilling its duty under Article 11 of the *DSU* in this case? USA

Brazil's Comment:

232. Because the United States has refused to cooperate in producing the most precise data concerning the amounts of contract payments to upland cotton producers, the Panel should (1) first draw adverse inferences from the US refusal to cooperate, and (2) use the best information available in making its determination.[464] Brazil presents the factual and legal basis permitting the Panel to make findings based on reasonable assumptions in its separate 28 January Comments and Requests Regarding US Data. These separate comments address most of the points raised in the extensive – and largely unresponsive – US answer to Question 256.[465] Additional points are set out below.

233. First, there is relevant WTO jurisprudence that provides a legal basis for the Panel to draw inferences from the best information available in the record in order to comply with the requirements of Article 11 of the DSU.[466] For example, in the *US – Wheat Gluten* case, the panel requested that the United States supply it with certain information that had been redacted from the public version of a

---

[461] US 22 December 2003 Answers to Questions, para. 182.

[462] In the context of the peace clause arguments, the United States argued that it could not control the amount of budgetary outlays under the programmes.

[463] Brazil's 20 January 2004 Answers to Additional Questions, paras. 18-22 (with further references).

[464] Brazil's 28 January 2004 Comments and Requests Regarding US Data, Section 6.

[465] *See* also Brazil's 28 January 2004 Comments and Requests Regarding US Data, Section 11.

[466] Brazil's 9 October 2003 Closing Statement, paras. 2, 9 (*citing* Panel Report, *Argentina – Textiles and Apparel*, WT/DS56/R, para. 6.39).

USITC Report, but despite several requests, the United States refused to submit the information.[467] The panel decided that while having access to all the requested information from the United States would have furnished a more extensive basis for its examination and have facilitated an objective assessment of the facts, there were other facts of record that the panel was required to include in its "objective assessment".[468] Ultimately, the panel determined that the United States violated provisions of the Agreement on Safeguards on the basis of the available factual record.[469] When the United States appealed this decision, the Appellate Body affirmed the panel, stating that "where a party refuses to provide information requested by a panel, that refusal will be one of the relevant facts of record, and indeed, an important fact, to be taken into account in determining the appropriate inference to be drawn".[470] The Appellate Body further indicated that it "deplored the conduct of the United States" in refusing to cooperate and provide information that was within its exclusive control.[471]

234. Another example of a panel using the best information available when a Member refused to provide documents within its exclusive control is the *Argentina – Textiles and Apparel* case. In that case, the United States requested Argentina to produce complete original customs documents of all footwear imports to demonstrate that Argentina was imposing and requiring payment of specific duties in excess of its bound duty rates of 35 per cent *ad valorem*.[472] Argentina refused to provide the complete (or any) documents.[473] The United States then provided examples of customs documents, which Argentina contested on a variety of authenticity and relevance grounds.[474] The panel rejected these Argentine arguments and found that "the United States has provided *sufficient evidence*".[475] In so holding, the panel noted that "[i]n situations where direct evidence is not available, relying on inferences drawn from relevant facts of each case facilitates the duty of international tribunals in determining whether or not the burden of proof has been met".[476] The panel further held that there is a requirement for collaboration of the parties in the presentation of the facts and evidence to the panel, and emphasized especially the role of the respondent in that process.[477]

235. Applying these concepts to the allocation issues involved in the peace clause portion of this dispute indicates that the Panel has more than sufficient evidence in the record to support a reasonable estimate of the amount of contract

---

[467] Appellate Body Report, *US – Wheat Gluten*, WT/DS166/AB/R, para. 168.
[468] Panel Report, *US – Wheat Gluten*, WT/DS166/R, para. 8.12.
[469] *Ibid.*
[470] Appellate Body Report, *US – Wheat Gluten*, WT/DS166/AB/R, para. 174.
[471] Appellate Body Report, *US – Wheat Gluten*, WT/DS166/AB/R, para. 171.
[472] Panel Report, *Argentina – Textiles and Apparel*, WT/DS56/R, para. 6.54.
[473] Panel Report, *Argentina – Textiles and Apparel*, WT/DS56/R, para. 6.56.
[474] Panel Report, *Argentina – Textiles and Apparel*, WT/DS56/R, para. 6.33.
[475] Panel Report, *Argentina – Textiles and Apparel*, WT/DS56/R, para. 6.65 (emphasis added).
[476] Panel Report, *Argentina – Textiles and Apparel*, WT/DS56/R, para. 6.39.
[477] Panel Report, *Argentina – Textiles and Apparel*, WT/DS56/R, para. 6.40.

payment support provided to upland cotton in MY 1999-2002.[478] Brazil detailed its views concerning the appropriate allocation methodology for purposes of the peace clause.[479] Faced with the US refusal to provide the data necessary to calculate the precise amount of support to upland cotton from the US contract payments using Brazil's (and the US) allocation methodology, Brazil offered extensive circumstantial evidence in support of its alternative so-called "14/16th methodology".[480] The Panel may properly draw adverse inferences that the United States data would, if produced, have shown that Brazil's 14/16th methodology undercounted the amount of support to upland cotton.[481] Such an adverse inference supports the other extensive evidence that the 14/16th methodology provides a reasonable estimate.[482]

236. Turning to its claims of serious prejudice and threat thereof, Brazil remains of the firm view that neither Part III of the SCM Agreement nor GATT Article XVI requires an exact determination of the amount of subsidies involved.[483] Rather, Brazil must demonstrate their *effects*.[484] Nevertheless, and as an alternative legal argument, Brazil presented extensive evidence concerning the *amounts as well as the effects* of each challenged subsidy. This is the same evidence Brazil used to demonstrate the amount of support to upland cotton.

237. The United States asserts that Brazil has to allocate all contract payments received by an upland cotton producing farm over the total value of that farm's sales.[485] However, even though the United States alone is in exclusive control of the information that would permit such an allocation, it has refused to produce that information. Even if it would be Brazil's burden to establish this fact, the United States has done everything to frustrate Brazil's ability to do so. In particular, the United States first wrongly asserted that data on plantings of farms was not available to it and – after Brazil demonstrated that this was incorrect[486] – refused to produce the evidence.[487]

---

[478] Brazil recalls that the United States has invoked the peace clause of Article 13 of the Agreement on Agriculture. As demonstrated by Brazil, the peace clause is in the nature of an affirmative defense. And even if the Panel were to disagree, Brazil established a *prima facie* case of inconsistency of the US measures with Article 13(b)(ii) of the Agreement on Agriculture. Neither the claim nor the measures to which it relates are outside the Panel's terms of reference, within the meaning of the Appellate Body decision in *Japan – Agricultural Products*, paras. 129-130.

[479] Brazil's 20 January 2004 Answers to Additional Questions, paras. 43-55.

[480] These facts are summarized in Annex 1 to Brazil's 9 October 2003 Closing Statement, but are also contained in a number of Brazil's earlier submissions to the Panel, beginning with its 24 June 2003 First Submission. *See* also Brazil's 18 November 2003 Further Rebuttal Submission, Sections 2.1 and 2.4; Brazil's 2 December 2003 Oral Statement, Sections 5.1 and 5.3.

[481] Brazil's 28 January 2004 Comments and Requests Regarding US Data, Section 6.

[482] *Ibid.*

[483] *See* Brazil's comment on Question 243, above.

[484] *See inter alia* Brazil's 2 December 2003 Oral Statement, paras. 4-6 (and the references cited therein).

[485] *See* US 22 December 2003 Answers to Questions, paras. 185-186, 10-11, 160-164.

[486] Brazil's 18 November 2003 Further Rebuttal Submission, Section 2.2; Exhibits Bra-368 – Bra-369.

[487] *See* generally Brazil's 28 January 2004 Comments and Requests Regarding US Data.

238. Indeed, even if the Panel were of the view that the US allocation methodology would provide the best means of evaluating the amount of support to upland cotton, the refusal of the United States to produce the requested data prevents the Panel from applying that methodology. In the face of this lack of cooperation, the Panel is required to apply some other methodology to estimate the amount of contract payment support, *i.e.,* Brazil's 14/16th methodology, or some variant thereof. To hold otherwise would obviously penalize Brazil, who sought the information, *inter alia*, for the purpose of demonstrating that the US methodology would reveal amounts of support similar to those estimated by Brazil's own 14/16th methodology.

239. It is ironic that among the evidence that supports Brazil's 14/16th methodology is the incomplete summary data provided by the United States. Brazil attempted to use that data to perform a simplified version of the (improper) US allocation methodology.[488] Brazil does not believe, as the Panel's question suggests, that it can make reasonable assumptions using this methodology based on the fragmented summary data provided by the United States. Nevertheless, although Brazil cautions against the use of its results, and although this methodology is not relevant for purposes of the peace clause, Brazil notes that these results are only marginally smaller than the results of Brazil's own 14/16th methodology.[489]

240. Thus, contrary to the US 22 December 2003 arguments[490], there is evidence provided by Brazil in the record on which the Panel can rely in making an objective assessment of the facts and in deciding on Brazil's claims under Part III of the SCM Agreement and GATT Article XVI (as well as under Article 13(b)(ii) of the Agreement on Agriculture). Brazil has also met its burden of proof in establishing a *prima facie* case concerning its claims of inconsistency of the US measures with these provisions.

IX. ADDITIONAL QUESTIONS POSED ON 23 DECEMBER 2003 AND 12 JANUARY 2004

257. The Panel takes note of the Appellate Body Report in *United States – Sunset Review of Anti-Dumping Duties on Corrosion-Resistant Carbon Steel Flat Products from Japan* (DS244), which was circulated to WTO Members on 15 December 2003. The Panel is aware that this report has yet to be adopted by the Dispute Settlement Body. Nevertheless, the Panel asks the parties to respond to the following related questions.

(a) In tht report, the Appellate Body cautioned against the "mechanistic" application of the so-called "mandatory/discretionary distinction" and stated that the import of this distinction may vary from case to case (para. 93). For the Appellate Body, the question of

[488] Brazil's 28 January 2004 Comments and Requests Regarding US Data, Section 10.
[489] *Ibid.*
[490] US. 22 December 2003 Answers to Questions, paras. 185-186.

whether a measure is mandatory or not is relevant "if at all" only as part of the assessment of whether the measure is, as such, inconsistent with particular obligations. How, if at all, are these statements and the related findings concerning the mandatory/discretionary distinction in that Appellate Body Report relevant to:

(i) the legal standard and elements Brazil sets out to establish its export and prohibited subsidy claims under the provisions of the *Agreement on Agriculture* and Articles 3.1(a) and (b) of the *SCM Agreement*, concerning: BRA

- Step 2 payments (see, *e.g.* paras. 244-245 & 250 Brazil's first written submission; Panel Question 109 and parties' responses/comments thereon); and

- export credit guarantee programmes: GSM-102, GSM-103 and SCGP (see, *e.g.,* para. 90 Brazil's oral statement at second Panel meeting).

(ii) the legal standard and elements Brazil sets out to establish its serious prejudice and "threat of serious prejudice" claims, and in particular, its designation of marketing loan; crop insurance; counter-cyclical payments; direct payments and Step 2 as "mandatory"? BRA

(iii) the legal standard and elements Brazil sets out to establish its "*per se*" "serious prejudice" claims (*e.g.* Brazil's 9 September further submission, para. 417 *ff*; US oral statement at second Panel meeting, para. 86 *ff.)*? BRA

(b) How and to what extent are the legal and regulatory provisions cited in paras. 415 and 423 of Brazil's 9 September further submission "normative" in nature and treated as binding within the US legal system (see, *e.g.,* para. 99 of the Appellate Body Report)? Does your response differ depending on whether the payments are dependent upon market price conditions? BRA

(c) Does Brazil challenge as "mandatory" the "subsidies" themselves, the subsidy programmes or the legal/regulatory provisions for the grant or maintenance of those subsidies, or something else? BRA

(d) Does the "requirement" upon the CCC to make available "not less than" $5.5 billion annually in guarantees have a normative character and operation? (see, e.g. Brazil's response to Panel Question 142; Exhibit BRA-297, 7 USC 5641(b)(1); 7 USC 5622(a) & (b); paragraph 201 of US 18 November further rebuttal submissions). Is this requirement "mandatory"? If so, how does the CCC have "discretion" not to make this amount of guarantees available in a given year? USA

(e) Does the US agree that, under the Budget Enforcement Act of 1990, the Office of Management and Budget classifies the export credit guarantee programmes as "mandatory" (see Brazil's response to

Panel Question 142, para. 89)? Does this exempt the programmes from the requirement to receive new Congressional budget authority before it undertakes new guarantee commitments (*e.g.* Exhibit BRA-117 (2 USC 661(c)(2))? USA

Brazil's Comment:

241. Brazil makes several observations with respect to the United States' 20 January 2004 responses to Questions 257(d) and 257(e).

242. First, the evidence discussed in the Panel's questions and the US responses is only relevant to a determination whether the United States is in compliance with Article 10.1 of the Agreement on Agriculture *with respect to scheduled products*. For unscheduled products, the Appellate Body held that it is inconsistent with Article 10.1 to provide *any* export subsidies.[491] Brazil has demonstrated that CCC guarantees were extended for unscheduled products during the period 1992-2003. Having also demonstrated that the CCC programmes constitute export subsidies (under Articles 1.1 and 3.1(a) of the SCM Agreement, and under item (j)), Brazil has therefore established that the United States has circumvented its export subsidy commitments with respect to unscheduled products, in violation of Article 10.1. Brazil has also demonstrated that CCC guarantees continue to be available for unscheduled products.[492] Since it is inconsistent with Article 10.1 to provide *any* export subsidies, the availability of CCC guarantees leads to a *threat* of circumvention of the US export subsidy commitments.

243. Second, the test to determine whether the United States is threatening to circumvent its export subsidy commitments with respect to scheduled products is *not* whether the CCC guarantee programmes are "mandatory" as opposed to "discretionary."[493] Rather, to determine whether export subsidies result in, or threaten to lead to, circumvention of the United States' export subsidy commitments, the test set out by the Appellate Body in *US – FSC* is whether there is a "mechanism in the measure" for CCC to "stem[], or otherwise control[], the flow of" CCC export credit guarantees.[494]

244. Under this test, the *threat* of circumvention is not abated simply because, as the United States notes, the CCC is not actually required to *issue* the "not less

---

[491] Appellate Body Report, *US – FSC*, WT/DS108/AB/R, para. 150.

[492] Exhibit Bra-299 ("Summary of FY 2003 Export Credit Guarantee Program Activity," USDA, covering GSM-102, GSM-103 and SCGP). For 1999-2002, *see also* Exhibit Bra-73 ("Summary of Export Credit Guarantee Program Activity," USDA, covering GSM 102, GSM 103 and SCGP for US fiscal years 1999-2003). For 1992-1998, *see* Exhibit US-41.

[493] The Panel will recall that in addition to its threat of circumvention claims with respect to scheduled products, Brazil has also demonstrated that the United States has used the CCC guarantee programs to circumvent its export subsidy commitments with respect to rice (a scheduled product). *See* Exhibit Bra-300 (Calculation on US Rice Exports Benefiting from GSM 102, GSM 103 and SCGP). The United States has not rebutted this evidence.

[494] Appellate Body Report, *US – FSC*, WT/DS108/AB/R, para. 149. Brazil's 27 October 2003 Answers to Questions, para. 88; Brazil's 18 November 2003 Further Rebuttal Submission, para. 257; Brazil's 2 December 2003 Oral Statement, paras. 90-91; Brazil's 20 January 2004 Answers to Additional Questions, para. 13.

than $5,500,000,000 in credit guarantees" that it must, as a matter of law, *make available* every year.[495] The threat arises because, year-on-year, the CCC announces its plans to extend over $6 billion in guarantees, as it did for fiscal year 2004.[496] It is required to do so by law.[497] It is, moreover, altogether exempt from any ceiling on the amount of guarantees it extends, and from the normal requirement that it receive new budget authority before undertaking new guarantee commitments (the programmes' "mandatory" status under US law "does not effectively constrain credit activity").[498] The CCC uses that exemption liberally, increasing allocations throughout the fiscal year to meet the needs of US exporters.[499]

245. Even if the CCC does not reach its goal of issuing over $6 billion in guarantees by year end, the fact that US law tells it that it *must* make available *at least* this amount, the fact that it sets its sights on and actually announces this amount, and the fact that nothing in US law sets any upward bound on the amount of guarantees it can issue, communicates a threat that it will circumvent its export subsidy commitments. Even if the CCC does not reach its goal of issuing $6 billion in export credit guarantees, foreign competitors of US farmers see that it has announced its intent to do so, that it has the authority to do that and an unlimited amount more, and that there is no "mechanism in the measure" for CCC to "stem[], or otherwise control[], the flow of" CCC export credit guarantees.[500]

246. Moreover, foreign competitors of US farmers have seen how, as an historical matter, the United States has applied the CCC guarantee programmes to surpass its quantitative export subsidy reduction commitments – even when falling short of its announced intent to issue $6 billion in guarantees. Brazil has

---

[495] Brazil is aware of no other provision of US law that provides a floor, and not a corresponding ceiling, for support to US industry.

[496] Exhibit Bra-296 ("USDA Announces $2.8 Billion in Export Credit Guarantees," FAS Press Release, 30 September 2003).

[497] Brazil's 18 November 2003 Further Rebuttal Submission, para. 261, *citing* Exhibit Bra-297 (7 U.S.C. § 5641(b)(1); 7 U.S.C. § 5622(a), (b)). *See also* Brazil's 2 December 2003 Oral Statement, para. 91, *citing* Exhibit Bra-366 (7 U.S.C. § 5622 note, "Promotion of Agricultural Exports to Emerging Markets, para. (a) ("The Commodity Credit Corporation shall make available for fiscal years 1996 through 2002 not less than $1,000,000,000 of direct credits or export credit guarantees for exports to emerging markets under section 201 or 202 of the Agricultural Trade Act of 1978 (7 U.S.C. 5621 and 5622), in addition to the amounts acquired or authorized under section 211 of the Act (7 U.S.C. 5641) for the program.")). *See also* Exhibit Bra-367 (Section 3203 of the 2002 FSRI Act (extending mandate to 2007)).

[498] Exhibit Bra-295 (2004 US Budget, Federal Credit Supplement, Introduction and Table 2 (CCC Export Loan Guarantee Programme classified as "Mandatory" in Table 2, and in the "Introduction," the Office of Management and Budget states that Table 2 provides "the program's BEA classification under the Budget Enforcement Act (BEA) of 1990 as discretionary or mandatory"); Exhibit Bra-117 (2 U.S.C. § 661(c)(2)) (exempting CCC programmes from appropriations requirement); Exhibit Bra-185 (Congressional Budget Office Staff Memorandum, "An Explanation of the Budgetary Changes under Credit Reform," April 1991, p. 7 (for quote provided in text above)).

[499] Brazil's 27 October 2003 Answers to Questions, para. 95, *citing* the archived list of USDA press releases announcing supplemental allocations extended throughout fiscal year 2003 (http://www.fas.usda.gov/excredits/exp-cred-guar.asp).

[500] Appellate Body Report, *US – FSC*, WT/DS108/AB/R, para. 149.

demonstrated how this threat materialized for one product – rice – in fiscal years 2001, 2002 and 2003 (despite the fact that the CCC did not reach its announced intent of handing out $6 billion in guarantees in any of those years).[501] Foreign producers' fears that the threat will materialize in other years for other products are legitimate, and the threat is therefore tangible (regardless whether or not the CCC meets its goal of handing out $6 billion in guarantees in any given year).

247. Merely having what the United States claims is the unwritten, administrative discretion to "tamp down the actual issuance of guarantees" would not be enough under this test.[502] The reason the Appellate Body in *US – FSC* looked for an *affirmative "mechanism in the measure"* subject to an Article 10.1 claim that would stem or control the flow of subsidies, rather than merely accepting as sufficient the unwritten administrative discretion to do so, is that only when such a mechanism exists, will foreign competitors of US farmers know with a degree of assurance that the threat of circumvention is not real. The purpose of the mechanism, in other words, is to diminish the threat.(Had this not been the Appellate Body's intent, it would simply have stuck to the traditional mandatory/discretionary formula it has used elsewhere and that the United States asserts applies in the analysis of an Article 10.1 claim.)

248. In any event, the "discretionary elements" that the United States asserts[503] abate the threat posed by its annual announcement that it will issue over $6 billion in CCC export credit guarantees are an illusion, for at least two reasons.[504]

249. First, the United States has offered no evidence that the CCC may reject "any individual application"[505] (much less that there is a "mechanism" to do so in order to avoid circumvention of US export subsidy commitments). As Brazil has

---

[501] Exhibit Bra-300 (Calculation on US Rice Exports Benefiting from GSM 102, GSM 103 and SCGP). The United States has never rebutted Brazil's showing. The CCC announced guarantee allocations of $5.762 billion in 2001, $6.158 billion in 2002, and $6.247 billion in 2003, while granting guarantees in the amount of $3.227 billion in 2001, $3.388 billion in 2002, and $3.223 billion in 2003. *See* Exhibit US-41.

[502] US 20 January 2004 Answers to Questions, para. 3.

[503] US 20 January 2004 Answers to Additional Questions, para. 3.

[504] Brazil has elsewhere explained the CCC's authority to undertake an inquiry into whether particular countries are creditworthy, and the possibility that this inquiry could end up reducing the amount of CCC guarantees, does not prevent a conclusion that nothing "stem[s], or otherwise control[s], the flow of" CCC guarantees. Brazil's 27 October 2003 Answers to Questions, para. 92. Under the United States' FSC measure, US authorities were permitted to undertake a factual inquiry into, among other things, whether the foreign-source income of the foreign corporation was "effectively connected with the conduct of a trade or business within the United States." Appellate Body Report, *US – FSC*, WT/DS108/AB/R, para. 16. This authority, and the possibility that the factual inquiry could limit the amount of income that would qualify for the FSC exemption, did not prevent the Appellate Body from concluding that nothing in the FSC measure "stem[ed], or otherwise control[led], the flow of" FSC benefits, leading to a threat of circumvention of the United States' export subsidy reduction commitments.

[505] US 20 January 2004 Answers to Additional Questions, para. 3. The United States has not offered any support for its assertion that CCC has the authority "to suspend the issuance of expert credit guarantees under any particular allocation". In any event, Brazil demonstrates *infra* that the allocation process does not remotely abate the threat that the United States will circumvent its *quantitative* export subsidy reduction commitments.

previously noted, the CCC guarantee programmes are classified as "mandatory" under US law.[506] The Congressional Budget Office ("CBO") and the Congressional Research Service ("CRS") (legislative branch agencies charged with servicing the US Congress) have both noted the inability of executive branch agencies charged with implementing mandatory programmes to deny support to eligible borrowers.[507] The United States cites a non-programme specific document for a generic principle that mandatory and discretionary classifications under the Budget and Enforcement Act "'do not determine whether a programme provides legal entitlement to a payment or benefit'".[508] Speaking specifically with respect to USDA mandatory programmes, however, the CRS states that "'[e]ligibility for mandatory programmes is written into law, and any individual or entity that meets the eligibility requirements is entitled to a payment as authorized by the law'".[509]

250. Second, the "discretionary elements" cited by the United States do not in any way abate the threat that the United States will circumvent its export subsidy commitments for scheduled products:

- The existence of eligibility criteria does not abate the threat. The focus for deciding whether a measure is discretionary is on whether it provides government officials with the discretion to implement the measure in a WTO-consistent manner.[510] Objective conditions, such as objective eligibility criteria, are not appropriately considered in determining whether a measure gives an implementing official "discretion" to act in a WTO-consistent fashion. For example, the FSC measure payments were only available where the income concerned was of foreign origin. Despite the fact that non-foreign sourced income would thus be excluded from FSC benefits, the measure was still found to threaten the circumvention of export subsidy commitments. Similarly, CCC guarantees are only available if an exporter meets the eligibility criteria

---

506 Exhibit Bra-295 (2004 US Budget, Federal Credit Supplement, Introduction and Table 2 (CCC Export Loan Guarantee Program classified as "Mandatory" in Table 2, and in the "Introduction", the Office of Management and Budget states that Table 2 provides "the programme's BEA classification under the Budget Enforcement Act (BEA) of 1990 as discretionary or mandatory").

507 *See* Exhibit Bra-117 (2 U.S.C. § 661(c)(2)); Exhibit Bra-185 (Congressional Budget Office Staff Memorandum, "An Explanation of the Budgetary Changes under Credit Reform," April 1991, p. 7 and Table 2); Exhibit Bra-186 (Congressional Research Service Issue Brief for Congress, "Agriculture and the Budget," IB95031 (16 February 1996), p. 3).

508 US 20 January 2004 Answers to Additional Questions, para. 7.

509 Exhibit Bra-186 (Congressional Research Service Issue Brief for Congress, "Agriculture and the Budget," IB95031 (16 February 1996), p. 3). The United States made a similar error in its 30 September 2003 Further Submission, at paragraph 156, when it cited the very same generic, non-agency-specific document (Circular A-11) for the principle that "the ability of CCC to issue guarantees is constrained by the apportionment process ..." As Brazil has demonstrated, the CCC programs are exempt from the requirement that to receive new Congressional budget authority before undertaking new guarantee commitments. *See* Exhibit Bra-117 (2 U.S.C. § 661(c)(2)).

510 Appellate Body Report, *US – 1916 Act*, WT/DS136/AB/R, para. 100.

set out in 7 C.F.R. § 1493.30.[511] The fact that a CCC official cannot legally issue a CCC guarantee to a non-eligible exporter does not make the CCC programmes "discretionary".

- The authority to limit guarantees given for exports to particular "destination[s]" and the authority to employ "exposure limits applicable to individual bank obligors"[512], like the authority to determine that particular destination countries are uncreditworthy and are ineligible for guarantees[513], do not reduce the threat of circumvention. The United States' export subsidy commitments are undertaken on a quantitative basis, and not on a destination or individual bank basis. Removing particular destination countries or banks from the list of those countries or banks eligible for CCC guarantees is utterly irrelevant to the CCC programmes' absolute activity levels – CCC can simply shift those guarantees to other countries and banks.
- Nor does the authority to limit the "time within which export must occur"[514] reduce the threat of circumvention. A requirement that the export that is the subject of a guarantee occur within a certain period of time following issuance of the guarantee only matters if the guarantee is issued in the first place; the requirement does nothing to control the flow of those guarantees or to abate the threat that they will circumvent the US export subsidy commitments.
- Nor does the allegedly commodity-specific allocation process that the United States cites[515] reduce the threat of circumvention. More than 95 per cent of allocations are made on a country-specific basis only, with less than 5 per cent of 2003 allocations made on a scheduled product-specific basis.[516] And the press release announcing initial allocations for 2004 contains no product-specific allocations.[517] More importantly, the allocations are made on a *monetary* basis, which provides virtually no assurance that the United States will not surpass its *quantitative* export subsidy re-

511 Exhibit US-6.

512 US 20 January 2004 Answers to Additional Questions, para. 3.

513 *See* US 30 September 2003 Further Submission, para. 154.

514 US 20 January 2004 Answers to Additional Questions, para. 3.

515 US 20 January 2004 Answers to Additional Questions, para. 3. *See also* US 30 September 2003 Further Submission, para. 155.

516 *See* Brazil's 27 October Answers to Questions, para. 99, note 136 and Exhibit Bra-299 ("Summary of FY 2003 Export Credit Guarantee Programme Activity," USDA, covering GSM-102, GSM-103 and SCGP (Total GSM 102, GSM 103 and SCGP allocations for fiscal year 2003 are listed as $6.025 billion, with product-specific allocations for scheduled products as follows: $200 million for wheat to Korea; $85 million for wheat to Pakistan; and, $10 million for vegetable oils for Tunisia.). *See also* Brazil's 18 November 2003 Further Rebuttal Submission, para. 261 (second bullet point).

517 Exhibit Bra-296 ("USDA Announces $2.8 Billion in Export Credit Guarantees," FAS Press Release, 30 September 2003).

duction commitments.[518] Brazil has demonstrated how this threat materialized for one product (rice)[519]; the threat that it might happen in some years for other products is therefore tangible.

251. Thus the "discretionary elements" cited by the United States do not abate the threat of circumvention of its export subsidy commitments. The United States erroneously states that "Brazil's own approach would require a showing that the programmes mandate that the premium rates will be insufficient to cover long-term operating costs and losses of the programmes".[520] The Panel will recall Brazil's demonstration that the United States has exported quantities of scheduled products in excess of US quantitative reduction commitments.[521] Thus, under Article 10.3 of the Agreement on Agriculture, the burden falls on the United States to prove that those excess quantities of scheduled products did not receive "export subsidies," within the meaning of Article 10.1. The burden is on the United States to show, in its own words, that the CCC programmes mandate that premium rates will be *sufficient* to cover long-term operating costs and losses of the programmes, within the meaning of item (j), *and* that CCC guarantees do not constitute financial contributions that confer benefits and are contingent on export, with the meaning of Articles 1.1 and 3.1(a) of the SCM Agreement.

252. But whomever bears the burden, Brazil has shown that the CCC does not have the discretion to charge fees that will enable it to meet its long-term operating costs and losses. Both USDA's Inspector General and the US General Accounting Office have noted the CCC's failure to change its premium rates or to reflect credit risk in those rates – *and in particular the maximum one-per cent premium rate imposed by US law*[522] – as evidence of a failure and inability to cover costs and losses.[523] There is no affirmative "mechanism" in place to stop the CCC programmes from constituting export subsidies under item (j), and in fact the fee ceiling imposed by US law is a mechanism that ensures that the programmes will operate as export subsidies.

253. Moreover, Brazil has demonstrated that the CCC export credit guarantee programmes confer "benefits" *per se*, within the meaning of Article 1.1(b) of the SCM Agreement (as well as that they are financial contributions and are contingent on export), and therefore that they constitute *per se* export subsidies for the purposes of Article 10.1.[524] Among other reasons (*e.g.*, the regulations for the CCC programmes, and a comparison to non-market benchmarks established by

518 Brazil's 27 October 2003 Answers to Questions, para. 100.

519 Exhibit Bra-300 (Calculation on US Rice Exports Benefiting from GSM 102, GSM 103 and SCGP).

520 US 20 January 2004 Answers to Additional Questions, para. 4.

521 Brazil's 2 December 2003 Oral Statement, para. 78; Brazil's 24 June 2003 First Submission, para. 265.

522 US 11 August 2003 Answers to Questions, para. 180. *See also* Exhibit Bra-297 (7 U.S.C. § 5641(b)(2)).

523 Brazil's 22 December 2003 Answers to Questions, paras. 63-64.

524 *See, e.g.*, Brazil's 18 November 2003 Further Rebuttal Submission, paras. 233-241.

the US Export-Import Bank)[525], Brazil has made this *per se* showing by demonstrating that CCC export credit guarantees are unique financing instruments for agricultural commodity transactions that are not available on the commercial market for terms longer than the marketing cycles of the eligible commodities.[526] Far from an affirmative "mechanism" to prevent CCC guarantees from constituting export subsidies, guarantees under the CCC programmes constitute export subsidies *per se*.

254. Everything about the CCC programmes aggravates and legitimizes the fear foreign competitors of US farmers have that the programmes will be used to circumvent the United States' export subsidy commitments. Brazil has demonstrated that under Articles 1.1 and 3.1(a) of the SCM Agreement, and item (j), guarantees under the programmes constitute *per se* export subsidies. The CCC issues these export subsidies free from the normal budgetary constraints placed on federal spending. The only constraint placed on the programmes is one that in fact encourages fear of circumvention – the obligation the US Congress has placed on the CCC to make available *a minimum* of $6.5 billion of CCC guarantees every year.[527] While the United States considers CCC's failure to actually grant $6.5 billion in guarantees in a given year as significant to its defense, it misunderstands the obligation included in Article 10.1. Article 10.1 prohibits the *threat* of circumvention. Foreign competitors of US farmers see and fear the unchecked authority US farmers and the CCC have to circumvent US export subsidy commitments. Their fear is legitimate, since that unchecked authority has been used in the past to circumvent those commitments.[528]

255. There is no affirmative "mechanism in the measure" that will stem or control the flow of CCC guarantees in a way that will abate the threat of circumvention of the US export subsidy commitments with respect to scheduled products. To abate the fear that makes the threat real, foreign competitors need to see a mechanism in place that will keep the United States from using the CCC programmes to provide export subsidies that surpass the US reduction commitments. The nature of the obligation in Article 10.1 – the prohibition of a *threat* – is such that it cannot be met with a showing that there is mere discretion to avoid surpassing those commitments. That the Appellate Body failed to apply the traditional mandatory/discretionary distinction in interpreting the standard required by Article 10.1 demonstrates its understanding that to prevent a measure from

---

[525] This evidence is summarized at paras. 231-241 of Brazil's 18 November 2003 Further Rebuttal Submission.

[526] *See* Brazil's 24 June 2003 First Submission, paras. 289-292; Brazil's 22 July 2003 Oral Statement, para. 116; Brazil's 11 August 2003 Answers to Questions, paras. 139-140, 152-157, 183-187; Brazil's 22 August 2003 Rebuttal Submission, paras. 103-105; Brazil's 22 August 2003 Comments, paras. 92-93, 109-113; Brazil's 27 August 2003 Comments on US Rebuttal Submission, paras. 68-80; Brazil's 7 October 2003 Oral Statement, para. 72; Brazil's 18 November 2003 Further Rebuttal Submission, paras. 230-242; Brazil's 2 December 2003 Oral Statement, para. 79.

[527] For citations, *see* Brazil's 2 December 2003 Oral Statement, para. 91.

[528] Exhibit Bra-300 (Calculation on US Rice Exports Benefiting from GSM 102, GSM 103 and SCGP).

posing a threat of circumvention, there needs to be some affirmative mechanism in place to reduce the legitimate fear of circumvention.

258. Please submit a detailed explanation of the method by which one could calculate total expenditures to producers of upland cotton under the four relevant programmes on the basis of the data which it seeks. BRA

ANNEX I-14

COMMENTS OF THE UNITED STATES ON THE ANSWERS OF BRAZIL TO FURTHER QUESTIONS FROM THE PANEL TO THE PARTIES FOLLOWING THE SECOND PANEL MEETING

(28 January 2004)

A. Terms of Reference

194. Does the United States maintain its position stated in response to the Panel's Question No. 67 that "it would not be appropriate for the Panel to examine payments made after the date of panel establishment"? If so, please explain why. Can Brazil comment on this statement? BRA, USA

1. Brazil's answer conflates two issues: the measures a Panel is to examine and the evidence a Panel may examine. As stated in the US response, Brazil has challenged certain statutory measures "as such"; Brazil has also challenged certain "payments" as measures. With respect to payments, it is only those payments made through panel establishment that can be "specific measures at issue" between the parties. Payments made after panel establishment necessarily had not been made as of the time of establishment; therefore, those "measures" did not exist and cannot have been within the Panel's terms of reference as set out by the DSB.

2. The situation here is different from that in *Chile – Price Bands*[1] where the question was whether an amendment made to a measure that both parties agreed were within the panel's terms of reference had altered the "essence" of the measure such that it was no longer a measure within the panel's terms of reference. Here, the question concerns measures (payments) that it is without dispute did not exist at the time of panel establishment. Accordingly, the request for a panel could not have "identified" non-existent measures, nor could Brazil have consulted on measures "affecting" (present tense) the operation of a covered agreement. To find these measures to be within the Panel's terms of reference would therefore be in contravention of Articles 4 and 6 of the DSU. It was Brazil's choice to request establishment of the Panel part way through marketing year 2002; thus, Brazil's timing sets the parameters for what payments are properly before the Panel.[2] In this connection, we note that Brazil has finally conceded the correctness of the US view that this Panel's terms of reference cannot expand beyond their scope of the date of panel establishment. In its answer to the Panel's Question 247 (paragraph 149), Brazil states:"Thus, the 'matter' before the Panel has not changed (*and cannot*) since the establishment of the Panel" (emphasis

---

[1] WT/DS207/AB/R.

[2] Past panels have examined measures subject to a dispute as they exist on the date of panel establishment. *See, e.g., Panel Report, India - Quantitative Restrictions on Imports of Agricultural, Textile and Industrial Products*, WT/DS90/R, adopted 22 September 1999, paras. 5.159-5.163.

added). Brazil should of course also have acknowledged that, despite this statement, it has in fact attempted to change the matter before the Panel.

3. This is not to say that a Panel may not examine evidence that is developed after panel establishment.[3] In fact, the United States would largely agree with Brazil's statement that "to the extent that 'payments' made since 18 March 2003 are evidence, the Appellate Body and panels have repeatedly found that evidence generated after the establishment of the panel can be used by [panels] in their objective assessment of the facts under DSU Article 11."[4] The Panel should carefully consider the import of this statement by Brazil, given the existence of three telling pieces of evidence that Brazil has sought to minimize or neglected:

- First, Brazil largely ignores the undisputed fact that no marketing loan payments have been made since 19 September 2003; thus, given expected prices, US outlays will be dramatically lower in marketing year 2003.
- Second, Brazil seeks to minimize the fact that futures prices indicate that the market expects cotton prices to remain high through marketing years 2003 and 2004.
- Third, and perhaps most disconcerting, Brazil has neglected to inform the Panel that, with respect to its preferred baseline approach, FAPRI has produced a (preliminary) November 2003 baseline that revises projected prices significantly upwards as compared to the outdated baseline on which Mr. Sumner's economic analysis relies.

4. The first piece of evidence demonstrates not only that marketing loan payments will be sharply lower in marketing year 2003 than in previous years, but fatally undercuts Brazil's economic analysis. The Panel will recall that in Brazil's economic analysis, the marketing loan programme alone accounted for almost 43 per cent of the effect of removal of all challenged US subsidies. Given that no marketing loan payments are being made and that futures prices and the November 2003 FAPRI baseline suggest that no marketing loan payments will be made over the remainder of marketing year 2003, the evidence does not support Brazil's argument that US marketing loans for upland cotton create a threat of serious prejudice.

5. The second piece of evidence is that futures prices indicate that the market expects cotton prices to remain high through marketing years 2003 and 2004. The table below shows settlement prices on 27 January 2004, for contracts through marketing year 2004.

---

[3] *See, e.g., Japan – Measures Affecting the Importation of Apples*, WT/DS245/R, para. 4.15 (15 July 2003) (rejecting Japan's preliminary ruling request to strike certain affirmative evidence developed and submitted after the date of panel establishment but no later than during the first panel meeting).

[4] Brazil's Answer to Question 194, para. 5.

New York Cotton Exchange, Cotton No. 2, 27 January 2000[5]	
Contract	**Settlement (cents per pound)**
March 2004	73.76
May 2004	75.06
July 2004	75.90
October 2004	68.25
December 2004	69.05
March 2005	71.05
May 2005	71.70
July 2005	72.40

6. The following table of futures prices for December 2004 upland cotton contracts further demonstrates that price expectations have risen over time, and market participants expect cotton prices to remain high through December 2004.

Futures Prices for December 2004 Cotton

Month ending	Open for the Month	High for the Month	Low for the Month	Close for the Month	Average Close for the Month
12/31/2002	60.63	62.20	60.49	60.50	61.34
1/31/2003	61.25	62.50	60.50	62.70	61.69
2/28/2003	62.90	63.00	61.30	62.87	62.53
3/31/2003	62.90	63.25	61.70	62.45	62.57
4/30/2003	62.40	64.00	62.00	62.45	62.69
5/31/2003	62.50	64.00	60.58	60.75	62.60
6/30/2003	60.50	64.60	59.00	65.25	62.55
7/31/2003	66.90	66.90	63.32	62.85	65.29
8/31/2003	62.90	63.25	60.70	63.68	61.95
9/30/2003	63.95	66.95	62.20	66.25	64.99
10/31/2003	65.75	71.00	64.80	68.85	67.72
11/30/2003	68.85	70.00	62.50	65.65	67.54
12/31/2003	67.50	68.45	63.25	68.28	65.60
1/22/2004	68.40	69.70	67.62	69.62	68.78

Source: New York Board of Trade, NY Cotton Exchange

7. Third, Brazil has not provided the Panel with any information relating to the most recent FAPRI November 2003 baseline. This preliminary baseline further undermines Brazil's economic analysis, which was predicated on projections of continued low cotton prices. As noted with respect to the cessation of marketing loan payments and high futures prices, that low-cotton-price projection on which Mr. Sumner relies has proven to be dramatically off-base. The November 2003 baseline now recognizes that fact.

- For example, the FAPRI November 2002 baseline used by Mr. Sumner projected an A-index of 50.7 cents per pound for marketing year 2003.
- The actual A-index in 2004 (through 22 January) has varied between a low of 75.45 cents per pound on 2 January to a high of

5 Exhibit US-142.

76.95 cents per pound on 22 January 2004 – that is, *roughly 50 per cent higher* than the FAPRI November 2002 projection.

8. The price outlook for cotton has improved considerably since publication of the November 2002 FAPRI baseline used by Dr. Sumner to estimate the effects of subsidies on US cotton production. The table below shows that projections for the Adjusted World Price are as much as *54.1 per cent higher*, or 20 cents per pound, for marketing year 2003 in the November 2003 baseline as under the November 2002 baseline.

FAPRI's Upwards Revisions to Adjusted World Price Baseline Projections

Year	Adjusted World Price (cents/lb)			
	Nov 2002 (Sumner)	Jan 2003	Nov 2003 1/	Increase from Sumner Nov02 baseline to Nov03
2003/04	37.22	44.8	57.36	54.1 %
2004/05	39.83	45.4	50.96	27.9 %
2005/06	41.94	46	50.82	21.2 %
2006/07	43.6	46.7	50.35	15.5 %
2007/08	45.48	48	49.24	8.3 %
Average	41.61	46.18	51.75	24.4 %

1/ Source: FAPRI Baseline, November 2003 (Exhibit US-132)

The chart below sets out the same data graphically, showing how much FAPRI's projections have been revised upwards since the November 2002 baseline on which Mr. Sumner's analysis relies.

9. As a result of this large upwards revision in FAPRI's projected adjusted world price, FAPRI's estimated marketing loan gains have been reduced considerably.

- Under the November 2003 baseline, *the estimatedmarketing loan gain for marketing year 2003 is now zero*, compared to almost 15 cents per pound under the November 2002 baseline used by Dr. Sumner.
- For marketing year 2004, the estimated marketing loan gain under the November 2003 baseline is 1.04 cents per pound, *a reduction of 91.5 per cent* from the 12.17 cents per pound estimated marketing loan gain in the November 2002 baseline used by Dr. Sumner.
- In fact, over the five-year period from marketing year 2003 to marketing year 2007, the average marketing loan gain is estimated in the November 2003 baseline as 1.32 cents per pound, *87.3 per cent lower* than the 10.39 cents per pound average using the November 2002 baseline on which Dr. Sumner relied.

FAPRI's Downwards Revisions to Its Marketing Loan Gain Baseline Projections

Year	Estimated marketing loan gain[1/] (cents/lb)			
	Nov 2002 (Sumner)	Jan 2003	Nov 2003 2/	Decrease from Sumner Nov02 baseline to Nov03
2003/04	14.78	7.2	0	100.0 %
2004/05	12.17	6.6	1.04	91.5 %
2005/06	10.06	6	1.18	88.3 %
2006/07	8.4	5.3	1.65	80.4 %
2007/08	6.52	4	2.76	57.7 %
Average	10.39	5.82	1.32	87.3 %

1/ The estimated marketing loan gain is the difference, if positive, between the loan rate (52 cents per lb) and the Adjusted World Price.

2/ Source: FAPRI Baseline, November 2003 (Exhibit US-132)

10. Recall that the marketing loan programme accounted for more than 42 per cent of the estimated effects of removing all US subsidies over MY 1999-2007 on production under the model developed by Dr. Sumner.[6] Thus, updating the model to the November 2003 baseline would virtually eliminate the estimated effect of the marketing loan programme and significantly reducing the overall estimated effect on production. Any remaining effects would largely be attributed to direct payments under Dr. Sumner's flawed model, with which we strongly disagree.

11. In addition, the FAPRI baseline from November 2002 projected 50.7 cents per pound for the A-Index for marketing year 2003 and the January 2003 baseline projected 58.4 cents per pound for the A-index for marketing year 2003. The FAPRI November 2003 projection for the MY2003 A-Index is 70.9 cents per pound, *40 per cent higher* than the FAPRI November 2002 projections used by Dr. Sumner. Even this revision could be low as the actual A-index for January 2004 (through 22 January) has varied between a low of 75.45 cents per pound on January 2 to a high of 76.95 cents per pound on 22 January 2004. We also note that FAPRI's November 2002 projections that Dr. Sumner employed did not show, through marketing year 2012, the A-Index *ever* rising as high as current prices.

FAPRI Baseline Projections for A-Index *(cents per pound)*

A-Index	Nov 2002 (Sumner)	Jan 2003	Nov 2003 1/	Increase from Sumner Nov02 baseline to Nov03
2003/04	50.7	58.4	70.9	39.8%
2004/05	53.4	58.8	64.5	18.9%
2005/06	55.8	59.4	64.3	15.2%
2006/07	57.6	60.1	63.8	10.8%
2007/08	59.6	61.5	62.7	5.2%

1/ Source: FAPRI Baseline, November 2003 (Exhibit US-132)

6 *See* Brazil's Further Submission, Annex I, table 1.4.

12. The current high cotton prices and market expectations of continued high prices are crucially relevant because, as mentioned, marketing loan payments will not be made if cotton prices are above the loan rate of 52 cents per pound and, further, counter-cyclical payments will not be made if the season average farm price is above 65.73 cents per pound (the target price of 72.5 cents minus the direct payment rate of 6.67 cents). The weighted average farm price for August-November was 62.4 cents per pound, as reported by USDA on 11 January 2004.[7]

13. Without even referencing the US critique of the modelling used by Brazil with respect to the challenged US measures, this evidence relating to prices indicates that Brazil's economic analysis is founded on price projections that are almost 40 per cent below actual prices; thus, the economic analysis put forward by Brazil does not support a finding of threat of serious prejudice. Furthermore, we recall that Brazil has argued that the 2002 Act increased the support provided to upland cotton producers, threatening continued high levels of production, exports, and price suppression. And yet, US acreage declined in both MY2002 and MY2003, and prices have steadily recovered from their MY2001-2002 trough to five-year highs. Market participants expect those high prices to continue. Thus, the evidence does not support the view that the effects of challenged US subsidies are significant price suppression.

B. ECONOMIC DATA

196. Please provide the latest data for the 2002 marketing year on payments under the marketing loan, direct payments, counter-cyclical payments, user marketing certificate (step 2) programmes and export credit guarantee programmes. BRA, USA

14. In its reply, Brazil makes several unfounded accusations and misrepresentations of fact. In this comment, the United States attempts to disentangle fact from fiction for the Panel.

15. Brazil asserts that through its December 18, 2003 letter, "the United States has finally confirmed – after asserting the contrary repeatedly to Brazil and then to the Panel – that it has collected complete planted acreage, contract base acreage, contract yields, and even payment data that would allow it to calculate with relative precision the amount of direct and counter-cyclical payments made to current producers of upland cotton in MY 2002." There are several errors in this passage. First, the United States recalls that it was the United States itself at the second session of the first panel meeting that brought to the Panel's and Brazil's attention the planting reporting requirement that was introduced by Section 1105 of the 2002 Act (7 USC 7915). Thus, the United States did not "finally confirm[]" the maintenance of planting data on 18 December.

---

7 *World Agricultural Supply and Demand Estimates*, USDA, WAOB, WASDE-406, 11 January 2004.

16. Second, the United States never asserted that it did not have contract base acreage and contract yield information. The United States explained that it did not track decoupled payments by recipients' production and thus did not maintain information on the payments made for upland cotton base acres to upland cotton producers. That statement remains true today. In fact, while Brazil's statement asserts that "planted acreage, contract base acreage, contract yields, and ... payment data" can be used to calculate the amount of decoupled payments "made to current producers of upland cotton," this information would allow the calculation of decoupled payments made to farms that reported *planting* upland cotton. As stated, the United States does not collect information relating to whether a farm *produces* upland cotton. Therefore, the data referenced by Brazil would allow calculation of payments made to upland cotton "planters," and in fact the United States has provided the contract data to perform this calculation on 18 and 19 December 2003.

17. Brazil claims that it "cannot calculate direct payment and counter-cyclical payment figures" because it was not provided (ignoring that Brazil bears the burden of proof in this dispute) "farm-specific identifying numbers, thus rendering any matching of farm-level information on contract payments with information on farm-specific plantings impossible." This statement was indecipherable to the United States until the Panel insisted that Brazil explain its proposed methodology for calculating those payments in Question 258. The United States comments on this proposed methodology, which lacks any basis in the Subsidies Agreement, any WTO agreement, or in economic logic, in its comment on Brazil's answer to Question 258.

18. It is, of course, ironic to read Brazil' s suggestion that only the "unique farm number (or a substitute number protecting the alleged confidentiality of farmers) would allow any matching" since *the United States expressly asked Brazil at the second panel meeting whether it could act to protect the privacy interests of US cotton producers*, perhaps by obscuring farm numbers. The Panel Chairman also inquired of Brazil whether obscuring the farm numbers would be acceptable, *but Brazil refused to agree to any such step, insisting that all of the information, including farm numbers, be provided as set out in Exhibit BRA-369.* Thus, it is Brazil that refused to allow "a substitute number protecting the ... confidentiality of farmers" – or any other step to maintain farmer confidentiality – to be used. The United States again notes Brazil's reference to "a private US citizen making a simple FOIA request," who was in fact a member of Brazil's delegation, and reminds Brazil for the third time of the US request for assistance in curing the breach of privacy that resulted from providing that planting information.

19. We also note that in Brazil's response, Brazil references several payments that were not included in the Panel's question, namely, crop insurance payments, cottonseed payments, and "other payments." Brazil does not state for what year these payments apply.

20. With regards to crop insurance payments[8], we note that the data provided by Brazil for crop insurance net indemnities with respect to upland cotton in 2002 is incorrect.[9] However, the only crop insurance payments within the scope of Brazil's panel request are payments to "upland cotton producers, users, and exporters."[10] Thus, Brazil is once again attempting to broaden the scope of this dispute to measures beyond its panel request, and the Panel should reject that effort.

21. With respect to cottonseed payments, the United States recalls the panel's communication of 8 December 2003 in which it stated that "[t]he Panel intends to rule that cottonseed payments made under the Agricultural Assistance Act of 2003 are not within its terms of reference." Thus, Brazil's citation to the amount of cottonseed payments made under this Act are not only outside the scope of the question but also outside the scope of this dispute. With respect to "other payments," the United States recalls its preliminary ruling request that these payments are not with the Panel's terms of reference.[11]

22. With respect to direct and counter-cyclical payments, Brazil continues to put forward erroneous figures before the Panel. Brazil fails to make any adjustment in the amount of payment to reflect the proportion of cotton planted acreage that is rented or owned. However, those "subsidies" to cotton producers that are the subject of Brazil's panel request must "benefit" producers.[12] Brazil itself has conceded that land rental rates as of marketing year 1997 – that is, one year after introduction of the decoupled production flexibility contract payments – reflect the capture of more than one-third of the subsidy by landowners. Finally, Brazil has not allocated these decoupled payments that are not tied to the produc-

---

[8] We also note that Brazil has insisted that crop insurance premium payments are "specific" subsidies within the meaning of Article 2 of the Subsidies Agreement because the crop insurance statute precludes coverage of livestock. *See, e.g.,* Brazil's Further Rebuttal Submission, para. 163. At one time there was such an exclusion, but as we have previously pointed out, it was removed. In fact, Brazil simply and repeatedly misquotes its own exhibit, which does not contain the "excluding livestock" language of the old statute. *See* Exhibit BRA-30, at 1-44 to 1-45 (extending coverage to enumerated products and "any other agricultural commodity, excluding stored grain, determined by the Board, or any one or more of such commodities, as the context may indicate").

[9] Total indemnity payments paid to upland cotton producers in 2002 was $400,686,555. Total upland cotton premiums were $317,610,012 of which the government provided premium subsidies of $194,111,641 and $123,498,371 was paid by producers. Thus, net indemnities (that is, indemnities minus producer-paid premiums) paid to upland cotton producers in 2002 was $277,188,184 ($400,686,555 minus $123,498,371), not $298.3 million as reported by Brazil.

[10] *See* WT/DS267/7, at 1 ("The measures that are the subject of this request are prohibited and actionable subsidies provided to US producers, users and/or exporters of upland cotton.").

[11] US Further Written Submission, Section II. The United States also recalls its point above, namely Brazil has conceded the correctness of the US view that this Panel's terms of reference cannot expand beyond their scope of the date of panel establishment. In its answer to the Panel's Question 247, Brazil states: "Thus, the 'matter' before the Panel has not changed (*and cannot*) since the establishment of the Panel." Brazil should also have acknowledged that, despite this assurance, it has in fact attempted to change the matter before the Panel.

[12] *See* Panel Report, *United States – Imposition of Countervailing Duties on Certain Hot-Rolled Lead and Bismuth Carbon Steel Products Originating in the United Kingdom*, WT/DS138/R, adopted 7 June 2000, paras. 6.65 and 6.66 (quoting and agreeing with *Canada – Aircraft* panel: "'A "benefit" does not exist in the abstract, but must be received and enjoyed by a beneficiary or a recipient. Logically, a "benefit" can be said to arise only if a person ... has in fact received something.'").

tion, use, or sale of any product across the total value of the recipient's production, the only allocation methodology set out in the Subsidies Agreement and, in fact, applied by Brazil itself for countervailing duty purposes.[13]

23. With respect to the export credit guarantee programmes, Brazil "estimates the amount of payments using the 'guaranteed loan subsidy' estimate FY 2003."[14] This figure is of course not a payment at all, but merely a prospective budgetary *estimate* calculated under the Federal Credit Reform Act of 1990. As the United States noted in its answer, for all cotton for fiscal year 2003 (October 2002 - September 2003), outstanding claims are $280,898, less than one-tenth of one per cent of the value of registrations – further evidence, specific to cotton export credit guarantees in particular, that premiums are more than sufficient to cover operating costs and losses.

199. What is the composition of the A-Index? We do note footnote 19 and, for example, Exhibit BRA-11, but please explain more in detail how this index is calculated. BRA

24. With respect to the explanations ofBrazil of the A-Index, we note that the A-Index is not a price for a "world market" for purposes of Article 6.3(c). As Brazil's answer puts it, the A-Index is an "average price," a "composite of quotations from the major producing regions around the world, much like a poll" (para. 11). The A-Index is also not a "price" in a "world market"; it is a Northern Europe-delivered price quote. We note the statement in paragraph 16 of Brazil's answer that "the average A-index price" in the week of export "would only be an estimate and would not necessarily reflect the price received by the US producers, or the prices received by the exporters." Finally, we note that there are 16 different quotes, and the A-Index consists of the average of the lowest 5. The fact that the prices differ also indicates that there is not one "world market" price. There is also a B-Index composed of upland cotton price quotes of lower quality growths, again suggesting that the A-Index is not a "world market price."

200. Concerning the chart on page 37 of Brazil's further rebuttal submission, why did Brazil use a futures price at planting time? Is this a relevant measure for assessing acreage response? BRA

25. Brazil asserts that US producers are largely unresponsive to market price movements and cites a chart provided in their oral statement of December 2 that showed cotton future prices and planted cotton acreage. However, using a simple cotton price is inappropriate to measure price responsiveness. Prices for cottons alternatives also fell from 1999 to 2002. A farmer cannot just consider cotton prices but must instead consider the opportunity cost at the time of planting. Operating costs being covered (as the United States has already shown the farmer expected to do in each year), he must decide which crop to plant, and this requires looking at the cotton price relative to alternatives. In fact, this is the ap-

[13] *See* US Comment on Brazil's Answer to Question 258 from the Panel.

[14] Brazil's Answer to Question 196 from the Panel, para. 9.

proach taken by FAPRI and Dr. Sumner in considering net returns of cotton versus other crops.[15]

26. When one considers movements of cotton futures versus the price of a substitute like soybeans, a far different picture emerges than the one promoted by Brazil in its response to question 200. The graph below uses the same planted area numbers and time period as Brazil. It shows planted area is price responsive when judged against the more appropriate ratio of cotton to soybeans harvest season futures prices at the time of planting.[16]

27. In the US *Comments Concerning Brazil's Econometric Model*, we point out that the correlation between planted acreage and the ratio of cotton futures to soybean futures is 0.69 over the 1996 to 2002 period. This compares to a correlation of 0.40 for lagged prices to planted acreage, and a *negative correlation* using Dr. Sumner's expected net return calculation and planted acreage. Thus, in contrast to statements by Brazil that futures prices are poor predictors of planted acreage, the correlation data suggest that the futures price ratios are better predictors of planted acreage than the arbitrary net return calculations as constructed by Dr. Sumner.

28. In conclusion, the United States has demonstrated that because the harvest season cotton futures price at planting was above the marketing loan rate (in MY99-01), farmers were planting for the market, not the loan rate. But it is simplistic for Brazil to put compare cotton plantings to futures and judge US farmers not to be price responsive. The United States has never claimed (nor would it) that cotton futures are the only variable that matters for purposes of planting decisions. The correlation data on cotton planted acres to the cotton / soybeans futures ratio shows that competing crops must be factored into any planted acreage analysis. Thus, if Brazil had been interested in presenting an accurate analysis to the Panel, it could have presented such data, or even incorporated alternative crops besides soy from each relevant growing region. Brazil preferred to put forward an analysis that could only serve to obscure the issue.

201. Is data available to show the proportion of US upland cotton production sold under futures contracts, and the prices under those contracts, at different times during the marketing year? If so, please provide summarized versions to the Panel. How does a futures sale impact the producer's entitlement to marketing loan programme payments? BRA, USA

29. As was pointed out in the US response to question 201, cotton producers' use of futures and option markets is high relative to other crops. Based on survey data from the 1996 USDA Agricultural Resource Management Study, it is estimated thatbetween 35 and 57 per cent of cotton farmers used a hedging instrument in 1996.(The ranges reflect a 95 per cent confidence interval.)In addition, an estimated 63 to 89 per cent of cotton farms used cash forward contracts in

[15] Indeed, our objections to their approach focuses on the use of lagged prices rather than futures prices as a proxy for producer price expectations.

[16] The cotton-soybeans futures price ratio is drawn from the US answer to question 175 from the Panel, para. 118.

1996.[17] These survey results suggest that even seven years ago a large proportion of cotton farmers either directly or indirectly priced their cotton off of organized futures and options markets.

30. Moreover, futures markets provide producers information regarding the future price outlook even if they do not hedge directly on the exchange. For example, the 16 January 2004 newsletter by cotton market analyst O. A.. Cleveland states:

> With December [futures contract price] exhibiting signals of breaking away from old crop prices, *hedging of new crop has increased.* Now above 69 cents, *December will need to move higher to prevent acreage loss to both soybeans and corn. A soybean/cotton ratio of9.5 to 1 is enough to begin moving some land from cotton to soybeans (November soybeans to December cotton). A 10 to 1 ratio accelerates the switch.* A September corn ratio of 4 to 1 over December cotton takes more cotton acreage. With both management and capital risk greatly reduced for both of these crops, relative to cotton, significant cotton acreage can be loss if cotton becomes less favourable. With world cotton carryover at a decade low, the new crop December must maintain its tie to the grain/oilseed complex instead of the old crop cotton contracts.[18]

Note that Dr. Cleveland refers not just to cotton futures but to the cotton to soybean ratio and the ratio between cotton futures and corn futures. He confirms not just the importance of cotton futures prices in guiding cotton planted acreage decisions but, more significantly, the relationship of cotton futures prices to the futures prices of competing crops like soybeans and corn.

31. Brazil has presented no evidence that any farmer ever planted based on "lagged prices" (or its "estimated adjusted world price"). Despite Brazil's criticisms of looking at December futures prices to gauge producer price expectations, farm publications are full of references (like that by O.A. Cleveland, above) to the use of December futures for upland cotton planting and hedging purposes. Consider USDA's "Weekly Cotton Market Review" of 9 January 2004.[19] It reported:

- "Most producers [in southeastern markets] have turned their focus to marketing the remainder of their 2003 crop and to *making initial preparations for planting the 2004 crop. Some producers inquired about forward contracts on 2004-crop cotton.* These inquiries were preliminary and no cotton was booked. Merchants offered

[17] A forward contract is defined as a cash market transaction in which two parties agree to buy or sell a commodity or asset under agreed-upon conditions. For example, a farmer agrees sell, and a ginner or warehouse agrees to buy, cotton at a specific future time for an agreed-upon price or on the basis of an agreed on pricing mechanism (such as a futures or options market). See Exhibit US-121, page 22.

[18] O.A. Cleveland Newsletter, January 16, 2004. Exhibit US-133.

[19] USDA, Weekly Cotton Market Review at 1-2 (January 9, 2004) (Exhibit US-139)

contracts in Georgia at *350 to 400 points off NY December futures*" (emphasis added).

Two weeks later, the most recent "Weekly Cotton Market Review" reported:[20]

- "Producers in Georgia booked a very light volume of 2004-crop cotton at 275 to 300 basis points off NY December futures."
- "Merchants continued to offer contracts in Georgia at 300 to 375 points off NY December futures."
- "Contracts in North Carolina were offered at 450 to 475 points off NY December futures."
- "Merchants offered forward contracts at 350 points off NY December futures [in south central markets]."

That is, as the United States has explained, producers are beginning to make planting decisions for MY2004 and are using the December futures price as a guide to their expected returns from planting cotton. A farmer in Georgia can currently lock in a price for the 2004 crop of approximately 65-66 cents per pound (27 Jan. 2004 December futures price of 69.05 cents per pound less 300 to 375 points), and farmers have begun to do just that. Thus, Brazil asserts that the US methodology of looking to the December futures price to gauge producer price expectations is far less valid than using the (outdated November 2002) FAPRI baseline, but cotton producers disagree. In the final analysis, it is producer decisions – and not FAPRI's nor Dr. Sumner's decision to use "lagged prices" – that must drive the Panel's analysis of the effect of removal of marketing loan payments.[21]

203. Please provide information concerning the organization, mandate, credentials and standing of FAPRI. BRA

32. The United States agrees with Brazil's general characterization of FAPRI as a preeminent research institution focused on providing comprehensive analysis of the food and agricultural system. As noted by Brazil in its answer, the United States takes issue with the modifications of the FAPRI model by Dr. Sumner. These differences are outlined in detail in the *US Comments Concerning Brazil's Econometric Model* of 22 December 2003. Chief among these differences is that manner in which Dr. Sumner modelled the effects direct and counter-cyclical payments. FAPRI allows for modest effects of direct payments on all crop acreage. Their result is consistent with the literature on decoupled

---

[20] USDA, Weekly Cotton Market Review at 1-2 (Jan. 23, 2004) (Exhibit US-140).

[21] We also note an argument by Brazil in paragraph 19 that farmers generate a combined revenue from the market and the marketing loan program that exceeds 52 cents per pound. Brazil's analysis is once again partial. The premise is that a farmer is able to sell when prices have *increased* relative to the price on the date they claimed the marketing loan gain. However, in reality, there is no guarantee that prices will have increased. It is equally possible that prices will fall *below* the price on the date when the claim was made. As Exhibit US-126 demonstrates, the margin fluctuates from month to month, with the value in several months even negative, implying that a farmer that did not sell his crop at the time he received the marketing loan payment earned *less than* the marketing loan rate.

payments, showing no or minimal effects on production.[22] By contrast, Dr. Sumner has included an arbitrary and completely *ad hoc* formulation that exaggerates the effects of these payments on acreage decisions. As compared to FAPRI's modelling, Dr. Sumner assumes and then finds effects some 50 times larger.[23]

33. The differences between the FAPRI baseline and Dr. Sumner's model were highlighted as well by Dr. Bruce Babcock, the economist who assisted Dr. Sumner in preparing the Annex I results. In a letter to Dr. Glauber, Dr. Babcock states, that the analysis of Dr. Sumner was "in no way an official FAPRI analysis and if FAPRI had done the analysis, FAPRI would have come up with different estimates of the effects of US cotton subsidies on world prices." Thus, to cloak Dr. Sumner's analysis in the reputation of"the award-winning FAPRI model" is grossly misleading. The differences between FAPRI and the Brazil analysis reflected in Annex I are substantial and, as detailed in the US Comments of 22 December, lead to the biased results presented by Brazil.

204. Which support to upland cotton is not captured in the EWG data referred to in Brazil's 18 November further rebuttal submission? BRA

34. In this answer on "support to upland cotton," Brazil makes reference to "contract payments from base acreage other than upland cotton" and the "allocation of these payments".[24] This answer makes clear that Brazil proposes that such payments with respect to non-upland cotton base acres can be "support to upland cotton." The United States comments on the methodology proposed by Brazil for allocating such payments, which lacks any basis in the Subsidies Agreement, any WTO agreement, or in economic logic, in its comment on Brazil's answer to Question 258. Here, we take issue with Brazil's attempt to amend this Panel's terms of reference to include such payments, and to do so at such a late stage in this proceeding.[25]

35. Nowhere in Brazil's consultation request or request for the establishment of this Panel does Brazil reference these payments under programmes unrelated to upland cotton. Accordingly these payments are not within this Panel's terms of reference. Moreover, Brazil's attempt to raise these payments at the very end of this proceeding deprives the United States of fundamental rights of due process. The United States, as well as all WTO Members, had a right, as of the date of Brazil's request for the establishment of this Panel, to know the "*specific*" measures at issue in this dispute.[26] Brazil cannot make vague allegations of "support" and then change at will the measures that it is challenging as its own position changes and to suit its convenience.

---

[22] *See* US Further Rebuttal Submission, paras. 81-82 (reviewing literature, which finds less than one per cent effect on production, even making unrealistic assumptions on wealth effects).

[23] *See* US Comments on Brazil's Economic Model, para. 20.

[24] Brazil's Answer to Question 204, para. 27.

[25] As previously noted, Brazil's answers to the Panel's questions contain an important concession: in its answer to the Panel's Question 247, Brazil states: "Thus, the 'matter' before the Panel has not changed (and cannot) since the establishment of the Panel."

[26] *See* DSU, Article 6.2.

36. Brazil's own submissions to this Panel demonstrate that Brazil did not consider these payments to be measures within the Panel's terms of reference. In particular, the measures Brazil has alleged are "support to upland cotton" govern both Brazil's serious prejudice claims as well as its Peace Clause analysis. That is, the same measures that are "support for upland cotton" under Brazil's subsidies claims must be the measures that Brazil claims are "support to a specific commodity" for purposes of the analysis under Article 13(b)(ii) of the support that current measures grant versus the support decided during the 1992 marketing year. However, by seeking to allocate to upland cotton "contract payments from base acreage other than upland cotton," Brazil directly contradicts the arguments it set forth in the Peace Clause phase of this dispute. For example, in response to Question 41 from the Panel, Brazil wrote:

> The*only US domestic support measures that Brazil is aware of that would meet the test of being 'support to upland cotton'are those that it listed for purposes of calculating the level of Peace Clause support* in its First Written Submission. In the view of Brazil, these non-green box domestic support measures are the measures that constitute "support to" upland cotton for the purpose of Article 13(b).[27]

The footnote to the first quoted sentence cited paragraphs 144, 148, and 149 of Brazil's first written submission. These paragraphs, in turn, contain the tables in which calculated that budgetary outlays it alleged were support to upland cotton; crucially, these tables list production flexibility contract payments, market loss assistance payments, direct payments, and counter-cyclical payments *for upland cotton base acres only.*[28]

37. Similarly, in response to Question 19, in which the Panel asked Brazil to identify "the measures ... in respect of which Brazil seeks relief," Brazil wrote:

> The first type of domestic support "measure" is the payment of subsidies for the production and use of upland cotton.... . Brazil has tabulated the different types of payments (i.e., the measures) made under these legal instruments in paragraphs 146-149 of its First Submission.[29]

Again, the referenced paragraphs list production flexibility contract payments, market loss assistance payments, direct payments, and counter-cyclical payments *for upland cotton base acres only.*[30]

38. Further, in explaining to the Panel why it did not allocate any portion of other payments notified by the United States to the WTO as non-product-specific, "some of which" (in the Panel's words) "presumably deliver support to upland cotton (e.g. state credit programmes, irrigation subsidies etc)," Brazil explained:

---

27 Brazil's Answer to Question 41 from the Panel, para. 58 (footnote omitted) (italics added).

28 *See* Brazil's First Written Submission, paras. 144, 148, 149.

29 Brazil's Answer to Question 19 from the Panel, para. 15.

30 *See* Brazil's First Written Submission, paras. 146-49.

> None[] of these other measures notified by the United States as non-product specific had *any upland cotton specific link* in terms of historic, updated, or present upland cotton acreage, present upland cotton production or prices, or upland cotton groups of insurance policies or *any other specific upland cotton provisions.*[31]

Of course, the same analysis applies to decoupled income support payments made with respect to base acres for wheat, corn, soy, oats, sorghum, barley, flax, sunflower, safflower, rice, rapeseed, mustard, canola, crambe, and sesame. *None* of these payments has any "upland cotton specific" link in terms of upland cotton acreage, production, prices, or "any other specific upland cotton provisions." Indeed, these other payments are related to acreage historically planted to these other crops and may be (in the case of counter-cyclical payments) related to current prices of these other crops, *not upland cotton*. It is for that reason, presumably, that Brazil did not identify any of these payments among the measures it challenged.

39. Indeed, an important element in Brazil's argument that the decoupled income support measures it challenged were *not* non-product-specific – and thus constitute "support to a specific commodity" – was that the challenged measures contained upland cotton-specific parameters. For example, with respect to counter-cyclical payments, Brazil wrote:

> For the purpose of calculating AMS, counter-cyclical payments (CCP) are 'product-specific' support for two main reasons:(i) they are not "support provided in favour of agricultural producers in general," and (ii) they are directly linked to *upland cotton-specific parameters* (current prices and historical acreage and yield).[32]

Brazil similarly argued that other decoupled income support measures were product-specific support in favour of upland cotton because they allegedly contain upland cotton-specific parameters.[33]

40. We also note that Brazil's request to the Panel to make rulings and recommendations does not reference any decoupled payments made with respect to non-upland cotton base acres. In fact, Brazil specifically stated that its "as such" challenge to "Sections of the 2002 FSRI Act and the referenced regulations thereto," including provisions relating to counter-cyclical payments and direct payments, were only made "to the extent that they relate to upland cotton."[34]

41. In sum, Brazil's arguments on the Peace Clause explicitly limited its claims with respect to decoupled income support measures to payments made with respect to upland cotton base acres. In fact, Brazil relied on the notion that such measures contained "upland cotton-specific" parameters to support its ar-

---

[31] Brazil's Answer to Question 41 from the Panel, para. 57 (italics added).

[32] Brazil's Answer to Question 44 from the Panel, para. 61 (italics added).

[33] *See, e.g.,* Brazil's First Written Submission, para. 60 ("Between MY 1998-2001, upland cotton producers thereby received an additional amount of money, which was calculated based on their respective share of total upland cotton base times the amount of budgetary outlays allocated for upland cotton.").

[34] Brazil's Further Submission, para. 471(vii).

gument that those measures were "support to upland cotton" rather than non-product-specific support.

42. Under its serious prejudice claims, however, Brazil now seeks to expand the challenged measures to include decoupled income support measures with respect to non-upland cotton base acres[35], despite repeatedly arguing that the challenged US subsidies provided $12.9 billion in support over marketing years 1999-2002, a figure based on payments made under specific programmes, *including decoupled income support with respect to upland cotton base acres only.*[36] Decoupled payments made with respect to non-upland cotton base acres would not be within the terms of reference of this dispute; Brazil as complaining party cannot unilaterally expand the terms of reference at the conclusion of a dispute and claim that additional programmes, other than those at issue throughout the dispute, are now also challenged measures providing "subsidies to upland cotton."[37]

209. It is understood that the data in the graph in paragraph 5 of the US oral statement are as at harvest time, while the data in the graph in paragraph 39 of Brazil's oral statement are as at planting time. Please explain why the trend of US acreage increase/decrease differs between these two graphs. BRA, USA

43. We note that Brazil acknowledges that a comparison of "planted to planted" area would be best. Harvested area can only be used as a proxy for planted area, and as indicated by the US data in the US Opening Statement of 2 December 2003, the two measures can diverge significantly. This divergence is especially important to note in light of Brazil's answer to Panel Question 210.

210. Are worldwide planted acreage figures available? BRA, USA

44. After noting in its response that consistent world-wide planting data for upland cotton are not available, Brazil continues to insist that world-wide harvested area data are a good proxy for planted area. Brazil offers a theoretical justification for using harvested area as a proxy for planted area (annual aban-

---

35 The United States notes that Brazil does not appear to seriously believe that these measures are within the Panel's terms of reference since Brazil has not presented the 1992 levels of support that would include these additional payments, which Brazil would have had to do to make the Peace Clause comparison.

36 We note that Brazil seeks to have it both ways. That is, it now argues that decoupled payments made with respect to non-upland cotton base acres can be allocated to, and become support to, upland cotton, yet at the same time, when it suits its purposes, it continues to argue that decoupled payments are support to upland cotton because of their alleged upland cotton-specific parameters. *See, e.g.,* Brazil 's Opening Statement at Second Panel Meeting, para. 60 ("[T]he 72.4 cent target price triggers CCP payments when *cotton* prices are lower – not corn, or soybeans prices – but *cotton.*").

37 Indeed, although Brazil attempted to argue at the second panel meeting that it sought information on payments made with respect to *non-upland cotton base acres* through the Annex V procedure that the DSB did not agree to initiate, Brazil itself stated in its first written submission that its Annex V request was *limited to upland cotton base acres*: "Brazil requested the United States during the Annex V procedure to provide information on the amount of the *total upland cotton base acreage and yield under the CCP (and DP) program.*" Brazil's First Written Submission, para. 68 (italics added). If so, this would be consistent with Brazil 's Peace Clause argumentation in this dispute that only payments on upland cotton base acres could be product-specific support for upland cotton.

donment will average out over all cotton producing countries and be relatively stable over time). But Brazil has no empirical evidence to support the theory and continues to mix "apples and oranges" in its charts. For example, we note the chart at paragraph 33 of Brazil's answers is misleading: it is not a chart of "Per cent Change in Planted Acres" as labelled. Rather, it compares changes in US *planted* area for upland cotton with changes in non-US *harvested* area. This comparison is not appropriate.

45. As noted in the US answers to Question 209 from the Panel, US planted and harvested area generally move in the same direction but occasionally move in opposite directions. We note that, once again, Brazil has relied on a period that begins with marketing year 1998 to present a biased analysis. The period 1998 - 2000 that Brazil focuses on in para. 33 was an unusual period for US cotton because of weather. As noted in the US Opening Statement of December 2 (para. 6), abandonment was especially high in 1998 and area rebounded sharply in 1999. The year 2000 was a year when US planted and harvested area moved in opposite directions.

US Planted and Harvested Upland Cotton Acres (1,000 acres)

Crop year	Planted acres	Harvested acres
1998	13,064	10,449
1999	14,584	13,138
2000	15,347	12,884

Source: USDA, National Agricultural Statistics Service, *Acreage*, various issues, as submitted inthe US Opening Statement of December 2 (para. 6).

46. Because foreign planted area data are not available, it is not possible to observe whether foreign planted and harvested area similarly diverged in these years. Therefore, using US planted area and foreign harvested area is a misleading comparison. Brazil uses its mislabelled chart to simplistically conclude that whenever US planted area moves in a divergent direction from foreign harvested area, the only reason must be because US subsidies insulate US upland cotton producers. That conclusion ignores any other possible factors that may affect area planted – for example, weather or competing crop prices – and is not supported by the data.

47. In para. 34, Brazil again complains that the US chart in the US Opening Statement of 2 Dec. (para. 6) is inappropriate. Brazil has it completely backwards. The US chart is the only appropriate comparison. We agree that a comparison of planted area data would be the best method, but the data are not available. Therefore, Brazil's conclusions based on a "planted versus harvested" comparison are not valid.

48. We again present a comparison of changes in US harvested area for upland cotton with changes in harvested area for the rest of the world.(These data are found in Exhibit US-63, but 2002 data are updated and estimated data for 2003-04 are included.)We note again the anomalous years of 1998 and 1999 for the US, where harvested area was sharply below planted area in 1998 because of

severe adverse weather but then planted (and harvested) area increased sharply in 1999 in reaction both to the previous year's high abandonment and to favourable prices relative to competing crops. For the years 2000 - 2002harvested area in the US and the rest of the world moved in tandem – declining in 2000, rising in 2001, and declining again in 2002. Brazil's claim of "distinctly different reactions"[38] are not supported by the data.

49. Brazil further claims that US area should have declined during the period 1999 - 2002. In fact, it is hard to discern any trend in US (or foreign) harvested area during this period. But since 1999, an admitted high year because of unique weather factors and favourable cotton prices relative to competing crops, US upland cotton area has generally declined. The new data provided for 2003 reinforce this conclusion: US area declined while the rest of the world, including Brazil, increased.

Harvested Area for Upland Cotton *(1,000 hectares and per cent change from previous year)*

Crop year	1998	1999	2000	2001	2002	2003(p)
US area	4,324	5,433	5,282	5,596	5,030	4,881
Foreign area	28,559	26,955	26,904	28,308	25,470	28,090
Brazil area	685	752	853	748	735	940
US (% change)	-20.3	25.6	-2.8	5.9	-10.1	-3.0
Foreign (% change)	0.5	-5.6	-0.2	5.2	-9.9	10.3
Brazil (% change)	-10.5	9.8	13.4	-12.3	-1.7	27.9

Sources: USDA, Foreign Agricultural Service, Production, Supply, and Distribution Database;World Agricultural Supply and Demand Estimates, World Agricultural Outlook Board, USDA, 11 January 2004. Exhibit US-63, with 2003 added.

50. The data show that US harvested cotton area moves consistently with the rest of the world, when there are not abnormal weather events. Brazil conceded as much (in para. 36) that US acreage movements were relatively consistent with the rest of the world. How could that be if US producers are insulated from price movements because of subsidies? In marketing year 2003, US cotton area declined 3 per cent while the rest of the world rose 10 per cent. These divergent results again suggest that cotton area around the world is affected by different factors and these need to be accounted for carefully. But a *decline* in US harvested acreage in marketing year 2003, following a decline in marketing year 2002, is certainly not consistent with Brazil's theory that the United States increased support in the 2002 Act and that these "higher" payments will result in US overproduction of cotton, threatening to cause serious prejudice.

51. In discussing how producers react to price signals, we would note recent trends in Brazil's cotton area. In MY2002, Brazil's harvested area declined about 2 per cent while the US and foreign cotton area dropped 10 per cent. In MY2003,

[38] Brazil's Answer to Question 210 from the Panel, para. 35.

Brazil's cotton area is estimated to have increased *28 per cent* while US cotton area fell 3 per cent. In fact, since the collapse in Brazil's cotton area in 1996, Brazil's cotton area has shown a much more consistent upward trend than US or foreign cotton area. We also note that in marketing years 1998, 1999, 2000 and 2001, Brazil's harvested area moved in the *opposite direction* from non-US cotton area. Those different responses, in absolute values, ranged from 11 per cent in MY1998 to 17.5 per cent in MY2001. In MY2002, Brazil's harvested area declined much less than the (non-US) rest of the world (1.7 per cent versus 9.9 per cent), and in MY2003 Brazil's harvested area is forecast to expand by far more than the (non-US) rest of the world (27.9 per cent versus 10.3 per cent). Thus, it would appear that, in terms of changes in harvested acres, Brazil deviates far more from the non-US rest of the world than does the United States.

52. Finally, in paragraph 35, even when Brazil' s misleading data do show a consistent decline between US planted and non-US harvested area, Brazil does not accept that US cotton producers were responding to market signals. Brazil simply claims that US cotton area should have declined more than it did.[39]

53. Brazil has tried to explain away similarities in acreage movements by asserting that Dr. Sumner's analysis suggests that US cotton acreage should have even been lower. Not only do we disagree with that analysis, but we note that it fails to explain why US and non-US harvested acreage moves commensurately from 1997-2002. If US producers were insulated from price movements, as Brazil claims, one would not expect US acreage to be highly correlated with acreage movements in the rest of the world. In fact, the data suggests the opposite; i.e., that US producers respond in similar fashion with cotton producers around the world.

213. What differences, if any, can be observed in the results of econometric models in the literature which use lagged prices and those which use futures prices to analyse the effect of prices on planting decisions? BRA, USA

54. Brazil points out that the statistical estimation literature in agricultural economics has used a variety of proxies for anticipated prices and revenue for the upcoming season. These include rational expectations in which many sources of information available to decision makers are combined and the expectations are consistent with the conditional forecasts of the model. Such models have strong theoretical grounding but have been impractical in most estimation situations.

---

[39] In paragraph 35, Brazil again tries to buttress its claims by arguing that US exports increased during a period when the US dollar was appreciating in value. The exchange rate analysis put forward by Brazil is incomplete and inadequate. Brazil has ignored the fact that cotton is a raw material for apparel and textile products. The increase in foreign demand for raw cotton drove an increase in US exports. For example, with a strong US dollar, imported cotton textile and apparel became relatively cheaper, thereby increasing demand for such products. Increased textile and apparel demand in the United States from the higher dollar resulted in increased demand for raw cotton by foreign textile and apparel manufacturers. Foreign use of cotton increased from 80.8 million bales in MY 1999 to 91 million bales in MY 2002. Foreign production, however, remained basically the same, 70.5 million bales in MY 1999 to 70.8 million bales in MY2002. Therefore, US exports were responding to demand that was not met by foreign production. Source: Cotton and Wool Situation and Outlook Yearbook, Economic Research Service, USDA, November 2003, pg. 32.

55. Models such as used by FAPRI, USDA and the Congressional Budget Office has been developed not for retrospective analysis but for *prospective* analysis. If one wants to project out over a period for which futures prices are not available, it makes sense to rely on lagged prices since the models will produce prices for a given year that can then be used as the price expectation for the following year.

56. Nonetheless, the use of lagged prices may result in biased results. Over the long term, where there is reasonable stability in markets, lagged prices function adequately as a proxy for price expectations. However, in those years, as in the period Brazil has pointed to here, when unexpected exogenous shocks such as China dumping stocks (late 1990s) and unexpected yields worldwide due to good weather conditions such as 2001, lagged prices are poor predictors of expected prices. Future prices, by contrast, are more efficient because they are based on more current information. Moreover, as we have argued elsewhere (see comments to question 200 and 201 above), producers base acreage decisions on futures markets. Where futures prices diverge from lagged prices, there is reason to believe that planted acreage decisions will diverge from forecast acreage from models based on lagged prices.

57. For example, during marketing years 2000, 2001, 2002, and 2003, lagged prices significantly understate the harvest season prices expected by producers as seen in the futures prices at the time of planting. The use of lagged prices thereby inflate the effect of the marketing loan rate. In fact, those lagged prices would have to be increased by 8-25 per cent, depending on the year, to equal the harvest season price actually expected by producers as indicated by the futures price.[40]

- For the period MY 1999-2003, when futures prices are used to gauge producer price expectations, only in MY 2002 were expected cash prices below the marketing loan rate.
- However, over that same period, when lagged prices are used as expected prices, the loan rate is higher than the expected price *in every year over this period* except MY1999.

Thus, it is a significant error for Brazil and Dr. Sumner to use lagged prices instead of the futures prices Brazil's own expert explained to be the more accurate gauge of farmers' price expectations. In fact, despite the hundreds of exhibits it has filed, Brazil has provided not one single piece of evidence that any farmers use or have ever used lagged prices to make planting decisions.

58. While the United States would agree with Brazil that it is impossible to know precisely what individual farmers' price expectations are, the United States (and Brazil's expert, Mr. McDonald) believe that futures prices provide the most current expectations of market participants. As such, futures prices incorporate the views of numerous market participants, including producers, regarding expectations of future market conditions. The United States disagrees with the approach used by Brazil in its analysis to rely solely on lagged prices and ignore information provided by futures prices. While it may be impractical to include

[40] US Further Rebuttal Submission, paras. 164-65.

futures prices in some models, modelling convenience is no justification to ignore these objective, market-based price expectations. The Panel cannot rely on Brazil's economic analysis that uses a proxy for expected prices that would have to be increased by up to 25 per cent to accurately reflect futures prices, the only objective data on the record reflecting actual price expectations of market participants. The biased results from using lagged prices do not assist the Panel in making an objective assessment of what is the effect of the US marketing loan programme.

59. Brazil ignores the fact that expected cash prices based on futures prices were above the loan rate from MY1999-2001, whereas the lagged price was below the loan rate for 2000-2002. That is, withdrawal of the marketing loan would not have greater acreage impacts because producers are planting for market prices, not loan rate.

215. Please expand or comment on the statement at paragraph 91 of the US further rebuttal submission that the counter-cyclical target price ceases to be paid when the farm price rises above 65.73 cents per pound. In this scenario, should the Panel disregard Direct Payments? BRA, USA

60. In the US response to question 211 (b), we demonstrate that market returns have exceeded variable costs for cotton producers in every year but one (2001) over the period of investigation. Brazil continues to argue that producers require direct payments to cover total costs of production, but this ignores the evidence that significant acreage is planted to cotton by cotton producers who have no cotton base acreage and hence are ineligible for cotton direct payments.

61. Brazil claims US producers will continue to plant upland cotton because they face no revenue risk, but this argument ignores the substantial evidence on record of huge acreage shifts, both on state level and within three categories of farms (i.e., those who plant cotton with cotton base; those who do not plant cotton but have cotton base; those farms who planted cotton but have no cotton base). Moreover, Brazil ignores the decline in plantings over last two years as other commodities have become more attractive and expected cotton prices less so. Finally, the claim that direct and counter cyclical paymentsremove risk of revenue loss runs contrary to theory on decoupled payments. Farmers will plant the crop that maximizes their expected revenue since the decoupled payment will be made whether they plant or not.

62. Brazil's argument that direct payments have significant effects on production runs counter to the empirical literature as well as running counter to the estimated effects from the FAPRI model that they purport to use. As pointed out in Dr. Glauber's literature review[41] and in the US discussion of direct payments in the US further submission and further rebuttal submission, empirical studies suggest that direct payments have only minimal effects on production. Indeed, as pointed out in the US Comments Concerning Brazil's Econometric Model of 22 December, the FAPRI baseline model (that is, the original FAPRI model as dis-

41 Exhibit US-23.

tinct from the model modified by Dr. Sumner) suggests that the effect of direct payments on cotton acreage is less than one per cent.

63. It is only when Dr. Sumner explicitly modifies the FAPRI model to *include* an *ad hoc* production specification for direct payments that Brazil obtains the tautological result that direct payments have a significant effect on cotton production.

216. How many times have upland cotton producers been able to update their base acres since 1984? How do upland cotton producers come to note the possibility of future updating? Please provide examples of relevant material. BRA, USA

64. In this answer the matter addressed has to do with base issues and whether farmers could or could not update their bases in the period that followed 1985. In our 22 December response we gave a full answer on that topic. We would note that in the US answer it is indicated that under the 1990 Act the running base provisions for cotton called for a five-year running average. This was an error. The running base period was a five-year period for other programme crops, but cotton and rice used a three-year period.

65. Brazil's contention that the United States has a base building policy is belied by Brazil's own recitation that there has been only one chance to add base cost-free (that is, without loss of benefits); that was in the 2002 Act, in which new crops were added to the programme mix, necessitating a recalculation. There is no guarantee nor any reason to believe that this will ever happen again. Brazil is simply speculating on the likelihood that updating could occur. What could happen in some cases is programme termination, such as that which occurred with the elimination of peanut quotas in the 2002 Act.

66. Brazil further speculates that some farmers could be upset by the new programme because they did not plant as much as they could have over 1998-2001 and that such farmers will now plant more than they would otherwise have. Brazil's speculation is devoid of any facts. In fact, the United States has pointed to planting data (for example, that submitted on December 18 and 19, 2003) that demonstrates just the opposite – that is, cotton plantings are declining. Further, Brazil's own scenario suggests that there was no such understood policy of base building – otherwise, why would any farmer be surprised? Farmers will always speculate on the shape of the future, but these speculations (for which Brazil has presented no evidence) cannot drive determinations of consistency or inconsistency of measures with WTO obligations.

67. Finally, to the extent that Members would wish to limit the ability of Members to choose a new "defined and fixed base period" for purposes of paragraph 6(a) of Annex 2 to the Agreement on Agriculture, they may do so as a result of the current Doha negotiations. However, no such limitation currently appears in the text, and Brazil is acting in contravention of Article 3.2 of the DSU in seeking to have a panel "add to or diminish" the rights and obligations of Members through dispute settlement. The United States would also note that Brazil's response to this question appears to assume that Members will not accept the US proposal for significant reductions in domestic support under the Doha

negotiations. The overall AMS reduction commitment would be relevant for the amount of support, including base acres, that a Member would provide.

D. EXPORT CREDIT GUARANTEES

220. What will be the relevance of Articles 9 and 10.1 of the Agreement of Agriculture to export credit guarantees when disciplines are internationally agreed? BRA

68. Brazil's response to this question demonstrates that Brazil continues to ignore the text of Article 10.2 itself. Article 10.2 is clear that once disciplines are internationally agreed, then Members undertake "to provide export credits, export credit guarantees or insurance programmes only in conformity therewith." No "amendment" to Articles 9 or 10 would be needed. Article 10.2 has already specified the obligations once the negotiations are completed. In this sense, Article 10.2 goes further than, for example, Articles XIII:2 and XV:1 of the GATS, which also call for negotiations to develop additional disciplines but do not on their face already commit Members to abide by the results of those negotiations.

69. Brazil mischaracterizes the views of the United States with respect to the role of the OECD and the interpretation of Article 10.2 of the *Agreement on Agriculture.* Brazil stated that "some participants [in the Uruguay Round negotiations] may have been seeking additional obligations regarding notification, consultation and information exchange, like those included in the OECD Arrangement on Officially Supported Export Credits for industrial products".[42] Brazil alluded to no other potential disciplines available under the OECD Arrangement. In its Closing Statement of 3 December 2003, the United States responded that Brazil minimizes the significance of Article 10.2 as reflecting:

> merely a banal compromise to accommodate potential 'additional obligations regarding notification, consultation, and information exchange.'Brazil implausibly asserts that the obvious transition between the language of the Draft Final Act that would have imposed significant substantive disciplines on export credit guarantees and the absence of such language in the Article 10.2 ultimately adopted can be fully explained as reflecting merely an agreement to work on such pedestrian disciplines as information exchange".[43]

70. Brazil, however, mischaracterizes the US statement as a dismissal of other disciplines that Brazil itself never mentioned: "permitted exceptions, matching of derogations, non-conforming non-notified items, and terms granted by countries that are not parties to the OECD Arrangement." [44]

71. Ironically, the United States – not Brazil – has emphasized the significance of the OECD in the interpretation of Article 10.2. During the Uruguay Round, WTO Members did not agree on disciplines to be applicable to export

---

[42] Opening Statement of Brazil, 2 December 2003, para. 74

[43] Closing Statement of the United States, 3 December 2003, para. 3.

[44] Answers of Brazil (22 December 2003), Question 220, para. 54.

credit guarantee programmes and therefore opted "to work toward the development of internationally agreed disciplines," as contemplated by the text of Article 10.2, in the appropriate forum of the OECD to achieve such disciplines. As the United States has pointed out, the OECD was the logical forum for such negotiations because of the institutional experience of that organization in the development of disciplines on officially supported export credits in the industrial sector.[45] Six years of negotiations continued there until 2001.

221. In respect of the table in paragraph 161 of the US August 22 rebuttal submission (concerning the cohort specific treatment of export credit guarantees), the Panel notes the subsequent US agreement (footnotes 82 and 96 in US further submission of 30 September 2003; footnote 160 in US 18 November further rebuttal submission) to Brazil's assertion (footnote 67 in Brazil's 27 August 2003 comments on US rebuttal submission) that the total figure net of re-estimates should be $230,127,023 instead of the figure which originally appeared ($381,345,059).

(c) The Panel notes that the CCC 2002 financial statement in Exhibit BRA-158 refers to annual "administrative" expenses of $4 million, and that the US has also referred to this figure in its submissions (e.g. US first written submission, paragraph 175). Please confirm whether the figures in the table in paragraph 161 of the US August 22 rebuttal submission (or a corrected version thereof) includes "administrative expenses", of approximately $4 million per year over the period 1992-2002, and explain why (or why not) this affects the substantive result.

72. Brazil quotes selective excerpts of 1998 testimony of then- General Sales Manager Christopher Goldthwait but misconstrues them to draw the absurd proposition that export credit premia cover only administrative expenses of the programme. These excerpts on their face not only do not say what Brazil claims - they contradict Brazil's claim. Both Brazil and the United States have noted that administrative expenses of the programme are between $3 and 4 million per year.[46] Premia collected, of course, consistently far exceed that amount.[47]

73. Moreover, Mr. Goldthwait's testimony does not state that premia cover *only* administrative expenses (even in the excerpt quoted by Brazil he twice says that the money collected is "more" than the amount of administrative expenses), and the actual figures for premia reveal the inaccuracy of Brazil's claim.

74. The testimony in Exhibit Bra-87 in fact supports the argument of the United States that it exercises considerable discretion in the administration of the programme and that contrary to Brazil's repeated mischaracterizations, CCC can "stem[], or otherwise control, the flow of" CCC export credit guarantees.[48]

---

45 US First Written Submission (11 July 2003), paras. 155-160

46 See, e.g., Oral Statement of Brazil (22 July 2003), para. 132.

47 Exhibit US-128.

48 The most recent invocation of Brazil's misapplied mantra appears in Brazil's Answer to Additional Question 257(c) (20 January 2004), para. 38

75. Then Undersecretary August Schumacher stated:

"On GSM we are continually revising the changing creditworthiness of these overseas buyers. We are extremely prudent in the use. We follow this very, very carefully. Without the [International Monetary Fund], we would be very reluctant to operate and allocate these GSM programmes as required by the Agricultural Trade Act of 1978.

"Actual credit packages are subject to interagency review. Overall, we will continue to achieve balance between our twin objectives of promoting US agricultural exports and operating Federal programmes such as the GSM with fiduciary responsibility to the taxpayers and to you in Congress."[49]

76. Further testimony not quoted by Brazil included the following:

Congressman Minge:

"I would like to ask if you could explain to us why you feel that this programme is one that will not expose the American taxpayer or the US Treasury to a loss, particularly if private sector lenders are competing with the Federal Government for repayment of their loans and these countries in Southeast Asia find their financial condition further deteriorates? Is this a risk that we are creating for the US Treasurer, or is this something you feel we are adequately protected on?"

Mr. Goldthwait:

"We developed our programme allocations by beginning with a country risk analysis. It is very much the same sort of analysis that a private bank will do in setting its ... confirmation line for transactions with a particular foreign country.

"We ... evaluate very carefully the financial situation of the country and the banks involved and the letters of credit that we will eventually guarantee in determining exactly how far further we can go and still remain prudent with the taxpayers'money."

Congressman Minge: "So you do not expect any greater exposure to loss here than you have had historically in the operation of the programme?"

Mr. Goldthwait: "We do not".[50]

223. Are the premium rates applicable to GSM 102, 103 and SCGP subject to regular review as to their adequacy in enabling the operating costs and losses associated with these programmes? If so, what criteria or benchmarks are taken into consideration for this purpose? Secondly, how do the premium rates applied compare with the implicit cost offorfaiting transactions and with premiums for export credit insurance? USA

---

49 Exhibit Bra-87, page 10.

50 *Ibid.*, page. 12.

77. Brazil asserts that "premium rates for the three CCC guarantee programmes are not subject to regular review".[51] This is incorrect. As the United States noted in its response to this question, premium rates are reviewed annually. They may or may not increase in any given year as a result of such annual review.

78. To avoid any potential misunderstanding the United States would also point out that the statutory cap on premia of one per cent applies only to GSM-102. Brazil correctly notes this in paragraph 66 of its December 22 answers, but paragraph 64 could be interpreted to imply that the cap similarly applies to GSM-103, which it does not.

227. The United States has indicated that Brazil continues to "mischaracterize" the amount of $411 million in the 2002 financial statement of the CCC, in Exhibit BRA 158, pp. 18 & 19. Can the United States please indicate how it believes this amount - referred to on p. 19 of the Exhibit as "Credit Guarantee Liability-End of Fiscal Year" - should be properly characterized? How, if at all, does it represent CCC operating costs or losses? USA

79. In addition to its own response to this question from the Panel, the United States would reiterate that the $411 million figure is an *estimate* and the "results of the reestimate process".[52] In addition, the $770 million in the 'subsidy allowance' is not an uncollectible amount. It is merely a loan loss *allowance* based on annual re-estimates reflected in the budget. It is obviously not an amount deemed uncollectible, because from 2001 to 2002, as reflected in the very next line of the financial statement, the number itself *declined* from $1.043 billion to $770 million.[53] Similarly, the figure applicable to pre-1992 credit guarantees in the column "allowance for uncollectible accounts" is itself only a prospective *allowance*, which may or may not ultimately correspond to actual uncollectability. As with the subsidy allowance noted above, in this case, too, the allowance declined from 2002 to 2003 by $389 million.[54]

80. Office of Management and Budget Circular A-11 defines "allowance" as follows:

> "Allowance means a lump-sum included in the budget to represent certain transactions that are expected to increase or decrease budget authority, outlays, or receipts but that are not, for various reasons, reflected in the programme details. For example, the budget might include an allowance to show the effect on the budget totals of a proposal that would affect many accounts by relatively small amounts, in order to avoid unnecessary detail in the presentations for the individual accounts. The President doesn't propose that Congress enact an allowance as such, but rather that it

[51] Answers of Brazil to Question 223 of the Panel (22 December 2003), para. 63.

[52] Rebuttal Submission of Brazil (22 August 2003), para. 109; US Further Submission (30 September 2003), fn. 94; See Exhibit Bra-158, Notes to Financial Statement, page 19.

[53] See Exhibit Bra-158, Notes to Financial Statement, p. 14.

[54] See Exhibit US-129, Notes to 2003 Financial Statement, p. 15.

modify specific legislative measures as necessary to produce the increases or decreases represented by the allowance."[55]

228. What accounting principles should the Panel use in assessing the long-term operating costs and losses of these three programmes? For example, if internal US Government regulations require costs to be treated differently to generally accepted accounting principles, is it incumbent on the Panel to conduct its analysis in accordance with that treatment? BRA, USA

81. Brazil incorrectly asserts that "US government's own accounting principles lead to a conclusion that premium rates are inadequate to meet the long-term operating costs and losses of the CCC guarantee programmes".[56] To the contrary, under current GAAP for Federal Entities, including the application of such principles related to the Federal Credit Reform Act of 1990, the programme reflects profitability for all of the first five cohorts (1992-1996). In addition, the cohort for 1999 is already showing profitability.[57] Exhibit US-128 also reflects the long-term profitability of the programmes.

82. The United States has every reason to believe this trend will continue with respect to more recent cohorts. Contrary to the assertions of Brazil, the United States is not "carefully selecting" or "cherry-picking" years that "did not lose money".[58] For the reasons set forth in US answers to Panel Questions 221(f), (g), (h), and (i)[59], chronologically more recent – not "carefully selected" – years are reflected unnecessarily negatively in the US budget.

E. SERIOUS PREJUDICE

229. What is the meaning of the words "may arise in any case where *one or several* of the following apply" (emphasis added) in Article 6.3 of the SCM Agreement? Please comment on the possibility that these words indicate that one of the Article 6 subparagraphs may not be sufficient to establish serious prejudice and that serious prejudice should be considered an additional or overriding criterion to the factors specified in the subparagraphs. BRA

83. Brazil states that "[t]he phrase 'one or several' must be read according to its ordinary meaning" and reads this phrase to mean "at least one." Brazil then states that it "disagrees with the possibility that the words *one or several* indicate that one of the Article 6.3 paragraphs may not be sufficient to establish serious prejudice".[60] However, Brazil's answer simply neglects to read *all* of "the words" quoted in the Panel's question (drawn from the chapeau of Article 6.3) according

---

55 OMB Circular A-11 (2003), Section 20.3, p. 20-2. http://www.whitehouse.gov/omb/circulars/a11/current_year/s20.pdf

56 Answers of Brazil to Panel Question 228 (22 December 2003), para. 68.

57 See Exhibit Bra-182 and US Answers to Panel Question 221(b) (22 December 2003, paras. 83-86.

58 See, e.g., Answer of Brazil to Panel Question 228 (22 December 2003), para. 73.

59 US Answers to Panel Questions (22 December 2003), paras. 91-104.

60 Brazil's Answer to Question 229 from the Panel, paras. 76-77.

to their ordinary meaning: "What is the meaning of the words'may arise in any case where *one or several* of the following apply" (emphasis added) in Article 6.3 of the *SCM Agreement*?" Crucially, Brazil simply neglects to read the words "may arise" according to their ordinary meaning.[61] The ordinary meaning of "may" is "have ability or power to; can"[62] and "to express possibility, opportunity, or permission".[63] Therefore, the ordinary meaning of the chapeau to Article 6.3 (that is, including the phrase "may arise" as well as "one or several") would be that there is a "possibility" or "opportunity" for serious prejudice in the sense of Article 5(c) to "arise" where one or more of the effects listed in Article 6.3 is found.[64]

84. Thus, when Brazil "disagrees with the possibility that the words *one or several* indicate that one of the Article 6.3 paragraphs may not be sufficient to establish serious prejudice," Brazil is not reading the chapeau of Article 6.3 according to the ordinary meaning of all of the words in the provision. Such a selective approach fails to read the treaty text according to the customary rules of interpretation of public international law. Indeed, if Article 6.3 had been intended to mean that any one of the subparagraphs would *necessarily* suffice to show serious prejudice, the text would have used obligatory language in favour of a finding of serious prejudice (such as, "serious prejudice ... shall arise in any case where at least one of the following apply").[65]

85. Brazil's discussion of various provisions of the Antidumping Agreement and Subsidies Agreement that contain language that no one factor can necessarily "give decisive guidance" towards a pertinent finding is inapt. That is, simply because the "may arise" language in the chapeau of Article 6.3 does not necessarily *preclude* a finding of serious prejudice where the effect in only one subparagraph has been demonstrated does not convert the "possibility" or "opportunity" that serious prejudice arise into an *obligation* to find serious prejudice. Rather, serious prejudice "may arise" or it may not, for example, where a panel concludes that one or more subparagraphs is technically met but the effect is not sufficient to cause serious prejudice.

86. Finally, we note Brazil's new argument that the "may arise" language "is necessary because while the facts may demonstrate that the effects of the subsidies *may* create the one, two, or three enumerated types of serious prejudice, these effects may not be actionable".[66] Brazil' s argument misunderstands the nature of the serious prejudice analysis. As stated above, the plain language of Article 6.3 establishes that demonstrating one or several of the effects of the

---

61 *See* Brazil 's Answer to Question 229 from the Panel, paras. 79-80 (setting forth no interpretation of "may arise" according to its ordinary meaning).

62 *The New Shorter Oxford English Dictionary*, vol. 1, at 1721 (1993 ed.).

63 *The Random House Dictionary of the English Language, Unabridged Edition* at 886 (1983).

64 *See* US Answer to Question 149 from the Panel, paras. 71-75.

65 Indeed, Article 6.1 demonstrates that Members knew how to create a presumption of serious prejudice: they did so by explicitly stating that, in certain cases, "[s]erious prejudice ... *shall* be deemed to exist" (italics added). Article 6.2, while providing a means to rebut that presumption, does not by its terms establish that serious prejudice "shall be deemed to exist" if one of the effects in Article 6.3 exists.

66 Brazil's Answer to Question 229, para. 80.

subparagraphs does not *necessarily* suffice to demonstrate serious prejudice. Thus, it is not the case that "serious prejudice" will arise where one of the effects is demonstrated but an "exemption" (in Brazil's words) in Article 6 applies; rather, the "exemptions" cited by Brazil preclude the very finding of "serious prejudice."

- For example, Brazil argues that the effect in Article 6.3(d) (an increase in world market share) may be demonstrated but may "not be actionable" because multilaterally agreed rules exist within the meaning of footnote 17. But the effect of footnote 17 is to remove certain primary products or commodities subject to such rules from the 6.3(d) analysis altogether.[67] Thus, no finding of "serious prejudice" for such a product would be possible.
- Neither does Article 6.7 support the conclusion that serious prejudice "may arise" but may not be actionable. Rather, that provision establishes that "[d]isplacement or impediment resulting in serious prejudice shall not arise under paragraph 3 where any one of the following circumstances exist"; that is, even where the effect of displacement or impediment is demonstrated under Article 6.3, a finding of serious prejudice is precluded ("shall not arise").
- Finally, Brazil points to Article 6.9 and claims that this provision "exempts serious prejudice that exists even where the requirements of Article 6.3 are fulfilled because the subsidies are exempt from action by virtue of the peace clause." Article 6.9 does not "exempt[] serious prejudice that exists," however. The text reads: "*This Article does not apply* to subsidies maintained on agricultural products as provided in Article 13 of the Agreement on Agriculture" (emphasis added). Because the entire "Article does not apply," no finding of "serious prejudice" is possible.[68]

87. Finally, we note that Brazil's argument that the "may arise" language is "necessary" because certain circumstances may exist in which a finding of serious prejudice is precluded would suggest that whenever an exception exists to a "shall" obligation, that obligation should be expressed using "may". For example, because there is an exception to the prohibition on export subsidies in Article 3.1 of the Subsidies Agreement, presumably Brazil would consider that the provision should have been written: "Except as provided in the Agreement on

[67] Footnote 17 to Article 6.3(d) follows the words "the effect of the subsidy is an increase in the world market share of the subsidizing Member in a particular subsidized primary product or commodity" and reads: "Unless other multilaterally agreed specific rules apply to the trade in the product or commodity in question."

[68] Brazil's argument echoes its erroneous interpretation of the "exempt from actions" language of the Peace Clause. Indeed, as the United States has pointed out, Brazil has never explained how it is that the Panel, if it ultimately determines that US measures are "exempt from actions" based on Articles 5 and 6 of the Subsidies Agreement, could nonetheless make findings on those claims without resulting in the DSB making rulings and recommendations with respect to those claims and measures. Given the automaticity in adoption of panel and Appellate Body reports, the only means by which Peace Clause-compliant US measures may be "exempt from actions" is for the Panel to decline to reach Brazil's claims based on those provisions specified in the Peace Clause.

Agriculture, the following subsidies, within the meaning of Article 1, [may] be prohibited." The use of "may" in place of "shall," however, changes the meaning of that provision from mandatory to permissive. Similarly, the use of "may" instead of "shall" in Article 6.3 means that there is a "possibility" or "opportunity" for serious prejudice to arise where one or more of the effects listed in Article 6.3 is found, rather than a certainty or necessity that serious prejudice have arisen.

232. How, if at all, should the Panel take into account the effects of other factors in its analysis of the effects of US subsidies under Article 6.3? If the Panel should compare the effects of other factors to establish the relative significance of one compared to others, how would this be done? What would be relevant "factors" for this purpose? BRA

88. Causation is a key issue in this dispute, and Brazil continues to gloss over this issue. The United States is interested to see Brazil argue that an econometric analysis by definition satisfies the causation requirements under the WTO.[69] Brazil's position in this dispute is at odds with its position in other disputes, such as *Steel*. Brazil appears to change its view on the correct approach to causation depending on whether it bears the burden or not. For example, Brazil now argues in its response to this question:"But the record shows that there is no legitimate basis to conclude that "other" supply and demand factors collectively (a) accounted for all of the declines in prices during the period of investigation or (b) meant that prices went as high as they would have even if no US subsidies had been provided." In other words, Brazil appears to claim that it is entitled to a finding in its favour on causation unless someone else (not Brazil) shows that other factors accounted for all the effects, rather than that Brazil must show that it is not attributing to the US measures at issue effects that are due to other factors. This is in error.

89. Brazil must establish that effect of the challenged subsidies was "significant price suppression" or an increase in world market share. Brazil has not established that it has accounted for "the effect of" other factors at play, even though it concedes that "[t]his world market share is the result of several key factors *including US subsidies*, weather effects in many countries, and exchange rate effects" (italics added). How then can Brazil claim that the effect of the subsidies is "significant"? That is, if Brazil itself argues that US subsidies were only one of "several key factors," its analysis must allow the Panel to distinguish the effects of these other factors. Brazil has not even attempted to explain what those effects were, nor did Brazil demonstrate that its economic model accounted for these factors.

90. Brazil did not answer the Panel's question about what relevant factors should be taken into account nor did it respond to the question about how this should be done. Brazil simply claims, through Dr. Sumner 's analysis, that it has taken various other factors into account. Until forced to respond to the US Further Submission of 30 Sept., Brazil had not acknowledged that any factor besides US subsidies had any effect on world cotton markets.

---

69 Brazil's approach would certainly simplify the causation discussion in numerous other disputes.

91. In paragraph 82, we find it curious that Brazil refers to the material on other factors presented by the United States[70] as covering "only" weak cotton demand, flat retail consumption, falling world incomes, increasing US textile imports, and China's releasing of stocks. Brazil also errs in referring to these as all "demand-related". For example, China's release of stocks affects the supply of cotton.(The US Further Submission also included an analysis of the effects of the strong US dollar on cotton prices.)These six factors were the "only" ones presented because they, in fact, provide a compelling explanation of the factors driving down world cotton prices at that time and encouraging the shift in US cotton use from domestic processing to export markets.

92. The Panel asks how it should take into account the effect of other factors. In paragraph 85, Brazil argues that *but for* the effect of US subsidies, world cotton prices would have been significantly higher. One could just as easily analyze and claim *but for* the effect of China's releasing 11.6 million bales of subsidized cotton onto world markets between 1999-2001 world prices would have been significantly higher. In other words, Dr. Sumner can claim his analysis accounts for various factors because he calibrated his model to actual data for the recent past, but Brazil' s analysis has not provided an explanation of the various events and actions at play that would allow the Panel to form a reasoned conclusion that the effects of US subsidies are not in fact the effects of these other factors.

93. Finally, in paragraph 87, Brazil's repeats oft-stated arguments about the presumed revenue-cost gap faced by US cotton producers using total costs of production. Brazil has not replied to US counter arguments that using *total average costs* is misleading and inappropriate. We refer the panel to the US further rebuttal submission, paras. 116-41, and the US answer to Question 211(b). As for Brazil's exchange rate argument, we refer the panel to the US answer to Question 210 above.

233. In Brazil's view, what is or are the "same market(s)" for the purposes of Article 6.3(c)? Does Brazil's view of "world market" imply that regardless of which domestic (or other) "market" is examined, price suppression will be identifiable? BRA

94. In this answer, Brazil continues to make serious interpretive errors with respect to Article 6.3(c). In addition, the evidence and arguments made by Brazil with respect to each of the "markets" it identifies do not satisfy the requirements of Article 6.3(c). The United States treats each of these issues in turn.

Brazil Misinterprets Article 6.3(c) and Fails to Bring Forward Evidence and Arguments to Establish Its Claims

95. The United States is gratified that in this answer Brazil finally appears to recognize that the "in the same market" language of Article 6.3(c) requires that Brazil make claims with respect to markets in which both Brazilian and US up-

70 US Further Submission, paras. 22 - 44.

land cotton are found.[71] This follows from the use of the words "same" and "market." "Market" means "[a] place or group with a demand for a commodity or service".[72] "Same" means "[i]dentical with what has been indicated in the preceding context" and "previously alluded to, just mentioned, aforesaid".[73] In the context of Article 6.3(c), the market that is "[i]dentical with what has been indicated in the preceding context" would be that market in which there is "significant price undercutting by the subsidized product as compared with the price of a like product of another Member" (the phrase immediately preceding the phrase on significant price suppression, depression, or lost sales). Thus, Brazil may only advance claims with respect to those markets in which US upland cotton and Brazilian cotton are both found .

96. Brazil continues to argue that there is a "world market" for upland cotton in which it may demonstrate significant price suppression, depression, or lost sales. However, the text and context of Article 6.3(c) do not support the view that Brazil may assert a generalized "world" price effect. First, the significant price suppression, depression, or lost sales must be "in the same market." As explained above, this "same market" would be the market in which both Brazilian and US cotton are found and there is significant price undercutting. In asserting that a "world" market can be this "same" market, Brazil renders the "same market" phrase inutile since the products of both the complaining and responding parties will always be in the "world." Consider that one of the effects under Article 6.3(c) is "lost sales in the same market." Brazil's interpretation would mean that a complaining party could advance a claim with respect to a lost sale anywhere in the "world," even if the responding party did not export to the market in which the lost sale occurred. Again, such a result would render the "in the same market" language meaningless.

97. Brazil's interpretation also does not make sense of important context for Article 6.3(c). Article 6.6 states that "[e]ach Member *in the market of which* serious prejudice is alleged to have arisen shall ... make available ... all relevant information ... as to the changes in market shares of the parties to the dispute as well as concerning *prices of the products involved*" (emphasis added). If the "world" could be a "market" for purposes of Article 6.3, which WTO Members should provide market data? Read literally, Article 6.6 would seemingly oblige *every* WTO Member to provide data on market share and prices since every Member would be a "Member in the market of which serious prejudice is alleged to have arisen." Annex V similarly suggests that the "same market" must be an actual market, be it that of the subsidizing Member or a third-country. For example, where Article 7.4 has been invoked "any third-country Member concerned" – for example, any Member in whose market significant price suppression is alleged to have occurred – "shall notify to the DSB" the organization responsible for responding to information requests and the procedures to be used to com-

[71] *See, e.g.*, Brazil's Answer to Question 233 from the Panel, para. 113 ("[T]hese indices are benchmarks for prices *in those 'same markets' where US and Brazilian cotton were exported ... .*") (emphasis added).

[72] *The New Shorter Oxford English Dictionary*, vol. 1, at 1699 (1993 ed.).

[73] *The New Shorter Oxford English Dictionary*, vol. 2, at 2678 (1993 ed.).

ply.[74] Furthermore, the information gathered during the information-gathering process "should include,*inter alia*, data concerning the amount of the subsidy in question (and, where appropriate, the value of total sales of the subsidized firms), *prices of the subsidized product, prices of the non-subsidized product, prices of other suppliers to the market*, changes in the supply of the subsidized product *to the market in question* and changes in market shares".[75] Again, these provisions suggest (as does Article 6.6) that Article 6.3(c) is directed at particular markets where competition exists between Brazilian and US upland cotton.

98. Because Brazil must demonstrate price suppression by US imports of Brazilian imports in the same market, Brazil must bring forward evidence and arguments on import volumes and prices. In numerous instances, Brazil has simply failed to present prices for Brazilian cotton and US cotton in an identified market, much less import volumes relating to the parties or other suppliers. This failure to present, *inter alia*, prices for each market sufficient to demonstrate price suppression is fatal to Brazil's claim with respect to each such market. The necessity of presenting price information for each market is suggested by the fact that each "same market" in which significant price suppression is alleged to occur is a market in which there is significant price undercutting. Article 6.6 refers to each Member "in the market of which serious prejudice is alleged to have arisen" providing the "prices of the products involved," also suggesting that prices for both Brazilian and US cotton must be examined. Further, Annex V, paragraph 5, states that a panel should examine "prices of the subsidized product, prices of the non-subsidized product, [and] prices of other suppliers *to the market.*"

There is No "World Market Price" for Upland Cotton that Can Be Significantly Suppressed

99. The preceding legal interpretation that the "same market" means a particular market in which competition between Brazilian and US cotton imports occurs is confirmed when one considers that nature of the "world price" that Brazil claims is significantly suppressed. This "world market price" turns out not to be a price at all but several "benchmarks" or indicia of prices. As Brazil states: "The record establishes that there is a "world market" for upland cotton and that the prices for that market are *reflected* in the *New York futures prices* and in the*A-index prices"*.[76] That is, this alleged "market" does *not* have or set any price for US and Brazilian upland cotton; rather, this "price" is "reflected" in not one, but two price indices, the NY futures price and A-index price.

100. Brazil must argue that the "world market price" is "reflected" in the NY futures and A-index because *neither* of these relates to an abstract "world market."

- Rather, the NY futures price relates to a New York-based exchange trading in contracts for future delivery with various physi-

[74] Subsidies Agreement, Annex V, para. 1.
[75] Subsidies Agreement, Annex V, para. 5.
[76] Brazil's Answer to Question 233 from the Panel, para. 91.

cal delivery points in the United States: Galveston, Houston, New Orleans, Memphis, or Greenville/Spartenburg (South Carolina).[77]

Indeed, Brazil concedes that "[w]hile the New York futures prices play a major role in *influencing markets*, the short term volatility of the futures market makes comparison with monthly or annual export prices more difficult".[78]

- The A-index "price" reflects delivery to Northern Europe of upland cotton with certain quality specifications (Middling,1-1/32 inch staple length). Further, the A-index is not a "price" but an average of the five lowest *price quotes* obtained by Cotlook, a private organization based in London, from various merchants of 15 cotton growths.

101. Thus, the A-index reflects price offers but does not reflect actual prices in Northern Europe of either Brazilian or US (or any other) upland cotton. The A-index relates to the Northern European market, not to the "world" market. In fact, the A-index, with its disparate price quotes from around the world, demonstrates that prices differ around the world, not that there is a uniform, harmonious "world" market price. The fact that Brazil points to *two* disparate price indices, which deviate significantly.[79] also demonstrates that there is not a "world market price" for upland cotton. Thus, neither the NY futures price nor the A-index are a "world market price" for upland cotton.

Brazil Cannot Demonstrate Significant Price Suppression in the United States Because There Were No Brazilian Imports

102. Brazil also identifies the US market as a "same market." However, Brazil does not advance any arguments nor evidence establishing that there were *any* Brazilian imports into the United States in marketing years 1999-2002. In fact, our information is that there have not been any imports of Brazilian cotton to the United States since marketing year 1996.[80] Neither (and perhaps for that reason) does Brazil present any arguments or evidence on Brazilian cotton prices in the United States. Thus, Brazil has failed to establish that the United States is a "same market" for purposes of Article 6.3(c).

Brazil's Effort to Expand the Scope of Its Claims and Arguments to 40 Third-Country Markets is Untimely

103. Brazil belatedly attempts to argue that it is alleging "significant price suppression" in 40 third-country markets; for only seven of these had Brazil previously even attempted to make argument. Brazil has not attempted to justify presenting this new affirmative evidence at this late stage in the proceeding, con-

---

77 *See* www.nybot.com (search No. 2 Cotton Futures Contract Specifications).

78 Brazil's Answer to Question 233 from the Panel, para. 93 (italics added).

79 *See* Brazil 's Answer to Question 233 from the Panel, para. 93 ("[P]rice oscillations of the A and B-index are much less pronounced than the futures market, but in the longer term they accompany the signs and trends coming from the futures market.").

80 *See* US Department of Agriculture trade statistics at www.fas.usda.gov/ustrade (search on Imports/HS-4 for Brazil).

trary to the Panel's working procedures. To do so prejudices the United States, which has necessarily participated in this dispute on the basis of the claims and arguments Brazil has previously set out, and would circumvent the notification obligations of the complaining party. For example, we note that in its request to the DSB to initiate the Annex V information-gathering process, which the DSB was not able to agree to in light of the Peace Clause issue, Brazil did not notify these 40 WTO Members that they were markets in which serious prejudice was alleged to have occurred. By not naming these markets at the outset of the dispute, but seeking to name them now, Brazil would preclude these Members from fulfilling their notification obligations under paragraph 1 of Annex V.

104. We also note that none of these 40 markets are listed in Brazil's request for rulings and recommendations from the Panel. That request, in pertinent part, reads: "The US subsidies provided during MY 1999-2002 caused and continue to cause serious prejudice to the interest of Brazil *by suppressing upland cotton prices in the US, world and Brazilian markets* for upland cotton in violation of Articles 5(c) and 6.3(c) of the SCM Agreement".[81] The United States is entitled to rely on Brazil's representations with respect to the scope of its claims and arguments.

105. Even in the markets that Brazil has raised in a timely manner, there are other suppliers into that market, and Brazil has failed to explain why any price suppression should be attributed to US sales rather than to sales from other countries. One cannot presume that US sales are the only factor that could cause any price suppression. Thus, with respect to these markets, Brazil has failed to establish a *prima facie* case on its claims.

Brazil Incorrectly Argues that Significant Price Suppression in All Markets Can Be Shown Through Suppression of "World Market Prices"

106. The foregoing considerations are dispositive of Brazil's claims with respect to significant price suppression in the same market. In this portion of its comment, the United States further examines the evidence and arguments Brazil has brought forward and points out that they do not establish the elements necessary to demonstrate a claim under Article 6.3(c).

107. Brazil argues that the US suppression of "world market prices" is transmitted to all markets as evidenced by the fact that price movements in individual markets are similar to the general trends of the A-index. Brazil alleges that the proof of the US suppression of the A-index is the results of Dr. Sumner's analysis and studies by USDA economists. The United States has already explained in great detail to the Panel the conceptual flaws of Dr. Sumner's analysis and will not repeat those here. Additionally, the USDA studies provided by Brazil to the Panel did not address impacts on the A-index or futures prices, but the impact of US programmes on US prices. While interesting academic exercises, moreover, those studies do not analyze the question before the Panel.[82]

---

[81] Brazil's Further Submission, para. 471(i).

[82] *See* US Answer to Question 212 from the Panel, paras. 48-55.

108. As a factual matter, the United States has provided evidence that disproves Brazil's allegation that the United States suppresses the A-index. Exhibit US-46 demonstrates that the low US quote (either Memphis or California) for the A-Index has rarely been one of the 5 low bids. If both US quotes are always above (but for one month) the 5 lowest quotes used in the A-Index, the United States cannot be suppressing the A-Index. Nevertheless, even if one were to follow the Brazilian approach, the data provided by Brazil does not provide evidence of price suppression by the United States.

109. As set out above, a generalized claim of price suppression is not contemplated by Article 6.3(c), which requires price suppression "in the same market" – that is, that market in which there is "significant price undercutting by the subsidized product as compared to the price of a like product of another Member." Thus, we proceed here to examine Brazil 's evidence with respect to those "same markets" identified in its answer.

Comparison based on Export Unit Values

110. Brazil begins its analysis by comparing US and Brazilian export unit values in various markets to the A-index. It should be noted that the proper analysis would be US and Brazilian market *prices* in the market in question. The export price does not represent the final selling price in the market in question. Given the short time the United States had to review all of this new data, the discussion here will focus on those countries included in the main text of the Brazilian response. To the extent that Brazil has provided data in its exhibits on various markets that it does not examine or explain, we do not consider that Brazil has advanced arguments with respect to such markets sufficient to carry its burden of establishing a *prima facie* case, and we ask the Panel to so find.

111. The fact that US or Brazil export prices to the seven markets, Argentina, China, India, Indonesia, Philippines, Portugal, and South Korea generally may have had movements similar to the A-Index does not demonstrate price suppression by the United States. In fact, Brazil does not in its main text show comparisons of US and Brazilian export unit values in each market (this is only provided in Exhibit BRA-386), much less other relevant market information, such as import prices from other suppliers or import volumes. This absence of relevant argument alone demonstrates that Brazil has not met its burden of establishing its price suppression claims. However, the United States has updated the Brazilian export unit value graphs to include data through November 2003 in order to set out a cursory analysis of each "same market" for the Panel.[83] On the whole, we find that it is the Brazilian price that undercuts the US price to these markets.

112. Brazil alleges price suppression in the Argentine market due to the United States. The data, however, does not support such a claim. As can be seen in the graph, the United States is an infrequent supplier to the Argentine market. For those time periods when no US imports were found in Argentina, there could be no price suppression by the US subsidized product of the prices of Brazilian cot-

[83] Exhibit US-134.

ton "in the same market." Of the 15 periods that both are in the market, the United States' export price was greater than Brazil's export price 8 times, below Brazil 6 times, and the same once.

113. Comparing US and Brazilian export unit values to China does not demonstrate price suppression by the United States. Brazil is not a frequent participant in the China market. For those time periods when no Brazilian imports were found in China, there could be no price suppression by the US subsidized product of the prices of Brazilian cotton "in the same market." From August 1999 to June 2003, Brazil only shipped to China in 13 months. Of these 13 months, Brazil's export unit value was below the US export unit value 8 times, above the US price 4 times, and the same once. Evidence of Brazilian price undercutting the US price is inconsistent with the argument that the United States suppresses Brazilian prices to the China market.

114. India was one of the few markets Brazil discussed in which there were a good number of months in which both parties supplied cotton. Of the 25 months in which both provided cotton, the US price was narrowly below the Brazil price in 12 months, was above Brazil in 12 months, and at the same level in 1 months. The time during which the US price was below the Brazil price was during the period April 2001 to December 2001, in which the high yields of MY2001 influenced. However, during August 2000 to January 2001 period, US unit values were high and were consistently undercut by Brazil by a large margin. This Brazilian undercutting led to a plunge in US unit values. We also note that US unit values appear to increase when Brazilian cotton is not in the market. Brazilian unit values, on the other hand, show very little change; this lack of price movement is not consistent with price suppression since the Brazilian price is unresponsive. As the graph shows, there is no systemic relationship between the US and Brazilian unit values to indicate that the United States is suppressing Brazilian prices to this market.

115. Indonesia also was another country in which both the United States and Brazil were active participants, and each had the low price about an equal number of times. However, the majority of times the US had a lower price occurred during MY2001, a period in which the United States had higher than expected yields which reduced US unit values while Brazil had lower than normal yields, driving up the price for Brazilian cotton. In MY2002, Brazil returned to general undercutting of US unit values, failing to follow US price increases in early 2003. There does not seem to be any support for price suppression in this market as the movements between the US and Brazilian export unit values are not the same. For example, during the period October 2000 to January 2001, US export unit values increased, whereas Brazil's export unit values declined. Again in the period December 2001 to June 2002, the wide swings in the Brazil price relative to the steady US movements demonstrate that US prices are not suppressing Brazil's.

116. Philippines is a market in which Brazil had sporadic shipments over the period. For those time periods when no Brazilian imports were found in Philippines, there could be no price suppression by the US subsidized product of the

prices of Brazilian cotton "in the same market." There were 19 months in which both parties supplied the Philippines. Part of the difference in price is probably due to the shipment sizes. As Exhibit BRA-383 reports, the quantities shipped are quite different between Brazil and the United States. Smaller shipments typically have higher per unit costs. Many of the months in which Brazil exhibited higher export unit values to the Philippines was during MY 2001, a year in which the US had higher than expected yields, driving down its price while Brazil had lower than expected yields, increasing its price.

117. Brazil and the United States overlapped in the Portuguese market in 27 months, a good number of samples. In all instances except for November 2003, the US unit value was greater than the Brazilian unit value, generally by a large margin. The fact the US unit value was greater than the Brazilian unit value is not consistent with price suppression by the United States. Even if there was a quality difference between the two, the spread between the two should be relatively constant. However, the movements of unit values do differ. When the US had big swings in the late 2000 and late 2001 early 2002, Brazil saw only modest changes in unit values. Since MY2003, US prices first increased and have slightly declined whereas Brazilian prices first declined and have been increasing slightly. The fact that the price movements are not consistent would weaken arguments that the United States is causing or threatens to cause price suppression to Brazil.

118. The final country market discussed directly in Brazil's response was South Korea. As the graph depicts, Brazil only supplied cotton to this market in one month. Since no Brazilian imports were found in South Korea over the complained of period, during those times there could be no price suppression by the US subsidized product of the prices of Brazilian cotton "in the same market."

Comparing Import Values ("Import Prices") to A-Index

119. Brazil continues its analysis by comparing average import prices to specific markets with the A-Index. As with the "export prices" these import prices are not the prices at which the product were sold but its value at the border of the importing country. Again a proper analysis would not use border valuation of the product but the actual market prices the product was sold. Also it is not clear how averaging import prices from the different sources would provide evidence that the United States has caused price suppression. In fact the various graphs provided by Brazil put in doubt their theory of world price transmission.

120. The yearly import price data in paragraphs 106-108 is too general to be of any assistance. Looking at the various graphs of monthly individual country import prices against the A-Index (paragraphs 106-107) also shows discrepancies between markets. For example, looking at the graph of Japan's prices against the A-Index, it is notable that their import prices never fell below 48 cents even though the A-Index fell to as low as 38 cents and that the gap between import prices and the A-Index were quite large when prices were falling but minimal when prices were rising. A similar pattern seems to have been present in Ecuador. On the face of it, these graphs would seem to imply that some mechanism

was at work to impede the transmission of declining "world market prices." This undermines Brazil' s assertion that price suppression can be shown in all third-country markets through alleged effects on a "world market price." The Hong Kong graph is exactly opposite in these respects from the Japanese and Ecuador graphs. This could mean that Hong Kong is less protected from world prices, but the great deal of inconsistency both within and between all of these graphs indicates the uncertainty surrounding Brazil's claims that "all these third country markets are heavily influenced by the A-Index and New York futures prices".

Comparison of Domestic Prices and the A-Index

121. Brazil then compares for a few countries in which it could get domestic prices, those domestic prices to the A-index. Again their analysis concludes that the A-index influences domestic prices in these markets and therefore, the United States is guilty of price suppression. We have explained that a claim of significant price suppression requires that US and Brazilian cotton be found "in the same market." In addition, there are problems with the connection between the A-Index and domestic prices as presented by Brazil. To demonstrate the problems with Brazil's analysis, the United States will look at the analysis on China.

122. We agree that China's domestic prices have always been significantly above the A-indexand tracked it rather well. Indeed we include a full series below including all the data currently available to us. This starts September, 1999 and runs through April 2003 (Southern China prices as reported by East-West Inc. a Beijing agricultural consulting group) . It is consistent with Brazil's data although Brazil's only starts in January 2001. These data reveal that China's domestic prices are not consistent with China's export and import prices.

123. China's export prices, as can be seen in Exhibit US-141, are well below the A-index during most of the time China exported heavily (MY 1999 through the first half of MY 20001, and the last quarter ofMY 2001 through the third quarter ofMY 2002). Contrary to Brazil's assertion in paragraph 113 that export prices from all suppliers move with the A-Index, more often than not China's export price did not, staying relatively flat during the periods from August 1999 to January 2001 and from February 2002 to July 2003. What is more, as can be seen from the China Prices graph in Exhibit US-141, China's export prices were significantly lower than the Chinese domestic price when China was exporting heavily.

124. The imports are different but still problematic. During those times when China has imported heavily, from the beginning of MY 2002 until the present, prices have tracked A-Index prices fairly well.

125. These data, not presented or explained by Brazil, show that Chinese domestic prices have some connection to the A-index but hardly the "heavily influenced" and "consistent" relationship Brazil asserts. As noted in the US further submission, the Chinese Government during this time had the goal of reducing their massive, undisclosed cotton stocks in a way that would insulate there cotton producers and processors from changes in prices. The aim was to maximize cot-

ton prices received by Chinese farmers while still insuring their cotton textile exports were competitive in world export markets. China sold as much as it could on the world market as long as the A-Index stayed at or above a trigger price around 50 cents a pound – hence the flat export price line until the stock situation was finally resolvedin late MY 2002.

Conclusion

126. Brazil has not done a proper analysis to support its price suppression claims. To demonstrate significant price suppression that leads to serious prejudice, Brazil must provide evidence showing that US prices in a given market are suppressing Brazilian prices in that market. Brazil has not presented and explained evidence on actual market prices of US and Brazilian cotton in third-country markets. Thus, Brazil has not established a *prima facie* case with respect to its price suppression claims. In fact, the market-by-market data presented above does not support a finding of significant price suppression by US cotton.

234. Does "significant" price suppression under Article 6.3(c) necessarily amount to "serious" prejudice within the meaning of Article 5(c)? Could the level of "significance" of any price suppression under Article 6.3(c) determine whether any prejudice under Article 5(c) rises to the level of "serious prejudice"? USA, BRA

127. Brazil's interpretation that whether price suppression is "significant"can only "be assessed with reference to the quality of the impacts of *whatever* level of price suppression exists on the producers of the like product" raises concerns. Brazil provides the example that even where "large amounts of price suppression" have been demonstrated, this might not be "significant" if the producers of the complaining party "had *de minimis* production, or no exports, and/or that the total value of lost revenue from suppressed prices was minimal".[84] The United States believes that the conditions of the producers of the complaining party would not enter into an analysis of whether a given level of price suppression is "significant." Brazil's interpretation would create, out of one legal standard ("significant price suppression"), different thresholds that would apply to different Members depending on their financial well-being. For example, a Member with a strong position in a given third-country market might not be able to utilize Article 6.3(c) (for significant price undercutting or significant price suppression or depression") simply on the basis that "the total value of lost revenue from suppressed prices was minimal" even if the level of price suppression was large. Conversely, a Member with a nascent exporting industry might not be able to utilize Article 6.3(c) if it "had *de minimis* production, or no exports," despite a desire to increase both production and exports. Neither scenario appears to fit with the text of Article 6.3(c).

128. In addition, Brazil fails to explain how the two different terms in the text of Article 6 ("serious prejudice" and "significant price suppression") result in

[84] Brazil's Answer to Question 234 from the Panel, para. 114.

there being only one and the same test for both terms. This would appear to render one of the terms superfluous, contrary to customary rules of treaty interpretation.

129. Finally, we note Brazil's reference to the impacts on "complaining party producers" of the like product. We take this to mean that, contrary to its earlier position, Brazil has now conceded that "adverse effects" to other Members are irrelevant for Brazil's claims. This follows from the text of the Subsidies Agreement. Under Article 5(c), no Member is to cause "serious prejudice *to the interests of another Member*," and a request for consultations under Article 7.2 "shall include a statement of available evidence with regard to ... serious prejudice *caused to the interests of the Member requesting consultations*."

235. Please comment on paragraphs 8, 9 and 10 of the US 2 December oral statement, in particular, why the average Brazilian price is shown as lower than the average US price. BRA

130. Brazil's answer to Question 235 does not refute the US evidence that Brazilian cotton prices undercut US prices from 1999-2002. Brazil does not go so far as to claim the United States undercut Brazil's prices – except in the Brazilian market, an argument that is based on prices that are not directly comparable, as will be discussed later. Instead Brazil argues that US and Brazilian prices exhibited an "absolute closeness" with Brazil's export prices sometimes higher and sometimes lower than US prices.

131. Except for their own market, Brazil does not provide data or analysis on country markets. Instead they examine aggregate data for forty markets that both the United States and Brazil exported to in MY1999 to MY 2002. As the United States explained in our comments on Question 233, this aggregate approach is not the proper method of analysis for price suppression claims under Article 6.3(c). However, even if we accept the Brazil approach, close analysis of the aggregated data presented inBrazil's responsefurther supports the US claim of-Brazilian undercutting by showing that consistently and on average Brazilian [unit values] prices were lower than those of the United States, even though there were periods when factors not related to subsidies led to lower US unit values.

Average Unit Value Comparison

132. First, Brazil in the graph following paragraph 121 compares the average unit values of Brazilian and US exports. It is this graph that Brazil uses to support its claim of "absolute closeness" between the two countries ' export prices and the absence of Brazil undercutting, but it simply does not do this. Of the 45 months when both the US and Brazil were exporting, Brazil prices were lower 25 months as opposed to the United States' 20. Further eight of the United States low-price months were in MY 2001, when good weather allowed the United States to realize record yields as opposed to sub-par yields for Brazil. The US yield of 790 kgs./hectare was 6 per cent above the five year average for MY 1999 to 2003.[85] Brazil's 1073/kgs/hectare for MY 2001 was 5 per cent below its

[85] Exhibit US-135.

1999-2001 average.[86] Also Brazil planting half a year later than the United States saw a much different price signal as cotton prices dropped sharply and soybean prices, themain alternative crop for both countries, rose slightly from February to August 2001.[87] The United States increased planted area by 6 per cent but Brazil reduced planted area by 12 per cent. US production consequently rose 18 per cent to 20.3 million bales in MY 2001, whereas Brazil's dropped to 18 per cent to 3.5 million bales. This naturally drove US export prices down compared to Brazil's. Brazilian prices followed the US prices down in the last half of MY 2001 and have stayed equal to or below US prices ever since.

133. Setting aside MY1999 and MY 2001 for the moment, two years that are not representative of normal conditions, Brazil prices undercut US prices in 18 of the 24 months for MY 2000 and MY 2002.[88] This is consistent with Brazilian production changes in the two years. In MY 2000 Brazil production increased 34 per cent while US barely 1 per cent from the year earlier. In MY 2002, Brazil production fell 2 per cent while US production fell 15 per cent.[89] So, even using Brazil's own methods we can see that Brazil undercut the United States in 2 of the 3 relevant marketing years and in that third year lower US prices are clearly related to yield and normalmarket price signals

134. The same conclusions are apparent when looking at the graph following paragraph 118 where Brazil looks at the aggregated weighted average of the 8 countries originally analyzed by the United States. Looking at the data available in this graph for MY 1999-2002, in 16 of 37 months when both countries exported to these countries, the United States price was higher 21 times as opposed to only 16 for Brazil. Six of the 16 periods when Brazil was higher came in MY 2001, consistent with the analysis above, and 6 came in MY 1999 whenresults were distorted because the volume of total Brazil exports was extremely small.

Looking at All US and Brazil Exports

135. To better look at the issue of Brazil's undercutting of US prices, it is appropriate to expand Brazil's analysis. Although Brazil emphasizes the closely interconnected world market, as noted before, their analysis looks only at data from countriesto which Brazil and the United States both exported. The graph below looks at unit values for the entirety of US and Brazilian exports during this period, which Brazil would argue is appropriate if in fact there is a "world price" that is transmitted with little interference to all cotton markets. The graph presents data obtained directly from the Foreign Agricultural Service/USDA web

86 *Ibid.*

87 The relevant futures prices ratio of cotton to soybean for Brazil in August 2001 was the May 2002 cotton and May 2002 soy which was 8.63. The relevant ratio for US farmers in February 2001 was the Dec 2001 cotton to Nov 2001 soybean which was 12.55. (New York Board of Trade and Chicago Board of Trade).

88 In MY 1999, Brazil only exported 12,000 bales of cotton compared to an average of 438,000 bales in MY 2000, MY 2001, and MY 2002. (See Exhibit US-135) As discussed in the preceding paragraph, MY 2001 was a year of atypical yields for both Brazil and the United States.

89 Exhibit US-135 (Production data)

site[90] and Brazilian customs data provided through the World Trade Atlas, a for-fee service that collects and enters in an easily accessible database official data from Brazil and numerous other countries (produced by Global Trade Information Service Inc.) showing value, quantity and unit values.[91] It also expands Brazil's data by incorporating data through November 2003.

136. This graph reenforces what was discussed above regarding Brazil's 40-same-markets data. In this case though, Brazil export unit values are lower than the United States in all but one of the 24 months in MY 2000 and MY2002. Although very similar to Brazil's graph, it is even clearer here that Brazil's export prices were consistently and often significantly lower than those of the United States. As the graph depicts, Brazil undercuts the United States during MY 2000, resulting in a decline in US unit values. In MY2001, both continued to decline because of record yields and slack demand. But at the beginning of MY2002, US export values rebound whereas Brazil's remain low, undercutting the US export values. In the start of MY 2003, US prices begin a sharp increase, but Brazilian prices decline slightly before making a slight increase resulting in an increased spread between the United States and Brazil.

Cumulative Average Values Using all the Data

137. Going further and looking at the cumulative weighted price as Brazil did in paragraph 120, but again using the entirety of US and Brazilian exports, the average US price for MY 1999-2002 was 47.59 cents per pound for the United States as compared to an average for Brazil of 44.70 (Brazil calculation was almost exactly the same at 44.65). This means the United States average export value during the period was 2.89 cents per pound (6 per cent) higher than that of Brazil. Looking at just the 40 markets, Brazil still found US prices were higher but by only 0.68 cents. This is an important point in itself when addressing the question of Brazil's price undercutting. This means the increased spread between average US and Brazilian prices when looking at all exports – as compared to just the 40 countries identified by Brazil – was due almost entirely to United States exporters being able to charge higher prices in markets where Brazil was not competing. This is clearly consistent with Brazil undercutting.

138. Looking at the cumulative averages for the atypicalMY 2001 when there were weather-related reasons for low US prices, Brazil's method showed a cumulative US average export price lower than Brazil's by 5.22 cents (44.05 for Brazil and 38.83 for the United States). Looking at the entirety ofexports, the difference was only 3.65 cents (44.14 for Brazil and 40.49 for the United States). In addition, a distortion in Brazil's cumulative analysis magnifies the importance of MY2001. Nearly 45 per cent of Brazil's exports during this 4-year period came in MY 2001.[92] By contrast, the United States only exported 30 per cent of its 4-year total in MY 2001.[93] This means the difference between the unit average

---

90 Exhibit US-136 (FAS US trade data)
91 Exhibit US-137 (WTA Brazilian trade data)
92 Exhibit US-135.
93 *Ibid.*

values is even further skewed. Looking at the difference in average unit values for years other than MY2001 (that is, in MY1999, MY2000 and MY2002 combined), the average unit valuefor the United States is 50.83. In Brazil it is 45.15. *US prices are higher by 5.68 per cent or almost 12 per cent.*

Prices in the Brazil Market

139. It is also misleading for Brazil to claim as they do in paragraph 130 that US cotton imported into Brazil undercuts domestic Brazilian cotton. This claim is based on comparing US FOB export prices to Brazil domestic prices. That is, it ignores Brazil's tariff on cotton imports as well as transportation and other costs incurred shipping cotton to Brazil, which would raise the US price significantly. The Brazilian tariff was 8 per cent in 1999 and 2000, 8.5 per cent in 2001, 10 per cent in 2002 and 9.5 per cent in 2003.[94] In all years except 1999, the difference between Brazil domestic and US export prices fell well short of even covering the tariff. In 1999 the difference of 10.27 per cent only exceeded the tariff by 2.27 per cent. Recent trader price quotes for transportation to Brazil exceed 10 cents a pound, more than offsetting the difference. In sum, Brazil's use of non-comparable prices cannot support a finding of price suppression, much less significant price suppression.

Price Suppression

140. Even using Brazil's method of looking at the average unit value of exports, rather than actual third-country domestic prices, strong evidence of Brazilian price undercutting exists – contrary to Brazil's arguments. Brazil's second line of argument is that price undercutting is irrelevant, arguing that it is not a question of undercutting but price suppression and that the global marketplace instantaneously translates subsidy-induced lower prices in the United States into lower prices world-wide. Brazil further contends that "prices in each of those 40 third country markets as well as the Brazilian and US market were already suppressed before any cotton was shipped by US or Brazilian exporters" (paragraph 131).

141. The price mechanism in cotton is relatively sophisticated, but Brazil's explanation is unrealistic. It says essentially that everyone in the market has perfect knowledge of the market and can adjust instantly. If over the period when US subsidies increased, they had a significant suppressing effect on world markets, this would have been manifested in the United States continually lowering prices to take more market share with other suppliers being forced to follow. It is implausible to assume that this would have occurred without some time lag between US and Brazilian prices that would have been evident in monthly export data – and yet, no such dynamic can be seen in the price data.[95]

---

[94] Source: Various USDA/FAS Attache Reports (available at: www.fas.usda.gov (search on Attache Reports, Brazil, Cotton, 1999-2003)).

[95] Prices take time to adjust. Suppliers are hesitant to lower prices particularly when they have not seen a reduction in their own costs and cannot be sure the prices will stay lower. They will be willing to allow stocks to build until the need to drop prices is inevitable. Similarly, customers will not im-

142. The fact that, other than in MY2001, US prices generally stayed above Brazilian prices indicates that is was not US subsidies, but other factors that drove down prices. The textile market was extremely competitive during this period. China's industry, operating in a tightly controlledmarket with access to cheap government stocks was pushing down prices. Also a sluggish world economy kept consumption growth in the same 1.5 to 1.75per cent annual growth range it had been in the previous 4 years despite markedly lower cotton prices. Processors ofraw cotton, other than those in China, demanded lower prices from suppliers in order to remain competitive with the Chinese. At the same time, the US textile and apparel industry was faced with increasing textile and apparel imports, domestic raw cotton use fell sharply, and US cotton growers and merchants had to turn to exports. The fact that US stocks grew significantly during this time also indicates that US suppliers were the price takers and not the price setters in this market.[96] Further, the shift in raw cotton consumption from the United States to other countries (much of which is shipped back to the United States in the form of cotton apparel) explains why US cotton exports increased as the US world market share was unchanged.

143. The point is reinforced by looking at the A-Index and the corresponding quotes for the United States and Brazil. Again one would expect that a US cotton industry with subsidized excess production to dispose of on export markets would have been consistently pricing below the average represented by the A-Index (the 5 lowest price quotes obtained by Cotlook CIF Northern Europe). But this is not the case as can be seen in the graph below of the A-Index and the US Memphis and California / ArizonaA-Index quotes.

- At no point during MY1999-2003 to date was the California / Arizona quote below the A-Index.
- Only once during MY1999-2003 to date, September 2002, was the Memphis quote below the A-Index.

144. Consistent with what was discussed before, a tightening of the gap between the A-Index and US quotes is apparent in MY 2001. However, Brazil aside, a number of countries had good weather and significantly increased area in that year so that US prices were still above the average as measured by the A-Index.

145. A parallel analysis can be made by comparing the US and Brazilian A-Index quotes (data from Brazil Exhibit 242). This graph is the same as that used by Brazil in paragraph 128 (although the last 3 data points are not in the exhibit). Again, US price quotes are well above Brazil quotes in marketing years

mediately switch since changing to a new unfamiliar supplier has costs particularly if the new lower prices do not continue. Additionally, as put forth by Brazil in its response to question 233 (para. 104), even if Brazilian suppliers and their customers had through the global pricing system perfect knowledge of US prices and their future direction, they would still have contractual commitments at higher prices that must be met and thus would delay the transmission of declines in price movements. Brazil, however, in its discussion ignored that this delayed transmission due to contracts also could bound a supplier to a lower price although spot prices are increasing.

[96] Exhibit US-135.

1999, 2000, 2002, and 2003 to date. In MY 2001 quotes grew closer, and for a few months the Memphis quote fell below the Brazilian.

- At all other times, the evidence demonstrates that Brazilian exporters were offering cotton at prices well below the US A-index quote.

146. Indeed, looking at the graph below comparing the A-Index to the Brazilian A-index quote, there are considerable periods, particularly in MY 2000, when Brazil was consistently quoting below the A-Index. This evidence of low price quotes by Brazilian exporters is consistent with the view that Brazilian price undercutting exerted downward pressure on prices.

237. Could a phenomenon that remains at approximately the same level over a given period of time be considered a "consistent trend" within the meaning of Article 6.3(d)? Do parties have any suggestions as to how to determine a "consistent trend", statistically or otherwise? BRA, USA

147. Although not entirely clear from Brazil's answer, Brazil appears to assert that as long as there is an increase in a Member's world market share over the preceding three-year average, the fact that the Member's world market share remains at approximately the same level could be compatible with a finding of an "increase" following a "consistent trend" within the meaning of Article 6.3(d). We would disagree. A flat world market share over a three-year period followed by a one-year increase would not demonstrate that the last year's "increase follows a consistent trend over a period when subsidies have been granted" (in the words of Article 6.3(d)). A flat "consistent trend" would not suffice since an "increase" could not "follow[] a [flat] consistent trend." In that situation, the "increase" would be deviating from, not following, the flat "consistent trend."

148. From a statistical standpoint, we would agree with Brazil's comment in paragraph 137 that due to the limited number of observations it is difficult to calculate a trend that is statistically significant. However, the United States strongly disagrees with the analysis presented by Brazil in the graphs accompanying paragraph 139. Note that if the trend line were calculated between 1986 and 2000 or 1996 to 2000, the trend line would be flat or slightly negative. As we have argued in the Second Submission to the Panel, the change in export share is due primarily to the decline in the US textile industry which resulted in almost two-thirds of US cotton being exported in 2002 compared to almost two-thirds milled domestically in 1998.

149. Indeed, if we observe the trend in the US market share as presented in our Second Submission to the Panel and in the Concluding statements to the panel of 8 October, the share of the world market for upland cotton supplied by US cotton has been flat over the period from marketing year 1999-2002. And of course Article 6.3(d) is talking about "the effect of the subsidy" which requires that it be the same subsidy at issue for each year of the "consistent trend".

244. What proportion of the 2000 cottonseed payments benefited producers of upland cotton, given that payments were made to first handlers, who were only obliged to share them with the producer to the extent that the

revenue from sale of the cottonseed was shared with the producer? (see 7 CFR §1427.1104(c) in Exhibit US-15). BRA

150. USDA did not require handlers of cottonseed to report their payments to producer, rather the payments went to first handlers. Handlers were allowed to settle up with their producers as they saw fit. The programme, however, *ipso facto*,did give the producers a basis for possible complaint against handlers who had effectively moved low seed prices back to their producers. If so, the remedy was lay in whatever civil remedies might be available in a particular jurisdiction.

151. It would appear that to the extent that the cost of low cottonseed prices were charged against the producer so as to create a duty for the handler to pass on the payment to the producer, the recovery by the producer would have been simply for higher ginning costs paid by the producer. That is, the producer would have suffered the loss to the extent the ginner charged more for ginning because the return to the ginner from the seed was too low.

152. Payments here are disaster-like in that the cost that was suffered and passed through to producers, to the extent that it was passed through, was after the fact. The season was long over and thus payments could not have induced the planting of the crop. In short, if there was a pass through, it was a wash to reflect higher ginning costs. Those costs were not associated with the marketing of upland cotton, but of cottonseed.

245. Can a panel take Green Box subsidies into account in considering the effects of non-Green Box subsidies in an action based on Articles 5 and 6 of the SCM Agreement? BRA, USA

153. Brazil and the United States agree that green box subsidies may not be taken into account in considering the effects of non-green box subsidies in an action based on Articles 5 and 6 of the Subsidies Agreement. Article 13(a)(ii) of the Agreement on Agriculture states that green box measures are "exempt from actions based on Article XVI of GATT 1994 and Part III of the Subsidies Agreement." We recall that previously in this dispute Brazil asserted that the phrase "exempt from actions" did not preclude the Panel from considering Brazil's serious prejudice claims but only from imposing remedies.[97] Nonetheless, in its answer, Brazil appears to have read this "exempt from actions" phrase to "*prohibit* ... the effects of these subsidies being included along with other effects of non-green box subsidies *in assessing Brazil's actionable subsidies claims"*.[98] Thus, Brazil here appears to read this phrase according to its ordinary meaning – that is, "not exposed or subject to" a "legal process or suit" or the "taking of legal steps *to establish a claim* or obtain a remedy".[99] This is the definition that the

[97] Brazil's Brief on Preliminary Issue Regarding the "Peace Clause" of the Agreement on Agriculture, para. 2 (5 June 2003) (interpreting "exempt from actions" to mean that "a complaining Member cannot receive authorization from the DSB *to obtain a remedy* against another Member's domestic and export support measures that otherwise would be subject to the disciplines of certain provisions of the Agreement on Subsidies and Countervailing Measures ... or Article XVI of GATT 1994") (emphasis added).

[98] Brazil's Answer to Question 245 from the Panel, para. 145.

[99] *See, e.g.,* Comments of the United States of America on the Comments by Brazil and the Third Parties on the Question Posed by the Panel, paras. 8-10 (June 13, 2003).

United States has advanced in this dispute, and the Panel should consider Brazil's answer to this question an endorsement of that definition.

246. Can a panel take prohibited subsidies into account in considering the effects of subsidies in an action based on Articles 5 and 6 of the SCM Agreement? BRA, USA

154. Brazil errs when it claims in its response to this question that "the Panel is required to take into account all non-green box subsidies, including prohibited subsidies in assessing Brazil's Article 5 and 6 claims under the SCM Agreement." The Panel has discretion in assessing Brazil's claims. The United States would note, for example, that Article 6.3(c) and (d) each refer to the "effect of the subsidy," which clearly permits the Panel to examine the effect of each subsidy individually.

247. Can the Panel take into account trends and volatility in market and futures prices of upland cotton after the date of establishment of the Panel? If so, how do they affect the analysis of Brazil's claim of a threat of serious prejudice? BRA, USA

155. The United States does not disagree that facts arising after the date of panel establishment may be taken into account, for example, in analyzing Brazil's threat of serious prejudice claim. As we have explained, as market prices have recovered strongly over marketing year 2003 (continuing their upwards trend since the trough reached in marketing year 2001), Brazil has jettisoned its proposed legal standard that the Panel examine whether there is a clearly foreseen and imminent likelihood of future serious prejudice. One could speculate that it has done so because the facts are no longer favourable – that is, high cotton prices will result in significantly lower budgetary outlays for two price-based measures (marketing loan payments and counter-cyclical payments) in marketing year 2003 than seen in previous years.

156. Brazil describes the task for the Panel "in an Article 5 and 6 claim" is to "assess[] whether present or threatened effects presently exist".[100] We would agree but note that Brazil has provided no basis to conclude that past subsidies, such as payments made for the 1999-2001 marketing years, that were fully expensed in past years could have "present ... effects [that] presently exist." To the contrary, to the extent that these subsidies are *not* allocated to future production – and the Panel will recall that Brazil itself has both expensed these payments for purposes of its Peace Clause calculation as well as recognized that these recurring subsidies payments would be expensed for countervailing duty purposes – no lingering effects can exist because the subsidies themselves are deemed to have been used up. Thus, the question before the Panel is whether present subsidies – that is, those made for marketing year 2002 through the date of panel establishment – were causing certain adverse effects to presently exist and whether the US laws and regulations in existence as of the date of establishment of the

[100] Brazil's Answer to Question 247 from the Panel, para. 150.

Panel threaten serious prejudice. Any payments not in existence as of the date of establishment are not measures within the Panel' s terms of reference.[101]

157. We also note that Brazil cites two reports in support of its arguments:*Argentina Footwear* and *Argentina Peaches*. Those citations are misplaced for several reasons. First, Brazil entirely ignores that both reports interpreted the *Agreement on Safeguards*, not the Subsidies Agreement, and that the two agreements have different texts. Brazil compounds the problem by failing to mention that the paragraphs it quotes in both reports dealt not with the issue of threat of injury, but with the issue of whether imports had "increased" (within the meaning of the Safeguards Agreement). Finally, while Brazil does acknowledge the existence of the Appellate Body report in *US Lamb*, it fails to point out that, in the context of a discussion of threat of serious injury under the Safeguards Agreement, in that report the Appellate Body made a finding that undercuts Brazil's position dramatically:

> Like the Panel, we note that the *Agreement on Safeguards* provides no particular methodology to be followed in making determinations of serious injury or threat thereof. However, whatever methodology is chosen, we believe that data relating to the most recent past will provide competent authorities with an essential, and, usually, the most reliable, basis for a determination of a threat of serious injury. The likely state of the domestic industry in the very near future can best be gauged from data from the most recent past. Thus, we agree with the Panel that, in principle, within the period of investigation as a whole, evidence from the most recent past will provide the strongest indication of the likely future state of the domestic industry.[102]

158. The strong recovery in market prices and futures prices demonstrate that there is no clearly foreseen and imminent likelihood of future serious prejudice. As we have previously seen with respect to the December 2004 future contract, price recovery has been sustained and steady; the contract average monthly close was 61.34 cents per pound in December 2002, and the current (as of 22 January 2004) monthly average close is 68.78 cents per pound. As a result of higher prices, US outlays are markedly down, with no marketing loan payments being made. In addition, the expectation of continuing high prices embodied in current future price suggests that no further marketing loan payments will be made this marketing year and that counter-cyclical payments will be dramatically lower.

159. In assessing the credibility of Brazil's argument that the baseline projections of FAPRI are more probative than futures prices, the Panel should recall the "testimony" of Brazil's own economic expert, Mr. MacDonald. Brazil has presented no evidence or analysis to suggest that FAPRI's baselines are more

---

[101] We recall once again that Brazil now admits that the matter before the Panel cannot change after establishment. Answer to Panel Question 247.

[102] Appellate Body Report, *United States – Safeguard Measures on Imports of Fresh, Chilled or Frozen Lamb Meat from New Zealand and Australia*, WT/DS177/AB/R, WT/DS178/AB/R, adopted 16 May 2001, para. 137 (footnote omitted).

accurate price projections than what the NY futures indicates; in fact, the United States has put before the Panel evidence showing that FAPRI's baseline projections have been far off the mark.

160. For corroboration, the Panel need only consider the marketing year 2003-2008 baseline projections made by FAPRI in November 2002, January 2003, and November 2003. The price outlook for cotton has improved considerably since publication of the November 2002 FAPRI baseline used by Dr. Sumner in his Annex I estimate of the effects of US subsidies on US cotton production.

- The table below shows that FAPRI's projections for the MY2003 Adjusted World Price (used for calculating the marketing loan payments) are as much as *20 cents per pound, or 54 per cent, higher* in the November 2003 baseline as under the November 2002 baseline.
- Even so, FAPRI's November 2003 projected Adjusted World Price is still almost 6 cents per pound lower than the current Adjusted World Price.[103]

161. As a result of these revisions, FAPRI's estimated marketing loan gains (the difference between the marketing loan rate and the estimated Adjusted World Price) are reduced considerably.

- Under the November 2003 baseline, the estimated marketing loan gain for 2003/04 is *zero*, compared to *almost 15 cents per pound* under the November 2002 baseline used by Dr. Sumner.
- Over the five-year period 2003/04 to 2007/08, the average marketing loan gain under the November 2003 baseline is estimated to be only *1.32 cents per pound.* This is compared to *10.39 cents per pound* using the November 2002 baseline used by Dr. Sumner.

FAPRI's Revised Price and Marketing Loan Gain Baseline Projections

Year	**Adjusted World Price (cents/lb)**			**Est. marketing loan gain 1/ (cents/lb)**		
	Nov 2002	**Jan 2003**	**Nov 2003 2/**	**Nov 2002**	**Jan 2003**	**Nov 2003 2/**
2003/04	37.22	44.8	57.36	14.78	7.2	0
2004/05	39.83	45.4	50.96	12.17	6.6	1.04
2005/06	41.94	46	50.82	10.06	6	1.18
2006/07	43.6	46.7	50.35	8.4	5.3	1.65
2007/08	45.48	48	49.24	6.52	4	2.76
Average	41.61	46.18	51.75	10.39	5.82	1.32

1/ The estimated marketing loan gain is the difference, if positive, between the loan rate (52 cents per lb) and the Adjusted World Price.

2/ Source: FAPRI Baseline, November 2003 (Exhibit US-132)

[103] The Adjusted World Price for January 23-29, 2004, is 63.25 cents per pound.

162. We also note the New York Cotton Exchange closing prices for 23 January 2004, showed the March 2004 contract at 75.94 cents, the May 2004 contract at 77.02 cents, and the July 2004 contract at 77.90 cents. Based on these futures prices, the latest (although preliminary) FAPRI baseline still appears to have projected near-term future cotton prices too low.

163. The marketing loan programme contributes to over 42 per cent of the estimated effects of removing subsidies on production under the model developed by Dr. Sumner.[104] As the November 2002 baseline projected significant marketing loan payments through 2008 whereas the November 2003 baseline projects no or minimal marketing loan payments, updating Dr. Sumner's model to the November 2003 baseline would significantly reduce the overall estimated effect of US payments on production. Any remaining effects would largely be those incorrectly attributed to decoupled income support payments under Dr. Sumner's flawed model.

164. Finally, in paragraph 154 of its answer, Brazil again tries to muddy the waters by referencing the wholly arbitrary "expected adjusted world price first mentioned in its opening statement at the second substantive meeting of the Panel with the parties. There, Brazil attempted to provide an alternative to the US futures analysis. Brazil's alternative was that farmers look to an "expected adjusted world price" when making planting decisions since the marketing loan programme benefits are ultimately determined by the Adjusted World Price. Whereas the United States has provided references to numerous sources that demonstrate farmers look to the futures prices in making planting decisions.[105] Brazil has not provided any evidence to support its assertion that farmers look to an "expected adjusted world price" in making planting decisions.

165. Without any sources to back up its assertion, Brazil implied that farmers could readily calculate an "expected adjusted world price" in making planting decisions.[106] According to Brazil, a farmer at planting time for MY 1999 would take the December 1999 futures price and subtract 18.5 cents to get the "expected adjusted world price" (which would then be compared to the marketing loan rate). Why 18.5 cents? For each of MY 1996-MY2002, Brazil calculated the difference between the December futures price and the average adjusted world price for that marketing year. Brazil then calculated the average of the differences for these 7 years as 18.5 cents.

166. As with Brazil's lagged price calculation, however, this formula has never been, nor could it ever be, applied by a farmer in real-life. First, calculating the "average adjusted world price" for a given year – say, MY 1999 – requires knowledge of the adjusted world prices that actually result in that year. Thus, a farmer making a planting decision for MY 1999 (that is, in January-March 1999) has no way of calculating the "average adjusted world price" for marketing year 1999 (1 August 1999 – 31 July 2000). Moreover, the same farmer making a

[104] *See* Brazil's Further Submission, Annex I, table 1.4.
[105] *See* US Answers to Questions 200 and 201.
[106] The methodology is set out in Brazil's opening statement at the second panel meeting and in Exhibits BRA-356 and BRA-357.

planting decision for MY 1999 could not possibly know the December futures prices for MY2000 - MY2002; nor could that farmer know the "average adjusted world price" for MY2000 - MY2002. Thus, that farmer could not have calculated the 18.5 cents per pound average for the "average adjusted world price," nor could he have calculated the "expected adjusted world price"[107]as set out by Brazil.[108] Thus, Brazil's critique of the US futures price approach to planting decisions is not only incorrect but grossly misleading.

167. Brazil's assertions relating to "lagged prices," "average adjusted world prices," and "expected adjusted world prices" are utterly irrelevant to an analysis of the effect of the marketing loan programme because they are simply not knowable by the farmer at the time of planting. In fact, the *only* parts of Brazil's spurious methodology that are objectively knowable at the time of planting – and undisputed facts on the record of this dispute – are (1) the December futures price at the time of planting and (2) the marketing loan rate. These are precisely the elements that make up the US analysis of the effect of the marketing loan programme.

249. The Panel notes that the definition of eligible "exporter" in 7 CFR 1427.104(a)(2) includes "a producer":

> **(a) How does this reconcile with Brazil's argument that Step 2 "export payments" do not directly benefit the producer? How, if at all, would this be relevant for an analysis of the issue of export contingency under the Agreement on Agriculture or the SCM Agreement? BRA**

168. In response to Brazil's statement that Step 2 "payments are conditional upon proof of export,"[109] the United States would simply remind the Panel that such payments are made to users of upland cotton upon demonstration of the use of cotton. Such use can be manifest either by opening the bale of cotton or by export. The programme is indifferent to whether recipients of the benefit of this subsidy are exporters or parties that open bales for the manufacture of raw cotton into cotton products. Indeed, to the extent a consumer that had intended to export instead opens the bale, then that consumer could still obtain the payment upon submission of the requisite documentation. This subsidy is therefore not contingent on export performance and is not an export subsidy.[110] The situation here is analogous to that in the Ad Note to Article III of the GATT 1994 which makes clear that just because a measure that covers all products evenly is applied in the case of imports (here exports) at the border, does not change it to a border measure.

169. As was pointed out in the *Opening Statement of the United States of America at the Second Session of the First Meeting of the Panel with the Parties*, Brazil's analysis of Step 2 payments exaggerates the effect of Step 2 payments on

---

[107] December futures - 7-year average of "average adjusted world price".

[108] *See* Brazil's Opening Statement at the Second Panel Meeting, paras. 44-47; Exhibit BRA-356, -357, -358; Brazil's Answer to Question 247, para. 154.

[109] Answers of Brazil to Question 249(a) (22 December 2003), para. 163.

[110] See, e.g., US First Written Submission (11 July 2003), paras. 127-135.

world prices. Because demand for cotton is more price responsive than supply, the incidence of processor subsidies like Step 2 accrue to supply rather than demand. That is, producers gain through higher prices paid to producers while world prices are relatively unaffected. This is consistent with a previous analysis of Step 2 by FAPRI in 1999 (Exhibit US-61). In that study, FAPRI estimated an average Step 2 payment of 5.3 cents per pound.(By way of contrast, the Step 2 payment rate in effect for January 23 - 29, 2004, is 1.62 cents per pound.)These payments resulted in an increase of the spot price of US cotton by 4 cents and a fall in the world cotton price of less than 0.5 cents.

170. While it is true as Brazil points out that the margin of difference that is required between the relevant delivered US price and the A index has been adjusted slightly by the 2002 farm bill, the Brazil answer shortchanges several aspects of the continued limitations on Step 2 payments. The statute continues to allow payments only when the deliveredUS price in Northern Europe is higher than the going local Northern European price, and only when that difference has existed for four weeks straight, and only when the prevailing local Northern European price (adjusted for price and location) is not more than 134 per cent of the US loan rate of 52 cents per pound. That figure, 134 per cent of the loan rate, would be about 69.6 cents, and the current adjustment for location and quality is about 13 cents per pound. This means that where the prevailing local N.E. price was more than about 82 cents, there would be no Step 2 payments irrespective of the amount of difference in the two prices that are otherwise compared to determine whether Step 2 payments are made. Also missing in the Brazil answer is a reference to reflect that the relief from the additional 1.25 cent differential is temporary as under current law that 1.25 cents will return on 1 August 2006.[111]

G. REMEDIES

250. Does Brazil seek relief under Article XVI of GATT 1994 in respect of expired measures? What type of recommendation would the Panel be authorized to make? (Brazil further submission, paragraph 471 (iii))BRA

171. In Brazil's answer, it states that it does not seek relief "under ... Article XVI of GATT 1994" in respect of "the legal instruments consisting of the 1996 US Farm Bill providing, *inter alia*, for production flexibility contract payments, as well as various emergency appropriation Acts in 1998-2001 providing, *inter alia*, for market loss assistance payments." However, Brazil also clarifies that "Brazil's claims under Articles 5(a) and 6(c) of the SCM Agreement do include the adverse effects today and in the future of subsidies *provided* under these ex-

[111] We have sought additional information on whether producers in the capacity of manufacturers or exporters ever receive Step 2 payments. As we indicated, this would only occur with very large producers, if at all. We have examined recent Step 2 payment lists, and they indicate that at the very best any such payments would be highly isolated. Cooperatives would not, in this sense, be considered "producers" since a cooperative does not, as such, have a risk in the crop during the growing season. Step 2 payments are never paid more than once for the same cotton and absent export are only paid in connection with the manufacturing process for breaking open bundles. A producer who simply bundled cotton just to break the bundle would not be eligible for the payment.

pired legal provisions".[112] Brazil's answer points out the difficulty in its approach to actionable subsidies.

172. As Brazil acknowledges, "a panel may *not* make a recommendation to the DSB that a Member bring a measure into conformity with its WTO obligations if that measure no longer exists." Simply put, if a measure does not exist at the time of panel establishment, then that "measure" is not part of the "matter" referred to the panel and cannot be within the panel's terms of reference. Furthermore, there is nothing to be brought into conformity. In this dispute, recurring subsidies "provided" (in Brazil's words) with respect to past years and fully expensed to those years no longer exist once a new marketing year, for which new recurring subsidies are paid, commences. Thus, not only did these measures (subsidies) for past marketing years (1999-2001) not exist at the time Brazil's panel request was filed and the panel established (during marketing year 2002), they do not exist today (half way through marketing year 2003) and cannot be the subject of any recommendation to be brought into conformity.[113]

173. For this reason, Brazil's insistence that its serious prejudice "claims ... do include the continuing adverse effects today and in the future of subsidies provided under these expired legal provisions" is troubling. Were the Panel to consider that expired subsidies have some continuing effect (and we note that Brazil has never explained how long those effects could be deemed to last nor how they would be distinguished from the present effects of current subsidies), "include" them as part of its analysis of Brazil's serious prejudice claims, and render a finding of present serious prejudice, the Panel could not recommend that these expired measures be brought into conformity. On the other hand, a recommendation that the adverse effects be removed would be of questionable use since those "effects" would have included the effects of expired measures. Thus, Brazil's claims of present serious prejudice should be limited to those measures that currently existed at the time of Brazil's panel request and panel establishment.

251. In light, inter alia, of Article 7.8 of the SCM Agreement, if the Panel were to find that any subsidies have resulted in adverse effects to the interests of another Member within the meaning of Article 5 of the SCM Agreement, should it make any recommendation other than the one set out in the first sentence of Article 19.1 of the DSU? BRA

174. The United States disagrees with Brazil's answer. There is no recommendation made "pursuant to Article 7.8 of the SCM Agreement." Rather, there is an obligation under Article 7.8 on a Member granting or maintaining a subsidy inconsistently with Article 5 to "remove the adverse effects or ... withdraw the subsidy" *after adoption* of the relevant reports "in which it is determined that any subsidy has resulted in adverse effects to the interests of another Member." Article 19.1 of the DSU addresses the entirely separate question of what recommen-

---

[112] Brazil's Answer to Question 250 from the Panel, para. 164 (emphasis added).

[113] This is so for all the reasons we have given earlier in this dispute, as well as for the reason that Brazil gives: the matter before a Panel "cannot" change after establishment. Brazil's Answers to Panel Question 247.

dations should be *in the report.*[114]1 We also note the contrast between Subsidies Agreement Articles 4.7 and 7.8 in that the text of Article 4.7 specifically authorizes the Panel to take an action ("shall recommend that the subsidizing Member withdraw the subsidy without delay")while Article 7.8 does not.

252. Without prejudice to any findings by the Panel, if the Panel were to find that any of the challenged measures constitute prohibited subsidies within the meaning of Article 3 of the SCM Agreement, what are the considerations that should guide the Panel in making a recommendation under Article 4.7 of the SCM Agreement relating to the time period "within which the measure must be withdrawn"? What should that time period be? BRA

175. In its answer, Brazil sets forth no considerations that could guide the Panel in making a recommendation under Article 4.7 relating to the relevant period of time, other than to say that the period should be 90 days. The United States understands that different time periods have been set by panels that have made findings of prohibited subsidies given the nature of the measure in question. For example, in several disputes in which it appears that solely administrative action would be necessary to withdraw the measure, it appears that panels have set 90-day periods. In the *United States – FSC* dispute, the panel found that withdrawal of the measure would require legislative action and provided an appropriate period of time. The time for appeal and adoption would also be a relevant consideration. The United States has explained on several occasions the intricacies of the US legislative process and the time needed to enact legislation, including in submissions to arbitrators acting under Article 21.3(c) of the DSU. No such arbitrator has ever concluded that a period as short as 90 days is a reasonable period of time for the United States to complete implementation of the DSB's recommendations and rulings where legislative action is needed.[115]

176. Brazil has challenged Step 2 payments, the export credit guarantee programmes, and FSC benefits to upland cotton as prohibited subsidies. Brazil has also asserted that these measures are "mandatory," such that officials have no discretion to implement the measures in a WTO-consistent fashion. While the United States does not accept Brazil's assertion, the United States would suggest that the 90-day period given with respect to measures requiring only administrative fixes would not be appropriate.

177. With respect to the FSC legislation, should the Panel find this to be inconsistent with US obligations under Article 3.2 of the SCM Agreement, it is not a practical possibility that the United States could withdraw the subsidy within 90 days, given that legislative action would be required. However, the United

[114] DSU Article 19.1 ("Where a panel or the Appellate Body concludes that a measure is inconsistent with a covered agreement, *it shall recommend that the Member concerned bring the measures into conformity with that agreement*.") (emphasis added; footnote omitted).

[115] The Panel may wish to refer, *inter alia*, to the 21.3(c) arbitrations conducted in the dispute *United States – Continued Dumping and Subsidy Offset Act of 2000* (WT/DS217/14, WT/DS234/22, award circulated 13 June 2003), to which Brazil was a party. Other such arbitrations include *United States - Anti-Dumping Measures on Certain Hot-Rolled Steel Products From Japan* and *United States - Antidumping Act of 1916*.

States notes that there already are bills before both houses of Congress that would repeal the FSC and that have been reported out of their respective committees. In the event of a prohibited subsidy finding, the United States should be given until the end of this year to complete the legislative process and enact this legislation into law.

H. MISCELLANEOUS

255. How does Brazil respond to US assertions concerning the circuit-breaker provision? (see US 2 December oral statement, paragraph 82). Does this mean that US subsidies cannot be "mandatory" for the purposes of WTO dispute settlement? BRA

178. The United States provides comments on the mandatory / discretionary analysis in its comments on Brazil's answer to question 257.

257. The Panel takes note of the Appellate Body Report in *United States – Sunset Review of Anti-Dumping Duties on Corrosion-Resistant Carbon Steel Flat Products from Japan* (DS244), which was circulated to WTO Members on 15 December 2003. The Panel is aware that this report has yet to be adopted by the Dispute Settlement Body. Nevertheless, the Panel asks the parties to respond to the following related questions.

> **(a) In that report, the Appellate Body cautioned against the "mechanistic" application of the so-called "mandatory/discretionary distinction" and stated that the import of this distinction may vary from case to case (para. 93). For the Appellate Body, the question of whether a measure is mandatory or not is relevant "if at all" only as part of the assessment of whether the measure is, as such, inconsistent with particular obligations. How, if at all, are these statements and the related findings concerning the mandatory/discretionary distinction in that Appellate Body Report relevant to:**

179. Brazil's response to question 257 begins with a general discussion of the Appellate Body report in *United States – Sunset Review.*[116] As reflected in the US answer to the same question, the United States agrees with the view expressed in paragraphs one and two of Brazil's response that the *United States – Sunset Review* report has no significant impact on this dispute and that the Appellate Body in *United States – Sunset Review* in fact undertook an analysis of whether the measure at issue in that dispute was mandatory based on a traditional "mandatory / discretionary" analysis. The language cited in the Panel's question was drawn from a separate section of the *United States – Sunset Review* report addressing the preliminary jurisdictional issue of what is a measure, and that question is not present here.

---

[116] Appellate Body Report, *United States – Sunset Review of Anti-Dumping Duties on Corrosion Resistant Carbon Steel Flat Products from Japan*, WT/DS244/AB/R (adopted 9 January 2004) ("*United States – Sunset Review*").

180. While the United States agrees that the *US–Sunset* report is not relevant to the analysis in this dispute, the United States nevertheless disagrees with Brazil's further characterizations of that report.

181. For example, in paragraph three of Brazil' s answer, Brazil addresses the Appellate Body discussion on the interpretation of a Member's domestic law. In its statement at the 9 January 2004, meeting of the DSB at which the report was adopted (attached as Exhibit US-138), the United States placed the Appellate Body statement which Brazil cites in its proper context, which is that the meaning of a domestic law must be determined based on applicable *domestic* legal principles of interpretation. It is simple error to conclude that a measure mandates behaviour by government officials of a Member if, under the domestic law of that Member, the behaviour is not mandated. Thus, Brazil's speculations in paragraph four of its answer that it is permissible to examine whether "the operation of a measure" creates requirements for government officials to act in a WTO-inconsistent manner is both groundless and meaningless. US officials are required to do what US laws require, and there is no principle of US law indicating that a law's "operation" requires anything.

182. Brazil elaborates on its discussion of the "operation of a measure" with a reference to the Appellate Body's discussion of "normative" requirements. However, the United States notes, as it did in its answer to Question 257(d), that the Appellate Body's discussion of an instrument's "normative" character came in the context of its analysis of whether an instrument can be a measure, and not the separate question of whether a measure mandates a breach of any WTO obligation. It is only this latter question that is before this Panel.

183. Likewise, the Appellate Body statement on protecting future trade which Brazil cites in paragraph five of its answer and analyzes in paragraph six came in the context of the Appellate Body's discussion of why certain instruments should be considered measures, and not in the Appellate Body's separate analysis of whether that measure mandates a WTO breach. Again, it is not disputed that the measures at issue in this case *are* "measures." Thus, as Brazil itself notes, the Panel "need not examine whether the subsidy measures that Brazil has challenged are mandatory as a preliminary jurisdictional matter," but should do so only in the context of determining whether the measures breach US obligations.[117]

(i) the legal standard and elements Brazil sets out to establish its export and prohibited subsidy claims under the provisions of the Agreement on Agriculture and Articles 3.1(a) and (b) of the SCM Agreement, concerning: BRA

- **Step 2 payments (see, e.g. paras. 244-245 & 250 Brazil's first written submission; Panel Question 109 and parties' responses/comments thereon); and**

184. Brazil has challenged Section 1207(a) of the 2002 Act providing for Step 2 payments as both a prohibited export subsidy under Subsidies Agreement Arti-

[117] *See* Brazil's Answer to Question 257 from the Panel, para. 2.

cle 3.1(a) and an import-substitution subsidy under Subsidies Agreement Article 3.1(b).[118] Brazil argues that the statute mandates payments inconsistent with WTO obligations and therefore is *per se* WTO inconsistent.[119]

185. The *United States – Sunset Review* Appellate Body report did not analyze or alter the mandatory/discretionary analysis that has been used in past WTO disputes. Thus, for purposes of Brazil's *per se* challenge to Section 1207(a) of the 2002 Act, the relevant issue is whether that measure mandates a violation of the WTO Agreement.[120] It does not, and therefore Brazil's *per se* claim must fail.

186. The United States has explained that "subject to the availability of funds (that is, the availability of CCC borrowing authority), Step 2 payments must be made to all those who meet the conditions for eligibility."[121] That is, the United States may not arbitrarily deny payment to eligible recipients when the price conditions for payment have been met. However, the absence of discretion given these conditions does not mean the measure mandate a violation of Articles 3.1(a), 3.1(b), and 3.2 of the Subsidies Agreement.

187. Brazil states that "US government officials are not provided with any flexibility under Section 1207(a) of the 2002 FSRI Act" and therefore "the Act violates Articles 3.3 and 8 of the Agreement on Agriculture, and Articles 3.1(a) and 3.1(b) of the SCM Agreement".[122] Whether or not US government officials have flexibility with regard to administration of the Step 2 programme, Step 2 subsidies can violate Articles 3.3 and 8 of the Agreement on Agriculture only if they constitute export subsidies. For the reasons summarized in the US Comment to Brazil Answer to Panel Question 249, Step 2 subsidies are not export subsidies.

188. The Step 2 subsidy payments are included in the Total Aggregate Measurement of Support reported by the United States. The United States has also remained within its domestic support reduction commitments as set forth in Part IV of its Schedule. Pursuant to Article 6.3 of the Agreement on Agriculture and Paragraph 7 of Annex 3 of that Agreement, the United States therefore "shall be considered to be in compliance with its domestic support reduction commitments." Under Article 6.3 a Member may choose to provide "amber box" support in any direct or indirect manner so long as that Member's "Current Total AMS

---

[118] Brazil's First Written Submission, para. 235 ("The measure Brazil challenges as a *per se* violation of the Agreement on Agriculture and the SCM Agreement is the Step 2 export payment program as set forth in Section 1207(a) of the 2002 FSRI Act."); *id.*, para. 331("The measure Brazil challenges is therefore Section 1207(a) of the 2002 FSRI Act, which mandates the payment of Step 2 domestic payments.").

[119] Brazil's First Written Submission, para. 250 ("Section 1207(a) of the 2002 FSRI Act mandates Step 2 export payments that are prohibited export subsidies within the meaning of SCM Agreement Article 3.1(a)."); *id.*, para. 341 ("The programme also constitutes a per se violation of ASCM Articles 3.1(b) and 3.2, because payments are mandatory under US law. Section 1207(a) of the 2002 FSRI Act gives no discretion to the US Secretary of Agriculture to apply the measure in a WTO consistent manner.").

[120] Appellate Body Report, *US – Anti-Dumping Act of 1916*, WT/DS136/AB/R, para. 88 (adopted 26 September 2000).

[121] US Answer to Question 109 from the Panel.

[122] Brazil's Answers to Question 257(a)(i) (20 January 2004), para. 8.

does not exceed the corresponding annual or final bound commitment level specified in Part IV of the Member's Schedule." Furthermore, the first words of Article 3 of the SCM Agreement render that article subject to the terms of the Agreement on Agriculture. The terms of Articles 3.1(a) and 3.1(b) of the SCM Agreement apply "except as provided in the Agreement on Agriculture".[123] Therefore, without regard to flexibility in operation of the Step 2 programme, to the extent the United States has not exceeded its domestic support reduction commitments, the Step 2 programme and its authorizing legislation do not constitute a *per se* violation of Article 3.1(a) or 3.1(b) of the Subsidies Agreement.[124]

- **export credit guarantee programmes: GSM-102, GSM-103 and SCGP (see, e.g., para. 90 Brazil's oral statement at second Panel meeting).**

189. With respect to export credit guarantee programmes, the United States will not reiterate its myriad points regarding the carve-out conferred by Article 10.2 of the Agreement on Agriculture and the data indicating that, in any event, premia are sufficient to cover long-term operating costs and losses.[125] We do note that, as Brazil recognizes, the programmes are currently below the 1 per cent cap on premiums. Because the United States has discretion to raise the fees to the cap, which along with other elements of discretion over provision of actual guarantees, creates a "discretionary" aspect to the programme that does not "mandate" WTO inconsistent measures.

190. However, the United States notes the disingenuous response of Brazil, in paragraph 16 of its response to Question 257(a)(i). On the one hand Brazil claims to have "looked at historical data concerning premiums collected and costs and losses incurred" to allegedly make its case under item(j), but in the very same paragraph it states that "Brazil does not agree with the United States that item(j) necessarily 'requires a certain retrospection.'" Brazil literally uses retrospection in an effort to make its case on this very point: "Brazil has demonstrated that, *retrospectively* [italics added], costs and losses incurred by the programmes exceeded premiums collected over a 10-year period".[126] The United States of course disagrees with the factual premise of the statement, but Brazil cannot credibly disagree that "a certain retrospection" is necessary for a proper analysis under item(j).

---

[123] See US First Written Submission (11 July 2003), paras. 138-145. See also, Answers of the United States to Panel questions 111-116 (22 August 2003), paras. 222-226; US Further Submission (30 September 2003), paras. 165-176.

[124] Step 2 payments are available to all users of domestic upland cotton within the United States, be they domestic users or exporters. Thus, payment is not contingent upon export performance, and Section 1207(a) does not mandate the grant or maintenance of a prohibited export subsidy within the meaning of Article 3.1(a).

[125] In the view of the United States, the relevant analysis under the Subsidies Agreement whether export credit guarantees are export subsidies could only be the cost-to-government approach set out in item (j) of the Illustrative List of export subsidies.

[126] Brazil's Answer to Question 257(c) (20 January 2004), para. 40.

(ii) the legal standard and elements Brazil sets out to establish its serious prejudice and "threat of serious prejudice" claims, and in particular, its designation of marketing loan; crop insurance; counter-cyclical payments; direct payments and Step 2 as "mandatory"? BRA

191. Brazil's answer does not explain the significance of assigning the "mandatory" label to challenged measures for purposes of its serious prejudice claim. Brazil has challenged certain statutory and regulatory provisions as *per se* inconsistent with Articles 5(c) and 6.3(c) and (d) of the Subsidies Agreement and Article XVI:1 and :3 of GATT 1994.[127] Brazil's challenge to these measures is "as such".[128] As explained above with respect to Section 1207(a) of the 2002 Act, under Brazil's *per se* challenge, the relevant issue is whether the challenged measures mandate a violation of the WTO Agreement.[129] They do not.

192. Both Brazil and the United States agree that, given certain conditions such as price levels, these challenged measures would be "mandatory" in the sense that the United States could not arbitrarily decline to provide them. However, for purposes of a mandatory / discretionary analysis, no WTO-inconsistency is mandated by those measures because serious prejudice does not necessarily result, even where there is no discretion not to provide payment.

- For example, a finding of serious prejudice based on Article 6.3(d) requires that there be an increase in the world market share of the subsidizing Member in a subsidized primary product and the increase follow a consistent trend over a period when subsidies have been granted. This finding cannot be made in the abstract but depends upon real-world conditions, such as the current and recent shares of the world market for upland cotton held by the United States.
- Similarly, a finding of serious prejudice based on Article 6.3(c) requires that there be "significant price suppression" in the "same market" where imports of both the complaining and responding party are found. This finding also cannot be made in the abstract but requires an examination of actual prices, import levels, and an analysis of the effects of challenged subsidies.

Thus, that certain US measures "mandate" payments given certain conditions (such as price levels) does not establish that these measures mandate a

127 Brazil's Further Submission, para 413 ("Brazil challenges as *per se* violations of Articles 5(c), 6.3(c), and 6.3(d) of the SCM Agreement, and Article XVI:1 and 3 of GATT 1994 selected mandatory provisions of the 2002 FSRI Act and the 2000 ARP Act, as they cause a threat of serious prejudice within the meaning of those provisions.").

128 Brazil's Further Submission, para. 471(vii) ("The following Sections of the 2002 FSRI Act and the referenced regulations thereto violate, as such, Articles 5(c), 6.3(c), 6.3(d) of the SCM Agreement and Articles XVI: 1 and 3 of GATT 1994 to the extent that they relate to upland cotton.").

129 Appellate Body Report, *US – Anti-Dumping Act of 1916*, WT/DS136/AB/R, para. 88 (adopted 26 September 2000).

WTO-inconsistency under a mandatory / discretionary analysis of Brazil's *per se* serious prejudice claim.

193. With respect to Brazil's threat of serious prejudice claims "that do not involve claims regarding the '*per se*' validity of the statutes," Brazil colloquially describes the 5 US subsidies in the Panel's question as "mandatory," but the mandatory / discretionary analysis is inapplicable to this threat claim. In this context, it is significant that certain of the challenged payments are not mandated if price conditions are not met. Thus, in evaluating the threat of serious prejudice resulting from these measures, the *likelihood* that price conditions will be satisfied must be taken into account.(For example, the price conditions have not been met for marketing loan payments since September 2003, and none are currently being made. Furthermore, farm prices have risen to the point that the counter-cyclical payment for marketing year 2003 is projected at one-third or less of its statutory maximum.)

194. Brazil argues that "a threat of serious prejudice under Articles 6.3 and 5(c) will be more likely to exist if the subsidies are mandatory" and that "there are no provisions in US law limiting the payments, and, thus, limiting the threat of prejudice." Putting aside the fact that the "circuit breaker" provision could serve to "limit[] the payments,"[130] Brazil's argument rests on the flawed notion that the absence of a "legal mechanism to limit the amount of potential subsidies that could be paid" necessarily creates a threat of serious prejudice. This proposed standard does not withstand scrutiny.

195. As the United States has noted[131], Brazil looks to the Appellate Body report in *United States – FSC*, but that report involved the "threat of circumvention" of export subsidies standard of Article 10.1 of the Agreement on Agriculture. Because agricultural export subsidies *are* subject to volume and value limits, it may be appropriate in that particular circumstance to conclude that the absence of a mechanism to control the flow of subsidies could threaten circumvention of those absolute commitment levels. However, the commitment in the case of Articles 5(c) and 6.3 is not to threaten serious prejudice – that is, not threaten a particular form of adverse *effect*. Whether a particular type and level of subsidy could threaten that effect necessarily depends upon a fact-intensive examination of, *inter alia*, the subsidy, the relevant market or markets, supply and demand factors, etc. Thus, the *FSC* standard for claims of "threat of circumvention" of export subsidy commitments is not relevant in this context.

196. Brazil's continued reliance on *EC – Sugar Export Subsidies* is misplaced. In that dispute, the panel found that as there was no legal mechanism to control the EC's sugar export subsidies, the subsidy constituted a permanent threat of instability. That panel, however, provided no basis for selecting that standard, which is not reflected in the text of the Subsidies Agreement or GATT 1994 Ar-

[130] Although the trigger for the circuit breaker provision is compliance with the United States' AMS commitments, the Secretary would appear to have discretion over what "adjustments in the amount of such expenditures" would be made. That is, the Secretary could determine to make adjustments in expenditures for one product or multiple products or decoupled income supports.

[131] *See, e.g.*, US Opening Statement at the Second Panel Meeting, paras. 83-85.

ticle XVI:1.[132] We further note that Brazil itself, when it first presented this report to the Panel, commented that "[t]he panel's conclusion was based on several key factual findings".[133] Thus, even that GATT panel report's finding of threat was based on the particular factual circumstances it reviewed, and that report would not support an abstract standard that the lack of a legal mechanism to control the flow of subsidies suffices to create a threat of serious prejudice.

(iii) the legal standard and elements Brazil sets out to establish its "per se" "serious prejudice" claims (e.g. Brazil's 9 September further submission, para. 417 ff; US oral statement at second Panel meeting, para. 86 ff.)? BRA

197. Given the way in which Brazil structured its answer, the United States directs the Panel's attention to its comment on Brazil's answer to question 257(a)(ii). We do note, however, that Brazil has not commented on or rebutted that portion of the US oral statement referred to in the Panel's question. There, we pointed out that Brazil had asserted that in either of two price circumstances, the United States is required to act in a manner inconsistent with US WTO obligations. The first price circumstance is that "both USDA's and FAPRI's baseline expect marketing loan and counter-cyclical payments to be made during the lifespan of the 2002 FSRI Act, i.e., through MY 2007. Thus, the circumstances that will exist during the lifespan of the 2002 FSRI Act are such that all of the five mandatory subsidies will be paid until MY 2007 and that they will threaten to cause serious prejudice".[134] Brazil avoids discussing the fact that market price developments during marketing year 2003 have already superseded this analysis by Brazil.

198. The second price circumstance Brazil posits is when prices are sufficiently high that only direct payments and crop insurance payments are made. Brazil has provided no analysis of the estimated effects of direct payments and crop insurance payments at such high market price levels – that is, its economic analysis is made using baseline prices that are *not* sufficiently high that only direct payments and crop insurance payments are made. Neither has Brazil responded to this criticism.

(b) How and to what extent are the legal and regulatory provisions cited in paras. 415 and 423 of Brazil's 9 September further submission "normative" in nature and treated as binding within the US legal system (see, e.g., para. 99 of the Appellate Body Report)? Does your response differ depending on whether the payments are dependent upon market price conditions? BRA

---

[132] Indeed, the GATT panel's conclusion that "the Community system and its application constituted a permanent source of uncertainty in world sugar markets and therefore constituted a threat of serious prejudice in terms of Article XVI:1" does not clarify any standard to distinguish subsidies that threaten serious prejudice from those that do not since any subsidy that has some production effect could be deemed to "constitute[] a permanent source of uncertainty." *See* GATT Panel Report, *EC – Sugar Exports II(Brazil),* L/5011, 27S/69, part V(g).

[133] Brazil's Further Submission, paras. 296-97.

[134] Brazil's Further Submission, para. 430.

199. As explained in the US answer to question 257(d), the Appellate Body's discussion of the "normative character and operation" of an instrument came in the context of its explanation of how to determine whether an instrument is a "measure" subject to challenge in dispute settlement. The Appellate Body distinguished this question from the separate question of whether the instrument, if a measure, mandates a breach of a WTO obligation under a "mandatory/discretionary" analysis. Since there is no dispute that the cited legal and regulatory provisions are "measures," the "normative" character of those measures is not at issue. Indeed, Brazil recognizes this in stating that, "[a]s used by the Appellate Body, the term 'normative' includes as a subcategory the group of measures that are mandatory, within the meaning of the traditional mandatory/discretionary distinction".[135] In other words, "normative" measures may or may not mandate a WTO-breach, as analyzed based on the "traditional mandatory / discretionary distinction."

200. Brazil further notes correctly that "[t]he focus for deciding whether a measure is mandatory or discretionary is on whether it provides government officials with the discretion to implement the measure in a WTO-consistent manner".[136] However, discretion is only one reason why a measure may not be found to mandate a breach of a WTO obligation. Here, Brazil's challenge is fact-dependent. There is no basis for presuming the existence of a particular set of facts, and hence no basis for presuming that measures mandate a breach of WTO obligations. Brazil erroneously denies the relevance of the conditions attached to payments.[137] For example, if, when those conditions are met, only *some* of the elements which establish a breach have been shown to exist, then there is no breach.

201. The United States has explained that, given the existence of certain conditions (for example, in the case of marketing loan payments, an adjusted world price less than 52 cents per pound), the five sets of measures Brazil challenges on a *per se* basis would mandate that payments be made. However, as set out in the US comment on Brazil 's answer to question 257(a)(ii), these measures do not mandate any inconsistency with the obligation not to cause serious prejudice because payment alone is not sufficient to establish a breach of the obligation. Even if all the conditions mandating payment have been met, one cannot simply presume that serious prejudice will result; it must also be demonstrated that the effect of the subsidy is one or more of the effects listed in Article 6.3 of the Subsidies Agreement and that serious prejudice results from such effect(s). Moreover, it cannot be disregarded that when those conditions have not been met, those payments will *not* be made and therefore cannot cause serious prejudice.

(c) Does Brazil challenge as "mandatory" the "subsidies" themselves, the subsidy programmes or the legal/regulatory provisions for the grant or maintenance of those subsidies, or something else? BRA

---

135 Brazil's Answer to Question 257(b), para. 24.
136 Brazil's Answer to Question 257(b), para. 27.
137 Brazil's Answer to Question 257(b), para. 29.

202. With respect to Brazil's arguments relating to its threat of serious prejudice claims, the United States refers the Panel to its comment on Brazil's answer to question 257(a)(ii). We do find it revealing that, as in its further rebuttal submission and its statements at the second panel meeting, Brazil makes no reference to the "clearly foreseen and imminent" standard it set forth in its further submission.[138] The absence is even more striking when one considers Brazil's argument that, "[h]aving established the existence of present serious prejudice from the actionable subsidies, demonstrating that such prejudice is 'clearly foreseen and imminent' from the effects of the same and even larger subsidies is not difficult".[139]

203. We would suggest that to argue that "such prejudice is 'clearly foreseen and imminent'" became much more difficult for Brazil as upland cotton prices recovered over the course of marketing year 2003. That is, the increase in prices had the simultaneous effect of reducing current outlays (for example, no marketing loan payments have been made since September and projected counter-cyclical payments have been reduced by two-thirds) and invalidating Brazil's (flawed) economic analysis for marketing years 2003-2007, which was based on an outdated FAPRI baseline projection that understates the MY2003 AWP by 54 per cent and overstates the estimated marketing loan gain by nearly 15 cents per pound (or 100 per cent). The 5-year high prices reached in marketing year 2003, and the high futures prices for the remainder of marketing years 2003 and for the marketing year 2004 crop, also severely undercut Brazil's rhetorical linking of the large amount of outlays in past marketing years with the extremely low prices experienced.

- That is, if US subsidies caused "significant price suppression" in marketing years 1999-2001, and Brazil claims that support under the 2002 Act has "*significantly increased*" from those levels[140], then how can prices have rebounded to 5-year highs?

Thus, Brazil has good reason not to focus the Panel's attention on actual market developments[141], which demonstrate that there is no "clearly foreseen and immi-

---

[138] *See, e.g.,* Brazil's Further Submission, para. 292 ("Prior to addressing the specifics of these three claims, Brazil sets forth two legal standards that could be used to analyze the threat of serious prejudice. The first is the standard established by the GATT Panels in *EC – Sugar Exports I (Australia)* and *EC – Sugar Exports II (Brazil)* of a "permanent source of uncertainty" requiring a demonstration that guaranteed subsidies by a large exporter have no effective production or export limitations. The second standard includes the same elements necessary to demonstrate present serious prejudice focusing on the likely effects of the subsidies in suppressing world prices and in increasing and maintaining a high level of world export market share.").

[139] Brazil's Further Submission, para. 308.

[140] *See* Brazil' s Further Submission, para. 309 ("The 2002 FSRI Act, along with the 2000 ARP Act, create a legal structure guaranteeing and mandating the payment of *significantly increased levels of spending* for the production, use and export of US upland cotton beyond the 1996 FAIR Act and special appropriation bills in 1998-2001.") (emphasis added).

[141] *See* Brazil's Further Submission, para. 308 ("The evidence presented by Brazil below is based on facts regarding the mandated and unlimited nature of the US subsidies, as well as on actual market conditions demonstrating the present and likely future effects of the US subsidies."). As the Panel will have noted, subsequent to Brazil's further submission, Brazil focused on the first half of this passage and sought to minimize the latter half.

nent" likelihood of future serious prejudice. To the contrary, there is a clearly foreseen and imminent likelihood of record cotton plantings in Brazil[142] and of continued high cotton prices in marketing year 2004.

204. With respect to Brazil's arguments relating to the export credit guarantee programmes, the United States refers the Panel to its comment on Brazil's answer to question 257(a)(i). In additions to those observations, the United States further notes that Brazil has not explained why premium rates at any particular level, let alone if they were significantly increased to the one per cent rate of GSM-102, will *necessarily* not be sufficient to cover long-term operating costs and losses. The United States has numerous mechanisms, such as evaluation of creditworthiness of particular countries and the establishment of individual bank limits, to insulate itself from "credit risks and meet costs".[143] Brazil does not suggest a "magic bullet" rate that would under *all* circumstances necessarily cover long-term operating costs and losses because it cannot, nor does it explain why the flexibility inherent in the operation of the export credit guarantee programme is necessarily less effective than some unknown rate.

205. With respect to Brazil's threat of circumvention claim against the CCC programmes "as such," this claim cannot stand. Assuming *arguendo* that Article 10.2 of the Agreement on Agriculture contrary to its terms did not obligate Members to work towards internationally agreed disciplines on export credit guarantees and thereafter provide export credits only in conformity with such disciplines, then the only way to judge whether the export credit guarantee programmes provide an export subsidy – and hence either circumvent US export subsidy reduction commitments or threaten to – is to look to item (j) of the Illustrative List. Under item (j), the relevant inquiry examines whether premiums are sufficient to cover long-term *operating* costs and losses. That is, it is the operating experience of the programmes that would matter. Thus, the programmes "as such" could not threaten circumvention.

206. Brazil argues in paragraph 39 that the export credit guarantee programmes themselves "confer 'benefits' *per se*." The United States has previously noted Article 10.2 provides the appropriate analysis for claims against export credit guarantee programmes for agricultural products. Were the Subsidies Agreement relevant to such programmes, the relevant test would be that of item(j) of the Illustrative List of Export Subsidies; the United States has shown that the export credit guarantee programmes meet that test. Further, we would note that Brazil has not demonstrated that any benefit is conferred by these programmes; in fact, Brazil has conceded that it "is not in a position to quantify the benefit to the recipients that has arisen from the application of the GSM 102 export credit guarantee programme to exports of US upland cotton between MY 1999-2002.[144] Neither has Brazil attempted to quantify any alleged benefit to recipients of export credit guarantees for any other agricultural products. Thus,

[142] Exhibit US-131 ("Brazil's Mato Grosso to triple winter cotton area," Reuters, 2004-01-20 ("Increased winter cotton planting will result in a record overall area.")).
[143] Brazil's Answer to Question 257(c) (20 January 2004), para. 40.
[144] Brazil's Answer to Question 140, para. 82.

Brazil may not obtain findings under Articles 1.1 and 3.1(a) of the Subsidies Agreement by virtue of Articles 10.2 and 21.2 of the Agreement on Agriculture, nor has Brazil established any *per se* inconsistency with Article 1.1 and 3.1(a).

258. Please submit a detailed explanation of the method by which one could calculate total expenditures to producers of upland cotton under the four relevant programmes on the basis of the data which it seeks. BRA

207. The Panel's question highlights Brazil's failure to provide its methodology prior to this late stage of the proceedings. The United States is gratified that the Panel's question has finally compelled Brazil to come forward and explain its methodology for allocating decoupled income support payments. Brazil states that it "appreciates the opportunity to describe to the Panel" this methodology, but Brazil needed no invitation to do so. In fact, as the complaining party alleging that certain decoupled income support payments are support to upland cotton for purposes of Article 13(b)(ii) of the Agreement on Agriculture and actionable subsidies for purposes of Articles 1, 5(c), 6.3, and 7 of the Subsidies Agreement, it has always been Brazil' s burden to make claims and arguments with respect to these measures. Rather, Brazil's answer demonstrates that Brazil's proposed methodology lacks any basis in the Subsidies Agreement, any WTO agreement, or in economic logic. Thus, the Panel should find that Brazil has not made a *prima facie* case of WTO inconsistency with respect to these measures.

208. Furthermore, Brazil's response demonstrates that it is attempting to add new measures to its claims in this proceeding, an attempt that is inconsistent with the Panel's terms of reference. Payments for programmes other than upland cotton are not within the terms of reference and are to be excluded from Brazil's claims. Brazil cannot now alter the terms of reference to add programmes for base acreage for other crops. As Brazil itself has admitted (in its response to question 247):"Thus, the 'matter' before the Panel has not changed (*and cannot*) since the establishment of the Panel" (emphasis added).

Brazil's Proposed Methodology is not Based on Any Text, Nor Does It Adequately Deal with Fundamental Subsidies Issues

209. By way of introduction, we recall the proper approach to attributing a non-tied (or decoupled) subsidy to particular products. The United States has explained that a complaining party in a serious prejudice dispute must demonstrate which product or products benefit from the challenged subsidy.[145] This requirement flows from several sources. First, Article 6.3 and provisions explaining it specifically identify certain effects – for example, displacement or impediment, significant price undercutting, suppression, or depression, and increase in world market share) – caused through a "subsidized product".[146] Thus, to de-

[145] *See, e.g.,* US Further Rebuttal Submission, paras. 6-17.

[146] For example, for purposes of a claim under Article 6.3(c) of the Subsidies Agreement, the "effect of the subsidy" must be "significant price undercutting" or "significant price suppression, price depression, or lost sales" caused by "*the subsidized product*." Article 6.5 confirms that price undercutting includes "any case in which such price undercutting has been demonstrated through a comparison of prices of the *subsidized product* with prices of a non-subsidized like product supplied to the same market." Similarly, under Article 6.3(d) "the effect of the subsidy" must be an increase in world

termine whether "the effect of the subsidy" is one of those listed in Article 6.3 requires a finding that upland cotton is a "subsidized product" with respect to that subsidy.

210. Second, a "subsidy" does not exist within the meaning of Article 1 of the Subsidies Agreement if a "benefit" is not conferred.[147] As Brazil is asserting the existence of serious prejudice with respect to upland cotton, the challenged subsidy must actually "benefit" cotton and not any other crop.

211. With respect to decoupled income support, a recipient need not produce upland cotton in order to receive payment. In fact, the recipient need not produce anything at all – hence, the support is "decoupled" from production requirements. Since decoupled income support payments do not, on their face, provide a "benefit" to upland cotton, the question of what products benefit from the subsidy arises.

212. Brazil now answers this question by inventing a methodology by which "excess" base acres – that is, base acres of a crop historically grown on the farm in excess of the planted acres of that crop in a given year – are allocated to other crops with "excess" planted acres(but only if they are "programme crops") – that is, planted acres in excess of the base acres of that crop historically grown on the farm. It is ironic to recall that Brazil criticized the US approach to this issue by writing that the "alleged requirement" to allocate untied subsidies across the total value of production on a recipient's farm "lacks any textual basis".[148]

- In fact, the Panel will search Brazil's answer to question 258 in vain for a *single citation* to a WTO provision that sets out or even indirectly supports its proposed allocation methodology.

213. The methodology explained by the United States, on the other hand, is rooted in the text and context of the Subsidies Agreement. As set out above, to establish that the effect of a subsidy is serious prejudice with respect to upland cotton, Brazil must identify the subsidized products– that is, the products that benefit from the payment and the portion of those payments that benefit upland cotton. Annex IV provides useful context in its methodology for calculating an *ad valorem* subsidization rate. An *ad valorem* subsidy rate is the quotient of a numerator (subsidy amount) and a denominator (value of the subsidized product). Thus, to perform the calculation, one must know what the subsidized product is.

- Paragraph 2 of Annex IV provides that "*the value of the product* shall be calculated as the *total value of the recipient firm's sales* in

market share "in a particular *subsidized primary product or commodity*." Finally, under Articles 6.4 and 6.3(b), pursuant to which Brazil is not claiming serious prejudice, the "change in relevant market shares" involves an examination of the "relative shares of the market" of the non-subsidized like product and "*the subsidized product*."

[147] *See* Panel Report, *United States – Imposition of Countervailing Duties on Certain Hot-Rolled Lead and Bismuth Carbon Steel Products Originating in the United Kingdom*, WT/DS138/R, adopted 7 June 2000, paras. 6.65 and 6.66 (quoting and agreeing with *Canada – Aircraft* panel: "'A "benefit" does not exist in the abstract, but must be received and enjoyed by a beneficiary or a recipient. Logically, a "benefit" can be said to arise only if a person ... has in fact received something.'").

[148] Brazil's Further Rebuttal Submission, para. 103.

the most recent 12-month period, for which sales data is available, preceding the period in which the subsidy is granted"(footnotes omitted & italics added).

- Paragraph 3 of Annex IV modifies the general principle of paragraph 2, providing that "[w]here the subsidy is *tied to the production or sale of a given product*, the value of the product shall be calculated as the *total value of the recipient firm's sales of that product* in the most recent 12-month period, for which sales data is available, preceding the period in which the subsidy is granted" (italics added).

Thus, "[w]here the subsidy is [not] tied to the production or sale of a given product," the general methodology of paragraph 2 applies. Because the "value of the [subsidized] product" is the "total value of the recipient firm's sales," it follows that the subsidized product is the entirety of what the recipient sells. To determine the share of the subsidy that is attributable to upland cotton, one would multiply the value of the payment by the share of the total value of production accounted for by upland cotton. Brazil does not deny that both the EC and Brazil apply this very methodology for purposes of their domestic countervailing duty procedures[149], nor that Brazil has proposed that Members adopt this very methodology as a "guideline" on calculating the amount of the subsidy.[150]

214. Brazil can only assert that the allocation methodology set out in Annex IV of the Subsidies Agreement and applied by Brazil itself and the EC for purposes of their countervailing duty procedures "are irrelevant to Article 6.3 claims".[151] And yet, *some* allocation methodology for purposes of Article 6.3 is necessary to deal with non-tied (decoupled) payments – to assert otherwise is to deny the relevance of the "subsidy" definition of Article 1 as well as those provisions of Article 6 contingent on the existence of a "subsidized product". However, Brazil's proposed methodology is not even based on a Subsidies Agreement text, nor based on *its own* procedures for determining the subsidized product that benefits from a non-tied (decoupled) payment. One could reasonably ask how Brazil's own countervailing duty procedures could deal with non-tied subsidies in one way while Brazil proposes a contradictory approach for purposes of its serious prejudice claims, given that both situations are faced with the same issues of whether a subsidy benefits a particular product.

215. In judging the credibility of Brazil's proposed methodology in comparison to the methodology explained by the United States, the Panel may wish to compare the sources that Brazil and the United States, respectively, have drawn upon:

---

149 *See* Brazil's Opening Oral Statement at the Second Panel Meeting, para. 4.

150 Paper by Brazil, Countervailing Measures: Illustrative Major Issues, TN/RL/W/19, at 6 (7 October 2002) ("If the benefit of a subsidy is limited to a particular product, the denominator should reflect only sales [production/exports] of that product. If this is not the case, the denominator should be the recipient's total sales.").

151 Brazil's Opening Statement at the Second Panel Meeting, para. 4.

Comparison of Allocation Methodologies for Non-Tied (Decoupled) Payments		
Party	**Methodology**	**Interpretive and Other Sources**
Brazil	Payments for base acres for historically grown crop are attributed to current plantings of that crop, if any; payments for base acres in excess of plantings are attributed to all crops planted in excess of base acres for that historically grown crop by the proportion of a crop's excess planted acres to total excess planted acres	None[152]
United States	Payments that are not tied to the production or sale of a given product are attributed to all the products the recipient produces; the subsidy benefits a particular product by its share of the total value of production	SCM Agreement, Article 1.1(a); Articles 6.3, 6.4, 6.5; Annex IV, paras. 2-3 CVD practice, Brazil and EC Brazilian CVD proposal[153]

Simply put, Brazil has pointed to nothing in the WTO agreements that would support its approach to the allocation of non-tied (decoupled) payments.

216. Finally, Brazil's argument that the Annex IV methodology*cannot* apply to claims of serious prejudice does not withstand scrutiny. Although the provision to which Annex IV relates – Article 6.1(a) – is no longer in effect, it may still be relevant for purposes of interpreting the Subsidies Agreement. For example, in *United States – Countervailing Measures (EC)*, the Appellate Body relied on Annex IV as context in interpreting another provision of the Subsidies Agreement.[154] Similarly, in *United States – FSC: Article 22.6*, Arbitrator cited the *expired* Articles 8 and 9 as "helpful ... in understanding the overall architecture of the Agreement with respect to the different types of subsidies it sought and seeks to address".[155]

217. There is a difference between looking to the expired provisions of Article 6.1 for a legal obligation (for example, the presumption created by a 5 per cent *ad valorem* subsidization rate) and looking to the provisions of Annex IV for a methodology, or logical approach to identifying the subsidized product. In the former case, it is precisely the expiry of the provision that indicates that the presumption created by that rule no longer has effect. In the latter case, unless there is some basis to draw a negative implication from the expiry of the rule in Article 6.1, the methodology can be examined for its underlying logic. If the methodology fits with pertinent subsidies concepts, it may provide useful guidance in determining the product that benefits from the subsidy. In this regard, we note Brazil's statement that the Annex IV methodology existed only because "[n]egotiators wanted to be certain that if such a presumption [of serious prejudice] was created [by virtue of Article 6.1(a)], the precise *level* of subsidization was carefully calculated".[156] To the extent that the Panel agrees that it must "be certain" that the non-tied subsidies at issue benefit upland cotton and that "the

152 *See* Brazil' s Answer to Question 258, paras. 43-55.

153 US Further Rebuttal Submission, paras. 9-13.

154 WT/DS212/AB/R, para. 112.

155 WT/DS108/ARB, note 56.

156 Brazil's Further Rebuttal Submission, para. 103.

precise level of subsidization [must be] carefully calculated," we suggest that Annex IV provides the appropriate methodology.

Brazil's Allocation Methodology Does Not Make Economic Sense

218. The foregoing discussion suffices to show that Brazil's allocation methodology has no basis in the Subsidies Agreement. As Brazil has not demonstrated, for each challenged decoupled payment (production flexibility contract, market loss assistance, direct, and counter-cyclical payments), what is the subsidized product nor what is the benefit to upland cotton, Brazil cannot and has not made a *prima facie* case with respect to these payments. That is, Brazil cannot begin to demonstrate "the effect of the subsidy" if it has not shown the subsidy benefit and the subsidized product.

219. It may be of interest to the Panel, however, that Brazil's allocation methodology does not make economic sense. In essence, Brazil's approach arbitrarily assigns payments for base acreage to particular planted acres, as if the current crop was "planted on" base acreage, even though "base acres" do not correspond to any physical acres on a farm; they are a mere accounting concept. At the same time, however, any "excess" base acres are assigned to crops that have "excess" planted acres. This methodology leads to situations in which a particular crop could be subsidized at different rates, depending on whether it is planted on "excess" acreage or base acreage. It leads to situations in which a particular crop could receive a greater subsidy than another crop that accounts for more acreage on the farm. It also allocates payments only to certain "programme" crops, ignoring the fact that the subsidy recipient may grow crops for which no base acreage exists and may engage in other types of production. Neither situation makes sense from an economic perspective, and neither results from the correct (Annex IV) methodology explained above.

220. The first situation is one in which a particular crop, such as upland cotton, could be subsidized at different rates, depending on what type of acreage it is "planted on." For example, consider a farm with 200 base acres, 100 of cotton and 100 of soybeans, and 200 planted acres, 150 of cotton and 50 of soybeans. According to Brazil's proposed methodology, 100 base acres of cotton are allocated to 100 acres of planted cotton, leaving 50 planted acres of cotton; similarly, the 50 of the 100 base acres of soybeans are allocated to the 50 base acres of soybeans, leaving 50 "excess" soy base acres that can be allocated to the 50 "excess" cotton planted acres. However, this allocation methodology results in two different rates of subsidization for cotton acreage. The 100 cotton acres deemed to be "planted on" cotton base acreage is subsidized at the rate corresponding to decoupled payments for upland cotton base acres while the 50 cotton acres deemed to be "planted on" soy base acreage is subsidized at the rate corresponding to decoupled payments for soy base acres.[157] There is no rationale for deeming one acre of cotton to receive one subsidy and deeming the next acre of cotton to receive an entirely different subsidy. These decoupled payments are not tied to

[157] *See, e.g.*, Brazil's Answer to Question 258, para. 48 (Sample Farm 4: 160 planted acres of cotton are allocated 100 base acres of cotton and 60 base acres of rice).

production of a particular commodity; in fact, the "upland cotton" base acreage could now be "planted to" soybeans or nothing at all. In economic terms, money is fungible, and payments received through decoupled payments are deemed to subsidize whatever the recipient chooses to produce. As all of the recipient's production is the "subsidized product," the subsidy should be neutrally allocated to all of those products.

221. The second situation is one in which a particular crop that is with "excess" plantings could receive a greater subsidy than another crop that accounts for more acreage on the farm. For example, consider a farm with 200 base acres of soybeans and none of cotton and with 75 planted acres of cotton and 50 planted acres of soybeans. Seventy-five base acres of soybeans are attributed to the 75 planted acres of soybeans, and "[p]ayments on any further base acreage for [that] programme crop[is] allocated to the crops for which planted acres exceed base acres".[158] Since cotton is the only crop "for which planted acres exceed base acres, payments for 125 base acres of soybeans are allocated the 50 acres of cotton.[159] This produces the anomalous result that the lesser planted crop (upland cotton, with 50 planted acres) would be deemed to receive a greater subsidy than the crop with greater planted acreage (soybeans, with 75 planted acres). If the same farm decided to plant 75 acres of soybeans and only *one* acre of cotton, again, all of the "excess" base acres would be allocated to the one acre of cotton. Again, this result makes no economic sense since the farm "allocated" its plantings 75 to 1, soy over cotton. The allocation of payments not tied to production of a particular commodity should reflect the recipient's decisions on what production to undertake.

222. Brazil's erroneous methodology also allocates payments only to certain "programme" crops, for which base acreage exists.[160] This ignores the fact that the subsidy recipient may grow crops for which no base acreage exists and may engage in other types of production. A farmer's activities and plantings are not restricted to "programme" crops. In the production flexibility contract era, farmers who planted cotton did not just plant wheat, oats, rice, corn, sorghum, and barley. They also planted other crops, like peanuts, sugar, soybeans, and perhaps tobacco. They may have also planted fruits and vegetables on any acreage exceeding their base acreage. They may have produced hay or had livestock operations on the farm. The possibilities are numerous. Given the myriad production activities that a payment recipient could (and did) choose to undertake, there is no basis to allocate non-tied (decoupled) payments solely to programme crops and not to the entirety of a farm's production.

223. In sum, these illogical results follow from a methodology in which payments on "excess" base acreage are allocated only to those crops for which plantings "exceed" their base. If Brazil believes a decoupled payment is capable of

---

158 Brazil's Answer to Question 258, para. 48.

159 *See, e.g.,* Brazil's Answer to Question 258, para. 51 (Sample Farm 5: 140 planted acres of cotton are allocated payments for 160 base acres (100 cotton, 40 wheat, 20 rice).

160 *See, e.g.,* Brazil's Answer to Question 258, para. 50 ("In Brazil's methodology, payments available for allocation – *i.e.,* not allocated to the program crop itself – are pooled and allocated proportionally to the remaining program crop acreage.").

allocation when base acreage "exceeds" planted acreage, Brazil must concede that the payment is not tied to production, use, or sale of particular commodity. However, the same consideration must apply to those payments with respect to base acreage for which there is an equal amount of planted acres – that is, those legally indistinguishable payments on "non-excess" base acres are not tied to production, use, or sale of a particular commodity either. Thus, one, consistent allocation methodology must apply to the entire amount of a recipient's decoupled payments. Brazil's erroneous allocation methodology does not provide that. The methodology set out in Annex IV and also applied by Brazil for purposes of its countervailing duty procedures under Part V of the Subsidies Agreement does.

Implications of Brazil's Erroneous Methodology for Subsidies Claims and Peace Clause

224. As Brazil's answer makes perfectly clear, and as it had previously stated[161], Brazil rejects the allocation methodology for non-tied (decoupled) payments suggested, *inter alia*, by Annex IV to the Subsidies Agreement. That is, Brazil has refused to acknowledge that such payments must be allocated across the total value of the recipient's production. Therefore, as the United States suggested in its answer to question 256, Brazil has not advanced claims and arguments that would allow the Panel to determine the subsidy benefit to upland cotton. It follows that Brazil has failed to make a *prima facie* case that decoupled income support payments cause or threaten to cause serious prejudice.

225. Brazil's refusal to adopt a proper methodology for determining the subsidy benefit and subsidized product also has important implications for its Peace Clause arguments. The Panel will recall that Brazil argued that "support to a specific commodity" in the Peace Clause proviso could only be gauged by using budgetary outlays. However, calculating the subsidy benefit to upland cotton is indispensable – on Brazil's approach – to determining the "support to" upland cotton. To the extent that Brazil has not utilized the correct methodology, its Peace Clause calculation of the support to upland cotton from decoupled payments is erroneous.

226. In addition, the fact that Brazil seeks to attribute upland cotton decoupled payments made for "excess" base acres is an important point. Brazil acknowledges that these decoupled payments are not tied to production, and therefore can be attributed across production. Our difficulty with Brazil's approach, is that it claims the attribution is only made to crops with "excess" acreage. As explained above, there is no basis for attributing part of a payment to only some crops planted on the farm, rather than attributing the entire value of such payments across all production. Thus, Brazil has not established that US domestic support measures breach the Peace Clause, and the US domestic support measures are entitled to Peace Clause protection.

[161] Brazil's Further Rebuttal Submission, paras. 103-05; Brazil's Opening Statement at the Second Panel Meeting, para. 4.

227. Brazil's answer also highlights that decoupled income support payments do not grant "support to a specific commodity" within the meaning of Article 13(b)(ii). Brazil has asserted that such support can be any support that benefits upland cotton. Thus, Brazil would seek to allocate decoupled payments to the products on the farm as set out in its methodology. However, Brazil's approach is incompatible with important Agreement on Agriculture concepts. As is clear from Brazil's answer, a payment made with respect to base acreage historically planted to one crop can be support to that crop *and* support to any other "programme" crop at the same time. Such a result is inconsistent on its face with the ordinary meaning of "support to a specific commodity" since such a payment would in fact be'support to multiple commodities.'

228. In addition, Brazil's approach would render nugatory non-product-specific support for purposes of the Peace Clause. Brazil has argued that the decoupled income support payments it challenges are not non-product-specific support because they are not support to producers "in general." And yet, the recipients of decoupled payments *are* producers "in general" because they are free, with limited exceptions, to plant any commodity and are free, without exception, to undertake other agricultural activities. Thus, they are producers generally of whatever products they choose to produce. By asserting that the allocation of such non-product-specific support to the commodities a recipient produces renders such payments "support to a specific commodity," Brazil reads non-product-specific support out of the scope of the Peace Clause. If non-product-specific support could simply be allocated to a recipient's production and thereby become support to each specific commodity produced, there would simply be no reason to have a category of non-product-specific support in the Agreement on Agriculture.

229. In fact, the Agreement on Agriculture does not permit an interpretation that would allocate all non-product-specific support to specific commodities. First, the precise definition of product-specific support in Article 1(f) ensures that support that is *not* "provided for an agricultural product in favour of the producers of the basic agricultural product" must be categorized as non-product-specific ("support provided in favour of agricultural producers in general"). Second, paragraph 1 of Annex 3 establishes that non-product-specific support must be kept separate from product-specific support for purposes of AMS calculation.[162] Brazil has stated that "support to a specific commodity" under the Peace Clause may be measured either using budgetary outlays or an "AMS-like methodology using rules in Annex 3".[163] Therefore, since Annex 3 specifically provides that non-product-specific support must be kept separate from product-specific support, non-product-specific support must also be kept separate from "support to a specific commodity" for purposes of the Peace Clause analysis. Brazil may not allocate non-product-specific decoupled payments to certain products for Subsidies Agreement purposes and then, on that

---

[162] Agreement on Agriculture, Annex 3, para. 1 ("Support which is non-product-specific shall be totalled into one non-product-specific AMS in total monetary terms.").

[163] Brazil's Rebuttal Submission, para. 87.

basis, assert that such allocated payments are "support to a specific commodity" for Peace Clause purposes. The product-specific / non-product-specific categories in the Agreement on Agriculture are *sui generis* and may not be rendered inutile by the application of Subsidies Agreement concepts (subsidy, benefit, subsidized product) not used in nor directly applicable to the Peace Clause.

List of Exhibits

US131	Brazil's Mato Grosso to triple winter cotton area2004-01-20 20:10:01 GMT (Reuters), By Inae Riveras
US132	Chart, US Crops Cotton supply and utilization, and Baseline
US133	Statement By O A Cleveland 1/16/04
US134	Charts of US and Brazilian Export Unit Values to 7 Destinations
US135	Production, Yield, Trade, and Stocks Data, MY99-02
US136	USDA/FAS US trade data, MY99-03
US137	World Trade Atlas official Brazilian trade data, MY99-03
US138	Statement of the United States at the DSB (9 January 2004) on adoption of the reports in *United States- Sunset Review of Anti-Dumping Duties on Corrosion-Resistant Carbon Steel Flat Products for Japan*
US139	USDA Weekly Cotton Market Review 1/9/04
US140	USDA Weekly Cotton Market Review 1/23/04
US141	Charts of Chinese (Domestic, Import, Export) Prices vs. A-Index
US142	NY Board of Trade, NY Cotton Exchange, 27 January 2004 futures data

ANNEX I-15

BRAZIL'S COMMENTS AND REQUESTS REGARDING DATA PROVIDED BY THE UNITED STATES ON 18/19 DECEMBER 2003 AND THE US REFUSAL TO PROVIDE NON-SCRAMBLED DATA ON 20 JANUARY 2004
(28 January 2004)

TABLE OF CONTENTS

Table of Cases

Short Title	Full Case and Citation
EC – Sugar Exports I (Australia)	GATT Panel Report, *European Communities – Refunds on Exports of Sugar Complaint by Australia,* L/4833 – 26S/290, adopted 6 November, 1979.
EC – Sugar Exports II (Brazil)	GATT Panel Report, *European Communities – Refunds on Exports of Sugar Complaint by Brazil,* L/5011 – 27S/69, adopted 10 November 1980.
US – Gasoline	Appellate Body Report, *United States – Standards for Reformulated and Conventional Gasoline*, WT/DS2/AB/R, adopted 20 May 1996.
EC – Hormones	Appellate Body Report, *European Communities - Measures Concerning Meat and Meat Products (Hormones),* WT/DS26/AB/R, adopted 13 February 1998.
Australia – Salmon	Panel Report, *Australia – Measures Affecting Importation of Salmon,* WT/DS18/R, adopted 6 November 1998.
EC – Bananas	Panel Report, *European Communities – Regime for the Importation, Sale and Distribution of Bananas – Recourse to Arbitration by the European Communities under Article 22.6 of the DSU*, WT/DS27/ARB, adopted 9 April 1999.
Brazil – Aircraft	Panel Report, *Brazil – Export Financing Programme for Aircraft,* WT/DS46/RW, adopted 28 August 2000.
Indonesia – Automobiles	Panel Report, *Indonesia – Certain Measures Affecting the Automobile Industry,* WT/DS54/R, adopted 23 July 1998.-
Argentina – Textiles and Apparel	Panel Report, *Argentina – Measures affecting Imports of Footwear, Textiles, Apparel and Other Items*, WT/DS56/R, adopted 22 April 1998.
Canada – Aircraft	Panel Report, *Canada – Measures affecting the Exports of Civilian Aircraft,* WT/DS70/R, adopted 20 August 1999.
Canada – Aircraft	Appellate Body Report, *Canada – Measures affecting the Exports of Civilian Aircraft,* WT/DS70/R, adopted 20 August 1999.
Japan – Agricultural Products	Appellate Body Report, *Japan – Measures Affecting Agricultural Products,* WT/DS76/AB/R, adopted 19 March 1999.
Korea – Dairy Safeguards	Appellate Body Report, *Korea – Definitive Safeguard Measure on Imports of Certain Dairy Products*, WT/DS98/AB/R, adopted 12 January 2000.
Canada – Dairy	Appellate Body Report, *Canada – Measures Affecting the Importation of Milk and the Exportation of Dairy Products,* WT/DS103/AB/R, adopted 27 October 1999.
Canada – Dairy (21.5) (II)	Appellate Body Report, *Canada – Measures Affecting the Importation of Milk and the Exportation of Dairy Products,* WT/DS103/AB/RW, adopted 17 January 2003.
US – FSC	Appellate Body Report, *United States – Tax Treatment for "Foreign Sales Corporation",* WT/DS108/AB/R, adopted 20 March 2000.
Australia – Leather	Panel Report, *Australia – Subsidies Provided to Producers and Exporters of Automotive Leather,* WT/DS126/R, adopted 16 June 1999.
Australia – Leather (21.5)	Panel Report, *Australia – Subsidies Provided to Producers and Exporters of Automotive Leather,* WT/DS126/RW, adopted 11 February 2000.
US – 1916 Act	Appellate Body Report, *United States – Anti-Dumping Act of 1916,* WT/DS136/AB/R, adopted 26 September 2000.

Short Title	Full Case and Citation
US – Wheat Gluten	Panel Report, *United States – Definitive Safeguard Measures on Imports of Wheat Gluten from the European Communities,* WT/DS166/R, adopted 19 January 2001.
US – Wheat Gluten	Panel Report, *United States – Definitive Safeguard Measures on Imports of Wheat Gluten from the European Communities,* WT/DS166/R, adopted 19 January 2001.
Chile – Agricultural Products (Price Band)	Appellate Body Report, *Chile- Price Band System and Safeguard Measures Relating to Certain Agricultural Products,* WT/DS207/AB/R, adopted 23 October 2002.
US – CVD's on EC Products	Appellate Body Report, *United States – Countervailing Duties on EC Products,* WT/DS212/AB/R, adopted 8 January 2003.
Canada – Aircraft II	Panel Report, *Canada – Measures Affecting the Export of Civilian Aircraft,* WT/DS222/R, adopted 19 February 2002.
EC – Sardines	Appellate Body Report, *European Communities – Trade Description of Sardines,* WT/DS231/AB/R, adopted 23 October 2002.
EC – Sardines	Panel Report, *European Communities – Trade Description of Sardines,* WT/DS231/R, adopted 23 October 2002.
Japan – Apples	Appellate Body Report, *Japan – Measures affecting the Importation of Apples,* WT/DS245/AB/R, adopted 10 December 2003.

1. INTRODUCTION AND SUMMARY

1. Brazil and the Panel have repeatedly requested information from the United States regarding the amount of four different types of contract payments to upland cotton producers. The Panel requested this information *five* months ago, in August 2003, and again in October 2003, in December 2003 and, finally, in January 2004. Brazil first requested this information in November 2002. This information is relevant to the "peace clause" portion of the dispute. It would have permitted the Panel to determine with considerable accuracy the amount of support provided to upland cotton from PFC, market loss assistance, direct and counter-cyclical payment subsidies. After repeatedly denying for over *thirteen* months that it even collected or maintained the payment information, the United States finally acknowledged in its 18/19 December 2003 and 20 January 2004 Letters to the Panel that USDA collected, compiled, and organized all data that would permit an allocation of the amount of contract payments received by producers of upland cotton for MY 1999-2002. Regrettably, even after admitting it has this highly relevant information, the United States refuses to produce the data. Accordingly, Brazil has no choice but to request the Panel to draw adverse inferences from the refusal of the United States to produce this data.

2. In this document, Brazil first describes in Section 2 the factual background and the purposes behind its various requests for contract payment information. In Section 3, Brazil details exactly what the United States produced (and did not produce) on 18/19 December 2003 when it "scrambled" farm-specific data and refused to produce other types of data. Brazil then addresses in Section 4 the *post hoc* and invalid US arguments that the farm-specific information is

"confidential" under US law. In Section 5, Brazil sets forth the relevant WTO jurisprudence interpreting Article 13.1 of the DSU, which requires Members to produce even confidential information when so requested by panels. In Sections 6-8, Brazil then makes its request for the Panel to draw adverse inferences that the withheld information would show contract payments higher than those estimated in Brazil's 14/16th methodology, and that, therefore, the Panel should find that the United States has no peace clause protection. In Sections 9 and 10, Brazil attempts to use the summary information provided by the United States on 18/19 December 2003, together with a number of assumptions, to apply Brazil's methodology for calculating the amount of the contract payments, as well as to perform the methodology advanced by the United States. The results of this analysis each support the amount of allocated payments, as calculated using Brazil's 14/16th methodology. Finally, in Section 11, Brazil demonstrates that the *Japan – Agricultural Products* decision relied on by the United States is inapplicable.

2. BRAZIL'S REQUEST FOR INFORMATION AS POSED BY THE PANEL ON 8 DECEMBER 2003 AND 12 JANUARY 2004

3. Brazil's request for information is set out in Exhibit Bra-369. Brazil requested "farm-specific data to determine the amount of cotton planted on contract base acreage during marketing year 1999-2002." The purpose of Brazil's request for contract acreage and planted acreage data for each farm producing upland cotton was to obtain actual data to permit as exact an allocation as possible of contract payments (from both upland cotton as well as other programme crop base acreage) to current producers of upland cotton. This farm-specific base and planting information (together with requested yield base information) would have permitted the calculation of the amount of support to upland cotton from contract payments by combining two different components of support:(a) *upland cotton* contract payments to current producers of upland cotton, and (b) *other crop* contract payments to current producers of upland cotton. These payments would then be allocated to the current plantings of upland cotton on the farm and, finally, aggregated.[1] This would help the Panel in determining the amount of contract payments that constitute "support to" upland cotton, within the meaning of Article 13(b)(ii) of the Agreement on Agriculture, and to decide on the peace clause. Finally, to a large extent, the requested information would have also permitted the Panel to apply the (incorrect) US-proposed methodology for calculating the amount of "benefit" from these subsidies to current upland cotton producers.

---

1 *See* Brazil's 20 January 2004 Answers to Additional Questions, paras. 43-55.

4. Brazil first requested this information in November 2002.[2] The Panel requested it in August, October, and December 2003, as well as in January 2004.[3] Faced with repeated US denials that it "maintained" such information, Brazil offered its so-called "14/16th" methodology during the peace clause phase of this dispute.[4] Because Brazil conclusively learned in late November 2003 (*inter alia via* the rice FOIA request[5]) that the United States had falsely stated that it did not maintain contract and planted acreage information for each farm, it sought the information detailed in Exhibit Bra-369 to confirm further its 14/16th methodology, which was already supported by a large amount of circumstantial evidence. In effect, Brazil sought to *replace* the 14/16th methodology with a methodology using actual farm-specific data that would provide precise information that the Panel could rely on in making its determination of the amount of support to upland cotton.[6] There is no question that the information withheld by the United States would have been the best information for allocating contract payments that constitute support to upland cotton.

5. Based on its experience working with the data produced in the rice FOIA request, Brazil knew how easy it is to use the computerized farm-specific data to perform the necessary calculations and present the evidence in a summary form. As the Panel could see from the computerized rice data displayed during the meeting on 3 December 2003, this farm-specific data permits the ready calculation of the amount of contract payment support provided to upland cotton producers. Brazil had an entire team ready on 18 December 2003 (and on 20 January 2004) to perform these operations quickly. Brazil had intended to present the evidence in a *summary* form (obviously not in a farm-specific form) for its Answers to Questions on 22 December 2003. But as described below, unlike

[2] Exhibit Bra-101 (Questions for the Purpose of Consultations, Questions 3.4, 3.5, 3.13, 3.14 and 11.2). Brazil has made a similar request during the Annex V procedure, during which the United States refused to participate (Exhibit Bra-49 (Brazil's Questions for the Purpose of the Annex V Procedure, Questions 3.8 – 3.10)). Brazil reiterated its request in note 411 of its 24 June 2003 First Submission.

[3] 25 August 2003 Communication from the Panel, Question 67*bis*; 13 October 2003 Communication from the Panel, Question 125(9); 8 December 2003 Communication from the Panel, second bulled point; 12 January 2004 Communication from the Panel, p. 1.

[4] Brazil's 11 August 2003 Answers to Questions 60 and 67.

[5] Brazil's request in Exhibit Bra-369 was modeled on a very similar request regarding rice made by a private US citizen who received rice farm-specific information as set out in Exhibit Bra-368. The rice FOIA request resulted in the production of farm-specific acreage information showing (a) the amount of rice contract acreage and (b) the amount of planted rice acreage for the entirety of rice farms between MY 1996-2002. (As noted in Exhibit Bra-368 (Second Statement of Christopher Campbell – Environmental Working Group, para. 6), more than 99.5 per cent of rice acreage planted is accounted for in the data provided in response to this FOIA request. The data on rice base acreage is naturally complete.) This farm-specific information allowed the easy tabulation of precise aggregate amounts of payments received by current rice producers between MY 1999-2002. Brazil presented the non-confidential *aggregate* rice information to the Panel in Exhibit Bra-368. This aggregated data demonstrates the absurdity of the US claim that the rice (or cotton) *aggregate* data is somehow "confidential."

[6] Brazil's 20 January 2004 Answers to Additional Questions, paras. 43-55. Brazil also sought the information to rebut the US argument that under its "value" allocation methodology that the amount of support to upland cotton would be much smaller.

USDA's response to the rice FOIA request, the United States intentionally "scrambled" the farm-specific information to make it useless for purposes of the comparison sought by the Panel and Brazil, i.e., for calculating the allocated contract payment figures (which the Panel had requested the United States to provide, *inter alia*, in response to Question 67*bis* on 27 August 2003).

6. On 12 January 2004, the Panel again requested the United States to produce the data, and offered the United States the option to (1) produce the data using "substitute farm numbers which still permit data-matching," and (2) to arrange for special confidentiality procedures.[7] In its 20 January 2004 Letter to the Panel, the United States refused again to provide the information.[8]

3. THE UNITED STATES 18/19 DECEMBER 2003 AND 20 JANUARY 2004 RESPONSES TO THE PANEL'S AND BRAZIL'S REQUEST FOR INFORMATION9

7. The first and fundamental conclusion from the US 18 December 2003 Letter and the accompanying data is that the United States admits, for the first time, that it collects, maintains, and can readily analyze whether every farm planting upland cotton is doing so on contract base acreage. It admits that it knows how many farms planted upland cotton in MY 1999-2002.[10] It admits that it knows the amount of acreage for each farm that planted upland cotton.[11] It admits that it knows the number of upland cotton contract acres planted to upland cotton.[12] It admits that it knows the amount of non-upland cotton contract

---

7 *See* 12 January 2004 Communication from the Panel.

8 *See* US 20 January 2004 Letter to the Panel, p. 3.

9 Brazil notes that the United States provided the MY 2002 data on 19 December (one day after the deadline set by the Panel). When Brazil refers to the 18 December data, any such reference includes the MY 2002 data provided on 19 December.

10 *See* Electronic PFC and DCP Summary Files provided by the United States on 18 and 19 December 2003 respectively. These files contain summarized data based on farm-specific data that is grouped in three categories: (1) farms producing upland cotton and holding upland cotton base, (2) farms not producing upland cotton but holding upland cotton base, and (3) farms producing upland cotton but not holding upland cotton base. Categories (1) and (2) would be relevant in this respect.

11 *See* Electronic Planted Acreage Files for MY 1999-2001 and MY 2002 provided by the United States on 18 and 19 December 2003 respectively offering farm-specific information but no farm-identifying information. *See* also Electronic PFC and DCP Summary Files provided by the United States on 18 and 19 December respectively offering summary information.

12 This information would result from matching the farm-specific information on contract acreage and planted acreage. The United States withheld the farm identification number for the acreage information so that Brazil and the Panel are unable to match the information provided and to generate this information. However, the United States performed this exercise as can be seen from the electronic PFC and DCP Summary Files provided by the United States on 18 and 19 December 2003 respectively. Had the United States not matched the information, it would have been impossible to group the farms into the three categories for which summary information is provided: (1) farms planting upland cotton and holding upland cotton contract base acreage, (2) farms not planting upland cotton but holding upland cotton contract base acreage, and (3) farms planting upland cotton and not holding upland cotton contract base acreage.

acreage planted to upland cotton.[13] And it admits that it knows the yield information for each farm with contract acreage.[14] Indeed, it admits that it knows the amount of contract payments received by each current producer of upland cotton.[15]

8. In other words, the United States *knows* today, and it knew on 18 December 2003 and on 20 January 2004, exactly how many dollars of contract payments were paid to producers of upland cotton during MY 1999-2002. Moreover, the United States, at a minimum, had the information necessary to make all payment calculations for MY 1999-2001 in November 2002 when Brazil first requested it.[16] And the United States had this information for MY 1999-2002 in August 2003, in October 2003, in December 2003, and in January 2004 when the Panel requested its production.[17]

9. The Panel can readily see from the US three-page description of the data it presented on 18 December 2003 that the data provided prevents any farm-specific analysis that would permit the calculation under either of the allocation methodologies advanced by the parties in this dispute. On page 2, the United States states that it is producing "*second*, a farm-by-farm file (with particular farm identification information) with all the requested data (plus additional data regarding payment quantities) *but not including planted acres and cropland.*"[18] Further, the United States states that it is producing "[t]hird, farm-by-farm files for planted acres ... *with the order of the farms scrambled in order to prevent any matching of farms.*"[19] In short, the United States admits that it does not "provide planted acreage information associated with an individual farm."[20] Translated, this means that neither the Panel nor Brazil can use the provided information to calculate the amount of contract payments made to *all* farms producing upland cotton and allocate the support to upland cotton. Brazil has explained this briefly in its 22 December 2003 Answers to Questions.[21]

10. While the United States provided a considerable amount of farm-specific data, the fact that it scrambled the data on plantings made any matching of contract base and current planting data impossible, and renders all data useless for purposes of producing any conclusive figures under any legitimate allocation

---

13 This results from the information discussed in the previous note. It is the residual category of the amount of upland cotton planted in any marketing year minus the amount planted on upland cotton base.

14 *See* Electronic PFC and DCP Files including yield information. The United States used the farm-specific yield information to provide summaries of payment units for each crop in each of the three categories for the contained in the PFC and DCP Summary Files provided on 18 and 19 December 2003 respectively.

15 This would be the result of multiplying the farm-specific payment units for each programme crop on each farm that plants upland cotton by the respective payment rate for the programme crop in that marketing year.

16 Brazil's 18 November 2003 Further Rebuttal Submission, paras. 36-40.

17 Brazil's 18 November 2003 Further Rebuttal Submission, paras. 36-41.

18 US 18 December 2003 Letter to the Panel, p. 2 (emphasis and underlining added).

19 *Ibid.*

20 US 18 December 2003 Letter to the Panel, p. 2.

21 Brazil's 22 December 2003 Answers to Questions, para. 7.

methodology. Admitting this, the United States then provides aggregate data for three groups of farms:(1) those planting upland cotton and having at least some upland cotton base acreage, (2) those not planting upland cotton but having at least some upland cotton base acreage, and (3) those planting upland cotton and not holding upland cotton base.[22] The United States appears to consider that this summary data could serve as a substitute for the farm-specific information.[23] This is fundamentally wrong.

11. The United States states as follows in its 20 January 2004 Letter to the Panel:

> [T]he information relevant to the Panel's assessment *would not be farm-specific data* but rather some *aggregation* of data to permit this "assessment of ... total expenditures." As noted above, the United States has provided both farm-specific and aggregated contract data that would permit an assessment of total expenditures of decoupled payments to farms planting upland cotton. [24]
>
> Further, the United States has provided both farm-specific and aggregated contract data that would permit the Panel to make the assessment it identifies, that is, an assessment of total expenditures of decoupled payments to farms planting upland cotton. [25]

12. Both the Panel's 12 January 2004 Communication and Exhibit Bra-369 are clear that the United States was required to produce farm-specific information, on the basis of which the allocation of contract payments as support to upland cotton could be performed. The Panel's 12 January 2004 Communication states:

> [T]he Panel requests the United States to provide the *same data* that it agreed to provide in its letters dated 18 and 22 December 2003 but in a format which permits matching of *farm-specific* information on contract payments with *farm-specific* information on plantings. The Panel considers it both necessary and appropriate to

22 *See* Electronic PFC and DCP Summary Files provided by the United States on 18 and 19 December 2003 respectively.

23 US 20 January 2004 Letter to the Panel, p. 2. ("the United States notes that it has previously provided data that permits calculation of "total expenditures" for all decoupled payments made to farms planting upland cotton with respect to historical base acres (whether upland cotton base acres or otherwise). In particular, for the production flexibility contract payment era, we provided a farm-by-farm file ("Pfcby.txt") with base acreage and yield data for all programme crops for all "cotton farms" as defined in BRA-369 and data file ("Pfcsum.xls") that aggregated this data for ease of use. The "programme payment units" field allows for easy calculation of "total expenditures" to farms planting upland cotton in any given year by multiplying payment units by the applicable payment rate. Similarly, for the direct and counter-cyclical payment era, the United States provided a farm-by-farm file ("Dcpby.txt") with base acreage and yield data and an aggregate data file ("Dcpsum.xls"). Again, the "programme payment units" field allows for easy calculation of total expenditures by multiplying payment units by the applicable payment rate. Thus, the data already provided by the United States to Brazil and the Panel would permit an assessment of total expenditures of decoupled payments to farms planting upland cotton.") (notes omitted).

24 US 20 January 2004 Letter to the Panel, p. 3-4 (emphasis added).

25 US 20 January 2004 Letter to the Panel, p. 4.

seek this information in a suitable format in order to undertake its mandate to assist the DSB in discharging its responsibilities under the DSU and the covered agreements.[26]

13. There is a fundamental reason why the US summary (non-farm specific) data does *not* allow for an allocation of support to upland cotton in any given marketing year. To obtain undistorted results, any allocation calculation has to be done on the basis of *individual farms*. Aggregating farm-specific data does not generate the correct amount of contract payments to be allocated to upland cotton. On the contrary, using the aggregate data provided by the United States to allocate payments will inevitably trigger distortions of the results due to an aggregation problem. This problem is illustrated by considering two cotton farms with the following combination of upland cotton base and current upland cotton plantings.

	Farm 1	**Farm 2**
Cotton Base	99 acres	1 acre
Cotton Plantings	1 acre	99 acres
Aggregate Cotton Base	100 acres	
Aggregate Cotton Plantings	100 acres	
Suggested Aggregate Cotton Plantings on Cotton Base	100 acres	
Actual Cotton Plantings On Cotton Base	1 acre	1 acre
Real Aggregate Cotton Plantings on Cotton Base Acreage	2 acres	

Farm 1 plants 99 acres of upland cotton and has 1 upland cotton base acre. Farm 2 plants 1 acre of upland cotton and has 99 upland cotton base acres. In the aggregate, there are 100 acres of upland cotton planted and 100 upland cotton base acreage – a perfect match suggesting that 100 per cent of the upland cotton is planted on upland cotton base. The underlying farm-specific data reveals, however, that this is not the case. Both farms only plant 1 upland cotton acre on upland cotton base. Thus, the real aggregate upland cotton planting on upland cotton base is only 2 acres – not 100 acres. The remaining upland cotton acreage may be planted on some other crop base acreage – as the information requested by the Panel and Brazil would have established.

14. This example demonstrates that using aggregate data to allocate contract payments distorts the results, possibly to a considerable extent. Without non-scrambled farm-specific data (exclusively controlled by the United States), it is impossible to assess how severe this problem is. More importantly, the same aggregation problem arises when other crop plantings and crop base acreages are considered. This increases the possible distortion that stems from the analysis of aggregate data and makes any judgement as to the direction of the distortion (over- or under-stating the results) impossible.

15. It follows from the discussions above that it is also necessary to have farm-specific data for any allocation exercise. It is only these farm-specific data that allow for farm-specific payment allocations, which, in turn, can be aggre-

[26] 12 January 2004 Communication from the Panel, p. 1 (emphasis added).

gated to "total expenditures."[27] Contrary to the US assertions,[28] aggregate data will not suffice. In sum, despite its numerous assertions on 18 December 2003 and 20 January 2004 to the contrary, the United States failed to provide the requested data.

16. In addition to not providing usable farm-specific planted acreage data, the United States also refused to provide other information requested by the Panel and Brazil.

17. First, the Panel and Brazil also requested the United States to produce farm-specific data on the amount of other contract crop base acreage on farms producing upland cotton with *no* upland cotton base acreage. But the United States refused to provide this information – even in summary form.[29] Although the United States claims otherwise in its 20 January 2004 Letter,[30] the summary files, in fact, do *not* contain data on contract payments to farms that plant upland cotton but do not have upland cotton base.[31] The fact that farms do not have any contract base for upland cotton cannot mean that no such farms have any base acreage whatsoever, which the US-produced data appears to suggest. To the contrary, at least some of these farms are likely to have contract base for other crops, such as rice, corn, and wheat, among others. Because the United States withheld that information, Brazil and the Panel would need to make assumptions on the amount of contract payments received by farms in this third category. Any such assumptions necessarily distort the resulting allocation of contract payments that constitute support to upland cotton.

18. It appears that the reason for the US refusal to provide even summary data on non-upland cotton contract base acreage for these farms stems from the erroneous US argument that Brazil has only challenged upland cotton contract payments made to current producers of upland cotton.[32] The United States concludes, therefore, that it is inappropriate for Brazil to allocate contract payments made to producers of upland cotton producing on other types of base acreage.[33] This refusal is based on an entirely flawed legal argument. In fact, the Panel's terms of reference include the following broad references to contract payments:

> Subsidies and domestic support provided under [the 2002 FSRI Act] ... related to ... direct payments, counter-cyclical payments ... that provide direct or indirect support to the US upland cotton industry.[34]
>
> Subsidies and domestic support provided under [the 1996 FAIR Act] ... relating to ... production flexibility contract payments ...

27 12 January 2004 Communication from the Panel, p. 1.

28 US 20 January 2004 Letter to the Panel, p. 2-4.

29 *See* Electronic PFC and CCP Summary Files provided by the United States on 18 and 19 December 2003 respectively (Information on contract base of farms in the third category).

30 US 20 December Letter to the Panel, p. 2.

31 *See* Electronic PFC and CCP Summary Files provided by the United States on 18 and 19 December 2003 respectively (Information on contract base of farms in the third category).

32 US 2 December 2003 Oral Statement, para. 31.

33 *Ibid.*

34 WT/DS267/7, p. 2.

providing direct or indirect support to the US upland cotton industry.[35]

Subsidies provided under the [1998-2001 Appropriation Acts, i.e., market loss assistance subsidies][36]

19. These terms of reference in Brazil's request for the establishment of a panel are not limited in any way to contract payments made on upland cotton base acres. Brazil listed *contract payments* (unqualified) providing support to the US upland cotton industry, *not upland cotton contract payments* providing support to the US upland cotton industry. Indeed, the reference to "indirect" subsidies is more than broad enough to encompass any type of payment, including payments made from non-upland cotton base acreage. In addition, Brazil's allocation methodology always has included payments made to producers of upland cotton on non-upland cotton base acreage.[37] In short, the US argument ignores the Panel's terms of reference, evidences a misunderstanding of Brazil's allocation methodology, and a misunderstanding of the Panel's and Brazil's requests for information.[38] (As with the other data the United States refuses to produce, Brazil discusses, in Section 5 below, how this constitutes a violation of the US obligations under Article 13.1 of the DSU to cooperate in a panel proceeding.[39])

20. Second, the United States has not provided the requested data for *market loss assistance payments* received by the farms listed for MY 1999-2001. Therefore, the Panel and Brazil would have to make assumptions about the amount of market loss assistance payments that constitute support to upland cotton, based on the information about PFC payments that constitute support to upland cotton. This might distort the results. Further, since market loss assistance payments were also made for soybean base (that otherwise was not eligible to receive PFC payments), this allocation methodology may significantly underestimate the amount of market loss assistance payments that constitute support to upland cotton.[40] In its 20 January 2004 Letter, the United States appears to recognize that market loss assistance payments were within the scope of the Panel's request.[41] It also implies that it has provided the information – at the very least on an aggregate basis.[42] The fact, however, remains that it has not done so.[43]

---

35 *Ibid.*

36 *Ibid.*

37 Brazil's 22 August 2003 Rebuttal Submission, Section 2.2 and particularly paras. 32, 38, 42; Brazil's 27 October 2003 Answers to Questions, para. 40; Brazil's 18 November 2003 Further Rebuttal Submission, paras. 2, 17, 50.

38 Exhibit Bra-369 (Brazil's Request to the United States for Farm-Specific Planting and Base Acreage Data).

39 *See* Section 5.

40 The Electronic DCP Summary File demonstrates that farms growing upland cotton in MY 2002 (categories I and III) also grow a significant amount of soybeans, this would have been eligible for a considerable amount of market loss assistance payments in MY 1999-2001 (for which no such data is available).

41 US 20 January 2004 Letter to the Panel, p. 2.

42 US 20 January 2004 Letter to the Panel, p. 2 ("In particular, for the production flexibility contract payment era, we provided a farm-by-farm file ("Pfcby.txt") with base acreage and yield data for all programme crops for all "cotton farms" as defined in BRA-369 and data file ("Pfcsum.xls") that

21. Third, Brazil notes that the 19 December 2003 US data concerning MY 2002 does not contain any information regarding the amount of direct and counter-cyclical payments made on peanut base.[44] As with the missing information on market loss assistance payments (specifically the soybean payment information), the missing data on peanut contract payments for MY 2002 would cause lower aggregate payments allocated as support to upland cotton.[45] It follows that any such figures would lead to understating the real support to upland cotton by an amount unknown to Brazil.

22. The United States asserts that the summary data it provided allows for the "easy calculation" of "total expenditures of decoupled payments to farms planting upland cotton."[46] This is simply not true. The table below presents Brazil's calculations of total contract payments to farms that actually produce upland cotton in as far as they were "easy" to perform.[47] The table also reflects the holes in the US summary data described above. These holes prevent any "easy," or even "difficult," calculation of the amount of contract payments to upland cotton farms. Only by making a number of assumptions, as detailed in Sections 9 and 10 below, can the incomplete summary data be used.

---

aggregated this data for ease of use.[42] The "programme payment units" field allows for easy calculation of "total expenditures" to farms planting upland cotton in any given year by multiplying payment units by the applicable payment rate. Similarly, for the direct and counter-cyclical payment era, the United States provided a farm-by-farm file ("Dcpby.txt") with base acreage and yield data and an aggregate data file ("Dcpsum.xls").[42] Again, the "programme payment units" field allows for easy calculation of total expenditures by multiplying payment units by the applicable payment rate.").

43 *See* Electronic PFC Summary File, which contains no information on soybean base for market loss assistance payments and no information on possible discrepancies between PFC base and market loss assistance base for the other PFC crops.

44 Exhibit US-112.

45 The President of the National Cotton Council testified to Congress in 2001 that he grew primarily cotton and peanuts. Exhibit Bra-41 (Congressional Hearing, "The Future of the Federal Farm Commodity Programmes (Cotton)," House of Representatives, 15 February 2001, p. 2). Peanuts are generally grown in the Southern states of the United States, where also cotton is grown. Therefore, it is likely that many cotton farms have also peanut base, which is a high per-acre payment base.

46 US 20 January 2004 Letter to the Panel, p. 3-4.

47 Brazil has omitted the third category of farms, for which the United States has presented data (farms not planting upland cotton but holding upland cotton base), as those farms do not produce upland cotton. Therefore, any contract payments received by these farms cannot be "support to" upland cotton.

Subsidy Programme	Farms Planting Cotton and Holding Cotton Base	Farms Planting Cotton and Not Holding Cotton Base[1]	Total Payments
Marketing Year 1999			
PFC Payments MLA Payments[2]	$695,912,510[48] ?	? ?	? ?
Marketing Year 2000			
PFC Payments MLA Payments[2]	$650,579,667[49] ?	? ?	? ?
Marketing Year 2001			
PFC Payments MLA Payments[2]	$520,230,908[50] ?	? ?	? ?
Marketing Year 2002			
Direct Payments[3] CCP Payments[3]	$619,049,305[51] $1,062,580,729[52]	? ?	? ?

[1] The United States has not provided any information on contract payments to farms that plant upland cotton, but do not hold any upland cotton base in its summary files.

[2] The United States has not provided specific information on market loss assistance payments. In particular, any information on soybean payments to upland cotton farms is missing.

[3] Brazil recalls that the United States withheld information on peanut base payment, thus, these figures are in all likelihood understated.

23. As the Panel can readily see, the only "easy to calculate" payment figures are the PFC, DP and CCP payments figures to farms planting upland cotton and holding upland cotton base (with the DP and CCP payment figures being understated due to the peanut base issue). The other payment figures relating to all market loss assistance payments, and to farms that plant upland cotton but hold only non-upland cotton base cannot be calculated, because the United States produced no data.

24. These calculations are, however, only one step to allocating the amount of contract payments that are actually support to "upland cotton." As Brazil has detailed above, any allocation of "support to" upland cotton has to be performed on a farm-specific basis, to avoid aggregation problems. Any calculation using the US summary data will further distort the results by due to its incompleteness, as demonstrated by the table above.

25. In sum, the fundamental shortcomings in the scrambled and incomplete data provided by the United States on 18 and 19 December 2003 render it unusable for purposes of Brazil's allocation methodology, discussed below,[53] and, for that matter, any allocation methodology.

26. While the United States argued in its 20 January 2004 Letter that the summary data it provided was useful for calculating the amount of contract acre-

---

[48] *See* Exhibit Bra-424 (Allocation Calculations Based on US Methodology and US Summary Data) for the details of the calculation. (Also provided electronically as 'allocation calculations.xls').

[49] *Ibid.*

[50] *Ibid.*

[51] *Ibid.*

[52] *Ibid.*

[53] *See* Section 3 below.

age that constitutes support to upland cotton[54], the Panel must realize that this is – at best – "second-best" evidence, which, due to all the shortcomings just discussed, only allows for distorted calculation results, heavily depending on assumptions.

27. Nevertheless, because the redacted, scrambled and incomplete US data is what was produced, Brazil has attempted to use it.[55] In particular, in Section 9, Brazil has attempted to use the summary data provided by the United States on 18 and 19 December 2003 to allocate contract payments that constitute support to upland cotton, within the meaning of Article 13(b)(ii) of the Agreement on Agriculture.[56] Due to the limitations of the data discussed above, Brazil was required to make a number of critical assumptions. None of Brazil's assumptions would have been necessary had the United States produced the requested complete farm-specific information within its exclusive control. Therefore, Brazil cautions against the use of these results. However, Brazil offers these calculations as further circumstantial evidence that its 14/16th methodology is reasonable.

28. In Section 10, Brazil has also attempted to use the US data to perform the US-proposed methodology of allocating contract payments over the total value of the crops produced on the farms producing upland cotton.[57] Brazil strongly disagrees with the US position that such an allocation is required under Part III of the SCM Agreement and GATT Article XVI.[58] Similarly, although Brazil

---

54 US 20 January 2004 Letter to the Panel, p. 2.

55 Brazil notes that the data provided by the United States appears to be complete, as shown by the following table:

MY	Contract Acres (US Data)	Contract Acres (USDA)	Percentage	Planted Acres (US Data)	Planted Acres (USDA)	Percentage
1999	16,416,399.4	16.4 million	100 %	14,572,963.5	14.584 million	99.92 %
2000	16,306,696.2	16.3 million	100 %	15,388,002.9	15.347 million	100.26 %
2001	16,245,896.4	16.2 million	100 %	15,463,934.5	15.499 million	99.77 %
2002	18,558,304.2	not yet reported	-	13,541,505.9	13.714 million	98.74 %

Sources:

Contract Acres (USDA): Exhibit Bra-394 (Agricultural Outlook Tables, USDA, November 2003, Table 19.

Planted Acres (USDA): MY 1999-2001: Exhibit Bra-4 ("Fact Sheet: Upland Cotton," USDA, January 2003, p. 4); MY 2002: Exhibit US-95. Contract Acres (US Data) and Planted Acres (US Data) are taken from the Electronic PFC and DCP Summary Files provided by the United States on 18 and 19 December respectively.

56 *See* Section 9 below. Brazil has applied publicly available information on the payment rates for the contract crops in the marketing yeas concerned (*see* Exhibit Bra-394 (Agricultural Outlook Tables, USDA, November 2003, Table 19).

57 *See* Section 10 below.

58 *See* Brazil's 18 November 2003 Further Rebuttal Submission, Section 3.5 and Brazil's 2 December 2003 Oral Statement, Section 3.

cautions against relying on Brazil's results from applying the US-proposed methodology[59] due to the limitations of the data and the resulting assumptions it had to make, the results would indicate that Brazil's 14/16th methodology generates fairly similar results.

4. THE US ASSERTIONS OF CONFIDENTIALITY ARE BASELESS

29. The United States attempts to justify its "scrambling" of the acreage data on the grounds that it is "confidential" data barred by the US Privacy Act.[60] A close examination of the facts, including the federal court precedent that binds USDA's administrative actions, shows that the farm-specific acreage data requested by the Panel and Brazil are not confidential.[61]

30. The primary basis for the US confidentiality assertion is an 11 April 2002 USDA FOIA decision concerning *FOOS Farm* (Exhibit US-104). This non-appealed USDA decision stands for the fairly narrow proposition that a FOIA request for a single farm's planting records is an invasion of privacy rights of that farm's operator. In that decision, USDA found that the "release of the number of acres farmed by FOOS Farms would not contribute significantly to public understanding of the operations and activities of FSA."[62]

31. As the USDA *FOOS Farm* decision in Exhibit US-104 demonstrates, there is clearly a difference between a FOIA request for a single farm's acreage data and an across-the-board request for all acreage information – such as that set out in Brazil's 3 December request, and in the rice FOIA request. USDA – and USTR – are bound by US federal court decisions that made exactly this distinction. The leading case is US district court decision in *Washington Post v. United States Department of Agriculture,* 943 F. Supp. 31 (D.D.C. 1996).[63] In that case, the federal court rejected USDA's arguments that the Privacy Act prevented it from producing information on the US cotton programme, including over $1 billion in marketing loan payments, Step 2 payments, and deficiency payments, among others, to US cotton farmers. The court found that there were no violations of privacy rights of US cotton farmers from the "disclosure of names, addresses, and payments that commodity programme recipients received."[64] A close reading of the decision highlights the illegitimacy of the *post hoc* US assertions of confidentiality raised in this dispute. Consider the following passages from the decision:

> The nature of the list [names, addresses, amount of subsidies] sought by plaintiff in this case does not create the same sort of personal privacy concerns or invite the kind of unwarranted intrusion

[59] *See* Section 10 below.
[60] US 18 December 2003 Letter to the Panel, p. 1-2.
[61] *See* also 12 January 2004 Communication from the Panel, p. 1.
[62] Exhibit US-104, p. 2.
[63] Cited in Exhibit US-104, p. 2.
[64] Exhibit Bra-418 (Washington Post v. United States Department of Agriculture, 943 F.Supp. 31 (D.D.C. 1996, p. 5).

> that would justify nondisclosure. The only individualized information that would be ascertainable from the release of the list is that a particular individual grows cotton, the address of the farm where the cotton is grown and where the subsidy is received, and how much of a subsidy that cotton farmer received in 1993. *It might also be deduced from the amount of the subsidy how much cotton the producer grew in 1993.* The Court is unable to discern, nor have defendants persuasively explained, how any of this relatively generic information about thousands of similarly situated business people could constitute clearly unwarranted invasions of their personal privacy. *Indeed, it is precisely because the list is so large and the information so generic that the impact on privacy interests are so small.*[65]

32. The court went on to note that there was a strong public interest in the disclosure of the information, rejecting USDA's arguments that the data "pertaining to the cotton programme recipients would not shed any light on the workings of the agency and that therefore there is no public interest in its disclosure." [66]The court found (in language that is particularly applicable to this WTO dispute) that "a significant public interest lies in shedding light on the workings of the Department of Agriculture and the administration of this massive subsidy programme, and plaintiffs have persuasively demonstrated how the release of the recipients names, addresses and subsidy amounts could illuminate the USDA's actions."[67] Thus, despite the Privacy Act of 1974, the court ordered USDA to turn over the farm-specific information.

33. A 1999 US federal court decision in *Hill v. United States Department of Agriculture* found there was a privacy interest in instances where the FOIA request sought information on loans made to an individual borrower. Citing the *Washington Post* case, the court reasoned that because the information related to the finances of one closely-held family corporation and not to "tens of thousands of otherwise indistinguishable business people," it found the corporation had a significant privacy interest.[68]

34. In light of this precedent, it is not surprising that USDA's FOIA office in Kansas City (which is USDA's only FOIA office for such data) agreed on 14 November 2003 to provide complete contract base and acreage data in relation to rice. This is because that request covered *all* rice planted acreage and all rice contract acreage. Pursuant to the reasoning in the *Washington Post* case, USDA's FOIA representatives necessarily must have determined that because the request

---

65 Exhibit Bra-418 (Washington Post v. United States Department of Agriculture, 943 F.Supp. 31 (D.D.C. 1996, p. 3)(emphasis added). None of the information at issue this case is stigmatizing, embarrassing, or dangerous; it does not expose these cotton farmers to creditors and nothing about the success or failure of the farm or the wealth or poverty of the recipient.

66 Exhibit Bra-418 (Washington Post v. United States Department of Agriculture, 943 F.Supp. 31 (D.D.C. 1996, p. 3).

67 Exhibit Bra-418 (Washington Post v. United States Department of Agriculture, 943 F.Supp. 31 (D.D.C. 1996, p. 4).

68 Exhibit US-104 *citing Hills v USDA* decision.

did not focus on an individual producer's farm, the interests of the public in understanding and evaluating the operation of the contract payment schemes outweighed any privacy interests. Otherwise, the rice data would never have been released. The *post-hoc* attempt by the United States on 18 December 2003 and 20 January 2004 to argue that this information was provided by "mistake" is simply not credible.

35. Brazil notes, further, that the United States provided no evidence that any mandatory provisions of US law or regulations prevent the production of acreage information. The United States incorrectly argues that the Privacy Act of 1974 prohibits the release of planted acreage information for individual farms.[69] But nothing in the text of the Privacy Act cited by the United States requires this. Indeed, the fact the federal court in *Washington Post* ordered the production of farm-specific payment data shows the fallacy of this US arguments. The *Washington Post* decision teaches that the Privacy Act of 1974 does not function as an inviolate shield to protect individual crop planting data with no exception other than the written permission of each US farmer, as the United States incorrectly asserts.

36. In fact, the only reference to acreage reports is in what the United States incorrectly characterizes as a "long-standing policy" set out in FSA's FOIA Handbook.[70] But this FOIA "policy" does not constitute a US law mandating confidentiality of planted acreage information. It is only guidance to FOIA officers that obviously can be disregarded by the USDA Secretary or other implementing officials in individual cases. The release of the rice information by USDA's FOIA office on 14 November 2003 demonstrates that this policy guidance is not mandatory. In fact, the statutory FOIA requirements, as interpreted by the US federal courts (as in the *Washington Post* decision) clearly take priority over any internal USDA policy guidance documents. The United States is not barred by any provision of US law, either on its face or as interpreted by US courts, from providing the information requested by the Panel.

37. The evidence cited by the United States in support of its refusal to provide the requested data does not, therefore, support its conclusion that the data cannot be released.[71] In effect, the US government has attempted to create, *post-hoc*, a new mandatory policy for the purposes of this dispute. This blatant attempt to prevent the Panel and Brazil from gaining access to information that was readily supplied to a private US citizen in the case of rice was rejected by the Panel in its 12 January 2004 Communication. Unfortunately, the United States' 20 January 2004 Letter continues this approach.

38. Finally, Brazil notes that even if the USDA FOIA policy "guidance" were set out in a mandatory US statute, the United States could still provide the information requested by the Panel and Brazil without "scrambling" it. As the Panel has noted in its 12 January 2004 Communication, there would have been various

---

69 US 18 December 2003 Letter to the Panel, p.2.

70 Exhibit US-106.

71 *Similarly* 12 January Communication from the Panel, p. 1.

options available to the United States to produce the information in a manner that would have protected the confidentiality rights of US farmers. Brazil made it clear in its 22 December 2004 Answers to Questions that a substitute number protecting the alleged confidentiality rights of farmers would be acceptable.[72] Since neither Brazil nor the Panel has any interest in an individual farm's identity, providing the requested information in such a manner would have provided Brazil and the Panel with the payment information that they have long sought.

39. In its 20 January 2004 Letter, the United States now asserts that no farm-specific data was actually requested, as the Panel has only sought to determine the total amount of contract payments to farms producing upland cotton.[73] However, both the Panel's 12 January 2004 Communication and Exhibit Bra-369 are clear that the United States was required to produce farm-specific information, on the basis of which the allocation of contract payments as support to upland cotton could be performed. And as Brazil has demonstrated above,[74] the initial allocations have to be performed on a farm-specific level to avoid any aggregation problems.

40. The United States did not even provide a complete summary of the data resulting from the farm-specific comparison between planted and contract acreage on an *aggregate* basis.[75] Such summary aggregate information is, of course, not confidential, since it could never reveal the names of any producers, their farms, or the location of the farms. Of course, such a summary document is not a perfect substitute for the complete farm-specific data requested by the Panel. But the US failure to present this obviously non-confidential data highlights its continuing non-justifiable concealment of key information from the Panel and Brazil.

41. Had the United States been willing to cooperate on this issue, it could have either provided the data, as the Panel's 12 January 2004 Communication and Brazil's 22 December Answers to Questions[76] suggested, using a dummy farm number or a consolidated single file for contract and planted acreage (with no farm number),[77] or clarified with Brazil whether there could be a way to address the US confidentiality concern, including throught special procedures for confidential information, as foreseen by Articles 13 and 18 of the DSU.[78] Instead, the United States has simply chosen to refuse to produce the information.

---

[72] Brazil's 22 December 2003 Answers to Questions, para. 7.

[73] US 20 January 2004 Letter to the Panel, p. 3.

[74] *See* Section 3.

[75] Of course, since the United States fails to provide other requested data, even the summary data of the farm-specific data has huge gaps. For example, the United States does not provide data on contract base on farms that have no upland cotton base but may have other crop contract base. Further, the United States does not provide any MY 2002 data on peanut base on whichever type of farm, thus triggering an understatement of the actual support to upland cotton from contract payments, calculated under any allocation methodology. Finally, the United States does not provide information on market loss assistance payments during MY 1999-2001.

[76] Brazil's 22 December 2003 Answers to Questions, para. 7.

[77] The United States was aware that neither Brazil nor presumably the Panel was interested in the farm serial number *per se*.

[78] The Panel has suggested that in its 12 January 2004 Communication as well.

42. Lastly, the United States' 18 December 2003 Letter dramatically calls for Brazil to "return" the rice FOIA request data that was requested and received by a private US citizen.[79] Yet, US federal courts have held that "once records are released, nothing in FOIA prevents the requester from disclosing the information to anyone else."[80] Thus, under US law, the rice data is in the public domain. However, in the spirit of cooperation, Brazil notes that it understands that neither it, nor any person in or formerly in its delegation, or which provided statements to the Panel, currently retains any of this now-public data released by USDA pursuant to its FOIA authority. Moreover, the only information from the rice request used by Brazil in this dispute is set out in Exhibit Bra-368, which reflects *aggregated* data gleaned from the farm-specific comparisons of rice contract acreage with rice planted acreage. Brazil assumes that even the United States would agree that this aggregated data is not confidential.

5. THERE IS NO BASIS UNDER WTO RULES FOR THE UNITED STATES TO WITHHOLD PLANTED ACREAGE INFORMATION ON THE BASIS OF CONFIDENTIALITY

43. As described in Section 4 above, the effect of the "scrambling" of planted acreage and contract acreage data by the United States amounts to withholding information specifically requested by the Panel. Further, the failure of the United States to provide any non-cotton base acreage for the third category of farms,[81] and the failure of the United States to produce any information on market loss assistance payments and peanut direct and counter-cyclical payments, also amounts to withholding the information requested by the Panel.

44. In its 20 January 2004 Letter, the United States now makes the additional argument that it can no longer provide the requested information in an anonymous format,[82] using either a dummy farm number, or providing a consolidated file that would contain both contract acreage and planted acreage, but no farm serial number.[83] According to the United States, this is because it has already provided contract acreage with farm serial numbers, and that, with the additional information requested by the Panel, Brazil would be able to deconstruct the "confidential" farm serial number.[84] This argument is irrelevant, because the United States has an obligation to produce the information, even if it is "confidential."

45. The United States asserts that, pursuant to the US Privacy Act, it cannot release so-called "confidential" farm-specific planted acreage information associated with a particular farm.[85] Nevertheless, despite the alleged bar of the US

---

[79] The United States reiterates its request in its 20 January 2004 Letter to the Panel, p. 3.

[80] *Swan v. SEC,* 96 F.3d 498, No. 95-5376, slip. Op. at 4 *cited in Washington Post,* Exhibit Bra-418, p. 2.

[81] Those that produce upland cotton, but do not have upland cotton contract acreage.

[82] This was suggested by the Panel in its 12 January 2004 Communication.

[83] As suggested by Brazil in its 22 December 2004 Answers to Questions, para. 7.

[84] US 20 January 2004 Letter to the Panel, p. 3.

[85] US 18 December 2003 Letter to the Panel, p. 2.

Privacy Act, the United States produced farm-specific information concerning the contract acreage designating it as "confidential due to its sensitive nature."[86] The United States never explained how it could produce *contract payment information* on a farm-specific basis, which would be protected by WTO confidentiality procedures, but not *farm-specific acreage information*. If the WTO confidentiality procedures are good enough for one set of confidential data, then they must be good enough for another set of "confidential" data.

46. But even accepting, *arguendo*, that the US acreage data is confidential under US law, there is no basis for the United States to argue or assert that the confidentiality of this information would not be protected in these WTO proceedings. Paragraph 3 of the Panel's working procedures states that "Members shall treat as confidential information submitted by another Member to the Panel which that Member has designated as confidential." These working procedures, like DSU Articles 13.1 and 18.1, require information designated as confidential by the United States to be protected as such by both the Panel and Brazil. Nothing in the Panel's working procedures or any other DSU rule suggests that the United States should be concerned that its information would not be protected. Certainly, nothing suggests that the United States may unilaterally withhold or redact requested information on confidentiality grounds. Indeed, the Panel notes in its 12 January 2004 Communication that this information "can be protected under the DSU and our working procedures."[87] Brazil fully agrees.

47. Brazil notes that the US 18 December 2004 Letter also did not request the adoption of any special confidentiality procedures. Nor did the United States attempt to contact Brazil prior to 18 December 2003 to discuss whether Brazil would agree to special procedures for the protection of the allegedly confidential information – procedures that Brazil has agreed to repeatedly in past disputes involving business confidential information.[88] The United States has similarly participated in many earlier WTO disputes in which it has agreed to such procedures.[89] Nor has the United States presented evidence or argument suggesting that existing WTO confidentiality provisions would not fully protect the confidentiality of planted acreage information. It goes without saying that Brazil would have treated such information in a confidential manner, consistent with its obligations under the Panel's working procedures, and Articles 13.1 and 18.1 of the DSU.

48. There is no legal basis under WTO rules for the United States to withhold this information following the Panel's August 2003, October 2003, 3 December 2003 and 12 January 2004 requests that it produce this information. These requests to the United States to produce the information requested by Brazil in

---

[86] US 18 December 2003 Letter to the Panel, p. 3.

[87] 12 January 2004 Communication from the Panel.

[88] Panel Report, *Brazil – Aircraft*, WT/DS46/R, para. 1.10; Panel Report, *Canada – Aircraft*, WT/DS70/R, paras. 9.57 – 59.

[89] Panel Report, *EC – Bananas (22.6) (US)*, WT/DS27/ARB, para. 2.5 (as requested specially by the United States); Panel Report, *Australia – Leather,* WT/DS126/R, para. 4.1; Panel Report, *Australia – Leather (21.5)*,WT/DS126/RW, para. 3.2; Panel Report, *US – Wheat Gluten*, WT/DS166/R, para. 3.1; Panel Report, *Canada – Aircraft*, WT/DS70/R, para. 9.54-56.

Exhibit Bra-369 were made pursuant to the Panel's authority under DSU Article 13.1.

49. The Appellate Body and panels have held that a Member is *required* to provide information – including confidential business information – upon a request made under DSU Article 13.1. The Appellate Body in *Canada – Aircraft* found that WTO Members "are … under a duty and an obligation to 'respond promptly and fully' to requests made by panels for information under Article 13.1 of the DSU."[90] The obligation in DSU Article 13.1 is not limited to only non-confidential information. Indeed, Article 13.1 explicitly anticipates the production of confidential information, providing that "confidential information which is provided shall not be revealed without formal authorization from the individual, body, or authorities of the Member providing the information." As the Appellate Body stated in *Canada – Aircraft*:

> [t]o hold that a Member party to a dispute is not legally bound to comply with a panel's request for information relating to that dispute, is, in effect, to declare that Member legally free to preclude a panel from carrying out its mandate and responsibility under the DSU. So to rule would be to *reduce to an illusion and a vanity the fundamental right of Members to have disputes arising between them resolved through the system and proceedings for which they bargained in concluding the DSU.*[91]

50. The "refusal by a Member to provide information requested of it" has been found by the Appellate Body to "undermine seriously the ability of a panel to make an objective assessment of the facts and the matter, as required by Article 11 of the DSU."[92] The obligation to provide information has been deemed a "requirement for collaboration of the parties in the presentation of the facts and evidence to the panel."[93] Panels have found that "the most important result of the rule of collaboration appears to be that the adversary is obligated to provide the tribunal with relevant documents which are in its sole possession."[94]

51. In *US – Wheat Gluten*, the Appellate Body reaffirmed this "obligation" and "duty" under DSU Article 13.1 to produce all information requested, including information designated as "business confidential." In that case, the United States only agreed to produce to the panel, but not to the EC, information redacted from the public version of a USITC report in a safeguard investigation. The panel in that case proposed three different special procedures for business confidential information, but the United States still refused to make the information available to the EC. The panel indicated that the information withheld "would have facilitated our objective assessment of the facts in this case, and of the matter before us."[95] On appeal, the Appellate Body reaffirmed the "obligation" and "duty" of Members to produce all information, including business con-

---

90 Appellate Body Report, *Canada – Aircraft*, WT/DS70/AB/R, para. 187 (emphasis added).
91 Appellate Body Report, *Canada – Aircraft*, WT/DS70/AB/R, para. 189 (emphasis added).
92 Appellate Body Report, *Canada – Aircraft*, WT/DS70/AB/R, para. 189.
93 Panel Report, *Argentina – Textiles and Apparel,* WT/DS56/R, para. 6.40.
94 *Ibid.*
95 Panel Report, *US – Wheat Gluten*, WT/DS166/R, para. 8.12.

fidential information, to panels when requested under DSU Article 13.1. In affirming the panel's ruling, the Appellate Body stated that it "deplore[d] the conduct of the United States" in refusing to produce business confidential information.[96]

52. The panel in *Canada – Aircraft* similarly emphasized the obligation of a Member under DSU Article 13.1 to provide "highly sensitive business confidential information,"[97] as well as information that Canada claimed was governed by a "Cabinet privilege."[98] Similar to what the United States did in "scrambling" the key information in this case, Canada argued that while it could not provide the confidential "Cabinet privilege" documents, it could provide a summary of the criteria the Government used to award one particular contribution.[99] However, the panel rejected the utility of this proffered information, finding that the information provided by Canada was not sufficient to rebut Brazil's *prima facie* case that Canada had provided export subsidies.[100] In addition, as with the "scrambled" information provided by the United States, the panel noted the uselessness of business confidential information "redacted" by Canada. The panel found it had been so heavily redacted that it was "simply of no value to the panel."[101]

53. As in *Canada – Aircraft,* the US "scrambling" of contract and acreage data effectively "redacted" the information requested by the Panel to such an extent that it cannot be relied on. In addition, the United States' offer to provide "summary" data tabulating the incomplete "scrambled" acreage data on the one hand, and the contract acreage on the other hand, should be rejected by the Panel. As in *Canada – Aircraft*, a party refusing to cooperate under Article 13.1 should not be permitted to selectively present evidence while withholding evidence within its exclusive control that is far more directly relevant. As the panel found in *Canada – Aircraft,* "Canada has outright refused (on the basis of Cabinet privilege) to provide what in the Panel's view are the most relevant of the documentation that it requested regarding the five contributions identified by Brazil."[102] Data permitting the linking of contract and acreage data is similarly the most relevant of the documentation requested by the Panel.

54. The US refusal to provide *certain* allegedly confidential information in this dispute without even seeking special confidentiality provisions[103] (while

---

96 Appellate Body Report, *US – Wheat Gluten*, WT/DS166/AB/R, para. 171.

97 Panel Report, *Canada – Aircraft*, WT/DS70/R, para. 9.293 (Canada's description).

98 Panel Report, *Canada – Aircraft*, WT/DS70/R, para. 9.294.

99 *Ibid.*

100 Panel Report, *Canada – Aircraft*, WT/DS70/R, para. 9.345.

101 *Ibid.*

102 *Ibid.*

103 In addition to DSU Article 13.1, DSU Article 18.2 provides procedures concerning the protection of confidential information. In addition, Article 12.1 of the DSU permits panels to adopt working procedures in addition to those established in the DSU. This would provide private business interests with adequate protection for their business information, if it is considered of sensitive nature. If the US concern was indeed confidentiality, it could have requested the Panel to arrange for the proper procedures to deal with the information the US claims has such a high confidential status, that it cannot be provided to the Panel or Brazil under normal business confidential information procedures.

providing other information it designates as confidential) is completely inconsistent with its arguments before the Appellate Body in *Canada – Aircraft*. In that appeal, the United States argued that "the need for additional procedures for protecting business confidential information is extremely important, because it goes to the viability of WTO dispute settlement as a vehicle for preserving the rights and obligations of Members."[104] Moreover, the United States argued that the application of procedures for protecting business confidential information promotes important objectives, because Members' rights and obligations under the covered agreements can only be preserved if due process is accorded to both the complaining party and the responding party.[105] The United States maintained that "the demands of due process are not satisfied, however, if the absence of such procedures precludes a Member from properly making its case."[106]

55. Finally, while it argues in this case that the 1974 Privacy Act allegedly prevents it from providing the acreage information *in any form,* the United States maintained in *Canada - Aircraft* that "a Member's national laws do not provide a basis for depriving another Member of its rights under the WTO Agreement."[107] In that case, the EC – as a third party – argued that requiring its officials to sign a non-disclosure form as part of special confidentiality procedures set up by the *Canada – Aircraft* panel would violate their duties of disclosure under EC law. In response, the United States argued that the EC's claim that "its officials would be unable, under their staff regulations, to accept the undertaking proposed 'should not be allowed.'"[108]

56. In conclusion, there is no justification under WTO rules for the United States to refuse to produce all of the information sought by the Panel in August 2003, October 2003, and on 3 December 2003 and 12 January 2004. The continuing refusal to provide this highly-relevant information is clear evidence of non-cooperation.

6. THE PANEL SHOULD DRAW ADVERSE INFERENCES FROM THE US FAILURE TO COOPERATE

57. In light of the US failure, in response to the Panel's four requests for information on the amount of contract payments provided to *current* producers of upland cotton, to provide information within its exclusive control, Brazil requests the Panel to draw the following adverse inferences:

- That the application of Brazil's methodology[109] for allocating PFC, MLA, CCP, and DP payments to current producer of upland cotton

Therefore, such procedures could have addressed the US concerns about the confidential nature of the information withheld. The United States has not done so.

104 Appellate Body Report, *Canada – Aircraft*, WT/DS70/AB/R, para. 137.

105 Appellate Body Report, *Canada – Aircraft*, WT/DS70/AB/R, para. 139.

106 *Ibid.*

107 Appellate Body Report, *Canada – Aircraft*, WT/DS70/AB/R, para. 140.

108 Appellate Body Report, *Canada – Aircraft,* WT/DS70/AB/R, paras 135, 140.

109 *See* Brazil's 20 January 2004 Answers to Additional Questions, paras. 43-55.

in each of the marketing years 1999-2002 using data exclusively within the control of the United States would have resulted in payments that were higher than those estimated by Brazil's 14/16th methodology.

- That the application of the US methodology for allocating PFC, MLA, CCP, and DP payments to current producer of upland cotton in each of the marketing years 1999-2002 using data exclusively within the control of the United States would have resulted in payments that were as high or higher than those estimated by Brazil's 14/16th methodology.
- That the information withheld by the United States would have been detrimental to its arguments that PFC, MLA, DP, and CCP payments are not support to upland cotton, within the meaning of Article 13(b)(ii) of the Agreement on Agriculture, or alternatively, "non-product-specific" support.

58. The legal basis for the Panel's drawing *adverse* inferences is found in the Appellate Body's decision in *Canada – Aircraft*, where it found that "the authority to draw adverse inferences from a Member's refusal to provide information belongs *a fortiori* also to panels examining claims of prohibited export subsidies. Indeed, that authority seems to us an ordinary aspect of the task of all panels to determine the relevant facts of any dispute involving any covered agreement: a view supported by the general practice usage of international tribunals."[110] The Appellate Body in *Canada – Aircraft* stated that "if we had been deciding the issue that confronted the panel [when referring to the drawing of adverse inferences] we might have concluded that the facts of the record did warrant the inference that the information Canada withheld included information prejudicial to Canada."[111] The Appellate Body based its "adverse inferences" holding on an interpretation of the DSU and the SCM Agreement, as well as on support from the following international law jurisprudence:

- In *The Corfu Channel Case*, where the International Court of Justice stated that "... the victim of a breach of international law is often unable to furnish direct proof of facts giving rise to responsibility. Such a State should be allowed a more liberal recourse to inferences of fact and circumstantial evidence. This indirect evidence is admitted in all systems of law, and its use is recognized by international decisions."[112]
- *Case Concerning Military and Paramilitary Activities In and Against Nicaragua,* where on the basis of the facts before it, the

[110] Appellate Body Report, *Canada – Aircraft*, WT/DS70/AB/R, para. 202; *See* also "Evidence Before International Tribunals," D.V. Sandifer, Revised Edition, University Press of Virginia 1975, p.153.

[111] Appellate Body Report, *Canada – Aircraft*, WT/DS70/AB/R, para. 205.

[112] The Corfu Channel Case, 1949, ICJ, 4, p.18, *cited* in Appellate Body Report, *Canada – Aircraft,* WT/DS70/AB/R; note 128.

International Court of Justice found that it could reasonably infer that certain aid had been provided from Nicaraguan territory.[113]

- *Case Concerning the Barcelona Traction, Light and Power Company Limited,* where Judge Jessup, in his separate opinion, opined that "... if a party fails to produce on demand a relevant document which is in its possession, there may be an inference that the document if brought, would have exposed facts unfavourable to the party... ."[114]
- In *William A. Parker (USA) v. United Mexican States*, the Mexican-United States General Claims Commissions stated that "in any case where evidence which would probably influence its decisions is peculiarly within the knowledge of the claimant or of the respondent Government, the failure to produce it, unexplained, may be taken into account by the Commission in reaching a decision."[115]

59. In *US – Wheat Gluten*, the Appellate Body provided additional guidance on the drawing of adverse inferences, noting that the complaining party must identify which facts support a particular inference and what inferences the Panel should have drawn from those facts.[116]

60. In view of these legal standards, Brazil sets forth and references the facts which support the drawing of these three adverse inferences it has requested.

61. First, at the time it refused to produce the requested information on 20 January 2004, the United States was aware of the following key facts:(1) it knew Brazil's latest estimates using the 14/16th methodology,[117] (2) it knew the results of the EWG database tabulations,[118] and (3) it had access to all farm-specific contract, yield, payment and planted acreage data in a centralized database that would have permitted a calculation of the total amount of support under a variety of methodologies, including that advocated by the United States. These facts support the drawing of the first two (adverse) inferences requested by Brazil.

62. Second, the United States was fully capable of calculating the amount of payments allocable to current US producers of upland cotton. As an initial matter, the data would allow for an exact payment total of the amount of *upland cotton* contract payments received by *upland cotton* farmers. Thus, without using any allocation methodology for non-upland cotton payments, the United States knows the exact amount of all these cotton-specific payments. Further, the

---

113 Case Concerning Military and Paramilitary Activities, 1986 ICJ 14, p. 82-86, paras. 152, 154-156, *cited* in Appellate Body Report, *Canada – Aircraft,* WT/DS70/AB/R; note 128.

114 Case Concerning the Barcelona Traction, Light and Power Company Limited, 1970 ICJ 3, p. 215, para. 97, *cited* in Appellate Body Report, *Canada – Aircraft,* WT/DS70/AB/R; note 128.

115 Reports of International Arbitral Awards, Vol. IV, 35, p.39, *cited* in Appellate Body Report, *Canada – Aircraft,* WT/DS70/AB/R; note 128.

116 Appellate Body Report, *US – Wheat Gluten*, WT/DS166/AB/R, para. 176.

117 Set out in Brazil's 22 December 2003 Answers to Question, para. 8.

118 Brazil's 18 November 2003 Further Rebuttal Submission, Section 2.1. *See* also Brazil's 28 January 2004 Comments on US Answers, paras. 20-22.

United States was fully instructed on how Brazil calculated the support attributable to rice in Exhibit Bra-368, Tables 2-3 and accompanying data. Further, throughout the briefings on the different allocation methodologies, the United States left no doubt that it was fully aware of how to calculate the amount of payments using a number of different methodologies, including Brazil's 14/16th methodology, as well as the methodology advocated by the United States itself.[119] Given this knowledge, opportunity, and capability, the Panel may infer that the United States knew the amount of payments resulting from the application of both the Brazilian as well as their own allocation methodologies. These facts support the drawing of the first two (adverse) inferences.

63. Third, the consistently misleading information provided by the United States concerning its possession of data regarding acreage and payment information for contract payments is another fact supporting the drawing of all three adverse inferences. Brazil first requested this information in November 2002, and then repeatedly through December 2003. The Panel made similar requests. It is uncontested that the United States government, through USDA's Kansas City Administrative Office and its database, collected, organized and maintained in a centralized database all of the data that would be responsive to Brazil's and the Panel's requests. The United States now argues it did not "maintain" information on the amount of contract payments paid to current producers of upland cotton.[120] The ordinary meaning of the word "maintain" is "practice habitually," "observe," "cause to continue (a state of affairs, a condition, an activity)."[121] The rapid response of USDA's Kansas City office to the rice FOIA request provides compelling evidence of habitual practice of the US government in "maintaining" both contract and planted acreage information.[122] In sum, the pattern of misrepresentations supports the finding that the United States sought to hide this information and to mislead Brazil and the Panel, because it knew that the requested information would be harmful to its defence.

64. Fourth, a major issue in this dispute has been whether the US contract payments are support to upland cotton, or alternatively, as the United States argued, whether they are "non-product-specific support." As the United States knew on 20 January 2004, a key element of Brazil's proof of support to upland cotton is demonstrating the extent to which the allegedly "decoupled" contract payments are actually paid to current producers of upland cotton. Brazil has pro-

---

[119] US 18 November 2003 Further Submission, paras. 11-17; US 2 December 2003 Oral Statement, paras. 23-24, 26-28.

[120] US 22 December 2003 Answers to Questions, paras. 6-11.

[121] New Shorter Oxford Dictionary, 1993 edition, p. 1669.

[122] The current WTO rules do not permit Brazil to recover the enormous costs it has incurred in this dispute to prove circumstantially what the United States had in its possession for the past 15 months. The Panel should consider that, if the misrepresentations made by the United States in this proceeding had been made in US Federal Courts, they would have resulted in the award of significant attorney's fees and costs in a US Federal Court. *See e.g.,* Federal Rule of Civil Procedure 26(g)(2)(A), (3) (sanctions include reasonable expenses including attorney's fees due to misleading certification of accuracy of discovery responses).

vided extensive circumstantial evidence demonstrating this link.[123] The refusal of the United States to provide the information provides the basis for the Panel to infer that the United States knew this information would be detrimental to its argument that these payments were not linked to current cotton production.

65. In deciding whether to draw any adverse inferences, the Panel may wish to consider the precedential impact of the US refusal to cooperate. If a Member can easily block a panel's request for information without any consequences, it will provide a clear roadmap for avoiding subsidy and other WTO disciplines in the future. It will also encourage parties to a future dispute to obfuscate and refuse to provide requested evidence. The WTO dispute settlement system will simply cease to function over the long run unless there are consequences that follow from a Member's non-cooperation. In short, the US lack of cooperation, in the words of the Appellate Body in *US – Wheat Gluten*, is to be "deplored," rather than rewarded.[124]

66. Finally, any adverse inferences drawn by the Panel become part of the evidence on the basis of which the Panel must make an objective assessment of the facts under DSU Article 11. Among the best available "facts" are the adverse inferences themselves. The Appellate Body in *Canada – Aircraft* held that "a panel must draw inferences on the basis of all of the facts of record relevant to the particular determination to be made,"[125] and that "[w]here a party refuses to provide information requested by a panel, that refusal will be one of the relevant facts on record, and indeed an important fact, to be taken into account in determining the appropriate inference to be drawn."[126]

7. THE US REFUSAL TO PROVIDE THE INFORMATION REQUESTED RENDERS BRAZIL'S 14/16TH METHODOLOGY THE MOST ACCURATE INFORMATION ON RECORD CONCERNING THE AMOUNT OF SUPPORT TO UPLAND COTTON FROM CONTRACT PAYMENTS

67. Since the United States has not provided the data, the best available information before the Panel is Brazil's so-called "14/16th" methodology. This information is the most accurate proxy for the amount of contract payments that constitute support to upland cotton. By this methodology, Brazil has made the assumption that all upland cotton is planted on upland cotton base. Or, put differently, for each acre planted to upland cotton an average contract payment in the amount of an upland cotton contract payment is received. Accordingly, Brazil has adjusted the amount of upland cotton contract payments made in any marketing year by the ratio of the acreage actually planted to upland cotton and

123 *See e.g.* Brazil's 9 October Closing Statement, Annex I, although later submissions provided considerable additional information such as Brazil's 18 November Further Rebuttal Submission, Sections 2.1, 3.1 and 3.7.5.

124 Appellate Body Report, *US – Wheat Gluten*, WT/DS166/AB/R, para. 171.

125 Appellate Body Report, *Canada – Aircraft*, WT/DS70/AB/R, para. 204.

126 *Ibid.*

the upland cotton contract payment base acreage in that marketing year.[127] For MY 2002, the original ratio was about 14/16th,[128] therefore the name of the methodology. In fact, Brazil has used a different adjustment factor for each marketing year.[129]

68. Brazil has demonstrated with circumstantial evidence that current upland cotton producers need contract payments to generate sufficient returns to remain economically viable.[130] Brazil has also demonstrated that current producers of upland cotton need high per-acre contract payments (such as those provided for upland cotton, rice, peanut or corn base) to cover the cost of upland cotton production.[131] Thus, in the absence of the withheld data, it is fair to assume that some upland cotton was planted on base acreage with higher payments than upland cotton base (*e.g.,* rice[132]), and some was planted on base acreage yielding lower contract payments than upland cotton base (*e.g.,* corn). These phenomena would, on average, cancel each other out, so that one can reasonably assume that the average planted upland cotton acre received a contract payment in the amount of an upland cotton contract payment.[133]

69. In addition, the incomplete EWG data supports the conclusion that most US upland cotton is planted on upland cotton base.[134] Three quarters of all upland cotton base payments are paid to producers of upland cotton.[135] The EWG data further demonstrates that the great majority of both contract payments and marketing loan payments received by upland cotton producers are for upland cotton.[136] Thus, while part of the contract payment support to upland cotton comes from non-upland cotton contract payments, any over- or under-counting resulting from Brazil's "14/16th" methodology would be minimal.

70. Finally, in making this factual finding, the Panel should also take into account, as a fact of record, the adverse inferences outlined in Section 6 above, which fully support a finding that Brazil's 14/16th methodology is correct. In addition, the Panel should take into account the adverse inference that the US allocation methodology would have resulted in contract payments at least as high as those in Brazil's 14/16th methodology. However, in making its objective assess-

---

[127] Since planted acreage in all marketing years is below the base acreage, this amounts to a downward adjustment of the total payments made in relation to upland cotton base acreage.

[128] The final planted acreage figure provided by the United States in a later stage of this dispute required a slight adjustment to the figure: *see* Brazil's 22 December 2003 Answers to Questions, para. 8.

[129] *See* Brazil's 11 August 2003 Answers to Questions, Notes to Table at paras. 97 and 130.

[130] These facts are summarized in Annex 1 to Brazil's 9 October 2003 Closing Statement but are contained in a number of Brazil's earlier submissions to the Panel beginning on 24 June 2003. *See* also Brazil's 18 November Further Rebuttal Submission, Sections 3.1 and 3.7.5.

[131] Brazil's 22 August 2003 Rebuttal Submission, paras. 30-34 and 39-44; Brazil's 27 October 2003 Answers to Questions, paras. 14-24 and Brazil's 2 December 2003 Oral Statement, paras 26-27.

[132] Brazil notes that the data provided by the United States does not contain any information on peanut base payments, which would also be a high per-acre payment crop.

[133] Brazil's 18 November 2003 Further Rebuttal Submission, paras. 50-51.

[134] Brazil's 18 November 2003 Further Rebuttal Submission, paras. 22-28. *See* also Brazil's 28 January 2004 Comments on US Answers, paras. 20-22.

[135] Brazil's 18 November 2003 Further Rebuttal Submission, paras. 23-24.

[136] Brazil's 18 November 2003 Further Rebuttal Submission, para. 26.

ment of the facts, the Panel should reject the partial information proffered by the United States in its 18 and 19 December 2003 Letter and reflected in various submissions.[137] As in *Canada – Aircraft*, this heavily redacted information, which excludes the most relevant information requested, should be ignored.

8. BRAZIL'S INTENDED METHODOLOGY FOR ALLOCATING CONTRACT PAYMENTS AS SUPPORT TO UPLAND COTTON

71. Brazil intended to use the data requested from the United States to calculate the amount of contract payments that constitute "support to" upland cotton,[138] within the meaning of Article 13(b)(ii) of the Agreement on Agriculture.[139] In its 20 January 2004 Answers to Additional Questions, Brazil provided more detailed information concerning its allocation methodology.[140] Brazil emphasizes that it intended to apply this methodology since early on in this dispute, but was prevented from doing so due to (1) the US denial that the data existed and (2) the US refusal to provide the data requested by the Panel and Brazil.[141] Only because of the US argument that it did not have the information requested and – after demonstrating the incorrectness of that argument – because of the US refusal to provide the information, Brazil suggested to apply its so-called "14/16th" methodology as a proxy.

---

[137] *E.g.,* in note 12 of the 22 December 2003 US Answers to Questions the United States asserts that only 30.7 per cent of cropland on US upland cotton farms was planted to upland cotton in MY 2002. This figure is however misleading, as the United States has classified as "upland cotton farm" not only farms that currently grow upland cotton, but also farms that historically grew upland cotton (and, therefore, have upland cotton base) yet have stopped to do so. This is an inappropriate categorization. By contrast, in paragraph 186 of its 22 December 2003 Answers to Questions, the United States provides the correct figure of 48 per cent of cropland on farms actually producing upland cotton is planted to upland cotton. The Panel should not allow the United States to selectively use its data (which cannot be checked), but not allow the Panel or Brazil to receive the data needed to calculate the amount of support to upland cotton from the contract payments.

[138] Brazil's 18 November 2003 Further Rebuttal Submission, paras. 3, 17-19, 47-49; Brazil's 2 December 2003 Oral Statement, para. 2 and Exhibit Bra-369 (Brazil's Request to the United States for Farm-Specific Planting and Base Acreage Data).

[139] Brazil notes that it is its position that the peace clause is an affirmative defence and that it is the burden of the United States to demonstrate that its current support to upland cotton does not exceed the support decided during 1992 (*see inter alia* Brazil's 22 July 2003 Oral Statement, paras. 5-11). The United States has not lived up to its burden of proof and has repeatedly failed to provide the data that would allow the Panel and Brazil to calculate the exact amount of support to upland cotton.

[140] Brazil's 20 January 2004 Answers to Additional Questions, paras. 43-55.

[141] *See inter alia* Brazil's 9 October 2003 Closing Statement, paras. 2-9, in particular para. 2, 6 and 9; Brazil's 18 November 2003 Further Rebuttal Submission, paras. 2-3, 17, 32 and 47-51.

9. USING THE PROBLEMATIC AND INCOMPLETE US 18 / 19 DECEMBER 2003 AGGREGATE DATA FOR ALLOCATING CONTRACT PAYMENTS AS SUPPORT TO UPLAND COTTON DOES NOT CONTRADICT BRAZIL'S 14/16TH METHODOLOGY

72. In this Section, Brazil presents its results from applying a simplified version of its methodology applied to the US summary data. Brazil incorporates all of its reservations it has expressed regarding this data.[142] Brazil further recalls its various arguments why contract payments constitute support to specific commodities.[143] Therefore, contract payments are principally allocated to the programme crops covered, as suggested by Brazil's methodology presented in its 20 January 2004 Answers to Additional Questions.[144]

73. As the record demonstrates, none of four types of contract payments[145] is truly "decoupled," given the production of programme crops by the farms holding contract payment base. To the contrary, they are intended to and, in fact, do provide support for the production of programme crops. This is particularly true in the case of high per-acre payment crops, such as upland cotton and rice.[146] Therefore, Brazil allocates contract payments to the programme crops covered. This approach is reasonable, since contract payments are eliminated, for instance, if fruits and vegetables are grown. In sum, Brazil maintains its position – supported by all third parties[147] – that the support from contract payments that can be allocated to upland cotton is product-specific support within the meaning of the Agreement on Agriculture.[148]

74. Although Brazil could not use the data provided by the United States for its intended purpose, Brazil has attempted to apply a similar but less complex allocation methodology[149] to the aggregate data provided by the United States.[150] The summary data provided by the United States groups farms in three different categories and provides aggregate data for these categories:(1) those farms planting upland cotton and holding upland cotton contract base acreage, (2) those farms not planting upland cotton but holding upland cotton contract base acreage, and (3) those farms planting upland cotton and not holding upland cotton

---

142 *See* Section 3.

143 *See inter alia* Brazil's 9 October 2003 Closing Statement, Annex 1.

144 Brazil's 20 January 2004 Answers to Additional Questions, paras. 43-55.

145 PFC, market loss assistance, direct and counter-cyclical payments.

146 *See inter alia* Brazil's 9 October 2003 Closing Statement, Annex I for a summary of these arguments.

147 *See* Brazil's 22 August 2003 Rebuttal Submission, para. 13 for further references.

148 *See e.g.* Brazil's 22 August 2003 Rebuttal Submission, paras. 13-23 and 24-52 for evidence and arguments concerning the four contract payments.

149 Due to the limitations of the data provided by the United States, Brazil had to simplify its suggested methodology (Brazil's 20 January 2004 Answers to Additional Questions, paras. 43-55) so as to enable its application to aggregate rather than farm-specific data.

150 Brazil notes that as explained above, the farm-specific data provided by the United States does not allow for matching the contract payment data with the data on current plantings of contract programme crops. Therefore, Brazil could only use the summary data for this allocation exercise.

contract base acreage.[151] For purposes of this analysis, only the aggregate data concerning farms in category (1) and (3) are of interest, as only those farms actually plant upland cotton. Brazil discusses below how it has calculated the contract payment support to upland cotton for each of these categories.

75. Due to the summary nature of this data, Brazil had to make several critical assumptions that would not have been necessary had the United States provided usable non-scrambled farm-specific data rather than summary data and "scrambled" farm-specific data. These assumptions are set out below.

76. First, Brazil had to assume that no "aggregation problem" exists with the US summary data. Brazil's example in Section 3 above demonstrates that basing calculations on aggregate rather than farm-specific data can distort the results to a considerable extent. Without usable non-scrambled farm-specific data, it is impossible to avoid this problem – although Brazil does not know how severe the problem is in the case of upland cotton contract payments. Using the US aggregate base acreage data and aggregate planting data to allocate contract payments will most likely trigger distortions of the results due to the allocation problem.

77. It bears repeating that a proper allocation calculation has to be done on the basis of individual farms to obtain undistorted results. Only aggregating farm-specific allocations of contract payments as support to upland cotton generates the correct total amount of contract payments to be allocated to upland cotton.

78. Further critical assumptions are discussed in the course of the description of the allocation methodology used, as set out below.

79. *First, Brazil has considered the data for upland cotton planted on farms that also have upland cotton base.* As indicated in Brazil's allocation approach,[152] as a first step in these calculations, Brazil has assigned all aggregate upland cotton base payments received by farms producing upland cotton and holding upland cotton base as support to upland cotton – yet only up to the share of upland cotton base acreage that was actually planted to upland cotton.[153] The monetary value of contract payments to these farms was calculated by multiplying the payment units for a crop base (as provided by the United States) by the payment rate for that crop in the marketing year in question.[154] For MY 1999-2001, all upland cotton PFC payments to farms producing upland cotton and holding upland cotton base were allocated as support to upland cotton, because the aggregate acreage planted to upland cotton by that group of farms exceeded their aggregate upland cotton base acreage.[155] For MY 2002, only a percentage

[151] *See* Electronic PFC and DCP Summary Files provided by the United States on 18 and 19 December 2003 respectively.

[152] Brazil's 20 January 2004 Answers to Additional Questions, paras. 43-55, in particular para. 47 discussion of Sample Farms 1-3.

[153] Brazil's 20 January 2004 Answers to Additional Questions, paras. 44-48.

[154] Exhibit Bra-394 (Agricultural Outlook Tables, USDA, November 2003, Table 19).

[155] *See* Exhibit Bra-419 (Allocation Calculations Based on Brazil's Methodology and US Summary Data). (Also provided electronically as 'allocation calculations.xls').

of total upland cotton direct and counter-cyclical payments was allocated as support to upland cotton, because upland cotton acres planted by farms holding upland cotton base were below their updated upland cotton base for that marketing year.[156] The percentage of payments allocated corresponds to the ratio of aggregated upland cotton planted acreage to aggregated upland cotton base acreage for the group of farms producing upland cotton and holding upland cotton base.[157] It follows that in MY 2002 for this group of farms no further direct or counter-cyclical payments from other crops were allocated.

80. Since for MY 1999-2001 upland cotton acreage planted by farms that also had upland cotton base exceeded that base, additional PFC payments paid on other crop base were allocated as support to upland cotton. As discussed in Brazil's methodology,[158] PFC payments for other crops were primarily allocated as support for these crops – up to the share of contract acreage planted to the respective crop – in a manner identical to the above described first step for upland cotton. Any further payments stemming from contract acreage not planted to the respective base crop were pooled and allocated as additional support to those contract crops whose aggregate planting exceeded their aggregated base acreage.[159]

81. Second, Brazil has analyzed the US summary data concerning *upland cotton that has been planted on farms without upland cotton base*. Unfortunately, the United States did not provide the requested information (even in summary form) regarding the amount of contract acreage that existed on those farms.[160] The second critical assumption Brazil, therefore, must make is that, for each upland cotton acre planted on a farm without upland cotton base, contract payments were received in an amount identical to the average per-acre payment allocated to upland cotton planted by the first group of farms. This assumption triggers further uncertainty about the reliability of the results, because it assumes that this group of farms receives contract payments in an equal manner as compared to group planting upland cotton and holding upland cotton base.[161]

---

156 *Ibid.*

157 *Ibid.*

158 Brazil's 20 January 2004 Answers to Additional Questions, para. 48 discussing Sample Farm 4.

159 *See* Brazil's 20 January 2004 Answers to Additional Questions, paras. 49-55 discussing Sample Farms 5-7. For MY 1999 and 2000, only upland cotton plantings exceeded the crop base acreage, thus, all additional payments were allocated to upland cotton. For MY 2001, also oats and sorghum were planted on more acreage than their respective contract base ("overplanted"), thus, triggering additional payments being allocated pursuant to the crop's share of the total acreage being "overplanted." *See* Exhibit Bra-419 (Allocation Calculations Based on Brazil's Methodology and US Summary Data). (Also provided electronically as 'allocation calculations.xls').

160 *See* Electronic PFC and DCP Summary Files provided by the United States on 18 and 19 December 2003 respectively. Considering the fact that US upland cotton producers needed contract payments to produce upland cotton in an economically viable manner, it is simply not realistic to assume that there were farms without any kind of contract acreage planting upland cotton. *See* Sections 4 and 5 rejecting the US reasoning for not providing the data.

161 Brazil also recalls that the US data for MY 2002 does not contain any information concerning the amount of direct and counter-cyclical payments made on peanut base (Exhibit US-112). Thus, the missing peanut contract payments for MY 2002 are also missing in the calculation of the amount of

82. Third, since the United States has not provided any information on the amount of market loss assistance payments received by any farm producing upland cotton – the United States did not even provide aggregate information – Brazil has assumed[162] that any allocation of market loss assistance payment as support to upland cotton would have to be made in the same manner as the allocation of PFC payments in the marketing year in question.[163]

83. Combining the resulting PFC, market loss assistance, direct and counter-cyclical payments from these calculations yields the following amount of contract payments that would be considered support to upland cotton.

MY	1999	2000	2001	2002
PFC Payments	$619,336,990.11	$564,607,044.52	$456,554,286.78	-
MLA Payments[164]	$616,320,738.53	$601,042,809.61	$630,594,516.48	-
DP Payments	-	-	-	$464,596,092.01
CCP Payments	-	-	-	$1,025,653,053.34

84. For purposes of comparison, Brazil presents below its results based on the "14/16th" methodology:[165]

MY	1999	2000	2001	2002
PFC Payments	$547,800,000	$541,300,000	$453,000,000	-
MLA Payments	$545,100,000	$576,200,000	$625,700,000	-
DP Payments	-	-	-	$454,500,000
CCP Payments	-	-	-	$935,600,000

As the Panel can see, Brazil's figures based on the 14/16th methodology are consistently *below* the results using the US summary data provided on 18 and 19 December 2003. It follows that the results of this methodology using the flawed US summary data, at the very least, do not contradict Brazil's 14/16th methodology. Judging from these results, it appears that, even having in mind all the limi-

direct and counter-cyclical payments that constitute support to upland cotton. It follows that these figures are understated by an amount unknown to Brazil.

162 Brazil recalls that market loss assistance payments are made on the same basis as PFC payments – with the exception that market loss assistance payments were also made for soybeans.

163 *See* note to the summary table below. This assumption leads to an understatement of the resulting payments, since market loss assistance payments also covered soybean production in additional to any PFC payment base. Thus, just relying on PFC payments as a proxy leaves out a potential significant amount of money that may have supported upland cotton.

164 The amount of market loss assistance payments has been calculated by applying the ratio of allocated PFC payments (as calculated) to upland cotton PFC payments as provided in Exhibit Bra-4 ("Fact Sheet: Upland Cotton," USDA, January 2003, p. 6) to the amount of upland cotton market loss assistance payments as provided by the same source.

165 The figures in this table are reproduced from Brazil's 9 September 2003 Further Submission, Table 1. MY 2002 data is taken from the updated figures presented by Brazil in its 22 December 2003 Answers, para. 8.

tations of the US data as discussed above,[166] Brazil's methodology is rather conservative compared to an allocation based on the US summary data, which the United States seems to endorse as a valid base for calculating support to upland cotton.[167]

10. APPLICATION OF THE US-PROPOSED ALLOCATION METHODOLOGY TO THE US SUMMARY DATA

85. Brazil recalls that its allocation methodologies offered so far and their results are provided in the context of the peace clause analysis under Article 13(b)(ii) of the Agreement on Agriculture.[168] The United States has criticized Brazil's 14/16th methodology and asserts that, for purposes of Brazil's claims under Articles 5(c) and 6.3 of the SCM Agreement, Brazil has to allocate contract payments to farms producing upland cotton over the entire sales of those farms.[169] (On the other hand, the United States maintains that any such allocation is not warranted for purposes of the peace clause[170] – an entirely untenable position, as Brazil explains in its 28 January 2004 Comments on the US 22 December 2003 Answers to Questions.[171])

86. Despite its serious misgivings about the proposed US methodology, Brazil sets forth below its analysis of the US methodology. Since the United States provided on 18/19 December 2003 some limited summary data on the production composition of upland cotton farms, Brazil has attempted to offer an estimate using the US allocation methodology. As described below, Brazil has been required to make several assumptions, given the shortcomings in the data and due to the US refusal to provide data in support of its own methodology.

87. Brazil notes that for MY 2002, the United States collected and has access to information on *all acreage planted to any crops*, including non-programme crops, produced by farmers receiving contract payments and marketing loan payments.[172] The United States has never produced this information to the Panel

---

166 Brazil notes that some of the limitations result in distortions in different directions. The omission of peanut base information tends to lower the amount of payments allocated. The missing information on market loss assistance payments has an unknown effect and so does the aggregation problem. The missing information on base acreage of farms that produce upland cotton but have no upland cotton base could slightly overstate results – however, Brazil cautions that this effect may not be too strong, as the mount of upland cotton planted on such farms is very limited.

167 US 20 January 2004 Letter to the Panel, p. 2.

168 Brazil maintains that no allocation methodology is warranted under Part III of the SCM Agreement. Rather, it is the effect of the subsidies that is the subject of scrutiny.

169 *See e.g.* US 7 October 2003 Oral Statement, para. 17; US 18 November 2003 Further Rebuttal Submission, paras. 11-17; US 2 December 2003 Oral Statement, para. 24; US 22 December 2003 Answers to Questions, paras. 11, 159-164, 184.

170 US 22 December 2003 Answers to Questions, paras. 159-164.

171 *See* Brazil's 28 January 2004 Comment on US Answer to Question 243. *See* also Brazil's 2 December 2003 Oral Statement, paras. 4-6. Brazil strongly disagrees that this is a required or appropriate methodology under Part III of the SCM Agreement or under GATT Article XVI (or even under Article 13(b)(ii) of the Agreement on Agriculture). The US arguments in that respect are not supported by any Vienna Convention interpretation of these provisions.

172 Brazil's 18 November 2003 Further Rebuttal Submission, para. 41.

or Brazil in any form (either as summary or farm-specific data). Thus, while the United States asserts that the Panel should apply a particular methodology, it refuses to provide the information that would permit the Panel to calculate the payments under the US methodology.

88. But the information requested by Brazil on all different types of contract crop plantings during MY 1999-2002 would go a long way towards permitting the calculation of the value of all crop production, as well as the calculation of the value of upland cotton produced in relation to other crops produced. This is because most cotton farms producing upland cotton specialize in the production of upland cotton as opposed to other crops, and only produce a limited amount of other crops and almost no livestock.[173]

89. Brazil notes that among the selected information provided by the United States is the amount of total cropland on farms producing upland cotton.[174] The following table shows the percentage of total cropland and the percentage of total programme cropland that is planted to upland cotton (and other programme crops) on upland cotton producing farms, i.e., farms in category (1) and (3).[175]

	MY 1999	**MY 2000**	**MY 2001**	**MY 2002**[176]
	Total Cropland 30,628,557.4 acres	Total Cropland 31,090,742.9 acres	Total Cropland 30,635,774.0 acres	Total Cropland 28,141,085.2 acres
	Total Programme Cropland 21,388,415.0 acres	Total Programme Cropland 22,552,704.4 acres	Total Programme Cropland 22,793,179.7 acres	Total Programme Cropland 22,753,369.8 acres
Programme Crop	Percentage of Total Cropland on the Farm Planted to That Crop			
	Percentage of Total Programme Cropland on the Farm Planted to That Crop			
Planted to Upland Cotton	47.58 per cent	49.49 per cent	50.48 per cent	48.12 per cent
	68.13 per cent	68.23 per cent	67.84 per cent	59.51 per cent
Planted to Wheat	8.95 per cent	10.60 per cent	8.58 per cent	10.36 per cent
	12.82 per cent	14.61 per cent	11.54 per cent	12.82 per cent
Planted to Oats	0.28 per cent	0.32 per cent	0.61 per cent	0.56 per cent
	0.40 per cent	0.44 per cent	0.82 per cent	0.69 per cent

---

173 Brazil's 27 October 2003 Answers to Questions, paras. 7-13. While the exclusion of tiny livestock production on upland cotton farms from the allocation of contract payments might slightly understate the resulting contract payments allocated to upland cotton, any such over counting would be outweighed by the missing data on peanut contract payments made to farms that results in an undercounting of the contract payments allocated to upland cotton.

174 *See* Electronic PFC and DCP Summary Files provided by the United States on 18 and 19 December 2003 respectively.

175 Farms planting upland cotton and holding upland cotton base and farms planting upland cotton without holding upland cotton base. Farms not planting upland cotton are excluded from these calculations, as they are entirely irrelevant for purposes of this dispute. They are simply not upland cotton farms, they only have been in the past.

176 Brazil has not indicated the percentages for other oilseeds, as the figures were so small.

	MY 1999	MY 2000	MY 2001	MY 2002[176]
Planted to Rice	1.72 per cent	1.35 per cent	1.77 per cent	1.50 per cent
	2.46 per cent	1.86 per cent	2.38 per cent	1.86 per cent
Planted to Corn	4.94 per cent	5.37 per cent	4.90 per cent	6.35 per cent
	7.07 per cent	7.41 per cent	6.59 per cent	7.86 per cent
Planted to Sorghum	6.17 per cent	5.21 per cent	7.87 per cent	6.13 per cent
	8.83 per cent	7.19 per cent	10.58 per cent	7.58 per cent
Planted to Barley	0.20 per cent	0.19 per cent	0.18 per cent	0.18 per cent
	0.29 per cent	0.26 per cent	0.25 per cent	0.22 per cent
Planted to Soybeans	no information, as no PFC programme crop	no information, as no PFC programme crop	no information, as no PFC programme crop	7.48 per cent
				9.26 per cent
Total Programme Farmland as a Percentage of Total Cropland	69.83 per cent	72.54 per cent	74.40 per cent	80.85 per cent

90. As demonstrated by this table, US farms planting upland cotton are specialized in that crop. Upland cotton plantings account for 50 per cent of their cropland and for between 60 and 70 per cent of the land devoted to programme crops. Important alternative crops planted by upland cotton farms are wheat, corn, sorghum, soybeans and rice. About 20 per cent of the cropland on farms producing upland cotton is devoted to non-programme crops or to no crops.[177] As detailed below, Brazil has conservatively assumed that the value of the crops produced on this 20 per cent of farmland is the average per-acre value of production of non-programme crops in that marketing year in the entire United States, as reported by USDA.[178]

91. Performing the US-invented allocation methodology, Brazil starts again by considering the group of farms that produce upland cotton and have upland cotton base acreage. As a first step, Brazil has calculated the total amount of contract payments received by these farms by multiplying the contract payment units provided in the US summary files by the payment rates applicable to the crop in any given marketing year.[179] The resulting payments have been summed up.

92. As a second step, Brazil has calculated the value of the programme crop production on farms producing upland cotton and holding upland cotton base. To estimate the value of the programme crop production on these farms,[180] Brazil has multiplied the acreage planted to a crop by its average yield in the United

177 The lower figures for MY 1999-2001 are explained by the fact that soybeans were not a contract programme crop.

178 This most certainly overstates their value for the farms under scrutiny, as it includes uses for the production of tobacco, greenhouse crops and other high value crops not likely produced on cotton farms. The result is an allocation of contract payments to upland cotton that is too low.

179 Payment rates are published by USDA, *see* Exhibit Bra-394 (Agricultural Outlook Tables, USDA, November 2003, Table 19).

180 Brazil recalls that the United States has only provided information on programme crop production on upland cotton farms.

States and the average price received by US farmers for that crop in any given marketing year.[181] As the United States has not provided any specific information on what upland cotton farms plant on the remainder of the cropland not devoted to the programme crops, Brazil had to make several assumptions. First, Brazil assumed that the per-acre value of these non-contract programme crops equals the average per-acre value of total US non- contract programme crop production, excluding fruits and vegetables.[182] Brazil has, therefore, calculated the total value of non-contract payment crops as the total value of US crops minus the value of programme crops and fruits and vegetables for each marketing year between MY 1999-2002.[183] The resulting figure has been divided by the total US cropland[184] (minus cropland devoted to fruits[185] and vegetables[186] and programme crops[187]).[188] The per-acre value thereby generated has been multiplied by the acreage not planted to programme crops on category (1) farms,[189] resulting in a figure for the total value of non-contract programme crops produced on the group of farms that produce upland cotton and hold upland cotton base.[190]

93. Following these preparatory steps, it is now possible to allocate contract payments that constitute support to upland cotton. Summing up the value of all crops produced on the farm provides the total value of the production on farms that produce upland cotton and hold upland cotton base. Dividing the value of the upland cotton crop by the value of all crops provides the adjustment factor to be applied to the total contract payments received by that group of farms.[191] This concludes the allocation for all group (1) farms.

94. Turning to farms in group (3), the Panel will recall that these farms plant upland cotton, but do not hold upland cotton base. The Panel will further recall that the United States has not provided any information concerning contract payments for this group of upland cotton farms.[192] This US refusal renders any precise calculations for the third group of farms impossible. Therefore, Brazil has assumed that farms producing upland cotton but not holding upland cotton

---

[181] MY 1999-2002 yields and farm prices for programme crops are published by USDA, *see* Exhibit Bra-420 (Agricultural Outlook Tables, November 2003, Table 17).

[182] Brazil considers this exclusion justified due to the elimination of contract payments if fruits and vegetables are planted.

[183] Exhibit Bra-421 (ERS Briefing Room: Farm Income and Costs: US Farm Sector Cash Receipts from Sales of Agricultural Commodities, USDA).

[184] Exhibit Bra-106 ("United States State Fact Sheet," ERS, USDA, 15 July 2003, p. 2). The figure represents the total amount of US cropland pursuant to the 1997 census. This is the latest figure available to Brazil. However, since the total of US cropland can be presumed to not vary too greatly, this may be a reasonable assumption.

[185] Exhibit Bra-422 (Fruits and Tree Nuts Yearbook, USDA, October 2003, Table A-2).

[186] Exhibit Bra-423 (Vegetables and Melons Yearbook, USDA, July 2003, Table 3).

[187] Exhibit Bra-420 (Agricultural Outlook Tables, USDA, November 2003, Table 17).

[188] *See* Exhibit Bra-424 (Allocation Calculations Based on US Methodology and US Summary Data) for the details of the calculation. (Also provided electronically as 'allocation calculations.xls').

[189] Farms that produce upland cotton and hold upland cotton base.

[190] *See* Exhibit Bra-424 (Allocation Calculations Based on US Methodology and US Summary Data) for the details of the calculation. (Also provided electronically as 'allocation calculations.xls').

[191] *Ibid.*

[192] *See* Electronic PFC and DCP Summary Files provided by the United States on 18 and 19 December 2003 respectively.

base receive per acre of upland cotton the same amount of allocated contract payments as farms producing upland cotton and holding upland cotton base.[193]

95. Since the United States has not provided any information on the amount of market loss assistance payments received by any farm producing upland cotton – the United States did not even provide aggregate information[194] – Brazil has assumed that any allocation of market loss assistance payment as support to upland cotton would have to be made in the same manner as the allocation of PFC payments in the marketing year in question.[195]

96. Contract payments allocated in both groups of upland cotton farms are aggregated. The results of this calculation are reported in the table below:

MY	**1999**	**2000**	**2001**	**2002**[196]
PFC Payments	$477,692,236.06	$473,744,959.03	$333,295,919.25	-
MLA Payments[197]	$475,365,812.83	$504,317,124.58	$460,349,590.68	-
DP Payments	-	-	-	$416,216,862.44
CCP Payments	-	-	-	$714,424,543.18

97. For purposes of comparison, Brazil presents below its results based on the "14/16th" methodology:[198]

193 *See* Exhibit Bra-424 (Allocation Calculations Based on US Methodology and US Summary Data) for the details of the calculation. (Also provided electronically as 'allocation calculations.xls').

194 *See* Section 3.

195 *See* note to the summary table below. Brazil recalls that market loss assistance payments were made for soybeans in addition to the PFC crops. This increases the total amount of market loss assistance payments that would be allocated to upland cotton. Solely using the PFC payments as a basis, undercounts Brazil's results by an unknown amount. Brazil also recalls that the US data for MY 2002 does not contain any information concerning the amount of direct and counter-cyclical payments made on peanut base (Exhibit US-112). Thus, the missing peanut contract payments for MY 2002 are also missing in the calculation of the amount of direct and counter-cyclical payments that constitute support to upland cotton. It follows that these figures are understated by an amount unknown to Brazil.

196 Brazil also recalls that the US data for MY 2002 does not contain any information concerning the amount of direct and counter-cyclical payments made on peanut base (Exhibit US-112). Thus, the missing peanut contract payments for MY 2002 are also missing in the calculation of the amount of direct and counter-cyclical payments that constitute support to upland cotton. It follows that these figures are understated by an amount unknown to Brazil.

197 The amount of market loss assistance payments has been calculated by applying the ratio of allocated PFC payments (as calculated) to upland cotton PFC payments as provided in Exhibit Bra-4 ("Fact Sheet: Upland Cotton," USDA, January 2003, p. 6) to the amount of upland cotton market loss assistance payments as provided by the same source.

198 The figures in this table are reproduced from Brazil's 9 September 2003 Further Submission, Table 1. MY 2002 data is taken from the updated figures presented by Brazil in its 22 December 2003 Answers, para. 8.

MY	1999	2000	2001	2002
PFC Payments	$547,800,000	$541,300,000	$453,000,000	-
MLA Payments	$545,100,000	$576,200,000	$625,700,000	-
DP Payments	-	-	-	$454,500,000
CCP Payments	-	-	-	$935,600,000

98. As the Panel can readily see, even using the methodology proposed by the United States as relevant under Part III of the SCM Agreement results in amounts of support to upland cotton from contract payments that, accounting for the shortcomings of the US data, are roughly equivalent to the figures produced by Brazil's 14/16th methodology. Brazil cautions against the direct use of these results, as they may be tainted by the assumptions Brazil had to make due to the refusal of the United States to provide data that would render possible performing the allocation that the United States asserts is called for under Part III of the SCM Agreement.[199] In particular, the data withheld on MY 2002 peanut contract payments to farms producing upland cotton would have increased the amount of contract payments allocated to upland cotton. Other shortcomings of the data are discussed above.

11. THE *JAPAN – AGRICULTURAL PRODUCTS* DECISION IS INAPPOSITE

99. The United States claims that the Appellate Body's decision in *Japan – Measures Affecting Agricultural Products* would have prevented the Panel from using the information the United States refused to provide to calculate the amount of contract payments across the "total value of the recipient's production."[200] However, this Appellate Body decision is inapposite.[201]

100. In *Japan – Agricultural Products*, the complaining party (the United States) did not "claim" in its request for establishment of a panel that there was an alternative SPS testing "measure" (determination of sorption levels) that was less trade restrictive.[202] Rather, the request for establishment "claimed" that testing by product (not variety) was sufficient to achieve Japan's appropriate level of protection. The panel, based on expert testimony and *not* on any arguments or evidence presented by the United States, found a violation of SPS Article 5.6 based on the alternative (sorption levels) testing "measure." This decision was taken despite a US argument to the panel that "it is not within the scope of the

---

[199] Again, Brazil notes that this allocation is not required under Part III of the SCM Agreement and GATT Article XVI:3. Both provisions deal with the effect of subsidies, and not their amount or subsidization rate.

[200] US 20 January 2004 Letter to the Panel, p.4.

[201] *See* also Brazil's 28 January 2004 Comments on Question 256.

[202] WT/DS76/2.

Panel's terms of reference to make findings with respect to the comparative efficacy of alternative treatments proposed by technical experts."[203]

101. On appeal, the Appellate Body reversed the panel's finding. Noting that a panel has authority under DSU Article 13.1 to request information, it found that "this authority cannot be used by a panel to rule in favour of a complaining party which has not established a *prima facie* case of inconsistency based on specific legal claims asserted by it." The Appellate Body found the panel had erred in relying on expert information and advice as the basis for a finding of inconsistency with SPS Article 5.6, "since the United States did not establish a *prima facie* case of inconsistency with Article 5.6 based on claims relating to the 'determination of sorption levels.'"[204]

102. The factual situation in this dispute is entirely different from that in *Japan –Agricultural Products*. Brazil's "claim" in relation to the withheld data is, first, that the United States does not enjoy peace clause protection because, *inter alia*, the non-green box contract payments provide support to upland cotton in excess of the level of support decided by the United States in MY 1992.[205] The "measures" impacted by the withheld data are PFC, market loss assistance, direct and counter-cyclical payment subsidies provided under the 1996 FAIR Act and the 2002 FSRI Act,[206] which fall squarely within the Panel's terms of reference. The withheld data is also relevant to Brazil's actionable subsidy "claims" to establish the volumes of subsidies provided for US upland cotton production.[207] Further, the withheld data is relevant to support Brazil's arguments that the contract payments are "support to upland cotton," because most of the upland cotton base payments are paid to current producers of upland cotton. Finally, the withheld data is relevant to provide the factual basis for Brazil to rebut US arguments that the US preferred "value" methodology for allocating payments results in much lower benefits to upland cotton.[208] Brazil notes that the Panel's 12 January 2004 request falls squarely within these various Brazilian claims and arguments when it states that "[d]isclosure is sought to permit an assessment of the total expenditures of PFC, MLA, CCP and direct payments by the US Federal Government to upland cotton producers in the relevant marketing years."[209]

103. The implication in the US citation to the *Japan – Agricultural Products* decision is that the Panel's 8 December 2003 and 12 January 2004 request may be designed to establish a "claim" never advanced by Brazil. This suggestion is

---

[203] Appellate Body Report, *Japan-Agricultural Products,* WT/DS76/AB/R, note 79.

[204] Appellate Body Report, *Japan-Agricultural Products,* WT/DS76/AB/R, para. 130.

[205] This is a claim in the alternative because, as Brazil has argued, it is the United States burden of proof to establish that it enjoys peace clause protection. *See e.g.* Brazil's 24 June 2003 First Submission, paras. 110-121; Brazil's 22 July 2003 Oral Statement, paras. 5-11; Brazil's 11 August 2003 Answers to Questions, paras. 48-51; Brazil's 22 August 2003 Comments, paras 42-45.

[206] The market loss assistance payments were based on various appropriations bills.

[207] Brazil has argued that the exact amounts of the subsidies are not legally relevant (contrary to the US arguments) but rather that the "effects" of the subsidies are what is at issue in claims under Article 6.3 of the SCM Agreement.

[208] *See* Section 10 above.

[209] 12 January 2004 Communication from the Panel, p. 1.

obviously contrary to the factual record outlined above. Moreover, it reveals a profound misunderstanding of the difference between a "claim" and an "argument." The Appellate Body in *EC –Hormones* held that there is a distinction between legal claims reflected in a panel's terms of reference, and arguments used by a complainant to sustain its legal claims. The Appellate Body ruled that "nothing in the DSU limits the faculty of a panel freely to use arguments submitted by any of the parties – *or to develop its own legal reasoning* – to support its own findings and conclusions of the matter under its consideration."[210] Numerous panel reports have narrowly interpreted "claims" to involve only legal claims and have freely permitted complaining parties to advance arguments not expressly reflected in a panel request.[211] A close reading of the Appellate Body's decision in *Japan – Agricultural Products* shows that it was based on the fact that the United States had not advanced legal "claims" relating to an alternative SPS "measure." The fact that the United States had also not made legal "arguments" on its non-claim only reinforced the underlying reasoning.[212]

104. This United States suggestion that the Panel's request of 8 December 2003 and 12 January 2004 would improperly make the case for Brazil is totally baseless. In the *Japan – Agricultural Products* case, the United States did not seek the expert information to support a "claim" or "measure" within the Panel's terms of reference. By contrast, Brazil *repeatedly* sought the information withheld by the United States for fourteen months. Further, the Panel's 8 December 2003 and 12 January 2004 requests incorporated Brazil's request of 3 December 2003, as set out in Exhibit Bra-369. Brazil, as a litigating party, has no independent right to request information from the United States;that must be conducted through the Panel's authority under DSU Article 13.1. Thus, the US assertion that somehow the Panel (and not also Brazil) is seeking evidence to support a "measure," "claim" or even "argument" never advanced by Brazil is fallacious.

105. Indeed, the United States cautions that the Panel "must take care not to use the information gathered under [the] authority [of DSU Article 13.1] to relieve a complaining party from its burdens of establishing a *prima facie* case." [213]This is a curious argument given the fact that the United States has refused to produce information the Panel found was "necessary and appropriate … in order to undertake its mandate to assist the DSB in discharging its responsibilities under the DSU and the covered agreements."[214] Brazil must ask how the Panel is to

---

210 Appellate Body Report, *EC – Hormones*, WT/DS26/AB/R, para. 156 (emphasis added).

211 Panel Report, *EC – Sardines*, WT/DS231/R, paras. 7.142-145 ("…Peru's requests for findings were actually just summations of its arguments and not claims."); Appellate Body Report, *Korea – Dairy Safeguards*, WT/DS98/AB/R, paras. 139-140 ("…EC reliance on the OAI report during the rebuttal stage of the panel proceeding to be a new argument rather than a new claim, and therefore, did not exclude it."); Panel Report, *Australia – Salmon*, WT/DS18/R, paras. 8.24-8.25 (Panel considered that "this 'new claim' to be a new argument, not a new claim.").

212 Appellate Body Report, *Japan-Agricultural Products*, WT/DS76/AB/R, para 130 (Appellate Body, after ruling the Panel erred noted that "The United States did not even *argue* that the 'determination of sorption levels' is an alternative measure which meets the three elements under Article 5.6").

213 US 20 January 2004 Letter to the Panel, p. 4.

214 12 January 2004 Communication from the Panel, p. 1.

even evaluate the evidence to "take care not to use" the information, if it does not even have it?

106. Finally, Brazil notes that this is the first dispute involving interpretations of the peace clause, as well as many provisions in Part III of the SCM Agreement. Brazil obviously does not know how the Panel will resolve many interpretative issues. A good example is the issue of the relevant allocation methodology under the peace clause, or whether subsidies challenged under Part III of the SCM Agreement are required to be allocated at all, and if so, by what methodology. Brazil believes strongly that the US methodology is not supported by any textual or legitimate contextual basis. But in order to "cover all the bases," and conscious of the absence of any remand procedures, Brazil has presented – or has attempted to present in the case of the withheld US data – considerable evidence to provide the Panel with the basis to make the factual determinations supporting any possible legal interpretation of these not previously interpreted WTO provisions. As demonstrated by Brazil's analysis in Section 3, above, the information withheld by the United States has deprived the Panel and Brazil of the opportunity to use the most accurate and complete information possible – even to apply the inappropriate US methodology for allocating contract payments.[215]

12. CONCLUSION

107. In sum, the United States has refused to provide the information concerning the amount of contract payments made to current producers of upland cotton. There are no legitimate confidentiality concerns that would prevent the United States from producing the data. And even if there were, confidentiality procedures under Article 13.1 of the DSU and/or the Panel's working procedures could have addressed these concerns.

108. Therefore, Brazil asks the Panel to draw adverse inferences (listed in Section 6) and conclude that the withheld information would have been adverse to the US defence in this case. Furthermore, Brazil asks the Panel to use the best information available, including the adverse inferences, to find that the figures Brazil has estimated under its so-called 14/16th methodology are supported by the evidence in the record. Brazil also notes that its attempts to apply the flawed and incomplete US summary data to both a simplified version of its own and the US approach yields results that further confirm the results of Brazil's 14/16th methodology.

[215] *See* Brazil's 28 January comment on Question 256.

ANNEX I-16

COMMENTS OF THE UNITED STATES ON COMMENTS BY BRAZIL ON US COMMENTS CONCERNING BRAZIL'S ECONOMETRIC MODEL

(28 January 2004)

I. INTRODUCTION

1. The United States wishes to rebut Brazil's response to the US 22 December 2003 Comments Concerning Brazil's Econometric Model. Our aim is to make clear the fundamental flaws in Brazil's analysis that invalidate its claims. In the following section, we lay out the erroneous approach Dr. Sumner took in modelling the effects of cotton payments. We believe that our rebuttal provides convincing evidence why the Panel should reject this model as supporting a finding of serious prejudice. Moreover, Dr. Sumner's rebuttal fails to allay our concerns regarding technical issues and lack of transparency with the model. These concerns are laid out in Section III.

II. US CONCERNS WITH THE SUMNER MODEL

2. The United States reiterates the following concerns it has with Brazil's approach to its economic analysis in this dispute:

(c) Dr. Sumner continues to imply that his model is essentially the FAPRI model. It is not. Dr. Sumner has made significant modifications to the FAPRI model. The fact that Dr. Sumner's model is "in no way a FAPRI model"is acknowledged by Dr. Babcock in his letter to staff members of the Senate and House of Representatives (Exhibit US-114).

(d) The ways in which Dr. Sumner has modelled decoupled payments (including Production Flexibility Contract payments, Market Loss Assistance payments, Direct payments and Counter cyclical payments), crop insurance payments, and export credit guarantees differ sharply from the FAPRI model and are not based on empirical studies. These *ad hoc* modifications contribute to the large effects on production and other variables obtained by Dr. Sumner when he simulates the removal of cotton subsidies. We argue that the effects are thus largely tautological with no empirical grounding.

(e) In particular, Dr. Sumner's results differ sharply from the economics literature on the effects of decoupled payments on production. As we have argued in numerous submissions, Dr. Sumner's treatment of decoupled payments (particularly from Annex I on pages 16-21) is neither a "standard" feature of other models, nor is it as "consistent" with USDA work in the area as repeated citations of that work might suggest. There has been considerable work done by the USDA and other researchers on such programmes, both theoretical and empirical, which acknowledges the programmes may have some minimal impact on production. However, the research concludes that the impact appears negligible (less than 1 per cent of acreage). As we pointed out in our *Comments Concerning Brazil's Econometric Model of 22 December 2003*, similar results are obtained by FAPRI (less than 0.3 per cent impact on cotton acreage). In contrast, Dr. Sumner's model produces results suggesting cotton acreage impacts as high as 15.9% - that is, more than 50 times larger than what the FAPRI model would indicate.

(f) Likewise, we disagree with Dr. Sumner's modelling of the crop insurance programme. We take issue with how the subsidies were calculated and how they affect production. In particular, we have argued that most cotton production has been insured at coverage levels less than 70 per cent and thus it is likely that any production effects are minimal. Moreover, we have noted that Dr. Sumner has failed to take into account the potential effects of moral hazard on input use and crop yields that potentially offset any impacts on area.

(g) We also take issue with how Dr. Sumner modelled export credit guarantees. In our previous comments, we have argued that Dr. Sumner's formulation is entirely *ad hoc*. He has essentially assumed an effect.

(h) As for marketing loans and deficiency payments, we would agree that such programmes are potentially production distorting when expected market prices fall below loan rates. However, we have argued that the use of lagged prices, while a modelling convenience for large scale models such as FAPRI and the model used by Dr. Sumner, nonetheless introduce potential biases that can overstate effects when futures market prices differ substantially from lagged prices, as they did in 2001 and 2002.

(i) Lastly, as we point out in our *Comments on Answers of Brazil to Questions from the Parties following the Second Panel Meeting,* calibrating Dr. Sumner's model to the November 2002 FAPRI baseline exaggerates the effects of price-based programmes such as marketing loans, counter-cyclical payments and Step 2 payments. The price outlook for cotton has improved considerably since publication of the November 2002 FAPRI baseline used by Dr. Sumner to estimate the effects of subsidies on US cotton production. Improving price forecasts suggest minimal marketing loan outlays over 2003-12.

3. We will briefly summarize our points below.

Dr. Sumner's treatment of decoupled programmes is unconventional and not based on theory or empirical evidence

4. Dr. Sumner's treatment of decoupled payments (particularly from Annex I on pages 16-21) is neither a "standard" feature of other models, nor is it as "consistent" with USDA work in the area as repeated citations of that work might suggest. There has been considerable work done by the USDA and other researchers on such programmes, both theoretical and empirical, which acknowledges the programmes may have some impact on production, and that those impacts depend in part on farmers' expectations (Westcott et al., 2002).[1] However, the research concludes that the impact appears negligible.

5. Dr. Sumner, on the other hand, uses a stylized logic to come up with the estimates for the impact of production flexibility contract (PFC) payments that have neither empirical nor theoretical grounding. He cites, then ignores, recent USDA empirical work showing that decoupled payments have only a small impact (ERS 2003).[2] He justifies this, in part, by saying that the analysis looked at all programmes, while he is looking only at cotton. However, in both their inception and administration, these programmes must be considered as a whole. Treating part of the overall programmes as though they were a "cotton programme" distorts the programmes. It is widely accepted that these programmes have whole farm impacts rather than crop specific impacts—the payments received do not have crop-specific impacts. Furthermore, the impact is much smaller than Dr. Sumner has estimated; the whole farm impact is, at its upper estimate,perhaps one-quarter to one-fifth the impact he cites for cotton alone. He thus vastly overstates the impact of these payments on cotton production.[3]

6. Dr. Sumner argues that market loss assistance (MLA) payments have a larger effect on area than do PFC payments despite the fact that MLA payments were paid on the identical payment base as the PFC payments. Moreover, MLA payments were authorized by Congress on a *post hoc* basis as emergency supplemental payments. Supplemental legislation authorizing each of these payments was passed several months after planting for the crop year in question had occurred. Dr. Sumner included these payments in his acreage equations and asserts that producers had expectations that they would receive market loss assistance payments at the time of planting. If producers had expectations of payment, then they also knew that they would be eligible to receive such a payment regardless of what crop they planted. Indeed, they could choose not to plant and still be eligible for the payment. This would argue that market loss assistance

---

1 Westcott, P., Young, C.E., and Price, M., USDA, ERS, The 2002 Farm Act, Provisions and Implications for Commodity Markets, Economic Research Service, November 2002. (*See* Exhibit BRA-42)

2 USDA, ERS, Decoupled Payments: Household Income Transfers in Contemporary US Agriculture, M.E. Burfisher and J. Hopkins, Eds. USDA ERS AER Number 822. February 2003. (*See* Exhibit US-53)

3 As we pointed out in our *Comments Concerning Brazil's Econometric Model of 22 December 2003*, similar results are obtained by FAPRI (less than 0.3 per cent impact on cotton acreage). In contrast, Dr. Sumner's model produces results suggesting cotton acreage impacts as high as 15.9% - that is, more than 50 times larger than what the FAPRI model would indicate.

payments, like production flexibility contract payments, direct payments, and counter-cyclical payments, are decoupled from planting decisions and should not be included in an acreage response equation.[4]

7. Like other direct payments, counter-cyclical payments are based on historical production rather than actual production. The fact that the payment rate is tied to current prices does not mean that payments are less decoupled from current production. Indeed, as economists have shown, producers can hedge counter-cyclical payment rates using options markets, thus converting a counter-cyclical payment into a fixed direct payment.[5]

8. Lastly, empirical evidence supports the decoupled nature of these payments. As reported in the US Answer to Panel Question 125(5), a preliminary review of data from the Farm Service Agency shows that 47 per cent of upland cotton farms eligible for decoupled income support payments planted no cotton in marketing year 2002. This number is consistent with the Environmental Working Group data presented by Brazil in its further rebuttal submission that showed the per cent of farms receiving only contract payments in 2000, 2001, and 2002.[6] Thus, Brazil and the United States would agree that the data support the notion that decoupled income support is, in fact, decoupled from production decisions since nearly half of historic upland cotton farms no longer plant even a single acre of cotton.

9. As was shown in Exhibit US-95, enrolled upland cotton base acreage exceeded planted acreage by over 5.1 million acres. Thus, planted acres accounted for less than 73 per cent of total base acres in 2002,[7] supporting the decoupled-from-production nature of direct and counter-cyclical payments. The ratio of planted acreage to base acreage varies considerably by region, ranging from about 40 per cent of eligible base in the West to almost 93 per cent of eligible base in the Southeast. The data also support the notion that rather than being required to base planting decisions on acreage base allocations, producers were able to exercise their planting flexibility, clearly choosing to plant other crops instead of cotton.

Dr. Sumner's analysis of the US crop insurance programme ignores effects of moral hazard on yields

10. As we have documented in our previous submissions, crop insurance subsidies are generally available for most crop producers and hence do not give a

---

[4] Dr. Sumner has argued that base updating provisions of the 2002 Farm Bill effectively relink direct payments to production, but as we have shown in Dr. Glauber's presentation at the Second Panel Meeting in December 2004, the economics argue the opposite and the empirical evidence suggests that concerns that producers are planting cotton in expectation of future base updating are unfounded.

[5] Anderson, C.G. "Consider "Hedging" Strategies to Enhance Income Beyond Farm Programme Payments" Texas A&M University, Extension Economics, October 2002 (*See* Exhibit US-54)

[6] Brazil's Further Rebuttal Submission, para. 23.

[7] We note that these numbers are similar to the Environmental Working Group data that show that 73.6 per cent of total contract payments in marketing year 2002 were on farms that also received marketing loan payments.

specific advantage to one crop over another. Thus, their effects are not commodity specific, and have no or minimal impacts on cotton markets.

11. Moreover, crop insurance purchases by cotton growers have generally been at lower coverage levels than for other row crops. This was particularly the case before 2002 when less than 5 per cent of insured cotton acres were insured at coverage levels greater than 70 per cent. Over 2002-03, roughly 90 per cent of cotton acreage insured was at coverage levels of 70 per cent or less. This supports the notion that crop insurance has had minimal effects on production.

12. Lastly, the economic literature on the effects of crop insurance on production is clearly mixed. While many studies like the ones cited by Brazil have suggested crop insurance subsidies may have a slight effect on acreage, the effects on production are less clear. If crop insurance encourages moral hazard problems like those cited by Brazil, crop yields will be adversely affected as producers attempt to increase crop insurance indemnities. If moral hazard and adverse selection problems are severe, they could potentially have a negative effect on production.[8]

Impacts attributed to the export credit guarantee programme are unsubstantiated

13. Neither Brazil nor Dr. Sumner has offered empirical analysis as to how much or whether the export credit guarantee programme actually affects exports. As demonstrated in Bra-313, Dr. Sumner imposed an *ad hoc* reduction in US export estimates of 500,000 bales (using the National Cotton Council testimony as his sole economic foundation), which correspondingly reduced US prices, which correspondingly both reduced US acreage and slightly increased exports - cutting into the initially imposed 500,000 bale shift.

The effects of marketing loans depend on underlying assumptions regarding price expectations

14. As we have argued elsewhere, we agree with the statement of Dr. Collins that marketing loan payments are *potentially* production- and trade-distorting.[9] The United States has consistently notified upland cotton marketing loan payments as cotton-specific amber box payments in its WTO Domestic Support notifications. The issue in this dispute is not whether marketing loan payments are potentially production- and trade-distorting, but the degree to which they have actually distorted production and trade in a particular year, given market prices and other relevant factors.

---

8 The Economic Research Service study cited by Dr. Sumner (Young et al. 2001) only examines the effects of crop insurance subsidies on acreage. The authors assume that yields are unaffected when they simulate production effects. Recent studies by Smith and Goodwin (1996), Babcock and Hennessy (1996) and Goodwin and Smith (2003) suggest that farms with more insurance tend to use less inputs like fertilizer and pesticides and vice versa. This demonstrates a potential moral hazard problem with crop insurance that suggests that crop insurance participation may have a negative effect on yields. Lower yields may well offset the marginal effects on crop area.

9 *See* US Answers to Questions of the Panel to the Parties following the Second Meeting of the Panel, 22 December 2004, para. 74.

15. The degree of distortion caused by the marketing loan programme depends on the relationship of the expected harvest price to the loan rate at the time of planting. If the expected price is below the loan rate, the loan rate may provide an incentive to plant cotton because farmers will receive a government payment for the difference between the loan rate and the adjusted world price. For this reason, we believe that the marketing loan programme was more distorting in 2002 when expected cash prices were below loan rates at planting than in 2001, when expected cash prices were higher than loan rates at the time of planting. However, as explained previously, the observed decline in upland cotton planted acreage in marketing year 2002 was commensurate with the decline in futures prices over the previous year.

16. In this dispute two approaches have been advocated in determining farmers' expectations about prices. Brazil and its economic consultant have used lagged prices as the mechanism to gauge farmers' expectations about prices. Dr. Sumner wrote:

> Of course, it is impossible to know precisely what individual growers expect. I have adopted the long-standing approach of FAPRI, and other models[,] to approximate these expectations by using the current year final realized market prices as the expectation for the following season's price.[10]

The lagged prices used by Brazil and its economic consultant can, at best, be an approximation of farmers' price expectations. That is because the lagged prices used in Brazil's analysis incorporate pricing information that occurs *after US farmers make their planting decision* (that is, prices from April through July of a given marketing year, when planting decisions are taken in the January to March period). Therefore, by necessity, farmers cannot be looking at a lagged price that incorporates prices that do not yet exist.

17. The United States, on the other hand, has advocated the use of futures prices, a market- determined expectation of prices. It is evident from the use of futures and options markets by cotton producers[11] and from numerous market reports available to producers that producers look to futures markets rather than lagged prices for information regarding future cash prices.

18. Furthermore, economic literature supports this view. For example, in his classic paper on rational price expectations, Muth (Exhibit US-48) argued that there is little evidence that expectations based on past prices are economically meaningful. Additionally, in a 1976 paper Gardner (Exhibit US-49) contended that the future price for next year's crop is the best proxy for expected price.

19. As we have repeatedly argued, the use of lagged prices may result in biased results. Over the long term, where there is reasonable stability in markets, lagged prices function adequately as a proxy for price expectations. However, in those years, as in the period under investigation here, when unexpected exoge-

---

10 Brazil's Further Submission, Annex I, para. 18.

11 *See* US Answers to Questions of the Panel to the Parties following the Second Meeting of the Panel, 22 December 2004, para. 58.

nous shocks such as China dumping stocks and unexpected yields worldwide due to good weather conditions, lagged prices are poor predictors of expected prices. Future prices, by contrast, are more efficient because they are based on more current information.

20. For example, during marketing years 2000, 2001, 2002, and 2003, lagged prices significantly understate the harvest season prices expected by producers as seen in the futures prices at the time of planting. The use of lagged prices thereby inflate the effect of the marketing loan rate. In fact, those lagged prices would have to be increased by 8-25 per cent, depending on the year, to equal the harvest season price actually expected by producers as indicated by the futures price.[12] For the period MY 1999-2003, only MY 2002 exhibits expected prices below the marketing loan rate when using futures prices. However, over that same period, when lagged prices are used as expected prices, the loan rate is higher than the expected price *in every year over this period* except MY1999. Thus, it is a significant error for Brazil and Dr. Sumner to use lagged prices instead of the futures prices Brazil's own expert, Mr. MacDonald, explained to be the more accurate gauge of farmers' price expectations.

Harvest Futures Prices at Planting Time Compared to "Lagged Prices"(cents per pound)					
	MY1999	MY2000	MY2001	MY2002	MY2003
Futures Price[1]	60.27	61.31	58.63	42.18	59.6
Expected Cash Price[2]	55.27	56.31	53.63	37.18	54.6
Lagged Prices[3]	60.2	45	49.8	29.8	44.5
Difference	-4.93	11.31	3.83	7.38	10.1

[1] February New York futures price for December delivery.
[2] Futures price minus 5 cent cash basis.
[3] Prior crop year average farm price, weighted by monthly marketings.[13]

21. Looking more specifically at Dr. Sumner's analysis in Annex I provides further evidence of the bias of lagged prices relative to future prices. Consider the 2002 crop year. In the Sumner analysis, area response to the removal of the cotton loan programme results in a 36 per cent reduction in US planted area – the largest single effect for any of the years considered in his analysis. Based on lagged prices, price expectations for 2002 were 29.8 cents per pound, a 40 per cent reduction from 2001 levels. Yet, the futures market data suggests a far smaller reduction in expected price. December futures prices taken as the average daily closing values in February 2002 averaged 42.18 cents per pound, a 28 per cent drop from year earlier levels. Based on Dr. Sumner's range of supply response elasticities of 0.36 to 0.47, a decline of this magnitude would suggest a drop in acreage of 10 to 13 per cent from the preceding year. In fact, actual US cotton acreage dropped 12 per cent (from 15.5 million acres in 2001 to 13.7 million acres in 2002), suggesting acreage levels entirely consistent with world market conditions and price expectations. Thus, in marketing year 2002, lagged

---

12 US Further Rebuttal Submission, paras. 164-65.
13 Exhibit US-90.

prices would significantly overestimate the decline in plantings in the absence of a marketing loan rate.

22. While the United States would agree with Brazil that it is impossible to know precisely what individual farmers' price expectations are, the United States argues that futures prices provide the most current expectations of market participants. The United States disagrees with the approach used by Brazil in its analysis to rely solely on lagged prices and ignore information provided by futures prices. While it may be impractical to include futures prices in some models, modelling convenience is no justification for ignoring these objective, market-based price expectations, and the biased results from using lagged prices do not assist the Panel in making an objective assessment of what is the effect of the US marketing loan programme.

Use of the November 2002 baseline exaggerates the effects of the removal of subsidies

23. The price outlook for cotton has improved considerably since publication of the November 2002 FAPRI baseline used by Dr. Sumner to estimate the effects of subsidies on US cotton production. As we show in the *US Response to Brazil's Answers to the Questions of the Panel of the Parties Following the Second Meeting of the Panel,* FAPRI projections for the Adjusted World Price are as much as 20 cents per pound higher in the November 2003 baseline as under the November 2002 baseline.

24. As a result, estimated marketing loan gains are reduced considerably. Under the November 2003 baseline, the estimated marketing loan gain for 2003/04 is zero, compared to almost 15 cents per pound under the November 2002 baseline. Over the five year period 2003/04 to 2007/08, the average marketing loan gain is estimated to be 1.32 cents per pound. This is compared to 10.39 cents per pound utilizing the November 2002 baseline used by Dr. Sumner in his estimates.

25. Under Dr. Sumner's model, the marketing loan programme contributes to over 42 per cent of the estimated effects of removing subsidies on production (*see* Annex 1, table 1.4). Thus, updating the model to the November 2003 baseline would significantly reduce the estimated effect on production, with the remaining effects largely attributed to direct payments under Dr. Sumner's flawed model, with which we strongly disagree.

26. In addition, the FAPRI baseline from November 2002 projected 50.7 cents per pound for the A-Index for marketing year 2003 and the January 2003 baseline projected 58.4 cents per pound for the A-index for marketing year 2003. FAPRI's November 2003 preliminary baseline projection for the A-Index is 70.9 cents per pound, 40 per cent higher than the FAPRI projections used by Dr. Sumner.[14] The actual A-index was 76.1 cents per pound on January 15, 2004. In fact, FAPRI's November 2002 projections (through 2012/13) did not show the A-

14 *Cotton: World Markets and Trade*, Foreign Agricultural Service, USDA. January 2004, Table 8, pg. 20.

Index ever rising as high as current prices. The current high cotton prices and market expectations of continued high prices are crucially relevant because, as mentioned, marketing loan payments will not be made if cotton prices are above the loan rate of 52 cents per pound and, further, counter-cyclical payments will not be made if the season average farm price is above 65.73 cents per pound (the target price of 72.5 cents minus the direct payment rate of 6.67 cents). The weighted average farm price for August-November was 62.4 cents per pound, as reported by USDA on 11 January 2004.[15]

Conclusions

27. Brazil's estimates of the impact of US subsidies on world cotton markets have rested largely on the basis of Dr. Sumner's flawed model. As we pointed out in our *Comments on Brazil's Econometric Model*, Dr. Sumner's model is not the FAPRI model. The modifications he has made are *ad hoc*; rather than being based on empirical research as is claimed, they are, in fact, at odds with the empirical literature.

III. TECHNICAL COMMENTS ON BRAZIL'S REBUTTAL

28. Brazil's explanations of exactly what was done to the FAPRI/CARD model have been stated and restated by Brazil at least three times to this point.

29. With each new statement, different clarifications are made, different variables used. In Annex I, Brazil submitted its economic analysis of the impacts of the US cotton programme. In Bra-313, Brazil provided more detail about its original economic analysis, in light of its seeming inability to provide the Panel with the actual model used. Finally, in its submission of 20 January 2004, Brazil informs the Panel that its Annex I discussion was a "simple heuristic discussion"[16] with Bra-313 explaining how the "heuristic explanation in Annex I was operationalized" and rationalizes the fact it did not use the baseline it stated it did in Annex I as "necessary recalibration."[17] These *post hoc* rationalizations of Annex I differ dramatically from oral statements delivered to the Panel on 7 October 2003.[18]

---

15 *World Agricultural Supply and Demand Estimates*, USDA, WAOB, WASDE-406, 11 January 2004.

16 *See* para. 58, Brazil's Comments on US Model Critique, 20 January 2004.

17 *See* para. 3, Brazil's Comments on US Model Critique, 20 January 2004.

18 "For more detail on these equations and the discussion of the incentives provided, please refer to my written description of the model in Annex I. My Annex I statement discusses in detail the analysis of the production enhancing impacts of the US supply side subsidies." Oral Statement of Dr. Sumner, 7 October 2003, para. 11. The United States read these and other statements, and the failure of Brazil to deliver its Annex I analysis, as indication that Brazil meant what it said in Annex I. The US was unaware that the document in which Dr. Sumner "discusses in detail the analysis" was, in fact, a "simple heuristic discussion." That revelation is no doubt a surprise to the Panel, as well.

Brazil further confuses the impact of its elasticity modifications

30. Brazil clings to its repeated representations that its model uses "*exactly the same elasticities of supply and demand that are also used in the FAPRI model*,"[19] yet, in its latest iteration of what is really included in its analysis, Brazil seems to be saying something different:

> ***As I will demonstrate, the differences between the two sets of estimates of the United States is primarily due to differences in the magnitude of elasticities of supply the United States used, as compared to the elasticities that I actually used. The United States applied time-varying, linear elasticities because this is what is suggested by the FAPRI linear modelling framework. My Annex I results of the effects of these listed programmes are, however, based on a constant elasticity structure."*** [20] ***[emphasis supplied]***

31. This current claim contradicts documentation in Annex I, oral statements made before the Panel, and Bra Exhibit-313. Table I.1 of Annex I clearly presents time-varying elasticities. This time-varying approach is again reported in equation (4) – (6) of Exhibit-313. Dr. Sumner's equations clearly indicate that the supply elasticity changes depending on the year *t*.

32. The United States remains convinced that neither it nor the Panel can be fully sure of whether the elasticities used by Brazil were "exactly the same" as those used in the FAPRI model as Brazil stated on 7 October, or whether those elasticities were based on a different structure entirely, as Brazil states in its 20 January 2004 submission. Brazil has never submitted a simple table showing a comparison of the elasiticities.

33. Finally, the United States does not agree with Dr. Sumner that the time-varying, linear elasticities, which would be consistent with the FAPRI modelling framework, lead to a dramatic underestimation of the effects. The United States stands firm by its belief that FAPRI has it right and that Dr. Sumner's approach leads to a dramatic overestimation of the impacts.

Calibration vs. manipulation vs. mislabelling[21]

34. The United States pointed out that Brazil stated that its analysis in Annex I was based on the FAPRI November 1 baseline, when it, in fact, was not. Now, Brazil confirms that those baseline numbers were, in fact, "necessarily recalibrated" by Dr. Sumner in order to conform to his use of the CARD International model - a use that is not consistent with FAPRI's modelling and a use that decidedly was not made clear to the Panel in Annex I,[22] contrary to Brazil's assertions

---

[19] Oral Statement of Dr. Sumner, 7 October 2003, para. 20. A similar comment was made at least twice in Annex I.

[20] *See* para. 71, Brazil's Comments on US Model Critique, 20 January 2004.

[21] *See* para. 24 and subsequent paragraphs in Brazil's 20 January submission.

[22] In paragraph 3 of Annex I, Dr. Sumner states that he used "the international model and parameters used in two recent publications from [CARD]…." He goes on to state that the "approach used here is standard and has been applied by the USDA Economic Research Service in their analysis of

in paragraph 24 of its recent submission. Ultimately, Brazil passes off this significant discrepancy as "confusion" in the "labelling of the baseline used in Annex I."[23] This continues a pattern of carelessness in modelling and analysis that has added significantly to the burden in discerning underlying data and model constructs in order to appropriately evaluate the validity of Brazil's proffered results.[24]

Crop Insurance programme results

35. The United States continues to disagree with Dr. Sumner's characterization of the crop insurance programme presented in paragraphs 31-33. The United States does not accept Dr. Sumner's logic that $1 from the crop insurance programme that is paid in the event of a crop failure would have the same production impact as $1 of benefit that is tied directly to the production decision. While the United States does not accept Dr. Sumner's logic, we are puzzled by his operational implementation of the acreage impacts. Dr. Sumner argues that FAPRI's net returns specification includes the value of the crop insurance programme by reducing variable costs of production. Based on this first step of reasoning, it is unclear to the United States why Dr. Sumner did not implement his scenario by simply increasing the costs of production in the FAPRI baseline by the amount of the per-acre benefit that he calculates. Such an approach would have produced smaller acreage impacts.

Replicating history and predicting the future

36. In paragraphs 43-56, Dr. Sumner develops a lengthy discussion regarding his view of the use of simulation models. Dr. Sumner dismisses a US concern that Dr. Sumner's analysis does a very poor job of explaining the movement in cotton acreage in the United States. Dr. Sumner appears to assert that policy simulation models do not attempt to "forecast the future." From a layman's point of view, it seems surprising that a model that changes the past and then estimates how that change would have resulted in a different future can be said to not be an attempt to forecast the future.

---

the FSRI Act of 2002….," citing the Westcott study. However, one of the two studies referenced in footnote 4 did not use the CARD International Cotton Model; it used FAPRI's full international model. Similarly, the study referenced in footnote 5 also used FAPRI's full international model. It is clear by reviewing paras. 3-11 of Annex I (particularly footnote 10) and Dr. Sumner's Oral Statement of 7 October 2003, that Brazil's documents manifestly led the Panel to believe it was using a broad, multi-commodity international model in its analysis. Only later did Brazil clearly admit it did not use such a model and that all competing crops were not included in its international analysis.

[23] *See* para. 42, Brazil's Comments on US Model Critique, 20 January 2004.

[24] The United States notes also that with each discovered discrepancy, Brazil has supposedly rerun its analysis to demonstrate that none of its misstatements has had any appreciable affect on the Sumner model results and asserts this demonstrates the "robustness" of the Sumner model. As noted in the introductory statements to this submission, every economic result ascribed to a FAPRI-type analysis by Brazil contains the same flawed assumptions originally introduced by Dr. Sumner, apart from the few corrections Brazil has made. It is no surprise that each rerun of the same basic construct would reveal the same basic results.

37. From an economic point of view, the analysis doesn't really change. Economists who develop structural models employ a number of techniques for validating the accuracy and reliability of a model. One of those techniques is testing the ability of the model to simulate actual historical outcomes. In such an historical simulation, the model is solved for each year of a historical period and predicted values for the exogenous variables are compared to the actual data. Not only is the model evaluated based on its ability to approximate historical values, but also on its ability to capture the turning points in the observed values, i.e. determine if the model's predicted values for a variable move in the same direction as the actual values from one year to the next.

38. The process of model validation involves testing the performance of the model over the historical period that corresponds to the timeframe used for the statistical estimation of parameter values, i.e. the in-sample period. In addition, the model will also be tested over a historical period outside of the estimation period. This is referred to as out-of-sample validation. If a model does not perform well under these validation methods, then particular components or equations within the system are evaluated and re-specified.

39. It does not appear that Dr. Sumner employed any of these standard techniques for validating the robustness of his model. It is doubtful that his model, with its modified acreage equations, would pass this common test. However, despite the lack of documented validation of the model, Dr. Sumner nevertheless proceeds to use the model and treats the results as credible.

40. Dr. Sumner's "simple illustration" provided in paragraph 50 does not address the true issue and is not relevant to the example of US cotton. The United States has repeatedly shown that the overriding economic signals that have affected cotton acreage have been the expected prices of cotton and relevant competing crops.

41. To conclude our response to Dr. Sumner's arguments in paragraphs 43-56, it is abundantly clear that Dr. Sumner can produce no meaningful empirical validation for his approach. His results are based on forced outcomes that are the results of his *ad hoc* modelling specifications.

Inconsistent descriptions of "full net revenue"

42. In paragraph 63, Dr. Sumner states that "full net revenue including all programme payments" form the basis for his model specification. He states that he does not understand how the United States made such a mistaken assumption. Dr. Sumner's current claim is in direct contradiction to his documentation in Exhibit Bra-313.

43. On page 2, in equation (2) and the subsequent paragraph of Exhibit Bra-313, Dr. Sumner clearly states that his net revenue includes only the farm price and the marketing loan and not the full programme payments. Then, in equations (4) - (6), the net revenue, which presumably is the same as specified in equation (2), is again denoted as being a portion of the denominator in his determination of the impacts of the programme in question. The United States maintains its assertion that the full programme payments should have been in the denominator

of the function. Neither the United States nor the Panel can be certain of Dr. Sumner's exact approach because his explanation changes with each submission.

Incorrect assertions

44. Dr. Sumner's criticisms in paragraph 65 of the calculations provided by the United States are unfounded.

45. The claim in paragraph 65 that the Southern Plains revenue of $109.04 does not include marketing loan benefits is patently incorrect. The Panel and Dr. Sumner need only to look in cell AO236 of the Equations sheet of the file FINAL US2003CropsModel WORKOUT.xls and they will find that the value of net revenue from the market and the marketing loan is $109.04. All subsequent critiques on this issue put forth by Dr. Sumner are obviously incorrect because of his error reading the spreadsheets submitted by Brazil.

46. Dr. Sumner attempts to invalidate the US criticisms in paragraph 69-70 by claiming that the numbers are not the ones reported in Annex I. He indicates that the numbers were generated by the United States, but that is incorrect. The United States properly references the source of the acreage impacts as being the file FINAL US2003CropsModel WORKOUT.xls. More specifically, the data come from rows 721-771 of the Equations sheet and are the first-round impacts reported in the model. These are appropriately compared to first-round impacts calculated in the US critique.

Marketing loan and step 2 impacts

47. Given Brazil's efforts to misstate the US position on marketing loan and step 2 impacts in paragraphs 8 and 9, the United States refers the Panel to its earlier discussion included in section G (paragraphs 152, et seq.) in the US Further Rebuttal Submission, 18 November 2003 where the United States stresses the need for the Panel to investigate the actual decisions facing producers making their planting decisions. The United States has also not altered its position regarding the step 2 programme. The US submission of 22 December 2003 was directed at its critique of Dr. Sumner's economic modelling. While the US has indicated to the Panel its belief that the FAPRI model is not the best measure of impacts of the marketing loan or step 2 programmes, it did not specifically criticize Brazil's analytical method in this regard as Brazil apparently did not make significant changes to the FAPRI model on these points - as it did in virtually every other aspect of its analysis.

Annex I results have never been independently confirmed

48. The models used and outputs obtained by Brazil and submitted to the Panel were not retained by Brazil's employed experts.[25] The record remains incomplete with respect to Dr. Sumner's adaptations.

---

[25] *See* Letter dated October 31, 2003 from Dr. Bruce Babcock to Dr. Dan Sumner, submitted to the Panel by Brazil on 5 November 2003.

49. The United States has found that the current submission by Dr. Sumner is fraught with many of the same types of errors contained in his previous submissions. He disputes numbers that are taken directly from files that either he or Dr. Babcock has provided to the Panel. He continues to provide contradictory explanations and documentation of his methodology. Furthermore, detailed electronic verification of his calculations used in Annex I have never been provided to the United States or the Panel. Dr. Sumner has repeatedly claimed that he has provided all information to the Panel. That is obviously not the case, since new information, such as the regional crop insurance numbers, were just provided in this most recent submission.

Impacts attributed to the export credit guarantee programme are unsubstantiated

50. The United States is surprised that, despite repeated opportunities to offer some degree of economic support to the 500,000 bale impact Brazil attributes to the US export credit guarantee programme, Brazil has still not done so.[26] Worse, Brazil still refers to its estimates of the impact of this programme as "conservative." As the United States indicated in its critique of the Sumner model, the figures bandied about regarding acreage impacts of the export credit guarantee programme on cotton are anything but conservative.

51. In the September 9 Brazil Submission before the Second Session of the First Panel Meeting, (paragraphs 192-194), Brazil implied that Dr. Sumner's export estimates with respect to the export credit guarantee programme were more conservative than the unsubstantiated estimate it cites from the National Cotton Council (the "NCC"). Paragraph 194 of that submission acts as if the NCC estimate of a possible 3 cent per pound US price impact and Dr. Sumner's estimate of a .57 cent per pound *world* price impact are somehow independent analyses - and demonstrate Dr. Sumner's conservative approach. However, as demonstrated in Bra-313, all Dr. Sumner did was force a reduction in the US export estimates of 500,000 bales (*using the NCC testimony as his sole economic foundation*), which correspondingly reduced prices in the US, which correspondingly both reduced US acreage and slightly increased exports - cutting into the initially imposed 500,000 bale shift.

52. The "different" price estimates were, in fact, estimates of two different sets of prices - US and world. Brazil inappropriately characterized Dr. Sumner's results as being conservative relative to the NCC estimate. (*see* para. 192, Brazil's Further Submission to the Panel, 9 September 2003) Later when the Panel raised a question about the results, Dr. Sumner somehow forced a full 500,000 bale decline in US exports, ignoring the impacts of price response. (*See*, *e.g.*, Bra-325, last category of tables - export credit guarantee with fixed 500,000 bale impact.)In that response, Brazil also maintained the stance that these two "analyses," neither demonstrating economic foundation, were somehow independent,

---

[26] Other than citing congressional testimony offered by the National Cotton Council, a US trade association that operates on behalf of the US cotton industry.

while fairly clearly demonstrating that Dr. Sumner merely took the NCC testimony and imposed a 500,000 bale demand shift.

53. Neither Brazil nor Dr. Sumner have ever offered any analysis at all as to how much or whether the export credit guarantee programme actually affects exports. They took someone else's word for it, with no demonstrated economic foundation - much the same approach Brazil has asked the Panel to take with respect to important aspects of the Annex I model.

Conclusions

54. Dr. Sumner's economic analysis should not be relied upon by the Panel as credible support for any findings on the effect of challenged US cotton subsidies. Brazil offers Dr. Sumner's model results as evidence that *but for* the US cotton programmes, US cotton acreage would have declined and world prices would have increased. In order to support this claim, Brazil and Dr. Sumner had to make significant modifications to a previously well-respected econometric system. The United States has demonstrated the weakness inherent in those modifications and the failure of Brazil to independently validate those modifications. Throughout its submissions, Brazil has claimed that nebulous factors such as a producer's "anticipation of policy change" are legitimate pillars on which to base Dr. Sumner's modifications to the FAPRI model. Brazil has pushed this questionable logic despite the fact that FAPRI itself has refused to ascribe the type of impacts forced on its model by Brazil. When confronted by the United States and pointedly questioned about the particulars of its approach, Brazil has been unable to advance convincing, supportable or even consistent explanations of its analysis.

55. As stated previously, while the US has demonstrated fatal flaws in Brazil's arguments on subsidy identification, causation, and its actionable subsidies claims, it is clear to the United States that *but for* the significant modification and adaptation of the FAPRI model carried out by Brazil and Dr. Sumner, acreage impacts attributed to the US cotton programme by that economic model would be far less than reported in Annex I. Brazil has offered nothing in its critique to change the US view of the failure of Brazil's evidence to prove this aspect of its claim.

ANNEX I-17

BRAZIL'S RESPONSE TO THE PANEL'S QUESTIONS
11 February 2004

Table of Cases

Short Title	Full Case and Citation
EC – Hormones	Arbitrator Report, *EC – Measures Concerning Meat and Meat Products (Hormones)*, WT/DS26/15, WT/DS48/13, circulated 29 May 1998.
Brazil – Aircraft	Panel Report, *Brazil – Export Financing Programme for Aircraft*, WT/DS46/R, adopted 20 August 1999.
Canada – Aircraft	Panel Report, *Canada – Measures Affecting the Export of Civilian Aircraft*, WT/DS/70, adopted 20 August 1999.
Korea – Alcoholic Beverages	Arbitrator Report, *Korea – Taxes on Alcoholic Beverages*, WT/DS75/16 and WT/DS84/14, circulated, 4 June 1999.
US – FSC	Panel Report, *United States – Tax Treatment for "Foreign Sales Corporation"*, WT/DS108/R, adopted 20 March 2000.
Australia – Leather	Panel Report, *Australia – Subsidies Provided to Producers and Exporters of Automotive Leather*, WT/DS126/R, adopted 16 June 1999.
US – 1916 Act	Arbitrator Report, *US – Anti-Dumping Act of 1916*, WT/DS136/11 and WT/DS162/14, circulated 28 February 2001.
Canada – Automotive Industry	Panel Report, *Canada – Certain Measures Affecting the Automotive Industry*, WT/DS139/R and WT/DS/142/R, adopted 19 June 2000.
US – Section 110	Arbitrator Report, *United States – Section 110(5) of the US Copyright Act*, WT/DS160/12, circulated 15 January 2001.
US – Hot-Rolled Steel	Arbitrator Report, *US – Hot-Rolled Steel from Japan*, WT/DS184/13, circulated 19 February 2002.
US – Byrd Amendment	Arbitrator Report, *US – Continued Dumping and Subsidy Offset Act*, WT/DS217/14 and WT/DS234/22, circulated 13 June 2003.
Canada – Aircraft II	Panel Report, *Canada – Measures Affecting the Export of Civilian Aircraft*, WT/DS222/R, adopted 19 February 2002.

276. The Panel notes the parties' responses and comments relating to Question No. 252 concerning the time period within which any prohibited measure must be withdrawn within the meaning of Article 4.7 of the *SCM Agreement*. Please supplement your original response, taking into account the particular nature of each alleged prohibited subsidy measure(i.e. "Step 2" payments under Section 1207(a) of the 2002 FSRI Act, export credit guarantee programmes and the ETI Act) and the functioning of the US legal and regulatory system in respect of these measures.

Brazil's Answer:

1. Brazil thanks the Panel for the opportunity to supplement its 22 December 2003 response to Question 252.[1] As Brazil has previously noted, the three prohibited subsidies at issue in this dispute (Step 2 payments, CCC export credit guarantees and ETI Act subsidies) all involve mandatory measures requiring changes to the statutes that provide for these prohibited subsidies.

2. The ordinary meaning of the phrase "without delay" in Article 4.7 of the SCM Agreement is "as quickly as possible." While the text does not state "immediately," neither does it use a qualifier such as "reasonable delay." The term implies a certain sense of urgency. And it suggests that implementing governments must move more quickly to implement prohibited subsidies measures than other types of measures. In particular, the phrase "without delay" requires a faster implementation than the "reasonable period of time" provisions of Article 21.3 of the DSU. Article 21.3 provides that if it is "*impracticable* to comply immediately with the recommendations and rulings, the Member shall have a *reasonable* period of time in which to do so" (emphasis added). The use of terms "impracticable" and "reasonable" suggest a less urgent approach to implementation in DSU Article 21.3 than in Article 4.7 of the SCM Agreement. This is exactly how the provisions of DSU Article 21.3 have been interpreted by a number of arbitrators, as discussed below.

3. The context of Article 4.7 of the SCM Agreement strongly supports a more rapid implementation for prohibited subsidy measures than for other measures. First, there are special expedited dispute settlement procedures in Articles 4.4-4.6 of the SCM Agreement for prohibited subsidy disputes. Why would the drafters have cut the time for litigating prohibited subsidy cases in half, if they had expected "business as usual" in the implementation phase by using the same "reasonable period" implementation provisions of DSU Article 21.3? The "special rule and procedure" status of Article 4.7 of the SCM Agreement in DSU Annex 2 is also significant. This special status must be given meaning by the Panel. To simply treat implementation according to the "reasonable period of time" standard of DSU Article 21.3, as the United States argument suggests[2],would effectively denude the "without delay" standard in Article 4.7 of any "special" status.

4. The"prohibited" status of subsidies covered by Articles 3 and 4 of the SCM Agreement suggests that the object and purpose of prohibited subsidy disciplines is to create significant disincentives for Members to continue providing such subsidies. These provisions demonstrate that negotiators determined that special dispute settlement and implementation procedures were required for prohibited subsidies because of their particularly trade-distorting nature. The object and purpose of Articles 3 and 4 would be frustrated if the phrase "without delay" were interpreted to permit a Member to take as long as normally required to implement any legislative changes. Each day that a prohibited subsidy, such as Step

[1] *See* Brazil's 22 December 2003 Answers to Questions, para. 167.

[2] *See* US 28 January 2004 Comments, paras. 175-177.

2 payments, continues to be provided is a day in which trade is distorted. This is particularly true given the recent fall in cotton futures prices.[3]

5. There is only one precedent applying the Article 4.7 "without delay" provision to prohibited subsidy measures requiring legislative changes. In the *US – FSC* dispute, the Panel found 1 October 000 (15 months after the interim report was issued) to be the appropriate "without delay" period.[4] However, the facts of *US – FSC* highlight the reason for such a long period of implementation. In that case, the Panel found that legislation repealing a *tax* break had to be enacted *before* the start of the next US fiscal (*i.e.,* tax) year. The Panel found that in view of the likely appeal of its report and the timing of the fiscal year, 1 October 2000 would be the earliest possible implementation date and, thus, a period of time constituting "without delay".[5]

6. Unlike the FSC measure, the export credit guarantee and Step 2 subsidies at issue in this dispute are not tax breaks determined (retrospectively) on the basis of annual income and in force for a fiscal year. Step 2 payments and export credit guarantees are also not paid on the basis of marketing years or any other time period. Instead, the beneficiaries of these two types of prohibited subsidies receive financial contributions that confer benefits on a *transaction-by-transaction* basis. Therefore, the United States cannot claim that there is a need to wait to enact legislation before a "fiscal year", as was required in the *US – FSC* dispute.[6]

7. Although the DSU Article 21.3 standard requires a less rapid legislative response than Article 4.7 of the SCM Agreement, the decisions of various arbitrators provide a useful reference point for the Panel's interpretation of Article 4.7. The now standard language in almost all arbitrators' reports under DSU Article 21.3 is that implementation must occur in the shortest period possible within the *normal* legal system of a Member.[7] DSU Article 21.3(c) implementation need not employ "extraordinary legislative procedures".[8] In other words, under DSU Article 21.3, an implementing Member's legislative process need not move faster than it would *normally* operate in moving legislation through its legal system.[9]

8. But the Panel's role is to interpret the meaning of Article 4.7 of the SCM Agreement and to give meaning to the term "without delay" as a special provision *apart* from DSU Article 21.3. This does not require the Panel to find that there is a conflict between the provisions. Rather, the Panel must prevent Article 4.7 from being totally absorbed within the meaning of DSU Article 21.3, as that

---

[3] http://www.nybot.com (click on cotton and then futures). As of 10 February 2004, the futures price for the March 2004 contract had fallen to 64.96 cents from a high of 86 cents in October 2003.

[4] Panel Report, *US – FSC*, WT/DS108/R, para. 8.8.

[5] *Ibid.*

[6] *Ibid.*

[7] Arbitrator Report, *EC – Hormones*, WT/DS26/15, para. 26. *See* also Arbitrator Report, *US – Section 110*, WT/DS160/12, para. 31.

[8] Arbitrator Report, *US – Section 110*, WT/DS160/12, para. 32; Arbitrator Report, *Korea – Alcoholic Beverages*, WT/DS75/16, para. 42.

[9] Arbitrator Report, *US – Section 110*, WT/DS160/12, para. 32.

latter provision has been interpreted by numerous arbitrators. Any interpretation of Article 4.7 that would not give it special and independent meaning by instead adopting a "business as usual" approach to implementation for prohibited subsidy measures would render that provision inutile.

9. In determining what "without delay" means for the United States' implementation obligations in this case, Brazil notes that various arbitrators have emphasized that the US Congress has considerable flexibility to enact legislation quickly.[10] The United States has confirmed this fact.[11] Indeed, the United States enacted the FSC replacement measure in less than eight months after the adoption of the panel report in *US – FSC*.[12] Arbitrators applying DSU Article 21.3(c) have found that the United States must be given the right to use "normal" legislative procedures, and therefore granted the United States between 10[13] and 15[14] months for implementation requiring legislative changes. But Article 4.7 of the SCM Agreement is not a "normal" procedure – it is a special one. And it requires special efforts of implementing legislators to act more quickly than may be "normal".

10. The record shows that Step 2 payments are prohibited subsidies that are paid upon proof of export shipments or domestic use by US textile mills. Eliminating this prohibited subsidy requires no complex word play or textual wrangling. Rather, it simply involves the repeal of Section 1207(a) of the 2002 FSRI Act. Therefore, Brazil considers that 90 days after the adoption of the Panel Report by the DSB should be considered to be "without delay".[15]

11. With respect to the CCC export credit guarantee programmes, the Panel should specify that within six months after the adoption of the Panel Report, the prohibited subsidies must be withdrawn by enacting the necessary changes to the statutes and regulations providing for GSM 102, GSM 103 and SCGP. These changes would have to result in CCC guarantees being provided on market terms and at premium rates that are adequate to cover the long-term operating costs and losses of the programmes. Due to the more complex nature of the implementation with respect to the CCC export credit guarantee programmes, Brazil consid-

---

[10] Arbitrator Report, *US – Section 110*, WT/DS160/12, para. 38; Arbitrator Report, *US – 1916 Act*, WT/DS136/11, para. 43; Arbitrator Report, *US – Byrd Amendment*, WT/DS217/14, para. 32.

[11] Arbitrator Report, *US – Section 110*, WT/DS160/12, para. 38.

[12] Arbitrator Report, *US – 1916 Act*, WT/DS136/11, para. 43.

[13] Arbitrator Report, *US – 1916 Act*, WT/DS136/11, para. 45.

[14] Arbitrator Report, *US – Hot-Rolled Steel*, WT/184/13, para. 40. Brazil notes that this case also involved changes to the regulations that could only be adopted after the underlying statute had been changed by Congress. Therefore, the arbitrator considered a period of more than 10 months to be "reasonable."

[15] The period of 90 days is also consistent with the specification of earlier panels that "without delay" generally means 90 days. *See* Brazil's 22 December 2003 Answers to Questions, para. 167. *See* Panel Report, *Brazil – Aircraft*, WT/DS46/R, para. 8.5; Panel Report, *Canada – Aircraft*, WT/DS70/R, para. 10.4; Panel Report, *US – FSC*, WT/DS108/R, paras. 8.7-8.8; Panel Report, *Australia – Leather*, WT/DS126/R, paras. 10.6-10.7, Panel Report, *Canada – Automotive Industry*, WT/DS139/R and WT/DS142/R, paras. 11.6-11.7, and Panel Report, *Canada – Aircraft II*, WT/DS222/R, para. 8.4.

ers a period of time of six months to be consistent with the "without delay" obligation.

12. With respect to the ETI Act, the United States has repeatedly indicated that implementation is underway and that "bills are before both houses of Congress that would repeal the FSC and that have been reported out of their respective committees."[16] In view of the implementation process, which has already begun, and the text of Article 4.7 of the SCM Agreement requiring the withdrawal of the prohibited subsidies "without delay", the Panel should specify that, with respect to the ETI Act, "without delay" means a period of 90 days. This represents an appropriate period of time that would be consistent with the "without delay" obligation to withdraw the ETI Act.

16 *See* most recently: US 28 January 2004 Comments, para. 177. *See* also US 11 July 2003 First Submission, para. 189 and US 11 August Answers to Questions, paras. 229-230.

ANNEX I-18

UNITED STATES' RESPONSE TO THE PANEL'S QUESTIONS

11 February 2004

259. With respect to the Privacy Act of 1974, 5 U.S.C. 552a:

(a) Whose interests are protected under section 552a(b) in light of the definition of "individual" in section 552a(a)(2)? Do all payment recipients, including corporations and organizations, have Privacy Act rights? If not, is the United States prevented by its domestic law from releasing such of the information requested on 12 January 2004 as relates to payment recipients without Privacy Act rights? Please explain with references to case law.

1. We appreciate the Panel's interest in the Privacy Act interests that the United States Department of Agriculture is obligated, under US domestic law, to protect. Farm-specific planting data is one such protected interest[1], and was one since long before the inception of this dispute. We discuss this point further in response to question 259(c) below.

2. Under the Privacy Act of 1974, generally, "[n]o agency shall disclose any record which is contained in a system of records by any means of communication to any person ... ". 5 U.S.C. 552a(b). The statute provides a criminal penalty for any agency employee who willfully discloses protected records knowing that disclosure is prohibited.5 U.S.C. 552(a)(I)(1). A "record" is defined as "any item, collection, or grouping of information about an individual that is maintained by an agency" (5 U.S.C. 552a(a)(4)), and an "individual" is defined as "a citizen of the United States or an alien lawfully admitted for permanent residence" (5 U.S.C. 552a(a)(2)). Therefore, courts have held that the rights of the Privacy Act of 1974 do not extend to corporations or organizations. *See, e.g., Dresser Industries v. United States*, 596 F.2d 1231 (5th Cir. 1979). While corporations do not have a personal privacy interest, closely held corporations are an exception in that the release of information about the corporation is tantamount to a release of information on the individuals involved.

3. With respect to planting information of non-closely held corporations, courts have heldthat information voluntarily received from a corporation is to be withheld under exemption (4) of the Freedom of Information Act (FOIA), 5 U.S.C. 552 (5 USC (b)(4)), if it is not the type of information that would customarily released by the corporation to the public. *See also*, *Center for Auto Safety v. National Highway Traffic Safety Administration*, 244 F.3d 144, 147 (DC Cir. 2001). This is the case with respect to plantings. Furthermore, the Trade Secrets Act, 18 U.S.C. 1905, prohibits the release of any information that falls within the

[1] We discuss below an exception to this principle for farms owned by corporations other than closely held corporations.

exemption from disclosure provided by 5 U.S.C. (b)(4) unless otherwise permitted by law. *CNA Financial Corp. v. Donovan*, 830 F.2d 1132, 1151-1152 (D.C. Cir. 1987).

4. The 1999-2001 plantings information of non-closely held corporations was voluntarily submitted. For 2002 and beyond the reports are required by statute. Thus, such data could presumably be released for non-closely held corporations (it would still be protected under the Privacy Act for individuals and closely-held corporations). However, determining which farms are non-closely corporations would require examining, on a case by case basis, the circumstances of each operation. That would requirethe consideration in county offices across the cotton-growing country of some 200,000 files.

5. As explained in the US letter of 20 January 2004, Brazil's insistence on receipt of contract payment and planting data identified by farm number is unnecessary to resolution of the issues in this dispute. Instead, to the extent any of this information is relevant to this dispute, given Brazil's arguments, aggregation of payment data would provide information in the appropriate format, and aggregation would moreover be consistent with US law. The Panel has now requested aggregated data, and as explained elsewhere in today's submissions the United States is working to provide that.

(b) The Panel notes that data concerning the four relevant programmes, in particular, payment amounts, identified by specific farms, is freely available on the internet. Please explain why that data can be disclosed but the requested planted acreage data cannot. Do individual recipients have Privacy Act rights with respect to their entrepreneurial activity? Please explain with references to case law.

6. The Panel is correct to distinguish between information on government activity and government payments, and individual activity, in particular individual entrepreneurial activity. Indeed, there are long-standing and well-recognized distinctions in the United States between, on the one hand, government-generated information and conclusions formed by the government itself (such as payment amounts, bases, and yields), and, on the other hand, the private reportings of farmers (such as plantings) which do not generate any payments and which are submitted for compliance purposes only. Filings of the latter kind have long been recognized in US agricultural law as being private in nature. *See, e.g.*, 7 USC 1373 and 7 USC 1502(c) (protecting such filings under the terms of the Agricultural Act of 1938 and in the crop insurance context).[2]

7. The interrelationship between the Privacy Act of 1974 and the FOIA requires an analysis balancing the privacy interest of the individual with the "core purpose" of FOIA which is to "shed light on an agency's performance of its statutory duties". *United States Department of Justice v. Reporters Committee for Freedom of the Press*, 489 US 749 (1989). Information that does not directly

[2] It would be odd, to say the least, to say that such planted acreage information would be protected for crop insurance purposes but then releaseable by some other avenue.

disclose government operations cannot be factored into the balance. *Reporters Committee*, 489 US at 775.

8. Information concerning planted acreage does not demonstrate anything regarding the government's operation – it only demonstrates what a producer is doing. Accordingly it is protected from disclosure. By contrast, information regarding payment amounts relate to the government's implementation of farm programmes, and this outweighs any privacy interest on the part of the producer.[3]

9. With respect to the final part of the Panel's question, while there is a split of authority in US courts as to whether individuals have Privacy Act rights with respect to their entrepreneurial activities, the Department of Agriculture has determined that an individual acting in an entrepreneurial capacity is protected by the Privacy Act of 1974. *See Metadure Corporation v. United States*, 490 F. Supp. 1368 (S.D.N.Y. 1980); *Campaign for Family Farms v. Glickman*, 200 F.3d 1180 (8th Cir. 2000).

(c) Please provide any further available evidence of the USDA's long-standing policy that planted acreage information will not be released.

10. Exhibit US-144 is a notice dated December 1, 1998, from the Acting Administrator of the Farm Service Agency ("FSA") to all FSA employees setting out "FSA's policy on information that can be released" to the public and "exclusions to FSA's policy on releasing lists of names and addresses. Page 2 of the notice states that "[a]creage, production data, and other producer-related information, without any personal identifiers attached, may be released when grouped ... unless the request would be able to identify an individual producer from the information provided".

11. Exhibit US-143 is a 18 September 1998, memorandum from the Director of the Legislative Liaison Staff for FSA, to State Offices. In this document, the author seeks to correct any misunderstandings that may have arisen after the *Washington Post* district court decision regarding what information may be releaseable under the Freedom of Information Act. The memorandum makes clear that, unlike the payment data at issue in that case, planted acreage information is not releaseable information under FOIA.

12. The Panel will see from these document that the positions taken by the Department of Agriculture here predate this dispute by several years.

260. On 27 August 2003, in its response to Question No. 67 bis, the United States indicated that "it does not maintain information on the amount of expenditures made under the cited programmes to US upland cotton producers". On 12 January 2004, the Panel requested the United States to provide information "to permit an assessment of the total expenditures of PFC,

---

3 This sort of weighing process was the basis of the decision in *Washington Post Company v. United States Department of Agriculture*, 943 F.Supp. 31 (D.D.C. 1996). There, the court found some privacy interest in payment information, but found that interest to be both minimal and outweighed by a "substantial" public interest in identifying "fraud and conflict of interest". 943 F. Supp. at 37.

MLA, CCP and direct payments by the US Federal Government to upland cotton producers in the relevant marketing years". On 20 January 2004, the United States informed the Panel that "the data already provided by the United States to Brazil and the Panel would permit an assessment of total expenditures of decoupled payments to farms planting upland cotton". Is the latest statement responsive to the Panel's request? If so, how can it be reconciled with the first statement?

13. It is important to distinguish between information on *plantings* and information on *production*. The United States maintains some information on plantings, but does not maintain information on individual farm production. The 27 August 2003 statement concerned production, while the 20 January 2004 statement concerned plantings. Brazil has all of the payment data and, for every "cotton farm" (as defined in Exhibit BRA-369), all of the yield data and all of the base data. In addition, the summary files that the United States prepared also present total cropland data for these "cotton farms". However, the United States does not maintain information on whether farms that planted cotton produced (i.e., harvested) that cotton or abandoned it. For cotton, abandonment rates can be significant.

261. Please confirm that each record in the actual planting database relates to a specific farm (Filenames: rPFCplac and rDCPplac in Exhibits US-111 and US-112). For example, in the data from rDCPplac:

> **First line:**
> **Field9;Field16;Field22;Field28;Field34;Field40;Field46;Field52;Field58;Field64;Field70Field76;Field82;Field88;Field94;Field100**
>
> **Second line:**
> **237.10;23059.80;5566.20;0.00;0.00;0.00;0.00;0.00;0.00;0.00;0.00;0.00;0.00;0.00;0.00;0.00**
>
> **Does the second line represent data on plantings by the same farm?**

14. Yes, we can confirm that the panel's understanding of the files is correct. That is, for the detailed farm-by-farm text files, each farm was given its own line, with fields separated by semi-colons. The last field would not be followed by any mark; rather, after the last field for a given farm, a new line was started, indicating a new farm entry.

262. The Panel has noted the two CD-ROMs delivered by the US in the evening of 23 December 2003. They are marked "US-111" and "US-112" respectively, but the contents actually do not correspond to the indication. The Panel also takes note of the US letter dated 28 January 2004 and the CD-ROM delivered together with it. For the record, please clarify the correct CD-ROMs and provide corresponding descriptions of their contents with exhibit numbers.

15. The United States originally prepared and submitted six data files. The files designated "PFCby.txt" (the base acreage and yield file for the PFC pay-

ment era)[4] and "DCPby.txt" (the base acreage and yield file for the DCP payment era)[5] set out all base acres for each "programme crop" on every identified farm and the associated programme yield. For the Panel's and Brazil's convenience, the United States also calculated the payment units (bushels or pounds) for each "programme crop".

16. The United States also provided farm-by-farm planted acreage information, with farm-identifying information removed, in the files "PFCplac.txt" (planted acreage for the PFC payment era)[6] and "DCPplac.txt" (planted acreage for the DCP payment era).[7] The United States has explained that, under US law, it could not provide the farm-by-farm planted acreage information in a format that would permit identification of a specific farm.[8]

17. Finally, to assist the Panel and Brazil in interpreting the voluminous data provided, the United States prepared and submitted summary files setting out aggregate cropland, base acreage, base yield, payment units, and planted acreage. These summaries were labeled "PFCsum.xls" (for the PFC payment era) and "DCPsum.xls" (for the DCP payment era).

18. On 28 January 2004, the United States submitted revised data files to the Panel that corrected for certain programming errors that inevitably resulted in the rush to provide nearly 220 megabytes of data within the limited time available to reply to Brazil's request for data. As set out in the US letter of 28 January, the file names are identical to those previously submitted but with an "r" preceding the original file name. Thus, the files are now titled "rDcpsum.xls" (aggregate data file), "rDcpby.txt' (farm-by-farm base and yield data file), "rDcpplac.txt" (planted acres file), "rPfcsum.xls" (aggregate data file), "rPfcby.txt" (base and yield data file), and "rPfcplac.txt" (planted acres file).

19. In Exhibit US-145 that is being submitted today, the United States sets out the contents of the four revised farm-by-farm ".txt" files (that is, not the summary files) that were submitted to the Panel on 28 January 2004, on CD-ROM.(We note that, in each of the four ".txt" files, the fields are separated by colons and field labels are set out within the file, with each farm having its own line, just as in the corresponding ".txt" files submitted on 18 and 19 December 2003.)These four revised files follow the same fields and formats as the files originally submitted on 18 and 19 December 2003. As explained on 28 January, those revised electronic files were prepared and submitted after the United States became aware of certain errors in the original data files submitted.

---

4 A description of the file contents for the "PFCby.txt" file was submitted as Exhibit US-109.

5 We note that Exhibit US-111 set out a description of the file contents (by field number and heading) for the "DCPby.txt" file. Any marking of a CD-ROM delivered on 23 December 2003, as "Exhibit US-111" was therefore in error.

6 A description of the file contents for the "PFCplac.txt" file was submitted as Exhibit US-110.

7 We note that Exhibit US-112 set out a description of the file contents for the "DCPplac.txt" file. Therefore, any marking of a CD-ROM delivered on 23 December 2003, as "Exhibit US-112" was in error. We apologize for any confusion that may have been caused.

8 *See* US Letter to Panel of 18 December 2003; US Letter to Panel of 20 January 2004; US Answers to Questions 259(a), (b), (c) from the Panel (11 February 2004).

263. The Panel has noted that the United States' response to Question No. 214 refers to Exhibits US-117 and US-118. Are these the correct documents to which the United States intended to refer in that response? If not, please provide a copy of regulations regarding the marketing loan programme and loan deficiency payments published at 58 Federal Register 15755, dated 24 March 1993.

20. The exhibits submitted in response to Question 214 were in error. A copy of the 24 March 1993, Federal Register notice is attached as Exhibit US-263. The United States regrets any inconvenience its error may have caused.

264. The Panel asks the United States to clarify certain aspects of Exhibit US-128:

(a) Is the Panel correct in understanding that - as Brazil asserts in footnotes 290 and 291 of Brazil's 28 January 2004 comments on US responses to questions - Exhibit US-128, all data are presented on a cohort-specific basis? If so, please also present the information originally requested by the Panel in another chart containing programme (as opposed to cohort-specific) activity by fiscal year.

21. The data presented in Exhibit US-128 is presented on a cohort-specific basis. However, a cohort by definition reflects activity related to guarantees issued within a specific fiscal year. Exhibit US-128 also presents such data with respect to each of the individual programmes (GSM-102, GSM-103, and SCGP), as well as their cumulative totals. This data reflects actual performance of the programmes, unlike the data in the US budget to which Brazil alludes in its footnote 290, which, as the United States has repeatedly explained, are based on estimates and re-estimates required under the Federal Credit Reform Act of 1990.

22. Although the data in Exhibit US-128 is already presented by programme (as well as cumulatively), the United States infers from the Panel's question that it nevertheless would like to see a different presentation of the same data. Accordingly, Exhibit US-147 presents the same data, except Columns D (Claim Payments), E (Claims Recovered), F (Claims Rescheduled), G (Claims Outstanding), L (interest collected on claims recovered), and M (interest collected on reschedulings) are presented on a chronological basis (i.e., instead of applying the particular activity back to the cohort of the guaranteerelated to such activity, the cash-flows are set out in the fiscal year in which they occurred).

(b) Does the US agree with the statement in paragraph 135 of Brazil's 28 January 2004 comments on US responses to questions that the difference between the $1,148 billion in the chart at para. 165 of Brazil's 11 August answers to questions and the $666 million amount in Exhibit US-128 ($1.75 billion) closely corresponds to the total "Claims rescheduled" figure reported by the US in Exhibit US-128 (column F)?

23. The United States is examining the cited figures and expects to be able to provide an answer within the same period as its response to the Panel's supplemental request for information.

(c) Does the US agree that from the formula in column G (that is: (Column (D) minus (E) minus (F)), it follows that a rescheduled claim no longer constitutes an outstanding claim at the moment the terms of the re-scheduling are agreed and that a rescheduling is treated as 100 per cent recovered, as Brazil states in footnote 292 of Brazil's 28 January 2004 comments on US responses to questions?

24. The Panel's understanding is correct. However, other than interest collected on reschedulings, Exhibit US-128 does not reflect the receipt of payments under the reschedulings. Consequently, no principal paymentsreceived under reschedulings are reflected in Exhibit US-128. As the principal amounts rescheduled are set forth in Column F and subtracted from Claims Outstanding in Column G, to include such principal payments as received would constitute double-counting.

(d) Is the Panel correct in understanding that the amount of $888,984,792.04 in column F in Exhibit US-128 under "ALL" for 1992 represents the total continuing amount of unrecovered claims for the 1992 cohort, and that the amount of 387,692,219.39 represents the total continuing amount of unrecovered claims for the 1993 cohort, etc? Please indicate and substantiate how much principal and/or interest has actually been paid/recovered/rescheduled annually 1992-2003 in respect of each of the amounts shown in Columns D, E & F in the table.

25. The Panel's understandingis not correct. The figures in column F to which the question refers do *not* reflect a continuing amount of unrecovered claims. As reflected in the response to question 264(c) these figures do not in any way reflect payment performance under the reschedulings themselves and therefore do not reflect a "continuing amount of unrecovered claims". Although Column M of Exhibit US-128 reflects interest collected on reschedulings, neither payment of original principal nor payments of capitalized interest are reflected in Exhibit US-128. Column M reflects only payments of interest on such original principal or on such capitalized interest.

26. Exhibit US-148 reflects, with respect to the same data as originally included in Exhibit US-128, principal and interest "paid/recovered/rescheduled" annually for 1992-2003, on a chronological cash basis.

265. In connection with the US response to Question No. 225, please also provide amounts actually "written off" and "forgiven" annually for each post-1992 cohort, with annual details of country and amount (principal/interest).

27. The response to Question 225 was intended to be comprehensive. CCC financial records indicate that no amounts have been "written off" or "forgiven" with respect to any post-1992 cohort.

266. What are the precise terms, conditions and duration of each rescheduling reflected in column F in Exhibit US-128?

28. Exhibit US-153 summarizes the principal terms, conditions, and duration of each rescheduling reflected in column F in Exhibit US-128. In each instance in which a Paris Club Agreed Minute is noted, the terms of the US rescheduling adhere to the multilateral terms agreed within the Paris Club. In no instance does the debt owed the United States and rescheduled in accordance with Paris Club terms pertain exclusively to debt arising from CCC export credit guarantee transactions.

267. Is the Panel correct in understanding that "interest collected on reschedulings" in Column M in Exhibit US-128 refers not to amounts that have been actually collected by the CCC but rather to interest capitalized in conjunction with the rescheduling? If so, what are the terms, conditions and duration of the arrangements pertaining to these amounts?

29. The Panel's understanding is *not* correct. As noted in the response to Question 264(d),Column M of Exhibit US-128 reflects only interest collected on reschedulings. It does not reflect either payment of original principal nor payments of capitalized interest. At the inception of a rescheduling some outstanding interest may be capitalized or interest may be capitalized during the term of the rescheduling. Such capitalized interest is not itself reflected in any way in Exhibit US-128. Column M reflects only payments of interest on original principal or on such capitalized interest.

268. Concerning Column N in Exhibit US-128, please elaborate upon "Interest earned from US Treasury on uninvested funds". What is the source and authority for these funds and for the interest thereon to be part of the CCC total revenues? What are the terms, conditions and duration of the arrangements pertaining to these amounts?

30. Section 505(c) of the Federal Credit Reform Act (2 USC Section 661d(c)) applies to "Treasury transactions with financing accounts". In relevant part, it provides:

> The Secretary of the Treasury shall borrow from, receive from, lend to, or pay to the financing accounts such amounts as may be appropriate. The Secretary of the Treasury may prescribe forms and denominations, maturities, and terms and conditions for the transactions described above, except that the rate of interest charged by the Secretary on lending to financing accounts [...] and the rate of interest paid to financing accounts on uninvested balances in financing accounts shall be the same as the rate determined pursuant to [2 USC section 655(b)] [.....]This subsection shall apply to transactions related to direct loan obligations or loan guarantee commitments made on or after October 1, 1991 [...] Cash balances of the financing accounts in excess of current requirements shall be maintained in a form of uninvested funds and the Secretary of the Treasury shall pay interest on these funds.

31. Such section 655(b) provides: "In estimating net present values, the discount rate shall be the average interest rate on marketable Treasury securities of

similar maturity to the cash flows of the direct loan or loan guarantee for which the estimate is being made."

32. Exhibit US-149 is Treasury Financial Manual I TFM 2-4600 (December 2003). This document, promulgated by the US Department of Treasury, prescribes Treasury reporting instructions for Federal credit programme agencies in accordance with Federal credit reform legislation. Section 4640 of that document addresses "Interest on Uninvested Funds". That section provides, in part: "Uninvested funds in the financing account consist of fund balances with Treasury from borrowings and/or offsetting collections that have not been disbursed. This balance earns interest from Treasury as determined by the disbursement-weighted average interest rate or single effective rate for each cohort in the financing account."

33. Agencies must report interest revenue and expense separately. Interest income becomes part of the cash balance in the financing account and is available to fund future disbursements.

269. The Panel notes the table submitted by the US in its answer to Question No. 224 (CCC Financing Account Payments of Interest on Borrowings from Treasury and Interest Earned on Uninvested Funds). Is the Panel correct in understanding that the figures in this table correspond to the "ALL" figures in Columns I and N of Exhibit US-128?

34. Yes. Column I of Exhibit US-128 corresponds to "Interest on Borrowings" found in the table associated with the response to Question 224, and Column N corresponds to "Interest Earned" in that same table.

270. With respect to Column I in Exhibit US-128,("Interest paid on borrowing from US Treasury") and Note 8, p. 25 of Exhibit US-129:

(i) please provide the total annual amounts (interest bearing and non-interest bearing) borrowed by the CCC from the US Treasury (annually since 1992), as well as the terms, conditions, interest rate (where applicable) and duration of such borrowing. Please provide details of any other amount borrowed by the CCC from the US Treasury during this period that may not have formed part of the regular annual borrowings.

35. The Panel's Question 270 in its various sub-parts suggests that the Panel may have a misunderstanding regarding the scope of Note 8, p. 25 of Exhibit US-129. As the Panel is aware, CCC has extensive domestic and foreign operations. Note 8 reflects Debt to the Treasury with respect to myriad activities of CCC, the preponderance of which is associated with borrowings from Treasury to carry out programmes other than the export credit guarantee programmes.

36. Column I of Exhibit US-128 sets forth the total annual amount of interest paid on borrowing from the US Treasury with respect to GSM-102, GSM-103, and SCGP for the periods described. All references to "non-interest bearing" debt or repayments in Note 8, p. 25 of Exhibit US-129are unrelated to the export credit guarantee programmes.

(ii) Please explain the nature of "CCC's permanent indefinite borrowing authority from Treasury" referred to in Note 8, p. 25 of Exhibit US-129.

37. This borrowing authority does not apply to the export credit guarantee programmes. Similar to "non-interesting bearing" debt or repayments noted in the preceding response, "CCC's permanent indefinite borrowing authority from Treasury" is not available with respect to export credit guarantee programmes and activities and has not been available since the advent of the Federal Credit Reform Act of 1990. It has therefore not been available with respect to any cohorts from 1992 to the present.

38. The permanent indefinite borrowing authority to which the question and Note 8, p. 125 of Exhibit US-129 refer is available to finance and carry out many (but not all) activities of the CCC, including, for example, certain domestic commodity and conservation programmes, but not including the export credit guarantee programmes. CCC may incur realized losses in the course of carrying out such other activities, and such net realized losses are restored through the annual Federal appropriations process.

(iii) What determines the level of CCC export credit guarantee borrowing (interest-bearing and non-interest-bearing)? Is the interest-free borrowing up to the amount of unreimbursed realized losses?

39. As noted in the preceding responses no "non-interest bearing" or "interest-free" borrowing is available with respect to the export credit guarantee programmes.

40. Generally speaking, the principal determinant of the level of CCC export credit guarantee financing will be the estimated programme activity in a particular fiscal year. Budget authority is based on estimates of all anticipated programme activity such as dollar value of guarantees projected to be issued, premia to be collected, payments to be received, and claims to be paid. Infrequently, borrowing from Treasury is also used if CCC has insufficient cash on hand to pay claims.

(iv) Why are repayments applied to non-interest bearing notes first, as indicated at Note 8, p. 25 of Exhibit US-129?

41. As noted in the previous responses, activity with respect to non-interest bearing notes is wholly unrelated to the export credit guarantee programmes.

271. Note 8, p. 25 of Exhibit US-129 states that "In fiscal year 2003, CCC was fully reimbursed for its prior year net realized losses." Please indicate the amounts of prior year net realized losses (annually, since 1992) for which the CCC has been fully reimbursed.

42. As indicated in the responses to Questions 226 (22 December 2003) and 272 below, such reimbursement is unrelated and inapplicable to the CCC export credit guarantee programmes since the inception of the Federal Credit Reform Act of 1990, which corresponds to fiscal year 1992. The table comprising Exhibit US-152 displays CCC net realized losses and all appropriations to restore

those losses for fiscal years 1992 through 2003, but the United States hastens to reiterate that these figures have no relation to the export credit guarantee programmes. Such reimbursements for net realized losses do not include any portion attributable or allocable to the export credit guarantee programmes.

272. With respect to the US response to Question No. 226, is the Panel correct in understanding that the reflection of write-offs as part of the operating loss of the CCC which in turn was replenished through the annual appropriations process ended with the entry into force of the FCRA in fiscal year 1992? If not, what amounts have been replenished through this process annually since fiscal year 1992?

43. The Panel's understanding is correct.

273. With respect to the US response to Question No. 225, what criteria does the CCC apply to "independently determine" that a debt is uncollectible? For post-1992 cohorts, what are these uncollectible amounts (annually) and how, if at all, are such "uncollectible amounts" shown in Exhibit US-128?

44. With respect to post-1992 cohorts, no amounts have been determined uncollectible and therefore none are reflected in Exhibit US-128.

45. The determinations of uncollectability reflected in the response to Question No. 225, were based on the following facts. In the Argentine case, two private sector banks entered Argentine insolvency proceedings and were subsequently liquidated. CCC, after collecting a portion of the outstanding debt, received advice from the US Embassy that CCC would never receive further collection. Accordingly, the outstanding debt was written off. In the case of the Russian debt, certain debt of a private sector bank was not included in Paris Club rescheduling of debt of the former Soviet Union. The Russian Federation was therefore not liable for this debt. CCC received payments from the private sector bank but made an internal error in properly accounting for these payments. Certain late interest was not paid as a result, and CCC opted to deem such amount uncollectible. CCC has so far been unable to locate records pertaining to the Nigerian write-off.

274. The Panel notes the US statement in the US response to Question No. 81 that"All rescheduled claims are currently performing " and that "all payments due up to this point under [rescheduling] agreements have been received". However, the Panel also notes Exhibit US-129 (in particular, Note 5 on p. 22) and Brazil's reference thereto in Brazil's 28 January comments on the US response to Question No. 222. In this connection:

(a) How does the US respond to Brazil's statement in Brazil's 28 January comments that Exhibit US-129 confirms that rescheduling of export credit guarantee receivables cover both principal and interest, thereby confirming that not all of the rescheduled debt performs and that additional interest charges were also rescheduled?

46. The United States would first point out that the references to reschedulings in Note 5, p. 22, of Exhibit US-129 are not limited to reschedulings associ-

ated with the export credit guarantee programmes, nor to post-1991 transactions. The substantial majority of the amounts rescheduled by CCC pertain to activities related to the P.L. 480 foreign food assistance programme.

47. Brazil misinterprets Exhibit US-129, Note 5, p. 22. Citing that reference, Brazil states:"Indeed, the CCC's Financial Statement for FY 2002 and 2003 confirm that rescheduling of export credit guarantee receivables covered both principle [*sic*] and interest, thereby confirming that not all of the rescheduled debt performs and that additional interest charges were also rescheduled."[9] Brazil is presumably referring to the second full paragraph of that page 22, particularly its second sentence. The full paragraph reads as follows:

> Direct credit and credit guarantee principal receivables under rescheduling agreements as of 30 September 2003 and 2002, were $7,532 million and $7,494 million, respectively. During fiscal years 2003 and 2002, CCC entered into agreements with debtor countries to reschedule their delinquent debt owed to CCC. These reschedulings totalled $591 million in delinquent principal and $196 million in delinquent interest during fiscal year 2003, and $152 million in delinquent principal and $55 million in delinquent interest during fiscal year 2002.

48. The second sentence refers primarily to delinquent debt under original obligations, not under outstanding reschedulings. All rescheduled export credit guarantee debt is currently performing.

(b) In Note 5 on p. 22 of Exhibit US-129, what is the definition of "non-performing"? What is the meaning of "delinquent"? What is the current principal balance and amount of interest of the three CCC export credit guarantee programme "receivables"in a non-performing status (individually and together, for GSM 102, GSM 103 and SCGP))? What is the amount of interest on non-reporting "receivables"?

49. Page 4 of Note 1 (Significant Accounting Policies) of Exhibit US-129 provides in relevant part under the paragraph entitled "Interest Income on Direct Credits and Credit Guarantees":"A non-performing direct credit or credit guarantee receivable is defined as a repayment schedule under a credit agreement, with an installment payment in arrears more than 90 days.""Delinquent" would apply to anything past due.

50. With respect to post-1991 cohorts, the principal balance of non-performing credit guarantee receivables as of 30 September 2003 is as follows:

GSM-102:	$181 million
GSM-103:	- 0 -
SCGP:	21 million
Total:	$202 million

9 Brazil's Comments on US 22 December Answers (28 January 2004), para. 135.

With respect to pre-1992 cohorts:

GSM-102:	$2,237 million
GSM-103:	11
SCGP:	-not applicable-
Total:	$2,248 million

51. With respect to the last question, the United States assumes that the Panel intended to refer to "non-performing 'receivables', rather than "non-reporting 'receivables'". The interest receivable on "non-performing 'receivables' is $146 million and is entirely related to pre-1992 GSM-102 principal.

(c) The Panel notes the US reference to the "Paris Club" in US response to Question No. 225. What is the P.L. 480 programme referred to in Note 5 on p. 22 of Exhibit US-129 (including the Paris Club debt reduction process and the HIPC Initiative) ? To what extent is the P.L. 480 programme and Paris Club process relevant to the export credit guarantee programmes at issue in this dispute? Please identify and give the amounts of all CCC export credit guarantee debt subject to the P.L. 480 debt reduction (or other similar) process since 1992.

52. The P.L. 480 programme is a foreign food-aid programme, under which assistance can be provided on either a grant or concessional financing basis. That programme is wholly distinct from the export credit programmes at issue in this dispute. Consequently, no CCC export credit guarantee debt overlaps with debt subject to P.L. 480 debt reduction. As the United States has noted in its prior submissions, virtually all of the rescheduling of debt in connection with the CCC export credit guarantee programmes is done in concert with a multilateral Paris Club debt rescheduling process. In addition, some debt has also been forgiven under the HIPC initiative. With reference to the United States' response to Question 225, all of the debt in the table reflecting "debt forgiveness" in paragraph 114 was associated with the Paris Club (Poland, Former Yugoslavia) or HIPC (Honduras, Tanzania, Yemen).

(d) Can the US explain the process referred to in the second column of Note 5 on p. 22("CCC is awaiting an apportionment from the Office of Management and Budget before the transaction can be completed. Until such time, however, there is a 100% subsidy allowance established against the relevant debt as of 30 September 2003.") Please provide details of all such "apportionments" relating to the three export credit guarantee programmes in fiscal years 1992-2003.

53. The transaction to which the cited reference applies involves an agreement between the United States and Pakistan to reduce debt incurred under the P.L. 480 programme, which is not within the scope of this dispute. It involves only P.L. 480 direct credits and does not involve any of the export credit guarantee programmes. It therefore does not involve transactions under federal credit reform provisions applicable to the export credit guarantee programmes. The cited reference is intended to note that although a debt reduction agreement had been signed, the requisite documentation from the Office of Management and

Budget authorizing such reduction on the books of CCC had not yet been received as of the statement date.

54. The procedure in the above P.L. 480 instance is distinct from that which would apply in the case of export credit guarantee apportionments. The response of the United States to Panel Question 225 indicated three cases of debt "write-off" and five cases of debt forgiveness. Seven of those eight cases involved pre-1992 debt. Under the Federal Credit Reform Act of 1990, an apportionment is ordinarily not necessary with respect to pre-1992 transactions. In fact, only one such apportionment has ever occurred, and that was in fiscal year 1992 to establish the particular budgetary account (the "liquidating account") under which the budgetary accounting occurs forall activity associated with pre-1992 transactions. That apportionment did not reflect any debt reduction or write off.

55. The only other instance was the write-off of $13,000 owed from the Former Soviet Union/Russia. This particular write-off did not involve a sufficiently large amount to require an apportionment. The Office of Management and Budget database rounds to the nearest million dollars, and therefore the write-off of $13,000 would not alter the relevant entries in the database for the particular budgetary account (the "financing account") applicable to post-1991 cohort transactions.

275. Please provide evidence (or cite relevant portions of the record) that the premium rates for the export credit guarantee programmes are "reviewed annually" as stated in US 28 January comments on response to Question No. 223 (see also US 22 December response to Question No. 107;Brazil's 28 January 2004 comments on responses to Question No. 223.).

56. Exhibit US-150 is comprised of the two most recentinternal USDA documents entitled "Annual Review of Fees for USDA Credit Programmes," dated 25 March 2003, and 8 April 2002, respectively. In addition, Exhibit US-151 are Sections I and II of US Office of Management and Budget Circular No. A-129, dated November 2000, entitled "Policies for Federal Credit Programmes and Non-Tax Receivables". Section II.2.b mandates such annual review.

List of Exhibits

64 Memorandum from Larry Mitchell, USDA Farm Services Agency, to Various FSA Offices, Administrators, and Divisions on Release of Restricted Information under the Freedom of Information Act (18 September 1998)

65 USDA Farm Services Agency, Notice INFO-16: Releasing Lists of Names and Addresses in Response to Requests Under FOIA (1 December 1998)

66 Contents of 4 corrected data files submitted on 28 January 2004

67 USDA, Commodity Credit Corporation, 58 Federal Register 15755-15756 (24 March 1993).

68 Data in response to Panel Question 264(a): Exhibit US-128 on a Fiscal Year/ Cash Basis

69 Data in response to Panel Question 264(d): Claim Payments/ Recoveries/ Reschedulings on a Fiscal Year/ Cash Basis

70 United States Department of the Treasury Financial Manual I TFM 2-4600 (December 2003)

71 "Annual Review of Fees for USDA Credit Programmes", 25 March 2003 and 8 April 2002.

72 United States Office of Management and Budget Circular No. A-129 (November 2000), Table of Contents, General Information, Appendix A, Sections I and II.

73 Commodity Credit Corporation Realized Losses and Appropriations to Restore Such Losses for Fiscal Years 1992-2003

74 Summary of Principal Terms, Conditions, and Duration of Each Rescheduling Reflected in Column F of Exhibit US-128

Partially Corrected Calculations Allocating Decoupled Payments for Upland Cotton Base Acres to Upland Cotton Using Incomplete Annex IV Methodology

ANNEX I-19

COMMENTS OF THE UNITED STATES ON COMMENTS OF BRAZIL
11 February 2004

I. INTRODUCTION

1. The United States thanks the Panel for providing a new deadline for comments on Brazil's comments on the data submitted by the United States on 18 and 19 December 2003.[1] The 48-page document filed by Brazil on 28 January 2004, goes far beyond a comment on that data or even its application to Brazil's invented allocation methodology for determining "support to" upland cotton. Instead, those "comments" on the US data present an attack on the good faith of the United States in responding to Brazil's requests for data, a lengthy attempt to re-write the history of this dispute, an inaccurate explanation of US domestic law regarding privacy interests in planting data, a request for the Panel to draw "adverse inferences" despite the fact that Brazil could have requested aggregated data that would not have implicated privacy interests, a rather circumspect application of its invented allocation methodology to the US data, and an inadequate application of the Annex IV allocation methodology[2] to the US data. Because Brazil has seen fit to raise and argue so many issues in its comments, the United States will necessarily address those in these comments. In these comments, we proceed as follows.

2. *First*, we put the issue of the use of the US data in its proper context. Brazil has asserted that decoupled income support payments must be allocated to upland cotton only for purposes of the Peace Clause and not for purposes of its serious prejudice claims. However, the allocation of a subsidy benefit is only mentioned in the Subsidies Agreement. The Agreement on Agriculture not only does not contain any allocation methodology, it also defines a category of support ("non-product-specific support") that consists of unallocated payments "to producers in general". Thus, Brazil gets it completely backwards:the text and context of the Peace Clause demonstrate that support is *not* to be allocated for purposes of the Peace Clause test while the text and context of Articles 5 and 6 of the Subsidies Agreement demonstrate that subsidies not tied to production of a given product (such as decoupled income support) *are* to be allocated to all of the products the recipient sells for purposes of serious prejudice claims.

3. *Second*, we explain the implications of Brazil's erroneous analysis and arguments, and in particular its express disavowal of any allocation methodology for purposes of its serious prejudice claims on decoupled income support pay-

[1] Brazil's Comments and Requests Regarding Data Provided by the United States on 18/19 December 2003 and the US Refusal to Provide Non-Scrambled Data on 20 January 2004 (28 January 2004) ("Brazil's Data Comments").

[2] *Agreement on Subsidies and Countervailing Measures*, Annex IV, paras. 2-3 ("Subsidies Agreement").

ments. Brazil has failed to make a *prima facie* case on these claims; therefore, no serious prejudice findings may be made with respect to these measures, and these payments may not be included in an analysis of whether the effect of the challenged US subsidies has been serious prejudice to Brazil's interests.

4. *Third*, although the foregoing points should end the analysis, we nonetheless examine Brazil's application of its invented methodology to the US-supplied data. We recall that this Brazilian methodology has no basis in the text or context of the WTO agreements. Neither does Brazil's methodology make economic sense. It does, however, allow Brazil to allocate decoupled payments exclusively or nearly exclusively to upland cotton. Thus, Brazil's invented allocation methodology can be described as an attempt to inflate the support to be allocated to upland cotton.

5. *Fourth,* the United States examines Brazil's cursory attempted application of the Annex IV methodology to the US-supplied data. We recall that Brazil expressly disavowed the applicability of that methodology. Brazil neither sought nor presented data to permit the Annex IV methodology to be applied. In fact, Brazil requested data relevant solely to its invented methodology, meaning there is no data before the Panel that would permit the Annex IV methodology to be applied. Finally, the calculations presented by Brazil reflect a misunderstanding of the plain meaning of that methodology and contain a number of erroneous assumptions that bias Brazil's results upwards.

6. *Fifth*, we correct Brazil's serious misrepresentations with respect to the data it requested and point out that the United States responded to that request as drafted and to the fullest extent permissible under US law. Thus, there is no basis to draw an inference, adverse or otherwise, from the inability to provide certain information that is not relevant to an analysis of Brazil's legal claims.

II. BRAZIL MISUNDERSTANDS THE RELEVANT ANALYSES FOR THE PEACE CLAUSE AND FOR ITS SERIOUS PREJUDICE CLAIMS

A. ***Brazil's Allocation Methodology is Inconsistent with the*** *Definition of Product-Specific Support in the Agreement on Agriculture and, Therefore, Cannot be Used for Peace Clause Analysis*

7. As has been evident since the parties' first submissions, Brazil and the United States have offered fundamentally differing interpretations of Article 13(b)(ii) of the Agreement on Agriculture and in particular the Peace Clause proviso which reads: "provided that such measures do not grant support to a specific commodity in excess of that decided during the 1992 marketing year." The differences between the parties' approaches can be seen in the way they interpret the phrase "product-specific support" and apply that interpretation to decoupled income support payments.

8. Brazil argues that decoupled income support payments are not "truly 'decoupled'" since some recipients do produce programme crops, that "the support from contract payments that can be allocated to upland cotton is product-specific support within the meaning of the Agreement on Agriculture," and that Brazil's approach – "to allocate contract payments to the programme crops covered" – is "reasonable".[3] However, as the United States demonstrated in its comment on Brazil's answer to question 258, Brazil points to *no text* in the Peace Clause, the Agreement on Agriculture, nor any WTO agreement that supports its allocation methodology[4], nor does that methodology make economic sense.[5] Brazil may consider its approach to be "reasonable", but that does not make it based on any WTO provision.

9. As just one example, Brazil apparently would require that "decoupled support" *discourage* recipients from producing certain crops in order to be "decoupled" while at the same time Brazil complains that the payment restriction for planting fruits and vegetables means that the support is *not* "decoupled". Brazil cannot have it both ways. If support is decoupled, then there is no requirement to produce any particular commodity. If producers choose to exercise their flexibility and plant particular crops, that is perfectly consistent with the concept of decoupled support.

10. The lack of grounding of Brazil's methodology in the WTO agreements stems from its erroneous interpretation of "support to a specific commodity". Brazil has argued that any support that is not made "to producers in general" – which Brazil takes to mean "all" or "nearly all" – is not non-product-specific and therefore must be "product-specific". As the United States has pointed out before, not only does this reading of "in general" rely on an obsolete meaning[6], which therefore cannot be the ordinary meaning of the terms, but Brazil has consistently failed to read together the definitions of product-specific support and non-product-specific support in Article 1(a) of the Agreement on Agriculture. Read in conjunction with one another, non-product-specific support ("support provided in favour of agricultural producers in general") is a residual category of support that is not product-specific ("support ... provided for an agricultural product in favour of the producers of the basic agricultural product").

---

3 Brazil's Data Comments, para. 73. Brazil also argues: "As the record demonstrates, none of four types of contract payments is truly 'decoupled,' given the production of programme crops by the farms holding contract payment base. To the contrary, they are *intended to* and, in fact, do provide support for the production of programme crops." *Ibid.* Brazil has in fact provided no evidence of such "intent" nor could it since the opposite is true. These programmes are intended to be decoupled. Moreover, under the Peace Clause, the "intent" of a payment is irrelevant; it is also irrelevant what a recipient decides to do with a payment. Rather, the issue is whether the payment as "decided" is "support to a specific commodity" or "support provided in favour of agricultural producers in general".

4 US Comments on Brazil's Answers to Panel Questions Following the Second Panel Meeting, paras. 209-217 (28 January 2004) ("US January 28 Comments").

5 US 28 January Comments, paras. 218-23.

6 US Comments on Brazil's Rebuttal Submission, para. 23 (noting that definition of "in general" as "in a body; universally; without exception" was marked "obsolete" in *New Shorter Oxford English Dictionary*).

11. Brazil's statement in its 28 January comments that "the support from contract payments that can be allocated to upland cotton is product-specific support within the meaning of the Agreement on Agriculture"[7] is significant because *it confirms that both parties interpret "support to a specific commodity" in the Peace Clause as meaning "product-specific support"*. Thus, the question for the Panel is whether decoupled income support measures provide product-specific support or non-product-specific support. The definitions from Article 1(a) quoted above establish that support that is *not* "provided for a basic agricultural product in favour of the producers of the basic agricultural product" cannot be product-specific support.

> The very fact that Brazil must apply an *allocation* methodology to these decoupled income support payments to attempt to determine the "support to upland cotton" demonstrates that they are not product-specific support. Rather, they are support to whatever *products* (if any) the recipients produce, rather than "support for *a* basic agricultural product." In addition, the recipients are "producers in general" because they are not required to be "producers of *the* basic agricultural product" the support is "provided for".

12. While Brazil appears to be arguing that its allocation methodology conforms to the concepts of product-specific and non-product-specific support in the Agreement on Agriculture, in fact that methodology is flatly inconsistent with those concepts.[8] There is nothing in the Agreement that suggests that support may, at one and the same time, be both product-specific and non-product-specific. For example:

> In Article 1(a), these two terms are defined disjunctively (that is, product-specific support "or" non-product-specific support).
>
> In Article 6.4(a), *de minimis* levels of support not required to be included in a Member's Current Total AMS are separately given for "product-specific domestic support" and "non-product-specific domestic support."
>
> Under Annex 3, paragraph 1, "an Aggregate Measurement of Support (AMS) shall be calculated on a product-specific basis for each basic agricultural product", and, separately, "[s]upport which is non-product specific shall be totalled into one non-product-specific AMS in total monetary terms".

Despite the fact that product-specific and non-product-specific support are kept distinct in the Agreement on Agriculture, Brazil's allocation methodology necessarily collapses the two concepts.

13. For example, under Brazil's methodology decoupled income support "payments for other crops were primarily allocated as support for these crops – up to the share of contract acreage planted to the respective crop", but "[a]ny further payments stemming from contract acreage not planted to the respective

---

[7] Brazil's Data Comments, para. 73.

[8] *See* US 28 January Comments, paras. 225-29.

base crop were pooled and allocated as additional support to those contract crops whose aggregate planting exceeded their aggregated base acreage".[9] Brazil states that in marketing year 2001, cotton, "oats and sorghum were planted on more acreage than their respective contract base ('overplanted'), thus[] triggering additional payments being allocated pursuant to the crop's share of total acreage being 'overplanted'".[10]

> That is, decoupled income support payments for base acreage with respect to other programme crops (other than upland cotton, oats, and sorghum) would, under Brazil's approach in this dispute, first be "product-specific support" to each of those programme crops to the extent of planted acreage.
>
> Then, the payments on "excess" base acreage would be "product-specific" support simultaneously to upland cotton, oats, and sorghum.

Logically, then, such payments would be support to "four different commodities" (whichever happen to be 'underplanted'), not "support to a *specific* commodity". Further, payments allegedly supporting four different commodities would not be "provided for *a* basic agricultural *product* in favour of the producers of *the* basic agricultural *product*".

14. Thus, decoupled income support payments are support to "agricultural producers in general" – that is, support to recipients who may decide (as Brazil has confirmed) to produce any of multiple commodities in general. Because such payments are non-product-specific, they may not at the same time be deemed to be product-specific. Brazil's methodology for purposes of the Peace Clause would result in non-product-specific support being allocated to the specific products the recipients produce, contrary to the separation of these concepts in the Agreement on Agriculture. As Brazil concedes that "support to a specific commodity" refers to "product-specific support within the meaning of the Agreement on Agriculture"[11], it follows that decoupled income support payments must be deemed to be non-product-specific within the meaning of Article 1(a) of the Agreement on Agriculture and therefore not part of the Peace Clause test under Article 13(b)(ii).

B. Challenged US Measures do not Grant Support to a Specific Commodity in Excess of that Decided during the 1992 Marketing Year

15. As Brazil has conceded that the Peace Clause proviso refers to "product-specific support", the question for the Panel becomes: do challenged US measures grant product-specific support in excess of that decided during the 1992 marketing year? The United States has previously demonstrated in exhaustive detail that, removing non-product-specific support(that is, decoupled income

---

9 Brazil's Data Comments, para. 80.

10 Brazil's Data Comments, para. 80 fn. 159.

11 Brazil's Data Comments, para. 73.

support measures and crop insurance payments) from the Peace Clause comparison, US measures do not. We will not repeat the extensive arguments on this point, for example, relating to how the United States "decided" its support.

16. We do recall, however, that as the United States by design shifted the support it provided to its agricultural sector from product-specific amber box support (in the form of deficiency payments) to green box support (production flexibility contract payments and direct payments) and non-product-specific support (market loss assistance payments and counter-cyclical payments), the result was that the product-specific support to upland cotton declined substantially. The only way Brazil can overcome this fact is to argue that the only way to gauge "support to a specific commodity" is through budgetary outlays[12], which in the case of marketing loan payments will reflect through high outlays the record low cotton prices in marketing years 2001 and 2002 that the United States did not decide and could not control – as Brazil has conceded.[13]

17. As the United States has shown,[14] *any* measurement of the product-specific support for upland cotton that eliminates the effect of market prices and instead gauges the support "decided" by the United States demonstrates that upland cotton product-specific support was higher in marketing year 1992 than in any marketing year from 1999-2002. That is, whether the analysis is (as the United States believes is compelled by the Peace Clause text) the rate of support as decided in US measures,[15] or the upland cotton AMS measured through a price-gap methodology[16], or the "expected rate of per unit support" calculated by Brazil's expert[17], the result is the same: challenged US measures are not in breach of the Peace Clause.

---

[12] In making this argument, Brazil ignores the fact that "support" does not mean "budgetary outlays". In fact, Annex 3 recognizes that an "Aggregate Measurement of Support" for price-based support either shall or can be calculated using a price-gap methodology, which does not rely on budgetary outlays. *See, e.g.,* Agreement on Agriculture, Annex 3, para. 8 ("Budgetary outlays made to maintain this gap, such as buying-in or storage costs, shall not be included in the AMS."); *id.,* para. 10.

[13] *See* Brazil's Comments on US Answers, para. 66 fn. 49 (August 22, 2003) ("Brazil acknowledges that the United States could not possibl[y] determine its expenditures as they would depend to a certain extent on market prices that were also influenced by factors outside the control of the US Government.").

[14] *See, e.g.,* US Rebuttal Submission, paras. 110-30.

[15] In marketing year 1992, 72.9 cents per pound; in marketing years 1999-2001, 51.92 cents per pound; in marketing year 2002: 52 cents per pound. US Rebuttal Submission, paras. 110-13.

[16] In marketing year 1992, $1,079 million; in 1999, $717 million; in 2000, $484 million; in 2001, $264 million; and in marketing year 2002 (as of the date of panel establishment, March 18, 2003), $205 million. US Rebuttal Submission, paras. 114-17.

[17] In marketing year 1992, 60.05 cents per pound; in marketing year 1999, 53.79 cents per pound; in marketing year 2000, 55.09 cents per pound; in marketing year 2001, 52.82 cents per pound; and in marketing year 2002, 56.32 cents per pound. US Rebuttal Submission, paras. 120-22. Removing the 1999 and 2002 marketing year cottonseed payments the Panel has determined to be not within its terms of reference results in support of 52.82 cents per pound in marketing year 1999 and 55.71 cents per pound in marketing year 2002.

C. *Under the Subsidies Agreement, Allocation of a Non-Tied Subsidy is Necessary to Identify the Amount of Subsidy and the Subsidized Product*

18. Brazil seeks to allocate support not tied to the production of a specific commodity for purposes of the Peace Clause, despite the fact that the Agreement on Agriculture explicitly distinguishes and keeps separate product-specific and non-product-specific support. There is no mention of an allocation methodology in that Agreement because there is no need to allocate support – in fact, allocation is contrary to the very structure of the agreement. Ironically, Brazil then seeks *not* to allocate such a non-tied payment for purposes of its serious prejudice claims when there *is* an allocation methodology set out in Annex IV and when there *is* a need to identify the subsidized product as well as the subsidy amount. Brazil's approach ignores the text and context of Articles 5 and 6 of the Subsidies Agreement.[18]

19. Brazil has argued that it "strongly disagrees that this [Annex IV methodology for allocating non-tied payments] is a required or appropriate methodology under Part III of the SCM Agreement or under GATT Article XVI (or even under Article 13(b)(ii) of the Agreement on Agriculture)".[19] However, Brazil has not provided any basis to conclude that the term "subsidy" can mean one thing in the context of Articles 5 and 6 and another in Article 1.1 (subsidy requires a "benefit" to recipient), Article 14 ("calculation of the amount of a subsidy in terms of the benefit to the recipient") and Article 15.5 (causal link necessary between injury and the subsidized imports "through the effects of subsidies"), all of which suggest that an evaluation of "the effect of the subsidy" requires an identification of the "benefit" the subsidy is alleged to provide. Further, Brazil has not provided any basis to conclude that a "subsidized product" for purposes of Articles 6.3(c), 6.3(d), 6.4, and 6.5 can be read in isolation from the methodology for determining the "subsidization" of a "product" set out in Annex IV. Therefore, the Subsidies Agreement – and Part III in particular – calls for an "allocation methodology" to determine the products that benefit from a subsidy that is not tied to production or sale of a given product.

20. Brazil denies the applicability to the Peace Clause analysis of the Annex IV methodology for allocating non-tied payments across the value of the recipients' production. However, even had Brazil suggested that the Annex IV methodology could be used for Peace Clause analysis, its interpretation would be plainly wrong. First, the phrase "support to a specific commodity" means "product-specific support" – as Brazil has conceded – and thus must be interpreted in light of the terms product-specific support and non-product-specific support in the Agreement on Agriculture (as set out above). Second, the terms "support to a specific commodity" and "product-specific support" are not found in Part III of

[18] US Comment to Brazil's Answer to Question 258, paras. 209-17.

[19] Brazil's Data Comments, para. 85 n. 171.

the Subsidies Agreement, nor in Article 1 or Annex IV.[20] Neither are the terms "subsidy," "benefit," or "subsidized product" from the Subsidies Agreement found in the Peace Clause proviso or any supporting text. Thus, the plain language of the Peace Clause and Articles 5 and 6 indicate that these provisions refer to wholly different approaches and suggest that the methodology for allocating non-tied (decoupled) payments under the Subsidies Agreement may not be relevant under the Agreement on Agriculture. The definitions of product-specific support and non-product-specific support in Article 1(a) of the Agreement on Agriculture confirm that the Annex IV allocation methodology does not apply for purposes of the Peace Clause.

21. Thus, allocating a non-tied payment across the value of the recipient's production is not pertinent for Peace Clause purposes but is necessary for the Panel to be able to attempt to gauge "the effect of the subsidy" for purposes of Brazil's serious prejudice claims. We discuss Brazil's failure to bring forward evidence and arguments relating to this issue in the next section.

III. BECAUSE BRAZIL EXPRESSLY DISAVOWS ANY ALLOCATION METHODOLOGY FOR PURPOSES OF ITS SERIOUS PREJUDICE CLAIMS ON DECOUPLED INCOME SUPPORT PAYMENTS, BRAZIL HAS FAILED TO MAKE A *PRIMA FACIE* CASE ON THESE CLAIMS

A Brazil Has Presented No Evidence or Arguments Supporting the Annex IV Methodology to Allocate Decoupled Income Support Payments for Purposes of its Serious Prejudice Claims

22. As we have noted, because Brazil has chosen to include subsidies that are not tied to the production or sale of a given product within its serious prejudice claims, the Annex IV methodology is necessary to determine the subsidized product and the amount of the challenged non-tied subsidy that benefits upland cotton. Brazil recognizes that *some* allocation methodology is necessary to identify the decoupled income support payments within the scope of its panel request ("subsidies to producers, users, and/or exporters of upland cotton")[21] but relies on its wholly invented methodology (allocating decoupled payments for crop base in "excess" of planted acreage of the respective crop solely to those programme crops planted on less acreage that their respective base acreage). That methodology finds no support in the text or context of the Subsidies Agreement or any other WTO agreement.

23. The result is that Brazil has not provided the Panel with evidence or arguments sufficient to establish a *prima facie* case that the effect of such decoupled payments is to cause serious prejudice to the interests of Brazil. Brazil has

[20] The term "support" appears in Article 1.1(a)(2) of the Subsidies Agreement, which gives one definition of "subsidy" as "any form of income or price support in the sense of Article XVI of GATT 1994."

[21] WT/DS267/7, at 1.

never sought or presented evidence and made arguments that would allow the Panel to evaluate properly "the effect of the subsidy" (decoupled income support payments) – for example, to identify the "subsidized product" through the Annex IV methodology and the "subsidy" in terms of the "benefit" to those recipients named in Brazil's panel request. Logically, if Brazil has not even identified the subsidized product with respect to such payments or the amount of the challenged subsidy, the Panel cannot evaluate "the effects".

24. Indeed, Brazil expressly disavows any allocation or even identification of the size of the subsidy for purposes of its serious prejudice claims:

> "Brazil maintains that no allocation methodology is warranted under Part III of the SCM Agreement. Rather, it is the effect of the subsidies that is the subject of scrutiny."[22]
>
> "Brazil strongly disagrees that this is a required or appropriate methodology under Part III of the SCM Agreement or under GATT Article XVI (or even under Article 13(b)(ii) of the Agreement on Agriculture."[23]
>
> "Again, Brazil notes that this allocation is not required under Part III of the SCM Agreement and GATT Article XVI:3. Both provisions deal with the effect of subsidies, and not their amount or subsidization rate."[24]

25. Further, Brazil has never sought nor presented information relating to the total value of the recipients' sales as would be necessary to apply the Annex IV methodology to decoupled income support payments.[25] Brazil has only sought base and planted acreage information to support its own invented methodology (and only for Peace Clause purposes).[26]

26. In this dispute, then, Brazil cannot have made its *prima facie* case with respect to the effect of decoupled income support payments. To find otherwise would mean a complaining party in a serious prejudice case could satisfy its burden merely by asserting that some unidentified amount of payments are received by producers of the relevant product.

B. The Japan – Agricultural Products Appellate Body Report Confirms that in Such a Situation a Panel May not "Make the Case for a Complaining Party"

27. Brazil includes a discussion of the Appellate Body report in *Japan – Agricultural Products*, suggesting that the report is "inapposite" and that Brazil has advanced relevant claims and arguments such that the Panel could in no event

---

22 Brazil's Data Comments, para. 85 n. 168.

23 Brazil's Data Comments, para. 85 n. 171.

24 Brazil's Data Comments, para. 98 n. 199.

25 Subsidies Agreement, Annex IV, paras. 2-3 (for a subsidy not tied to the production or sale of a given product, the subsidized product is "the total value of the recipient firm's sales").

26 *See* Exhibit Bra-369; Brazil's Data Comments, para. 3 ("The purpose of Brazil's request for *contract acreage and planted acreage* for each farm producing upland cotton was ... .") (italics added).

relieve Brazil of its burden of establishing a *prima facie* case of inconsistency with WTO obligations. However, a careful reading of both Brazil's arguments as well as that report reveals that, were the Panel to seek and obtain data to apply, for purposes of its serious prejudice analysis, the allocation methodology set out in Annex IV of the Subsidies Agreement to the challenged decoupled income support payments, the Panel would be making Brazil's case for it.

28. We begin by examining Brazil's artfully drafted arguments. Brazil alleges that the US argument is that the *Japan – Agricultural Products* report "would have prevented the Panel from using the information the United States refused to provide to calculate the amount of contract payments across the 'total value of the recipient's production.'"[27] Brazil's assertion is wrong. First, the US argument is that the Panel may not seek and apply information to use the Annex IV methodology for decoupled income support payments because (as set out in the bulleted quotes above) Brazil has *expressly disavowed* any allocation or even identification of the size of the subsidy for purposes of its serious prejudice claims. As Brazil has brought forward no evidence or arguments to support findings on decoupled payments, it has not made its *prima facie* case.

29. Second, the United States has not "refused to provide" information to allocate decoupled payments according to the Annex IV methodology for the simple reason that *Brazil never sought this information.* Brazil merely asked for planted acreage and base acreage (and yield) information.[28] With respect to the farm-by-farm planted acreage data that the United States was unable under US law to provide in a format allowing matching with farm-specific base acreage data, that data is simply irrelevant for purposes of the Annex IV methodology. Thus, while the Panel has the authority under DSU Article 13 to seek information "as the panel considers necessary and appropriate", the inability of the United States to provide that data in the farm-by-farm format requested on 12 January 2004 is ultimately of no moment in this dispute since Brazil's allocation methodology using planted and base acreage data finds no support in any WTO text. The situation is quite different with respect to the Annex IV methodology that is found in the WTO agreements but that has been disavowed by Brazil.

30. Thus, it is Brazil that errs when it suggests that the Panel could seek and apply any information at all without making Brazil's case for it since Brazil has advanced relevant claims and arguments.[29] With respect to the allocation of non-tied (decoupled) payments across the total value of the recipients' sales for purposes of identifying the amount of the subsidy and the subsidized product, Brazil has not sought such information, has not made arguments to support use of that methodology, and has in fact argued that no allocation or identification of the subsidy amount is warranted under Part III of the Subsidies Agreement. Thus, the Panel would in fact be making Brazil's case for it were it to seek to apply the Annex IV methodology.

---

27 Brazil's Data Comments, para. 99.

28 *See* Exhibit BRA-369.

29 *See* Brazil's Data Comments, para. 103-04.

31. Appellate Body report. There, the Appellate Body reversed a panel finding of inconsistency with Article 5.6 of the *Agreement on the Application of Sanitary and Phytosanitary Measures* ("SPS Agreement") "because this finding was reached in a manner inconsistent with the rules on burden of proof".[30] Specifically, the Appellate Body found that "it was for the United States to establish a *prima facie* case ... of inconsistency with Article 5.6. Since the United States did not even claim before the Panel that the 'determination of sorption levels' is an alternative measure which meets the three elements under Article 5.6, we are of the opinion that the United States did not establish a *prima facie* case that the 'determination of sorption levels' is an alternative measure within the meaning of Article 5.6".[31]

32. Brazil argues that this reversal was based on the fact that "the complaining party (the United States) did not 'claim' in its request for establishment of a panel that there was an alternative measure (determination of sorption levels) that was less trade restrictive".[32] However, in making this argument, Brazil itself (as it later asserts of the United States) "reveals a profound misunderstanding of the difference between a 'claim' and an 'argument'".[33] The United States agrees with Brazil (and the Appellate Body report in *EC – Hormones*) that "there is a distinction between legal claims reflected in a panel's terms of reference, and arguments used by a complainant to sustain its legal claims". There is no question, however, that the United States advanced a legal *claim* that Japan's varietal testing measure was inconsistent with Article 5.6 of the SPS Agreement.[34] The issue was whether the United States had presented evidence and arguments relating to an alternative measure that satisfied its burden of making a *prima facie* case with respect to its Article 5.6 claim.[35] Thus, the Appellate Body concluded that "the Panel was correct to seek information and advice from experts to help it to understand and evaluate the evidence submitted and arguments made by the United States and Japan with regard to the alleged violation of Article 5.6" but the panel erred "when it used that expert information and advice for a finding of inconsistency with Article 5.6 since the United States did not establish a *prima facie* case of inconsistency with Article 5.6 based on claims relating to the 'determination of sorption levels'".[36]

---

30 WT/DS76/AB/R, para. 130.

31 WT/DS76/AB/R, para. 126.

32 Brazil's Data Comments, para. 100.

33 Brazil's Data Comments, para. 103.

34 *See, e.g.*, WT/DS76/AB/R, para. 123 ("In this dispute, the United States claimed that the varietal testing requirement is more trade restrictive than required to achieve Japan's appropriate level of protection and is, therefore, inconsistent with Article 5.6."); Panel Report, *Japan – Agricultural Products*, WT/DS76/R, paras. 1.2, 4.178, 8.64.

35 WT/DS76/AB/R, para. 124 ("As noted above, the United States argued that 'testing by product' is an alternative measure which meets the three cumulative elements under Article 5.6."); *id.*, para. 125 ("We note that the Panel explicitly stated that the United States, as complaining party, did *not specifically argue* that the 'determination of sorption levels' met any of the three elements under Article 5.6".).

36 WT/DS76/AB/R, para. 130.

33. A similar situation would occur here were the Panel to seek and apply information to apply the Annex IV methodology to decoupled income support payments.[37] Brazil has neither sought nor presented any evidence relating to the total value of the recipient firms' sales. Brazil has also not only *not* argued that the Annex IV methodology is necessary to identify the subsidized product and the subsidy benefit, Brazil has also continually argued against use of the Annex IV methodology since, in its view, no allocation of the payment or quantification of the benefit is warranted under Part III of the Subsidies Agreement. Thus, it would appear that Brazil has resisted making the necessary legal arguments and refused to submit any evidence relating a proper analysis of its claims.

34. With respect to Brazil's refusal to recognize the relevance of the Annex IV methodology for purposes of its serious prejudice claims, and its resulting refusal to present evidence and arguments with respect to the application of that methodology to its claims, the findings of the Appellate Body in *Japan – Agricultural Products* remain highly relevant:

> "Article 13 of the DSU ... suggest that panels have a significant investigative authority. However, this authority cannot be used by a panel to rule in favour of a complaining party which has not established a prima facie case of inconsistency based on specific legal claims asserted by it. A panel is entitled to seek information and advice from experts and from any other relevant source it chooses, pursuant to Article 13 of the DSU ... *to help it understand and evaluate the evidence submitted and the arguments made by the parties, but not to make the case for a complaining party*."[38]

In this case, Brazil has not submitted evidence and made arguments sufficient to make its case that the effect of decoupled income support payments is to cause serious prejudice to Brazil's interests. In fact, Brazil's arguments have seemingly been designed to prevent the Panel from ascertaining even what is the amount of the subsidy being challenged. In such a circumstance, Brazil has not established a *prima facie* case of inconsistency with Articles 5 and 6 of the Subsidies Agreement with respect to these payments, and the Panel cannot make findings of serious prejudice.

IV. BRAZIL'S INVENTED METHODOLOGY HAS NO BASIS IN THE WTO AGREEMENTS AND REPRESENTS AN EFFORT TO MAXIMIZE THE PAYMENTS ALLOCATED TO UPLAND COTTON

35. The foregoing analysis suffices to demonstrate that Brazil has not made a *prima facie* case under its serious prejudice claims with respect to decoupled income support measures. Simply put, based on the evidence and arguments brought forward by Brazil, the Panel cannot make findings on those measures

---

[37] *See* US Answer to Question 256 from the Panel, paras. 183-86 (22 December 2003).

[38] WT/DS76/AB/R, para. 129 (italics added).

under Articles 5 and 6 of the Subsidies Agreement (as well as GATT 1994 Article XVI) without making Brazil's case for it. In this section of these comments,we nonetheless examine Brazil's application of its invented methodology to the US-supplied data.

36. The United States has previously explained, both in these comments and in its comments to Brazil's answer to Question 258, that the Brazilian allocation methodology has no basis in the text or context of the WTO agreements.[39] We do not repeat that detailed critique of Brazil's invented methodology here, other than to note that Brazil seeks to *apply* an allocation methodology for purposes of Peace Clause – despite the fact that the definitions of product-specific support and non-product-specific support (and their application in the Agreement on Agriculture) do not permit any such allocation – while at the same time Brazil seeks to *deny* any allocation methodology for purposes of serious prejudice – despite the fact that an allocation methodology is set forth explicitly in Annex IV reflecting core Subsidies Agreement concepts relating to subsidy benefits and the subsidized product. Thus, Brazil invites the Panel to adopt a legally erroneous approach that does violence to the existing texts of the Agreement on Agriculture and the Subsidies Agreement.

37. We have also previously explained that Brazil's invented allocation methodology does not make economic sense. Decoupled payments by their nature provide income support not tied to the production or sale of any given commodity[40], therefore, there is no more reason to attribute $1 in income support to upland cotton production on a farm than there is to attribute that $1 in income support to production of any other product (soybeans, corn, etc.). Brazil's approach, however, makes just such an arbitrary attribution, producing illogical results:

> The same crop (for example, upland cotton) produced on a farm could be deemed to be subsidized at different rates. For example, planted acres of upland cotton up to the amount of upland cotton base acres will be deemed to be subsidized at a rate corresponding to decoupled payments for upland cotton base acres. Planted acres of upland cotton in excess of the amount of upland cotton base acres will be deemed to be subsidized at a different rate – perhaps higher if sufficient payments corresponding to base acres for other crops are available, perhaps lower or even zero if few or no payments for "excess" base acres are available. From an economic perspective, there is no basis to say that some income support dollars are going to a certain portion of the crop but not others.[41]
>
> In addition, because payments on all the "excess" base acreage are allocated to whatever programme crop has planted acres in excess of base acreage, the subsidization of the "excess" planted acreage

---

[39] *See, e.g.,* US Comments to Brazil's Answer to Question 258 from the Panel, paras. 207-29 (28 January 2004).

[40] *See, e.g.,* Brazil's First Written Submission, para. 51 (under direct payment program, the "amount of payment is not dependent upon current production" of any particular commodity).

[41] *See* US Comment on Brazil's Answer to Question 258, para. 221.

can be far higher than for other acres of that crop or for acreage of other crops that may be more heavily planted.(For example, if a farm has 100 base acres of soy, 10 planted acres of soy, and 1 planted acre of cotton, the 90 "excess" base acres of soy will be allocated to the 1 acre of cotton, resulting in a cotton subsidy and subsidization rate far higher than that for soy, despite the fact that soy plantings outstrip cotton plantings 10 to 1.)[42]

Brazil's approach simply ignores the existence of crops other than "programme crops", much less other farming or non-farm economic activities the subsidy recipient may undertake. Again, there is no economic reason to attribute income support payments to some (programme) crops but not others and some (crop production) economic activities but not others.[43]

38. Fundamentally, Brazil's approach is in error because it assumes that there is a tie between the decoupled payments and current plantings. Brazil attributes payments for base acres to currently planted crops by describing the current crop as "planted on" base acres. The reality is that there are no physical "base acres" on a farm; crop base is an accounting concept that is limited by the farm's cropland.(For example, the farm may have 100 base acres of upland cotton, but if it currently plants 100 acres of cotton, that cotton may physically be "planted on" any land on the farm.) But Brazil does not carry through its own concept of crops "planted on" base acres.

For example, in the example given above of a farm with 100 base acres of soy and current plantings of 10 acres of soy and 1 acre of cotton, under Brazil's approach, payments on the 90 "excess" base acres of soy are allocated to the 1 acre of upland cotton. But 1 acre of upland cotton could only be "planted on" 1 base acre of soy.

Thus, for planted acreage *up to* the crop's base acreage, Brazil uses the concept of a crop "planted on" base acreage. But for planted acreage *beyond* the crop's base acreage, Brazil would allocate more than (or less than) one base acre per planted acre. In the preceding example, the one acre of upland cotton could not be deemed to be "planted on" 90 acres of soy.

Brazil's allocation methodology thus is not even internally consistent.

39. Given that Brazil's invention allocation methodology has no basis in the text or context of the Peace Clause, much less in the Subsidies Agreement or any other WTO agreement, given that its methodology does not make economic sense, and given that its methodology is internally inconsistent, one is left to wonder how Brazil arrived at its methodology. One answer may be that Brazil developed this methodology because it allows Brazil to allocate certain decoupled payments exclusively or nearly exclusively to upland cotton. That is, Brazil's invented allocation methodology can be described as an attempt to maximize the

---

42 *Ibid.*

43 *See* US Comment on Brazil's Answer to Question 258, para. 222.

payments to be allocated to upland cotton, regardless of the legal or common-sense objections.

40. Consider the information set out in footnote 159 to paragraph 80 of Brazil's Data Comments. Brazil notes that "[f]or MY 1999 and 2000, *only upland cotton plantings exceeded the crop base acreage*; thus, *all additional payments were allocated to upland cotton* [italics added]. For MY 2001, also oats and sorghum were planted on more acreage than their respective contract base ('overplanted');thus, triggering additional payments being allocated pursuant to the crop's share of the total acreage being 'overplanted'". Restated, in marketing year 2001, all "excess" contract payments were allocated to upland cotton, oats, and sorghum, but the latter two crops accounted for only a small share of plantings on farms that planted upland cotton.[44]

> Thus, for cotton plantings up to the amount of cotton base, Brazil would allocate payments on upland cotton base acres to cotton.
>
> For cotton plantings in excess of the amount of cotton base, Brazil's allocation methodology results in all "excess" contract payments for programme crops being allocated to upland cotton in marketing years 1999-2000 and almost all "excess" contract payments being allocated to upland cotton in marketing year 2001.

In this way, Brazil seeks to maximize the payments being allocated to upland cotton, regardless of the illogic of its approach. The Panel should reject Brazil's legally erroneous and economically unsound approach to allocation issues.

41. Brazil attempts to apply its unsound methodology to the summary data provided by the United States on 18 and 19 December 2003.(We note that Brazil did not request the summary data in Exhibit BRA-369. The United States generated this summary in order to assist the Panel and Brazil in viewing the aggregated results.)Brazil asserts that "Using the US aggregate base acreage data and aggregate planting data to allocate contract payments will most likely trigger distortions of the results due to the allocation problem".[45] However, we note that Brazil does not explain to the Panel that the results using the aggregated data will likely be biased upwards, overstating the decoupled payments allocated to upland cotton.

42. In Brazil's allocation methodology, a farm that plants less acreage of upland cotton than its cotton base acreage must always produce a drop in support because some payments on upland cotton base acres will not be allocated to cotton. A farm that plants more cotton acreage than its cotton base acreage, on the other hand, may still enjoy support for the "excess" planted acres but only if there are also "excess" non-upland cotton base acres on the farm. However, when all of the base acreage and planted acreage data are aggregated, Farm A's cotton planted acreage in excess of upland cotton base acres may effectively be allo-

---

[44] *See* US Letter to Panel (January 28, 2004) (file rPFCsum.xls: for farms planting upland cotton in MY2001 upland cotton planted acreage was 15.5 million acres, oats planted acreage was 0.19 million acres, and sorghum planted acreage was 2.4 million acres).

[45] Brazil's Data Comments, para. 76.

cated support from Farm B's "excess base acreage" in another programme crop (or more than one). Thus, while Brazil is correct that applying its methodology to the summary data will not necessarily produce the same results as a farm-by-farm calculation, Brazil fails to recognize that the results presented by Brazil in paragraph 83 of its data comments applying its invented allocation methodology to the summary data are biased upwards.

43. In sum, the United States has shown that Brazil's allocation methodology is not based on any WTO agreement text, does not make economic sense, and is not internally consistent. Based on the categorical US rejection of Brazil's methodology, the Panel should take Brazil's statement that "Brazil's methodology is rather conservative compared to an allocation based on the US summary data, *which the United States seems to endorse as a valid base for calculating support to upland cotton*"[46] as another gross distortion by Brazil. Unlike Brazil, the United States has taken a consistent position in this dispute that "support to a specific commodity" means "product-specific support" and that such support must be gauged by looking at the support "decided" by a Member through its measures.

V. BRAZIL'S APPLICATION OF THE ANNEX IV METHODOLOGY TO THE US DATA IS INADEQUATE AND FLAWED

44. In this section, the United States examines Brazil's cursory application of the Annex IV methodology to the US-supplied data.[47] We note that Brazil's analysis is patently insufficient to carry Brazil's burden with respect to decoupled income support payments. First, Brazil has neither sought nor presented relevant data. Brazil requested data relevant only to its invented methodology, and there is no data before the Panel that would permit the Annex IV methodology to be applied. Brazil's complaint that the United States has "refuse[d] to provide" the information that would permit the Panel to calculate the payments under the US methodology[48] – while erroneous[49] – is also misplaced. It is not the United States' responsibility to make Brazil's *prima facie* case, and Brazil's argument reflects an impermissible effort to shift the burden onto the responding party.

45. Brazil has also not presented arguments sufficient to carry its burden. Brazil has repeatedly and expressly disavowed the applicability of the Annex IV methodology for purposes of identifying the subsidized product or quantifying the subsidy benefit for non-tied (decoupled) payments. Perhaps for that reason, the calculations presented by Brazil reflect a misunderstanding of the plain meaning of the Annex IV methodology and contain a number of erroneous assumptions that bias Brazil's results upwards.

---

46 Brazil's Data Comments, para. 84 (italics added).

47 *See* Brazil's Data Comments, § 10.

48 Brazil's Data Comments, para. 87.

49 For example, the United States has collected no information on "the recipient firm's sales" for marketing years 1999-2002.

46. Under the Annex IV methodology, a subsidy not tied to a particular product is allocated to all of the recipients' sales. That is, since money is fungible, the subsidy benefit is deemed to inure to all of the products the recipient produces; a neutral way of attributing the subsidy to particular products is according to their proportion of the firm's sales. Thus, allocating to upland cotton those Production Flexibility Contract (PFC) payments,Market Loss Assistance (MLA) payments, Direct Payments (DP) and Counter-Cyclical Payments (CCP) for upland cotton base acres would be done as follows:

PFC payments for upland cotton base * (cotton gross sales/total sales)

MLA payments for upland cotton base * (cotton gross sales/total sales)

DP payments for upland cotton base * (cotton gross sales/total sales)

CCP payments for upland cotton base * (cotton gross sales/total sales)[50]

The "total value of the recipient firm's sales" (Annex IV, para. 2) would include all economic activities by the firm (e.g., other farm and non-farm related activities). Thus, Brazil errs in limiting the denominator in its calculations to the estimated value of crops produced by the payment recipients.[51] Further, Brazil has presented no evidence relating to the total value of the recipient firm's sales that would permit the Annex IV methodology to be applied.

47. In its calculated apportionment, Brazil makes several errors that result in an overestimate of the payment value allocated to cotton. First, Brazil allocates decoupled payments for all crop base (e.g., wheat PFC payments, corn MLA payments) to upland cotton. As the United States has explained[52], Brazil impermissibly seeks to bring within the scope of this dispute payments that Brazil did not identify and that have not been at issue throughout this dispute.

48. In this regard, Brazil's argument that these programmes are within the Panel's terms of reference by virtue of the reference in Brazil's panel request to "payments ... providing direct or indirect support to the US upland cotton industry"[53] is not sustainable. Article 6.2 of the DSU requires that the panel request "identify the specific measures at issue". Brazil's statement fails to meet this requirement; indeed, Brazil affirmatively emphasizes that its list of payments is "unqualified", and that it "is more than broad enough to encompass any type of payment".[54] In other words, Brazil by its own admission has provided virtually no information that would allow identification of the specific measures at issue.

49. Moreover, to the extent that Brazil in any way qualifies this list, it does so based on *legal* conclusions. Rather than identifying the payment measures by describing their characteristics or by citing any specific provision of US law[55],

---

50 Arguably, one could include all economic activities by the firm (e.g., other farm and non-farm related activities.)

51 Brazil's Data Comments, paras. 85-98.

52 *See* US Comment on Brazil's Answer to Question 204 from the Panel, paras. 34-42 (28 January 2004).

53 Para. 18.

54 Para. 19.

55 Brazil's reference to payment programs provided under the 2002 FSRI Act, the 1996 FAIR Act, and the 1998 -2001 Appropriations Acts in no way provides the required specificity. These laws

Brazil seeks to draw into the scope of this dispute an uncircumscribed and unidentified list of measures limited only by whether the *legal* conclusion may be drawn that the measure provides "direct or indirect support to the US upland cotton industry". Brazil might just as well have stated that it was challenging, "any US law that is inconsistent with US WTO obligations." In neither case would the description allow an identification of which measure is subject to the case, and in neither case would it be possible to determine whether a measure is within the scope of the case until the legal issues in the dispute are fully adjudicated. Indeed, the Appellate Body has criticized a panel for blurring the distinction between legal claims and measures when it read the term "measures" as synonymous with alleged violations, and thereby failed to require identification of the specific measure at issue.[56]

50. The DSU requirement to allow identification of the measures at issue is not a hollow one, and panels have not hesitated to conclude that measures fall outside the scope of a dispute because they are not adequately described.[57] Brazil's "unqualified" panel request does not bring non-cotton contract payments into the scope of this dispute.

51. While decoupled payments for upland cotton base account for the majority of decoupled income support payments to farms that planted cotton, including total decoupled payments in the allocation overstates the value of decoupled payments to be allocated.

Decoupled payments:	1999[1]	2000[1]	2001[1]	2002
Payments on cotton base	515,280,580	482,302,565	387,870,741	1,520,701,136
Total payments	695,912,510	650,579,667	520,230,908	1,681,630,034
Cotton as per cent of total	74.0%	74.1%	74.6%	90.4%

1 Does not include Market Loss Assistance payments.

Source: Exhibit Bra-424; also provided electronically as "allocation calculations.xls"

52. Second, in calculating crop values for purposes of the total value of the recipient firm's sales[58], Brazil calculates crop values based on planted, not harvested, acreage. For cotton, abandonment rates can be significant. In the US response to Question 209 from the Panel, the United States demonstrated that harvested acreage differed significantly from planted acreage over the period 1999-2002. The use of the smaller harvested acreage figure would lower the total value of cotton by as much as 16 per cent from what Brazil calculated.[59]

provided for a myriad of payment programmes, and it is impossible through these references to determine the payment programmes Brazil now seeks to include within the dispute.

[56] Report of the Appellate Body, *Guatemala – Anti-Dumping Investigation Regarding Portland Cement from Mexico*, WT/DS60/AB/R, adopted 25 November 1998, para. 69.

[57] *See, e.g.,* Preliminary Ruling by the Panel, *Canada – Measures Relating to Exports of Wheat and Treatment of Imported Grain*, WT/DS276/12, circulated 21 July 2003, paras. 28, 32.

[58] *See* Subsidies Agreement, Annex IV, para. 2.

[59] Brazil inadvertently uses the all cotton crop yield in their calculations rather than the yield for upland cotton only.

Planted and Harvested Upland Cotton Acres (1,000 acres)

Crop year	Planted acres	Harvested acres	Abandoned acres	Rate of abandonment
1999	14,584	13,138	1,446	9.9%
2000	15,347	12,884	2,463	16.0%
2001	15,499	13,560	1,939	12.5%
2002	13,714	12,184	1,530	11.2%

Source: USDA, National Agricultural Statistics Service, *Acreage,* various issues.

53. Third, Brazil underestimates the value of crop sales on cotton farms. To calculate the value of programme crops, Brazil multiplies acres planted to that crop (as provided electronically by the United States on December 18 and 19) times average crop yield times average farm price. For cropland not planted to programme crops, Brazil "assumed that the value of the crops produced on this 20 per cent of farmland is the average per-acre value of production of non-programme crops in that marketing year in the entire United States, as reported by USDA"[60]. Brazil has claimed repeatedly that upland cotton production is "concentrated" in several US States[61], but now that the issue matters, Brazil ignores its long-standing position. Under Brazil's approach to the Annex IV methodology, it is the per-acre value of production in cotton-producing states that would be relevant (rather than including, say, the per acre value of production of crops grown in Alaska in its average).

54. To calculate the average per-acre value of non-programme crops, moreover, Brazil also excludes the value of all fruits, tree crops, vegetables and melons, arguing that their exclusion is justified on the basis that, if fruits or vegetables are grown, "contract payments are eliminated".[62] However, this argument ignores the fact that producers may grow such crops on any cropland on the farm in excess of the farm's base acreagewithout any effect on payments.[63] As previously noted by Brazil, non-programme base accounts for 20 per cent of total cropland on farms that planted cotton over the period or about 6 million acres. Ignoring fruits and vegetables thus underestimates the value of non-programme crops and, as a consequence, overestimates the per cent of total crop value accounted for by cotton.[64]

55. Fifth, as Brazil concedes,[65] in estimating the total value of crop sales, Brazil excluded sales of (high value) livestock and livestock products. We would

---

[60] Brazil's Data Comments, para. 90.

[61] *See, e.g.,* Brazil's Answer to Question 125(2)(a) from the Panel, para. 13 (27 October 2003).

[62] *See* Brazil's Data Comments, paras. 73, 92.

[63] *See, e.g.,* Brazil's First Written Submission, para. 45 (PFC payments are reduced or eliminated if fruits or vegetables are grown "on 'base acreage'" but not on total cropland).

[64] Brazil also appears to have inadvertently copied the incorrect acreage numbers for cotton planted on farms with no cotton base for 2000 and 2001. (The 1999 figure was copied to 2000 and 2001. From the spreadsheet "Raw Data 1999-2001" the correct numbers are:
1999 1,033,617.7
2000 1,222,180.1
2001 1,347,140.2

[65] Brazil's Data Comments, fn. 173.

also note that Brazil excluded any other farm-related income. Brazil has put no data on the record that would allow for these sales to be included in the Annex IV allocation.

56. Finally, Brazil fails to make any adjustment in the amount of payment to reflect the proportion of cotton planted acreage that is rented or owned.[66] However, those "subsidies" to cotton producers that are the subject of Brazil's panel request must "benefit" producers.[67] Brazil itself has conceded that land rental rates as of marketing year 1997 – that is, one year after introduction of the decoupled production flexibility contract payments – reflect the capture of more than one-third of the subsidy by landowners.[68] Thus, only those cotton producers who are also landowners of base acreage for which decoupled payments are made would benefit from those payments.[69]

57. The cumulative effect of these omissions and erroneous assumptions is to bias upwards Brazil's allocation of decoupled payments to upland cotton. In the following table, we have recalculated an estimated value of cotton production compared to the value of all crops produced on farms using corrected values for harvested acres, upland cotton yields, and per-acre value of non-programme crops.[70] Because Brazil has not put relevant data on the record, we have not been able to correct its calculations by including the value of all economic activities by the firm, for example, livestock and livestock products, other farm-related activities, and non-farm economic activities in the denominator. However, even without those necessary adjustments, the incomplete (undervalued) data show that cotton accounted for only about half of the total value of crop production on recipient farms planting upland cotton over the period.

---

[66] *See* US Answer to Question 195 from the Panel, paras. 6-11 (22 December 2003).

[67] *See* Panel Report, *United States – Imposition of Countervailing Duties on Certain Hot-Rolled Lead and Bismuth Carbon Steel Products Originating in the United Kingdom*, WT/DS138/R, adopted 7 June 2000, paras. 6.65 and 6.66 (quoting and agreeing with *Canada – Aircraft* panel: "'A "benefit" does not exist in the abstract, but must be received and enjoyed by a beneficiary or a recipient. Logically, a "benefit" can be said to arise only if a person ... has in fact received something.'").

[68] *See, e.g.*, Brazil's Further Rebuttal Submission, para. 154 ("[S]ome portion of the contract payments do find their way into increased rent and cost of land") (footnote omitted).

[69] Indeed, the 2002 Act implicitly recognized that decoupled income support payments ultimately benefit landowners by giving to the landowner the authority to choose whether to update his or her base acres on the farm. *See* 2002 Act, § 1101(a)(1) ("For the purpose of making direct payments and counter-cyclical payments with respect to a farm, the Secretary shall give an owner of the farm an opportunity to elect 1 of the following as the method by which the base acres of all covered commodities on the farm are to be determined."); *see also id.*, § 1101(b), 1101(c), 1101(e)(1), (3), (5) (Exhibit US-1).

[70] Further calculations are presented in Exhibit US-154..

Value of Upland Cotton as Per cent of All Crops on Farms Planting Upland Cotton

	1999	2000	2001	2002
Upland cotton	$3,056,169,795	$3,707,427,799	$2,554,264,280	$3,351,712,385
All crops	$5,940,836,757	$6,543,259,828	$5,277,060,069	$6,280,154,911
Per cent	51.4%	56.7%	48.4%	53.4%

58. In the table that follows, we present recalculated figures for decoupled payments on upland cotton base using the corrected value of upland cotton sales and per-acre value for non-programme crops in calculating the total value of crop sales to use in the denominator of the formula: decoupled payments received by recipient firms * (upland cotton gross sales / total crop sales). Again, contrary to Annex IV, paragraph 2, this calculation does not include in the denominator the value of *all* economic activities by the recipient firms. Nor have we adjusted the value of the decoupled payments for upland cotton base acres downwards to reflect the fact that two-thirds of cotton acreage is rented, not owned, and that landowners will capture the benefit of those payments for base acres on farms worked by tenants.

59. Nonetheless, the table shows that the "14/16" methodology proposed by Brazil, as well as the estimates purporting to apply the Annex IV methodology provided in section 10 of Brazil's data comments (reproduced below), are grossly inflated.

Partially Corrected Results of Calculations Allocating Decoupled Payments for Upland Cotton Base Acres to Upland Cotton Using Incomplete Annex IV Methodology

	1999	2000	2001	2002
PFC Payments	265,077,970	273,273,870	187,741,729	na
MLA Payments	263,787,006	290,909,042	259,309,589	na
DP Payments	na	na	na	253,021,210
CCP Payments	na	na	na	558,575,463
Total	528,864,975	564,182,912	447,051,318	811,596,673

Brazil's Erroneous Calculations Allocating Decoupled Payments for all Contract Base to Upland Cotton Using Incomplete Annex IV Methodology (Brazil's Data Comments, para. 96.)

	1999	2000	2001	2002
PFC Payments	$477,692,236	$473,744,959	$333,295,919	na
MLA Payments	$475,365,813	$504,317,125	$460,349,591	na
DP Payments	na	na	na	$416,216,862
CCP Payments	na	na	na	$714,424,543
Total	$953,058,049	$978,062,084	$793,645,510	$1,130,641,406
Minimum Per cent Overstated	**80.2**	**73.4**	**77.5**	**39.3**

Brazil's Allocation of Decoupled Payments for all Contract Base to Upland Cotton Using Its Erroneous 14/16 Methodology (Brazil's Data Comments, para. 97)

	1999	2000	2001	2002
PFC Payments	$547,800,000	$541,300,000	$453,000,000	na
MLA Payments	$545,100,000	$576,200,000	$625,700,000	na
DP Payments	na	na	na	$454,500,000
CCP Payments	na	na	na	$935,600,000
Total	$1,092,900,000	$1,117,500,000	$1,078,700,000	$1,390,100,000
Minimum Per cent Overstated	**106.7**	**98.1**	**141.3**	**71.3**

That is, when the results of Brazil's calculations are compared to the results obtained by the United States correcting for certain but not all of Brazil's errors and omissions, it appears that *Brazil dramatically overstates the decoupled payments that would be allocated to upland cotton* by 39.3 to 80.2 per cent for its incomplete Annex IV calculations and by 71.3 to 141.3 per cent for its erroneous 14/16 calculations.

60. Had Brazil put other data on the record necessary to apply the Annex IV methodology, for example, the value of any livestock and livestock products, other farm-related activities, and non-farm economic activities of recipient firms, moreover, *the decoupled payments allocated to upland cotton would be reduced even further*. Had Brazil further adjusted the value of the decoupled payments for upland cotton base acres downwards to reflect the capture of two-thirds of the benefit of those payments by landowners who are not cotton producers, *the decoupled payments allocated to upland cotton would be reduced even further*. Rather than confront the fact that the Annex IV methodology and Subsidies Agreement concepts would dramatically reduce the value of decoupled payments deemed to benefit upland cotton (and hence, would dramatically reduce the supposed "$12.9 billion" in support provided to upland cotton between marketing years 1999-2002), Brazil chose to argue that *no* allocation of non-tied payments is necessary and that *no* quantification of the subsidy benefit to upland cotton is necessary. Brazil also chose *not* to seek or put on the record information relevant to this determination. Thus, as explained earlier, Brazil has deliberately chosen a course of action that results in its failure to make a *prima facie* case on its serious prejudice claims with respect to decoupled payments.

VI. BRAZIL MISREPRESENTS BOTH THE SCOPE OF ITS OWN REQUESTS FOR DATA AS WELL AS THE US RESPONSE

61. Finally, in this portion of its comments, the United States responds to inaccurate assertions by Brazil relating to what information it sought and what information the United States provided. The United States also responds to Brazil's arguments that certain "adverse inferences" should be drawn from its inaccurate portrayal of what was requested and provided. The United States notes

that these issues are of relatively minor importance given that Brazil's allocation methodology, for which it sought farm-by-farm planted and base acreage data:

> (1) may not be applied for purposes of determining the product-specific support to upland cotton for purposes of the Peace Clause analysis because the methodology inappropriately conflates product-specific and non-product-specific support and
>
> (2) may not be applied for purposes of determining the subsidized product or the subsidy benefit for decoupled income support payments because that methodology has no basis in the WTO agreements and Brazil expressly disavows its use for purposes of its serious prejudice claims.

Nonetheless, we undertake this review of Brazil's assertions because Brazil grossly distorts the record of the dispute in an effort to make the United States appear uncooperative (at best). The truth is that the United States has expended an unprecedented amount of time and resources in responding to the fullest extent under US law to the requests for information made of it. Given our experience in WTO dispute settlement to date, we question whether other Members would have responded so fully and promptly to similarly burdensome requests.

A. Brazil Grossly Distorts the Record of This Dispute by Suggesting that the United States Has Failed to Cooperate

62. Brazil make a number of spurious accusations regarding US participation in this dispute and simple misstatements of the record. Although we regret the imposition on the Panel's time and attention, we do feel it necessary to set the record straight.

63. *Brazil First Asked for this Data in December 2003, Not November 2002*:First, Brazil asserts that it "first requested this information in November 2002".[71] "This information" refers to the request for information "set out in Exhibit BRA-369" for "contract acreage and planted acreage for each farm producing upland cotton".[72] Brazil's claim is false. There is no request in Exhibit BRA-101 (Brazil's consultation questions) for "contract acreage and planted acreage for each farm producing upland cotton". Further, there is no reference in Brazil's consultation questions to decoupled income support payments for non-upland cotton base acres. For example, Consultation Question 3.6 (not referenced by Brazil in footnote 2 of its data comments) was expressly directed at payments made "in connection with upland cotton for each of the marketing years 1992 through 2002". When the United States answered those questions by referring (where appropriate) to payments made with respect to upland cotton base acres, Brazil at no point asserted that it sought information with respect to "other crop contract payments".

64. *Brazil Misrepresents the Panel's Request for Information*:Second, Brazil asserts that the "Panel requested [this data] in August, October, and December

---

[71] Brazil's Data Comments, para. 4 (footnote referencing BRA-101 omitted).

[72] Brazil's Data Comments, para. 3.

2003, as well as in January 2004." The Panel well knows what it has requested, but the United States notes that the Panel's questions too did not request contract and planted acreage information. Question 67 *bis* in August 2003 requested information about annual amounts granted to upland cotton producers per pound and in total expenditures under each of the decoupled payment programmes, not information on planted or base acreage. As previously explained, the United States accurately answered that it does not maintain information on expenditures to upland cotton producers because the United States collects no farm-specific production (harvesting) data.[73] Question 125(9) in October 2003 requested, *inter alia*, information on any adjustments to make for decoupled payments for upland cotton base acreage, not for information on planted and base acreage. In its 8 December 2003, communication, the Panel did not request planted and base acreage information from the United States; rather, it stated that "the United States will be given until **18 December** to respond to *Brazil's request* made in Exhibit BRA-369".[74] Finally, the 12 January 2004, communication from the Panel *did* request the planted acreage and base acreage information as set out in Exhibit BRA-369, and the United States explained that it was not able to provide this information farm-by-farm under the US Privacy Act. Thus, Brazil misrepresents the facts when it asserts that the Panel has requested "this data" four times.

65. *Brazil Falsely Alleges that the United States Denied Having Certain Data*:Brazil then accuses the United States of "falsely stat[ing] that it did not maintain contract and planted acreage information for each farm".[75] As just explained, the United States did not "falsely state" that it did not maintain that information because it was not asked for that information until the Panel on 8 December 2003, invited it to respond to Brazil's request made in Exhibit BRA-369. In its 18 and 19 December 2003, replies to that request, the United States explained that under US law it could not provide (as Brazil specifically requested and insisted upon) planted acreage information together with base acreage and yield information and FSA farm numbers.

66. We also recall, as explained in the US comments on Brazil's answers[76], that it was the United States itself at the second session of the first panel meeting (that is, before "late November 2003" and the presentation of Exhibit BRA-369 at the second panel meeting) that brought to the Panel's and Brazil's attention the acreage reporting requirement that was introduced by Section 1105 of the 2002 Act (7 USC 7915). We trust that the fact that the United States *offered* this information to Brazil and the Panel will lay to rest the unwarranted suggestion that the United States sought to obscure it instead.

67. contract base acreage and yield information. The focus of the Panel's question 67 *bis* and Brazil's argumentation has naturally been on the amount of

---

[73] *See, e.g.,* US Answer to Question 195 from the Panel, paras. 6-11 (22 December 2003).

[74] The United States notes but does not understand the reference in fn.3 to paragraph 4 of Brazil's data comments to the "second bulleted point" in the Panel's December 8 communication; that bullet point referred to "a communication from the Panel concerning the FAPRI model".

[75] Brazil's Data Comments, para. 4.

[76] US Comment on Brazil's Answer to Question 196 from the Panel, paras. 15-18 (28 January 2004).

decoupled income support payments to upland cotton producers. The United States has explained that it does not track decoupled payments by recipients' production and thus does not maintain information on the payments made for upland cotton base acres (or any other base acres) to upland cotton *producers*. The farm-by-farm planted acreage and base acreage and yield data sought by Brazil in Exhibit BRA-369 and by the Panel in its request of 12 January 2004, does not provide information on the payments made to upland cotton *producers*. Rather, putting aside issues of the appropriate methodology to identify the amount of the subsidy, this planted and base information would allow the calculation of the amount of decoupled payments made to farms that reported *planting* upland cotton.

68. *Brazil Incorrectly Accuses the United States of Refusing to Provide Data on Non-Upland Cotton Base*:Brazil also argues that the United States "refused to provide" farm-specific data on the amount of other contract base acreage on farms producing upland cotton with no upland cotton base acreage.[77] The omission of non-upland cotton base acreage from the data submitted by the United States in December 2003 was inadvertent and the result of programming errors, as explained in the US letter of 28 January 2004 transmitting revised data files. Thus, Brazil's extensive protestations that the United States "withheld that information" are misplaced.

69. We do note, however, that the United States continues to believe that such decoupled payments for non-upland cotton base acreage are not within the Panel's terms of reference and that Brazil's effort to include these payments at the end of this proceeding would deprive the United States of fundamental rights of due process.[78] That such payments for non-upland cotton base acreage was not even considered by Brazil earlier in this proceeding is nowhere more clear than in Brazil's own words:

> "Brazil requested the United States during the Annex V procedure to provide information on the total amount of *upland cotton base acreage and yield* under the CCP (and DP) program."[79]

Indeed, the accuracy of Brazil's own description of its questions is amply supported by the text of those questions relating to "Deficiency Payments/Production Flexibility Contract Payments/Direct Payments":[80]

> "Please state the number of US upland cotton farms updating their *upland cotton base acreage* for the purposes of calculating Direct Payments under the 2002 FSRI Act. Please also provide the percentage of all US farmers producing upland cotton that updated *their upland cotton base acreage*."(Question 3.1 (italics added))

---

77 Brazil's Data Comments, para. 17.

78 *See* US Comments on Brazil's Answer to Question 204 from the Panel, paras. 34-42 (28 January 2004).

79 Brazil's First Written Submission, para. 68 (emphasis added). We note in passing that the DSB did not initiate the Annex V procedures and that Brazil's statement that it asked the United States questions "during the Annex V procedure" is therefore incorrect.

80 *See* Exhibit BRA-49 (Brazil's questions for purposes of the Annex V procedure).

> "Please state the annual amount of Deficiency Payments made by the US Government in connection with *upland cotton base* for each of the marketing years 1992 through 1996."(Question 3.4 (italics added))
>
> "Please state the annual amount of Production Flexibility Contract Payments made by the US Government in connection with *upland cotton base* for each of the marketing years 1996 through 2002."(Question 3.6 (italics added))
>
> "Please state the total amount of Direct Payments made by the US Government in connection with *upland cotton base* in marketing year 2002."(Question 3.7 (italics added))
>
> "Please state the amount of *upland cotton base acreage* and the *average upland cotton base yield* applicable on this acreage under the Production Flexibility Contract Payment Program."(Question 3.9 (italics added))· "Please state the amount of *upland cotton base acreage* and the *average upland cotton base yield* applicable on this acreage for the Direct Payment Program."(Question 3.10 (italics added))

Thus, Brazil's assertion that it has argued all along that decoupled payments for non-upland cotton base acres are challenged measures is flatly contradicted by its own questions set out above. Brazil sent these questions on 1 April 2003, a mere 14 days after the DSB established the panel to consider this matter. If Brazil had considered that payments for non-upland cotton base acreage were within the scope of this dispute, surely it would have requested information with respect to those payments as well. The sheer number of references to upland cotton base acreage and yields demonstrates Brazil's view, at the time of panel establishment, of the scope of the decoupled payments it challenged.[81]

70. *Market Loss Assistance Data Was Not Requested But Was Provided*:Brazil argues that the United States "has not provided the requested data for market loss assistance payments received by the farms listed for MY 1999-2001". Brazil's argument is confused. Exhibit BRA-369 requested planted acreage and base acreage (and yield) for marketing years 1999-2002, and the United States provided that, farm-by-farm. The base acreage did not differ for production flexibility contract payments and market loss assistance payments so there was no need to set out base data for market loss assistance payments separately.

71. It is ironic that Brazil would accuse the United States of failing to provide certain "data for market loss assistance payments" since Exhibit BRA-369 *did not even identify market loss assistance payments by name*. Instead, it defined "programme crop" as "any crop that was assigned base acreage and payment

[81] The United States has previously set out further evidence that decoupled payments for non-upland cotton base acres are not within the Panel's terms of reference and that Brazil did not consider these payments to be measures within the Panel's terms of reference. *See* US Comments to Brazil's Answer to Question 204 from the Panel, paras. 32-42 (28 January 2004).

yields under the Production Flexibility Contract (MY 1999-2001). Brazil inserts a question mark for MLA payments in its table at paragraph 22 of its comments, arguing that "[t]he United States has not provided any specific information on market loss assistance payments," but again Brazil ignores its own data request. Nowhere in Exhibit BRA-369 did Brazil request actual *payment* amounts for any of the decoupled income support programmes, and in any event Brazil well knows that market loss assistance payments were calculated in the same proportion as the production flexibility contract payments.[82]

72. *Soybeans Were Not Within Brazil's Data Request:*Next, Brazil argues that "since market loss assistance payments were also made for soybean base (that otherwise was not eligible to receive PFC payments), this allocation methodology [based on PFC payments] may significantly underestimate the amount of market loss assistance payments that constitute support to upland cotton".[83] The existence of soybeans market loss assistance payments is simply irrelevant to the data Brazil requested from the United States. Exhibit BRA-369 requested planted acreage and base acreage (and yield) information for "programme crops." Soybeans, however, were not a programme crop (or "contract commodity") under the 1996 Act[84], and no soybean base acreage was assigned to farms before marketing year 2002. In fact, in the very statutes that provided sections that provided for payments designated as marketing loss assistance, there were separate provisions for payments for soybeans in marketing years 1999 and 2000; these payments were not designated as market loss assistance and were provided for current soybeans producers (and oilseed producers of all types).[85] Contrary to market loss assistance payments, soybeans producers received payments not based on the farm history, but their own production history (as explained in the 8 June 2000 rule), no matter where they planted the soybeans. Thus, no soybeans data was included in the US response to Exhibit BRA-369 because no soybeans data was requested. Indeed, Brazil later implicitly concedes that soybeans data could *not* have been included in its request since soybeans were not a programme crop.[86]

73. *Peanuts Were Not Within Brazil's Data Request:*Finally, Brazil argues that "the 19 December 2003 US data concerning MY 2002 does not contain any

---

82 *See* Brazil's First Written Submission, para. 60 ("Between MY1998-2001, upland cotton producers thereby received an additional amount of money, which was calculated based on their respective share of total upland cotton base times the amount of budgetary outlays allocated for upland cotton.").

83 Brazil's Data Comments, para. 20.

84 *See* 1996 FAIR Act, § 102(5) (Exhibit BRA-28).

85 The 1999 crop soybean program was provided for by a statute, PL 106-78, enacted 22 October 1999. In fact, the USDA's programme rules were not issued until 8 June 2000, at 65 FR 36550. The amount provided in that statute was $475 million for all oilseeds, not just soybeans. As for the 2000 crop, the soybean payments were allowed by PL 106-224, in the amount of $500 million for all oilseeds, with rules that did not issue until 65 F.R. 5709 in November 2000. The amount paid was amplified for the 2000 crop by the addition of monies, long after, in PL 107-25, enacted in August of 2001. It is worth noting that all of these payments occurred well after plantings, again contradicting the contention of Brazil that non-upland cotton payments cause farmers to plant cotton.

86 *See* Brazil's Data Comments, para. 90 fn. 177 ("The lower figures for MY 1999-2001 are explained by the fact that soybeans were not a contract programme crop.").

information regarding the amount of direct and counter-cyclical payments made on peanut base". Brazil asserts that "the missing data on peanut contract payments for MY 2002 would cause lower aggregate payments allocated as support to upland cotton".[87] Again, Brazil makes assertions that do not follow from its own data request. The marketing year 2002 data contains no peanut information because no farm had peanut base in marketing year 2002; it follows that there were no payments made on any farm base. No peanut base existed for farms in marketing year 2002 because decoupled payments for peanut base acreage was brand new, and the base was not assigned by Section 1302 of the Farm Bill to a farm but to "historical peanuts producers". The statute did not require an assignment of the base acreage to a farm until the 2003 crop. In fact, the United States expressly noted in Exhibits US-111 (describing contents of farm-by-farm DCP base and yield file) and US-112 (describing contents of farm-by-farm DCP planted acres file) that "[p]eanut figures were not run as peanut bases were not farm-specific in 2002". Thus, the United States could not have provided farm-specific planted acreage and base acreage information with respect to peanuts because there was no peanuts base acreage for farms in marketing year 2002. Again, Brazil's complaints are without merit.

74. *Conclusion:Brazil's Accusations Are Spurious and Complicate the Panel's Task Needlessly*:In conclusion, the United States notes that not only has Brazil sought to put the United States in a difficult position through its overbroad data request and unreasonable approach to privacy issues under US law, but the lack of clarity in Brazil's approach has added considerable confusion to this proceeding. For example, Brazil at one and the same time faults the United States for not providing the farm-specific information as requested in Exhibit BRA-369 but then also faults it for not producing the information using "a substitute number protecting the alleged confidentiality rights of farmers."[88] Despite refusing to consider any deviation from BRA-369 at the second panel meeting, Brazil now asserts that the United States should have noticed a newfound flexibility in a passing reference within a Brazilian answer and on that basis produced an entirely new set of data. It was entirely reasonable for the United States to consider Exhibit BRA-369 as Brazil's request since Brazil's refusal to consider alternatives compelled the United States to make tremendous efforts to produce that requested information while simultaneously preparing answers to more than 50 panel questions and comments on Brazil's econometric evidence.(Further, as the United States explained in its 20 January 2004, letter to the Panel, the sheer number of fields involved in Brazil's request would make possible identification of specific farms based on a unique combination of planted and base acreage, even with substitute farm numbers.)

75. As another example, Brazil's request was so broad that (as set out above) Brazil itself appears not to have understood the precise scope of the information it requested. This continual overbroad argumentation wastes the time and re-

---

87 Brazil's Data Comments, para. 21.

88 *See* Brazil's Data Comments, paras. 38-39 (referencing Brazil's December 22 Answers to Questions, para. 7).

sources of the United States and the Panel that would be better spent on issues actually pertinent to this dispute. In addition, Brazil faults the United States for "misunderstanding [] Brazil's allocation methodology," when that methodology was not set out until Brazil filed its answer to Question 258 on 20 January 2004 – that is, more than one month after the United States provided the data requested in Exhibit BRA-369 (to the extent permissible under US law) and more than eight months into this proceeding. In this regard, Brazil's litigation tactics have impacted the ability of the United States to address Brazil's claims, arguments, and evidence and have complicated this Panel's task immensely and needlessly.[89]

B. US Law Prohibits Disclosing Planted Acreage Information Without the Prior Consent of the Farmer

76. The United States has explained in its letters dated 18 December2003, 19 December 2003, and 20 January 2004, that under US law it may not disclose planting information in which a farmer has a privacy interest. This has been consistent US Department of Agriculture policy and is not contradicted by the *Washington Post* district court decision referenced by Brazil (which dealt with disclosure of payment information – similarly, the United States has provided contract data on a farm-by-farm basis). The United States also explains these matters in more detail in its answer to Questions 259(a), (b), and (c).

77. Brazil's views on how US law operates in the FOIA context are not relevant to the US Department of Agriculture's statutory responsibility to respect the privacy interests of US farmers in the planted acreage data. However, Brazil's discussion of *Washington Post v. United States Department of Agriculture*, 943 F. Supp. 31 (D.D.C. 1996), does not support Brazil's arguments that the United States need not protect this data.

78. The US position on the privacy interests in plantings is not *post hoc* since, as we showed in the attachments to the US letter of 18 December 2003, the position on planted acres has been the same since at least 1997 – that is, after the *Washington Post* decision. Brazil neglects to mention that all that was at issue in the *Washington Post* case was crop *payments*, not farmer plantings. Hence, that case fit within the FOIA precept of disclosure of the activities of the government, which was what was of concern to the court. 943 F. Supp. at 33, 36. Plantings are quite a different matter, involving a farmer's activities, not that of the govern-

89 Indeed, the United States has cooperated in good faith in this dispute and expended extraordinary resources to do so, but Brazil put the United States in the position of violating US law or providing requested data. Brazil now seeks to have the Panel draw adverse inferences when its own request for information was over-broad in that Brazil could simply have asked the United States to apply its methodology (which, as of 3 December 2003, it had not yet disclosed, and would not until forced to do so by the Panel on 20 January 2004). The Panel should consider that it was Brazil at the second panel meeting that refused to cooperate and consider alternative means to request information that could have protected US farmers' privacy interests. If there is an "adverse inference" to be drawn, it may be that Brazil withheld its methodology until the end of the proceeding because it knew it could not withstand a full analysis and review and because Brazil sought to distract from Brazil's failure to provide evidence and data necessary to support its arguments based on its methodology.

ment. Moreover, such producer-supplied information, not government-generated, has long been recognized as having special privacy concerns. *See, e.g.*, 7 USC 1373 and7 USC 1502. Thus, under specific provision of the 1938 Act and provisions of the Crop Insurance Act, the US government has long considered plantings separate matters not subject to disclosure. A similar outcome results from an analysis under the Privacy Act and to some degree the Trade Secrets Act.

79. Regarding the rice matter, Brazil argues that "USDA's FOIA representatives necessarily must have determined that because the request did not focus on an individual producer's farm, the interests of the public in understanding and evaluating the operation of the contract payment schemes outweighed any privacy interests". However, the rice matter involved one office, and that disclosure was contrary to clearly established national policy. We have explained fully what the problem was and what FSA policy is. The concerns here are much greater than in the *Hill* decision, moreover, because the privacy interests of 200,000 farmers are involved.

C. There Is No Basis to Draw Any Inference, Much Less an "Adverse Inference"

80. Brazil has asked the Panel to draw certain adverse inferences from the alleged failure of the United States to cooperate fully and provide requested data. As noted in the US letter of 20 January and explained above, the United States did not have the authority to provide the farm-specific planting information in the format requested by the Panel's 12 January 2004. However, the United States did provide both farm-specific and aggregated contract data that would permit the Panel and Brazil to assess the total expenditures of decoupled payments to farms planting upland cotton.[90] Brazil itself admits that "the data provided by the United States appears to be complete" with respect to both contract acres and planted acres[91] – therefore, the willingness of the United States to provide information within the limits set by US law cannot be questioned. Further, the Panel on 3 February requested certain additional aggregated information, which therefore does not implicate privacy interests of farmers and which the United States is endeavouring to provide.

81. The situation here is thus very different from the one in *Canada - Aircraft* where the Appellate Body first opined that "a panel should be willing expressly to remind parties – during the course of dispute settlement proceedings – that a refusal to provide information requested by the panel may lead to inferences[92]

---

[90] The United States notes that it had no basis to provide any other aggregation of the data than that which it provided since it was not aware of Brazil's allocation methodology until Brazil filed its answer to Question 258 on 20 January 2004.

[91] Brazil's Data Comments, para. 27 fn. 55.

[92] The United States notes that in the same report the Appellate Body was careful to distinguish "adverse" inferences from other "inferences", remarking that: "We note, preliminarily, that the 'adverse inference' that Brazil believes the Panel should have drawn is not appropriately regarded as a punitive inference in the sense of a 'punishment' or 'penalty' for Canada's withholding of information. It is merely an inference which in certain circumstances could be logically or reasonably derived by a

being drawn about the inculpatory character of the information withheld."[93] There is no basis for an "inference" of any kind, adverse or otherwise.

82. This is particularly so in this dispute as the farm-specific planted and base acreage information was sought for purposes of Brazil's allocation methodology, which is without any textual basis in the WTO agreements. For purposes of Peace Clause, Brazil's methodology is inapplicable because Brazil concedes that "support to a specific commodity" means "product-specific support" – and yet, Brazil's allocation methodology would contradict the meaning of product-specific support and non-product-specific support set out in the Agreement on Agriculture. Further, Brazil's methodology is inapplicable for purposes of its serious prejudice claims because Brazil argues that no allocation of decoupled payments or identification of subsidy benefits or the subsidized product is necessary under Part III of the Subsidies Agreement. Further, the only allocation methodology set out in the Subsidies Agreement is that of Annex IV, for which the farm-specific planted and base acreage information would be irrelevant. Thus, there is no need to draw an inference of any sort in this dispute.

83. Brazil's proposed "adverse influences" also do not follow logically from the data before the Panel. Brazil first suggests that farm-by-farm data would have resulted in payments higher than Brazil's 14/16 methodology. However, Brazil cannot escape the fact that it has not brought forward evidence and arguments to support findings under the Annex IV methodology.

84. Second, Brazil suggests that the Annex IV methodology would have produced higher payments than Brazil's 14/16 methodology. The United States is not in exclusive possession of relevant information with respect to an Annex IV methodology, but the incomplete data and calculations above demonstrate that in fact the Annex IV methodology would produce a far *lower* subsidy amount than Brazil's 14/16 methodology.

85. Third, Brazil suggests that "the information withheld" by the United States "would have been detrimental" to US arguments that decoupled payments are non-product-specific support. As set out previously, the farm-by-farm planted acreage data that the United States could not provide under US law is simply irrelevant to the issue whether decoupled payments are "product-specific support". Brazil appears to overreach, moreover, in suggesting that a "detrimental" inference be drawn since the *Canada – Aircraft* report found that the inferences to be drawn were not punitive but factual in nature.

VII. CONCLUSION

86. Brazil has asserted that decoupled income support payments must be allocated to upland cotton only for purposes of the Peace Clause and not for purposes of its serious prejudice claims. However, Brazil's analysis is completely

panel from the facts before it." *Canada – Measures Affecting the Export of Civilian Aircraft*, WT/DS70/AB/R, adopted 20 August 1999, para. 200 ("*Canada – Aircraft*").

[93] *Canada – Aircraft*, WT/DS70/AB/R, para. 204.

backwards:the text and context of the Peace Clause demonstrate that support is *not* to be allocated for purposes of the Peace Clause test while the text and context of Articles 5 and 6 of the Subsidies Agreement demonstrate that subsidies not tied to production of a given product (such as decoupled income support) *are* to be allocated to all of the products the recipient sells for purposes of serious prejudice claims.

87. The implication of Brazil's erroneous analysis and arguments, and in particular its express disavowal of any allocation methodology for purposes of its serious prejudice claims on decoupled income support payments, is that Brazil has failed to make a *prima facie* case on these claims. As a result, no findings may be made with respect to these measures, and these payments may not be included in an analysis of whether the effect of the challenged US subsidies has been serious prejudice to Brazil's interests

List of Exhibits

ANNEX I-20

BRAZIL'S COMMENTS ON UNITED STATES 11 FEBRUARY 2004 ANSWERS TO ADDITIONAL QUESTIONS FROM THE PANEL FOLLOWING THE SECOND MEETING OF THE PANEL WITH THE PARTIES

18 February 2004

Table of Cases Cited

Japan – Apples	Appellate Body Report, *Japan – Measures affecting the Importation of Apples,* WT/DS245/AB/R, adopted 10 December 2003.

List of Exhibits

Dresser Industries v United States, 596 F.2d 1231 (5th Cir. 1979)	Exhibit Bra-425
Center for Auto Safety v National Highway Traffic Safety Administration, 244 F.3d 144 (DC Cir 2001)	Exhibit Bra-426
CNA Financial Corporation v Donovan, 830 F.2d 1132 (DC Cir 1987)	Exhibit Bra-427
United States Department of Justice at al. v Reporters Committee for the Freedom of the Press et al., 489 US 749 (1989)	Exhibit Bra-428
Metadure Croporation v United States, 490 F. Supp. 1368 (S.D.N.Y. 1990)	Exhibit Bra-429
Campaign for Family Farms v Glickman, 200 F.3d 1180 (8th Cir. 2000)	Exhibit Bra-430
Comparison of US and Brazil's Cash-Basis Accounting Methodologies for Purposes of the Item (j) Analysis	Exhibit Bra-431
Congressional Budget Office, Fact Sheet, row titled "Export Credit Guarantee Programme, Subsidy Account"	Exhibit Bra-432

259. With respect to the Privacy Act of 1974, 5 U.S.C. 552a:

(a) Whose interests are protected under section 552a(b) in light of the definition of "individual" in section 552a(a)(2)? Do all payment recipients, including corporations and organizations, have Privacy Act rights? If not, is the United States prevented by its domestic law from releasing such of the information requested on 12 January 2004 as relates to payment recipients without Privacy Act rights? Please explain with references to case law.

Brazil's Comment:

1. In its 11 February 2004 response, the United States repeats its assertion that (many of) US upland cotton farms' planting reports are protected by the US

Privacy Act and cannot be produced to the Panel and Brazil, even under confidentiality arrangements.[1] As explained below, the United States is wrong. But more fundamentally, as the United States has argued before other WTO panels, a WTO Member's domestic laws do not provide a basis for not complying with its obligation to cooperate in a WTO dispute settlement proceeding and to provide, if requested by a panel under DSU Article 13, any information – if necessary using special confidentiality procedures.[2] In sum, as Brazil established in its 28 January 2004 Comments and Requests Regarding US Data, there is no basis for the United States, citing confidentiality concerns, to withhold data from the Panel.[3]

2. The US 11 February 2004 response to this question confuses two fundamental questions. First, are there any Privacy Act rights of US upland cotton farms that would cover information about planted acreage that is gathered by the US government *via* mandatory or voluntary planting reports? And second, do these privacy rights prevail under the US Freedom of Information Act ("FIOA")) over the interest of the public in understanding the operations or activities of the US government. While the United States partly (yet falsely) addresses the first question, it ignores the second question.

3. The starting point for addressing these issues is the relationship of the Privacy Act and the FOIA. The Privacy Act, codified as 5 U.S.C. § 552a[4], protects "records maintained on individuals" by the US government, and prevents disclosure "to any person, or to another agency", with certain exceptions.[5] One of the exceptions listed reads: "unless disclosure would be ... (2) required under section 552 of this title".[6] 5 U.S.C. § 552 is the place where the FOIA is codified. It follows that the prohibition of disclosure of information on individuals provided for by the Privacy Act is subject to the requirements of the FOIA.

4. Returning to the first step, the United States admits that corporations are not covered by the Privacy Act.[7] This is confirmed by the case law cited by the United States (*Dresser Industries v United States*).[8] Yet, neither this case law, nor any other reference provided by United States, supports the United States' distinction between "normal" corporations and "closely held corporations."[9] Even if "closely held corporations" were covered by the Privacy Act – an assertion for which the United States does not offer any proof – they would have the

---

1 US 11 February 2004 Answers to Additional Questions, paras. 1-5.

2 *See* Brazil's 28 January 2004 Comments and Requests Regarding US Data, para. 55.

3 *See* Section 5 of Brazil's 28 January 2004 Comments and Requests Regarding US Data.

4 Exhibit US-107.

5 Exhibit US-107 (5 U.S.C. § 552a(b)).

6 Exhibit US-107 (5 U.S.C. § 552a(b)(2).

7 US 11 February 2004 Answers to Additional Questions, para. 2.

8 Exhibit Bra-425 (Dresser Industries v United States, 596 F.2d 1231 (5th Cir. 1979), p. 7 [**16]).

9 US 11 February 2004 Answers to Additional Questions, para. 8. As the party asserting this fact, the United States bears the burden of proving it. *See e.g.* Appellate Body Report, *Japan – Apples*, WT/DS245/AB/R, para. 157 ("It is important to distinguish, on the one hand, the principle that the complainant must establish a *prima facie* case of inconsistency with a provision of a covered agreement from, on the other hand, the principle that the party that asserts a fact is responsible for providing proof thereof.").

same status as private individuals, which are discussed below in Brazil's comment on the US 11 February 2004 response to Question 259(b).

5. The United States further refers to the District of Columbia Court of Appeals decision in *Center for Auto Safety v National Highway Traffic Safety Administration*[10] for the proposition that information voluntarily submitted to the US government by corporations may not be released if that information would not customarily be released by the corporation to the public.[11] However, the United States misquotes this decision. In fact, the decision states that the information was

> exempt from disclosure because the information was voluntarily submitted *and constituted confidential commercial information that was not customarily disclosed*. The ... information at issue had been disclosed in the past only when necessary, and always with a confidentiality agreement or protective order.[12]

Thus, the restriction only applies to confidential commercial information. While the United States asserts that "[t]his is the case with respect to plantings", the United States provides no evidence for this assertion.[13] The United States' assertion is simply wrong.

6. Planting information is always in the public domain – anyone can look at a field to determine to what crop it is planted. Most US farmland is connected by paved roads and is easily accessible to the public. Further, the Aerial Photography Field Office of USDA's Farm Services Agency exists to provide detailed aerial photographs of cropland.[14] The Office maintains aerial photographs of every square kilometre of cropland in the United States and updates the photographs on a regular basis.[15] Any person can order any aerial photograph by including a legal description of the area of interest in township, range, and section number or latitude and longitude coordinates.[16] The Aerial Photography Field Office indicated that scaled enlargements of photographs are made using specialized rectifying enlargers which maintains an accuracy greater than 99 per cent for most cropland in the United States.[17] The final rectified aerial photograph is, in effect, a photographic map accurately representing ground features. In fact, USDA's local FSA offices use the aerial photographs in verifying planting re-

---

10 Exhibit Bra-426 (Center for Auto Safety v National Highway Traffic Safety Administration, 244 F.3d 144 (DC Cir 2001)).

11 US 11 February 2004 Answers to Additional Questions, para. 3.

12 Exhibit Bra-426 (Center for Auto Safety v National Highway Traffic Safety Administration, 244 F.3d 144 (DC Cir 2001), p. 4 [*147]) (emphasis added).

13 As the party asserting this fact, the United States bears the burden of proving it. *See e.g.* Appellate Body Report, *Japan – Apples*, WT/DS245/AB/R, para. 157 ("It is important to distinguish, on the one hand, the principle that the complainant must establish a *prima facie* case of inconsistency with a provision of a covered agreement from, on the other hand, the principle that the party that asserts a fact is responsible for providing proof thereof.").

14 The Web-page of the Office is found at http://www.apfo.usda.gov.

15 *See* http://www.apfo.usda.gov.

16 *Ibid.*

17 *Ibid.*

ports (FSA 578 forms) required under various US farm programmes.[18] No Privacy Act warnings are shown on the order form or on the web-site where these photographs can be purchased.

7. By its very nature, planting information cannot be confidential commercial information that could always be protected by confidentiality arrangements. In that sense, planting information is very different from technical information about airbags used in cars, which was at issue in *Center for Auto Safety v National Highway Traffic Safety Administration.*[19]

8. This conclusion is supported by another appellate court decision in *CNA Financial Corporation v Donovan*, also cited by the United States.[20] Referring to the Trade Secrets Act, the court defined the scope of the exception in 5 U.S.C. § 552(b)(4) as only prohibiting the disclosure of commercial or financial information if disclosure "is likely to ... cause substantial harm to the competitive position of the person from whom the information was obtained", requiring "both a showing of actual competition and a likelihood of substantial competitive harm".[21] The United States has made no such showing with respect to planting information on upland cotton farms. Furthermore, the court held that "[t]o the extent that any data requested under FOIA is in the public domain, a submitter is unable to make any claim of confidentiality – a *sine qua non* of [5 U.S.C. § 552(b)(4)]".[22] None of the information requested by the Panel poses a significant threat to "cause substantial harm to the competitive position of the person from whom the information was obtained", in particular because, as demonstrated above, the information is, in fact, by its very nature not information that can remain confidential, but is in the public domain, and, indeed, offered for sale by USDA.[23] It follows that (non-closely held) upland cotton farms cannot invoke the Trade Secrets Act to prevent disclosure of planting information.

9. Since the United States characterizes information submitted to the US Government under mandatory terms to be releasable (*i.e.*, MY 2002 planting information),[24] and MY 1999-2001 planting information is not protected under the above rebutted US theory, there is nothing in the Privacy Act that would prevent the United States from producing farm-specific planting information for

---

18 *See* Brazil's 18 November 2003 Further Rebuttal Submission, para. 36.

19 Exhibit Bra-426 (Center for Auto Safety v National Highway Traffic Safety Administration, 244 F.3d 144 (DC Cir 2001), p. 3-4 [*146-*147]).

20 Exhibit Bra-427 (CNA Financial Corporation v Donovan, 830 F.2d 1132 (DC Cir 1987)).

21 Exhibit Bra-427 (CNA Financial Corporation v Donovan, 830 F.2d 1132 (DC Cir 1987), p. 23 [*1152]).

22 Exhibit Bra-427 (CNA Financial Corporation v Donovan, 830 F.2d 1132 (DC Cir 1987), p. 25 [*1154]).

23 The United States neither presents the legal provisions of the Trade Secrets Act nor explains any other pertinent information with respect to that Act. (*See* U.S. 11 February 2004 Answers to Additional Questions, para. 3.) Yet, as the party asserting this fact, the United States bears the burden of proving it. *See e.g.* Appellate Body Report, *Japan – Apples*, WT/DS245/AB/R, para. 157 ("It is important to distinguish, on the one hand, the principle that the complainant must establish a *prima facie* case of inconsistency with a provision of a covered agreement from, on the other hand, the principle that the party that asserts a fact is responsible for providing proof thereof.").

24 US 11 February 2004 Answers to Additional Questions, para. 4.

corporate farms using farm serial numbers or "dummy" numbers. At best, there is some ambiguity in the US law that should be resolved by the United States in favour of releasing the information, as required by its obligations under the DSU.

10. Second, even for the "individuals" covered by the protection of the Privacy Act, there is no legal basis to preclude the release of planting information. As noted above, the protection of the Privacy Act is conditional on the FOIA disclosure rules, which necessitate a weighing process between the privacy interest of the group of individuals and the public interest in the operations of the US Government. Under the applicable case law, this weighing process would be resolved in favour of disclosing the information, as discussed in Brazil's comment on the US 11 February 2004 response to Question 259(b), below.

11. In sum, none of the US Privacy Act arguments holds up to scrutiny. And none is relevant in the first place, since the United States is under an obligation to provide – possibly subject to special confidentiality procedures – information requested by the Panel under DSU Article 13, even if that information is confidential.

(b) The Panel notes that data concerning the four relevant programmes, in particular, payment amounts, identified by specific farms, is freely available on the internet. Please explain why that data can be disclosed but the requested planted acreage data cannot. Do individual recipients have Privacy Act rights with respect to their entrepreneurial activity? Please explain with references to case law.

Brazil's Comment:

12. In its 11 February 2004 response, the United States asserts that "[i]nformation concerning planted acreage does not demonstrate anything regarding the government's operation – it only demonstrates what a producer is doing".[25] Brazil strongly disagrees. Information about plantings of farms receiving contract payments provides important information about the extent to which the US contract payments provide support to specific commodities. US taxpayers, as in the *Washington Post* case, have a strong public interest in knowing how their tax dollars are being spent. In particular, such information would shed light on the question of how much upland cotton is planted on upland cotton base acreage – information that is important for the US public to assess whether the United States is in compliance with its obligations under the Agreement on Agriculture. As the aggregate information provided by the United States suggests, in MY 2002, 96 per cent of US upland cotton plantings took place on upland cotton base.[26]

13. If follows that the US citation to a US Supreme Court decision in paragraph 7 of the US 11 February 2004 response misses the point. Since planting information is a vital component for assessing the "the government's operation", it has to be part of the balance between "the privacy interest of the individual

---

[25] US 11 February 2004 Answers to Additional Questions, para. 8.

[26] *See* Brazil's 18 February Comments on US Comments, Annex A, para. 11.

with the 'core purpose' of FOIA".[27] And the US district court decision in *Washington Post v. United States Department of Agriculture* confirms that in cases, where "the information is so generic that the impact on privacy interests are so small"[28], the information has to be disclosed. This interpretation is, in fact, confirmed, rather then contradicted, by the US Supreme Court Decision in *United States Department of Justice v Reporters Committee For Freedom of the Press* ("Reporters Committee").[29]

14. The *Reporters Committee* decision concerns an individual person's FBI "rap sheet" that was requested under the FOIA. The Supreme Court rejected this request as outside the purpose of the FOIA, since it did not "contribut[e] significantly to the understanding *of the operation or activities of the government*" (emphasis in original).[30] By contrast, planting information of farms clearly contributes to the understanding of the operation of the US contract payments programmes. Providing this information would, thus, not only enhance the Panel's ability to make an objective assessment of the matter before it, but would also conform to "the basic purpose of the [FOIA,] to open agency action to the light of public scrutiny".[31]

15. The US Supreme Court decision in *Reporters Committee* states that "Congress exempted nine categories of documents from the FOIA's broad disclosure requirements".[32] These exemptions are codified at 5 U.S.C. § 552(b).[33] In this case, disclosure of the information is neither prevented by other laws (5 U.S.C. § 552(b)(3)), *i.e.,* the Trade Secrets Act (because the information does not constitute trade secrets as defined by US courts[34]), or the Privacy Act (which applies subject to the FOIA Act), nor by the separate exemption (5 U.S.C. § 552(b)(4) for trade secrets and commercial or financial information). Once again, since planting information could be collected from the public domain – or rather observed by any member of the public or, indeed, purchased from USDA – it cannot be deemed confidential. In fact, as the appeals court in *CNA Financial Corporation v Donovan* held, "[t]o the extent that any data requested under FOIA is in the public domain, a submitter is unable to make any claim of confidentiality – a *sine qua non* of [5 U.S.C. § 552(b)(4)]".[35]

---

27 US 11 February 2004 Answers to Additional Questions, para. 7.

28 Exhibit Bra-418 (Washington Post v United States Department of Agriculture, 943 Supp. 31 (D.D.C.) 1996, p. 3). *See* Brazil's 28 January Comments and Requests Regarding U.S. Data, paras. 31-34.

29 Exhibit Bra-428 (United States Department of Justice at al. v Reporters Committee for the Freedom of the Press et al., 489 US 749 (1989)).

30 Exhibit Bra-428 (United States Department of Justice at al. v Reporters Committee for the Freedom of the Press et al., 489 US 749 (1989), p. 15 [*775]).

31 Exhibit Bra-428 (United States Department of Justice at al. v Reporters Committee for the Freedom of the Press et al., 489 US 749 (1989), p. 15 [*774]).

32 Exhibit Bra-428 (United States Department of Justice at al. v Reporters Committee for the Freedom of the Press et al., 489 US 749 (1989), p. 6 [*755]).

33 Exhibit US-103.

34 *See* above.

35 Exhibit Bra-427 (CNA Financial Corporation v Donovan, 830 F.2d 1132, p. 25 [*1154]).

16. Moreover, 5 U.S.C. § 552(b)(7)(C) exempts information "compiled for law enforcement purposes, but only to the extent that the production of such ... information would ... (C) ... constitute an unwarranted invasion of personal privacy."[36] While acreage reports are partly mandatory to enforce the requirements of various US domestic support programmes[37], disclosure of planting information does not constitute an unwarranted invasion of personal privacy. In fact, the information could be gathered by simply checking the fields of a farm or by purchasing aerial photographs from the Aerial Photography Field Office of USDA's Farm Services Agency, as discussed above.[38] It is not difficult to determine the type of crop or the amount of acreage being planted to that crop from using high resolution colour aerial photographs. If a farmer growing crops can purchase from USDA high resolution and detailed aerial photographs of his next-door neighbour's farm to calculate that information, how can it be that this same farmer can claim a Privacy Act violation for his own planted acreage data? This evidence provides the common sense answer to the question whether acreage reports are, in fact, subject to the Privacy Act.

17. Thus, from the perspective of its "public domain" character, acreage information is even less confidential than payment information, which the district court in *Washington Post* decided must be released under FOIA.[39] Since acreage information sheds light on the performance of USDA and its adherence to the WTO obligations of the United States, any weighing of the limited privacy interests in planting information and the interest of the public in evaluating the work of USDA must be resolved in favour of the latter.

18. Finally, with respect to the "split of authority in US courts as to whether individuals have Privacy Rights with respect to their entrepreneurial activities"[40], it is clear that even if a privacy interest protected under the Privacy Act should exist with respect to the entrepreneurial activity in question, the FOIA takes precedence over that interest, as explained in Brazil's comment to the US 11 February 2004 response to Question 259(a), and in the *Washington Post* and *Reporters Committee* precedent. Concerning planted acreage information at issue between the parties, it is clear that the public interest in USDA's performance, including USDA adherence to the US obligations under the WTO Agreement, takes precedence over the privacy interests of US farmers in information that is potentially always in the public domain. Even assuming, *arguendo*, that there were some ambiguity in the meaning of the US domestic law applicable to the question of confidentiality and the release of planted acreage information, the United States should resolve the ambiguity in favour of releasing the information, as required by its obligations under the DSU.

---

36 Exhibit US-103.

37 *See* Brazil's 18 November 2003 Further Rebuttal Submission, Section 2.2.

38 *See* also http://www.apfo.usda.gov.

39 *See* Brazil's 28 January 2004 Comments and Requests Regarding US Data, paras. 31-33.

40 US 11 February 2004 Answers to Additional Questions, para. 9. The cases cited by the United States are reproduced as Exhibits Bra-429 (Metadure Croporation v United States, 490 F. Supp. 1368 (S.D.N.Y. 1990)) and Bra-430 (Campaign for Family Farms v Glickman, 200 F.3d 1180 (8th Cir. 2000)).

(c) Please provide any further available evidence of the USDA's long-standing policy that planted acreage information will not be released.

Brazil's Comment:

19. Brazil notes that it is not USDA's place to provide an authoritative interpretation of US law, including the Freedom of Information Act. Any "internal policy memorandum" cannot change the meaning of US law. Interpreting US laws is left to the US courts, which have issued rulings that would compel release of the planting, payment and contract payment base information.

20. Further, both Exhibits US-134 and US-144 refer to individual acreage information *in connection with names that cannot be released.* Brazil recalls that the Panel has requested farm-specific information with farm serial numbers (rather than names)[41], or, alternatively, farm-specific information using "dummy" farm numbers.[42] And Exhibit US-144 clarifies that "[a]creage, production data, and other producer-related information, without any personal identifier attached may be released". This language would certainly cover farm-specific information using "dummy" farm numbers.

21. Finally, whether there is a long-standing practice by USDA of not releasing farm-specific acreage data to the public is irrelevant to a WTO dispute. First, under DSU Article 13, the United States is required to provide even confidential information.[43] Second, any such information is not released to the public, and can – under WTO procedures – be protected as confidential information and be returned to the United States once this panel proceeding ends. Confidentiality procedures either under DSU Articles 13.1 and 18.1 or special confidentiality procedures under the Panel's working procedures can address any US concern that Brazil could match data provided by the United States with data publicly available to unveil the names of specific farmers and their plantings. In addition, any such concern would not exist had the United States provided a single file containing both base acreage and yields as well as planting information. Under these circumstances, no identification number, whether farm serial number or "dummy" number, would be necessary.

260. On 27 August 2003, in its response to Question No. 67 *bis*, the United States indicated that "it does not maintain information on the amount of expenditures made under the cited programmes to US upland cotton producers". On 12 January 2004, the Panel requested the United States to provide information "to permit an assessment of the total expenditures of PFC, MLA, CCP and direct payments by the US Federal Government to upland cotton producers in the relevant marketing years". On 20 January 2004, the United States informed the Panel that "the data already provided by the United States to Brazil and the Panel would permit an assessment of total expenditures of decoupled payments to farms planting upland cotton." Is

41 8 December 2003 Communication from the Panel.

42 12 January 2004 Communication from the Panel.

43 *See* Section 5 of Brazil's 28 January 2004 Comments and Requests Regarding US Data.

the latest statement responsive to the Panel's request? If so, how can it be reconciled with the first statement?

Brazil's Comment:

22. The US 11 February 2004 response to the Panel's Question continues a pattern of misrepresentation that has tainted the US statements on this issue during this entire dispute.[44] In its response, the United States draws the distinction between farms that plant upland cotton, for which the United States admits it has information, and farms that produce upland cotton, *i.e.,* farms that harvest the planted upland cotton, for which the United States asserts it does not have information.[45] Allegedly, this distinction between "planters" and "producers" of upland cotton explains the discrepancy between the two US statements referred to in the Panel's question. It does not.

23. In fact, the United States in its 11 February 2004 response engages in a play with words that hides its non-cooperation in this panel proceeding. Contract payments made to "planters" of upland cotton support the production of upland cotton and are, thus, "support to" upland cotton. This is true even if the planted upland cotton is in the end abandoned and not harvested. Indeed, the 2002 FSRI Act defines a "producer" as someone who "*shares in the risk of producing a crop* and is entitled to share in the crop available for marketing from the farm *or would have shared had the crop been produced*".[46] Thus, a person remains a "producer" even if the chances were against him or her in a given year and a planted crop failed.

24. In sum, the terms "producer" and "planter" of a crop are synonyms for purposes of defining "support to" a specific commodity. Any contract payments paid to producers/planters of upland cotton must be considered in allocating the "support to" upland cotton from contract payments – whether the crop planted on that farm was harvested or not.

25. It follows that the two US statements referred to in the Panel's question are *irreconcilable*.[47] Unfortunately, Brazil has to note that the United States continues its approach of trying to mislead the Panel and Brazil on the question of the amount of contract payments that constitute support to upland cotton. In its 11 February 2004 Comments on Brazil's 28 January 2004 Data Comments, the United States engages in a self-serving revisionist history.[48] What is left after the US rhetoric is one clear fact: that the United States has engaged in a highly successful effort over sixteen months to deny Brazil and the Panel information giving a definitive amount of the four contract payments paid to and received by producers of upland cotton during MY 1999-2002. Brazil and the Panel are still waiting for data that would allow a precise calculation of this support, either in a

---

[44] US 11 February 2004 Answers to Additional Questions, para. 13.

[45] US 11 February 2004 Answers to Additional Questions, para. 13. *See* also US 11 February 2004 Comments para. 67 and US 28 January 2004 Comments, para. 16 making the same argument.

[46] Exhibit Bra-29 (Section 1000(12) of the 2002 FSRI Act)(emphasis added).

[47] *See* also Brazil's 28 January 2004 Comments on Question 195, para. 6-9.

[48] US 11 February 2004 Comments, paras. 62-75.

farm-specific manner, as requested by the Panel on 8 December 2003 and 12 January 2004, or in the aggregate manner as requested by the Panel on 3 February 2004. Brazil notes that the Panel has granted the United States an extension until 3 March 2004 to provide this information.[49]

26. Brazil believes the Panel is well aware of the US refusal to provide payment information in the numerous forms in which that information has been requested.[50] In an effort to assist the Panel with making factual findings in its report regarding this issue, Brazil sets forth a chronology of the facts relating to these various requests. These facts need little, if any, commentary or argument from Brazil, as they speak for themselves:

- **22 November 2002**: Brazil files its First Set of Questions and Request for Production of Documents to the United States.[51] Question 3.6 stated: "*What was the annual amount of ... (ii) production flexibility contract payments and (iii) direct payments (as relevant given the particular time period) made by the US Government in connection with upland cotton for each of the marketing years 1992 through 2002.*" Question 11.1 stated: "*Please state the total amount of market loss assistance payments made to the US upland cotton industry in marketing years 1998 through 2001.*"[52]
- **3 December 2002:** During the consultations, the United States responded orally to Question 3.6 by referring Brazil to the "Fact Sheet: Upland Cotton" (Exhibit Bra-4) and to *www.fsa.usda.gov/dam/bud/bud1.htm*. In response to Question 11.1, the United States similarly referred Brazil to *www.fsa.usda.gov/dam/bud/bud1.htm*. The data in these documents represented the total amount of payment data provided to holders of upland cotton base but did not provide any information about contract payments made to the US "upland cotton industry", which Brazil defined in its consultation and panel requests as "US producers, users and/or exporters of upland cotton". Brazil used the data included in Exhibit Bra-4 and the above-referenced website as the basis for its tabulation of the contract payment amount included in Table 1 of its 24 June 2003 First Submission.
- **1 April 2003:** Brazil filed a questionnaire with the United States in the Annex V procedures.[53] Question 11.1 states: "*Please state the total amount of Market Loss Assistance payments made to the US upland cotton industry in marketing years 1998 through 2002.*" Question 13.1 states: "*Please state the total amount of Counter-Cyclical Payments made by the United States to US upland cotton*

[49] 16 February 2004 Communication from the Panel.

[50] The US 11 February 2004 Comments, para. 69 incorrectly assert that "this information" refers to contract acreage

[51] Exhibit Bra-101 (Questions for Purposes of the Consultations).

[52] Brazil defined "upland cotton industry" as "producers, users and/or exporters of upland cotton".

[53] Exhibit Bra-49 (Questions for Purposes of the Annex V Procedure).

farmers in marketing year 2002." The United States provided no information in response to these questions.

- **24 June 2003:** Brazil's 24 June 2003 First Submission states, at paragraph 214, that "*[i]n the absence of the requested information from the United States on actual DP and CCP payments related to the production of upland cotton* or to farms holding upland cotton base, Brazil has used conservative methodologies to estimate the amount of 2002 DP and CCP payments received by upland cotton producers". In addition, Brazil stated that it "reiterates its requests to the United States to provide it and the Panel with actual upland cotton base acreage for the DP and CCP programmes and will revise its estimates and levels of support for MY 2002 based on updated data".[54]
- **22 July 2003:** Brazil states in its 22 July 2003 Oral Statement at the first meeting with the Panel that "Brazil notes that it has presented the best available information that it has access to and that is not exclusively within the control of the United States."[55] Brazil further stated that "the United States never provided any answers to Brazil's Annex V questions [and] [a]ccordingly, Brazil requests the Panel to rule on questions of fact based on the best information available as submitted by Brazil".[56]
- **11 August 2003**: Brazil provides an estimate of the total budgetary outlays of contract payment using its 14/16th methodology in its 11 August 2003 response to Question 60, as explained in paragraph 97 and notes 2-5 to the table accompanying paragraph 97. Brazil further states in response to Question 83 that "The list of Annex V questions provided to the United States by Brazil is included in Exhibit Bra-49. … [G]iven the United States' failure to cooperate in the Annex V information gathering process, Brazil has and will present its case regarding peace clause issues and serious prejudice claims based on evidence available to it. If there are gaps in the evidence provided to the Panel by Brazil in support of its *prima facie* case, and those gaps are due to the United States' failure to cooperate with and participate in the Annex V process, Annex V, paragraph 6 provides that 'the panel may complete the record as necessary relying on the best information otherwise available.'"[57]
- **25 August 2003**: The Panel requests the United States in Question *67bis* to provide "the annual amount granted by the US Government in each of the 1999, 2000, 2001, and 2002 marketing years (as applicable) to US upland cotton producers ... in total expendi-

54 Brazil's 24 June 2003 First Submission, note 415.
55 Brazil's 22 July 2003 Oral Statement, para. 4.
56 *Ibid.*
57 Brazil's 11 August 2003 Answers to Questions, para. 190.

tures, under each of the following programmes: production flexibility contract payments, market loss assistance payments, direct payments and counter-cyclical payments."[58]

- **27 August 2003**: The United States provides a response to Question 67*bis* which states, *inter alia,* that the United States "does not maintain and cannot calculate this information"[59] and that it "does not maintain information on the amount of expenditures made under the cited programmes to US upland cotton producers".[60] The United States stated in paragraph 21 of its 27 August 2003 response that "Thus, the United States did not track total expenditures with respect to base acres of [1996 FAIR Act covered commodities] under the expired production flexibility contract payments and market loss assistance payments and does not track total expenditure with respect to base acres of [contract commodities] under the direct payments and counter-cyclical payments." Further, the United States stated in paragraph 28 of its 27 August 2003 response that "we are unable to provide to the Panel the total outlays under the cited programmes with respect to upland cotton base acreage."
- **7 October 2003**: The United States alleges that "Brazil has presented no evidence that the recipients of these decoupled payments on upland cotton base acres are, in fact, upland cotton producers".[61] And the United States alleges that Brazil's methodology is "merely a guess because Brazil has failed to demonstrate that the acres currently being used for upland cotton production are, in fact, upland cotton base acres. That is, Brazil has presented no evidence that the recipients of these decoupled payments on upland cotton base acres are, in fact, upland cotton producers".[62] The United States further alleges that Brazil has not substantiated the amount of contract payments to US upland cotton producers ("[I]t is for Brazil to establish who are the recipients of the subsidies and that the subsidies are properly attributed to upland cotton."[63] "Nor has [Brazil] demonstrated how much of the subsidy ... should be allocated to other products produced by the recipient, such as corn or soybeans."[64]).
- **8 October 2003:** The Panel orally asks the United States whether it collects or maintains information concerning the amount of contract payments received by upland cotton producers. The United

58 25 August 2003 Communication from the Panel.
59 US 27 August 2003 Comments and Answers to Additional Question, para. 20.
60 US 27 August 2003 Comments and Answers to Additional Question, para. 20.
61 US 7 October 2003 Oral Statement, para. 14.
62 US 7 October 2003 Oral Statement, para. 6.
63 US 7 October 2003 Oral Statement, para. 10.
64 US 7 October 2003 Oral Statement, para. 19.

States answered orally that it neither collected nor retained this information.

- **9 October 2003:** Brazil stated in its closing statement that it had "requested this information [*i.e.,* information concerning the amount of contract payments to upland cotton producers] more than a year ago in the consultation phase of this dispute but never received any information".[65] The United States, following its closing statement, informed the Panel and Brazil that the 2002 FSRI Act contained a reporting requirement for the United States to collect information on planted acreage, as a condition for recipients receiving direct payments and CCP payments.
- **13 October 2003:** The Panel asks the United States in Question 125(9) how to calculate upland cotton contract payments made to cotton producers and how to account for non-upland cotton contract payments made to producers of upland cotton.[66]
- **27 October 2003:** The United States responds to Question 125(9) by stating that it is for Brazil to prove the amount of contract payments (which the United States does not limit to upland cotton contract payments) that need to be allocated to upland cotton.[67] While referring to Annex IV, the United States declines to provide any data.[68]
- **18 November 2003:** Brazil requested the Panel to request the United States to produce information that would permit the calculation of a very precise amount of contract payment support to current producers of upland cotton.[69] Brazil further set forth evidence that USDA collects and maintains in a centralized database base acreage data and planted acreage data for all farms for MY 2002 and for almost all farms for the period MY 1999-2001.[70]
- **21 November 2003:** USDA's Kansas City FOIA office delivered to a private US citizen a completed analysis of farm-specific contract acreage data and planted acreage data for MY 1996-2002 regarding rice. The FOIA documentation indicates that the request was received on 30 October 2003, and that work was completed on 14 November 2003. The rice data showed that between 99.52 and 99.90 per cent of the farms producing rice in MY 1999-2002 completed planted acreage reports. The rice data provided by USDA

---

65 Brazil's 9 October 2003 Closing Statement, para. 2.

66 13 October 2003 Communication from the Panel.

67 US 27 October 2003 Answers to Questions, para. 23.

68 US 27 October 2003 Answers to Questions, para. 24.

69 Brazil's 18 November 2003 Further Rebuttal Submission, para. 48.

70 Brazil's 18 November 2003 Further Rebuttal Submission, paras. 33-48.

permitted the calculation of the exact amount of rice contract acreage that was planted to rice during MY 1996-2002.[71]

- **2 December 2003:** Brazil requests the United States to provide farm-specific information as set out in Exhibit Bra-369.
- **3 December 2003:** Brazil presented the results of the rice FOIA request to the Panel and provided a copy of the rice data to the Panel and the United States.[72]
- **8 December 2003:** The Panel requests the United States to provide the farm-specific information set out in Exhibit Bra-369. In Question 195, the Panel asked whether "the United States wish to revise its response to the Panel's Question No. 67*bis,* in particular, its statement that "the United States ... does not maintain information on the amount of expenditures made under the cited programmes to US upland cotton producers?"[73]
- **18 December 2003:** The United States produced scrambled farm-specific information for MY 1999-2001, contrary to Brazil's and the Panel's requested set out in Exhibit Bra-369.
- **19 December 2003:** The United States produced scrambled farm-specific information for MY 2002, contrary to Brazil's and the Panel's requested set out in Exhibit Bra-369.
- **22 December 2003:** The United States responds to Question 195 but does not "state the annual amount granted by the US government in each of the 1999, 2000, 2001 and 2002 marketing years to upland cotton producers ... in total expenditures under the [four contract payment programmes]", as requested by the Panel on 25 August 2003 in Question 67*bis*. The United States reasoned that it "does not collect production data based on actual harvesting figures reported by farmers".[74] The United States response did not offer any information regarding the amount of contract payments received by upland cotton farmers who planted upland cotton. Brazil indicated in its Answer to Question 196 that the scrambled information provided by the United States prevented it from calculating the amount of payments received by US upland cotton producers planting upland cotton on contract base acreage.[75]

---

71 Exhibit Bra-368 (Second Statement of Christopher Campbell – Environmental Working Group, 1 December 2003) and Exhibit Bra-369 as amended on 3 December 2003 (Brazil's Request to the United States for Farm – Specific Planting and Base Acreage Data, 3 December 2003).

72 *See* Exhibit Bra-368 (Second Statement of Christopher Campbell – Environmental Working Group, 1 December 2003) and Exhibit Bra-369 as amended on 3 December 2003 (Brazil's Request to the United States for Farm – Specific Planting and Base Acreage Data, 3 December 2003).

73 8 December 2003 Communication from the Panel.

74 US 22 December 2003 Answers to Questions, para. 6.

75 Brazil's 22 December 2003 Answer to Question 196.

- **12 January 2004:** The Panel requested farm-specific information from the United States indicating that "it considers it both necessary and appropriate to seek this information in a suitable format in order to undertake its mandate to assist the DSB in discharging its responsibilities under the DSU and the covered agreements".[76] The Panel further stated that "disclosure is sought to permit an assessment of the total expenditures of PFC, MLA, CCP, and direct payments by the US Federal Government to upland cotton producers in the relevant marketing years". The Panel requested the United States to produce the information by 20 January 2004.
- **20 January 2004:** The United States filed a letter with the Panel stating it would not produce non-scrambled farm-specific data requested by the Panel on 12 January 2004.[77] The United States did not provide total expenditure information for the four contract payments originally requested in Question 67*bis* and did not otherwise provide information that would "permit an assessment of the total expenditures" that constitute "support to" upland cotton under the four contract payments, as requested by the Panel on 12 January 2004. Brazil files a detailed description of its methodology allocating upland cotton and non-upland cotton contract payments as support to upland cotton.[78]
- **28 January 2004:** Brazil filed a request that the Panel draw adverse inferences from the United States refusal during the period November 2002 through January 2004 to produce information relating to the amount of contract payments received by upland cotton producers who planted upland cotton.[79] The United States provided revised scrambled farm-specific data.[80]
- **3 February 2004:** The Panel requested aggregated farm-specific information from the United States in a format similar to the rice FOIA request set out Exhibit Bra-369, and further requested that the United States produce planted information on crops on cropland covered by the acreage reports. The Panel gave the United States until 11 February 2004 to provide the requested data.[81] This aggregate data would allow a precise calculation of the amount of support to upland cotton from the US contract payments, whereas the US summary data produced on 18/19 December 2003 and the revised US summary data produced on 28 January 2004 does

[76] 12 January 2004 Communication from the Panel.
[77] US 20 January 2004 Letter to the Panel.
[78] Brazil's 20 January 2004 Answers to Additional Questions, paras. 43-55.
[79] Brazil's 28 January 2004 Comments and Requests Regarding US Data, Section 6.
[80] US 28 January 2004 Letter to the Panel.
[81] 3 February 2004 Communication from the Panel.

not.[82] The Panel also asked the United States (Question 260) how it reconciled its 27 August 2003 response (that it did not maintain data on contract payments to upland cotton producers) with its 20 January 2004 Letter to the Panel stating that it had provided such information.[83]

- **11 February 2004:** The United States indicated it was not in a position to respond to the Panel's 3 February 2004 request and stated that it needed an additional four weeks to provide the aggregated data.[84]
- **13 February 2004:** Brazil requested the Panel to deny the United States any additional time to respond to the Panel's 3 February 2004 request, noting that this request represented the fifth time that the Panel had requested the United States to provide total expenditure information regarding the amount of contract payments made to upland cotton producers.[85]
- **16 February 2004:** The Panel extended the deadline for the United States to provide the data requested on 3 February 2004 and clarified its request.[86]
- **3 March 2004:** The deadline for the United States to produce the data requested by the Panel on 3 February 2004.[87]

27. Brazil hopes that the United States will finally live up to its obligation under the DSU and provide data that would permit the calculation of the support to upland cotton from the US contract payments. In one form or another, these figures have been at issue in all stages of this dispute – from the first round of consultations until the latest submissions to the Panel 16 months later. During all this time, it has been clear to the United States that what Brazil and the Panel sought was information that would enable a determination of the amount of contract payments that actually benefit upland cotton production. To be clear, that means support that benefits farms that plant upland cotton and support that can be allocated to this upland cotton planting/production.

28. In case the United States should fail to produce the information by 3 March 2004, Brazil maintains its 28 January 2004 request to the Panel to draw adverse inferences from this failure of cooperation. Drawing adverse inferences is clearly warranted given the history of his dispute settlement proceeding.

---

[82] Brazil's 13 February 2004 Letter to the Panel. *See* also Brazil's 18 February 2004 Comments on US 11 February 2004 Comments on Brazil's 28 January 2004 Comments and Requests Regarding U.S. Data.

[83] 3 February 2004 Communication from the Panel.

[84] Cover Letter to US 11 February 2004 Answers to Additional Questions.

[85] Brazil's 13 February 2004 Letter to the Panel.

[86] 16 February 2004 Communication from the Panel.

[87] *Ibid.*

261. Please confirm that each record in the actual planting database relates to a specific farm (Filenames: rPFCplac and rDCPplac in Exhibits US-111 and US-112). For example, in the data from rDCPplac:

First line:
Field9;Field16;Field22;Field28;Field34;Field40;Field46;Field52;Field58;Field64;Field70;Field76;Field82;Field88;Field94;Field100

Second line:
237.10;23059.80;5566.20;0.00;0.00;0.00;0.00;0.00;0.00;0.00;0.00;0.00;0.00;0.00;0.00;0.00

Does the second line represent data on plantings by the same farm?

262. The Panel has noted the two CD-ROMs delivered by the US in the evening of 23 December 2003. They are marked "US-111" and "US-112" respectively, but the contents actually do not correspond to the indication. The Panel also takes note of the US letter dated 28 January 2004 and the CD-ROM delivered together with it. For the record, please clarify the correct CD-ROMs and provide corresponding descriptions of their contents with exhibit numbers.

263. The Panel has noted that the United States' response to Question No. 214 refers to Exhibits US-117 and US-118. Are these the correct documents to which the United States intended to refer in that response? If not, please provide a copy of regulations regarding the marketing loan programme and loan deficiency payments published at 58 Federal Register 15755, dated 24 March 1993.

264. The Panel asks the United States to clarify certain aspects of Exhibit US-128:

(a) Is the Panel correct in understanding that - as Brazil asserts in footnotes 290 and 291 of Brazil's 28 January 2004 comments on US responses to questions - Exhibit US-128, all data are presented on a cohort-specific basis? If so, please also present the information originally requested by the Panel in another chart containing *programme* (as opposed to cohort-specific) activity by fiscal year.

Brazil's Comment:

29. In paragraph 21 of its 11 February 2004 response, the United States suggests that Brazil's cash-basis accounting methodology for making an assessment under item (j), because it uses data included in the US budget, is "based on estimates and re-estimates" under the Federal Credit Reform Act ("FCRA"). This response is untruthful in the extreme.

30. None – absolutely none – of the data used for Brazil's cash-basis accounting methodology for making an assessment under item (j) is "based on estimates and re-estimates" generated for the purposes of the FCRA. As is evident from the chart included in paragraph 165 of Brazil's 11 August 2003 Answers (reproduced

in paragraph 129 of its 28 January 2004 comments), Brazil's cash-basis accounting methodology relies on data from the "actual", prior year column of the US budget. Moreover, the data input into Brazil's cash-basis accounting methodology is drawn from the "financing account" for the CCC programmes.[88] The US budget makes the following statement about the financing account:

> As required by the Federal Credit Reform Act of 1990, this *non-budgetary* account records all *cash flows* to and from the Government resulting from loan guarantees committed in 1992 and beyond. The amounts in this account are a means of financing and are *not* included in the *budget* totals.[89]

31. Whether presented on a cohort-specific (Exhibit US-128) or a fiscal year (Exhibit US-147) basis, Brazil notes that none – absolutely none – of the data provided by the United States is verifiable. The United States has provided *no* documentation (or even citations to documentation that could be independently collected and reviewed by the Panel) to back up its data. The Panel asked the United States for this supporting documentation in July 2003, in Question 78 to the United States. The United States has never provided the supporting documentation requested by the Panel. In contrast, Brazil has provided US government documents to back up each and every figure input into its cash-basis accounting methodology for making an assessment under item (j).[90]

(b) Does the US agree with the statement in paragraph 135 of Brazil's 28 January 2004 comments on US responses to questions that the difference between the \$1,148 billion in the chart at para. 165 of Brazil's 11 August answers to questions and the \$666 million amount in Exhibit US-128 (\$1.75 billion) closely corresponds to the total "Claims rescheduled" figure reported by the US in Exhibit US-128 (column F)?

Brazil's Comment:

32. The United States has failed to answer the Panel's question, stating that it will instead do so on a timeline of its own choosing.[91] The United States did not request additional time from the Panel, either in its 11 February 2004 response or in the cover letter to that response, but simply asserted in paragraph 23 of its response that it will take whatever additional time it needs.[92] In its letter to the

---

[88] The only exception is administrative expenses, which Brazil takes from the "programme account" included in the U.S. Budget. *See, e.g.,* Exhibit Bra-127 (2004 US Budget, p. 107 (line 00.09)). The US budget notes, however, that "administrative expenses are estimated on a cash basis", rather than a present value basis. *See, e.g.,* Exhibit Bra-127 (2004 US Budget, p. 108). *See also* Brazil's 22 July 2003 Oral Statement, para. 130 (and citations included at footnote 168). In any event, the United States and Brazil use virtually identical figures for the administrative costs of the CCC programs. *See* Exhibit Bra-431 (Columns 5(a) and 5(b)).

[89] *See, e.g.,* Exhibit Bra-127 (2004 U.S. Budget, p. 109 (emphasis added)).

[90] *See* exhibits cited in Brazil's 11 August 2003 Answers, para. 165 and Brazil's 28 January 2004 Comments, para. 129.

[91] US 11 February 2004 Answers, para. 23.

[92] In a letter to the Panel dated 16 February 2004, the United States similarly declares that it "will provide any other data in response to Question 264(b) within the time indicated (and sooner if the data can be collected and examined in less time)."

Panel dated 13 February 2004, Brazil noted that the United States had more than adequate time (8 days) to undertake the review necessary to answer the Panel's question. After receiving the fiscal-year cash-basis accounting data included in Exhibit US-147, it took Brazil one hour to prepare a spreadsheet – included as Exhibit Bra-431 – that zeroes in on and identifies the reason that Brazil's cash-basis accounting methodology concludes that the operating costs and losses for the CCC export credit guarantee programmes have exceeded income over the period 1993-2002 by $1.083 billion, while the United States' cash-basis accounting methodology concludes that income for the CCC export credit guarantee programmes has exceeded operating costs and losses over the period 1993-2002 by $536 million.

33. In its 16 February 2004 ruling, the Panel did not respond to Brazil's request that it deny the United States' efforts to decide at what pace it wishes to offer responses to the Panel's questions. Brazil requests that if the United States, whenever it deems it convenient, eventually offers a response to Question 264(b), the Panel reject that response as not timely filed. If the Panel accepts the United States' response, Brazil reserves the right to comment.

34. In any event, the spreadsheet included as Exhibit Bra-431 confirms the assertion Brazil made in paragraph 135 of its 28 January 2004 Comments, which is that the difference between the results arrived at using the Brazilian versus the US cash-basis methodology (a difference of $1.6 billion) is largely due to the United States' treatment of rescheduled claims (listed by the United States as $1.58 billion). As confirmed by the United States in paragraph 24 of its 11 February 2004 response to Question 264(c), the United States' methodology treats defaulted guarantees that have been rescheduled as 100 per cent recovered at the moment the terms of the rescheduling are agreed.

35. Brazil, in contrast, treats rescheduled claims as receivables. Under Brazil's methodology, receivables resulting from rescheduling are treated just like any other receivable – receivables resulting from rescheduling are only treated as recovered incrementally, to the extent, in a given year, some increment of the rescheduled debt is actually collected (in column 2(a) of Exhibit Bra-431). This fundamental difference in approach is the reason that the "claims outstanding" recorded by the United States (in column 4(b) of Exhibit Bra-431) and Brazil (in column 4(a) of Exhibit Bra-431) differ by $1.6 billion – the only significant difference revealed in the comparison included in Exhibit Bra-431.

36. As Brazil has previously demonstrated, it is not actuarially appropriate to treat defaulted guarantees that have been rescheduled as 100 per cent recovered at the moment the terms of the rescheduling are agreed.[93] Brazil and the United States agree that a default that has been rescheduled is properly treated as a re-

[93] *See* Brazil's 28 January 2004 Comments, paras. 135-137; Brazil's 27 August 2003 Comments, para. 64; Brazil's 22 August 2003 Comments, para. 99; Brazil's 11 August 2003 Answers, para. 162; Brazil's 22 July 2003 Oral Statement, para. 122.

ceivable[94], but as the CCC itself has acknowledged in its financial statements, not all receivables are considered *collectible*, let alone actually *collected.*[95]

37. The United States' methodology itself recognizes that defaulted guarantees that have been rescheduled are only collected over time (if at all). While the United States treats the *principal* amounts of rescheduled debt as an immediate, 100 per cent recovery that is passed through as a dollar-on-dollar reduction of the amount of claims outstanding in the year the terms of the rescheduling are agreed, it also tracks massive (and ever increasing) amounts of *interest* collected on reschedulings (column M in Exhibit US-147). Interest is collected on the rescheduled debt because significant amounts of principal remain outstanding on that rescheduled debt. It is not legitimate, therefore, for the United States to treat that rescheduled debt as recovered at the moment it is rescheduled, since it is not actually recovered at that moment.

38. In fact, no evidence suggests that CCC will collect the rescheduled principal that remains outstanding. In column F of Exhibit US-147, the United States states that $1.64 billion of defaulted CCC guarantees have been rescheduled over the period 1992-2003. Yet as of 30 November 2003, the United States reports in Exhibit US-153 that the principal outstanding on these reschedulings amounts to $1.58 billion. *This means that over the period 1992-2003, the CCC has only collected $60 million, or 3.6 per cent, of the $1.64 billion in defaulted CCC guarantees that have been rescheduled. Over 96 per cent of defaulted CCC guarantees that have been rescheduled over the period 1992-2003 remain outstanding.*

39. This demonstrates precisely why it is not legitimate for the United States to treat rescheduled debt as recovered at the moment it is rescheduled. The record does *not* suggest that the CCC will collect this rescheduled debt – in fact, the record shows that the CCC hardly collects any of the principal on its rescheduled debt. Rescheduled debt is nothing more than a receivable, and should be treated as recovered only incrementally, as portions of that debt are, in fact, recovered. This is how Brazil has treated rescheduled debt in its own cash-basis accounting methodology for making an assessment under item (j) (column 2(a) of Exhibit Bra-431).

40. Even if rescheduled debt could, as an actuarial matter, be considered 100 per cent recovered at the very moment the terms of the rescheduling are concluded but before the rescheduled debt is in actual fact collected, the United States appears to have triple-counted portions of the CCC reschedulings. The Panel will recall that under the United States' cash-basis accounting methodology for making an assessment under item (j), the entire amount of the approximately

---

94 *See* US 11 August 2003 Answers, para. 155.

95 Exhibit Bra-158 (US Department of Agriculture, Office of Inspector General, Financial and IT Operations, Audit Report, *Commodity Credit Corporation's Financial Statements for Fiscal Year 2002*, Audit Report No. 06401-15-FM (December 2002), Notes to the Financial Statements, p. 14); Exhibit US-129 (US Department of Agriculture, Office of Inspector General, Financial and IT Operations, Audit Report, *Commodity Credit Corporation's Financial Statements for Fiscal Years 2003 and 2002*, Audit Report No. 06401-16-FM (November 2003), Notes to the Financial Statements, p. 15).

$1.6 billion in rescheduled debt (in column 3(b) of Exhibit Bra-431) is subtracted from the amount of claims outstanding (in column 4(b) of Exhibit Bra-431) in the year the terms of the rescheduling are agreed. Over $636 million of the approximately $1.6 billion in reschedulings listed in Exhibit US-153 and column 3(b) of Exhibit Bra-431, however, appears to have been "[p]reviously [r]escheduled" (*see* the last two entries in Exhibit US-153, concerning CCC guarantees to Russia). It already is not legitimate for the United States to treat rescheduled debt as recovered at the moment it is rescheduled, since the record shows that the CCC has only collected 3.6 per cent of that rescheduled debt. But to allow the United States to reduce claims outstanding multiple times for successive reschedulings of the very same underlying defaults is unacceptable.

(c) **Does the US agree that from the formula in column G (that is: (Column (D) minus (E) minus (F)), it follows that a rescheduled claim no longer constitutes an outstanding claim at the moment the terms of the re-scheduling are agreed and that a rescheduling is treated as 100 per cent recovered, as Brazil states in footnote 292 of Brazil's 28 January 2004 comments on US responses to questions?**

Brazil's Comment:

41. Brazil notes the United States acknowledgment, in paragraph 24 of its response, that under the US cash-basis accounting methodology for making an assessment under item (j), a rescheduled claim no longer constitutes an outstanding claim as of the moment the terms of the rescheduling are agreed. Please see Brazil's comment on the United States' response to Question 264(b), which demonstrates that it is not legitimate for the United States to treat rescheduled debt as recovered at the moment it is rescheduled, since the record shows that the CCC has only collected 3.6 per cent of that rescheduled debt.

42. Additionally, Brazil notes the United States' statement, at paragraph 24 of its 11 February 2004 response, that "no principal payments received under reschedulings are reflected in Exhibit US-128". It is hardly surprising that the United States does not treat principal payments on rescheduled debt as recovered principal (under column 2(b) of Exhibit Bra-431), incrementally and year-on-year as they are actually recovered, since the United States already subtracts 100 per cent of rescheduled debt from claims outstanding (column 4(b) of Exhibit Bra-431) immediately, in the year the terms of the rescheduling are agreed.

(d) **Is the Panel correct in understanding that the amount of $888,984,792.04 in column F in Exhibit US-128 under "ALL" for 1992 represents the total continuing amount of unrecovered claims for the 1992 cohort, and that the amount of 387,692,219.39 represents the total continuing amount of unrecovered claims for the 1993 cohort, etc? Please indicate and substantiate how much principal and/or interest has actually been paid/recovered/rescheduled *annually* 1992-2003 in respect of each of the amounts shown in Columns D, E & F in the table.**

Brazil's Comment:

43. Please see Brazil's comment on the United States' response to Question 264(b), which demonstrates that it is not legitimate for the United States to treat rescheduled debt as recovered at the moment it is rescheduled, since the record shows that the CCC has only collected 3.6 per cent of that rescheduled debt.

44. As noted in Brazil's comment on the US response to Question 264(c), it is evident that the US methodology does not "reflect payment performance under the reschedulings themselves"[96] (under column 2(b) of Exhibit Bra-431), since the United States already subtracts 100 per cent of rescheduled debt from claims outstanding (column 4(b) of Exhibit Bra-431) immediately, in the year the terms of the rescheduling are agreed.

265. In connection with the US response to Question No. 225, please also provide amounts actually "written off" and "forgiven" annually for each *post*-1992 cohort, with annual details of country and amount (principal/interest).

Brazil's Comment:

45. The United States notes, in paragraph 27 of its response, that "CCC financial records indicate that no amounts have been 'written off' or 'forgiven' with respect to any post-1992 cohort." Brazil makes two observations.

46. First, Brazil notes that the Federal Credit Reform Act took effect for the 1992 cohort. Thus, the Panel's question was likely meant to refer to "each post-199*1* cohort". Brazil hopes that the United States understood the Panel's question to include the 1992 cohort.

47. Second, Brazil makes the obvious point that defaults need not be "written off" or "forgiven" to constitute an operating cost or loss for the purposes of item (j). Defaults (or other operating costs and losses) that remain on the books are just as relevant to an assessment under item (j) as they would be if they were "written off" or "forgiven".

266. What are the precise terms, conditions and duration of each rescheduling reflected in column F in Exhibit US-128?

Brazil's Comment:

48. While the Panel asked for the "precise terms, conditions and duration of each rescheduling", the United States has provided "summarized" data[97], without any documentary evidence as support.

267. Is the Panel correct in understanding that "interest collected on reschedulings" in Column M in Exhibit US-128 refers not to amounts that have been actually collected by the CCC but rather to interest capitalized in conjunction with the rescheduling? If so, what are the terms, conditions and duration of the arrangements pertaining to these amounts?

[96] US 11 February 2004 Answers, para. 25.

[97] US 11 February 2004 Answers, para. 28.

Brazil's Comment:

49. Please see Brazil's comment on the United States' response to Question 264(b), which demonstrates that it is not legitimate for the United States to treat rescheduled debt as recovered at the moment it is rescheduled, since the record shows that the CCC has only collected 3.6 per cent of that rescheduled debt.

50. As noted in Brazil's comment on the US responses to Questions 264(c) and 264(d), it is hardly surprising that the US methodology does not "reflect ... payment of original principal"[98] (under column 2(b) of Exhibit Bra-431), since the United States already subtracts 100 per cent of rescheduled debt from claims outstanding (column 4(b) of Exhibit Bra-431) immediately, in the year the terms of the rescheduling are agreed.

268. Concerning Column N in Exhibit US-128, please elaborate upon "Interest earned from US Treasury on uninvested funds". What is the source and authority for these funds and for the interest thereon to be part of the CCC total revenues? What are the terms, conditions and duration of the arrangements pertaining to these amounts?

269. The Panel notes the table submitted by the US in its answer to Question No. 224 (CCC Financing Account Payments of Interest on Borrowings from Treasury and Interest Earned on Uninvested Funds). Is the Panel correct in understanding that the figures in this table correspond to the "ALL" figures in Columns I and N of Exhibit US-128?

270. With respect to Column I in Exhibit US-128, ("Interest paid on borrowing from US Treasury") and Note 8, p. 25 of Exhibit US-129:

> **(i) please provide the total annual amounts (interest bearing and non-interest bearing) borrowed by the CCC from the US Treasury (annually since 1992), as well as the terms, conditions, interest rate (where applicable) and duration of such borrowing. Please provide details of any other amount borrowed by the CCC from the US Treasury during this period that may not have formed part of the regular annual borrowings.**

Brazil's Comment:

51. The United States has not answered the Panel's question, which requested "the terms, conditions, interest rate (where applicable) and duration" of CCC borrowings from the US Treasury.

> **(ii) Please explain the nature of "CCC's permanent indefinite borrowing authority from Treasury" referred to in Note 8, p. 25 of Exhibit US-129.**

---

[98] US 11 February 2004 Answers, para. 29.

Brazil's Comment:

52. The United States' response inaccurately implies that CCC's authority to extend export credit guarantees is somehow limited by the budget appropriations process. As Brazil has frequently noted, US law expressly provides that the CCC export credit guarantee programmes are exempt from the requirement that they receive new Congressional budget authority before undertaking new guarantee commitments.[99] Moreover, any "subsidy" losses the programmes incur are funded "through a permanent, indefinite appropriation and not by annual appropriation".[100]

(iii) What determines the level of CCC export credit guarantee borrowing (interest-bearing and non-interest-bearing)? Is the interest-free borrowing up to the amount of unreimbursed realized losses?

(iv) Why are repayments applied to non-interest bearing notes first, as indicated at Note 8, p. 25 of Exhibit US-129?

271. Note 8, p. 25 of Exhibit US-129 states that "In fiscal year 2003, CCC was fully reimbursed for its prior year net realized losses." Please indicate the amounts of prior year net realized losses (annually, since 1992) for which the CCC has been fully reimbursed.

Brazil's Comment:

53. The United States' response inaccurately implies that CCC's authority to extend export credit guarantees is somehow limited by the budget appropriations process. As Brazil has frequently noted, US law expressly provides that the CCC export credit guarantee programmes are exempt from the requirement that they receive new Congressional budget authority before undertaking new guarantee commitments.[101] Moreover, any "subsidy" losses the programmes incur are funded "through a permanent, indefinite appropriation and not by annual appropriation".[102]

---

[99] *See* Exhibit Bra-117 (2 U.S.C. § 661(c)(2)); Exhibit Bra-185 (Congressional Budget Office Staff Memorandum, "An Explanation of the Budgetary Changes under Credit Reform," April 1991, p. 7 and Table 2); Exhibit Bra-186 (Congressional Research Service Issue Brief for Congress, "Agriculture and the Budget," IB95031 (16 February 1996), p. 3).

[100] US House of Representatives, Report 105-178, Agriculture, Rural Development, Food and Drug Administration, and Related Agencies Appropriations Bill, 1998, p. 90, available at: http://frwebgate.access.gpo.gov/cgi-bin/getdoc.cgi?dbname=105_cong_reports&docid=f:hr178.105.pdf.

[101] *See* Exhibit Bra-117 (2 U.S.C. § 661(c)(2)); Exhibit Bra-185 (Congressional Budget Office Staff Memorandum, "An Explanation of the Budgetary Changes under Credit Reform," April 1991, p. 7 and Table 2); Exhibit Bra-186 (Congressional Research Service Issue Brief for Congress, "Agriculture and the Budget," IB95031 (16 February 1996), p. 3).

[102] US House of Representatives, Report 105-178, Agriculture, Rural Development, Food and Drug Administration, and Related Agencies Appropriations Bill, 1998, p. 90, available at: http://frwebgate.access.gpo.gov/cgi-bin/getdoc.cgi?dbname=105_cong_reports&docid=f:hr178.105.pdf.

272. With respect to the US response to Question No. 226, is the Panel correct in understanding that the reflection of write-offs as part of the operating loss of the CCC which in turn was replenished through the annual appropriations process ended with the entry into force of the FCRA in fiscal year 1992? If not, what amounts have been replenished through this process annually since fiscal year 1992?

Brazil's Comment:

54. Brazil notes that under US law, any "subsidy" losses the CCC export credit guarantee programmes incur are funded "through a permanent, indefinite appropriation and not by annual appropriation".[103]

273. With respect to the US response to Question No. 225, what criteria does the CCC apply to "independently determine" that a debt is uncollectible? For post-1992 cohorts, what are these uncollectible amounts (annually) and how, if at all, are such "uncollectible amounts" shown in Exhibit US-128?

Brazil's Comment:

55. The United States notes, in paragraph 44 of its response, that "[w]ith respect to post-1992 cohorts, no amounts have been determined uncollectible ..." Brazil makes two observations.

56. First, Brazil notes that the Federal Credit Reform Act took effect for the 1992 cohort. Thus, the Panel's question was likely meant to refer to "each post-199*1* cohort". Brazil hopes that the United States understood the Panel's question to include the 1992 cohort.

57. Second, Brazil notes that CCC's financial statements record a $1.16 billion "subsidy allowance" for all post-1991 cohorts.[104] Under the FCRA, the subsidy allowance is recorded on a net present value basis, which means that it represents the cost CCC considers it will incur on post-1991 guarantee cohorts at the time those cohorts are closed. In other words, at the time all outstanding post-1991 cohorts close, the CCC considers that it will face $1.16 billion in uncollectible guarantees.[105]

274. The Panel notes the US statement in the US response to Question No. 81 that "All rescheduled claims are currently performing " and that "all

---

[103] US House of Representatives, Report 105-178, Agriculture, Rural Development, Food and Drug Administration, and Related Agencies Appropriations Bill, 1998, p. 90, available at: http://frwebgate.access.gpo.gov/cgi-bin/getdoc.cgi?dbname=105_cong_reports&docid=f:hr178.105.pdf.

[104] Exhibit US-129 (US Department of Agriculture, Office of Inspector General, Financial and IT Operations, Audit Report, *Commodity Credit Corporation's Financial Statements for Fiscal Years 2003 and 2002*, Audit Report No. 06401-16-FM (November 2003), Notes to the Financial Statements, p. 15).

[105] The Congressional Budget Office agrees, projecting positive subsidy estimates for every cohort during the period 2002-2013. Exhibit Bra-432 (Congressional Budget Office, Fact Sheet, row titled "Export Credit Guarantee Program, Subsidy Account," available at http://www.cbo.gov/factsheets/CCC&FCIC.pdf).

payments due up to this point under [rescheduling] agreements have been received". However, the Panel also notes Exhibit US-129 (in particular, Note 5 on p. 22) and Brazil's reference thereto in Brazil's 28 January comments on the US response to Question No. 222. In this connection:

(a) How does the US respond to Brazil's statement in Brazil's 28 January comments that Exhibit US-129 confirms that rescheduling of export credit guarantee receivables cover both principal and interest, thereby confirming that not all of the rescheduled debt performs and that additional interest charges were also rescheduled?

Brazil's Comment:

58. The United States has offered no documentary support for its assertion that the "substantial majority" of the reschedulings referred to in Note 5, p. 22 of Exhibit US-129 "pertain to activities related to the P.L. 480 foreign food assistance programme".[106]

59. Moreover, the United States has never offered *any* support for its repeated assertion that "[a]ll rescheduled export credit guarantee debt is currently performing."[107] In fact, in its comment on the US response to Question 264(b), Brazil demonstrated that CCC is not collecting over 96 per cent of the rescheduled principal that remains outstanding.[108] In column F of Exhibit US-147, the United States states that $1.64 billion of defaulted CCC guarantees have been rescheduled over the period 1992-2003. Yet as of 30 November 2003, the United States reports in Exhibit US-153 that the principal outstanding on these resched-

---

[106] US 11 February 2004 Answers, para. 46. As the party asserting this fact, the United States bears the burden of proving it. *See e.g.* Appellate Body Report, *Japan – Apples*, WT/DS245/AB/R, para. 157 ("It is important to distinguish, on the one hand, the principle that the complainant must establish a *prima facie* case of inconsistency with a provision of a covered agreement from, on the other hand, the principle that the party that asserts a fact is responsible for providing proof thereof.").

[107] US 11 February 2004 Answers, para. 48. *See also* U.S. 11 August 2003 Answers, para. 155. As the party asserting this fact, the United States bears the burden of proving it. *See e.g.* Appellate Body Report, *Japan – Apples*, WT/DS245/AB/R, para. 157 ("It is important to distinguish, on the one hand, the principle that the complainant must establish a *prima facie* case of inconsistency with a provision of a covered agreement from, on the other hand, the principle that the party that asserts a fact is responsible for providing proof thereof.").

[108] Moreover, the United States has never responded to reports by the U.S. General Accounting Office and testimony by GAO officials, submitted by Brazil, demonstrating that CCC rescheduling has historically been in arrears. *See* Brazil's 28 January 2004 Comments, para. 136; Brazil's 22 August 2003 Comments, para. 99. *See also* Exhibit Bra-181 (US General Accounting Office, Report to the Ranking Minority Member, Committee on Agriculture, Nutrition, and Forestry, US Senate, *Former Soviet Union: Creditworthiness of Successor States and US Export Credit Guarantees*, GAO/GGD-95-60 (February 1995), p. 50-52 and Table 2.6 (noting that in 1995 defaults on Russian and Former Soviet Union guarantees reached $2 billion by the end of 1993, and that despite repeated rescheduling agreements, those debts were not being repaid.); Exhibit Bra-152 (GAO, Statement of Allan I. Mendelowitz, Director, Trade, Energy and Finance Issues, National Security and International Affairs Division, before the Task Force on Urgent Fiscal Issues of the Committee on Budget of the US House of Representatives, *Status Report on GAO's Reviews of the Targeted Export Assistance Programme, the Export Enhancement Program, and the GSM-102/103 Export Credit Guarantee Programs*, GAO/T-NSIAD-90-53, 28 June 1990, p. 14 (noting that historically, the majority of GSM support that is rescheduled is "in arrears.").

ulings amounts to $1.58 billion. This means that over the period 1992-2003, the CCC has only collected $60 million, or 3.6 per cent, of the $1.64 billion in defaulted CCC guarantees that have been rescheduled. Over 96 per cent of defaulted CCC guarantees that have been rescheduled over the period 1992-2003 remains outstanding.

(b) In Note 5 on p. 22 of Exhibit US-129, what is the definition of "non-performing"? What is the meaning of "delinquent"? What is the current principal balance and amount of interest of the three CCC export credit guarantee programme "receivables" in a non-performing status (individually and together, for GSM 102, GSM 103 and SCGP))? What is the amount of interest on non-reporting "receivables"?

(c) The Panel notes the US reference to the "Paris Club" in US response to Question No. 225. What is the P.L. 480 programme referred to in Note 5 on p. 22 of Exhibit US-129 (including the Paris Club debt reduction process and the HIPC Initiative) ? To what extent is the P.L. 480 programme and Paris Club process relevant to the export credit guarantee programmes at issue in this dispute? Please identify and give the amounts of all CCC export credit guarantee debt subject to the P.L. 480 debt reduction (or other similar) process since 1992.

(d) Can the US explain the process referred to in the second column of Note 5 on p. 22 ("CCC is awaiting an apportionment from the Office of Management and Budget before the transaction can be completed. Until such time, however, there is a 100% subsidy allowance established against the relevant debt as of September 30, 2003.") Please provide details of all such "apportionments" relating to the three export credit guarantee programmes in fiscal years 1992-2003.

Brazil's Comment:

60. Although the United States asserts that the reference in the Panel's question is to a single transaction related to the P.L. 480 food aid programme[109], and further asserts that the "apportionment" procedure cited in the Panel's question does not apply to the CCC export credit guarantee programmes[110], the United States offers *no* support for these assertions.[111]

61. In any event, Brazil makes the obvious point that defaults need not be "written off" to constitute an operating cost or loss for the purposes of item (j). Defaults (or other operating costs and losses) that remain on the books are just as

[109] US 11 February 2004 Answers, para. 53.

[110] US 11 February 2004 Answers, para. 54.

[111] As the party asserting this fact, the United States bears the burden of proving it. *See e.g.* Appellate Body Report, *Japan – Apples*, WT/DS245/AB/R, para. 157 ("It is important to distinguish, on the one hand, the principle that the complainant must establish a *prima facie* case of inconsistency with a provision of a covered agreement from, on the other hand, the principle that the party that asserts a fact is responsible for providing proof thereof.").

relevant to an assessment under item (j) as they would be if they were "written off".

275. Please provide evidence (or cite relevant portions of the record) that the premium rates for the export credit guarantee programmes are "reviewed annually" as stated in US 28 January comments on response to Question No. 223 (see also US 22 December response to Question No. 107; Brazil's 28 January 2004 comments on responses to Question No. 223.).

Brazil's Comment:

62. Even if the CCC does undertake the annual premium rate review asserted by the United States, the US Department of Agriculture's Inspector General noted in 2000 and 2001 that "the fees CCC charges for its GSM-102 and GSM-103 export credit guarantee programmes have not been changed in 7 years and may not be reflecting current costs".[112] Brazil has demonstrated that since 1993, only two changes have in fact been made to the GSM 102 fee schedule.[113]

63. Brazil makes several observations regarding Exhibit US-150, which purports to include memoranda concerning the 2003 and 2002 annual reviews of fees for the CCC export credit guarantee programmes.

64. First, page 2 of the 2003 memorandum shows that "offsetting fees" for GSM 102, GSM 103 and SCGP, both "historical[ly]" and for FY 2004, do not cover the "subsidy", within the meaning of the FCRA. As the Panel will recall, under the net present value accounting methodology endorsed by the US Congress and the President in the FCRA, a positive subsidy indicates a judgment that when the cohorts close, the CCC programmes will "lose money."[114] At page 3 of the memorandum, a major heading reinforces the point that the programmes are losing money, reading as follows: "JUSTIFICATION FOR NOT COVERING THE SUBSIDY COST OF THE PROGRAMME."

65. Second, Exhibit US-150 reinforces Brazil's claim that the CCC programmes confer "benefits" *per se*, within the meaning of Article 1.1(b) of the SCM Agreement, and therefore that they constitute *per se* export subsidies for the purposes of Article 10.1.[115] With other evidence (*e.g.*, the regulations for the CCC programmes, and a comparison to non-market benchmarks established by

---

[112] Exhibit Bra-153 (US Department of Agriculture Office of Inspector General Financial and IT Operations Audit Report of the Commodity Credit Corporation's Financial Statements for Fiscal Year 2000, Audit Report No. 06401-14-FM (June 2001), p. 31). *See also* Exhibit Bra-154 (US Department of Agriculture Office of Inspector General Great Plains Region Audit Report of the Commodity Credit Corporation's Financial Statements for Fiscal Year 2001, Audit Report No. 06401-4-KC (February 2002), p. 49 ("[T]he fees CCC charged for its GSM-102 and GSM-103 export credit guarantee programs have not been changed for many years and may not be reflecting current costs.").

[113] *See* Brazil's 11 August 2003 Answers, para. 167 (second bullet point).

[114] Exhibit Bra-121 (US General Accounting Office ("GAO"), Report to Congressional Committees, "Credit Reform: US Needs Better Method for Estimating Cost of Foreign Loans and Guarantees," GAO/NSIAD/GGD-95-31, December 1994, p. 20) ("GAO/NSIAD/GGD-95-31")).

[115] *See*, *e.g.*, Brazil's 28 January 2004 Comments, para. 253; Brazil's 18 November 2003 Further Rebuttal Submission, paras. 233-241.

the US Export-Import Bank)[116], Brazil has made this *per se* showing by demonstrating that CCC export credit guarantees are unique financing instruments for agricultural commodity transactions that are not available on the commercial market for terms longer than the marketing cycles of the eligible commodities.[117] Pages 3-4 of the 2003 memorandum included in Exhibit US-150 reinforce Brazil's claim, by stating that fees for the CCC programmes are set not according to market benchmarks, but are instead set according to policy considerations. According to page 3 of the memorandum, "[s]etting prices is a policy matter, sometimes governed by statutory provisions and regulations, and other times by managerial or public policies". While it is fundamental that pricing for market-based financial instruments takes account of the risks involved in a transaction, the memorandum notes, at page 4, that "current fees for GSM-102, GSM-103, and SCGP are not risk-based", and that "[i]f the fees were changed to a risk-based system, this would most likely exceed [the statutory fee cap of] 1 per cent ..."[118]

276. The Panel notes the parties' responses and comments relating to Question No. 252 concerning the time period within which any prohibited measure must be withdrawn within the meaning of Article 4.7 of the *SCM Agreement*. Please supplement your original response, taking into account the particular nature of each alleged prohibited subsidy measure (i.e. "Step 2" payments under Section 1207(a) of the 2002 FSRI Act, export credit guarantee programmes and the ETI Act) and the functioning of the US legal and regulatory system in respect of these measures.

---

[116] This evidence is summarized at paragraphs 231-241 of Brazil's 18 November 2003 Further Rebuttal Submission.

[117] *See* Brazil's 24 June 2003 First Submission, paras. 289-292; Brazil's 22 July 2003 Oral Statement, para. 116; Brazil's 11 August 2003 Answers to Questions, paras. 139-140, 152-157, 183-187; Brazil's 22 August 2003 Rebuttal Submission, paras. 103-105; Brazil's 22 August 2003 Comments, paras. 92-93, 109-113; Brazil's 27 August 2003 Comments on US Rebuttal Submission, paras. 68-80; Brazil's 7 October 2003 Oral Statement, para. 72; Brazil's 18 November 2003 Further Rebuttal Submission, paras. 230-242; Brazil's 2 December 2003 Oral Statement, para. 79.

[118] Regarding the statutory one-per cent fee cap, *see* US 11 August 2003 Answers, para. 180. *See also* Exhibit US-150 (Annual Review of Fees for USDA Credit Programmes, March 25, 2003, p. 4 ("Section 211(b)(2) of the Agricultural Trade Act of 1978, as amended, caps the current fees at 1 per cent for ... GSM-102 and SCGP.")).

ANNEX I-21

COMMENTS OF THE UNITED STATES TO THE 11 FEBRUARY 2004 ANSWERS OF BRAZIL TO PANEL QUESTION 276

18 February 2004

Question 276. "The Panel notes the parties' responses and comments relating to Question No. 252 concerning the time period within which any prohibited measure must be withdrawn within the meaning of Article 4.7 of the SCM Agreement. Please supplement your original response, taking into account the particular nature of each alleged prohibited subsidy measure (i.e. "Step 2" payments under Section 1207(a) of the 2002 FSRI Act, export credit guarantee programmes and the ETI Act) and the functioning of the US legal and regulatory system in respect of these measures."

1. The United States appreciates this opportunity to comment on the response of Brazil to Panel question 276, posed on 3 February 2004. As an initial matter, the United States notes that the question poses a hypothetical situation: that any of the measures at issue in this dispute might be found to be a prohibited subsidy. The United States of course has explained that Brazil has not shown that any of the measures at issue is a prohibited subsidy. That being said, the United States offers the following comments on Brazil's response.

2. Of note, in its response Brazil has recognized that its previous answer to Question 252 from the Panel was inadequate. In full, that answer provided: "Brazil suggests that the Panel follow the precedent of all previous WTO panels that made findings of prohibited subsidies and specify that the measure must be withdrawn within 90 days."[1] Brazil has now revised – from 90 days to six months – its recommendation to the Panel of the time period that would constitute withdrawing "without delay" subsidies allegedly provided by the export credit guarantee programmes. However, Brazil's response sets out a faulty analysis of the meaning of "without delay" in Article 4.7 as applied in previous reports and therefore identifies what would be inappropriately short time periods for withdrawal of the measures at issue if they were prohibited subsidies, which they are not.

3. Article 4.7 of the *Agreement on Subsidies and Countervailing Measures* ("Subsidies Agreement") establishes that "[i]f the measure in question is found to be a prohibited subsidy, the panel shall recommend that the subsidizing Member withdraw the subsidy without delay. In this regard, the panel shall specify in its recommendation the time-period within which the measure must be withdrawn". The Agreement does not further define "without delay", although Brazil concedes that the "text [of Article 4.7] does not state 'immediately'".[2]

---

[1] Brazil's Answer to Question 252 from the Panel, para. 167 (22 December 2003) (footnotes omitted).

[2] Brazil's Answer to Question 276 from the Panel, para. 2.

4. Past panels have dealt with the meaning of the term "without delay," and have concluded that this involves an examination of the nature of the changes to be effected and the domestic legal process involved. For example, in *Canada – Certain Measures Affecting the Automotive Industry*, the panel found that "in examining what time-period would represent withdrawal 'without delay' in a particular case, we consider that we may take into account the nature of the steps necessary to withdraw the prohibited subsidy".[3] Similarly, in *Australia – Subsidies Provided to Producers and Exporters of Automotive Leather*[4], the panel found that "the nature of the measures and issues regarding implementation might be relevant" to the time period for withdrawal of the subsidies".[5]

5. The analysis by these panels is similar to that undertaken by arbitrators under Article 21.3 of the *Understanding on Rules and Procedures Governing the Settlement of Disputes* ("DSU") in considering the period of time for a Member to implement DSB recommendations and rulings. There, arbitrators have also considered that Article 21.3 calls for an analysis of the nature of the changes to be effected and "the shortest period possible within the legal system of the Member to implement the recommendations and rulings of the DSB".[6] Thus, in practical terms, the "reasonable period of time" standard of DSU Article 21.3 has been interpreted to mean something akin to without "delay" ("procrastination; lingering; putting off"[7]).

6. DSU Article 21.3 is part of the context of Article 4.7. Brazil attempts to distinguish Article 4.7 of the Subsidies Agreement from Article 21.3 of the DSU.[8] However, Brazil argues that a key difference is that Article 21.3 uses the term "reasonable". Brazil thus appears to argue that under Article 4.7 any time period specified should not be reasonable. The United States agrees that there are differences between Article 4.7 of the Subsidies Agreement and Article 21.3 of the DSU. But those differences do not amount to a requirement that panels require unreasonable actions. Rather, one key difference is that DSU Article 21.3(c) provides arbitrators with a "guideline" that the "reasonable period of time" to implement panel or Appellate Body recommendations "should not exceed 15 months from the date of adoption of a panel or Appellate Body report" whereas Article 4.7 does not.[9]

---

3 WT/DS139/R, WT/DS142/R, paras. 11.6-11.7 (adopted as modified 19 June 2000) (italics added).

4 WT/DS126/R, paras. 10.4-10.7 (adopted 16 June 1999).

5 *See also* the panel reports in the *Aircraft* disputes between Canada and Brazil, in which the panels took into account the nature of the measures and the procedures which may be required to implement the panels' recommendations.

6 Report of the Arbitrator, *United States – Continued Dumping and Subsidy Offset Act of 2000*, WT/DS217/14, WT/DS234/22, para. 42 (13 June 2003) (quotation marks and footnote omitted) (citing 3 previous reports of arbitrators).

7 *The New Shorter Oxford English Dictionary*, vol. 1, at 623 (1993 ed.).

8 Brazil's response to Question 276, para. 2.

9 In the earliest arbitrations under Article 21.3(c), arbitrators viewed the guideline as meaning that each party bore the burden of proof that the reasonable period of time should depart from the 15 months period, which would be a significant difference from Article 4.7. That approach has now

7. In the current dispute, the measures at issue all involve legislation and any change would require legislative action. Brazil has proposed that withdrawal "without delay" should be considered to mean withdrawal within 90 days for allegedly prohibited subsidies under the Step 2 programme and the ETI Act and withdrawal within 6 months for alleged export subsidies under the export credit guarantee programmes. However, Brazil's proposed time periods are not supported by considerations relating to the nature of the measures at issue nor the US legislative process that would be necessary to effect changes to those measures.

8. Specifically, Brazil concedes that statutory changes would be necessary to withdraw the allegedly prohibited subsidies at issue in this dispute.[10] However, the panel reports Brazil cites as support for the proposition that "without delay" generally means 90 days dealt with subsidies that required *only executive or administrative action* to withdraw:[11]

> In Canada – Certain Measures Affecting the Automotive Industry, the panel found: "we note that the [challenged measures] are both Orders-in-Council, and as such are acts of the executive, and not the legislative branch of government. The amendment of an act of the executive branch can normally be effectuated more quickly than would be the case if legislative action were required."[12] The report further notes that "in those disputes involving a prohibited subsidy in which legislative action was not required, panels have specified a time-period of 90 days".[13]
>
> In Australia – Subsidies Provided to Producers and Exporters of Automotive Leather,[14] taking into account that the dispute involved payments made under a grant contract between the Australian Government and a private company, the panel recommended that the measures be withdrawn within 90 days.
>
> In Canada – Export Credits and Loan Guarantees for Regional Aircraft,[15] involving executive action concerning financing provided by Canada for particular transactions, the panel found that "Canada should withdraw the export subsidies within 90 days ("without delay").

evolved into the practice described above of the shortest possible period of time within the legal system of the Member to implement the recommendations and rulings of the DSB.

10 Brazil's Answer to Question 276 from the Panel, para. 10 (11 February 2004) (eliminating Step 2 "simply requires the repeal of Section 1207(a) of the 2002 FSRI Act); *id.,* para. 11 (for export credit guarantee programmes, "the prohibited subsidies must be withdrawn by enacting the necessary changes to the statutes and regulations providing for GSM102, GSM 103, and SCGP"); *id.,* para. 12 (90 days "represents an appropriate period of time ... to withdraw the ETI Act").

11 Brazil's Answer to Question 276 from the Panel, para. 10 n.15.

12 WT/DS139/R, WT/DS142/R, paras. 11.6-11.7 (adopted as modified 19 June 2000) (italics added).

13 *Ibid.,* para. 11.7 n. 910 (citing panel reports in *Australia – Leather*, *Brazil – Aircraft*, and *Canada – Aircraft*).

14 WT/DS126/R, paras. 10.4-10.7 (adopted 16 June 1999).

15 WT/DS222/R, paras. 8.1-8.4 (adopted 19 February 2002).

> In Brazil – Export Financing Programme for Aircraft, with respect to payments under the interest rate equalization component of PROEX,[16] the panel report found that, "taking into account the nature of the measures and the procedures which may be required to implement our recommendation," Brazil should withdraw the measures within 90 days.[17]
>
> In Canada – Measures Affecting the Export of Civilian Aircraft,[18] with respect to certain executive action concerning financing and funds provided to the Canadian civil aircraft industry, the panel report found that, "[t]aking into account the procedures that may be required to implement our recommendation", Canada should withdraw the measures within 90 days.

Thus, in every panel report in which the "without delay" time period has been set as 90 days, only executive action (and not statutory amendment) has been necessary. Thus, these reports offer little guidance to the Panel, other than to indicate that 90 days would *not* be an adequate time period, given that Brazil recognizes that legislation would be required to modify the measures in dispute.

9. Brazil notes, almost in passing, that "[t]here is only one precedent applying the Article 4.7 'without delay' provision to prohibited subsidy measures requiring legislative changes"[19]: the panel report in *United States – FSC*.[20] However, Brazil fails to quote or discuss that panel report's discussion of the "without delay" language, which would seem to be particularly relevant given that Brazil has challenged the ETI Act – the successor to the FSC programme – in this dispute. Brazil erroneously cites this report as supporting the proposition that "without delay" generally means withdrawal within 90 days[21], but there is no discussion of a 90-day period in the report.

10. Upon finding that the FSC scheme provided export subsidies inconsistent with Article 3.1(a) of the Subsidies Agreement, the *FSC* panel first recommended, "pursuant to Article 4.7 of that Agreement, that the DSB request the United States to withdraw the FSC subsidies without delay".[22] The panel examined what should be its recommendation with respect to the time-period within which the measure must be withdrawn. The panel noted that the time period specified "must be consistent with the requirement that the subsidy be withdrawn 'without delay'". The panel then went on to find, and recommend:

> Given that the implementation of the Panel's recommendation will require legislative action (a fact recognized by the European

[16] PROEX was being maintained by provisional measures issued by the Brazilian Government on an monthly basis, and the financing terms for which interest rate equalization payments were made were set by Ministerial Decrees. WT/DS46/R, paras. 2.1, 2.3 (adopted 20 August 1999).

[17] *Ibid.*, paras. 8.2-8.5.

[18] WT/DS70/R, paras. 10.3-10.4 (adopted as modified 20 August 1999).

[19] Brazil's Answer to Question 276 from the Panel, para. 5 (11 February 2004).

[20] Panel Report, *United States – Tax Treatment for "Foreign Sales Corporations"*, WT/DS108/R (adopted 20 March 2000) ("*United States – FSC*").

[21] Brazil's Answer to Question 276 from the Panel, para. 10 n.15 (11 February 2004).

[22] *United States – FSC*, WT/DS108/R, para. 8.3.

> Communities), that the United States fiscal year 2000 starts on 1 October 1999, and that this report is not scheduled for circulation to Members until September 1999 (and, if appealed, might not be adopted until as late as early spring 2000), it is not in our view a practical possibility that the United States could be in a position to take the necessary legislative action by 1 October 1999. That being so, and acting in good faith, there is no way that this could be described as a 'delay.' However, this objective timing constraint would not be present with effect from the following fiscal year (2001), which commences on 1 October 2000. As this would be the first practicable date by which the United States could implement our recommendation, it satisfies the 'without delay' standard found in Article 4.7. Accordingly, we specify that FSC subsidies must be withdrawn at the latest with effect from 1 October 2000.[23]

Brazil recognizes that statutory changes would be necessary to modify the measures at issue in this dispute. However, Brazil fails to discuss the various considerations identified by the *FSC* panel report, such as the potential date of circulation of the Panel's report and the effect of appeal on the timing of adoption. Neither does Brazil discuss whether there would be a "practical possibility" of legislative action within its suggested time periods.

11. With respect to the potential date of circulation, the Panel's current schedule provides for the final report to be issued to the parties on 19 May. Circulation to all Members would be upon translation into the official WTO languages. Conservatively assuming one month for completion of translation of what may be a very lengthy panel report, the report would be circulated in mid-June. Panel reports may not be considered for adoption until 20 days after they have been circulated to all Members[24] – approximately early July. If the Panel report is appealed, the Appellate Body report will likely be issued 90 days from the notice of appeal[25] – approximately early October. The Appellate Body report would be adopted (unless the DSB decides by consensus not to adopt it) within 30 days of circulation[26] – approximately early November.

12. The current US Congress is scheduled to adjourn on 1 October 2004. Accordingly, no legislative action would be possible until after the new Congress convenes in 2005 and organizes itself. The United States has previously stated that, in the event of a prohibited subsidy finding, it should be given until the end of "this year" to complete the legislative process. However, given the probable time line for this dispute noted above, that is not a possibility.

13. Once the new Congress convenes and organizes (a process that we would not expect to be completed before mid-February), any legislation would then

---

[23] *United States – FSC*, WT/DS108/R, para. 8.8.

[24] DSU Article 16.1.

[25] See *Statistical Information on Recourse to WTO Dispute Settlement Procedures: Background Note by the Secretariat*, Job(03)/225, circulated 11 December 2003, Section IV.B and Table 8.

[26] DSU Article 17.14.

need to proceed through the legislative process. In the United States, this involves the following.[27]

The US Legislative Process

14. Under the United States system of constitutional government, any changes to a federal statute must be enacted by the US Congress, which sets its own procedures and timetable. The Executive branch of the US Government has no control over these procedures and timetable. Securing the enactment of legislation in the US Congress is a complex and lengthy process. Moreover, only a small fraction of the thousands of bills introduced in each Congress ever become law. This indicates that the process of obtaining the votes necessary to enact legislation is difficult and time-consuming. Viewed in this light, there is no "practical possibility" that this process will take, as Brazil suggests, 3 months for the Step 2 programme and ETI Act and 6 months (including time for administrative action) for the export credit guarantee programmes.

15. The power to legislate is vested in the United States Congress, which has two chambers, the House of Representatives and the Senate. Both chambers must approve all legislation in identical form, before it is sent to the President of the United States for signature or other action. Only after presidential approval does proposed legislation become law. Proposed legislation that will become public law usually takes the form of a "bill". From the time that a bill is introduced in Congress to the time that it is approved by both chambers, it will have passed through at least ten steps. These ten steps include: (1) the bill is introduced in the House of Representatives or the Senate by a member of Congress; (2) the bill is referred to a standing committee or committees having jurisdiction over the subject matter of the bills, which may also refer the proposed legislation to various subcommittees; (3) the merits of the bill are considered by a subcommittee, which may include public hearings; (4) when hearings are completed, the subcommittee meets to "mark-up" the bill (make changes and amendments) prior to deciding whether to recommend (or "report") the bill to the full committee; (5) the full committee (considering the subcommittee's report) may conduct further study and hearings and then votes whether to report the bill, either as originally introduced without amendment, or as revised, to the full House; (6) the House considers the bill on its merits and, after voting on amendments, the House immediately votes on the bill itself with any adopted amendments; (7) if the bill is passed, the bill must be referred to the Senate, which, following its own legislative process and consideration, may approve the bill as received, reject it, ignore it, or change it; (8) if the Senate amends the bill or passes its own similar but not identical legislation, a conference committee is organized to reconcile differences between the House and Senate versions; (9) if the committee reaches agreement on a single bill, a "conference report" must be approved by

[27] A more detailed description of the US legislative process may be found in paragraphs 21-35 of the Submission of the United States in the Arbitration under Article 21.3(c) of the DSU in the dispute *United States – Continued Dumping and Subsidy Offset Act of 2000*, WT/DS217 & 234 (13 April 2003) (available at http://www.ustr.gov/enforcement/briefs.shtml).

both chambers, in identical form, or the revised legislation dies; and (10) after the bill proposed by the conference committee is approved by both chambers, it is sent to the President for approval. Most bills that are introduced do not survive this process to become law, and those that do are likely to have been significantly amended along the way.

16. In addition, Brazil has recognized that a finding that the programmes are prohibited export subsidies would necessarily require "changes to the statutes and regulations" providing for the programmes.[28] The regulatory changes could not be made until after the legislative changes are finalized. Thus, the time period that would constitute withdrawal "without delay" would have to allow for both legislative and regulatory changes.

17. No panel report considering Article 4.7 has ever awarded a period of less than three months. Moreover, panels have found that "[t]he amendment of an act of the executive branch can normally be effectuated more quickly than would be the case if legislative action were required".[29]

18. Indeed, in a recent arbitration under DSU Article 21.3(c) in a dispute where compliance by the United States involved both legislative and regulatory action, the arbitrator concluded that 15 months was the reasonable period of time for implementation.[30]

19. In light of the foregoing considerations, under the hypothetical situation that any of the measures at issue would be a prohibited subsidy, the United States suggests that a panel recommendation that the measure be withdrawn 15 months after adoption of the DSB recommendations and rulings would be "without delay" in the circumstances of this dispute.

---

[28] Brazil's Answer to Question 276 from the Panel, para. 11.

[29] *Canada – Certain Measures Affecting the Automotive Industry*, WT/DS139/R, WT/DS142/R, paras. 11.6-11.7.

[30] Award of the Arbitrator, *United States – Anti-Dumping Measures on Certain Hot-rolled Steel Products from Japan: Arbitration under Article 21.3(c) of the DSU*, WT/DS184/13, circulated 19 February 2002.

ANNEX I-22

BRAZIL'S COMMENTS ON UNITED STATES 11 FEBRUARY COMMENTS ON BRAZIL'S 28 JANUARY "COMMENTS AND REQUESTS REGARDING DATA PROVIDED BY THE UNITED STATES ON 18/19 DECEMBER 2003 AND THE US REFUSAL TO PROVIDE NON-SCRAMBLED DATA ON 20 JANUARY 2004"

18 February 2004

TABLE OF CONTENTS

Table of Cases

EC – Hormones (US, Canada)	Arbitrator Report, *European Communities – Measures Concerning Meat and Meat Products (Hormones)*, WT/DS26/ARB and WT/DS48/ARB, circulated 12 July 1999.
EC – Bananas (Ecuador)	Arbitrator Report, *European Communities – Regime for Import, Sale and Distribution of Bananas*, WT/DS27/ARB, circulated 9 April 1999.
EC – Bananas (US)	Arbitrator Report, *European Communities – Regime for Import, Sale and Distribution of Bananas*, WT/DS27/ARB/ECU, circulated 24 March 2000.
Brazil – Aircraft	Arbitrator Report, *Brazil – Export Financing Programme for Aircraft*, WT/DS46/ARB, circulated 28 August 2000.
Japan – Agricultural Products	Appellate Body Report, *Japan – Measures Affecting Agricultural Products,* WT/DS76/AB/R, adopted 19 March 1999.
US – FSC	Arbitrator Report, *United States – Tax Treatment for "Foreign Sales Corporations"*, WT/DS108/ARB, circulated 30 August 2002.
US – Sheet/Plate from Korea	Panel Report, *United States – Anti-Dumping Measures on Stainless Steel Plate in Coils and Stainless Steel Sheet and Strip from Korea*, WT /DS179/R, adopted 1 February 2001.
Canada – Aircraft II	Arbitrator Report, *Canada – Export Credits and Loan Guarantees for Regional Aircraft*, WT/DS222/ARB, circulated 17 February 2003.
US – Lumber CVD Final	Appellate Body Report, *United States – Final Countervailing Duty Determination with Respect to Certain Softwood Lumber from Canada*, WT/DS/257/AB/R, not yet adopted.

1. INTRODUCTION

1. Brazil sets forth its response to the US 11 February 2004 Comments on Brazil's 28 January Comments and Requests regarding the US Data ("US 11 February 2004 Comments"). Brazil demonstrates in Sections 2 and 3 that the US critique of any methodology for tabulating "support to a specific commodity" is based on (1) a faulty legal interpretation that only subsidies tied to the production of a specific commodity can be counted for the purposes of Article 13(b)(ii) of the Agreement on Agriculture, and (2) a faulty factual assumption that the non-

green box US contract payments did not provide support to maintain US production of upland cotton between MY 1999-2002. In Section 5, Brazil responds to the US 11 February 2004 Comments by demonstrating that applying Brazil's and the US methodologies (along with two slight variations thereof) to the incomplete and inadequate US summary data (including the most recent 28 January 2004 data) demonstrates that the US budgetary expenditures in MY 1999-2002 exceed the level of support decided in MY 1992. Finally, Brazil responds to a number of other points raised by the US 11 February 2004 Comments in Sections 4, and 6-10.

2. THE US CRITIQUE OF BRAZIL'S METHODOLOGY IS BASED ON THE FLAWED US INTERPRETATION OF "SUPPORT TO A SPECIFIC COMMODITY" AND, ALTERNATIVELY, "NON-PRODUCT SPECIFIC SUPPORT"

2. The United States' 11 February 2004 Comments challenging Brazil's methodology for counting contract payments are premised on a faulty interpretation of Article 13(b)(ii) of the Agreement on Agriculture. The US comments continue the US interpretation that the Panel can only count as "support" in MY 2002 those non-green box subsidies that *require* the production of upland cotton.[1] But this leaves behind a number of subsidies that significantly and directly support production of upland cotton. As Brazil has previously argued, the Panel is required to count under Article 13(b)(ii) as "support to upland cotton" for MY 1999-2002 *all* identifiable non-green box support to upland cotton that supports, either directly or indirectly, the production or sale of upland cotton.[2]

2.1 US 11 February 2004 Comments Improperly Interpret the Phrase "Support to a Specific Commodity"

3. The United States argues that no allocation methodology can be applied by the Panel under Article 13(b)(ii) of the Agreement on Agriculture. This US argument is based on the US 11 February 2004 Comments that "support to" means support "tied to" the production of a specific commodity.[3] In evaluating this argument the Panel should examine the ordinary meaning of the phrase "support to a specific commodity" in Article 13(b)(ii). The word "support" is defined as "the action of preventing a person from giving way or of backing-up a person or group; assistance, backing".[4] "Support" does not mean or require, as the US comments suggest, an "incentive" or "encouragement" to produce. The SCM Agreement Annex IV, paragraph 3 phrase "tied to the production or sale of a [specific commodity]" is not found in Article 13(b)(ii). Rather, the word "support" has a more general sense of "backing up" a group of agricultural farmers

1 *See* US 11 August 2003 Answer to Question 38, para 81.
2 Brazil's 22 August 2003 Rebuttal Submission, para. 14-16.
3 Brazil's 11 February 2004 Comments, paras. 7-9.
4 New Shorter Oxford Dictionary, Volume II, p. 3152 (first definition).

producing a specific commodity. For example, subsidies that cover costs of production when a farmer chooses to grow a crop, "back up" or "support" that farmer. While some non-green box subsidies at issue in this dispute may create a greater *incentive* to produce (*i.e.*, marketing loan, counter-cyclical payments, or crop insurance subsidies) than other subsidies (PFC or direct payments), all of these subsidies at issue in this dispute "support" production of upland cotton because they cover (or contribute to) the costs of production of a crop.

4. The distinction between "support for production" and "incentive for" (or "tied to") production becomes relevant only when examining the *effects* these subsidies have in causing serious prejudice, within the meaning of Part III of the SCM Agreement. Brazil and the United States agree that the contract payments, which do not *require* production, create less direct *incentives* to produce than, *e.g.*, marketing loan payments, Step 2 payments and crop insurance subsidies. But it is improper to impose an "incentive to" or "tied to" production test when counting up the non-green box "support" to a specific commodity under Article 13(b)(ii) of the Agreement on Agriculture. As noted above, the meaning of the phrase "support to" is a far broader concept. Indeed, the *chapeau* of Article 13(b)(ii) confirms this broader meaning of "support," because it includes all types of non-green box measures, without regard to whether they create direct production incentives.

5. The United States' comments continue to repeat the flawed mantra that "support to a specific commodity" means exactly the same thing as "product-specific support".[5] Negotiators presumably knew what they intended when they used the very particular term "product-specific support". They used the term repeatedly in the Agreement on Agriculture, and even defined "non-product-specific support" in Article 1(a) – yet they declined to use "product-specific support" in Article 13(b)(ii). Accepting *arguendo* the US narrow interpretation of "product-specific"[6], one reason may be that the "support to a specific commodity" phrase was *not* intended to mean *only* support that is tied to *one product*, but rather is intended to include *all* support that is *provided*, either directly or indirectly, to *a product*. The term "specific" clarifies that Article 13(b)(ii) focuses on any support to an individual commodity, not a *group* of commodities such as "grains"[7] or even all commodities. In fact, the notion of a "specific commodity" is very analogous to the "like product" in, *inter alia*, Articles 5 and 6 of the SCM Agreement and Article XVI of GATT 1994 – provisions that are expressly referenced in Article 13(b)(ii) of the Agreement on Agriculture.

6. The United States argues that the Panel is prohibited from even including as "support to" upland cotton, let alone applying *any* allocation methodology to, any non-green box domestic support measure.[8] This would be true even where a measure may provide billions of dollars of support to producers of a "specific

---

5 US 11 February 2004 Comments, paras. 11-14.

6 Brazil disagrees with the US interpretation, as set out in Section 2.2, *infra*.

7 Brazil's 11 August 2003 Answer to Question 42, paras. 59-60.

8 US 11 February 2004 Comments, para 36 (arguing that "support to a specific commodity" really means "product-specific support").

commodity". This, of course, is based on the US view that only support directly tied to the production of a specific product is covered by Article 13(b)(ii).[9] But because Article 13(b)(ii) captures *all* non-green box domestic subsidies that support a commodity, it may require the application of an allocation methodology for many trade- and production-distorting domestic support measures that may provide support to more than one commodity. The issue under Article 13(b)(ii) is whether a particular commodity receives "backing" or "support" from a domestic support measure. But the sole fact that multiple commodities are supported by a single type of (trade- and production-distorting) measure does not mean that the "support" or backing suddenly disappears when tabulating the amounts of support for the purpose of Article 13(b)(ii).

7. Applying a methodology such as that proposed by Brazil is consistent with the object and purpose of Article 13(b)(ii) – to capture all identifiable non-green box trade distorting subsides that "support" upland cotton production. To allow huge amounts of trade- and production-distorting support – such as the almost $1 billion in counter-cyclical payments received by almost every upland cotton farmer in MY 2002 – to remain uncounted renders any disciplines during the implementation period inutile. Were this the intention of negotiators, as the United States argues, then it would certainly have been stated explicitly – with language such as "exempt from actions ... provided that measures *which are paid upon the production of* a specific commodity do not grant support to a specific commodity in excess of that decided during the 1992 marketing year". Or with language such as "exempt from actions ... provided that *measures are directed only at a specific commodity* do not grant support ... ." It would have been simple to include these explicit phrases limiting support measures to only subsidies tied to production. But no such limitations were made in the *sui generis* provisions of Article 13(b)(ii).

8. In rejecting the narrow US "required production" test for "support to" in Article 13(b)(ii), the Panel must also reject the US criticisms of Brazil's methodology for calculating support to upland cotton. This is because the US challenge to Brazil's methodology is premised on incorporating into Article 13(b)(ii) the test that the only trade and production distorting support that can be counted is support that is *de jure* "tied to the production or sale of a given product". Yet, this "tied to the production" language is found only in Annex IV, paragraph 3 of the SCM Agreement – not Article 13(b)(ii) of the Agreement on Agriculture.

2.2 The US 11 February 2004 Comments Improperly Interpret the Phrase "Product-Specific"

9. Brazil has argued, *in the alternative*, that the contract payments would also be considered to be "product-specific" support if the term "product-specific" had actually been used in the text of Article 13(b)(ii).[10] Brazil argued

[9] US 11 August 2003 Answers to Question 38, para. 81.

[10] Brazil's 11 August 2003 Answers to Questions 40-41; Brazil's 11 August 2003 Rebuttal Submission, paras. 24-52.

that the meaning of "product-specific" AMS must be governed by the only term providing some guidance to what it means – the definition of "non-product-specific support" in Article 1(a) of the Agreement on Agriculture.[11] Because the United States raised this issue in its 11 February 2004 Comments,[12] Brazil addresses it below, referencing Brazil's earlier arguments.

10. As a preliminary matter, however, Brazil must correct an error in the US 11 February 2004 Comments. The United States falsely asserts that Brazil has "conceded that 'support to a specific commodity' refers to 'product-specific support'".[13] The alleged "concession" by Brazil[14] becomes the foundation for the US arguments in paragraphs 11-17 of the US 11 February 2004 Comments.

11. As the Panel knows, Brazil argued extensively – and correctly – in the peace clause phase of this dispute that the phrase "support to a specific commodity" is *not* the same as "product-specific support".[15] Brazil's earlier arguments noted that under the facts of this case, all of the non-green box support payments challenged by Brazil as "support to a specific commodity" would also be considered "product-specific support", within the meaning of Article 1(a) of the Agreement on Agriculture.[16] However, this argument was only made in the alternative, to demonstrate that, even under the incorrect US theory, the amount of "product-specific" support for upland cotton in MY 1999-2002 exceeded the level of "product-specific" support for upland cotton decided in MY 1992.

12. The US 11 February 2004 Comments now go so far as to argue that *any* allocation methodology under Article 13(b)(ii) – which it argues means "product-specific" support – is prohibited by the Agreement on Agriculture.[17] One interpretative guide to determine whether support is "product-specific" is found in the definition of "non-product-specific support" in Article 1(a) of the Agreement on Agriculture. Brazil demonstrated that only non-product specific support is actually defined and that it includes "support provided in favour of agricultural producers *in general*".[18] The United States asserts that Brazil's definition of "general" is obsolete and that "general" means any support provided to more than

---

11 Brazil's 11 August 2003 Answers to Questions 40-41; Brazil's 22 August 2003 Rebuttal Submission, para. 19.

12 US 11 February 2004 Comments, paras. 11-14.

13 *Ibid.*

14 The text of the alleged "concession" made by Brazil is "In sum, Brazil maintains its position – supported by all third parties – that the support from contract payments that can be allocated to upland cotton is product-specific support within the meaning of the Agreement on Agriculture." What the United State neglects to note in its "concession" assertion is that Brazil then cited to its 22 August 2003 Rebuttal Submission, paras. 3-23 and 24-52, where Brazil argued exactly the same position it has set forth in these comments. Therefore, there was no "concession" or otherwise by Brazil.

15 Brazil's 22 August 2003 Rebuttal Submission, paras. 13-22. Brazil's 22 July 2003 Oral Statement, paras. 13-26. Brazil's 24 July 2003 Closing Statement, para. 8.

16 Brazil's 22 August 2003 Rebuttal Submission, paras. 13-52. Brazil's 22 August 2003 Comments on US Answers to Questions 38-39, paras. 48-53, Question 43, para. 58.

17 US 11 February 2004 Comments, paras 11 and 36 ("the definitions of product-specific support and non-product specific support (and their application in the Agreement on Agriculture) do not permit any such allocation … ".).

18 Brazil's 11 August 2003 Answers to Questions 40-41.

one commodity.[19] But this is a tortured reading of the term "in general". "Non-obsolete" definitions of "general" include "relating to a whole class of objects" and "*not* partial, local or sectional".[20] As with the so-called "obsolete" definition criticized by the United States, these definitions fully support the ordinary meaning of "non-product-specific" support as support provided to a broad range of producers covering a wide variety of agricultural products, not simply more than one, as the United States argues.

13. Further context for the existence of some sort of an allocation methodology in the Agreement on Agriculture is Annex 3, paragraph 7, which provides that "[m]easures directed at agricultural processors shall be included *to the extent that such measures benefit* the producers of the basic agricultural products". This use of the term "benefit" is very similar to the notion of "support" as used in Article 13(b)(ii). The assessment of the extent to which measures directed at agricultural processors benefit producers of a particular product necessitates a delineation of support that actually benefit upstream agricultural producers. This requires an allocation methodology.

14. Further, the narrow US interpretation is contradicted by Annex 3, paragraphs 7, 8, 12 and 13 of the Agreement on Agriculture, which include as "product-specific" many types of domestic support not tied to the production of a particular commodity.[21] Nor do the Agreement on Agriculture citations in paragraph 12 of the US 11 February 2004 Comments provide guidance as to where to draw the line for "non-product specific support".

15. While future negotiators may decide to clarify exactly what "product-specific" means in future revisions of the Agreement on Agriculture, the present text does not provide the "hard and fast" "production-requirement" subsidy rules advanced by the United States in this dispute. Indeed, Brazil notes that all commenting third parties in this dispute have stated their belief that the US counter-cyclical payments and crop insurance subsidies were "product-specific".[22] This suggests that the United States' trading partners do not agree that there is a "production-requirement" test for "product-specific support". Consistent with these third party views, there is nothing in the text of the Agreement on Agriculture to support a finding that "product-specific" is determined solely by the *de jure* form of the payment or by whether the payment is tied to the production of the crop. Nor does the Agreement on Agriculture support the US hard and fast "tied to production" test. Absent such guidance, the determination of whether agricultural support is specific or "general" is a *factual* issue that must be decided on a case-by-case basis.

---

[19] US 11 February 2004 Comments, para. 10.

[20] New Shorter Oxford Dictionary, Volume I, p. 1073 (definitions 1, 3, 4).

[21] Brazil's 22 August 2003 Rebuttal Submission, paras. 17-18 (illustrating that many non-green box measures considered as "product-specific" support do not contain "tied-to" production requirements). The United States never rebutted this argument.

[22] *See* New Zealand's 11 August 2003 Answer to Third Party Question 15; Argentina's 11 August 2003 Answer to Third Party Question 15 and 23 July 2003 Oral Statement, para. 8; EC's 11 August 2003 Answer to Third Party Question 15 *See* also Exhibit Bra-144 (G/AG/R/31, paras. 29-32).

16. The US 11 February 2004 Comments further state that "product-specific" and "non-product-specific" are disjunctive, and that Article 6.4 of the Agreement on Agriculture requires *de minimis* levels of support to be categorized into "product-specific" and "non-product-specific".[23] This is true, but begs the question of how and when to draw the line between product-specific and non-product-specific support. For example, the United States has argued that MY 2002 counter-cyclical payments for upland cotton are non-product specific.[24] But in MY 2002, upland cotton counter-cyclical payments of almost $1 billion were received by producers holding only 1.7 per cent of US farmland.[25] Brazil agrees with the EC, New Zealand, and Argentina that such payments are "partial, local or sectional" to particular US producers. [26] They are not provided "in general" to a broad group of US producers. Thus, they should be allocated as "product-specific support," including for purposes of an Article 6.4 *de minimis* analysis.

17. The United States argues that a single type of domestic support measure cannot be both "product-specific" and "non-product-specific" support.[27] Once again, the answer to this question would depend on the facts of the case. For example, if 95 per cent of the expenditures of a so-called decoupled payment ended up in the pockets of farmers producing a single commodity (such as upland cotton counter-cyclical payments), these facts would support the finding of product-specific support for that commodity. Whether the other nine commodities eligible to receive a similar type of payment were also receiving product-specific support would have to be decided on a case-by-case basis. Similarly, if a decoupled payment programme gave farmers the flexibility to grow four different crops, but these crops represented only 10 per cent of total commodity production in that Member, then the support for each of these crops might be considered to be "product-specific".

18. In sum, the use of the term "in general" in Article 1(b) of the Agreement on Agriculture implies that this is a question of fact, the answer to which depends on a host of factors, not a simplistic and non-textually based "tied to production" rule, as advanced by the United States. Any other interpretation would write text into the Agreement on Agriculture that is not there and was not agreed to by Members. As the comments of the EC, New Zealand and Argentina in this dispute vividly illustrate, there is not an universal understanding that product-specific support means only domestic support that is *de jure* tied to production. By defining "non-product-specific support" using the "in general" language, Members provided flexibility to examine, on an case-by-case basis, whether the domestic support was so linked to a handful of products that it could not be considered "non-product specific support".

---

23 US 11 February 2004 Comments, para. 12.

24 US 22 August 2003 Rebuttal Submission, paras. 86-88.

25 Brazil's 11 August 2003 Answers to Question 44, para. 62 (first and next to last bullets).

26 *See* New Zealand's 11 August 2003 Answer to Third Party Question 15; Argentina's 11 August 2003 Answer to Third Party Question 15 and 23 July 2003 Oral Statement, para. 8; EC's 11 August 2003 Answer to Third Party Question 15 *See* also Exhibit Bra-144 (G/AG/R/31, paras. 29-32).

27 US 11 February 2004 Comments, paras. 13-14.

19. Finally, Brazil does not believe that the Panel, in this dispute settlement proceeding, is required to interpret "product-specific" support to resolve the now-expired peace clause provisions of Article 13(b)(ii). The concept of "product-specific" continues to be a significant issue with respect to ongoing negotiations and in future interpretations of Members' obligations to comply with their "total AMS" requirements. Brazil's claims in this dispute do not challenge the "total AMS" of the United States. Brazil has never claimed that "AMS" must be interpreted in this dispute. The interpretative issues relating to the peace clause can and should be resolved by interpreting the terms actually used in that provision – "support to a specific commodity" – not by interpreting the term "product-specific" that the United States now seeks to substitute in place of a carefully negotiated text.

3. BRAZIL'S METHODOLOGY IS SUPPORTED BY UNDISPUTED EVIDENCE THAT THE CONTRACT PAYMENTS WERE ESSENTIAL TO MAINTAIN UPLAND COTTON PRODUCTION BETWEEN MY 1999-2002, AND, THUS, ARE SUPPORT TO UPLAND COTTON

20. The US critique of Brazil's methodology rests not only on an incorrect legal interpretation of "support to a specific commodity," but more fundamentally on its false assumption that contract payments do not support the production of upland cotton. This factual assumption permeates *all* of the 32 pages of the US 11 February 2004 Comments. It is articulated by asserting that the contract payments are "decoupled" or "not tied to" the production of upland cotton. Ultimately, the combination of these flawed legal interpretations and factual assumptions result in the equally flawed US assertion that its Annex IV methodology is the only way to allocate contract payments (albeit only for purposes of Part III of the SCM Agreement).

21. In evaluating which methodology to use to count contract payment as "support to cotton", the starting point is the necessary fact that all the contract payments at issue are non-green box support.[28] For example, direct payments and counter-cyclical payments are not properly considered "decoupled income support", within the *chapeau* of paragraph 6 of Annex 2 of the Agreement on Agriculture.[29] This means that each of the contract payments is linked (or coupled), to some extent, to the production of one or more agricultural commodities. In addition, prior to applying the methodology, it must have been determined that the non-green box measures are "support to a specific commodity".

22. Having demonstrated these first two steps, the next question is the "amount of the support" to a specific commodity. This is a factual question and requires assessing *to what extent* a particular non-green box subsidy supports or

---

[28] The Panel would not be able to count these programmes for purposes of Article 13(b)(ii) unless they are out of the green box, and thus, "non-green box" support.

[29] *See e.g.* Brazil's 24 June 2003 First Submission, Section 3.2.7 and 3.2.8; Brazil's 22 August 2003 Rebuttal Submission, Section 2.1.

maintains the production of a specific commodity or commodities. This initially requires an examination of the legal structure of the support mechanism. But more importantly, it requires an examination of the record evidence concerning the extent to which the payments *de facto* support or maintain the production of a specific commodity. Applied to this case, it means that the stronger the requirement for the contract payments to maintain (*i.e.,* cover the costs of) production of upland cotton, the more appropriate it is to use a methodology that treats each dollar of payments received directly by producers of upland cotton as "support to" upland cotton.

23. The US "Annex IV" methodology assumes that all four contract payments are not tied in any significant way to the production of upland cotton. The primary evidence relied on by the United States are the legal provisions of the 1996 FAIR Act and the 2002 FSRI Act, which permit "producers" to grow other crops (except fruits, vegetables and wild rice) and still receive the contract payments. The United States argued that the legally permitted "decoupled" form of the support requires the payment to be spread out over the entire value of a farm's production.[30] It is this assumption that underpins the US Annex IV methodology.

24. Calculating the amount of contract payments that is "support" to upland cotton by allocating the benefit of those payments across total production of farms receiving the payments might make sense *if* the four contract payments had, *in fact*, no significant role in maintaining the production of upland cotton. But the US methodology runs headlong into the overwhelming weight of the evidence showing a direct and significant link between "producers" receiving upland cotton contract payments and "producers" planting upland cotton. Brazil produced extensive evidence showing the link between these contract payments and the maintenance of upland cotton production.[31] Consider the following key uncontested facts:

- 96 per cent of MY 2002 upland cotton acreage was planted on farms that hold upland cotton base.[32] This demonstrates that the overwhelming majority of current US upland cotton production is planted on upland cotton base and shows that, in fact, direct and counter-cyclical payments are directly linked to current production.
- US upland cotton producers would have lost $332.79 per acre between MY 1997-2002 if they had not received upland cotton con-

30 *See* US 11 February 2004 Comments, para. 37-38.

31 Brazil's 9 October 2003 Closing Statement, Annex I (Summary of Evidence Demonstrating that Upland Cotton Producers in MY 1999-2002 Produced Upland Cotton on Upland Cotton, Rice, or Peanut Base Acreage); *see also* Brazil's 27 October 2003 Answers to Question 125(a), paras. 7-25; Brazil's 18 November 2003 Further Rebuttal Submission, Sections 2.1 and 3.1; Brazil's 2 December 2003 Oral Statement, paras. 25-27.

32 *See* Annex A, Section 1, para. 16. This figure might be slightly overstated by possible aggregation problems. However, Brazil notes that the total amount of upland cotton base on farms planting upland cotton and holding upland cotton base exceeds MY 2002 plantings by 800,000 (13.8 million acres v 13 million acres), suggesting that any aggregation problem for MY 2002 is not significant.

tract payments.[33] This demonstrates the critical role contract payments play in sustaining *production* of upland cotton during MY 1999-2002.

- Without direct and counter-cyclical payments in MY 2002, the average US cotton farmer would have lost 14.36 cents per pound. With these two payments, they earned a "profit" of 4.2 cents per pound with the cotton DP and CCP payments.[34]
- Producers growing crops on upland cotton acreage receive much higher per acre payments than all other "covered commodities", except rice. The higher per acre payments are directly related to the higher costs to produce cotton compared to other crops.[35] This fact highlights the *expectation* that former producers would continue to be present producers.[36] This is an expectation that is a reality, since 96 per cent of upland cotton farmers do plant upland cotton on high per-acre payment upland cotton base acreage.
- Upland cotton producers in MY 2002 received $446.8 million in upland cotton direct payments, representing a subsidization rate of 13.1 per cent.[37]
- Upland cotton producers in MY 2002 received $986.4 million in upland cotton counter-cyclical payments, representing a subsidization rate of 28.9 per cent. [38]
- The amount of US planted cotton acreage has shown only relatively small shifts over the past ten years regardless of market price movements, confirming the influence of the contract payments in maintaining large volumes of production.[39] This evidence is consistent with NCC testimony and USDA data showing that most upland cotton farmers do not shift out of specializing in upland cotton production towards the production of other crops to any great extent.[40]
- NCC officials repeatedly stated that their cotton farmer members cannot produce upland cotton without contract payments, and they

---

33 Brazil's 2 December 2003 Oral Statement, paras 25-27 *and* Exhibit Bra-353.

34 Brazil's 22 August 2003 Rebuttal Submission, paras. 39-41.

35 Brazil's 18 November 2003 Further Rebuttal Submission, para. 70 and Exhibit Bra-324 (NCC Chairman's Report by Kenneth Hood, 24 July 2002, p. 2)..

36 *See* Brazil's 9 September 2003 Further Submission, para. 344 and Exhibit Bra-109 (Testimony (Full) of Robert McLendon, Chairman, NCC Executive Committee, before the House Agriculture Committee, National Cotton Council, p. 5-7) arguing for higher upland cotton loan rates and "decoupled commodity payment rate[s]."

37 *See* Annex A, Section 1, Table 1.5. *See* Table 3.8 for the total value of the upland cotton crop on all farms producing upland cotton.

38 *Ibid.*

39 *See* Brazil's 27 October 2003 Answers to Questions, paras. 35-36; Brazil's 18 November 2003 Further Rebuttal Submission, paras. 81-88.

40 Brazil's 9 October 2003 Closing Statement, Annex I (Summary of Evidence Demonstrating that Upland Cotton Producers in MY 1999-2002 Produced Upland Cotton on Upland Cotton, Rice, or Peanut Base Acreage, paras. 9-12.

have always treated contract payments as an integral part of an overall subsidy package of support for upland cotton production.[41]

25. In addition to the above, the provisions of the 2002 FSRI Act are evidence that upland cotton contract payments were intended to support the production of upland cotton. First, Section 1104(c)(1)(F) of the 2002 FSRI Act sets a "target price" for upland cotton of 72.4 cents per pound, which guarantees high revenues in much the same way that deficiency payments worked before MY 1996. This upland cotton-specific "target price" was requested by the NCC in 2001 and exists to support upland cotton – not the production of other crops. The cotton target price results in much higher per acre counter-cyclical payments for upland cotton than other crops (except rice). Second, Sections 1103(a) and 1104(a) require payments to current producers growing on covered crop base acreage. In other words, Congress intended that only farmers actually planting crops (or sharing the risk of planting a crop if one would have been produced) would directly receive the payments. Third, Section 1103(b) of the 2002 FSRI Act establishes very high direct payment rates for upland cotton base relative to other "covered commodities"[42]

26. The facts set out above are crucial for understanding why the US "Annex IV" methodology rests on a completely false assumption. That assumption is that US producers of upland cotton do not need or rely on the full amount of upland cotton payments to cover their long-term losses from the production of *upland cotton*. The United States implements this assumption by proposing that the *only* methodology that can be used is one that would spread the entire amount of the contract payments across the total value of an upland cotton farmer's production. But the record shows conclusively that most upland cotton farmers simply could not produce upland cotton profitably in MY 1999-2002 without using all contract payments they demanded and received for their upland cotton production.

27. The US 11 February 2004 Comments argue that Brazil's methodology for counting support to upland cotton makes "no economic sense".[43] But it is the US Annex IV methodology, as applied to contract payments to US upland cotton producers, that makes no economic sense. For example, if upland cotton farmers were, in fact, using these payments to support unprofitable dairy, livestock, or fish farming operations, then they would have lost money on their upland cotton production. The fact that US producers were able to grow any upland cotton at all in MY 2002 after four straight years of huge "losses" (totalling $872 per acre by MY 2002,[44] comparing production costs and market revenue) demonstrates conclusively the production-sustaining effects of these subsidies.[45] Indeed, the continued high levels of plantings in MY 2002 despite these losses are strong

---

41 Exhibits Bra-3, 108, 109, 111 and 252. Brazil's 9 October 2003 Closing Statement, Annex I (Summary of Evidence Demonstrating that Upland Cotton Producers in MY 1999-2002 Produced Upland Cotton on Upland Cotton, Rice, or Peanut Base Acreage, paras. 14-19.

42 *See* Exhibit Bra-29 (2002 FSRI Act).

43 US 11 February 2004 Comments, para. 37.

44 Brazil's 27 October 2003 Answers to Questions, paras. 35-36

45 Without contract payments, US producers would have lost $332.79 per acre over the 6-year period. Brazil's 2 December 2003 Oral Statement, paras. 25-27 *and* Exhibit Bra-353.

evidence that upland cotton producers did in fact (a) receive, and (b) use upland cotton contract payments to sustain their upland cotton production during MY 1999-2002. If not, US upland production would have been far lower, as farmers simply could not have survived economically. Thus, the US assumption in its "Annex IV" methodology that producers did not need or use upland cotton payments to sustain high-cost upland cotton production is simply wrong.

28. By contrast, Brazil's methodology properly reflects the economic reality of the key role these payments played in sustaining US upland cotton production in MY 1999-2002. Brazil, like the NCC, believes that the contract payments were necessary for the maintenance and the survival of US upland cotton production during MY 1999-2002.[46] In keeping with the key role that upland cotton contract payments played in sustaining upland cotton production, the principal element of Brazil's methodology focuses only on upland cotton contract payments made to producers of upland cotton. Such "cotton to cotton" payments represent the vast bulk of contract payments received by upland cotton producers. For example, under Brazil's methodology, 99.1 per cent of the MY 2002 direct payments received by upland cotton producers were upland cotton payments.[47] Similarly, under Brazil's methodology, 99.8 per cent of the MY 2002 counter-cyclical payments received by upland cotton producers were upland cotton payments.[48] Treating all of these "cotton to cotton" payments as support to upland cotton is fully supported by the essential role these cotton payments play in sustaining US upland cotton production.

29. The second (and relatively minor) part of Brazil's methodology is to account for the non-upland cotton contract payments received by current upland cotton producers. These non-upland cotton base payments represented a tiny 0.9 per cent in MY 2002 of the total direct payments allocated to upland cotton under Brazil's methodology, and 0.2 per cent in MY 2002 of the counter-cyclical payments allocated to upland cotton under Brazil's methodology. This small part of Brazil's methodology first pools any contract payments received for base acres not planted to their respective base crop and then distributes them as support to these contract payment crops according to their share of total "overplanted" base acreage on the farm.

30. The facts show that it is appropriate for Brazil to allocate these payments over the plantings of the other "covered commodities" produced by an upland cotton producer. Brazil demonstrated that, for each of the marketing years from 2000-2002, an upland cotton producer growing upland cotton on *non*-contract acreage would have suffered considerable losses.[49] Even growing on non-upland cotton (except rice) base acreage would have resulted in losses during most of the period of investigation.[50] Therefore, the relatively few upland cotton produc-

46 Brazil's 24 June 2003 First Submission, para. 1.

47 *See* Annex A.2, Tables 2.9, 2.21 and 2.21.

48 *See* Annex A.2, Tables 2.9, 2.20 and 2.21.

49 Brazil's 27 October 2003 Answers to Question 125(c), paras. 15-25; Brazil's 22 August 2003 Rebuttal Submission, paras. 39-44, and 30-31.

50 *Ibid.*

ers planting on some other type of base acreage needed and relied on the non-upland cotton payments to come close to making a profit. Without such payments, the average producer would have not been able to sustain upland cotton production.

31. In addition, the allocation across all contract crops (as opposed to all farm products produced) is justified by the evidence of the "specific" nature of the "covered commodity" payments. The United States never contested Brazil's evidence or argument that the contract payments are "specific" subsidies within the meaning of the SCM Agreement. For example, the United States never rebutted evidence that the 2002 FSRI Act "covered commodities" represented only 24 per cent of the value of US farm receipts (and 30 per cent of US farm acreage) in MY 2002, and that the 1996 FAIR Act "programme crops" represented less than 14 per cent of the value of US crops (and 22 per cent of the acreage) during MY 1999-2001.[51] Nor did the United States ever rebut any of the numerous statements of the users and recipients of the contract payments – the NCC – that they needed and received contract payments to survive.[52]

32. In sum, the proper allocation methodology under Article 13(b)(ii) of the Agreement on Agriculture must be consistent with the extent to which the domestic support payments directly maintain the production of a specific commodity. Brazil's methodology reflects the crucial role that each of the four contract payments plays in maintaining the production of US upland cotton. By contrast, the US "Annex IV" methodology assumes incorrectly that these payments do not support upland cotton any more than they support catfish farming or other production activities on an upland cotton farm. For the above reasons, Brazil requests that the Panel reject the US arguments, and adopt Brazil's methodology for allocating the contract payments.

4. A METHODOLOGY TO COUNT CONTRACT PAYMENTS IS APPROPRIATE BASED ON THE TEXT OF ARTICLE 13(B)(II) OF THE AGREEMENT ON AGRICULTURE

33. The United States criticizes Brazil's methodology (and presumably any other methodology) because it is not based in the "text" of the peace clause or the Agreement on Agriculture.[53] Instead, the United States argues that the Panel should use Annex IV of the SCM Agreement as the basis for its calculation of the amount of the contract payments.[54]

---

51 Brazil's 22 August 2003 Rebuttal Submission, paras. 24-25; Brazil's 9 September Further Submission, paras. 46, 55.

52 *See e.g.* Brazil's 22 July 2003 Oral Statement, paras 52-53, 58-60; Brazil's 24 June 2003 First Submission, para. 1; Brazil's 18 November 2003 Further Rebuttal Submission, para. 25, 70, 102.

53 US 11 February 2004 Comments, para. 8.

54 The United States argues that its methodology can only be used in connection with Part III of the SCM Agreement, not the Agreement on Agriculture. (*See e.g.* US 11 February 2004 Comments, paras. 2, 86).

34. Article 13(b)(ii) of the Agreement on Agriculture does not provide explicit guidance on how to count up the amount of support for contract or any other type of payments.[55] But that does not mean that no counting methodology can be used. The absence of explicit guidance on implementing more general provisions has not stopped WTO panels or parties from proposing and using methodologies to tabulate the amount of subsidies, costs, and volumes of trade impacted.

35. The Panel only need to look as far as the export credit guarantee arguments in this dispute as an example. Item (j) establishes that export credit guarantee programmes constitute export subsidies if they are operated at premium rates that are inadequate to cover the long-term operating costs and losses of the programmes.[56] There is no explicit methodology provided in the text of item (j) that would define how to apply this provision. Yet, the United States has repeatedly argued for the application of a cash-basis accounting methodology to tabulate the amount of costs and losses.

36. Similarly, DSU Article 22.7 requires any suspension of concessions to be "equivalent to the level of nullification or impairment". As with Article 13(b)(ii) of the Agreement on Agriculture, this requires the tabulation of amounts – in the case of Article 22.7, the amounts of trade impacted through the non-implementation of WTO-inconsistent measures. Again, there is no methodology provided in Article 22.7 to assess the level of nullification or impairment. Nevertheless, arbitrators, at the urging, *inter alia,* of the United States, have applied DSU Article 22.7 using a variety of methodologies developed on a case-by-case basis to assess the level of nullification or impairment.[57]

37. Finally, other provisions of the WTO Agreement similarly require WTO Members, as a practical matter, to implement general obligations by applying different valuation and allocation methodologies under general Anti-Dumping Agreement and the SCM Agreement rules.[58]

38. The United States argues that only Annex IV of the SCM Agreement offers any useful context. While it derides Brazil's methodology as being "invented", a close look at the text of Article IV reveals that it is ill-equipped to address the tabulation of support issue before the Panel. Annex IV, which is enti-

---

[55] Nor does Annex IV, as discussed in Section 4 below.

[56] Brazil also claims that the export credit guarantee programmes constitute export subsidies under the terms of Articles 1.1. and 3.1(a) of the SCM Agreement.

[57] Arbitrator Report, *EC – Bananas (US)*, WT/DS27/ARB; Arbitrator Report, *EC – Bananas (Ecuador)*, WT/DS27/ARB; Arbitrator Report, *EC – Hormones (US, Canada)*, WT/DS26/ARB and WT/DS48/ARB; Arbitrator Report, *Brazil – Aircraft*, WT/DS46/ARB; Arbitrator Report, *US – FSC*, WT/DS108/ARB; Arbitrator Report, *Canada – Aircraft II*, WT/DS222/ARB.

[58] *See e.g.* Appellate Body Report, *US – Lumber CVDs Final*, WT/DS257/AB/R, paras. 155-166 (Appellate Body affirmed panel's finding that a "pass-through" methodology analysis must be performed by investigating authorities to determine the amount of subsidies benefiting down-stream purchases of subsidized products; this was despite the fact that no specific methodology for pass through was explicitly set out in Articles 10 and 32.1 of the SCM Agreement); Panel Report, *US – Sheet/Plate from Korea*, WT /DS179/R, paras. 6.135-36 (finding USDOC methodology applying multiple averaging periods during the investigation appropriate to implement "fair comparison" standard of Article 2.4 of the Anti-Dumping Agreement).

tled "Calculation of the Total *Ad Valorem* Subsidization (Paragraph 1(a) of Article 6)" deals – as the title indicates – with the calculation of subsidization rates, within the meaning of Article 6.1(a) of the SCM Agreement. However, the "support to cotton" question before this Panel is *not* establishing an *ad valorem* subsidization rate, but rather the calculation of the *amount of support* to upland cotton, within the meaning of Article 13(b)(ii) of the SCM Agreement.

39. But setting aside the problem that Annex IV deals with calculation of a subsidization rate, the US contract payments at issue in this dispute are *de facto* tied to upland cotton production. Thus, Annex IV paragraph 3 would be implicated, *i.e.,* the subsidization rate is determined by *dividing the total amount of the tied contract payment* subsidies by the total value of upland cotton sales. But this presupposes that the amount of the payments subsidies is known. Thus, Annex IV does not answer the crucial question how to determine the amount of the *de facto* tied contract payments that constitute support to upland cotton. Instead, it only offers a methodology to calculate the *subsidization rate* for known amounts of subsidies.

40. Indeed, Annex IV itself recognizes that there are holes in its provisions, stipulating in footnote 62 to Annex IV that "[a]n understanding among Members should be developed, as necessary, on matters which are not specified in this Annex or which need further clarification for purposes of paragraph 1(a) of Article 6". One such matter could have been the scope of the meaning of "tied to the production or sale of a given product". Must the "tie to production" be *de jure* as the United States argues, or *de facto* as Brazil asserts? But no understanding or clarification of this, or any other issue relating to Annex IV, was agreed to by Members prior to the expiration of Annex IV in 2000.

41. Thus, Annex IV does not assist the Panel in determining the amount of support to upland cotton, within the meaning of Article 13(b)(ii) of the Agreement on Agriculture. Contrary to the US arguments, paragraph 2 of Annex IV is inapplicable because the subsidies at issue are *de facto* tied to upland cotton production. Further, paragraph 3 of Annex IV does not provide any guidance on how to calculate the amount of the subsidy which is the goal of the Article 13(b)(ii) exercise.

42. In conclusion, it is incorrect to assert that the absence of any specific methodology precludes the Panel from applying one for the purposes of Article 13(b)(ii). It is also incorrect to claim that Annex IV provides definitive guidance, because it could only be useful for establishing a rate of subsidization, and not for calculating the amount of the subsidy. Thus, as with its item (j) analysis, the Panel needs to adopt a reasonable methodology to be applied for purposes of the peace clause in assessing the amount of support to upland cotton from the four contract payment programmes. This methodology must reflect the facts in the record and be consistent with the text, context and object and purpose of Article 13(b)(ii). As Brazil has argued, its methodology – or some variant of its methodology such as the cotton-to-cotton methodology – is reasonable given the key

role that contract payments played in the maintenance of upland cotton production during MY 1999-2002.[59]

5. THE EVIDENCE IN THE RECORD SUPPORTS A FINDING, UNDER ANY METHODOLOGY, THAT THE UNITED STATES' LEVEL OF SUPPORT PROVIDED IN MY 1999-2002 EXCEEDED THE AMOUNT OF SUPPORT DECIDED IN MY 1992

43. Brazil responds in this section to the US 11 February 2004 Comments asserting that Brazil has not established that the amount of "support to upland cotton" in MY 1999-2002 is greater than the support decided in MY 1992.[60] Brazil's basic response to these arguments is that even if the United States does not produce the farm-specific information by 3 March 2004, the Panel has before it sufficient evidence, including the evidence of any adverse inferences, to establish the amount of four contract payments for MY 1999-2002. The less-than-ideal data analyzed below confirms, in the first instance, Brazil's 14/16th methodology. Moreover, even if the Panel were to rely directly on the figures generated below from the application of Brazil's methodology, the US Annex IV methodology and a variation of each of those methodologies to the incomplete US data,[61] these figures support a finding that the US support to upland cotton in MY 1999-2002 exceeded the level decided in MY 1992.

44. Brazil's analysis of the data below is necessary because Brazil's 28 January 2004 original analysis of the incomplete US data submitted on 18/19 December 2003 did not include additional data the United States recognized[62] it failed to produce on 18/19 December 2003, and subsequently produced on 28 January 2004. Brazil has made certain adjustments to respond to criticisms of the United States. Further, to assist the Panel, Brazil presents the calculations from a minor variation of Brazil's methodology and of the US Annex IV methodology. In the final analysis, these various methodologies are "tools" (not "claims") that assist the Panel in making an objective assessment of the US data and other evi-

---

[59] *See* Section 3, *supra*. The fact that the great majority of upland cotton is planted on upland cotton base (86.34 per cent in MY 1999, 82.05 per cent in MY 2000, 80.10 percent in MY 2001 and 96.17 per cent in MY 2002) lends considerable support for this conclusion. These amounts are calculated as the share of upland cotton production planted on farms holding upland cotton base (up to the amount of upland cotton base) of total upland cotton plantings. MY 1999-2001 data are taken from category "1" farms and total upland cotton planting from the rPFCsum.xls file provided by the United States on 28 January 2004. Data for MY 2002 is taken from "Enrolled in Cotton PFC and planted cotton" farms and total upland cotton plantings from the rDCPsum.xls file provided by the United States on 28 January 2004.

[60] *See* US 11 February 2004 Comments, paras. 15-17. This section also responds to the US comments that Brazil has not established a *prima facie* case of the amount of the contract payment subsidies for the purpose of its serious prejudice claims.

[61] Brazil recalls that even the revised US summary data produced on 28 January 2004 suffers from aggregation problems and falls short of enabling the Panel and Brazil to account for soybean market loss assistance and peanut direct and counter-cyclical payments in its allocations. *See* Section 3 of Brazil's 28 January 2004 Comments and Requests Regarding US Data.

[62] US 28 January 2004 Letter to the Panel and accompanying CD-Rom.

dence before it for purposes of making a peace clause finding (and, if the Panel deems this necessary, the amount of subsidization for Brazil's serious prejudice claims).

45. Below, Brazil presents its updated results of the two methodologies applied in Sections 9 and 10 of its 28 January 2004 Comments and Requests Regarding US Data. This update is based on the revised US data provided by the United States on 28 January 2004.[63] For detailed calculations, Brazil refers the Panel to Annex A to this submission.

Cotton-to-Cotton Methodology

46. Brazil first presents the results of using a slight variation of Brazil's methodology. Brazil notes the US arguments that only upland cotton contract payments could be included in any "support to" upland cotton. Counting only upland cotton payments would undercount the amount of contract support, as Brazil argues in Section 9, *infra.* [64] But even though it undercounts the amount of support, a methodology that examines only "cotton-to-cotton" payments is supported by the evidence in the record described in Section 3 *supra*, including the fact that in MY 2002 96 per cent of upland cotton was planted on upland cotton base acreage.[65]

47. Brazil sets out the results of examining only the upland cotton contract payments received by producers planting upland cotton for MY 1999-2002 in Table 1.5 below:[66]

Annex A Table 1.5

Cotton-to-Cotton Methodology [67]				
MY	PFC Payments	MLA Payments	Direct Payments	CCP Payments
1999	$515,310,673.4	$512,801,043.5	-	-
2000	$482,422,346.0	$513,554,489.0	-	-
2001	$387,916,892.8	$535,792,287.0	-	-
2002	-	-	$446,796,377.9	$986,357,993.8

48. As Brazil described in its 28 January 2004 Comments, the results of this analysis may be distorted somewhat because the revised US summary data does

[63] *See* US 28 January Letter to the Panel.

[64] US 11 February 2004 Comments, paras. 47-51. *See* also US 28 January 2004 Comments, paras. 34-52, 208.

[65] Calculated as the share of upland cotton production planted on farms holding upland cotton base (up to the amount of upland cotton base) of total upland cotton plantings. MY 1999-2001 data are taken from category "1" farms and total upland cotton planting from the rPFCsum.xls file provided by the United States on 28 January 2004. Data for MY 2002 is taken from "Enrolled in Cotton PFC and planted cotton" farms and total upland cotton plantings from the rDCPsum.xls file provided by the United States on 28 January 2004.

[66] This is because only in MY 2002 was less acreage planted to upland cotton than the total amount of upland cotton base acreage held by farms producing upland cotton and holding upland cotton base. In MY 1999-2001, the amount of upland cotton acreage slightly exceeded the amount of upland cotton base. This phenomenon is the effect of the base update allowed for under the 2002 FSRI Act.

[67] For details of the calculations, see Annex A.1.

not control for aggregation problems.[68] However, given the fact that the United States can be deemed to know the amount of payments from a cotton-to-cotton match, any continued refusal of the United States to produce the data should permit the Panel to infer that the data outlined above is accurate.

Brazil's Methodology

49. Brazil also presents the results of applying its proposed methodology. However, given the absence of farm-specific information, Brazil can present only a modified version of its proposed methodology, as discussed in more detail in its 20 January 2004 Answers to Additional Questions[69] and applied in its 28 January 2004 Comments and Requests Regarding US Data.[70] The data presented below updates Brazil's earlier calculations by using the 28 January 2004 revised US summary data that includes information on contract payments to farms not holding upland cotton base but producing upland cotton.[71] The following table shows the results of applying Brazil's allocation methodology to the revised US summary data.[72]

Table 2.21

Brazil's Methodology				
MY	PFC Payments	MLA Payments	Direct Payments	CCP Payments
1999	$574,488,456.1	$571,690,622.7	-	-
2000	$538,079,545.3	$572,803,412.3	-	-
2001	$428,007,676.4	$591,165,829.7	-	-
2002	-	-	$450,924,339.1	$988,252,054.4

Modified US Annex IV methodology

50. Brazil also applied the revised US summary data to a modified "Annex IV" methodology allocating total contract payments to farms producing upland cotton over the value of *contract payment* crops produced on these farms. This methodology is based on two assumptions: first, contract payments are support only to contract payment crops; and second, contract payments are allocated pursuant to the value of these contract crops' production on upland cotton producing farms.

---

[68] Brazil notes that the US summary data requested by the Panel on 3 February 2004 (part (b) of the Panel's Request for Information under DSU Article 13) would not result in aggregation problems tainting the results, nor would farm-specific data withheld by the United States and requested by Brazil on 3 December 2003 and by the Panel on 8 December 2003, 12 January 2004 and 3 February 2004 (part (a) of the Panel's Request for Information under DSU Article 13).

[69] *See* Brazil's 20 January 2004 Answers to Additional Questions, paras. 43-55.

[70] *See* Section 9 of Brazil's 28 January 2004 Comments and Requests Regarding US Data.

[71] Calculations based on this data continue to suffer from aggregation problems and the missing information on soybean contract payments and peanut direct and counter-cyclical payments to farms producing upland cotton. (*See* Section 3 of Brazil's 28 January 2004 Comments and Requests Regarding US Data).

[72] For details of the calculations, see Annex A.2.

51. Brazil believes that this methodology is not appropriate because it improperly undercounts the amount of support provided to maintain the production of upland cotton. Nevertheless, the analysis of this methodology permits the Panel to assess the impact of different assumptions on the amount of contract payments allocated. Further, because the "cotton-to-cotton" and "Brazil's" methodologies are supported by the strong link between contract payments and maintaining upland cotton production, the same evidence would more than support the modified Annex IV methodology. The following table shows the results of this allocation methodology. Brazil notes these figures are understated due to the fact that the United States did not provide any data concerning soybean market loss assistance payments and peanut direct and counter-cyclical payments.[73]

Annex A Table 3.10

Modified Annex IV Methodology				
MY	PFC Payments	MLA Payments	Direct Payments	CCP Payments
1999	$576,544,351.0	$573,736,505.1	-	-
2000	$546,052,507.2	$581,290,893.0	-	-
2001	$399,648,260.3	$551,995,696.4	-	-
2002	-	-	$431,923,303.9	$722,082,667.7

US Annex IV Methodology

52. Finally, Brazil has applied the revised US summary data to the US-proposed methodology – updating the calculations presented in Section 10 of Brazil's 28 January 2004 Comments and Requests Regarding US Data. The data presented here updates Brazil's earlier calculations by using the 28 January 2004 revised US summary data that includes information on contract payments to farms not holding upland cotton base but producing upland cotton.[74] The following table shows the results of applying the US-proposed allocation methodology to the revised US summary data.[75]

Annex A Table 4.8

US Annex IV Methodology				
MY	PFC Payments	MLA Payments	Direct Payments	CCP Payments
1999	$440,061,035.8	$437,917,881.4	-	-
2000	$432,996,788.7	$460,939,354.1	-	-
2001	$304,243,319.2	$420,222,029.1	-	-
2002	-	-	$383,057,256.1	$640,389,168.2

[73] For details of the calculations, see Annex A.3.

[74] Calculations based on this data continue to suffer from aggregation problems and the missing information on soybean contract payments and peanut direct and counter-cyclical payments to farms producing upland cotton. (*See* Section 3 of Brazil's 28 January 2004 Comments and Requests Regarding US Data).

[75] For details of the calculations, see Annex A.4.

53. For purposes of comparison, Brazil reproduces the results of its "14/16th" methodology, as presented to the Panel at paragraphs 8 of Brazil's 22 December 2003 Answers to Questions and Brazil's 9 September 2003 Further Submission.

Results of Brazil's 14/16th Methodology				
MY	PFC Payments	MLA Payments	Direct Payments	CCP Payments
1999	$547,800,000	$545,100,000	-	-
2000	$541,300,000	$576,200,000	-	-
2001	$453,000,000	$625,700,000	-	-
2002	-	-	$454,500,000	$935,600,000

54. Brazil notes that the results from each of the four methodologies applied to the revised US summary data suffer from shortcomings due to the incomplete and non-farm-specific data. Brazil would have to re-calculate all of these numbers if the United States produces the actual data on 3 March 2004. As it stands, the data currently available undercounts the support under each of the methodologies (except the cotton-to-cotton), because no information on soybean market loss assistance payments and peanut direct and counter-cyclical payments to farms producing upland cotton was provided by the United States. Further, due to the manner in which the US data is provided, distortions from the aggregation of farm-specific data possibly over- or under-state the results, as discussed in Section 6 below. Therefore, Brazil remains of the view that in the absence of complete farm-specific aggregated data, the Panel should rely on Brazil's 14/16th methodology.

55. While Brazil does not believe that the Panel should rely on either the two Annex IV-type methodologies, or even the "cotton-to-cotton" methodology, it is noteworthy that all four of the methodologies show that the United States does not enjoy peace clause protection.[76] The table below shows the results of the comparison of US support to upland cotton decided in MY 1992 with US support to upland cotton provided in MY 2002. Under any methodology, the US support to upland cotton in MY 2002 exceeds the support decided in MY 1992 considerably – by at least $464 million.

[76] Only under methodology (4) in MY 2000 is the support provided in that marketing year below the support decided in MY 1992.

Budgetary Outlays For Upland Cotton MY 1992, 2002[77]

Year / Programme	1992	2002 (1)	2002 (2)	2002 (3)	2002 (4)	2002 (5)
	- $ million -					
Deficiency Payments	1017.4	None	none	none	none	none
Direct Payments	none	466.8	450.9	432.9	383.1	454.5
CCP Payments	none	986.4	988.3	722.1	640.4	935.6
Marketing Loan Gains and LDP Payments[78]	866	898	898	898	898	898
Step 2 Payment	207	415	415	415	415	415
Crop Insurance	26.6	194.1	194.1	194.1	194.1	194.1
Cottonseed Payments	none	50	50	50	50	50
Total	**2,117.0**	**2,990.3**	**2,996.3**	**2,711.1**	**2,580.6**	**2,947.2**

(1) Cotton-to-Cotton Methodology
(2) Brazil's Methodology
(3) Modified Annex IV Methodology
(4) US Annex IV Methodology
(5) Brazil's 14/16th Methodology

56. Brazil presents the tabulations for MY 1999-2001 in Annex B. These data show that the United States also exceeds the MY 1992 limits under each of the four methodologies (except for methodology (4) in MY 2000) and under Brazil's 14/16th methodology.[79]

6. THE US CRITIQUE OF BRAZIL'S ALLOCATION METHODOLOGY IS BASELESS

57. Brazil recalls that its methodology allocates support paid for upland cotton base that is "planted to" upland cotton. It further allocates proportionally any other contract crop base payments that are not allocated to plantings of the respective contract payments crop.[80] Brazil's methodology, as well as the "cotton-to-cotton" methodology, generates results that are very close to Brazil's 14/16th methodology. This is not surprising since the 14/16th methodology is based on

[77] The table below reproduces the table at paragraph 73 of Brazil's 22 August 2003 Rebuttal Submission as updated by paragraph 8 of Brazil's 22 December 2003 Answers to Questions and paragraphs 12-14 of the US 22 December 2004 Answers to Questions. Step 2 and marketing loan payments have been updated in light of the US answer to Question 196. *See* US 22 December 2004 Answers to Questions, para. 12.

[78] "Other Payments" have been included in the marketing loan figures.

[79] Besides conclusively demonstrating that the US non-green box domestic support measures are not exempt from action by virtue of Article 13(b)(ii) of the Agreement on Agriculture, the table above, as well as the tables in Annex B, indicate the amount of subsidization of upland cotton by contract payments. Thus, should the Panel consider that an allocation methodology is warranted under Part III of the SCM Agreement, the record provides the factual basis for a finding that Brazil has met its burden of proof and established a *prima facie* case of the amount of subsidization.

[80] Brazil's 20 January 2004 Answers to Additional Questions, para. 43-55 and Brazil's 28 January 2004 Comments and Requests Regarding US Data, Section 9.

the assumption of very high percentages of upland cotton "planted on" upland cotton base acreage. All three of these methodologies reflect the economic reality in MY 1999-2002 that each allocated contract dollar received by upland cotton producers over a four-year period was needed to cover the costs of producing upland cotton. The fact that the vast majority of upland cotton was actually planted on upland cotton base is further confirmation of the reasonableness of these three methodologies.

58. Much of the US criticism of Brazil's methodology is tainted by the wrong assumption that contract payments provide "decoupled income support".[81] For example, the United States states, at paragraph 38 of its 11 February 2004 Comments, that "fundamentally, Brazil's approach is in error because it assumes that there is a tie between the decoupled payments and current production". The United States is correct – Brazil's methodologies do make that assumption, for the very good reason that that assumption reflects the economic cost realities and the cotton-to-cotton planting on the ground, discussed in Section 3 *supra.* Similarly, the United States claims, at paragraph 37 of its comments, that "decoupled payments by their nature provide income support not tied to the production or sale of any given commodity". But this ignores the vast weight of the evidence, which demonstrates the link between upland cotton production and upland cotton base acre payments (and other payments) in MY 1999-2002.

59. The United States raises a number of hypothetical "problems" with Brazil's methodology.[82] But the extent of any such problems, if any, can only be assessed by examining the actual farm-specific data. It is not credible for the United States to refuse to produce key farm-specific data and then speculate about potential problems for individual farms. Upon receipt of the US response to the Panel's request, Brazil looks forward to providing the Panel with such an analysis.

60. A principle complaint of the United States is that Brazil's allocation of *non-upland cotton contract payments* results in differential subsidization rates on different acres planted to upland cotton.[83] Similarly, the United States criticizes Brazil for potentially allocating more than one *non-upland cotton* base acre payments to one planted acre of upland cotton.[84] Both of these alleged problems with the allocation of non-upland cotton contract payments do not exist for MY 2002. This is because Brazil's methodology allocates for each planted acres of upland cotton only one upland cotton base acre payment.[85] In MY 2002, the vast majority of contract payments allocated as support to upland cotton are upland cotton contract payments. In MY 2002, 99.1 per cent of direct payments[86] and

---

81 *See inter alia* US 11 February 2004 Comments, paras. 37. *See* also US 28 January 2004 Comments, paras. 217, 219, 222-223.

82 US 11 February 2004 Comments, paras. 37-42.

83 US 11 February 2004 Comments, para. 37.

84 US 11 February 2004 Comments, para. 38-42.

85 The United States has not criticized Brazil's allocation of one payments on one contract payment base acres to one planted acre of cotton and the other contract payment crops. In other word, the United States accepts that the one-to-one allocation between planted and base acres.

86 *See* Annex A.2, Tables 2.9, 2.21 and 2.21.

99.8 per cent of the counter-cyclical payments[87] received by upland cotton producers were upland cotton contract payments. This is because the vast majority of upland cotton is grown on farms holding upland cotton base, which in MY 2002 exceeds acreage planted to upland cotton. Farms growing upland cotton but not holding upland cotton base accounted for only 0.9 and 0.2 per cent of total allocated direct and counter-cyclical payments respectively. Since the two main US criticisms affect only the allocation of non-upland cotton contract payments, they affect, at most, 0.9 per cent of the payments at issue for MY 2002.[88]

61. Brazil notes that the "cotton-to-cotton" methodology, discussed in Section 5, does not allocate any non-upland cotton base payments. Therefore, none of the US criticisms, at paragraphs 37-42 of its 11 February 2004 Comments, affects the "cotton-to-cotton" results for MY 1999-2002. Thus, these results reflect the worst case scenario of any alleged over-counting in Brazil's methodology. Comparing the results of both methodologies, reproduced in Section 5 and Annex B demonstrates that even under the "cotton-to-cotton" methodology the Unites States surpasses its peace clause limits. The tables below reproduce the results of both methodologies:

Cotton-to-Cotton Methodology (Table 1.5 of Annex A.1)

MY	PFC Payments	MLA Payments[89]	Direct Payments	CCP Payments
1999	$515,310,673.4	$512,801,043.5	-	-
2000	$482,422,346.0	$513,554,489.0	-	-
2001	$387,916,892.8	$535,792,287.0	-	-
2002	-	-	$446,796,377.9	$986,357,993.8

Brazil's Methodology (Table 2.21 of Annex A.2)

MY	PFC Payments	MLA Payments[90]	Direct Payments	CCP Payments
1999	$574,488,456.1	$571,690,622.7	-	-
2000	$538,079,545.3	$572,803,412.3	-	-
2001	$428,007,676.4	$591,165,829.7	-	-
2002	-	-	$450,924,339.1	$988,252,054.4

87 *See* Annex A.2, Tables 2.9, 2.20 and 2.21.

88 The United States has not criticized Brazil's allocation of one payments on one contract payment base acres to one planted acre of cotton and the other contract payment crops. In other word, the United States accepts that the one-to-one allocation between planted and base acres.

89 Market Loss Assistance Payments are calculated as PFC payments multiplied by the ratio of upland cotton market loss assistance payments to upland cotton PFC payments, as contained in Exhibit Bra-4 ("Fact Sheet: Upland Cotton", USDA, January 2003, p. 6). Since payment rates are not available directly, this ratio provides the information because both subsidies are paid based off the same payment units. Brazil notes that the market loss assistance payment amounts are understated by the non-allocated amount of soybean market loss assistance payments for which the United States has not produced any information.

90 *Ibid.*

62. As the Panel can readily see, the differences in the results of both methodologies are minor (with $118 million in MY 1999, $114 million in MY 2000, $95.5 million in MY 2001, and $5.7 million in MY 2002).

63. In addressing the specific US criticism affecting MY 1999-2001, Brazil notes that its methodology involves analysing the planting patterns and base acres of individual farms. Each farm is unique. Some farms will have greater base acres than planted acres and *vice versa.* Some farms will plant different crops than they used to establish their base acres, and, as in the case of most upland cotton farms, they will continue to plant upland cotton holding upland cotton base acres. Brazil's methodology accounts for all contract payments as support to contract crops planted on farms holding base. This means that some farms will have "extra" base acres payments that will need to be allocated over fewer planted acres of contract payments crops or *vice versa.* This reflects economic realities for farms that have many different combinations of base and planted acres.

64. The US comments, at paragraph 37 of its 11 February 2004 Comments, raise theoretical "arbitrary" attribution problems relating to "excess cotton acreage" or "excess" base acreage situations for a hypothetical farm. But the purpose of any methodology is not to determine the "subsidization" rate of a particular farm, but rather to assess, in the aggregate, the amount of payments. Of course, different farms will have different crop subsidization rates given the inherently unique base acreage and planting combinations. Therefore, Brazil's methodology, which is based on examining individual farm data, may result, in certain cases, in different crop subsidization rates for different farms. But this is neither remarkable nor illogical, as the United States claims, but rather reflects economic reality.

65. The United States further complains that Brazil allocates all "excess" contract payments in MY 1999-2000 and almost all "excess" contract payments in MY 2001 to upland cotton.[91] However, the data shows that in those three marketing years, all contract payment crops (except upland cotton) were planted to a degree that fell *short* of the base acreage for these crops. Thus, the simple fact that upland cotton farms during MY 1999-2001 increased their amount of upland cotton plantings at the expense of other contract payment crops suggests that some of the payments for these non-upland cotton base acres were devoted to supporting upland cotton production. This is reflected in Brazil's 28 January 2004 calculations (as well as in its updated calculations in Annex A.2). Brazil's calculations, therefore, reflect the reality of upland cotton production in those marketing years – production on upland cotton farms shifted to upland cotton and away from other contract payment crops. Brazil notes that no such "excess" upland cotton production exists in MY 2002. This appears to be – at the very least in part – a direct consequence of the base update aligning contract payments base with production trends during MY 1998-2001.[92] The re-linkage of produc-

[91] US 11 January 2004 Comments, paras. 40.

[92] Brazil notes that part of the phenomenon also results from reduced upland cotton plantings.

tion meant that more current upland cotton production takes place on base acreage than during MY 1999-2001.

66. Finally, the United States asserts that the aggregation problems inherent in the US summary data will necessarily *increase* the amount of payments allocated to upland cotton.[93] This criticism is again an ironic assertion by a party that has refused to provide the very data that would answer this criticism. Whether the aggregation problem leads to an upward or downward error in estimating the amount of support to upland cotton is a factual question that cannot be answered in the abstract, as suggested by the United States.[94] Indeed, the effect of the aggregation problem is that upland cotton contract payments on farms that have "excess" upland cotton base are treated as upland cotton payments to farms that have "excess" upland cotton plantings.[95] Whether such a treatment leads to over- or under-counting depends entirely on what the amount of support allocated to the "excess" planted upland cotton acres would be, which can only be derived with using farm-specific data. Only if it is lower then the support for an upland cotton base acre (allocated due to the aggregation effect) would the aggregation problem lead to over-counting. And this is a factual, not a theoretical question. The amount of support allocated to the "excess" acres planted to upland cotton could rank from zero (no contract payments available for allocation on that farm) to an amount that exceeds the upland cotton per-acre payment rate (for instance, rice base or payments for more than one base acre). Again, it bears repeating, that there will be no "aggregation problems" if the United States produces complete farm-specific data on 3 March 2004.

67. In sum, Brazil maintains that, in view of the *de facto* tied nature of the US contract payments at issue, Brazil's methodology is a reasonable means of calculating the support to upland cotton. As for some of the US criticisms that might affect the results (except for MY 2002), Brazil will control for these effects once the United States provides aggregate data in the manner requested by the Panel. Yet, Brazil is of the firm view that none of the US criticisms will meaningfully affect its results.

7. THE US CRITIQUE OF BRAZIL'S APPLICATION OF THE IMPROPER ANNEX IV METHODOLOGY IS BASELESS

68. Brazil has earlier demonstrated, in Section 4 above, the inability of Annex IV of the SCM Agreement to provide useful guidance regarding the calculation of the amount of the contract payments that constitute support to upland cotton. Brazil further demonstrated that the entire premise behind the US attempt to use an Annex IV-like methodology is wrong, since contract payments during MY 1999-2002 were *de facto* tied to the production of upland cotton.

---

93 US 11 January 2004 Comments, para. 42.

94 *Ibid.*

95 *See* Brazil's 28 January 2004 Comments and Requests Regarding US Data, para. 13-15.

69. Nevertheless, as an alternative argument, Brazil attempted in its 28 January 2004 Comments to apply the Annex IV paragraph 2 non-tied subsidy allocation methodology to the US summary data. As a preliminary matter, Brazil notes that the United States has never presented any data in support of its methodology.[96] Instead, the United States has repeatedly argued that it is not its "burden" to establish the amount of contract payments under its own methodology. The United States has gone even further and refused, to date, to provide the data that would permit the calculation of its "across the value of total production on the farm" methodology. As a result, Brazil had to make a number of assumptions to fill the data gaps. The United States has reserved its energy regarding its methodology for a spirited critique of Brazil's attempt to apply the US methodology. Brazil responds to these to these arguments, and the incorrect US calculations, below.

70. First, the United States challenges, in paragraph 51 of its 11 February 2004 Comments, the use of non-upland cotton base acreage payments. This criticism is incorrect, since the Panel must make an objective assessment of the amount of "support to" upland cotton under Article 13(b)(ii), including support provided from non-upland cotton base payments. Therefore, Brazil's inclusion of all contract payments in its calculation was proper. Brazil sets out its arguments in Section 9 *infra*.[97] Consequently, all of the US calculations at paragraphs 59-60 of the US 11 February 2004 Comments are incorrect, because they exclude all non-upland cotton payments.[98]

71. Second, the United States criticizes Brazil for not having included all farm and non-farm income of a farm into its calculations.[99] There is no legitimate basis to include social security and stock market investment income in any payment calculation.[100] Brazil has earlier responded to similar US arguments in cost of production discussions.[101] The focus of Article 13(b)(ii) is on tabulating the amount of *agricultural* domestic support to a specific commodity.

72. Third, the United States claims that Brazil should have included the value of livestock raised by upland cotton farmers. The United States has provided no

---

96 As the party asserting this fact, the United States bears the burden of proving it. *See e.g.* Appellate Body Report, *Japan – Apples*, WT/DS245/AB/R, para. 157 ("It is important to distinguish, on the one hand, the principle that the complainant must establish a *prima facie* case of inconsistency with a provision of a covered agreement from, on the other hand, the principle that the party that asserts a fact is responsible for providing proof thereof.").

97 *See* also US 11 January 2004 Comments, paras. 46-50.

98 Otherwise, all figures seem to reflect Brazil's calculations.

99 US 11 January 2004 Comments, paras. 46, 55 and note 50.

100 Brazil has addressed the US argument that off-farm income may be responsible for closing the gap between upland cotton market revenue and production costs in paragraph 28 of its 2 December 2003 Oral Statement.

101 US 18 November 2003 Further Rebuttal Submission, paras. 111, 137. Brazil is further puzzled by the fact that the United States argues for inclusion of off-farm income over which contract payments have to be allocated. In its 18 November 2003 Further Rebuttal Submission, the United States argued that off-farm income (such as social security benefits) could be support to upland cotton (para. 111). It follows that the United States would argue that social security benefits support the production of upland cotton, while contract payments support social security benefits.

data to support its own methodology or its implied assertion that livestock production is a major component of upland cotton farms' production. However, the record supports Brazil's decision not to include any livestock value. A USDA 1997 ARMS study on costs of production on cotton farms showed that only between 0-6 per cent (depending on the category and location) of US upland cotton farms specialize in livestock production.[102] Since no significant amount of livestock production is found on upland cotton farms, distortions in Brazil's results, if any, would be very minor.

73. The United States also raises several issues with respect to Brazil's calculation methodology. The United States correctly points out that Brazil should have used yields on planted acreage, rather than applying yields on harvested acreage to all acreage planted.[103] Brazil has corrected for this in its updated analysis, set out in Annex A.4 – albeit only for its calculation of the value of upland cotton production.[104] Since yield information on planted acreage for other crops is not available to Brazil – assuming that the US allegation is correct and the yield data in Exhibit Bra-420 is, indeed, based on harvested acres – Brazil continues to apply this data with respect to planted acreage for other crops. Any bias caused by this inaccuracy will naturally *overstate* the value of the non-upland cotton crop production on upland cotton farms[105] and, thus, undervalue the amount of contract payments constituting support to upland cotton.[106]

74. The United States also criticizes Brazil's exclusion of fruits and vegetables from the calculation of the value of non-contract payment crop plantings.[107] However, the contract payment programmes themselves exclude fruits and vegetables as possible beneficiaries of that support, by prohibiting the growing of these crops on base acres. There is no legitimate reason to assume that these payments could be support to fruits and vegetables.[108] In any event, Brazil notes

---

[102] Exhibit Bra-16 ("Characteristics and Production Costs of US Cotton Farms", USDA, October 2001, Appendix Tables 1-4 p. 23-26).

[103] US 11 February 2004 Comments, para. 52 note 59.

[104] US 11 February 2004 Comments, para. 52 and accompanying table.

[105] This is because the upland cotton value is correct, whereas all the values of all other crops are overstated, reducing the share of the upland cotton value of total crop production on the farm.

[106] The United States also asserts, at paragraph 53 of its 11 February 2004 Comments, that Brazil should have used state-by-state data in the determination of the value of sales from non-contract payment crops. Brazil is puzzled by this US argument, as it was the United States that withheld the farm-specific data, including data that would have enabled Brazil to use state-by-state figures on non-contract payment crop plantings for the calculation of the value of non-contract payment crop plantings. The US summary data simply does not allow for a proper weighting of any state-by-state values of non-contract payments crop plantings, if such data were indeed available. Similarly, the US reference to farming in Alaska is irrelevant. Any value of production in that state would not meaningful affect aggregates for the United States. In fact, it would be the US burden to produce data that would allow for the application of its proposed methodology. As the party asserting a fact, the United States bears the burden of proving it. *See e.g.* Appellate Body Report, *Japan – Apples*, WT/DS245/AB/R, para. 157 ("It is important to distinguish, on the one hand, the principle that the complainant must establish a *prima facie* case of inconsistency with a provision of a covered agreement from, on the other hand, the principle that the party that asserts a fact is responsible for providing proof thereof.").

[107] US 11 January 2004 Comments, para. 54.

[108] *See* Section 6 above. *See* also Brazil's 28 January 2004 Comments and Requests Regarding US Data, paras. 92. Brazil's 20 January 2004 Answers to Questions, para. 73.

that the United States required reporting of fruits, vegetables and wild rice acreage on all farms receiving contract payments from MY 1999-2002 and that the Panel has requested this information.[109] Thus, the extent of any distortions, if any, can only be assessed when the actual data is reviewed.

75. Finally, the United States repeats its flawed arguments that contract payments have to be reduced by about two-thirds to reflect the fact that only upland cotton farms that own their land in fact benefit from contract payments.[110] Brazil refers the Panel to its 28 January 2004 Comments for its arguments on this issue.[111]

76. In sum, none of the US criticisms summarized at paragraphs 57 and 60 of its 11 February 2004 Comments withstand close scrutiny. Brazil's calculations under the US Annex IV methodology, based on the incomplete non-farm-specific data, are not biased.[112] By contrast, all of the calculations presented by the United States in its 11 February 2004 Comments were improperly based on upland cotton contract payments only.[113]

8. BRAZIL HAS ESTABLISHED, IN THE ALTERNATIVE, THE AMOUNT OF CONTRACT PAYMENTS FOR PURPOSES OF ITS SCM SERIOUS PREJUDICE CLAIMS

77. The United States 11 February 2004 Comments continue the US argument that there is an explicit allocation requirement in Part III of the SCM Agreement "for determining the 'subsidization' of a product set out in Annex IV."[114] The US Comments also argue that "Brazil has expressly disavowed any allocation methodology for purposes of its serious prejudice claims on decoupled income support payments [and has] failed to make a *prima facie* case on these claims."[115] Both assertions are incorrect.

78. Brazil has argued that Part III of the SCM Agreement does not require detailing the precise amount of the subsidies or a subsidization rate.[116] But it has presented evidence and argument, in the alternative, regarding the size and subsidization rate of the subsidies it has challenged.[117] For the four contract pay-

---

[109] 3 February 2004 Communication from the Panel.

[110] US 11 February 2004 Comments, paras. 56, 60; *See* also US 28 January 2004 Comments, para. 22.

[111] Brazil's 28 January 2004 Comments, paras. 192-214.

[112] For instance, Brazil has used yields on harvested acres for all non-upland cotton planted acres, thereby significantly overstating the value of the non-upland cotton production and understating the amount of support allocated to upland cotton. In fact, Brazil's calculations are conservative.

[113] US 11 February 2004 Comments, paras. 58-59.

[114] US 11 February 2004 Comments, paras. 20.

[115] US 11 February 2004 Comments, paras. 22-24.

[116] *See e.g.,* Brazil's 11 February 2004 Comments on US Answers to Questions Posed by the Panel Following the Second Substantive Meeting of the Panel, paras. 196-197, 216; Brazil's 18 November 2003 Further Rebuttal Submission, paras. 97-107; Brazil's 2 December 2003 Oral Statement, paras 3-5.

[117] *See e.g.,* Brazil's 11 February 2004 Comments on US Answers to Questions Posed by the Panel Following the Second Substantive Meeting of the Panel, para.216; Brazil's 2 December 2003 Oral

ments, the subsidy quantities are those amounts generated for the purposes of the "peace clause" analysis. The amount of a subsidy for purposes of establishing "support to a specific commodity" for purposes of Article 13(b)(ii) is the same amount for Brazil's serious prejudice claims. This conclusion is supported by the fact that the phrase "domestic support" in the Agreement on Agriculture is the same as "subsidy" in the SCM Agreement (assuming the elements of a subsidy for the "support" have been established). Thus, Brazil has offered the contract payment quantities (as well as the other subsidies) established in the peace clause phase of the proceedings as the "amount of subsidization," to the extent this is required, in the serious prejudice phase of the proceedings.

9. THE UNITED STATES IMPROPERLY SEEKS TO LIMIT THE SCOPE OF THE NON-GREEN BOX SUPPORT MEASURES TO BE EXAMINED FOR DETERMINING THE AMOUNT OF SUPPORT FOR PURPOSES OF THE PEACE CLAUSE

79. The United States' 11 February 2004 Comments argue that the Panel cannot examine any evidence of payments received by upland cotton producers growing upland cotton on non-upland cotton base acreage, because Brazil's request for the establishment of a panel ("Brazil's panel request") violates DSU Article 6.2.[118] There is no factual or legal merit to these arguments.

80. First, the Panel's obligation is to conduct an objective assessment of the facts and arguments before it. The issue of the *amount* of contract payments is a key issue that is part of the broader question of the *amount* of support to upland cotton under Article 13(b)(ii) of the Agreement on Agriculture. This broader issue is ultimately the key legal question and it is clearly within the Panel's terms of reference. Determining the amount of support requires an objective assessment by the Panel as to the amount of non-green box support to producers and users of upland cotton in MY 1992 and MY 1999-2002. It requires the Panel to include all support to upland cotton from the evidence before it – regardless of whether Brazil's panel request is broad enough to encompass all of the same subsidies for the purpose of its serious prejudice claims. For example, the fact that the Panel has ruled that certain cottonseed payments are not within its terms of reference for purposes of Brazil's serious prejudice claims does not mean that these same subsidies cannot be counted as "support to upland cotton" for the purposes of the peace clause. The amount of these payments is within the Panel's terms of reference in order to resolve the peace clause issues, because they are "support to" upland cotton. Indeed, identical payments made in MY 1999 have been notified by the United States as "product-specific" upland cotton support.[119]

Statement , para. 5; Brazil's 9 September 2003 Further Submission, Table 1 (setting out the amount and rate of subsidization of each of the four contract payment subsidies based on the 14/16th Methodology).

118 US 11 February 2004 Data Comments, paras. 47-50.

119 *See* Exhibit Bra-47 (G/AG/N/USA/43, p. 20).

81. Second, with respect to the new US Article 6.2 assertion, Brazil notes that the US comments acknowledge that Brazil's panel request is broad enough to cover the contract payments received by upland cotton producers.[120] But the United States now claims the request is *too* broad claiming it "provides virtually no information that would allow identification of the specific measure at issue".[121] This argument is both untimely[122] and contradicted by Brazil's request.

82. Brazil's request complied fully with DSU Article 6.2 by identifying the specific measures at issue. Brazil's request (1) identified by name the specific laws providing for contract payments, *i.e.,* the 1996 FAIR Act, the 2002 FSRI Act, and the 1998-2001 appropriation acts for market loss assistance payments, (2) identified by name the specific payments, *i.e.,* PFC, market loss assistance, direct and counter-cyclical payments, which were required to be paid from those laws, (3) identified by name the specific recipients of those payments, *i.e.,* upland cotton producers, and (4) identified the specific time period when those payments were made, *i.e.,* MY 1999-2007. Yet, the United States would read into DSU Article 6.2 a requirement to go to a further level of detail and identify the *sub*-category (*i.e.,* payments on non-upland cotton and on upland cotton base acreage) of the specific measures that were identified (contract payments to upland cotton producers). This would impose an unprecedented and unjustified level of detail in a panel request that is not required by DSU Article 6.2.

83. In sum, it is undisputed that Brazil's panel request covered all types of contract payments to upland cotton producers, not just those based on upland cotton base acreage. Thus all types of contract payment provided to upland cotton producers, as properly allocated, are support to upland cotton that are well-within the Panel's terms of reference.

84. Finally, the United States now claims that its due process rights were somehow violated because Brazil did not present its methodology for allocating contract payments when it filed its first submission on 24 June 2004.[123] This is simply not credible. Brazil did not realize until early November 2003 that the United States had inaccurately denied for almost one year that it did not have specific information that would allow the computation of the amount of contract payments received by upland cotton producers planting upland cotton.[124] With-

---

[120] US 11 February 2004 Comments, para. 48.

[121] *Ibid.*

[122] Brazil notes that the United States did not make this assertion even at the Panel meeting of 2-3 December 2004 even though Brazil's 18 November 2003 Further Rebuttal Submission unequivocally stated that non-upland cotton contract payments were included when calculating the amount of contract support payments. *For example*, in Brazil's 18 November 2003 Further Rebuttal Submission, Brazil stated in paragraph 16 in presenting the EWG data that "the best evidence that would permit the Panel to calculate the most precise amount of support to upland cotton from these contract payments is (sic) amount of upland cotton (*and other*) contract acreage that is planted to upland cotton". The footnote to this statement indicated that "*these payments include all contract payments for upland cotton base acreage and payments for other crop base acreage that are received by US producers of upland cotton.*" (emphasis added).

[123] *See* US 16 February 2004 Letter to the Panel.

[124] *See* Brazil's 18 February 2004 Comments on US Answers to Questions, para. 26 (setting out the chronology of Brazil's and the Panel's requests for information).

out farm-specific data, there is no basis to develop, let alone apply, Brazil's methodology. Brazil could only develop a methodology to apply to actual data when it received the EWG data in mid-November, and when it then sought farm-specific data from the United States.[125] This methodology then would be applied to *actual* data, and replace Brazil's 14/16th methodology. Thus, it is disingenuous in the extreme for the United States to claim now[126] that Brazil should have presented its methodology on 24 June 2003. Any delay in the United States receiving notice of Brazil's methodology is due directly to the regrettable pattern of US misrepresentations in this dispute beginning in December 2002.[127] In any event, the United States' due process rights have hardly been violated, since they have had more than sufficient opportunity to comment on Brazil's methodology.[128] Unfortunately, Brazil cannot say the same, since it has not been able to apply its methodology because the United States has not produced farm specific data requested by the Panel on several occasions.

10. THE UNITED STATES ARGUMENTS CONCERNING VARIOUS ISSUES RELATED TO THE AMOUNT OF SUPPORT "DECIDED" IN MY 1992 COMPARED TO THE AMOUNT SUPPORTED IN MY 1999-2002 ARE WITHOUT MERIT

85. Brazil briefly responds to several arguments that the US level of support decided in MY 1999-2002 was less than that decided in MY 1992. The United States first argues that because it could not know in MY 1992 what its exact expenditures would be, it is inappropriate to use a budgetary outlay methodology for calculating the amount of support to upland cotton.[129] Brazil will not repeat all of its arguments concerning the meaning of "decided" and "support pro-

---

[125] *See* Brazil's 18 November 2003 Further Rebuttal Submission, para 16.

[126] The United States points to questions raised by Brazil in the Annex V procedures – questions the United States refused to answer. US 11 February 2004 Data Comments, para. 69. While Brazil focused some of its questions on upland cotton base acreage, it also focused on total market loss assistance and CCP payments to the US upland cotton industry and US upland cotton farmers in Questions 11.1 and 13.1. Exhibit Bra-49 (Questions for Purpose of Annex V Procedure). Similarly, Brazil's questions 3.6 in the consultations focused on total amount of PFC and DP to "upland cotton" for marketing years 1992-2002, and question 11.1 asked for the "total amount of market loss assistance payments made to US upland cotton industry in marketing years 1998 through 2001". Exhibit Bra-101 (Questions for Purposes of the Consultations). Obviously, Brazil is not precluded from seeking information or arguing that "support to upland cotton" also included payments to upland cotton producers on non-cotton base acreage. No party is required to cast in stone its arguments concerning a never-before interpreted WTO Agreement in responding to hundreds of questions, exhibits, and more than a thousand pages of arguments. Given the 10 months of briefing in this extraordinary panel proceeding – and the US refusal to provide requested information – it is disingenuous for the United States to claim that Brazil is prevented from further elaborating on its methodologies for allocating contract payments.

[127] Given the refusal of the United States for the past sixteen months to produce information regarding contract payments, it is incredible for the United States to argue that Brazil "has provided virtually no information that would allow identification of the specific measures at issue". US 11 February 2004 Comments, para. 48.

[128] *See* US 11 February 2004 Comments, paras 35-43.

[129] US 11 February 2004 Comments, para. 16.

vided".[130] However, the United States cannot deny that when it passed the implementing Uruguay Round legislation and Congress approved the SAA in late 1994, it was well aware of all, or the vast majority of, the budgetary support for upland cotton provided in MY 1992. Had the United States been concerned about the certainty of its peace clause "protection", it would not have been difficult for Congress, in the 1996 FAIR Act or even the 2002 FSRI Act, to include a "circuit breaker" provision directing the USDA Secretary to stop funding of any upland cotton budgetary outlays in excess of the 1992 levels. Such a provision would have allowed the United States to ensure that it remained protected by the peace clause throughout the implementation period.[131]

86. Furthermore, the United States asserts that under any methodology of calculating "support to upland cotton", it provided support in MY 1999-2002 below the level of support decided in MY ^1992.[132] The United States performs this legal magic by (1) making $4.7 billion in contract payments[133], including a billion dollars of CCP upland cotton payments in MY 2002 alone, simply disappear, (2) assuming that $5.5 billion[134] in marketing loan payments were never made by applying a price-gap support methodology it never actually used or notified,[135] and (3) imposing its "statute of limitations" calculation to end MY 2002 payments on 18 March 2002.[136] Brazil has addressed all of these creative attempts to cover-up billions of dollars in support payments and will not repeat them here.

11. THE UNITED STATES COMMENTS REGARDING THE APPELLATE BODY'S *JAPAN – AGRICULTURAL PRODUCTS* DECISION ARE MISPLACED

87. Brazil has studied the US comments regarding *Japan – Agricultural Products*[137] carefully and believes Brazil's initial analysis of the decision largely addresses the points raised in the US comments.[138] The United States continues to incorrectly interpret *Japan – Agricultural Products* by confusing "claims"

---

[130] Brazil's 22 August 2003 Rebuttal Submission, paras. 68-87; Brazil's 22 July 2003 Oral Statement, paras. 27-36.

[131] Of course, the United States was not required to enact such a measure, because the "peace clause" does not create an obligation on Members to bring their laws into conformity, since it is in the nature of an affirmative defence.

[132] US 11 February 2004 Comments, para. 17 and accompanying notes.

[133] This figure is based on Brazil's 14/16th methodology, but all other methodologies performed in Annex A generate very similar amounts of support to upland cotton from the four contract payment programmes.

[134] *See* Brazil's 2 December 2003 Oral Statement, Section 5.2.

[135] *See* US 22 August 2003 Rebuttal Submission, paras. 114-119. *See* Brazil's response in its 27 August 2003 Comments, paras. 10-16 and Brazil's 28 January 2004 Comments, paras. 29-36.

[136] US 11 August 2003 Answer to Questions, para. 69, 133-134; US 22 August 2003 Rebuttal Submission, para. 115 note 145. *See* Brazil's response in its 22 August 2003 Rebuttal Submission, paras. 88-96; 22 August 2003 Comments, para. 33; Brazil's 2 December 2003 Oral Statement, paras. 7-10.

[137] US 11 February 2004 Comments, paras 27-34.

[138] Brazil's 28 January 2004 Comments and Requests Regarding US Data, paras. 99-106.

with "arguments". The United States argues in paragraph 33 of its 11 February 2004 Comments that because Brazil allegedly has not *argued* that Annex IV is the proper methodology, the Panel cannot request information from the United States relevant to the application of that methodology.[139] But *Japan – Agricultural Products* stands for the proposition that a Panel cannot make a "claim" for a party, *i.e., a legal claim* that would be required to be set out in a request for the establishment of a panel. It does not stand for the proposition that a panel is prevented from requesting information from a party that would be relevant to determine the merits of *arguments* made by that same party.

88. Further, the United States' entire premise in relying on *Japan – Agricultural Products* is wrong. In its 28 January 2004 Comments and Requests Regarding US Data, Brazil has made an "argument," *in the alternative*, regarding a methodology proposed by the United States. The Panel's 3 February 2004 request for information on non-contract acreage crops grown by upland cotton producers was entirely consistent with the United States' suggestion of the US Annex IV methodology and with Brazil's attempt in its 28 January 2004 comments to apply the US Annex IV methodology. The United States responded to Brazil's argument on 11 February 2004. There is no doubt that receipt of the non-contract acreage crops grown on cotton farms would allow a more precise tabulation of the amount of payments using the Annex IV methodology. Thus, the Panel's various requests are fully consistent with the holding by the Appellate Body in *Japan – Agricultural Products* that a "panel is entitled to seek information ... to help it understand and evaluate the evidence submitted and the arguments made by the parties."[140]

---

[139] US 11 February 2004 Comments, para. 33.

[140] WT/DS76/AB/R, para. 129.

ANNEXES A: CALCULATIONS OF THE "SUPPORT TO" UPLAND COTTON USING VARIOUS METHODOLOGIES AND ANNEX B: PEACE CLAUSE COMPARISONS

ANNEX A

Calculation of Contract Payment Support to Upland Cotton

1. In this Annex, Brazil sets forth the details of its calculation of contract payments that constitute support to upland cotton, within the meaning of Article 13 of the Agreement on Agriculture. All of Brazil's calculations are based on the revised US summary files produced on 28 January 2004 and other USDA documents provided as exhibits to the Panel. Brazil explains its calculations either in the narrative of this annex or in the footnotes accompanying the tables.

1. Upland Cotton Contract Payments Only

2. The calculations in this section are based on the presumption that only upland cotton contract payments would be relevant for calculating support to upland cotton. As Brazil has explained in the main text of these comments, Brazil strongly opposes the US arguments that all non-upland cotton contract payments have to be excluded from the calculation of support to upland cotton. All contract payments, including those made on non-upland cotton base acreage, are properly within the Panel's terms of reference. Further, the Panel needs to include all contract payments, including those made on non-upland cotton base acreage, in its objective evaluation of the applicability of the peace clause exemption. Nevertheless, Brazil provides below the necessary calculations for allocating only upland cotton contract payments as "support to" upland cotton.

3. These calculations are performed in two different manners: First, the total amount of upland cotton contract payments to farms actually producing upland cotton is calculated. Second, the amount of upland cotton contract payments to farms actually producing upland cotton is adjusted pursuant to the amount of upland cotton actually produced by farms holding upland cotton base. Under this approach, only upland cotton payments for upland cotton base acres that are actually planted to upland cotton would be considered support to upland cotton. Since plantings of upland cotton on farms also holding upland cotton base exceed the upland cotton base acreage in MY 1999-2001,[1] the adjustment only affects MY 2002 figures.[2]

4. The first step is performed by multiplying the amount of upland cotton payments units on farms producing upland cotton and holding upland cotton

[1] *See* rPFCsum.xls and rDPCsum.xls files provided by the United States on 28 January 2004.

[2] Both approaches exclude any non-upland cotton contract payments received by farms that produce upland cotton and (1) hold upland cotton base, or (2) do not hold upland cotton base (but possible other base).

base[3] (as reported by the United States in its 28 January 2004 summary files) by the applicable payment rate for upland cotton in each of the marketing years 1999-2002.

Table 1.1

Upland Cotton Contract Payments to Farms Producing Upland Cotton and Holding Upland Cotton Base				
MY	Programme	Payment Units[4]	Payment Rate[5] (cents per pound)	Subsidy Amount[6]
1999	PFC Payments	6,539,475,550.8	7.88	$515,310,673.4
2000	PFC Payments	6,581,478,117.7	7.33	$482,422,346.0
2001	PFC Payments	6,476,075,004.9	5.99	$387,916,892.8
2002	Direct Payments	7,107,791,953.5	6.67	$474,089,723.3
	CCP Payments	7,622,807,085.5	13.73	$1,046,611,412.8

5. The table below summarizes the total amount of upland cotton contract payments received by farms producing upland cotton and holding upland cotton base.

Table 1.2

Total Upland Cotton Contract Payment Amounts on Farms Producing Upland Cotton and Holding Upland Cotton Base[7]				
MY	PFC Payments	MLA Payments[8]	Direct Payments	CCP Payments
1999	$515,310,673.4	$512,801,043.5	-	-
2000	$482,422,346.0	$513,554,489.0	-	-
2001	$387,916,892.8	$535,792,287.0	-	-
2002	-	-	$474,089,723.3	$1,046,611,412.8

6. For purposes of comparison, Brazil reproduces the results of its "14/16th" methodology, as presented to the Panel at paragraphs 8 of Brazil's 22 December 2003 Answers to Questions and Brazil's 9 September Further Submission.

---

3 These farms are called "1" in the rPFCsum.xls file and "Enrolled in Cotton PFC and planted cotton" in the rDCPsum.xls file. Presumably the latter should be called "Enrolled in Cotton DCP and planted cotton."

4 Payment Units for MY 1999-2001 are taken from category "1" farms from the rPFCsum.xls file provided by the United States on 28 January 2004. Payment Units for MY 2002 are taken from the rDCPsum.xls file provided by the United States on 28 January 2004.

5 Exhibit Bra-394 (Agricultural Outlook Tables, USDA, November 2003, Table 19).

6 Subsidy Amount = Payment Units * Payment Rate.

7 *See* Table 1.1 for the underlying calculations.

8 Market Loss Assistance Payments are calculated as PFC payments multiplied by the ratio of upland cotton market loss assistance payments to upland cotton PFC payments, as contained in Exhibit Bra-4 ("Fact Sheet: Upland Cotton," USDA, January 2003, p. 6). Since payment rates are not available directly, this ratio provides the information because both subsidies are paid based off the same payment units. Brazil notes that the market loss assistance payment amounts are understated by the non-allocated amount of soybean market loss assistance payments for which the United States has not produced any information.

Table 1.3

Results of Brazil's 14/16th Methodology				
MY	PFC Payments	MLA Payments	Direct Payments	CCP Payments
1999	$547,800,000	$545,100,000	-	-
2000	$541,300,000	$576,200,000	-	-
2001	$453,000,000	$625,700,000	-	-
2002	-	-	$454,500,000	$935,600,000

7. As the Panel can see, the results of this methodology are not considerably different from the results of Brazil's 14/16th methodology.

8. In a second step, Brazil adjusts the above calculated subsidy amount pursuant to the amount of upland cotton actually planted on farms holding upland cotton base. These calculations are possible distorted due to the aggregation problems discussed in Brazil's 20 January 2004 Comments and Requests Regarding US Data.[9] The adjustment factor is calculated as the ratio of upland cotton planted acreage to upland cotton base acreage (capped a 1).

Table 1.4

Adjustment Factor to Be Applied to Upland Cotton Contract Payments to Farms Producing Upland Cotton and Holding Upland Cotton Base				
MY	Upland Cotton Planted Acreage[10]	Upland Cotton Base Acreage[11]	Ratio[12]	Adjustment Factor[13]
1999	13,540,382.7	12,581,724.8	1.07619	1
2000	14,170,477.5	12,625,168.7	1.12239	1
2001	14,118,952.4	12,386,499.4	1.02176	1
2002	13,022,668.9	13,818,215.2	0.94243	0.94243

9. The table below includes the amount of contract payments that would constitute "support to" upland cotton, if only payments for upland cotton base acreage that is actually planted to upland cotton were considered.

---

9 *See inter alia* Brazil's 28 January 2004 Comments and Requests Regarding US Data, paras. 13-15.

10 Upland Cotton Planted Acreage for MY 1999-2001 are taken from category "1" farms from the rPFCsum.xls file provided by the United States on 28 January 2004. Upland Cotton Planted Acreage for MY 2002 is taken from "Enrolled in Cotton PFC and planted cotton" farms from the rDCPsum.xls file provided by the United States on 28 January 2004.

11 *Ibid.*

12 Ratio = Upland Cotton Planted Acreage / Upland Cotton Base Acreage.

13 The Adjustment Factor equals the Ratio of Upland Cotton Planted Acreage to Upland Cotton Base Acreage capped at 1. This means all upland cotton contract payments are deemed to be support to upland cotton if more (or equal) upland cotton is planted than there is upland cotton base. If upland cotton plantings are short of upland cotton base, only the respective ratio is considered to be support to upland cotton.

Table 1.5

Cotton-to-Cotton Methodology				
MY	PFC Payments	MLA Payments[14]	Direct Payments	CCP Payments
1999	$515,310,673.4	$512,801,043.5	-	-
2000	$482,422,346.0	$513,554,489.0	-	-
2001	$387,916,892.8	$535,792,287.0	-	-
2002	-	-	$446,796,377.9	$986,357,993.8

10. For purposes of comparison, Brazil reproduces the results of its "14/16th" methodology, as presented to the Panel at paragraphs 8 of Brazil's 22 December 2003 Answers to Questions and Brazil's 9 September Further Submission.

Table 1.6

Results of Brazil's 14/16th Methodology				
MY	PFC Payments	MLA Payments	Direct Payments	CCP Payments
1999	$547,800,000	$545,100,000	-	-
2000	$541,300,000	$576,200,000	-	-
2001	$453,000,000	$625,700,000	-	-
2002	-	-	$454,500,000	$935,600,000

11. The results of this methodology are only marginally below the results of Brazil's 14/16th methodology, although this methodology would assume that upland cotton produced on farms that do not hold upland cotton base would not receive any contract payments at all, and that upland cotton contract payments on farms that produce upland cotton and hold base would only allocated up to the share of contract acreage that is actually planted to upland cotton. The reason for the close similarity between the 14/16th methodology and the cotton-to-cotton methodology results is that the overwhelming majority of upland cotton is planted on upland cotton base (86.34 per cent in MY 1999, 82.05 per cent in MY 2000, 80.10 per cent in MY 2001 and 96.17 per cent in MY 2002).[15]

---

[14] Market Loss Assistance Payments are calculated as PFC payments multiplied by the ratio of upland cotton market loss assistance payments to upland cotton PFC payments, as contained in Exhibit Bra-4 ("Fact Sheet: Upland Cotton," USDA, January 2003, p. 6). Since payment rates are not available directly, this ratio provides the information because both subsidies are paid based off the same payment units. Brazil notes that the market loss assistance payment amounts are understated by the non-allocated amount of soybean market loss assistance payments for which the United States has not produced any information.

[15] Calculated as the share of upland cotton production planted on farms holding upland cotton base (up to the amount of upland cotton base) of total upland cotton plantings. MY 1999-2001 data are taken from category "1" farms and total upland cotton planting from the rPFCsum.xls file provided by the United States on 28 January 2004. Data for MY 2002 is taken from "Enrolled in Cotton PFC and planted cotton" farms and total upland cotton plantings from the rDCPsum.xls file provided by the United States on 28 January 2004.

2. Brazil's (Simplified) Allocation Methodology

12. In this section of Annex A, Brazil provides an update of its calculations in Section 9 of its 28 January 2004 Comments and Requests Regarding US Data taking into account the revised summary data produced by the United States on 28 January 2004. Brazil has discussed its methodology in considerable detail in its 20 January 2004 response to Question 258[16] and has applied it in Section 9 of its 28 January 2004 Comments and Requests Regarding US Data. Brazil recalls that its methodology considers as support to a particular crop all crop contract payments for that crop that are made for base acres actually planted to that crop. All remaining support is pooled and allocated as support to contract crops according to their share of total "overplanted" contract crop acreage on a farm.

13. While the revised US summary data provided on 28 January 2004 neither addresses the aggregation problems resulting from the particular manner in which the United States produced its summary data,[17] nor the shortcomings in terms of soybean market loss assistance payments and peanut direct and counter-cyclical payments, the United States provides information on contract base of farms that plant upland cotton, but do not hold upland cotton base. To reflect this additional information, Brazil has updated its earlier calculations.[18]

14. In a first step, Brazil analyses farms that plant upland cotton and hold upland cotton base. By marketing year, the following four tables provide, first, by crop the total amount of contract payments received by farms that produce upland cotton and hold upland cotton base.

---

[16] Brazil's 20 January 2004 Answers to Additional Questions, paras. 43-55.

[17] No such aggregation problem exists with respect to the summary data as requested by the Panel on 3 February 2004.

[18] Since there are also minor changes to the summary data on farms that plant upland cotton and hold upland cotton base, Brazil has recalculated all of the figures presented in Section 9 of its 28 January 2004 Comments and Requests Regarding US Data following the very same calculation methodology.

Table 2.1

MY 1999 PFC Payments by Crop for Farms Producing Upland Cotton And Holding Upland Cotton Base				
Crop	Programme	Payment Units[19]	Payment Rate[20] (US$ per unit)	Subsidy Amount[21]
Upland Cotton	PFC Payments	6,539,475,550.8	0.0788	$515,310,673.4
Wheat	PFC Payments	95,664,040.0	0.6370	$60,937,993.5
Oats	PFC Payments	4,237,510.4	0.0300	$127,125.3
Rice	PFC Payments	1,737,257,447.2	0.0128	$22,236,895.3
Corn	PFC Payments	161,779,123.3	0.3630	$58,725,821.8
Sorghum	PFC Payments	85,161,081.8	0.4350	$37,045,070.6
Barley	PFC Payments	6,144,577.9	0.2710	$1,665,180.6

Table 2.2

MY 2000 PFC Payments by Crop for Farms Producing Upland Cotton And Holding Upland Cotton Base				
Crop	Programme	Payment Units[22]	Payment Rate[23] (US$ per unit)	Subsidy Amount[24]
Upland Cotton	PFC Payments	6,581,478,117.7	0.0733	$482,422,346.0
Wheat	PFC Payments	97,234,507.3	0.5880	$57,173,890.3
Oats	PFC Payments	4,307,676.7	0.0280	$120,614.9
Rice	PFC Payments	1,835,587,326.3	0.0118	$21,659,930.5
Corn	PFC Payments	160,180,015.1	0.3340	$53,500,125.0
Sorghum	PFC Payments	85,770,731.7	0.4000	$34,308,292.7
Barley	PFC Payments	6,408,296.1	0.2510	$1,608,482.3

[19] Payment Units for MY 1999 are taken from category "1" farms from the rPFCsum.xls file provided by the United States on 28 January 2004.

[20] Exhibit Bra-394 (Agricultural Outlook Tables, USDA, November 2003, Table 19). Rice payment units are expressed in US$ per pound rather than in US$ per hundredweight as reported in that exhibit (*i.e.*, divided by 220.46).

[21] Subsidy Amount = Payment Units * Payment Rate.

[22] Payment Units for MY 2000 are taken from category "1" farms from the rPFCsum.xls file provided by the United States on 28 January 2004.

[23] Exhibit Bra-394 (Agricultural Outlook Tables, USDA, November 2003, Table 19). Rice payment units are expressed in US$ per pound rather than in US$ per hundredweight as reported in that exhibit (*i.e.*, divided by 220.46).

[24] Subsidy Amount = Payment Units * Payment Rate.

Table 2.3

MY 2001 PFC Payments by Crop for Farms Producing Upland Cotton And Holding Upland Cotton Base				
Crop	Programme	Payment Units[25]	Payment Rate[26] (US$ per unit)	Subsidy Amount[27]
Upland Cotton	PFC Payments	6,476,075,004.9	0.0599	$387,916,892.8
Wheat	PFC Payments	92,731,181.0	0.4740	$43,954,579.8
Oats	PFC Payments	4,096,334.8	0.0220	$90,119.4
Rice	PFC Payments	1,963,467,470.7	0.0095	$18,652,941.0
Corn	PFC Payments	154,693,661.2	0.2690	$41,612,594.9
Sorghum	PFC Payments	82,952,147.8	0.3240	$26,876,495.9
Barley	PFC Payments	5,564,922.0	0.2060	$1,146,373.9

Table 2.4

MY 2002 Direct and Counter-Cyclical Payments by Crop for Farms Producing Upland Cotton And Holding Upland Cotton Base				
Crop[28]	Programme	Payment Units[29]	Payment Rate[30] (US$ per unit)	Subsidy Amount[31]
Upland Cotton	DP Payments	7,107,791,953.5	0.0667	$474,089,723.3
	CCP Payments	7,622,807,085.5	0.1373	$1,046,611,412.8
Wheat	DP Payments	68,412,316.3	0.5200	$35,574,404.5
	CCP Payments	70,209,721.9	0.0000	$0
Oats	DP Payments	3,202,016.5	0.0200	$64,040.3
	CCP Payments	3,227,085.9	0.0000	$0
Rice	DP Payments	1,972,478,301.5	0.0107	$21,105,517.8
	CCP Payments	2,133,694,144.3	0.0075	$16,002,706.1
Corn	DP Payments	118,220,781.7	0.2800	$33,101,818.9
	CCP Payments	132,055,130.0	0.0000	$0
Sorghum	DP Payments	63,545,759.2	0.6300	$40,033,828.3
	CCP Payments	64,258,624.9	0.0000	$0
Barley	DP Payments	4,494,711.7	0.2400	$1,078,730.8
	CCP Payments	4,663,526.3	0.0000	$0
Soybeans	DP Payments	32,002,425.3	0.4400	$14,081,067.1
	CCP Payments	35,163,355.6	0.0000	$0

---

[25] Payment Units for MY 2001 are taken from category "1" farms from the rPFCsum.xls file provided by the United States on 28 January 2004.

[26] Exhibit Bra-394 (Agricultural Outlook Tables, USDA, November 2003, Table 19). Rice payment units are expressed in US$ per pound rather than in US$ per hundredweight as reported in that exhibit (*i.e.,* divided by 220.46).

[27] Subsidy Amount = Payment Units * Payment Rate.

[28] Brazil has not calculated the amounts of payments for other minor oilseeds, as the figures were so small and payment rates were not available to Brazil. Any distortion resulting from this omission would only reduce the amount of contract payments that are considered support to upland cotton.

[29] Payment Units for MY 2002 are taken from category "Enrolled in Cotton PFC and planed cotton" farms from the rDCPsum.xls file provided by the United States on 28 January 2004.

[30] Exhibit Bra-394 (Agricultural Outlook Tables, USDA, November 2003, Table 19). Rice payment units are expressed in US$ per pound rather than in US$ per hundredweight as reported in that exhibit (*i.e.,* divided by 220.46).

[31] Subsidy Amount = Payment Units * Payment Rate.

15. The next four sets of calculations indicate the amount of base and planted acreage for each crop and the amount of crop contract payments allocated to each crop as well as the amount of contract payments available for allocation to other crops. They finally also indicate the amount of contract payments that constitute support to upland cotton on farms that plant upland cotton and hold upland cotton base.[32]

Table 2.5

MY 1999 Farms Producing Upland Cotton And Holding Upland Cotton Base (PFC Payment Allocation)				
Crop	Contract Acres[33]	Planted Acres[34]	Subsidy Allocated[35]	Subsidy Available for Allocation[36]
Upland Cotton	12,581,724.8	13,540,382.7	**$515,310,673.4**	$0.0
Wheat	3,071,118.0	2,363,687.3	$46,900,953.1	$14,037,040.4
Oats	110,232.9	72,349.1	$83,436.1	$43,689.2
Rice	466,080.3	451,264.0	$21,530,003.1	$706,892.2
Corn	2,214,514.8	1,306,755.6	$34,653,322.9	$24,072,498.9
Sorghum	1,809,835.7	1,747,475.2	$35,768,629.3	$1,276,441.4
Barley	119,385.9	59,080.0	$824,040.9	$841,139.7

16. Since planted acreage exceeds base acreage only for upland cotton, the entire amount of 1999 PFC payments available for allocation (**$40,977,701.8**) is allocated to upland cotton. Therefore the amount of PFC payments that constitute support to upland cotton on farms planting upland cotton and holding upland cotton base in MY 1999 is **$556,288,375.2**.[37]

---

32 Additional PFC payments will be allocated as support to upland cotton on farms that produce upland cotton but do not hold upland cotton base, as discussed below.

33 Contract Acres for MY 1999 are taken from category "1" farms from the rPFCsum.xls file provided by the United States on 28 January 2004.

34 Planted Acres for MY 1999 are taken from category "1" farms from the rPFCsum.xls file provided by the United States on 28 January 2004.

35 The subsidy allocated is the entire amount of contract payments for that crop if planted acreage exceeds or equals base acreage. The subsidy allocated is amount of contract payments for that crop adjusted by the ratio of planted acreage to base acreage if planted acreage is below base acreage. (*see* Table 2.1 for the calculation of the total MY 1999 PFC payment by crop).

36 The amount of subsidy available for allocation to other contract payment crops is the residuum of crop contract payments that has not been allocated to the respective crop because planted acreage was below base acreage.

37 Additional PFC payments will be allocated as support to upland cotton on farms that produce upland cotton but do not hold upland cotton base, as discussed below.

Table 2.6

MY 2000 Farms Producing Upland Cotton And Holding Upland Cotton Base (PFC Payment Allocation)				
Crop	Contract Acres[38]	Planted Acres[39]	Subsidy Allocated[40]	Subsidy Available for Allocation[41]
Upland Cotton	12,625,168.7	14,170,477.5	**$482,422,346.0**	$0.0
Wheat	3,127,581.2	2,866,488.2	$52,400,967.8	$4,772,922.5
Oats	112,722.9	80,100.4	$85,708.4	$34,906.5
Rice	491,929.7	350,319.2	$15,424,743.7	$6,235,186.8
Corn	2,201,781.0	1,439,083.7	$34,967,672.9	$18,532,452.1
Sorghum	1,833,506.9	1,458,672.4	$27,294,448.5	$7,013,844.2
Barley	124,232.0	55,138.4	$713,899.3	$894,583.0

17. Since planted acreage exceeds base acreage only for upland cotton, the entire amount of 2000 PFC payments available for allocation (**$37,483,895.1**) is allocated to upland cotton. Therefore the amount of PFC payments that constitute support to upland cotton on farms planting upland cotton and holding upland cotton base in MY 2000 is **$519,906,241.1**.[42]

---

[38] Contract Acres for MY 2000 are taken from category "1" farms from the rPFCsum.xls file provided by the United States on 28 January 2004.

[39] Planted Acres for MY 2000 are taken from category "1" farms from the rPFCsum.xls file provided by the United States on 28 January 2004.

[40] The subsidy allocated is the entire amount of contract payments for that crop if planted acreage exceeds or equals base acreage. The subsidy allocated is amount of contract payments for that crop adjusted by the ratio of planted acreage to base acreage if planted acreage is below base acreage. (*see* Table 2.2 for the calculation of the total MY 2000 PFC payment by crop).

[41] The amount of subsidy available for allocation to other contract payment crops is the residuum of crop contract payments that has not been allocated to the respective crop because planted acreage was below base acreage.

[42] Additional PFC payments will be allocated as support to upland cotton on farms that produce upland cotton but do not hold upland cotton base, as discussed below.

Table 2.7

MY 2001 Farms Producing Upland Cotton And Holding Upland Cotton Base (PFC Payment Allocation I)				
Crop	Contract Acres[43]	Planted Acres[44]	Subsidy Allocated[45]	Subsidy Available for Allocation[46]
Upland Cotton	12,386,499.4	14,118,952.4	**$387,916,892.8**	$0.0
Wheat	2,948,042.9	2,235,873.5	$33,336,312.8	$10,618,267.0
Oats	105,068.0	155,272.1	$90,119.4	$0.0
Rice	530,490.2	437,596.1	$15,386,625.9	$3,266,315.1
Corn	2,149,751.1	1,272,872.9	$24,638,919.5	$16,973,675.4
Sorghum	1,785,775.2	2,228,624.6	$26,876,495.9	$0.0
Barley	106,907.6	53,286.2	$571,389.8	$574,984.1

18. The total amount of PFC payment that is available for allocation over crops whose planted acreage exceeds their base acreage is allocated as detailed in the following table:

Table 2.8

MY 2001 Farms Producing Upland Cotton And Holding Upland Cotton Base (PFC Payment Allocation II)				
Crop	(Contract Acres[47]) – (Planted Acres[48])	Share of Total Overplanted Base[49]	Total Subsidy Available for Allocation[50]	Additional Subsidy Allocated[51]
Upland Cotton	1,732,453.0	77.85 per cent	$31,433,241.7	**$24,469,312.4**
Oats	50,204.1	2.26 per cent	$31,433,241.7	$709,086.9
Sorghum	442,849.4	19.89 per cent	$31,433,241.7	$6,254,842.3
Total	2,225,506.5	100 per cent	$31,433,241.7	$31,433,241.7

[43] Contract Acres for MY 2001 are taken from category "1" farms from the rPFCsum.xls file provided by the United States on 28 January 2004.

[44] Planted Acres for MY 2001 are taken from category "1" farms from the rPFCsum.xls file provided by the United States on 28 January 2004.

[45] The subsidy allocated is the entire amount of contract payments for that crop if planted acreage exceeds or equals base acreage. The subsidy allocated is amount of contract payments for that crop adjusted by the ratio of planted acreage to base acreage if planted acreage is below base acreage. (*see* Table 2.3 for the calculation of the total MY 2001 PFC payment by crop).

[46] The amount of subsidy available for allocation to other contract payment crops is the residuum of crop contract payments that has not been allocated to the respective crop because planted acreage was below base acreage.

[47] Contract Acres for MY 2001 are taken from category "1" farms from the rPFCsum.xls file provided by the United States on 28 January 2004.

[48] Planted Acres for MY 2001 are taken from category "1" farms from the rPFCsum.xls file provided by the United States on 28 January 2004.

[49] *See* "Total" in the preceding column.

[50] The figures in this column represent the total of the amount of MY 2001 PFC payments available for allocation as calculation in the "Subsidy Available for Allocation" column of Table 2.7.

[51] Additional Subsidy Allocated = Share of Total Overplanted Base * Total Subsidy Available for Allocation.

19. The amount of PFC payments that constitute support to upland cotton on farms planting upland cotton and holding upland cotton base in MY 2001 is **$412,386,205.2.**[52,53]

20. Since in MY 2002, the amount of upland cotton acreage (13,022,668.9 acres[54]) on farms that planted upland cotton and held upland cotton base was below the amount of upland cotton base (13,818,215.2[55]), no additional contract payments would be allocated. Instead, the amount of support to upland cotton is calculated by multiplying the amount of upland cotton direct and counter-cyclical payments on these farms by 0.94243.[56] The table below shows the amount of payments allocated as support to upland cotton.

Table 2.9

MY 2002 Allocated Upland Cotton Direct and Counter-Cyclical Payments			
	Total Payments[57]	Share To Be Allocated[58]	Payments Allocated[59]
Direct Payments	$474,089,723.3	94.243 per cent	**$446,796,377.9**
CCP Payments	$1,046,611,412.8	94.243 per cent	**$986,357,993,8**

21. In a second step, Brazil analyses farms that plant upland cotton but do not hold upland cotton base. By marketing year, the following four tables provide, first, by crop the total amount of contract payments received by farms that produce upland cotton and hold upland cotton base.

52 Calculated as the sum of the two bolded figures in Tables 2.7 and 2.8.

53 Additional PFC payments will be allocated as support to upland cotton on farms that produce upland cotton but do not hold upland cotton base, as discussed below.

54 Taken from category "Enrolled in Cotton PFC and planted cotton" farms from in rDCPsum.xls provided by the United States on 28 January 2004.

55 *Ibid.*

56 This figure represents the share that upland cotton planted acreage constitutes of upland cotton base acreage.

57 *See* Table 2.4 for the calculation of the total upland cotton MY 2002 direct and counter-cyclical payments.

58 This figure represents the share that upland cotton planted acreage constitutes of upland cotton base acreage – calculated based on data taken from "Enrolled in Cotton PFC and planted cotton" farms column from in rDCPsum.xls provided by the United States on 28 January 2004.

59 Payments Allocated = Total Payments * Share To Be Allocated.

Table 2.10

MY 1999 PFC Payments by Crop for Farms Producing Upland Cotton But Not Holding Upland Cotton Base				
Crop	Programme	Payment Units[60]	Payment Rate[61] (US$ per unit)	Subsidy Amount[62]
Upland Cotton	PFC Payments	0	0.0788	$0
Wheat	PFC Payments	20,027,129.9	0.6370	$12,757,281.7
Oats	PFC Payments	801,406.4	0.0300	$24,042.2
Rice	PFC Payments	579,443,200.3	0.0128	$7,416,873.0
Corn	PFC Payments	34,650,665.6	0.3630	$12,578,191.6
Sorghum	PFC Payments	12,138,759.1	0.4350	$5,280,360.2
Barley	PFC Payments	551,544.3	0.2710	$149,468.5

Table 2.11

MY 2000 PFC Payments by Crop for Farms Producing Upland Cotton But Not Holding Upland Cotton Base				
Crop	Programme	Payment Units[63]	Payment Rate[64] (US$ per unit)	Subsidy Amount[65]
Upland Cotton	PFC Payments	0	0.0733	$0
Wheat	PFC Payments	22,244,808.9	0.5880	$13,079,947.6
Oats	PFC Payments	952,045.1	0.0280	$26,657.3
Rice	PFC Payments	633,534,085.0	0.0118	$7,475,702.2
Corn	PFC Payments	36,445,141.6	0.3340	$12,172,677.3
Sorghum	PFC Payments	12,928,302.9	0.4000	$5,171,321.2
Barley	PFC Payments	558,190.5	0.2510	$140,105.8

60 Payment Units for MY 1999are taken from category "3" farms from the rPFCsum.xls file provided by the United States on 28 January 2004.

61 Exhibit Bra-394 (Agricultural Outlook Tables, USDA, November 2003, Table 19). Rice payment units are expressed in US$ per pound rather than in US$ per hundredweight as reported in that exhibit (*i.e.,* divided by 220.46).

62 Subsidy Amount = Payment Units * Payment Rate.

63 Payment Units for MY 2000 are taken from category "3" farms from the rPFCsum.xls file provided by the United States on 28 January 2004.

64 Exhibit Bra-394 (Agricultural Outlook Tables, USDA, November 2003, Table 19). Rice payment units are expressed in US$ per pound rather than in US$ per hundredweight as reported in that exhibit (*i.e.,* divided by 220.46).

65 Subsidy Amount = Payment Units * Payment Rate.

Table 2.12

MY 2001 PFC Payments by Crop for Farms Producing Upland Cotton But Not Holding Upland Cotton Base				
Crop	Programme	Payment Units[66]	Payment Rate[67] (US$ per unit)	Subsidy Amount[68]
Upland Cotton	PFC Payments	0	0.0599	$0
Wheat	PFC Payments	22,428,260.7	0.4740	$10,630,995.6
Oats	PFC Payments	942,768.1	0.0220	$20,740.9
Rice	PFC Payments	777,335,099.0	0.0095	$7,384,683.4
Corn	PFC Payments	38,743,300.2	0.2690	$10,421,947.8
Sorghum	PFC Payments	13,988,512.5	0.3240	$4,532,278.1
Barley	PFC Payments	583,440.6	0.2060	$120,188.8

Table 2.13

MY 2002 Direct and Counter-Cyclical Payments by Crop for Farms Producing Upland Cotton But Not Holding Upland Cotton Base				
Crop[69]	Programme	Payment Units[70]	Payment Rate[71] (US$ per unit)	Subsidy Amount[72]
Upland Cotton	DP Payments	0	0.0667	$0
	CCP Payments	0	0.1373	$0
Wheat	DP Payments	8,301,576.6	0.5200	$4,316,819.8
	CCP Payments	8,541,723.9	0.0000	$0.0
Oats	DP Payments	161,464.9	0.0200	$3,229.3
	CCP Payments	164,737.2	0.0000	$0.0
Rice	DP Payments	495,586,654.0	0.0107	$5,302,777.2
	CCP Payments	498,858,849.4	0.0075	$3,741,441.4
Corn	DP Payments	16,302,167.4	0.2800	$4,564,606.9
	CCP Payments	18,440,044.0	0.0000	$0.0
Sorghum	DP Payments	5,944,728.1	0.6300	$3,745,178.7
	CCP Payments	5,882,846.2	0.0000	$0.0
Barley	DP Payments	127,254.2	0.2400	$30,541.0
	CCP Payments	129,400.5	0.0000	$0.0
Soybeans	DP Payments	1,732,743.1	0.4400	$762,407.0
	CCP Payments	1,855,963.7	0.0000	$0.0

[66] Payment Units for MY 2001 are taken from category "3" farms from the rPFCsum.xls file provided by the United States on 28 January 2004.

[67] Exhibit Bra-394 (Agricultural Outlook Tables, USDA, November 2003, Table 19). Rice payment units are expressed in US$ per pound rather than in US$ per hundredweight as reported in that exhibit (*i.e.,* divided by 220.46).

[68] Subsidy Amount = Payment Units * Payment Rate.

[69] Brazil has not calculated the amounts of payments for other minor oilseeds, as the figures were so small and payment rates were not available to Brazil. Any distortion resulting from this omission would only reduce the amount of contract payments that are considered support to upland cotton.

[70] Payment Units for MY 2002 are taken from category "Not Enrolled in Cotton PFC and planed cotton" farms from the rDCPsum.xls file provided by the United States on 28 January 2004.

[71] Exhibit Bra-394 (Agricultural Outlook Tables, USDA, November 2003, Table 19). Rice payment units are expressed in US$ per pound rather than in US$ per hundredweight as reported in that exhibit (*i.e.,* divided by 220.46).

[72] Subsidy Amount = Payment Units * Payment Rate.

22. The next four sets of calculations indicate the amount of base and planted acreage for each crop and the amount of crop contract payments allocated to each crop as well as the amount of contract payments available for further allocation to other crops. They finally also indicate the amount of contract payments that constitute support to upland cotton on farms that plant upland cotton but do not hold upland cotton base.[73]

Table 2.14

MY 1999 Farms Producing Upland Cotton But Not Holding Upland Cotton Base (PFC Payments)				
Crop	Contract Acres[74]	Planted Acres[75]	Subsidy Allocated[76]	Subsidy Available for Allocation[77]
Upland Cotton	0	1,032,580.8	**$0**	$0
Wheat	664,033.9	377,929.2	$7,260,697.5	$5,496,584.2
Oats	20,442.4	12,284.9	$14,448.2	$9,594.0
Rice	133,161.8	74,642.6	$4,157,458.7	$3,259,414.3
Corn	495,800.2	205,429.0	$5,211,626.2	$7,366,565.4
Sorghum	224,604.4	141,533.7	$3,327,401.1	$1,952,959.1
Barley	13,086.9	3,021.1	$34,504.7	$114,963.8

23. Since for none of the non-upland cotton crops planted acreage exceeds base acreage, the entire amount of 1999 PFC payments available for allocation (**$18,200,080.9**[78]) is allocated to upland cotton.[79]

[73] Additional PFC payments will be allocated as support to upland cotton on farms that produce upland cotton and hold upland cotton base, as discussed above.

[74] Contract Acres for MY 1999 are taken from category "3" farms from the rPFCsum.xls file provided by the United States on 28 January 2004.

[75] Planted Acres for MY 1999 are taken from category "3" farms from the rPFCsum.xls file provided by the United States on 28 January 2004.

[76] The subsidy allocated is the entire amount of contract payments for that crop if planted acreage exceeds or equals base acreage. The subsidy allocated is amount of contract payments for that crop adjusted by the ratio of planted acreage to base acreage if planted acreage is below base acreage. (*see* Table 2.10 for the calculation of the total MY 1999 PFC payment by crop).

[77] The amount of subsidy available for allocation to other contract payment crops is the residuum of crop contract payments that has not been allocated to the respective crop because planted acreage was below base acreage.

[78] Sum of "Subsidy Available for Allocation" in Table 2.14.

[79] Additional PFC payments will be allocated as support to upland cotton on farms that produce upland cotton and hold upland cotton base, as discussed above.

Table 2.15

MY 2000 Farms Producing Upland Cotton But Not Holding Upland Cotton Base (PFC Payments)				
Crop	Contract Acres[80]	Planted Acres[81]	Subsidy Allocated[82]	Subsidy Available for Allocation[83]
Upland Cotton	0	1,217,550.3	**$0**	$0
Wheat	749,812.2	429,019.3	$7,483,940.6	$5,596,007.0
Oats	25,096.0	19,731.5	$20,959.1	$5,698.2
Rice	147,118.7	70,088.3	$3,561,472.9	$3,914,229.3
Corn	523,505.2	231,096.1	$5,373,505.8	$6,799,171.5
Sorghum	244,894.8	162,155.4	$3,424,154.6	$1,747,166.6
Barley	13,533.9	2,808.5	$29,074.2	$111,031.6

24. Since for none of the non-upland cotton crops planted acreage exceeds base acreage, the entire amount of 2000 PFC payments available for allocation (**$18,173,304.2**[84]) is allocated to upland cotton.[85]

[80] Contract Acres for MY 2000 are taken from category "3" farms from the rPFCsum.xls file provided by the United States on 28 January 2004.

[81] Planted Acres for MY 2000 are taken from category "3" farms from the rPFCsum.xls file provided by the United States on 28 January 2004.

[82] The subsidy allocated is the entire amount of contract payments for that crop if planted acreage exceeds or equals base acreage. The subsidy allocated is amount of contract payments for that crop adjusted by the ratio of planted acreage to base acreage if planted acreage is below base acreage. (*see* Table 2.11 for the calculation of the total MY 2000 PFC payment by crop).

[83] The amount of subsidy available for allocation to other contract payment crops is the residuum of crop contract payments that has not been allocated to the respective crop because planted acreage was below base acreage.

[84] Sum of "Subsidy Available for Allocation" in Table 2.15.

[85] Additional PFC payments will be allocated as support to upland cotton on farms that produce upland cotton and hold upland cotton base, as discussed above.

Table 2.16

MY 2001 Farms Producing Upland Cotton But Not Holding Upland Cotton Base (PFC Payments)				
Crop	Contract Acres[86]	Planted Acres[87]	Subsidy Allocated[88]	Subsidy Available for Allocation[89]
Upland Cotton	0	1,344,982.1	**$0**	$0
Wheat	716,566.2	393,648.9	$5,840,185.8	$4,790,809.8
Oats	23,851.4	32,464.5	$28,230.8	-$7,489.9
Rice	182,597.4	105,932.1	$4,284,152.0	$3,100,531.4
Corn	569,027.1	228,127.0	$4,178,232.8	$6,243,715.0
Sorghum	264,349.3	182,763.6	$3,133,488.4	$1,398,789.7
Barley	13,343.0	2,783.6	$25,073.6	$95,115.2

25. Since for none of the non-upland cotton crops planted acreage exceeds base acreage, the entire amount of 2001 PFC payments available for allocation (**$15,621,471.2**[90]) is allocated to upland cotton.[91]

---

86 Contract Acres for MY 2001 are taken from category "3" farms from the rPFCsum.xls file provided by the United States on 28 January 2004.

87 Planted Acres for MY 2001 are taken from category "3" farms from the rPFCsum.xls file provided by the United States on 28 January 2004.

88 The subsidy allocated is the entire amount of contract payments for that crop if planted acreage exceeds or equals base acreage. The subsidy allocated is amount of contract payments for that crop adjusted by the ratio of planted acreage to base acreage if planted acreage is below base acreage. (*see* Table 2.13 for the calculation of the total MY 2001 PFC payment by crop).

89 The amount of subsidy available for allocation to other contract payment crops is the residuum of crop contract payments that has not been allocated to the respective crop because planted acreage was below base acreage.

90 Sum of "Subsidy Available for Allocation" in Table 2.16.

91 Additional PFC payments will be allocated as support to upland cotton on farms that produce upland cotton and hold upland cotton base, as discussed above.

Table 2.17

MY 2002 Farms Producing Upland Cotton But Not Holding Upland Cotton Base (Direct Payments)				
Crop[92]	Contract Acres[93]	Planted Acres[94]	Subsidy Allocated[95]	Subsidy Available for Allocation[96]
Upland Cotton	0	518,837.0	**$0**	$0
Wheat	243,967.7	231,183.7	$4,090,616.8	$226,203.0
Oats	4,049.8	11,842.4	$3,229.3	$0.0
Rice	111,611.5	49,723.9	$2,362,433.6	$2,940,343.6
Corn	197,312.6	145,345.6	$3,362,408.3	$1,202,198.6
Sorghum	108,062.4	104,094.2	$3,607,650.6	$137,528.1
Barley	3,368.5	1,697.3	$15,388.8	$15,152.2
Soybeans	98,409.5	140,070.8	$762,407.0	$0.0

26. The total amount of MY 2002 direct payments that is available for allocation over crops whose planted acreage exceeds their base acreage is allocated as detailed in the following table:

[92] Brazil has not calculated the amounts of payments for other minor oilseeds, as the figures were so small and payment rates were not available to Brazil. Any distortion resulting from this omission would only reduce the amount of contract payments that are considered support to upland cotton.

[93] Planted Acres for MY 2002 are taken from category "Not Enrolled in Cotton PFC and planted cotton" farms from the rDCPsum.xls file provided by the United States on 28 January 2004.

[94] Contract Acres for MY 2002 are taken from category "Not Enrolled in Cotton PFC and planted cotton" farms from the rDCPsum.xls file provided by the United States on 28 January 2004.

[95] The subsidy allocated is the entire amount of contract payments for that crop if planted acreage exceeds or equals base acreage. The subsidy allocated is amount of contract payments for that crop adjusted by the ratio of planted acreage to base acreage if planted acreage is below base acreage. (*see* Table 2.14 for the calculation of the total MY 2002 direct payment by crop).

[96] The amount of subsidy available for allocation to other contract payment crops is the residuum of crop contract payments that has not been allocated to the respective crop because planted acreage was below base acreage.

Table 2.18

MY 2002 Farms Producing Upland Cotton But Not Holding Upland Cotton Base (Direct Payments)				
Crop	(Contract Acres[97]) – (Planted Acres[98])	Share of Total Overplanted Base[99]	Total Subsidy Available for Allocation[100]	Additional Subsidy Allocated[101]
Upland Cotton	518,837.0	91.298 per cent	$4,521,425.4	**$4,127,961.2**
Oats	7,792.60	1.371 per cent	$4,521,425.4	$61,999.3
Soybeans	41,661.30	7,331 per cent	$4,521,425.4	$331,464.9
Total	568,290.90	100 per cent	$4,521,425.4	$4,521,425.4

27. The total amount of 2002 direct payments that constitute support to upland cotton on farms that produce upland cotton but do not hold upland cotton base is therefore **$4,127,961.2**.[102]

[97] Contract Acres for MY 2002 are taken from category "Not Enrolled in Cotton PFC and planted cotton" farms from the rDCPsum.xls file provided by the United States on 28 January 2004.

[98] Planted Acres for MY 2002 are taken from category "Not Enrolled in Cotton PFC and planted cotton" farms from the rDCPsum.xls file provided by the United States on 28 January 2004.

[99] *See* Total in the preceding column

[100] The figures in this column represent the total of the amount of MY 2002 direct payments available for allocation as calculated in the "Subsidy Available for Allocation" column in Table 2.17.

[101] Additional Subsidy Allocated = Share of Total Overplanted Base * Total Subsidy Available for Allocation.

[102] Additional direct payments will be allocated as support to upland cotton on farms that produce upland cotton and hold upland cotton base, as discussed above.

Table 2.19

MY 2002 Farms Producing Upland Cotton But Not Holding Upland Cotton Base (CCP Payments)				
Crop[103]	Contract Acres[104]	Planted Acres[105]	Subsidy Allocated[106]	Subsidy Available for Allocation[107]
Upland Cotton	0	518,837.0	**$0**	$0
Wheat	243,967.7	231,183.7	$0	$0
Oats	4,049.8	11,842.4	$0	$0
Rice	111,611.5	49,723.9	$1,666,844.9	$2,074,596.5
Corn	197,312.6	145,345.6	$0	$0
Sorghum	108,062.4	104,094.2	$0	$0
Barley	3,368.5	1,697.3	$0	$0
Soybeans	98,409.5	140,070.8	$0	$0

28. The total amount of MY 2002 counter-cyclical payments that is available for allocation over crops whose planted acreage exceeds their base acreage is allocated as detailed in the following table:

Table 2.20

MY 2002 Farms Producing Upland Cotton But Not Holding Upland Cotton Base (CCP Payments)				
Crop	(Contract Acres[108]) – (Planted Acres[109])	Share of Total Overplanted Base[110]	Total Subsidy Available for Allocation[111]	Additional Subsidy Allocated[112]
Upland Cotton	518,837.0	91.298 per cent	$2,074,596.5	**$1,894,060.6**
Oats	7,792.60	1.371 per cent	$2,074,596.5	$28,447.6
Soybeans	41,661.30	7,331 per cent	$2,074,596.5	$152,088.3
Total	568,290.90	100 per cent	$2,074,596.5	$2,074,596.5

[103] Brazil has not calculated the amounts of payments for other minor oilseeds, as the figures were so small and payment rates were not available to Brazil. Any distortion resulting from this omission would only reduce the amount of contract payments that are considered support to upland cotton.

[104] Contract Acres for MY 2002 are taken from category "Not Enrolled in Cotton PFC and planted cotton" from the rDCPsum.xls file provided by the United States on 28 January 2004.

[105] Planted Acres for MY 2002 are taken from category "Not Enrolled in Cotton PFC and planted cotton" from the rDCPsum.xls file provided by the United States on 28 January 2004.

[106] The subsidy allocated is the entire amount of contract payments for that crop if planted acreage exceeds or equals base acreage. The subsidy allocated is amount of contract payments for that crop adjusted by the ratio of planted acreage to base acreage if planted acreage is below base acreage. (*see* Table 2.14 for the calculation of the total MY 2002 counter-cyclical payment by crop).

[107] The amount of subsidy available for allocation to other contract payment crops is the residuum of crop contract payments that has not been allocated to the respective crop because planted acreage was below base acreage.

[108] Contract Acres for MY 2002 are taken from category "Not Enrolled in Cotton PFC and planted cotton" farms from the rDCPsum.xls file provided by the United States on 28 January 2004.

[109] Planted Acres for MY 2002 are taken from category "Not Enrolled in Cotton PFC and planted cotton" farms from the rDCPsum.xls file provided by the United States on 28 January 2004.

[110] *See* Total in the preceding column

[111] The figures in this column represent the total of the amount of MY 2002 direct payments available for allocation as calculated in the "Subsidy Available for Allocation" column in Table 2.17.

[112] Additional Subsidy Allocated = Share of Total Overplanted Base * Total Subsidy Available for Allocation.

29. The amount of 2002 counter-cyclical payments that constitute support to upland cotton on farms that produce upland cotton but do not hold upland cotton base is therefore **$1,894,060.6.**[113]

30. In a third step, Brazil presents the total amount of contract payments received by farms that produce upland cotton that constitute support to upland cotton, whether or not these farms actually hold upland cotton base.[114]

Table 2.21

Total Contract Payment Support to Upland Cotton on Farms Producing Upland Cotton and Holding Upland Cotton Base				
MY	PFC Payments	MLA Payments[115]	Direct Payments	CCP Payments
1999	$574,488,456.1	$571,690,622.7	-	-
2000	$538,079,545.3	$572,803,412.3	-	-
2001	$428,007,676.4	$591,165,829.7	-	-
2002	-	-	$450,924,339.1	$988,252,054.4

31. For purposes of comparison, Brazil reproduces the results of its "14/16th" methodology, as presented to the Panel at paragraphs 8 of Brazil's 22 December 2003 Answers to Questions and Brazil's 9 September Further Submission.

Table 2.22

Results of Brazil's 14/16th Methodology				
MY	PFC Payments	MLA Payments	Direct Payments	CCP Payments
1999	$547,800,000	$545,100,000	-	-
2000	$541,300,000	$576,200,000	-	-
2001	$453,000,000	$625,700,000	-	-
2002	-	-	$454,500,000	$935,600,000

32. As the Panel can readily see, both methodologies produce quite similar results.

113 Additional counter-cyclical payments will be allocated as support to upland cotton on farms that produce upland cotton and hold upland cotton base, as discussed above.

114 These figures have been calculated as the sum of the contract payments allocated as support to upland cotton on farms that either hold or do not hold upland cotton base and produce upland cotton.

115 Market Loss Assistance Payments are calculated as PFC payments multiplied by the ratio of upland cotton market loss assistance payments to upland cotton PFC payments, as contained in Exhibit Bra-4 ("Fact Sheet: Upland Cotton," USDA, January 2003, p. 6). Since payment rates are not available directly, this ratio provides the information because both subsidies are paid based off the same payment units. Brazil notes that the market loss assistance payment amounts are understated by the non-allocated amount of soybean market loss assistance payments for which the United States has not produced any information.

3. Annex IV-Type Methodology Over Contract Crop Values Only

33. The calculations in this section apply an Annex IV-type allocation methodology to all contract payments received by farms that produce upland cotton, whether or not those farms hold upland cotton base. The approach is the same as in Section 10 of Brazil's 28 January Comments and Requests Regarding US Data. – with the sole exception that the allocation is performed only over the value of programme crops produced on the farm, rather than over the entire value of the upland cotton farms (crop) production.[116]

34. As a first step, Brazil tabulates the total amount of contract payments received by farms that produce upland cotton, as calculated in Section 2 above. The following four tables show the results of this calculation indicating the amount of contract payments by contract payment crop.

Table 3.1

Total Amount of MY 1999 PFC Payments			
Crop	Farms Holding Upland Cotton Base[117]	Farms Not Holding Upland Cotton Base[118]	Total PFC Payment[119]
Upland Cotton	$515,310,673.4	$0.0	$515,310,673.4
Wheat	$60,937,993.5	$12,757,281.7	$73,695,275.2
Oats	$127,125.3	$24,042.2	$151,167.5
Rice	$22,236,895.3	$7,416,873.0	$29,653,768.3
Corn	$58,725,821.8	$12,578,191.6	$71,304,013.4
Sorghum	$37,045,070.6	$5,280,360.2	$42,325,430.8
Barley	$1,665,180.6	$149,468.5	$1,814,649.1
Total	$696,048,760.5	$38,206,217.2	**$734,254,977.7**

Table 3.2

Total Amount of MY 2000 PFC Payments			
Crop	Farms Holding Upland Cotton Base[120]	Farms Not Holding Upland Cotton Base[121]	Total PFC Payment[122]
Upland Cotton	$482,422,346.0	$0.0	$482,422,346.0
Wheat	$57,173,890.3	$13,079,947.6	$70,253,837.9
Oats	$120,614.9	$26,657.3	$147,272.2
Rice	$21,659,930.5	$7,475,702.2	$29,135,632.7
Corn	$53,500,125.0	$12,172,677.3	$65,672,802.3
Sorghum	$34,308,292.7	$5,171,321.2	$39,479,613.9
Barley	$1,608,482.3	$140,105.8	$1,748,588.1
Total	$650,793,681.7	$38,066,411.4	**$688,860,093.1**

116 This calculation based on the revised 28 January 2004 US data is replicated in Section 4 below.

117 *See* Table 2.1 for the calculations resulting in these subsidy figures.

118 *See* Table 2.10 for the calculations resulting in these subsidy figures.

119 Sum of the two preceding columns

120 *See* Table 2.2 for the calculations resulting in these subsidy figures.

121 *See* Table 2.11 for the calculations resulting in these subsidy figures.

122 Sum of the two preceding columns

Table 3.3

Total Amount of MY 2001 PFC Payments			
Crop	Farms Holding Upland Cotton Base[123]	Farms Not Holding Upland Cotton Base[124]	Total PFC Payment[125]
Upland Cotton	$387,916,892.8	$0.0	$387,916,892.8
Wheat	$43,954,579.8	$10,630,995.6	$54,585,575.4
Oats	$90,119.4	$20,740.9	$110,860.3
Rice	$18,652,941.0	$7,384,683.4	$26,037,624.4
Corn	$41,612,594.9	$10,421,947.8	$52,034,542.7
Sorghum	$26,876,495.9	$4,532,278.1	$31,408,774.0
Barley	$1,146,373.9	$120,188.8	$1,266,562.7
Total	$520,249,997.7	$33,110,834.6	**$553,360,832.3**

Table 3.4

Total Amount of MY 2002 Direct and Counter-Cyclical Payments				
Crop[126]	Programme	Farms Holding Upland Cotton Base[127]	Farms Not Holding Upland Cotton Base[128]	Total DP and CCP Payments[129]
Upland Cotton	DP Payments	$474,089,723.3	$0.0	$474,089,723.3
	CCP Payments	$1,046,611,412.8	$0.0	$1,046,611,412.8
Wheat	DP Payments	$35,574,404.5	$4,316,819.8	$39,891,224.3
	CCP Payments	$0.0	$0.0	$0.0
Oats	DP Payments	$64,040.3	$3,229.3	$67,269.6
	CCP Payments	$0.0	$0.0	$0.0
Rice	DP Payments	$21,105,517.8	$5,302,777.2	$26,408,295.0
	CCP Payments	$16,002,706.1	$3,741,441.4	$19,744,147.5
Corn	DP Payments	$33,101,818.9	$4,564,606.9	$37,666,425.8
	CCP Payments	$0.0	$0.0	$0.0
Sorghum	DP Payments	$40,033,828.3	$3,745,178.7	$43,779,007.0
	CCP Payments	$0.0	$0.0	$0.0
Barley	DP Payments	$1,078,730.8	$30,541.0	$1,109,271.8
	CCP Payments	$0.0	$0.0	$0.0
Soybeans	DP Payments	$14,081,067.1	$762,407.0	$14,843,474.1
	CCP Payments	$0.0	$0.0	$0.0
Total	DP Payments	$619,129,131.0	$18,725,559.9	**$637,854,690.9**
	CCP Payments	$1,062,614,118.9	$3,741,441.4	**$1,066,355,560.3**

123 *See* Table 2.3 for the calculations resulting in these subsidy figures.

124 *See* Table 2.12 for the calculations resulting in these subsidy figures.

125 Sum of the two preceding columns

126 Brazil has not calculated the amounts of payments for other minor oilseeds, as the figures were so small and payment rates were not available to Brazil. Any distortion resulting from this omission would only reduce the amount of contract payments that are considered support to upland cotton.

127 *See* Table 2.4 for the calculations resulting in these subsidy figures.

128 *See* Table 2.13 for the calculations resulting in these subsidy figures.

129 Sum of the two preceding columns

35. In a second step the value of all contract payment crops produced on farms that also produce upland cotton is determined. Therefore, the total amount of acreage planted to each of the contract payment crops is multiplied by the average yield and the average farm price for the crop. This is shown in the following four tables.

Table 3.5

MY 1999 Value of Programme Crop Production on Upland Cotton Farms					
Crop	Crop Plantings on Farms Holding Upland Cotton Base[130]	Crop Plantings on Farms Not Holding Upland Cotton Base[131]	Average Yield[132]	Farm Price per unit[133]	Total Value[134]
Upland Cotton	13,540,382.7	1,032,580.8	536.095	$0.45	$3,515,621,790.4
Wheat	2,363,687.3	377,929.2	42.7	$2.48	$290,326,220.9
Oats	72,349.1	12,284.9	59.6	$1.12	$5,649,488.8
Rice	451,264.0	74,642.6	5,866	$0.027	$82,912,712.7
Corn	1,306,755.6	205,429.0	133.8	$1.82	$368,241,145.1
Sorghum	1,747,475.2	141,533.7	69.7	$1.57	$206,712,354.9
Barley	59,080.0	3,021.1	59.2	$2.13	$7,830,700.3
Total	19,540,993.90	1,847,421.30	-	-	$4,477,294,413.0

[130] Planted Acres for MY 1999 are taken from category "1" farms from the rPFCsum.xls file provided by the United States on 28 January 2004.
[131] Planted Acres for MY 1999 are taken from category "3" farms from the rPFCsum.xls file provided by the United States on 28 January 2004.
[132] Upland cotton yields per planted acre (adjusted for abandonment) are taken from Exhibit Bra-4 ("Fact Sheet: Upland Cotton," USDA, January 2003, p. 4). All other yields are taken from Exhibit Bra-420 (Agricultural Outlook Tables, November 2003, Table 17). If these yields should constitute yields on harvested acres (the USDA document relied on by Brazil does not provide this information), then the use of these figures would bias the results leading to lower allocations for upland cotton. No other yield figures are available to Brazil.
[133] Average farm prices are taken from Exhibit Bra-420 (Agricultural Outlook Tables, November 2003, Table 17).
[134] Total Value = (Crop Plantings on Farms Holding Upland Cotton Base + Crop Plantings on Farms Not Holding Upland Cotton Base) * Average Yield * Farm Price per Unit.

Table 3.6

MY 2000 Value of Programme Crop Production on Upland Cotton Farms					
Crop	Crop Plantings on Farms Holding Upland Cotton Base[135]	Crop Plantings on Farms Not Holding Upland Cotton Base[136]	Average Yield[137]	Farm Price per unit[138]	Total Value[139]
Upland Cotton	14,170,477.5	1,217,550.3	525.84	$0.498	$4,029,636,988.1
Wheat	2,866,488.2	429,019.3	42.0	$2.62	$362,637,645.3
Oats	80,100.4	19,731.5	64.2	$1.10	$7,050,128.8
Rice	350,319.2	70,088.3	6,281	$0.025	$67,139,462.6
Corn	1,439,083.7	231,096.1	136.9	$1.85	$422,998,087.0
Sorghum	1,458,672.4	162,155.4	60.9	$1.89	$186,558,900.6
Barley	55,138.4	2,808.5	61.1	$2.11	$7,470,572.3
Total	20,420,279.80	2,132,449.40	-	-	$5,083,491,784.8

135 Planted Acres for MY 200 are taken from category "1" farms from the rPFCsum.xls file provided by the United States on 28 January 2004.
136 Planted Acres for MY 2000 are taken from category "3" farms from the rPFCsum.xls file provided by the United States on 28 January 2004.
137 Upland cotton yields per planted acre (adjusted for abandonment) are taken from Exhibit Bra-4 ("Fact Sheet: Upland Cotton," USDA, January 2003, p. 4). All other yields are taken from Exhibit Bra-420 (Agricultural Outlook Tables, November 2003, Table 17). If these yields should constitute yields on harvested acres (the USDA document relied on by Brazil does not provide this information), then the use of these figures would bias the results leading to lower allocations for upland cotton. No other yield figures are available to Brazil.
138 Average farm prices are taken from Exhibit Bra-420 (Agricultural Outlook Tables, November 2003, Table 17).
139 Total Value = (Crop Plantings on Farms Holding Upland Cotton Base + Crop Plantings on Farms Not Holding Upland Cotton Base) * Average Yield * Farm Price per Unit.

Table 3.7

MY 2001 Value of Programme Crop Production on Upland Cotton Farms					
Crop	Crop Plantings on Farms Holding Upland Cotton Base[140]	Crop Plantings on Farms Not Holding Upland Cotton Base[141]	Average Yield[142]	Farm Price per unit[143]	Total Value[144]
Upland Cotton	14,118,952.4	1,344,982.1	607.25	$0.298	$2,798,361,319.1
Wheat	2,235,873.5	393,648.9	40.2	$2.78	$293,864,905.3
Oats	155,272.1	32,464.5	61.4	$1.59	$18,327,973.3
Rice	437,596.1	105,932.1	6,496	$0.019	$68,010,000.7
Corn	1,272,872.9	228,127.0	138.2	$1.97	$408,653,226.8
Sorghum	2,228,624.6	182,763.6	59.9	$1.94	$280,217,777.2
Barley	53,286.2	2,783.6	58.2	$2.22	$7,244,442.4
Total	20,502,477.80	2,290,701.80	-	-	$3,874,679,644.8

140 Planted Acres for MY 2001 are taken from category "1" farms from the rPFCsum.xls file provided by the United States on 28 January 2004.

141 Planted Acres for MY 2001 are taken from category "3" farms from the rPFCsum.xls file provided by the United States on 28 January 2004.

142 Upland cotton yields per planted acre (adjusted for abandonment) are taken from Exhibit Bra-4 ("Fact Sheet: Upland Cotton," USDA, January 2003, p. 4). All other yields are taken from Exhibit Bra-420 (Agricultural Outlook Tables, November 2003, Table 17). If these yields should constitute yields on harvested acres (the USDA document relied on by Brazil does not provide this information), then the use of these figures would bias the results leading to lower allocations for upland cotton. No other yield figures are available to Brazil.

143 Average farm prices are taken from Exhibit Bra-420 (Agricultural Outlook Tables, November 2003, Table 17).

144 Total Value = (Crop Plantings on Farms Holding Upland Cotton Base + Crop Plantings on Farms Not Holding Upland Cotton Base) * Average Yield * Farm Price per Unit.

Table 3.8

MY 2002 Value of Programme Crop Production on Upland Cotton Farms					
Crop[145]	Crop Plantings on Farms Holding Upland Cotton Base[146]	Crop Plantings on Farms Not Holding Upland Cotton Base[147]	Average Yield[148]	Farm Price per unit[149]	Total Value[150]
Upland Cotton	13,022,668.9	518,837.0	566.676	$0.445	$3,414,772,646.8
Wheat	2,685,236.6	231,183.7	35.3	$3.56	$366,500,706.3
Oats	145,601.7	11,842.4	56.7	$1.81	$16,158,015.7
Rice	373,548.5	49,723.9	6,578	$0.019	$53,252,747.8
Corn	1,641,968.8	145,345.6	130.0	$2.32	$539,054,023.0
Sorghum	1,621,276.2	104,094.2	50.7	$2.32	$202,944,967.9
Barley	49,167.3	1,697.3	54.9	$2.72	$7,595,509.0
Soybeans	1,966,061.6	140,070.8	38.0	$5.53	$442,582,662.5
Total	21,505,529.60	1,202,794.90	-	-	$5,042,861,279.0

36. The following table shows the share that the upland cotton value represents of the total value of contract payments crops produced on farms that also produce upland cotton.

Table 3.9

Percentage of Upland Cotton Value of Total Programme Crop Value[151]			
MY 1999	MY 2000	MY 2001	MY 2002
78.521 per cent	79.269 per cent	72.222 per cent	67.715 per cent

37. Finally, Brazil applies these percentages (the share of upland cotton value of total contract payment crop value) to the total amount of contract payments, as calculated in the first step. The resulting figures represent the total amount of contract payments that constitute support to upland cotton under this methodol-

[145] Brazil has not calculated the amounts of payments for other minor oilseeds, as the figures were so small and payment rates were not available to Brazil. Any distortion resulting from this omission would only reduce the amount of contract payments that are considered support to upland cotton.

[146] Planted Acres for MY 2002 are taken from category "Enrolled in Cotton PFC and planted cotton" farms from the rDCPsum.xls file provided by the United States on 28 January 2004.

[147] Planted Acres for MY 2002 are taken from category "Not Enrolled in Cotton PFC and planted cotton" farms from the rDCPsum.xls file provided by the United States on 28 January 2004.

[148] Upland cotton yields per planted acre (adjusted for abandonment) are taken from Exhibit Bra-4 ("Fact Sheet: Upland Cotton," USDA, January 2003, p. 4). All other yields are taken from Exhibit Bra-420 (Agricultural Outlook Tables, November 2003, Table 17). If these yields should constitute yields on harvested acres (the USDA document relied on by Brazil does not provide this information), then the use of these figures would bias the results leading to lower allocations for upland cotton. No other yield figures are available to Brazil.

[149] Average farm prices are taken from Exhibit Bra-420 (Agricultural Outlook Tables, November 2003, Table 17).

[150] Total Value = (Crop Plantings on Farms Holding Upland Cotton Base + Crop Plantings on Farms Not Holding Upland Cotton Base) * Average Yield * Farm Price per Unit.

[151] These figures have been calculated as "Total Value" of upland cotton divided by "Total Value" of all crops reported in Tables 3.5-3.8.

ogy. The following table shows the amount of support to upland cotton if an Annex IV-type methodology is applied to allocate the value of contract payments over the total value of contract crops produced on farms that also produce upland cotton.

Table 3.10

Total Contract Payments Allocated as Support to Upland Cotton[152]				
MY	PFC Payments	MLA Payments[153]	Direct Payments	CCP Payments
1999	$576,544,351.0	$573,736,505.1	-	-
2000	$546,052,507.2	$581,290,893.0	-	-
2001	$399,648,260.3	$551,995,696.4	-	-
2002	-	-	$431,923,303.9	$722,082,667.7

38. For purposes of comparison, Brazil reproduces the results of its "14/16th" methodology, as presented to the Panel at paragraphs 8 of Brazil's 22 December 2003 Answers to Questions and Brazil's 9 September Further Submission.

Table 3.11

Results of Brazil's 14/16th Methodology				
MY	PFC Payments	MLA Payments	Direct Payments	CCP Payments
1999	$547,800,000	$545,100,000	-	-
2000	$541,300,000	$576,200,000	-	-
2001	$453,000,000	$625,700,000	-	-
2002	-	-	$454,500,000	$935,600,000

4. US-Proposed Annex IV Methodology

39. In this section, Brazil provides updated calculations for allocating contract payments over the entire sales of crops produced on farms producing upland cotton.[154] In Section 3 of this annex, Brazil calculated the total amounts of contract payments received by farms producing upland cotton (Tables 3.1-3.4). Brazil also calculated the value of the contract programme crop production on farms producing upland cotton (Tables 3.5-3.8). To avoid repetition, Brazil refers to Panel to these calculations.

[152] These figures have been calculated by multiplying the percentage amount in Table 3.9 by the total amount of PFC, direct and counter-cyclical payments in Tables 3.1-3.4.

[153] Market Loss Assistance Payments are calculated as PFC payments multiplied by the ratio of upland cotton market loss assistance payments to upland cotton PFC payments, as contained in Exhibit Bra-4 ("Fact Sheet: Upland Cotton", USDA, January 2003, p. 6). Since payment rates are not available directly, this ratio provides the information because both subsidies are paid based off the same payment units. Brazil notes that the market loss assistance payment amounts are understated by the non-allocated amount of soybean market loss assistance payments for which the United States has not produced any information.

[154] Brazil's original calculations are contained in Section 10 of its 28 January 2004 Comments and Requests Regarding US Data.

40. While the revised US summary data provided on 28 January 2004 neither addresses the aggregation problems resulting from the particular manner in which the United States produced its summary data,[155] nor the shortcomings in terms of soybean market loss assistance payments and peanut direct and counter-cyclical payments, the United States provides information on contract base of farms that plant upland cotton, but do not hold upland cotton base. To reflect this additional information, Brazil has updated its earlier calculations.[156]

41. Allocating the total amount of contract payments over the entire sales of crops produced on farms that also produce upland cotton requires determining the value of the non-programme crop production on these farms. In a first step, Brazil calculates the amount of acreage planted to non-programme crops on farms that produce upland cotton.

Table 4.1

MY 1999 Non-Contract Payment Crop Acres on Upland Cotton Farms	
Total Acreage on Farms Holding Upland Cotton Base[157]	27,912,407.1 acres
Total Acreage on Farms Not Holding Upland Cotton Base[158]	2,716,150.3 acres
Total Acreage on Upland Cotton Farms[159]	30,628,557.4 acres
Total Contract Crop Acreage on Farms Holding Upland Cotton Base[160]	19,540,993.9 acres
Total Contract Acreage on Farms Not Holding Upland Cotton Base[161]	1,847,421.3 acres
Total Contract Crop Acreage on Upland Cotton Farms[162]	21,388,415.2 acres
Total Non-Contract Crop Acreage on Upland Cotton Farms[163]	**9,240,142.2 acres**

155 No such aggregation problem exists with respect to the summary data as requested by the Panel on 3 February 2004.

156 Since there are also minor changes to the summary data on farms that plant upland cotton and hold upland cotton base, Brazil has recalculated all of the figures presented in Section 10 of its 28 January 2004 Comments and Requests Regarding US Data following the very same calculation methodology.

157 Data taken from category "1" farms column in rPFCsum.xls file provided by the United States on 28 January 2004.

158 Data taken from category "3" farms column in rPFCsum.xls file provided by the United States on 28 January 2004.

159 Sum of the two above figures.

160 Sum of figures reported in Table 2.5.

161 Sum of figures reported in Table 2.14.

162 Sum of the two above figures.

163 Difference between "Total Acreage on Upland Cotton Farms" and "Total Contract Crop Acreage on Upland Cotton Farms."

Table 4.2

MY 2000 Non-Contract Payment Crop Acres on Upland Cotton Farms	
Total Acreage on Farms Holding Upland Cotton Base[164]	28,104,322.2 acres
Total Acreage on Farms Not Holding Upland Cotton Base[165]	2,986,458.7 acres
Total Acreage on Upland Cotton Farms[166]	31,090,780.9 acres
Total Contract Crop Acreage on Farms Holding Upland Cotton Base[167]	20,420,279.8 acres
Total Contract Acreage on Farms Not Holding Upland Cotton Base[168]	2,132,449.4 acres
Total Contract Crop Acreage on Upland Cotton Farms[169]	22,552,729.2 acres
Total Non-Contract Crop Acreage on Upland Cotton Farms[170]	**8,538,051.7 acres**

Table 4.3

MY 2001 Non-Contract Payment Crop Acres on Upland Cotton Farms	
Total Acreage on Farms Holding Upland Cotton Base[171]	27,412,998.5 acres
Total Acreage on Farms Not Holding Upland Cotton Base[172]	3,222,775.5 acres
Total Acreage on Upland Cotton Farms[173]	30,635,774.0 acres
Total Contract Crop Acreage on Farms Holding Upland Cotton Base[174]	20,502,477.8 acres
Total Contract Acreage on Farms Not Holding Upland Cotton Base[175]	2,290,701.8 acres
Total Contract Crop Acreage on Upland Cotton Farms[176]	22,793,179.6 acres
Total Non-Contract Crop Acreage on Upland Cotton Farms[177]	**7,842,594.4 acres**

[164] Data taken from category "1" farms column in rPFCsum.xls file provided by the United States on 28 January 2004.

[165] Data taken from category "3" farms column in rPFCsum.xls file provided by the United States on 28 January 2004.

[166] Sum of the two above figures.

[167] Sum of figures reported in Table 2.6.

[168] Sum of figures reported in Table 2.15.

[169] Sum of the two above figures.

[170] Difference between "Total Acreage on Upland Cotton Farms" and "Total Contract Crop Acreage on Upland Cotton Farms."

[171] Data taken from category "1" farms column in rPFCsum.xls file provided by the United States on 28 January 2004.

[172] Data taken from category "3" farms column in rPFCsum.xls file provided by the United States on 28 January 2004.

[173] Sum of the two above figures.

[174] Sum of figures reported in Table 2.7.

[175] Sum of figures reported in Table 2.16.

[176] Sum of the two above figures.

[177] Difference between "Total Acreage on Upland Cotton Farms" and "Total Contract Crop Acreage on Upland Cotton Farms."

Table 4.4

MY 2002 Non-Contract Payment Crop Acres on Upland Cotton Farms	
Total Acreage on Farms Holding Upland Cotton Base[178]	26,576,970.2 acres
Total Acreage on Farms Not Holding Upland Cotton Base[179]	1,564,115.0 acres
Total Acreage on Upland Cotton Farms[180]	28,141,085.2 acres
Total Contract Crop Acreage on Farms Holding Upland Cotton Base[181]	21,505,529.6 acres
Total Contract Acreage on Farms Not Holding Upland Cotton Base[182]	1,202,794.9 acres
Total Contract Crop Acreage on Upland Cotton Farms[183]	22,708,324.5 acres
Total Non-Contract Crop Acreage on Upland Cotton Farms[184]	**5,432,760.7 acres**

42. Brazil notes that the calculation of the average value of the production from a non-contract crop acre in the United States is unaffected by the new summary data provided by the United States on 28 January 2004. For ease of reference, Brazil reproduces the average values in the table below.

Table 4.5

Average Per-Acre Value from Production of Non-Contract Programme Crops in the United States[185]			
MY 1999	MY 2000	MY 2001	MY 2002
$150.28	$155.58	$154.92	$118.42

43. Multiplying the per acre value of non-contract crop production by the amount of acreage planted to non-programme crops provides the total value of this production, as shown in the table below.

Table 4.6

Total Value of Non-Contract Programme Crops Production on Upland Cotton Farms[186]			
MY 1999	MY 2000	MY 2001	MY 2002
$1,388,608,569.8	$1,328,350,083.5	$1,214,974,724.4	$643,347,522.1

---

178 Data taken from category "Enrolled in Cotton PFC and planted cotton" farms column in rDCPsum.xls file provided by the United States on 28 January 2004.

179 *Ibid.*

180 Sum of the two above figures.

181 Sum of planted acre figures on category "Enrolled in Cotton PFC and planted cotton" farms from rDCPsum.xls provided by the United States on 28 January 2004.

182 Sum of figures reported in Tables 2.17 and 2.18.

183 Sum of the two above figures.

184 Difference between "Total Acreage on Upland Cotton Farms" and "Total Contract Crop Acreage on Upland Cotton Farms."

185 *See* Exhibit Bra-424 (Allocation Calculations Based on US Methodology and US Summary Data). Brazil has provided this file also electronically as 'allocation calculations.xls' on 28 January 2004.

186 Total Value = "Average Per-Acre Value of Non-Contract Payment Crop Production in the United States" (as reported in Table 4.5) * "Total Non-Contract Crop Acreage on Upland Cotton Farms" (as reported in Tables 4.1-4.4).

44. These figures are added to the value of contract programme crops determined in Section 3 and presented below.

Table 4.7

Total Value of Crop Production on Upland Cotton Farms				
	MY 1999	MY 2000	MY 2001	MY 2002
Value of Contract Programme Crops[187]	$4,477,294,413.0	$5,083,491,784.8	$3,874,679,644.8	$5,042,861,279.0
Value of Non-Contract Payment Crops[188]	$1,388,608,569.8	$1,328,350,083.5	$1,214,974,724.4	$643,347,522.1
Total Value[189]	$5,865,902,982.8	$6,411,841,868.3	$5,089,654,369.2	$5,686,208,801.1
Upland Cotton Value[190]	$3,515,621,790.4	$4,029,636,988.1	$2,798,361,319.1	$3,414,772,646.8
Upland Cotton Value as a Percentage of Total Value[191]	59.933 per cent	62.857 per cent	54.981 per cent	60.054 per cent

45. Applying this percentage rate to the total amount of contract payments received by farms producing upland cotton generates the amount of contract payments that constitute support to upland cotton under this methodology. The figures are shown in the table below.

Table 4.8

Total Contract Payments Allocated as Support to Upland Cotton[192]				
MY	PFC Payments	MLA Payments[193]	Direct Payments	CCP Payments
1999	$440,061,035.8	$437,917,881.4	-	-
2000	$432,996,788.7	$460,939,354.1	-	-
2001	$304,243,319.2	$420,222,029.1	-	-
2002	-	-	$383,057,256.1	$640,389,168.2

46. For purposes of comparison, Brazil reproduces the results of its "14/16th" methodology, as presented to the Panel at paragraphs 8 of Brazil's 22 December 2003 Answers to Questions and Brazil's 9 September Further Submission.

---

187 *See* Tables 3.5-3.8.

188 *See* Table 4.6.

189 Sum of the two preceding figures.

190 *See* Tables 3.5-3.8.

191 Calculated by dividing "Upland Cotton Value" by "Total Value."

192 Calculated by applying the "Upland Cotton Value as a Percentage of Total Value" (reported in Table 4.7) to the total amount of contract payments reported in Tables 3.1-3.4.

193 Market Loss Assistance Payments are calculated as PFC payments multiplied by the ratio of upland cotton market loss assistance payments to upland cotton PFC payments, as contained in Exhibit Bra-4 ("Fact Sheet: Upland Cotton", USDA, January 2003, p. 6). Since payment rates are not available directly, this ratio provides the information because both subsidies are paid based off the same payment units. Brazil notes that the market loss assistance payment amounts are understated by the non-allocated amount of soybean market loss assistance payments for which the United States has not produced any information.

Table 4.9

Results of Brazil's 14/16th Methodology				
MY	PFC Payments	MLA Payments	Direct Payments	CCP Payments
1999	$547,800,000	$545,100,000	-	-
2000	$541,300,000	$576,200,000	-	-
2001	$453,000,000	$625,700,000	-	-
2002	-	-	$454,500,000	$935,600,000

ANNEX B

Peace Clause Comparisons MY 1999-2001 Under Various Allocation Methodologies Budgetary Outlays For Upland Cotton MY 1992, 1999[1]

Year	1992	1999 (1)	1999 (2)	1999 (3)	1999 (4)	1999 (5)
Programme	- $ million -					
Deficiency Payments	1017.4	none	none	none	none	none
PFC Payments	none	515.3	574.5	576.5	440.1	547.8
MLA Payments	none	512.8	571.7	573.7	437.9	545.1
Marketing Loan Gains and LDP Payments[2]	866	1,761	1,761	1,761	1,761	1,761
Step 2 Payment	207	422	422	422	422	422
Crop Insurance	26.6	169.6	169.6	169.6	169.6	169.6
Cottonseed Payments	none	79	79	79	79	79
Total	**2,117.0**	**3,459.7**	**3,577.8**	**3,581.8**	**3,309.6**	**3,524.5**

(1) Adjusted Total Upland Cotton Contract Payments to Farms Producing Upland Cotton and Holding Upland Cotton Base; (Under The Non-Adjusted Methodology, The Amount Would Be Identical)
(2) Brazil's Allocation Methodology
(3) Annex IV-Type Allocation Over Value of Contract Payment Crops Only
(4) US-proposed Methodology
(5) Brazil's 14/16th Methodology

[1] The table below reproduces the table at paragraph 73 of Brazil's 22 August 2003 Rebuttal Submission.

[2] "Other Payments" have been included in the marketing loan figures.

Budgetary Outlays For Upland Cotton MY 1992, 2000[3]

Year	1992	2000 (1)	2000 (2)	2000 (3)	2000 (4)	2000 (5)
Programme	- $ million -					
Deficiency Payments	1017.4	none	none	none	none	none
PFC Payments	none	482.4	538.1	546.1	433.0	541.3
MLA Payments	none	513.6	572.8	581.3	460.9	576.2
Marketing Loan Gains and LDP Payments[4]	866	636	636	636	636	636
Step 2 Payment	207	236	236	236	236	236
Crop Insurance	26.6	161.7	161.7	161.7	161.7	161.7
Cottonseed Payments	none	185	185	185	185	185
Total	**2,117.0**	**2,214.7**	**2,329.6**	**2,346.1**	**2,112.6**	**2,336.2**

(1) Adjusted Total Upland Cotton Contract Payments to Farms Producing Upland Cotton and Holding Upland Cotton Base; (Under The Non-Adjusted Methodology, The Amount Would Be Identical)
(2) Brazil's Allocation Methodology
(3) Annex IV-Type Allocation Over Value of Contract Payment Crops Only
(4) US-proposed Methodology
(5) Brazil's 14/16th Methodology

Budgetary Outlays For Upland Cotton MY 1992, 2001[5]

Year	1992	2001 (1)	2001 (2)	2001 (3)	2001 (4)	2001 (5)
Programme	- $ million -					
Deficiency Payments	1017.4	none	none	none	none	none
PFC Payments	none	387.9	428.0	399.6	304.2	453.0
MLA Payments	none	535.8	597.2	552.0	420.2	625.7
Marketing Loan Gains and LDP Payments[6]	866	2,609	2,609	2,609	2,609	2,609
Step 2 Payment	207	196	196	196	196	196
Crop Insurance	26.6	262.9	262.9	262.9	262.9	262.9
Cottonseed Payments	none	none	none	none	none	none
Total	**2,117.0**	**3,991.6**	**4,093.1**	**4,019.5**	**3,792.3**	**4,146.6**

(1) Adjusted Total Upland Cotton Contract Payments to Farms Producing Upland Cotton and Holding Upland Cotton Base; (Under The Non-Adjusted Methodology, The Amount Would Be Identical)
(2) Brazil's Allocation Methodology
(3) Annex IV-Type Allocation Over Value of Contract Payment Crops Only
(4) US-proposed Methodology
(5) Brazil's 14/16th Methodology

---

[3] The table below reproduces the table at paragraph 73 of Brazil's 22 August 2003 Rebuttal Submission.

[4] "Other Payments" have been included in the marketing loan figures.

[5] The table below reproduces the table at paragraph 73 of Brazil's 22 August 2003 Rebuttal Submission.

[6] "Other Payments" have been included in the marketing loan figures.

ANNEX I-23

COMMENTS OF THE UNITED STATES TO THE 18 FEBRUARY 2004 COMMENTS OF BRAZIL

3 March 2004

Introduction

1. The United States thanks the Panel for this opportunity to provide comments on the 18 February comments filed by Brazil relating to the data submitted by the United States on 18 And 19 December 2003. As an initial matter, the United States finds it odd that Brazil's 18 February comments advance a number of new arguments concerning the applicability of the Peace Clause at this late stage in the proceedings, long after the time when the Peace Clause portion of the dispute was supposed to have been concluded. This only demonstrates the shifting nature of Brazil's arguments and approach to the legal provisions at issue.

2. In these comments, we proceed as follows:

- First, the United States sets forth how Brazil's arguments on the use of the December data are mistaken because of Brazil's erroneous interpretation of the Peace Clause phrase "support to a specific commodity."
- Second, we rebut Brazil's argument that support to a specific commodity may be determined by an analysis of whether the payment in question "cover[s] (or contribute[s] to) the costs of production of a crop." Brazil's "costs of production" principle finds no support in the text of the Peace Clause or of any WTO agreement and in fact collapses when applied to its logical conclusion.
- Third, we demonstrate that Brazil's argument that decoupled income support payments are *de facto* tied to production is in error.
- Fourth, we explain that Brazil has not made a *prima facie* case under its subsidies claims with respect to decoupled payments because it has failed to advance evidence and arguments to allow for identification of the challenged subsidy and subsidized product.
- Fifth, we demonstrate that Brazil's various allocation methodologies, in addition to being irrelevant for Peace Clause Purposes and inapplicable for serious prejudice claims, are internally inconsistent and illogical and that its so-called "Annex IV" methodologies are in fact unrelated to the text of Annex IV.
- Finally, we conclude by noting that Brazil's interpretation of the Peace Clause and application of the December data would upset the balance of rights and obligations of members in the WTO agreements.

Brazil Misinterprets the Peace Clause[1] Phrase, "Support to a Specific Commodity"

3. We begin by noting that the entirety of section 2, and many other parts, of Brazil's comments are based on an argument that Brazil invents and falsely ascribes to the United States. Brazil seeks to paint the US interpretation of the Peace Clause proviso as "based on" an understanding that "'support to' means 'tied to' the production of a specific commodity" – that is, that "support to" in Article 13(b)(ii) of the Agreement on Agriculture means something like "tied to the production or sale of a given product" in paragraph 3 of Annex IV of the Subsidies Agreement.[2] Brazil's argument, however, is not based on any submission of the United States since the United States has never linked the Peace Clause to Annex IV. Indeed, in the US February 11 comments, we specifically noted that:

> [T]he terms "support to a specific commodity" and "product-specific support" are not found in Part III of the Subsidies Agreement, nor in Article 1 or Annex IV. Neither are the terms "subsidy," "benefit," or "subsidized product" from the Subsidies Agreement found in the Peace Clause proviso or any supporting text. Thus, the plain language of the Peace Clause and [Subsidies Agreement] Articles 5 and 6 indicate that these provisions refer to wholly different approaches and suggest that the methodology for allocating non-tied (decoupled) payments under the Subsidies Agreement may not be relevant under the Agreement on Agriculture. The definitions of product-specific support and non-product-specific support in Article 1(a) of the Agreement on Agriculture confirm that the Annex IV allocation methodology does not apply for purposes of the Peace Clause.[3]

Thus, contrary to Brazil's assertions, the United States is plainly *not* inappropriately attempting to interpret the phrase "support to" in the Peace Clause in light of the phrase "tied to" in Annex IV.[4] Having laid down a patently incorrect understanding of the US argument, Brazil proceeds never to address the true bases

---

[1] In paragraph 19 of Brazil's 18 February comments, Brazil in passing characterizes the Peace Clause as "now-expired". As the United States has explained earlier in this proceeding, the issue of the date of expiration of the Peace Clause is not at issue in this proceeding. Brazil accepts that the Peace Clause was in effect when the Panel was established. However, the United States has also explained that the Peace Clause has not yet expired for the United States or other Members whose relevant "year" began later in 1995, so Brazil's characterization is inaccurate as well.

[2] Brazil's 18 February Comments, para. 3.

[3] US February 11 Comments, para. 20 (footnote omitted).

[4] Similarly, we are puzzled by Brazil's lengthy argument in section 4 of its comments that it is the US position that "only Annex IV of the SCM Agreement offers any useful context" to finding some methodology to apply to decoupled payments for purposes of the Peace Clause analysis. Brazil's 18 February Comments, paras. 38-41. As set out above, the Peace Clause determination is made on the basis of its text in its context; the United States does not rely on Annex IV as context or otherwise for interpretation of the Peace Clause; and no methodology to allocate non-product-specific support to a specific commodity can be found in the Agreement on Agriculture.

for the US interpretation of the Peace Clause phrase "support to a specific commodity".

4. Although Brazil correctly suggests that the Panel should look to the ordinary meaning of the phrase "support to a specific commodity," it *only* provides a dictionary definition for one term in the phrase, "support" ("assistance, backing").[5] Brazil's reliance on "support" is misplaced. When Brazil states: "The issue under Article 13(b)(ii) is whether a particular commodity receives 'backing' or support' from a domestic support measure," Brazil fundamentally misunderstands the issue.[6] "Non-product-specific support" is also "support" to various agricultural commodities. The simple fact that it supports those commodities (on a non-specific basis) does not thereby convert that support into support to a "specific commodity" for purposes of Article 13(b)(ii). In addition, by solely defining "support," Brazil avoids the ordinary meaning of the phrase as a whole – that is, "assistance" or "backing" "specially ... pertaining to a particular" "agricultural crop"[7] – a meaning which runs directly contrary to Brazil's approach under which support to multiple commodities is at the same time support to particular commodities. Brazil not only fails to look to the ordinary meaning of *all* of the terms in this phrase[8], it also fails to read the phrase "support to a specific commodity" in light of any other provision of the Agreement on Agriculture (the most immediate context for the Peace Clause) that contains any of the terms "support," "specific," or "commodity".[9]

5. For example, the phrase "support to a specific commodity" contains elements found in the phrases product-specific and non-product-specific support – but Brazil denies that those concepts have any relevance to the Peace Clause.[10] Brazil also fails to discuss (and therefore presumably believes irrelevant) the similarities between the phrase "*support to a specific commodity*" and the phrases "*support* ... provided *for an agricultural product* in favour of the producers of the basic agricultural product" (Article 1(a)) and "*support for basic agricultural products*" (Article 1(h)), which, respectively, define and refer to product-specific support (without using those exact words). Brazil's interpretation of

---

5 Brazil's 18 February Comments, para. 3.

6 Brazil's 18 February Comments, para. 6.

7 *See* US First Written Submission, para. 77 (July 11, 2003) (citing dictionary definitions of each term).

8 According to the customary rules of interpretation of public international law, the Agreement is to "be interpreted in good faith in accordance with the ordinary meaning to be given to the terms of the treaty in their context and in the light of its object and purpose." *See* Vienna Convention on the Law of Treaties, Article 31 (General rule of interpretation).

9 *See, e.g.,* Agreement on Agriculture, Articles 1(a), 1(d), 1(f), 6.4, and Annex 3 (paras. 1 and 7).

10 Instead, Brazil claims that all of its arguments relating to product-specific support and non-product-specific support have been arguments "*in the alternative.*" Brazil also faults the United States for "falsely assert[ing] that Brazil has 'conceded that 'support to a specific commodity' refers to 'product-specific support.'" Brazil's 18 February Comments, paras. 9-10. The United States notes that the Brazilian statement previously referred to by the United States (that is, "the support from contract payments that can be allocated to upland cotton is product-specific support within the meaning of the Agreement on Agriculture", Brazil's 28 January Comments, para. 73) did *not* contain any indication that it was made "in the alternative". Nonetheless, in these comments, the United States proceeds as if Brazil's 18 February comments are its final position.

the Peace Clause phrase "support to a specific commodity", in addition to ignoring the ordinary meaning of the phrase as a whole, ignores relevant context as well – that is, those phrases in the Agreement on Agriculture that, because of their close similarities, must inform a valid interpretation.

6. As we have previously noted, "support to a specific commodity" must be read not only according to the ordinary meaning of the terms, but also in light of the structure of the Agreement on Agriculture. Brazil asserts that Members would have used the exact phrase "product-specific support" instead of "support to a specific commodity" if they had meant the two to be read as having the same meaning,[11] but Brazil sets up a false dichotomy. The Agreement elsewhere defines (Article 1(a)) and refers to (Article 1(h)) this concept without using that exact phrase. Indeed, the Agreement on Agriculture *nowhere* uses the exact phrase "product-specific support". A close approximation is the phrase "product-specific domestic support" in Article 6.4(a)(i); in Annex 3, paragraph 1, the term "product-specific" is used in the context of describing the AMS to be calculated for each basic agricultural product.[12] Despite the absence in the text of the exact phrase "product-specific support", even Brazil has no difficulty recognizing that such a concept exists in the Agreement on Agriculture; thus, that the exact phrase "product-specific support" was not used in the Peace Clause is no bar to finding that this is the correct interpretation of "support to a specific commodity".[13]

7. In addition, Brazil's suggestion that "support to a specific commodity" was intended to clarify that the Peace Clause test involves only "support to an individual commodity, not a *group* of commodities such as grains or even all commodities"[14], does not withstand scrutiny.

- First, the phrase "support to a commodity," without the use of the word "specific", conveys the same meaning as "support to an individual commodity" (Brazil's proffered interpretation); thus, Brazil's interpretation renders the use of the term "specific" inutile.
- Second, under Brazil's interpretation of the Peace Clause, support to "a group of commodities" or "even all commodities" could be support to a specific commodity because the payments may be allocated to an individual commodity depending on what the recipient produces. Thus, Brazil's own Peace Clause interpretation con-

---

11 Brazil's February 18 Comments, para. 5 ("Negotiators presumably knew what they intended when they used the very particular term 'product-specific support'. They used the term repeatedly in the Agreement on Agriculture, and even defined 'non-product-specific support in Article 1(a) – yet they declined to use 'product-specific support' in Article 13(b)(ii)".).

12 *See* Agreement on Agriculture, Annex 3, para. 1 ("Subject to the provisions of Article 6, an Aggregate Measurement of Support (AMS) shall be calculated on a product-specific basis for each basic agricultural product receiving market price support, non-exempt direct payments, or any other subsidy not exempted from the reduction commitment ('other non-exempt policies').").

13 For convenience sake, the United States will use the term "product-specific support" as a short-hand for the concept of support to a specific commodity, in contrast to "non-product-specific support".

14 Brazil's 18 February Comments, para. 5.

> tradicts this distinction between "support to an individual commodity" and support "to a group of commodities".

In addition, Brazil's suggestion that "the *chapeau* of Article 13(b)(ii) confirms this broader meaning of 'support,' because it includes all types of non-green box measures"[15], simply begs the question. "Domestic support measures that conform fully to the provisions of Article 6" (the language in the chapeau) may be either product-specific or non-product-specific, and even Brazil would agree that non-product-specific support is not "support to a specific commodity". Thus, just because a measure falls within the Article 13(b)(ii) chapeau does not assist in determining whether that measure provides "support to a specific commodity".

8. What may be most striking about the Brazilian critique of the US reading of the Peace Clause is that it nowhere presents nor rebuts the basis for the US interpretation. The basis for the US interpretation is set out plainly in the US February 11 comments:

> The lack of grounding of Brazil's methodology in the WTO agreements stems from its erroneous interpretation of "support to a specific commodity." ... . *Brazil has consistently failed to read together the definitions of product-specific support and non-product-specific support in Article 1(a) of the Agreement on Agriculture.* Read in conjunction with one another, non-product-specific support ("support provided in favour of agricultural producers in general") is a residual category of support that is not product-specific ("support ... provided for an agricultural product in favour of the producers of the basic agricultural product").[16]

Brazil nowhere addresses the US argument relating to the definition of product-specific support in Article 1(a) of the Agreement on Agriculture. In fact, whereas in Brazil's Peace Clause submissions it serially misquoted the definition of product-specific support in Article 1(a), dropping key words,[17] in its 18 February comments Brazil avoids that inconvenient definition *by simply never mentioning it.*[18] At the same time, however, Brazil relies heavily on the definition of non-product-specific support in Article 1(a).[19] Thus, once again, Brazil invites the Panel to commit legal error in interpreting the phrase "non-product-specific support provided in favour of agricultural producers in general" devoid of the context provided by the immediately preceding definition of product-specific support.

9. That Brazil's position is untenable is demonstrated by comparing Annex 3, entitled "Calculation of Aggregate Measurement of Support," with Article

---

15 Brazil's 18 February Comments, para. 4.

16 US 11 February Comments, para. 10 (emphasis added).

17 *See* US Rebuttal Submission, para. 82 (22 August 2003); US Comments on Brazil's Rebuttal Submission, para. 23 n.30 (27 August 2003).

18 *See, e.g.,* Brazil's February 18 Comments, para. 9 ("Brazil has argued that the meaning of 'product-specific' AMS must be governed by the only term providing some guidance as to what it means – the definition of 'non-product-specific support' in Article 1(a) of the Agreement on Agriculture".).

19 *See, e.g.,* Brazil's 18 February Comments, paras. 9, 12, and 18.

1(a), which defines "Aggregate Measurement of Support" or "AMS". Paragraph 1 of Annex 3 specifies that two different types of AMS shall be calculated:

- First, "an Aggregate Measurement of Support (AMS) shall be calculated *on a product-specific basis* for each basic agricultural product." Second, "[s]upport *which is non-product specific* shall be totalled into one non-product-specific AMS in total monetary terms".

Thus, Annex 3 distinguishes and calls for the separate calculation of non-product-specific support and product-specific support, which together comprise the AMS. Article 1(a), defining AMS, contains the identical distinction. While only non-product-specific support is identified by name, the structure of the AMS definition – which parallels Annex 3, paragraph 1 – demonstrates that product-specific and non-product-specific support together comprise the AMS:

- "'Aggregate Measurement of Support' and 'AMS' mean the annual level of support, expressed in monetary terms, [1] provided for an agricultural product in favour of the producers of the basic agricultural product *or* [2] non-product-specific support provided in favour of agricultural producers in general ... [bold and italics added]."[20]

That is, just as the calculation of AMS (which uses the term "product-specific") distinguishes product-specific from non-product-specific support, logically, so too does the definition of AMS (which does not use that term).[21] Thus, it is simply not credible for Brazil to refer to the definition of "non-product-specific support" in Article 1(a) but to ignore the immediately preceding definition of product-specific support.[22]

10. her, Brazil's discussion of the meaning of the term "in general" in the definition of non-product-specific support is disappointing because Brazil mischaracterizes the US position and presents the Panel with an interpretation that is not the ordinary meaning of the term. In so doing, Brazil renews a faulty argument advanced in its Peace Clause submissions. In case there were any confusion, the United States clarifies the issue here.

- Brazil has, in fact, never used a dictionary definition of "in general," the exact phrase in the definition of non-product-specific support. Rather, Brazil has attempted to define "in general" by providing definitions of the word "*general*" as "relating to a whole class of objects" and "*not* partial, local or sectional".[23] However, in

---

20 Agreement on Agriculture, Article 1(a).

21 *See also* Agreement on Agriculture, Article 6.4(a) (for purposes of *de minimis* support, distinguishing "product-specific domestic support" from "non-product-specific domestic support").

22 *See, e.g.,* Brazil's 18 February Comments, para. 12 ("One interpretive guide to determine whether support is 'product-specific' is found in the definition of 'non-product-specific support' in Article 1(a) of the Agreement on Agriculture. Brazil demonstrated that *only non-product-specific support is actually defined ...* .") (emphasis added).

23 Brazil's 18 February Comments, para. 12 (footnote omitted); Brazil's Answer to Question 40 from the Panel (para. 54) (defining "general" as "'including, involving, or affecting all or nearly all the parts of a (specified or implied) whole'").

the same dictionary from which Brazil quotes, there is a definition of "in general," which Brazil continues to avoid.[24]

- The definition of "in general" that comes closest to Brazil's use (for example, "including, involving, or affecting all or nearly all the parts of a (specified or implied) whole") is "in a body; universally; without exception." *However, that definition of "in general" is marked "obsolete" in Brazil's own dictionary.*[25]

- Thus, Brazil errs when it argues that the United States has asserted "that Brazil's definition of 'general' is obsolete". Rather, the United States has asserted that Brazil has advanced a reading of the phrase "*in general*" that employs an obsolete meaning.[26]

- In contrast, the non-obsolete definition of "in general" is "in general terms, generally".[27]

Thus, the ordinary meaning of "non-product-specific support provided in favour of agricultural producers in general" in Article 1(a) would be support *not* "specially ... pertaining to a particular"[28] product provided in favour of agricultural producers "generally".

11. Brazil uses its faulty definition of non-product-specific support to conclude that US decoupled payments are not non-product-specific. However, Brazil recognizes that decoupled income support payments do not require any production[29], a recipient may produce nothing at all or may produce any of numerous commodities. Thus, decoupled income support payments are non-product-specific because they do not "specially ... pertain[] to a particular" product and are support "generally" to producers of whatever commodities they choose to produce (if any).

12. We also pause to note that Brazil argues that the EC, New Zealand, and Argentina believe that decoupled income support in the form of counter-cyclical payments are product-specific.[30] However, Brazil points to nothing in the arguments of these third parties that differs from its own flawed interpretation, which

---

[24] *See* US Rebuttal Submission, para. 83 (22 August 2003).

[25] US Comments on Brazil's Rebuttal Submission, para. 23 (noting that the definition of "in general" as "in a body; universally; without exception" was marked "obsolete" in *The New Shorter Oxford English Dictionary*).

[26] US 11 February Comments, para. 10 ("As the United States has pointed out before, *not only does this reading of 'in general' rely on an obsolete meaning, which therefore cannot be the ordinary meaning of the terms*, but Brazil has consistently failed to read together the definitions of product-specific and non-product-specific support in Article 1(a) of the Agreement on Agriculture.") (emphasis added; footnote omitted).

[27] "In general" means "in general terms, generally" and "as a rule, usually." *The New Shorter Oxford English Dictionary*, vol. 1, at 1073 (1993 ed.).

[28] *The New Shorter Oxford English Dictionary*, vol. 2, at 2972 ("specific": second definition); *see also id.* (fifth definition: "Clearly or explicitly defined; precise, exact, definite.").

[29] Brazil's 18 February Comments, para. 4 ("Brazil and the United States agree that the contract payments, which do not *require* production .... .").

[30] Brazil's 18 February Comments, para. 15 & n.22, para. 16 & n. 26.

the United States has thoroughly rebutted. Moreover, Brazil now explicitly argues that the Peace Clause "may require the application of an allocation methodology for ... domestic support measures that may provide support to more than one commodity".[31]

- However, in the Peace Clause phase of this dispute, Brazil had asserted that "[t]he use of the word 'specific' [in "support to a specific commodity"] makes clear that AoA [Agreement on Agriculture] Article 13(b)(ii) addresses actionable subsidy challenges made on a product-by-product basis, *as opposed to* challenges regarding *support for multiple commodities*".[32]
- Further, we recall that the European Communities argued that "support which is provided to a number of crops cannot at the same time be considered 'support to a specific commodity'. Such support is 'support to several commodities' or 'support to more than one commodity'".[33]

Thus, the European Communities has set out an understanding of "support to a specific commodity" in the Peace Clause that *directly contradicts* Brazil's current allocation methodology. Had Brazil revealed (or conceived of) its allocation methodology during the Peace Clause phase of the dispute, the third parties would have been in a better position to provide their informed opinions as to Brazil's Peace Clause interpretation and characterization of particular measures.

13. We also note that the context to which Brazil cites in support of its allocation methodology for Peace Clause purposes lends no support to its interpretation. First, Brazil argues that "[f]urther context for the existence of some sort of an allocation methodology in the Agreement on Agriculture is Annex 3, paragraph 7".[34] However, even if this provision were to suggest "*some sort of* an allocation methodology" in the Agreement on Agriculture, it only applies to calculate AMS with respect to measures directed at processors and does not suggest any methodology that would allocate non-product-specific support as "support to a specific commodity." Brazil also suggests that paragraphs 7, 8, 12, and 13 of Annex 3 "include as 'product-specific' many types of domestic support not tied to the production of a particular commodity."[35] The United States has noted that it is Brazil that has put forward this "tied to the production" definition; the US position is that product-specific support means what Article 1(a) says it does: "support ... provided for an agricultural product in favour of the producers of the basic agricultural product." That said, none of the paragraphs cited by Brazil speak to an allocation of non-product-specific support as product-specific support. That is, whether measures referred to in those provisions are product-specific or non-

31 Brazil's 18 February Comments, para. 6.

32 Brazil's First Submission, para. 136 (24 June 2003) (emphasis added).

33 Oral Statement by the EC at the First Panel Meeting, para. 21. The same logic would apply to crop insurance payments: support is provided to multiple commodities through premium payments for approved insurance products. *See, e.g.,* US Rebuttal Submission, paras. 93-98 (22 August 2003).

34 Brazil's 18 February Comments, para. 13.

35 Brazil's 18 February Comments, para. 14.

product-specific must be determined on the basis of the definition found in Article 1(a).[36]

14. Finally, Brazil argues that "Article 13(b)(ii) of the Agreement on Agriculture does not provide explicit guidance on how to count up the amount of support for contract or any other types of payments. But this does not mean that no counting methodology can be used. The absence of explicit guidance on implementing more general provisions has not stopped WTO panels or parties from proposing and using methodologies to tabulate the amount of subsidies, costs, and volumes of trade impacted."[37] We disagree with Brazil's diagnosis and remedy.

- First, the Peace Clause is not a "general provision[]" lacking "explicit guidance on how to count up the amount of support." In fact, the Peace Clause provides "explicit guidance" through the phrase "support to a specific commodity". Read according to its ordinary meaning and in its context, this phrase refers to product-specific support as defined in Article 1(a) of the Agreement on Agriculture. The definitions in Article 1(a) establish a methodology by which product-specific support is included in "count[ing] up the amount of support" for Peace Clause purposes while non-product-specific is not.
- Second, given the balance struck in concluding the Uruguay Round between the need to achieve binding reduction commitments on agricultural support and the need of Members to be able to design measures to conform to those commitments – a point to which we return later – it is difficult to imagine that Members would have left the issue of how to calculate the "support to a specific commodity" for Peace Clause purposes undefined, putting the Panel in the difficult position of "proposing and using [a] methodolog[y]" on such a crucial issue. In fact, the Peace Clause provides a methodology for calculating that support. The *measures* to be included in the calculation are identified by the phrase "support to a specific commodity," as explained in the preceding bullet. The *unit of measure* to be used in the Peace Clause comparison is identified

---

36 For example, Brazil cites to paragraph 8 of Annex 3 on the calculation of "market price support". This provision refers to "the quantity of *production* eligible to receive the applied administered price"; assuming that "the applied administered price" relates to production of one product, such a measure would be product-specific. Paragraph 12 of Annex 3 refers to "[n]on-exempt direct payments which are based on factors other than price" being measured using budgetary outlays; paragraph 13 refers to the measurement of the value of other non-exempt direct payments; neither provision speaks to the distinction between non-product-specific support and product-specific support nor to the allocation of the former to the latter.

37 Brazil's 18 February Comments, para. 34.

> by the way in which the Member "decided" support during the 1992 marketing year.[38]

Thus, Members did not put the Panel in the untenable position of "adopt[ing] a reasonable methodology" with respect to its Peace Clause findings. Rather, they agreed to language that provides an explicit methodology both for the Panel's purposes as well as for the purposes of Members who wished to ensure their measures would conform to the Peace Clause. Neither Brazil's allocation "methodology [n]or some variant of its methodology" – however "reasonable" Brazil may believe those to be – can serve those purposes or find any basis in the Peace Clause and the Agreement on Agriculture.

15. Thus, we end where we began: the interpretation of the Peace Clause phrase "support to a specific commodity" we have provided is based on its ordinary meaning and in light of the context provided by relevant provisions of the Agreement on Agriculture,[39] in particular, the definition of product-specific support in Article 1(a). Brazil, on the other hand, does not read this phrase according to the ordinary meaning of all of its terms, ignores the context provided by those provisions of the Agreement on Agriculture that use the terms "support", "specific," and "commodity," ignores the definition of product-specific support in Article 1(a), and instead points to provisions that do not provide any relevant context.

16. The Panel may ask itself: can a methodology that (as Brazil's tortured allocation methodology would have it) results in a payment sometimes being considered as support to *no* commodity (if the recipient produces nothing), sometimes as support to *one* commodity (if the recipient has planted a number of acres of a crop at least equal to the number of recipient's base acres of that crop), or sometimes as support to *multiple* commodities (if the recipient plants fewer acres of any crop for which the recipient has base acres) provide any meaningful interpretation of the phrase "support to a specific commodity"? The United States believes that the answer is no. Brazil has, at best, appreciated the *reality* of the payments in question: they are paid to producers in any of the situations it has described. Such support is not "support to a specific commodity" under the ordinary meaning of the terms (assistance or backing specially pertaining to a particular agricultural crop) or the Article 1(a) definition (support provided for an agricultural product in favour of the producers of the basic agricultural products). Rather, it is non-product specific support (support not specially pertaining to a particular product provided in favour of agricultural producers generally).

Brazil's Costs of Production Approach to Determine Whether Payments are "Support to a Specific Commodity" Does Not Withstand Scrutiny

17. In the foregoing section, the United States set out the textual and contextual basis for reading the Peace Clause phrase "support to a specific commodity"

---

[38] Thus, in the case of the United States, the support "decided during the 1992 marketing year" was a rate of support provided by the target price for deficiency payments of 72.9 cents per pound and the marketing loan rate of 52.35 cents per pound. *See* US February 11 Comments, paras. 15-17.

[39] *See, e.g.,* Agreement on Agriculture, Articles 1(a), 1(d), 1(f), 6.4, and Annex 3 (paras. 1 and 7).

according to the definition of product-specific support in Article 1(a). We also pointed out that it is not the United States that has attempted to apply Subsidies Agreement concepts to the Peace Clause analysis as Brazil incorrectly asserted. Rather, it is Brazil that has attempted to apply an (incorrect) allocation methodology as might be relevant for purposes of actionable subsidies claims under the Subsidies Agreement to the Peace Clause analysis. In so doing, Brazil has asserted a principle for determining whether a subsidy provides support to a commodity – that is, whether "they cover (or contribute to) the costs of production of a crop"[40] – that is unworkable and illogical.

18. First, we note that Brazil defines "support" as relating to the recipient, but later elides this into support for a crop. For example, Brazil writes: "[T]he word 'support' has a more general sense of 'backing up' *a group of agricultural farmers* producing a specific commodity. For example, subsidies that cover costs of production when a farmer chooses to grow a crop, 'back up' or 'support' *that farmer*".[41] However, the Peace Clause text is "support to a *specific commodity*" not support to *farmers* producing a specific commodity. This distinction is also found in the Article 1(a) definition of product-specific support: "support ... provided *for an agricultural product* in favour of the producers of the basic agricultural product". The difference is that income support provided to farmers is not "support to a specific commodity" because the support is not "provided for an agricultural product" over any other; the farmer can (in Brazil's words), "choose[] to grow a crop", choose to grow no crop, or choose to grow multiple crops. Even if all recipients of a decoupled payment chose to produce one crop in particular, the payment would still not be support "for an agricultural product"; the support is "for" no specific product but rather is support not "specially ... pertaining to a particular" product that supports producers generally. It is those producers, in turn, who may choose to produce one crop in particular.

19. Brazil then, without further explanation, links the notion that support has a "sense" of backing up a farmer who "chooses to grow a crop" to the notion that such support is "support to a specific commodity" by asserting that "all of these subsidies at issue in this dispute 'support' production of upland cotton because they cover (or contribute to) the costs of production of a crop".[42] Brazil nowhere provides any basis in the text of the Peace Clause or the Agreement on Agriculture for this test. Neither does Brazil explain the necessary implications of its approach.

20. For example, if a decoupled payment is "support to a specific commodity" if it "cover[s] (or contribute[s] to) the costs of production of a crop" then the same payment will be product-specific for some producers but not others. Brazil has pointed to survey data from 1997 – that the United States has explained is technologically and structurally out-of date[43] – for the notion that average total costs of production for US producers are $0.73 per pound. On this basis, Brazil

40 Brazil's 18 February Comments, para. 3.
41 Brazil's 18 February Comments, para. 3 (italics added).
42 Brazil's 18 February Comments, para. 3.
43 US Further Rebuttal Submission, paras. 123-33.

has (incorrectly) claimed that decoupled payments were necessary to cover the gap between market revenue and costs. Putting aside the extensive US critique of Brazil's argument (such as its reliance on total costs instead of operating costs)[44], however, the out-of-date per pound total average cost on which Brazil relies is just that, an average. In claiming that all decoupled payments received by upland cotton producers (satisfying its complicated allocation methodology) are support to upland cotton, Brazil takes no account of the distribution of costs across farms. That is, some farms produce at costs below the average and some produce at costs above the average.[45] Brazil attempts no analysis of whether decoupled payments received by producers who produce cotton at costs below the average "cover (or contribute to) the costs of production of" upland cotton.

- However, *under Brazil's own rationale*, if the decoupled payments do *not* "cover (or contribute to) the costs of production of a crop", then those payments do not support production of that crop and *are not support to a specific commodity*.

Thus, those payments could not form part of Brazil's Peace Clause analysis, but Brazil has not accounted for this.

21. Consider further Brazil's argument that "[w]ithout direct and counter-cyclical payments in MY 2002, the average US cotton farmer would have lost 14.36 cents per pound. With these two payments, they earned a 'profit' of 4.2 cents per pound with the cotton DP and CCP payments".[46] But Brazil has asserted that payments are "support to a specific commodity" only if they "cover (or contribute to) the costs of production of a crop".

- Thus, *under Brazil's own rationale*, the 4.2 cents per pound of "profit" – that is, returns above and beyond total costs of produc-

---

[44] The United States has presented a detailed critique of Brazil's alleged costs of production vs. total revenue "gap" in paragraphs 105-41 of its further rebuttal submission of 18 November 2003. As further confirmation that Brazil's "average total costs of production" argument is wrong, we note that Brazil silently has de-emphasized its assertion that, to cover their high costs of production, upland cotton producers *must* have planted upland cotton "on" upland cotton, rice, or peanut base acreage to reap decoupled payments for these base acres. *See, e.g.,* Brazil's Closing Statement at the Second Session of the First Panel Meeting, Annex I (summary of evidence demonstrating that upland cotton producers in MY 1999-2002 produced upland cotton on upland cotton, rice, or peanut base acreage) (October 9, 2003). In fact, without having repudiated its earlier argument, Brazil's 28 January calculations demonstrate that Brazil's allocation methodology results in payments for many other programme crops being allocated to cotton. For example, for farms producing cotton and having cotton base, in marketing year 1999, payments for *wheat, oats, rice, corn, and sorghum* are allocated to cotton; in marketing year 2000, payments for *wheat, rice, corn, sorghum, and barley* are allocated to cotton; and in marketing year 2001, payments for *wheat, rice, corn, and barley* are allocated to cotton, oats, and sorghum. Brazil's 18 February Comments, Annex A, paras. 15-19 (Tables 2.5-2.8). That is, under Brazil's 20 January allocation methodology, upland cotton is allegedly "planted on" base acres for each of the programme crops just listed, not the cotton, rice, or peanut acres in Brazil's costs argument. Brazil has never explained the contradiction in its two arguments.

[45] For example, the 1997 study shows that in that year the 25 per cent of US cotton farms with the lowest cost (accounting for 36 per cent of cotton production) had average operating costs of $0.31 cents per pound and average total costs of $0.55 cents per pound. Exhibit BRA-16, at tbl. 2.

[46] Brazil's 18 February Comments, para. 24 (third bullet) (footnote omitted).

tion – that Brazil attributes to decoupled payments cannot be "support to" upland cotton.

Brazil, of course, fails to carry through its rationale to this extent because this would reduce the decoupled payments it has calculated as support to upland cotton under its own (incorrect) approach.

22. In addition, Brazil's argument that payments are "support to a specific commodity" only if they "cover (or contribute to) the costs of production of a crop" carried through to its logical end would not only run contrary to the definitions of product-specific support and non-product-specific support in Article 1(a) of the Agreement on Agriculture but would produce illogical results. Consider the situation of marketing loan payments for soybeans:

- In the US view, there is no question that these payments are "support to a specific commodity" within the meaning of the Peace Clause because they are "support ... provided for an agricultural product in favour of the producers of the basic agricultural product" (Article 1(a)).
- Under Brazil's rationale, however, marketing loan payments for soybeans might *not* be "support to" soybeans because they might not "cover (or contribute to) the costs of production of [that] crop".
- To determine whether, under Brazil's theory, those marketing loan payments for soybeans are "support to" soybeans or "support to" some other commodity (such as upland cotton) "requires an examination of the record evidence concerning the extent to which the payments *de facto* support or maintain the production of a specific commodity".[47]
- Under some combination of facts, then, marketing loan payments for soybeans could be deemed, under Brazil's theory, to be support to upland cotton (or some other commodity).

This cannot be the right result since, if the marketing loan payments provide any incentive to production (which will depend on the expected harvest season prices at planting), they provide an incentive to plant soybeans, not upland cotton (and if payments are made, they are made to producers of soybeans, not upland cotton). A correct reading of the Peace Clause does produce the right result since such payments are "support to a specific commodity," soybeans[48], regardless of "the record evidence concerning the extent to which the payments *de facto* support or maintain the production of a specific commodity".

---

[47] Brazil's 18 February Comments, para. 22; *see also id.*, para. 32 ("In sum, the proper allocation methodology under Article 13(b)(ii) of the Agreement on Agriculture must be consistent with the extent to which the domestic support payments directly maintain the production of a specific commodity.").

[48] Under Article 1(a), marketing loan payments for soybeans are "support ... provided for an agricultural product [soybeans] in favour of the producers of the basic agricultural product". Under the ordinary meaning of the terms "support to a specific commodity," marketing loan payments for soybeans are "assistance" or "backing" "specially ... pertaining to a particular" "agricultural product": soybeans.

23. Finally, as a factual matter, we would note that Brazil has not addressed the most telling data that contradicts its assertion that decoupled payments "directly maintain the production of" upland cotton. This is the significant amount of upland cotton acreage planted by farms without any upland cotton base acres.

- Under the 1996 Act, farms without any upland cotton base acres planted 1.0 million acres of upland cotton in marketing year 1999, 1.2 million acres of upland cotton in marketing year 2000, 1.3 million acres in marketing year 2001, and 1.5 million acres in marketing year 2002.[49]
- After new base acreages were established in the 2002 Act (for purposes of direct and counter-cyclical payments), farms without any upland cotton base acres planted 0.5 million acres of upland cotton in marketing year 2002.

Under Brazil's theory, none of these acres should have been planted since without decoupled payments for upland cotton base acres, these producers "would have lost $332.79 per acre between MY 1997-2002" and "would have lost 14.36 cents per pound" in marketing year 2002.[50] The fact that such large numbers of acres *were* planted without decoupled payments for upland cotton base acres demonstrates that, as a factual matter, US upland cotton producers can and do plant upland cotton without the allegedly indispensable decoupled payments for upland cotton base acres.[51]

24. Thus, the principle Brazil advances to determine whether and to what extent decoupled payments are support to a specific commodity – that is, whether they "cover (or contribute to) the costs of production of a crop" – must fail. This principle is not applied by Brazil to its logical ends because to do so would reduce the amount of support to upland cotton Brazil has calculated to upland cotton. Most importantly, Brazil's costs of production principle finds no support in the text of the Peace Clause or any WTO agreement (such as the definition of product-specific support in Article 1(a)). Thus, the Panel should reject Brazil's erroneous approach.

---

[49] US Letter to Panel (28 January 2004) (file "rPFCsum.xls": category 3 under column "cotton planted acres").

[50] Brazil's 18 February Comments, para. 24 (second and third bullets).

[51] The data submitted in response to the Panel's supplementary request for information further proves the point. In marketing year 2002, for example, the 52,504 farms in category B planted 7.0 million acres of upland cotton and had, in the aggregate, 5.4 million base acres of upland cotton; the 7,420 farms in category C planted 0.5 million acres of upland cotton and had 0 base acres of upland cotton. In marketing year 2001, the 61,854 farms in category B planted 10.0 million acres of upland cotton and had 6.4 million base acres of upland cotton; the 20,322 farms in category C planted 1.3 million acres of upland cotton and had no upland cotton base acres. In marketing year 2000, the 62,557 farms in category B planted 9.8 million acres of upland cotton and had 6.4 million base acres of upland cotton; the 18,001 farms in category C planted 1.2 million acres of upland cotton and had no upland cotton base acres. In marketing year 1999, the 59,793 farms in category B planted 9.0 million acres of upland cotton and had 6.0 million base acres of upland cotton; the 15,812 farms in category C planted 1.0 million acres of upland cotton and had no upland cotton base acres. *Under Brazil's theory, none of the tens of thousands of category B farms should have planted more upland cotton acres than their respective quantities of upland cotton base acres, and none of the tens of thousands of category C farms should have planted upland cotton at all.*

Brazil's Argument that Decoupled Income Support Payments Are *De Facto* Tied to Production Is Wrong

25. Brazil argues that the decoupled income support measures at issue in this dispute cannot be allocated across "the total value of the recipient firm's sales" under paragraph 2 of Subsidies Agreement Annex IV because the payments are "*de facto* tied to upland cotton production".[52] Brazil also argues that the amount of subsidies that support upland cotton cannot be determined under Annex IV, paragraph 3, and therefore "Annex IV does not assist the Panel in determining the amount of support to upland cotton, within the meaning of Article 13(b)(ii) of the Agreement on Agriculture".[53] On this latter point, we are in agreement with Brazil: as set out above, the Peace Clause establishes the relevant support through the ordinary meaning of the phrase "support to a specific commodity" in its context, not by way of Annex IV. Under a correct reading of the phrase "support to a specific commodity", *no* allocation methodology may be applied to allocate non-product-specific support as "support to a specific commodity". Here, however, we note that Brazil's argument relating to the alleged *de facto* tie of payments to production does not hold.

26. In fact, the evidence does not support Brazil's argument that decoupled income support payments are "tied to the production or sale of a given product".[54] These payments are received by recipients that may choose to produce no, one, or many different products. The evidence presented by the United States – fully consistent with the Environmental Working Group data presented by Brazil[55] – is that approximately 47 per cent of upland cotton farms eligible for decoupled income support payments planted no cotton in marketing year 2002.[56] Thus, payments are not "tied to the production or sale of a given product" since nearly half of the recipients do not plant even a single acre of cotton.

27. Brazil points to evidence that it asserts demonstrates the "crucial role that each of the four contract payments plays in maintaining the production of US upland cotton".[57] That is, Brazil argues that without the decoupled income support payments, many US producers would not have been able to continue producing cotton. However, Brazil's argument is not, as in Annex IV, that "the subsidy is tied to the production or sale of a given product", but rather that the production or sale of a given product is tied to the subsidy. The two statements are not equivalent. That an upland cotton farmer could not produce upland cotton without a subsidy payment (an argument which the United States has rebutted) does not mean that the payment is "tied to the production or sale of a given product" if recipients may produce or sell other than a given product. This is precisely

52 Brazil's 18 February Comments, para. 39.

53 Brazil's 18 February Comments, para. 41.

54 Subsidies Agreement, Annex IV, para. 3.

55 Brazil's Further Rebuttal Submission, para 23 (EWG data showed that 46, 45, and 45 per cent of farms receiving upland cotton contract payments received no marketing loan payments in 2000, 2001, and 2002, respectively).

56 US Oral statement at Second Panel Meeting, para. 56 (2 December 2003); US Answer to Panel Question 125(9).

57 Brazil's 18 February Comments, para. 32.

the case with respect to decoupled income support payments: there is no "tie" to the production or sale of upland cotton because payment recipients can choose not to produce upland cotton (or any other crop).

28. Thus, Brazil has not established that the decoupled income support payments are "*de facto* tied to upland cotton production"; rather, the facts that demonstrate that nearly half of the payment recipients choose not to plant upland cotton at all *de facto* contradict Brazil's argument.

Brazil Has Not Made a *Prima Facie* Case under its Subsidies Claims with respect to Decoupled Payments

29. The United States has previously explained that Brazil has not properly interpreted the Peace Clause proviso and has not demonstrated that the challenged US measures are in breach of the Peace Clause. This ends the analysis with respect to Brazil's subsidies claims under Subsidies Agreement Articles 5 and 6 and GATT 1994 Article XVI:1. However, even if the Panel were to look beyond the Peace Clause to Brazil's subsidies claims, Brazil has not established a *prima facie* case with respect to decoupled payments.[58]

30. Brazil now argues that, while "Part III of the Subsidies Agreement does not require detailing the precise amount of the subsidies", Brazil "has presented evidence and argument, in the alternative, regarding the size and subsidization rate of the subsidies challenged."[59] Brazil further claims that it "has offered the contract payment quantities (as well as the other subsidies) established in the peace clause phase of the proceedings as the 'amount of subsidization', to the extent this is required, in the serious prejudice phase". In light of Brazil's repeated disavowals of any need to identify the amount of the subsidy for purposes of its subsidies claims,[60] the United States does not believe that this and two other comments referenced by Brazil demonstrate that Brazil has argued and advanced evidence relating to identification of the challenged subsidy.[61]

---

[58] The United States has elsewhere explained that Brazil has not demonstrated serious prejudice, or threat thereof, from upland cotton marketing loan payments or any other challenged US measures. *See, e.g.,* US Further Rebuttal Submission, paras. 1-177; US Further Submission, paras. 16-133.

[59] Brazil's 18 February Comments, para. 78. The United States continues to be surprised by Brazil's denial of the significance of the amount of the subsidy for purposes of determining "the effect of the subsidy' under its serious prejudice claims. For example, had the DSB initiated the Annex V information-gathering process, that process would have been concerned, in part, with establishing "the amount of subsidization," Subsidies Agreement, Annex V, para. 2, and "the amount of the subsidy in question," *id.,* Annex V, para. 7. Brazil's position that "the effect of the subsidy" may be evaluated without identifying the amount of the subsidy is akin to saying that one can determine "the effect of eating" without knowing how much is being eaten.

[60] *See, e.g.*, US 11 February comments, para. 24.

[61] *See* Brazil's Comment on US Answer to Question 214 from the Panel, para. 216 (28 January 2003) ("Detailing the precise amount of the financial contribution ending up in the bank accounts of US upland cotton producers is not a legal pre-requisite to Brazil's actionable subsidy claims. If the Panel finds that Brazil is legally required to examine the exact *amount* of the subsidies in order to assess their 'effects,' ... Brazil refers the Panel to evidence and the allocation of the amount of 'support to upland cotton' it has presented in the peace clause portion of its various submissions. This evidence is part of the record pursuant to Brazil's alternative arguments and is offered as evidence of the amount of such subsidy payments."); Brazil's Opening Statement at the Second Panel Meeting, para.

31. Nonetheless, even if the Panel were to find that Brazil's comments dated 28 January 2004, and 11 February 2004 – that is, more than eight months into this dispute and after scheduled panel meetings and written submissions have been concluded[62] – advanced an argument in the alternative, Brazil still would not have made a *prima facie* case with respect to decoupled payments. As set out in the US 11 February comments[63], Brazil has never presented evidence nor made arguments that would allow the Panel to evaluate "the effect of the subsidy [decoupled income support payments]". In particular, Brazil has never presented information relating to the total value of the recipients' sales as would be necessary to determine the amount of these subsidies benefiting upland cotton that are not tied to the production or sale of a given product. The reason for this omission is simple: Brazil has never believed, nor does it today, that the Annex IV methodology is necessary or even relevant to identify the subsidy benefit and subsidized product.[64] Because Brazil believes Annex IV is irrelevant for the Peace Clause but has offered its Peace Clause calculations (again, in the alternative) "as evidence of the amount of such subsidy payments"[65], logically, Brazil must believe that Annex IV "does not assist the Panel in determining the amount of [the subsidy]".[66]

32. We do note that Brazil has argued that, "as an alternative argument, Brazil attempted in its 28 January 2004 Comments to apply the Annex IV paragraph 2 non-tied subsidy allocation methodology to the US summary data".[67] We later set out in more detail the infirmities in Brazil's calculations. Here, we note that, Brazil evidently believes that by liberally assigning the "in the alternative" label, it will be able to assert that it has advanced evidence and arguments relating to whatever methodology the Panel adopts. Such an approach speaks volumes to Brazil's confidence in its approach to its serious prejudice claims, but it is also

5 ("In any event, Brazil has demonstrated a collective subsidization rate averaging 95 per cent and subsidies in the amount of $12.9 billion.").

62 Article 12 and Appendix 3 of the DSU contemplates a process which all WTO dispute settlement proceedings must follow in order to ensure due process for the parties involved. Such a process requires that the parties "present the facts of the case, their arguments and their counter-arguments" before the first substantive meeting of the panel (*see* para. 4 of the Working Procedures of the Panel), present their case at the first substantive meeting of the panel (*see* para. 5 of the Working Procedures of the Panel), and then present their formal rebuttals by the second substantive meeting of the panel (*see* para. 6 of the Working Procedures of the Panel). In this regard, for Brazil to present new arguments for the first time now, or to use recently submitted US data to try to meet Brazil's initial burden of proof now, outside of the confines of the established panel process and without allowing the United States to provide counter-arguments or rebuttals, would appear contrary to the due process safeguards provided by the DSU and the Working Procedures of the Panel.

63 US 11 February Comments, paras. 22-34.

64 *See, e.g.,* Brazil's 18 February Comments, para. 38 ("[A] close look at the text of Annex IV reveals that it is ill-equipped to address the tabulation of support issue before the Panel."); *id.,* para. 41 ("Thus, Annex IV does not assist the Panel in determining the amount of support to upland cotton, within the meaning of Article 13(b)(ii) of the Agreement on Agriculture.").

65 *See* Brazil's Comment on US Answer to Question 214 from the Panel, para. 216.

66 Brazil's 18 February 18 Comments, para. 41 ("Thus, Annex IV does not assist the Panel in determining the amount of support to upland cotton, within the meaning of Article 13(b)(ii) of the Agreement on Agriculture.").

67 Brazil's 18 February Comments, para. 69.

not enough to meet its *prima facie* case. A party may not make an argument, even if "in the alternative", for the first time nine months into briefing in a dispute, in its 18 February "Comments on US 11 February Comments on Brazil's 28 January 'Comments and Requests Regarding Data Provided by the United States on 18/19 December 2003 and the US Refusal to Provide Non-Scrambled Data on 20 January 2004", in order to later claim to have carried its burden of making a *prima facie* case should the Panel decide to rely on this new argument. (The Panel will appreciate the irony that the party that has been complaining incessantly about delay in the proceedings has now been reduced to improperly trying to take advantage of that delay.) To allow this would deny the United States due process – as the entire dispute has been argued on other grounds and enormous amounts of time and resources have been devoted to defending against the arguments Brazil *did* make – and deprive the Panel of the opportunity to receive fully considered briefing with respect to those issues.

33. Finally, through its belated and patently inadequate arguments and evidence relating to Annex IV, Brazil has put the Panel in the inappropriate position of "mak[ing] the case for the complaining party" were it to base any serious prejudice findings on decoupled payment subsidies allocated using the Annex IV methodology. As we stated in the February 11 comments:

- "Brazil has neither sought nor presented any evidence relating to the total value of the recipient firms' sales. Brazil has also not only *not* argued that the Annex IV methodology is necessary to identify the subsidized product and the subsidy benefit, Brazil has also continually argued against use of the Annex IV methodology since, in its view, no allocation of the payment or quantification of the benefit is warranted under Part III of the Subsidies Agreement. Thus, it would appear that Brazil has resisted making the necessary legal arguments and refused to submit any evidence relating a proper analysis of its claims."[68]

Brazil chose to challenge decoupled income support payments not tied to production or sale of a given product but also chose not to seek, develop, and present evidence relating to the total value of the recipients' sales. In fact, Brazil has not presented evidence that would allow that methodology to be applied.[69] Therefore, due to its own litigation choices, Brazil has not established the amount of the challenged subsidies and therefore has not established a *prima facie* case that the effect of decoupled income support payments is to cause serious prejudice to Brazil's interests. The United States respectfully requests the Panel to so find.

34. The United States has reviewed Brazil's new comments regarding the *Japan – Agricultural Products* Appellate Body report and believes that Brazil continues to misread that report. In fact, Brazil does not address any of the facts relating to the "claims" and "arguments" made by the United States in that dis-

---

[68] US 11 February Comments, para. 33.

[69] *See* US 11 February Comments, paras. 44-60.

pute, instead relying on generalizations as to "the proposition" that that report "stands for".[70] The United States refers the Panel to its previous comments on this report for a more complete analysis.[71]

35. The United States does note that Brazil argues that any evidence sought by the Panel that would allow an Annex IV calculation to be made "was entirely consistent" with the US proposal of that methodology and Brazil's in the alternative argument. We have already shown that Brazil's "in the alternative" evidence and arguments are patently insufficient, and this was done without the need for additional information or the need to run any Annex IV calculations. Further, it requires no information to understand and evaluate the US rebuttal that Brazil had not brought forward evidence and arguments relating to the Annex IV methodology necessary for Brazil to identify the subsidy benefit and subsidized product. In other words, Brazil cannot use a US defence as rationale to insist that the Panel seek information and make all the Annex IV calculations necessary to make Brazil's *prima facie* case for Brazil.

Brazil's Various Allocation Methodologies, In Addition to Being Irrelevant for Peace Clause Purposes and Inapplicable for Serious Prejudice Claims, Are Internally Inconsistent and Illogical

36. The United States here addresses Brazil's revised, and in some cases new, allocation methodologies. Brazil advances all of these allocation calculations for purposes of the Peace Clause (and, in the alternative, to identify the amount of the challenged subsidies). For purposes of the Peace Clause, as set out above, the United States believes that no allocation methodology may be employed since the only relevant support is product-specific. For purposes of Brazil's serious prejudice claims, we have already explained that the Annex IV methodology would be necessary to identify the subsidy benefit and subsidized product for each of the challenged decoupled income support measures – and Brazil has not brought forward evidence and arguments to allow the Annex IV methodology to be used. Nonetheless, here we present certain additional comments on Brazil's allocation methodologies.

Brazil's Allocation Methodology Is Internally Inconsistent and Not Applied Consistently

37. In its February 18 comments, Brazil reaffirms that "its methodology allocates support paid for upland cotton base that is 'planted to' upland cotton. It further allocates proportionally any other contract crop base payments that are not allocated to plantings of the respective contract payments crop".[72] We note that Brazil inserted quotation marks around "planted to" in the phrase "upland cotton base that is 'planted to' upland cotton". The reason for this is, as the United States has explained, there are no physical "base acres" on a farm. Crop base acres are

[70] Brazil's 18 February Comments, para. 88.
[71] US 11 February Comments, paras. 31-34.
[72] Brazil's 18 February Comments, para. 57.

an accounting fiction that do not represent any particular acres on the farm.[73] Thus, base acres cannot be physically "planted to" any crop; this expression merely means that a quantity of acres has been planted that corresponds to (are equal to or less than) a farm's quantity of base acres. Thus, at the outset, there is no physical basis to say that decoupled payments for base acres of a crop must be "support to" that crop to the extent that the quantity of planted acres is less than or equal to the quantity of base acres – but that is exactly the first step in Brazil's flawed methodology.[74]

38. There is also no economic basis to conclude that (in Brazil's words) payments for base acres of a crop "planted to" that crop are support to that planted crop. Because a recipient of a decoupled income support payment is free to plant no crop, plant one crop, plant multiple crops, or engage in other economic activities, that payment is a subsidy to all of the recipient's economic activities (if any). Brazil's "planted to" approach does not take into account the fungible nature of money: if the payment recipient chooses to produce only upland cotton, that would be the sole "subsidized product", but if the recipient chooses to produce upland cotton and other products, all of those products are the "subsidized product" since the payment could have been applied to any of those activities. (In fact, recipients of decoupled payments *do* engage in a myriad of other activities; for example, in marketing year 2002, the 137,160 cotton farms falling in Category A as defined by the Panel (that is, that planted fewer cotton acres than their quantities of upland cotton base acres) planted over 1 million acres of fruits and vegetables and nearly 7 million acres of "other crops" as compared to nearly 6 million acres of upland cotton.)[75]

39. Further, we note that Brazil's reason for treating decoupled income support payments for upland cotton base acres as "support to" upland cotton was allegedly based on the *de facto* tie between such payments and upland cotton production. That is, Brazil argued that such payments were necessary to support or maintain upland cotton production.[76] But Brazil does not apply that analysis throughout its methodology.

- Brazil also allocates decoupled income support payments for non-upland cotton base acres *first* to the respective programme crops.[77]

---

73 US 11 February Comments, para. 38.

74 Applied to decoupled payments for upland cotton base acres, this first step in Brazil's methodology is the "cotton-to-cotton" alternative methodology set out by Brazil. *See, e.g.,* Brazil's 18 February Comments, Annex A, para. 3 ("Under this approach, only upland cotton payments for upland cotton base acres that are *actually planted to* upland cotton would be considered support to upland cotton.") (italics added). As set out in the text above, base acres are not "actually planted to" anything; thus, in addition to not accounting for the fungible nature of money, the cotton-to-cotton methodology is not based on any physical reality.

75 *See* file "DCP02-2W.xls" (Category A farms, "Total" row).

76 *See, e.g.,* Brazil's 18 February Comments, paras. 22-28.

77 *See, e.g.,* Brazil's February 18 Comments, Annex A, Tables 2.5-2.7; *id.,* Annex A, para. 15 n. 175 ("The subsidy allocated is the entire amount of contract payments for that crop if planted acreage exceeds or equals base acreage. The subsidy allocated is [the] amount of contract payments for that crop adjusted by the ratio of planted acreage to base acreage if planted acreage is below base acreage.").

- However, Brazil has made *no analysis* of whether such decoupled payments for *non*-upland cotton base acres support or maintain the production of the respective programme crop to which they are allocated by Brazil.

Therefore, *even under its own Peace Clause analysis*, Brazil has provided no basis to a key step in its allocation methodology – that is, the allocation of payments for non-upland cotton base acres first to the respective programme crops.

40. Brazil's current Peace Clause allocation methodology also directly contradicts its position earlier in this dispute. First, Brazil argued that all payments for upland cotton base acres were support to upland cotton. Then, Brazil amended its argument and asserted that, in order to cover their total costs, upland cotton producers must have planted upland cotton "on" upland cotton base acres. Subsequently, Brazil changed that argument to upland cotton must be "planted on" base acres for upland cotton, rice, or peanuts.[78] Thus, the latter two of these arguments were predicated on the notion that each planted acre of upland cotton corresponded to one base acre. Now, however, Brazil's allocation methodology could assign payments from multiple base acres to a single planted acre of upland cotton.[79]

41. Tellingly, Brazil has no response to this critique of its methodology, other than to assert that "they affect, at most, 0.9 per cent of the payments at issue for MY 2002"[80] and a vague statement that "[a]s for some of the US criticisms that might affect the results (except for MY2002), Brazil will control for these effects once the United States provides aggregate data in the manner requested by the Panel".[81]

- That is, Brazil has *no logical explanation* for the internal inconsistency in its methodology, that one upland cotton base acre should be allocated to one upland cotton planted acre while multiple non-upland cotton base acres could be allocated to one upland cotton planted acre.

This internal inconsistency suggests that Brazil's methodology is an effort to assign the maximum amount of payments to upland cotton, regardless of whether it provides any economically neutral method to allocate decoupled payments (as Annex IV, paragraph 2, does).

42. As the United States has previously pointed out, moreover, there is no economic reason to attribute decoupled income support payments to some crops (programme crops) but not others and some economic activities (programme

---

[78] *See, e.g.*, Brazil's Closing Statement at the Second Session of the First Panel Meeting, Annex I (summary of evidence demonstrating that upland cotton producers in MY 1999-2002 produced upland cotton on upland cotton, rice, or peanut base acreage) (9 October 2003).

[79] *See* US 11 February Comments, para. 38 (providing example of farm with 100 base acres of soy, 10 planted acres of soy, and 1 planted acre of cotton; under Brazil's methodology, the 1 acre of cotton would be "planted on" (receive payments related to) 90 base acres of soy).

[80] Brazil's 18 February Comments, para. 60.

[81] Brazil's 18 February Comments, para. 67.

crop production) but not others.[82] Brazil's 18 February calculations demonstrate the point. For farms with *no* upland cotton base acres, Brazil treats all upland cotton planted acres as "overplanted base" (that is, planted acres in excess of base acres) eligible for an allocation of the total subsidies available from "excess" base acres for other programme crops.[83]

- However, non-programme crops are in the *identical position* to upland cotton: that is, all non-programme crops also have base acreage equal to zero.[84]
- Even on Brazil's methodology, there is no reason (other than Brazil's assertion that it is so) to treat decoupled payments for non-upland cotton base acres as subsidizing upland cotton when a farm has overplanted its (zero) upland cotton base but *not* to non-programme crops that also (necessarily) have "overplanted" their base.

43. Finally, we note that, had Brazil desired to make its invented allocation methodology consistent with other arguments in its 18 February comments, it should have allocated "excess" base acres *not* to programme crops with "overplanted base" but rather to any crop (programme or not) produced by a payment recipient for which such payments "cover (or contribute to) the costs of production".[85] Where payments "cover (or contribute to) the costs of production," according to Brazil, payments *must* be "support to [that] specific commodity."[86] Further, if Brazil has *not* analyzed whether the challenged payments "cover (or contribute to) the costs of production" of other products produced by payment recipients, Brazil cannot assert that any payments must be "support to" one commodity over another since the payment might be necessary to "cover (or contribute to) the costs of production" of more than one product. That Brazil was unwilling to apply its "costs of production" principle throughout its allocation methodology suggests that Brazil's approach to Peace Clause interpretation has been a *post hoc* exercise in rationalization.

44. In sum, Brazil's allocation methodology is irrelevant to the Peace Clause because the only relevant support is product-specific. Unlike the Annex IV methodology, moreover, it is not a neutral and economically rational methodology for allocating a non-tied subsidy (such as decoupled payments) in order to

---

82 *See* US 11 February Comments, para. 37.

83 *See, e.g.,* Brazil's 18 February Comments, Tables 2.17 & 2.18 (upland cotton base acres: 0; upland cotton planted acres: 518,837.0; planted acres over which "excess" subsidy allocated: 518,837.0).

84 The data submitted in response to the Panel's supplementary request for information reveals that in marketing year 2002 (after base acres were established under the 2002 Act) farms planting upland cotton and having no upland cotton base acres planted substantial amounts of non-programme crop acreage, for example, 64,917 acres of fruits and vegetables, 9,664 acres of tobacco, and 169,480 acres of other crops. *See* "DCP02-2W.xls" file, Category C farms, "Total" row.

85 Brazil's 18 February Comments, para. 3.

86 Recall that it is for purposes of the Peace Clause that Brazil asserts its allocation methodology; in the alternative, Brazil argues that its Peace Clause methodology would also calculate the amount of the subsidy for its serious prejudice claims.

identify the subsidized product and the amount of the subsidy. Finally, it is internally inconsistent and even contradicts other arguments Brazil has put forward in this dispute, for example, its argument that a payment is "support to a specific commodity" if it "cover[s] (or contribute[s] to) the costs of production" of that commodity.

Brazil's "Annex IV" Methodologies Are Nothing Like the Methodology Set Out in Annex IV

45. Brazil presents two other methodologies, a "modified Annex IV" calculation and a "US Annex IV calculation". Neither of these methodologies could serve as a basis to identify the amount of subsidy and subsidized product for purposes of Brazil's serious prejudice claims. The correct methodology is neither a "modified" nor a "US" methodology; rather, it is the methodology set out in the text of Annex IV. That text establishes that, if a payment is not "tied to the production or sale of a given product," the subsidized product is all of the recipient firm's sales, and the subsidy for any one product is that product's share of "the total value of the recipient firm's sales".[87] Brazil does not use "the total value of the recipient firm's sales" in its "Annex IV calculations" and does not even attempt to calculate total sales of upland cotton producers. Thus, neither of these methodologies can fairly be called an "Annex IV" calculation.

46. With respect to Brazil's "modified Annex IV" methodology, we note that Brazil allocated total contract payments to farms producing upland cotton "over the value of *contract payment* crops produced on the farms" based on the assumption that "contract payments are support only to contract payment crops".[88] This approach is fundamentally inconsistent with Annex IV, paragraph 2, under which the subsidy is allocated over "the total value of the recipient firm's sales." Further, the United States has set out above a rebuttal of Brazil's assertion that decoupled income support payments could be considered "support only to contract payment crops". For example, such an approach ignores the fungible nature of money and contradicts Brazil's argument that payments are support to those crops whose costs are covered by the payments.

47. With respect to Brazil's "US Annex IV methodology," the United States has explained above that Brazil has not made a *prima facie* case with respect to decoupled payments because it has not presented evidence and arguments sufficient to allow an Annex IV calculation to be made. Brazil also has not corrected for errors in its calculations that the United States previously pointed out in its 11 February comments.

48. For example, Brazil's "US Annex IV methodology" errs in omitting the value of fruits and vegetables in calculating the total value of non-programme crop production. Brazil justifies this stance by asserting that fruits and vegetables could not possibly be "beneficiaries" of decoupled payments because they may not be grown on base acres. Again, this argument by Brazil ignores Annex IV,

[87] Subsidies Agreement, Annex IV, paras. 2-3.
[88] Brazil's 18 February Comments, para. 50.

paragraph 2, under which the subsidy is allocated over "the total value of the recipient firm's sales" and ignores the non-tied (decoupled) nature of these payments. The aggregate data submitted today demonstrates that, in marketing year 2002 alone, 1.2 million acres were planted to fruits and vegetables on farms that reported cotton base acreage.[89] As pointed out in the US comments of 11 February[90], excluding fruits and vegetables biases significantly downward the value of non-programme crop acreage. For example, the per-acre value of non-programme crops including fruits and vegetables was estimated at $281[91] for 2002 – that is, 138 per cent higher than the $118 per acre Brazil calculated when fruits and vegetables are excluded.[92]

49. Including fruits and vegetables in the total value of crop production gives a more accurate reflection of the share of upland cotton as a per cent of the total value of crop production on farms that planted upland cotton. As noted previously,[93] had Brazil included fruits and vegetables in the value of non-programme crop cropland, upland cotton would have accounted for approximately 48.4 per cent to 56.7 per cent of the total value of crop production on farms that planted cotton in 1999-2002.

50. Moreover, Brazil has not taken any account of the value of on-farm production other than crops, and has presented no data that would allow that calculation to be made. Again, Brazil's approach is inconsistent with Annex IV, paragraph 2, pursuant to which the subsidy is allocated over "the total value of the recipient firm's sales." Brazil asserts that its "decision not to include any livestock value" is supported by the 1997 ARMS cotton costs of production survey, but that survey only shows that a small number of cotton farms in the survey year "specialized" in livestock production. Brazil does not define what "specialization" in livestock production would entail, but it would seem that a farm may have sales of a product without "specializing" in that product. The evidence suggests that, had Brazil taken into account the value of non-crop on-farm production, the share of cotton as a per cent of total farm sales would be lower still. For example, in the 1997 ARMS cotton costs of production survey, the US Department of Agriculture found that, for 1997 when the value of cotton was high, cotton accounted for only 44.5 per cent of the total value of agricultural production on cotton farms.[94]

51. Brazil also fails to include off-farm economic activity, which can be substantial, in its calculation. Annex IV, paragraph 2, establishes that the non-tied subsidy is allocated over "the total value of the recipient firm's sales"; there is no basis in that provision to limit the sales over which the subsidy is allocated to *farm* sales. Brazil's refusal to apply the Annex IV methodology in full introduces

---

[89] *See* file "DCP02-2W.xls" ("Grand Total (Farms A - C)" row).

[90] *See* US 11 February Comments, para. 54.

[91] See Exhibit US-154.

[92] Brazil's 18 February Comments, Annex A, Table 4.5.

[93] *See* US 11 February Comments, para. 57.

[94] See Exhibit BRA-16, table 3.

yet another serious distortion in its calculation as cotton operations earn almost 30 per cent of income from off-farm sources.[95]

52. Finally, Brazil contests the notion that, in calculating the amount of subsidy benefiting upland cotton, it must take account of the fact that decoupled payments for base acres are capitalized into higher land values and cash rents, thus benefiting land owners, not necessarily those farming the land, referring the Panel to its 28 January comments.[96] There, Brazil asserts that it is for the United States to demonstrate that payments on rented acres are capitalized into rents, thus impermissibly seeking to shift its burden of establishing the amount of challenged subsidies to the United States as responding party. Brazil also cites aggregate state-level data on cash rents to show that average cash rents in some cotton-producing states increased by less than the rate of inflation over the 1996-2002 period.[97] Such analysis, however, ignores the aggregation bias introduced by averaging (1) cash rents from farmland *with* programme base with (2) cash rents from farmland *without* programme base.

53. We recall that Brazil has previously conceded that, as of marketing year 1997, 34 to 41 cents per dollar of production flexibility contract payments were capitalized into land rent.[98] Brazil now argues that there is no evidence that further (increased) shares of production flexibility contract payments were capitalized in subsequent years. The Commission on the Application of Payment Limitations for Agriculture, to which Dr. Sumner presented testimony, reached conclusions on this very issue, however, and Brazil submitted this report as Exhibit BRA-276. The United States was therefore disappointed to see that Brazil's exhibit was missing pages 89-122, which precisely includes the portion of Chapter 5 of the Report entitled "Effects of Further Payment Limitations on Farmland Values." We attach as Exhibit US-155 the missing pages from the report.

54. The analysis of the *Report of the Commission on the Application of Payment Limitations for Agriculture* directly contradicts Brazil's conclusion that cash rent data "do [not] appear to reflect to any considerable extent the effects of PFC or other contract acreage payments".[99] To the contrary, the Commission's Report explained:

> In early 1997, professional farm managers indicated that in areas where competition for rental land was intense, *PFC payments were almost immediately captured by landowners and reflected in rental rates and land values*. Given the intense competition for leased land in many areas, tenants operating on cash leases found their lease rates being bid up until the landowner had captured most of the tenant's share of PFC payments. Producers with share leases reported that some landowners reduced their share of expenses, re-

---

95 *See* US Further Rebuttal Submission, para. 137.

96 Brazil's 18 February Comments, para. 75.

97 *See* Brazil's Comments on US Answer to Panel Question 242, paras. 204-206 (28 January 2003).

98 Brazil's Answer to Question 179 from the Panel, para. 165 (27 October 2003); Brazil's Opening Statement at the Second Panel Meeting, para. 57.

99 Brazil's Comments on US Answer to Panel Question 242, para. 208 (28 January 2004).

> tained a larger crop share, or converted from share leases to cash leases. However, in areas where competition for rental land was less intense, tenants retained much of their PFC payments (Ryan et al). *Goodwin and Mishra estimate that each additional dollar per acre of PFC payments increased US average rents by $0.81 to $0.83 per acre during 1998-2000.*[100]

Thus, the missing pages from Brazil's own exhibit reports that, during 1998-2000, an estimated average of 81 to 83 per cent of production flexibility contract payments were captured by landowners through increased rent.[101] This conclusion is consistent with the US position that land owners capture the benefit of decoupled payments for base acres made to producers on rented land.[102] The Report also extends its conclusions to market loss assistance payments, direct payments, and counter-cyclical payments.[103]

55. We also note Brazil's argument that counter-cyclical payments could not be captured by landowners through increased rent because the payments are "triggered on a year-by-year basis depending on low prices for upland cotton", and a landowner "cannot know in what amount CCP payments will be made".[104] As noted, the Commission's Report does not support Brazil's position on counter-cyclical payments. However, Brazil does not draw the logical conclusion from its assertion: if that statement is true, then counter-cyclical payments cannot have effects on cotton farmers' planting decisions and production because farmers (and therefore landowners) cannot anticipate receiving those payments. On the other hand, to suggest that counter-cyclical payments *do* have production effects, Brazil has also argued that farmers *do* anticipate counter-cyclical payments being

---

[100] Exhibit US-155, at 106 (italics added).

[101] We also note that this information directly contradicts Brazil's previous argument that "contrary to the premise of the Panel's question [179], th[e] evidence suggests that PFC payments are somewhat, but not 'largely capitalized' into land rents". Brazil's Answer to Question 179 from the Panel, para. 165 (27 October 2003).

[102] Brazil also attempts to draw a distinction between land that is cash-rented versus share-rented. However, the Commission's Report describes a "non-operator landlord" as including those who "receiv[e] rent in the form of the crop produced on the land." Exhibit US-155, at 104. Thus, the Report's conclusions that the benefits of government payments largely accrue to non-operator landlords would appear to apply to owners who share-rent their land as well.

[103] *See, e.g.,* Exhibit US-155, at 106 ("Barnard et al. (2001) estimated that $62 billion or 20 per cent of the value of land producing the 8 major programme crops ... was due to PFC payments, market loss assistance, disaster payments, and marketing loan benefits."); *id.* at 106 ("The effects of farm commodity payments on cropland values vary geographically, reflecting differences in ... payments for crops eligible for direct and counter-cyclical payments and marketing loan benefits ... ."); *id.* at 111 ("Government payments in the form of direct payments, counter-cyclical payments, and marketing loan benefits affect the value of farmland and land rents. Several studies indicate that government payments in recent years have increased farmland values nationally by 15-25 per cent.")

[104] Brazil's Comments on US 22 December 2003 Answers, para. 209 (28 January 2003). Brazil goes on to say: "Further, as Brazil has demonstrated repeatedly, given the high non-land-related production costs involved in producing cotton, most US producers simply could not profitably produce cotton without CCP payments. Therefore, there is little, if any, basis for a non-producing landlord to demand increased rents to capture CCP payments". *Ibid.* The United States is puzzled by this assertion. It would appear that Brazil is saying that landlords would not charge higher rental rates because producers "could not profitably produce cotton without CCP payments". This is not our understanding of how landlords choose to set rental rates.

made.[105] If that is true, then Brazil's own evidence demonstrates that those payments will be capitalized. Brazil cannot have it both ways.

56. In sum, Brazil's two "Annex IV" methodologies are wholly inadequate because Brazil does not even attempt to apply the methodology actually set out in Annex IV: that is, to allocate the value of a non-tied subsidy across "the total value of the recipient firm's sales". Brazil has never sought nor presented the value of *total sales* of the recipients (upland cotton producers) of the challenged decoupled income support payments. Brazil's inadequate calculations cannot meet its burden of establishing a *prima facie* case on decoupled income support payments for purposes of its serious prejudice claims.

Conclusion: Brazil's Interpretation of the Peace Clause Would Upset the Balance of Rights and Obligations of Members in the WTO Agreements

57. Throughout this dispute, we have noted that Brazil's Peace Clause interpretation is without foundation in the text and context of that provision and would upset the balance of rights and obligations set out in the Agreement on Agriculture. Brazil asserts that "[h]ad the United States been concerned about the certainty of its peace clause 'protection,' it would not have been difficult for Congress, in the 1996 FAIR Act or even the 2002 FSRI Act, to include a 'circuit breaker' provision directing the USDA Secretary to stop funding any upland cotton budgetary outlays in excess of the 1992 levels".[106] Of course, the United States has disciplined itself to grant support not in excess of that decided during the 1992 marketing year by shifting away from the product-specific deficiency payments with high target prices under the 1990 Act and instead to provide a mix of decoupled income supports that are green box (direct payments) or non-product-specific (counter-cyclical payments) and product-specific marketing loan payments. But Brazil's assertion raises a number of questions:

- How could the United States have known how to cap the budgetary outlays under the decoupled income support measures to stay within the 1992 levels?
- How could the United States have known what payments would be considered "support to upland cotton" under Brazil's methodology, which only appeared on 20 January 2004?
- Which of Brazil's five in-the-alternative methodologies – the "cotton-to-cotton methodology", "Brazil's methodology", the "modified Annex IV methodology", the "US Annex IV methodology", or "Brazil's 14/16th methodology"[107] – should the United States have

[105] For example, in Dr. Sumner's model, acreage is a function of the net return to planting cotton, which includes prospective counter-cyclical payments. *See* Brazil's Further Submission, Annex I, para. 28 (equation (1)).

[106] Brazil's 18 February Comments, para. 85.

[107] *See, e.g.,* Brazil's 18 February Comments, para. 55. We note that the range of budgetary outlays Brazil calculates under these five in-the-alternative methodologies range from, for 2002 direct payments, $383.1 million to $466.8 million, and for 2002 counter-cyclical payments, from $640.4 million to $988.3 million.

been applying to ensure that budgetary outlays did not exceed the 1992 level?

Indeed, Brazil has ended this dispute taking the position that "the Panel needs to adopt a *reasonable* methodology to be applied for purposes of the peace clause in assessing the amount of support to upland cotton from the four contract payment programmes".[108] It is difficult to imagine how that standard could have been incorporated into the design of the challenged decoupled income support measures to ensure Peace Clause compliance.

58. The United States submits that the Peace Clause must be interpreted in a way that permits Members to comply in good faith – that is, Members must be able to tell if they will breach the Peace Clause or not. Putting legal interpretive issues aside, Brazil's budgetary outlays approach does not do that since, with price-based support such as marketing loan payments, the United States cannot "decide" market prices.[109] Brazil's allocation methodology also does not do that because the United States does not "decide" what a decoupled income support recipient chooses to produce (or not to produce).[110] Brazil's approach to Peace Clause issues would rob Members of the ability to design price-based and income support measures to conform to the Peace Clause and mean that Members could not know if they had complied with the Peace Clause until it was too late to do anything about it.

59. The United States has demonstrated that using any measurement that reflects the support "decided" by the United States – rather than factors (such as market prices) beyond the United States' control – US support to upland cotton in marketing years 1999-2002 has not exceeded the 1992 marketing year level.[111] The question then is whether the Panel will find that the United States has breached the Peace Clause simply because market prices were lower in some recent years than they were in 1992. We have demonstrated that the United States has disciplined itself to grant support not in excess of that decided during the 1992 marketing year.[112] Therefore, we are entitled to the protection of the Peace Clause and respectfully request the Panel to so find.

---

108 Brazil's 18 February Comments, para. 42 (italics added).

109 We have previously noted that "support" does not mean "budgetary outlays". US 11 February Comments, para. 16 n.12. In addition, it is ironic that Brazil criticizes the US interpretation on the grounds that the Peace Clause does not read "product-specific support" when the Peace Clause also does not read "budgetary outlays"; however, the latter *is* a defined term in Article 1(b) of the Agreement on Agriculture while the former is not, suggesting that Members' decision not to use "budgetary outlays" in the Peace Clause was deliberate.

110 As set out above, no allocation methodology can be applied to the Peace Clause as the only support that is relevant to that determination is support to a specific commodity, read according to its ordinary meaning and in context.

111 *See, e.g.*, US 11 February Comments, paras. 15-17.

112 Recognizing, as the United States believes is required by the Peace Clause text, that "decided" and "grant" cover only those parameters over which Members exercise control would also be consistent with this approach of allowing "good faith" compliance since it would permit Members to control whether their measures conformed to their obligations.

ANNEX I-24

RESPONSE OF THE UNITED STATES TO THE PANEL'S 3 FEBRUARY 2004 DATA REQUEST, AS CLARIFIED ON 16 FEBRUARY 2004

3 March 2004

Introduction

1. The United States is submitting today 8 data files, as requested by the Panel in its 3 February 2004, supplementary request for information, as clarified by the Panel's communication of 16 February 2004. The files are in an EXCEL format.

2. The data has been prepared in response to those letters, and has been prepared as well as possible in the time allotted, involving much time and effort. We first address how the files were derived and issues involved in their preparation, such as the handling of 1999 and 2000 crop soybeans and 2002 peanuts. Because of the peanut and soybean issues, there were in essence two runs of data, and both sets of data are presented.

3. In the first run, the United States ran the figures for 1999 and 2000 treating soybeans as a non-base crop, and thus one which would not effect any categorizations based on comparing plantings of total programme crops to total programme crop bases (such as those necessary to sort farms into B1, B2, and B3 categories). In the second run, soybeans were treated as a full programme crop for the Market Loss Assistance payments for those years in which oilseed payments were made (1999 and 2000) with an assigned base of zero for each farm as there were no farm bases for the soybean crops for 1999 and 2000.

4. Likewise, for peanuts, there were separate runs for 2002. In the first run, the peanut crops for Direct payments and Counter-cyclical payments were treated as a non-programme crop for categorization purposes. In the second run, peanuts were treated as a programme crop with a base of zero for each farm.

5. These two runs took into account the directive of the Panel of 16 February. There, the Panel instructed us to treat soybeans for Market Loss Assistance (MLA) as a programme crop and peanuts as a Direct and Counter-cyclical Payment (DCP) crop. As indicated, this did raise a question, one which is colored somewhat by a broader issue on the MLA payments themselves. There is no separate base acreage or yields for MLA purposes. And, the oilseed programmes for 1999 and 2000 were not farm based programmes. No farm had a soybean base for those years. Likewise, with peanuts, there was no farm base for 2002, the first year that peanuts became a programme crop. Bases were not assigned for peanuts until 2003 and could not be effective until that year. For 2002, the peanut programme was a producer-based programme. The same was true for soybeans in 1999 and 2000.

6. Finally, we also present the results of our efforts to identify any farms that would not have protectable privacy interests under the Privacy Act of 1974, as requested in item (a) of the Panel's 3 February supplementary request for information.

7. We then indicate how the files were put together and identify the files.

There were no Separate Market Loss Assistance Bases; Rather the Payments Were Made Proportionately to the Production Flexibility Contract (PFC) Payments

8. The market loss assistance payments (MLAs) were after the fact and simply supplemented payments that were made to a person under a PFC contract. There were no new contracts, bases, or yields. There were four MLA programmes. The first was for the 1998 crop. MLA programmes followed for the 1999, 2000 and 2001 crops, each under separate legislation, each after the fact – that is after the crop was planted and in supplement of payments already made under the PFC contracts.

9. To respond to the Panel's data request of 3 February 2004, the United States was called upon to give information for the PFCs and the MLAs. The data request was for base acreage with respect to farms that were in the programme. There were no bases as such for MLAs. The payments were proportional to what has been received in the PFC. The only slight difference was that for 2000, where Congress simply prescribed a rate, drawing from the previous statute for the previous crop. Thus, we have treated the request for MLA data (as explained below, soybeans aside) to be a request for the PFC data for the PFC year for which the PFC payment was supplemented by a particular MLA payment.

There Was No Soybean Farm Base for the 1999 and 2000 Market Loss Assistance Programme As There Were No Market Loss Assistance Programmes for Soybeans, and Oilseed Payments in those Years were Producer-Based, Not Farm-Based

10. Soybeans complicate the analysis. The United States reads the Panel's 16 February letter to indicate that for purposes of the data request, soybeans should be treated as an MLA crop. This presents an analytical problem because no farm had a soybean base. We note that the data files do contain for every category the soybean plantings for 1999 and 2000. (We note that there was no oilseed programme, and therefore no payments for soybeans, for 2001.)

11. As an initial matter, soybean payments for 1999 and 2000 were part of an overall oilseeds programme. There was no oilseed programme for the 2001 crop; therefore, there was no soybean payment of any kind for that year. There was never, even for 1999 and 2000, a base or yield for a farm for oilseeds in the PFC era.

12. For the PFC programme crops like cotton, the "farm" had a base. The "farm" had a yield. "Producers" on the farm received the payment even if they were not the same person who had produced the crops that produced the historic base or yield or had even been on the farm when the base or yield were created.

If the producer had an interest in several farms with base under the PFC programmes, the producer received several checks. The base acreage and yield derived from historical plantings on the farm.

13. In the oilseeds programme, it was completely different. The producer had a base. The producer had a yield. The farm had no base. The farm had no yield. For the 1999 programme, if the producer was on Farm X in 1999 and planted soybeans there, the producer could receive a payment based on plantings that the producer may have had on Farms A, B, C, and D in the historical period. Current producers on Farms A, B, C, and D, by contrast, would have no "base." In short, there was no base for soybeans for any farm for oilseeds payments for 1999 or 2000.

14. Thus, this is the problem in terms of the data request for the Panel: the request considers soybeans as a covered commodity for MLAs and seeks information for base acreage on "farms," but soybean base for 1999 and 2000 oilseed payments was producer-based, not farm-based. In order to be as responsive as possible, we have run the data two ways. First, for 1999 and 2000, we treat soybeans as a non-programme crop for purposes of categorizing the farms into subcategories (as explained in more detail below), but show the actual soybean plantings for all farms. In the second run, we treat soybeans as a programme crop and, for categorization purposes, treat all farms as having a soybean base of zero.

15. We respectfully refer the Panel to its 3 February 2004, letter. Category B farms are those with cotton "overplantings" – that is with more cotton plantings than cotton base. Category B2 farms are defined are those where, for all covered crops added together, the farm underplanted the total aggregated base. B3 is the mirror image of B2. It is where there was an aggregated overplanting for all programme crops taken together.

16. Assume the following plantings on Farm A:

Cotton	Base 10	Plantings 12
Rice	Base 5	Plantings 0
Soybeans	-	Plantings 5

If soybean plantings do not matter for categorization, then this farm is a B2 farm since the plantings for rice and cotton would be 12 and the total base would be 15. But if soybeans are counted and treated as having a zero base, then this farm is a B3 farm because the countable base would still be 15, but the plantings would now be 17. This would only be the case for MLA. Since soybeans, under the Panel's February 16 letter, would only be counted for MLAs, the farm would still be a B2 farm for purposes of the PFC calculations for the same year.

17. As we have indicated and set out further below, we have it covered both ways. We provide a file in which soybeans are treated as a covered commodity (for MLA purposes) with a farm base of zero. We also present a file in which soybeans are not considered a programme crop, in which the PFC and MLA figures are the same.

Farms Had No Peanut Base in 2002 Because the 2002 Peanut Programme was Producer-Based, Not Farm-Based

18. The Peanut programme presents the same problem for the 2002 Direct and Counter-cyclical Programme (DCP) as do soybeans for the 1999 and 2000 programmes, since it too was a producer-based, not a farm-based programme. There were no peanut bases for 2002 for any farm. The base was assigned to a producer for 2002. That producer had to be a "historical peanut producer" – someone who had produced peanuts in the base period. For the 2002 crop year, the producer received one check for all of the producer's base, calculated as the payment rate times the "payment acres of the historic cotton producer" times the "average peanut yield ... for the historic cotton producer."[1] However, starting in 2003, the base and yield had to be assigned by the historical producer to a farm of that producer's choice. The designated farm did not have to be a farm in which the producer had an interest, or one on which the producer had ever produced peanuts, or, for that matter, one on which anyone had ever produced peanuts or would ever produce peanuts in the future.

19. The distinction is perhaps best demonstrated by example. Assume that a farmer had in 1998-2001 produced peanuts on rented Farms A, B, and C. Assume that for 2002 the farmer decided to get out of farming altogether, and was living in retirement in Denver, Colorado, far outside the peanut belt and with no interest in any farm or any farm production anywhere. Under the terms of the 2002 Farm Bill, that historical producer would receive a payment based on that producer's base and that producer's yield. If that farmer happened to be a producer in 2002 on Farm D, that farmer would nonetheless receive payment based on his or her production on Farms A, B, and C in the base period. Producers in 2002 on Farms A, B, and C would receive nothing (unless they of course had their own producer base).

20. For 2003, however, the farmer living in Denver would have to pick a farm on which to place his base.

21. In short, there were no bases for any peanut farm in 2002, and the problem is the same as for soybeans. As for soybeans, the data was run both ways – that is, treating peanuts as a covered commodity for 2002 with a farm base of zero and not treating peanuts as a covered commodity.

How the Data was Compiled

22. The United States now explains the source of the data. We have previously mentioned the limitations of crop reports, which is from where all the planting data in the aggregations presented here are derived. Crop reports were not generally required until 2002, at which point they were required for persons seeking benefits for crops other than peanuts in the form of direct payments, counter-cyclical payments, or marketing loans. As for peanuts, similar reporting requirements apply where the payments are in connection with farms for which a

[1] 2002 Farm Bill, § 1303(c) (direct payments) (Exhibit US-1); *see id.* § 1304(e) (counter-cyclical payments).

base is assigned. Hence, the peanut reporting provision only begins to apply with the 2003 crop.

23. We note that the total number of acres accounted for in 2002 may exceed the total cropland numbers set out in the 18-19 December 2003 data, as corrected on 28 January 2004. Differences may result because: (1) farmers may have reported plantings of grass on noncropland; (2) there can be double-cropping in some areas; and (3) CRP acres may not have been reported and counted as available cropland.

The Categories of Farms for the Aggregated Data Files Responsive to Part "(b)" of the Panel's Request

24. We have sorted and aggregated the relevant farms into those categories set out in the 3 February supplementary request from the Panel. Category A farms are those for which the farms underplanted their cotton base. The panel also asked for farms that did not plant any other covered commodities and we have classified those as "A1" farms.

25. Category B farms are farms that overplanted their base. Subcategory B1 farms are farms that, in total for all base crops, planted exactly their covered commodity base, while B2 farms under-planted and B3 farms over-planted those total bases.

26. Category C farms planted cotton but had no base.

Data on Farms Without Privacy Interests Under the Privacy Act of 1974 As Set Out in Item (a) of the Panel's Request

27. We now address what was item (a) of the Panel's 3 February supplementary request for information. The Panel asked for information relating to those farms that do not have a privacy interest and thus who could potentially be subject to a detailed release of planted and base acreage information. This information appears to be of little interest to Brazil at this point as Brazil indicated in its 13 February letter that "because the United States apparently intends only to provide farm-specific information for far less than the total amount of farms (i.e., those that are not held by 'individuals') this information will be useless for calculating the exact amount of total contract payments."[2] By way of contrast, Brazil commented that, "[i]f the United States provides the complete information requested in part (b) of the 3 February 2004 Request, then most of Brazil's 28 January Data Comments would be rendered moot," and "[w]ith the actual and complete data, the Panel would be in a position to apply any methodology it deems acceptable."[3]

---

2 Brazil's 13 February 2004, Letter to the Panel, at 2.

3 Brazil's 13 February 2004, Letter to the Panel, at 5. Brazil further commented that "by producing the complete aggregated information, there would no longer be a need to draw adverse inferences." *Ibid.* In light of the filing today of a complete response to item (b) of the Panel's supplementary request, the United States welcomes Brazil's withdrawal of its request that the Panel draw adverse inferences in this dispute.

28. For non-closely held corporations, information *voluntarily* received from a corporation is to be withheld if it is not the type of information customarily released by the corporation to the public. *See Center for Auto Safety v. National Highway Traffic Safety Administration*, 244 F.3d 144 (D.C. Cir. 2001).

29. Such is the case with respect to plantings prior to 2002. It would therefore, be necessary to examine, on a case by case basis, the circumstances of each "corporate" farming operation to determine if it is a closely held corporation which might enjoy a privacy interest and if the information was voluntarily submitted and not the type of information customarily released by the corporation to the public.

30. Given the time available, we used the year 2002 when in all cases, crop reports were mandatory with the limits indicated above. The United States conducted an electronic sort of cotton farms to narrow the number of files to a manageable number, which we then examined on a farm-by-farm basis to see if they were closely-held corporations. The data file containing farm-by-farm base, yield, and planted acreage information for these farms is described below.

The Data Files

31. The United States is providing the following data files via CD-ROM. This information is sensitive, and we do not consent to the release of this information to the public domain. Therefore, as with the data submitted on 18 and 19 December 2003, as corrected on 28 January 2004, pursuant to paragraph 3 of the Panel's working procedures, we designate this information as confidential.

32. *File Name: PFC1999W.xls*: This file is the first 1999 PFC and MLA file treating soybeans as a non-base crop and showing soybeans plantings.

33. *File Name: PFC99-2W.xls*: This file is the second 1999 PFC and MLA file. Soybeans is treated as a crop with a zero base on all farms.

34. *File Name: PFC2000W.xls*: This file is the 2000 PFC and MLA files with soybeans treated as a non-base crop and showing soybeans plantings.

35. *File Name: PFC00-2W.xls*: This file is the 2000 PFC and MLA files treating soybeans as a crop with a zero base on all farms.

36. *File Name: PFC2001W.xls*: This file is the 2001 PFC and MLA file.

37. *File Name: DCP2002W.xls*: This file is the 2002 Direct and Countercyclical file with peanuts treated as a non-base crop and showing peanuts plantings.

38. *File Name: DCP02-2W.xls*: This file is the 2002 Direct and Countercyclical file with peanuts treated as a crop with a zero base on all farms.

39. *File Name: notclose.xls*: This is the result of the search for not closely held farms as described above. (Each line corresponds to one farm. The base, yield, and planting fields are set out in the file and are the same as those in the base/yield and planted acres data files provided on 28 January 2004 (as set out in Exhibit US-145).)

ANNEX I-25

UNITED STATES' RESPONSE TO QUESTION 264(B) DATED 3 FEBRUARY 2004 FROM THE PANEL TO THE PARTIES FOLLOWING THE SECOND MEETING OF THE PANEL

3 March 2004

264. The Panel asks the United States to clarify certain aspects of Exhibit US-128:

(b) Does the US agree with the statement in paragraph 135 of Brazil's 28 January 2004 comments on US responses to questions that the difference between the $1,148 billion in the chart at para. 165 of Brazil's 11 August answers to questions and the $666 million amount in Exhibit US-128 ($1.75 billion) closely corresponds to the total "Claims rescheduled" figure reported by the US in Exhibit US-128 (column F)?

1. The United States first notes that Exhibit US-128 portrays data on a cohort basis. The figures in Brazil's chart are on a fiscal-year basis, which do not necessarily correspond to figures on a cohort-basis. In addition, data reflected in Exhibit US-128 commence with the 1992 cohort and end with the 2003 cohort. In contrast, Brazil's chart commences with fiscal year 1993 and ends with fiscal year 2002.

2. Also, as indicated in response to question 264(c)[1], Exhibit US-128 does not reflect the receipt of principal payments under the reschedulings. Exhibit US-148 (column F) reflects approximately $205 million of principal collected on the reschedulings. As a theoretical matter, such "recovered principal" should be reflected in the budget line 88.40 that Brazil cites in its chart. Accounting research within the US Government suggests, however, that a significant portion of this amount has not in fact been reflected in that budget line.

3. Although the $1.75 billion number cited in the question and the $1.637 billion number pertaining to "claims rescheduled" are numerically of the same order of magnitude, for the reasons noted above, a direct comparison between Exhibit US-128 and Brazil's chart is not as appropriate or facile as Brazil would suggest. Nevertheless, as a general matter, the United States acknowledges that the most significant difference between the data reflected in Exhibit US-128 and the data in the Brazilian chart arises as a function of the standard accounting treatment of reschedulings by the Commodity Credit Corporation as no longer constituting an outstanding claim, but in fact a new direct loan.[2] This is consis-

---

[1] US Answers to Further Panel Questions Following Second Panel Meeting (11 February 2004), para. 24

[2] Under FASAB: Original Pronouncements, Version 3 (01/2004), a "direct loan" is defined as "a disbursement of funds by the government to a nonfederal borrower under a contract that requires the repayment of such funds within a certain time with or without interest. The term includes the purchase of, or participation in, a loan made by another lender. (Adapted from OMB Circular A-11)."

tent with standard commercial practice in accounting for refinancings and reschedulings.[3] Such treatment is reflected in column F of Exhibit US-128.

http://www.fasab.gov/pdffiles/vol1v3.pdf, p. 1290. Section 185.3 of OMB Circular A-11 defines "direct loan": "a disbursement of funds by the Government to a non-Federal borrower under a contract that requires repayment of such funds with or without interest. The term includes: [...] Financing arrangements that defer payment for more than 90 days [...]." Exhibit BRA-116 (section 185.3, page 185-6).

3 In a routine case, a lender upon rescheduling or refinancing a loan would extinguish the prior loan because payments are no longer due on the original schedule. The lender simultaneously would book the new rescheduled loan as the asset (receivable) pursuant to the terms of which payments would be received. Perhaps the most familiar illustration of this type of transaction is a home mortgage refinancing where the applicable interest rate and maturity are changed from the prior mortgage loan. Upon consummation of the refinancing, the original note and mortgage are deemed paid, and the new loan and its terms are booked as the new loan receivable.

ANNEX I-26

BRAZIL'S COMMENTS ON US 3 MARCH 2004 DATA
10 March 2004

TABLE OF CONTENTS

List of Exhibits

I. INTRODUCTION

1. Brazil thanks the Panel for the opportunity to comment on the US data produced on 3 March 2004. Section II of this submission provides Brazil's comments on the completeness and usability of the 3 March 2004 US data. In Section III, Brazil presents the results of its calculations applying the same allocation methodologies as used in Brazil's 18 February 2004 Data Comments. In Section IV, Brazil offers four tables comparing MY 1992 support to upland cotton with MY 1999-2002 support to upland cotton as determined under the four allocation methodologies.

2. Brazil's results – whether based off the 3 March 2004 US summary data or the earlier US 18/19 December 2003 or 28 January 2004 summary data – remain unchanged. Under any reasonable methodology for allocating contract payment support to upland cotton, the US support to upland cotton in MY 1999-2002 exceeds the support decided in MY 1992, within the meaning of Article 13(b)(ii) of the Agreement on Agriculture. Thus, the US domestic support measures challenged by Brazil in this dispute are not "exempt from actions" under the SCM Agreement and GATT Article XVI.

II. THE US 3 MARCH 2004 DATA REGARDING PART B OF THE PANEL'S 3 FEBRUARY 2004 REQUEST IS GENERALLY USABLE AND SHOULD BE RELIED ON BY THE PANEL

3. Given the US refusal to provide farm-specific data, the aggregated data provided by the United States on 3 March 2004 in response to part (b) of the Panel's 3 February 2004 Request is the best information available before the Panel. While certain problems with the US 3 March 2004 data remain (which particularly affect any value-based Annex IV-type allocation methodology), the Panel can and should rely on this data in making its peace clause determination. Thus, Brazil notes that it no longer considers that relying on its "14/16th" methodology would be appropriate.

4. With respect to part (b) of the Panel's 3 February 2004 Request, the United States appears to have provided complete summary base and complete summary planted acreage data covering all crops for which data was requested by the Panel and all farms covered by the Panel's request.

5. However, the United States has engaged in a completely incorrect reading of the Panel's request for data on Category A farms. The Panel defined Category A farms as "farms [that] had fewer *upland cotton planted acres* than upland cotton base acres".[1] Unfortunately, the United States read this request as covering all farms that had upland cotton base and planted less than their full upland cotton base to upland cotton or that planted no upland cotton at all.[2] There is no basis for any such interpretation. Farms with no planted acres do not have "fewer upland cotton planted acres" – which refers to a positive amount – they have none. Indeed, from the context of the Panel's 3 February 2004 Request is becomes clear that the entire purpose of the Panel's request was to facilitate the calculation of support to upland cotton, within the meaning of Article 13(b)(ii) of the Agreement on Agriculture. Neither Brazil, nor the United States, has ever argued that farms, which do not even plant upland cotton, receive any "support to upland cotton". Including these farms in the calculations would inevitably lead to major distortions, as the calculations are impacted by base and planted acreage on farms that are of no relevance to a determination of the "support to upland cotton".[3] Had the United States interpreted the Panel's request according to its ordinary meaning, or, alternatively, provided the farm-specific information requested by the Panel on 8 December 2003, 12 January 2004 and 3 February 2004 (as part (a) of the Panel's Request[4]), this would not have been a problem.

---

1 3 February 2004 Communication from the Panel, p. 1 (emphasis added).

2 This is apparent from the fact that the sum of all upland cotton base acres from Category A, B and C farms in the US 3 March 2004 summary data equals the amount of total upland cotton base in the United States. Logically, farms that gave up producing upland cotton must have been included in one of the categories and could only have been included in Category A. Indeed, this inclusion explains that large amount of upland cotton base relative to the upland cotton planted acreage on these farms.

3 Brazil notes that this problem does not affect the Cotton-To-Cotton Methodology, as discussed below.

4 Brazil notes that it is of the firm view that none of the farm-specific planting data requested by the Panel would be covered by the US Privacy Act.

6. Nevertheless, Brazil has been able to use the 28 January 2004 US summary data to largely correct for this erroneous inclusion of additional non-upland cotton producing farms in Category A. The 28 January 2004 US summary data contains a separate category for farms that hold upland cotton base but do not produce upland cotton. Brazil has used this aggregate information to subtract out of Category A data any base and planted acreage on farms that do not produce upland cotton.[5] However, this approach was not feasible for the US Annex IV Methodology, since the 28 January 2004 US summary data does not contain all the data items contained in the 3 March 2004 US summary data. In particular, specific data on planted acreage for non-contract payment crops is missing from the 28 January 2004 US summary data, limiting Brazil's ability to correct all Category A farm data items for the purposes of applying the data to the US Annex IV Methodology. Similarly, a correction was not feasible for soybean planted acreage during MY 1999-2001 and for peanut planted acreage in MY 2002, as discussed below. Thus, any remaining distortions that might result from the necessary exclusion of soybeans and peanuts of Brazil's calculations under Brazil's Methodology and under the Modified Annex IV Methodology are directly a result of the US erroneous inclusion of non-upland cotton producing farms in Category A (and its continued refusal to produce farm-specific data).

7. In addition, and again in contrast with the 28 January 2004 US summary data, the United States' 3 March 2004 response does not provide contract payment yields or payments units that would allow for a precise calculation of the total amounts of contract payments received by a category of farms. While Brazil recognizes that the Panel's 3 February 2004 Request does not ask for this information, the United States should have produced in good faith the information on payment units in order to avoid potential distortions (as it did when providing its 18/19 December 2003 and 28 January 2004 summary data). Brazil has been required, therefore, to use the contract payment yield information set out in the 28 January 2004 US summary data. Brazil believes this contract payment yield information to be a useful proxy and the potential distortions that might result from the use of this data to be relatively minor.[6]

8. The United States' 3 March 2004 summary data is furthermore inadequate because it does not permit the calculation of support from soybean market loss assistance payments and peanut direct and counter-cyclical payments. The

---

[5] Brazil has subtracted from the Category A summary data provided on 3 March 2004 the amount of planted and base acreage per covered commodity as reported in the 28 January 2004 US summary data for farms that hold upland cotton base but do not plant upland cotton. This calculation corrects for any erroneous inclusion of additional farms in Category A. Since the 28 January 2004 US summary data does not contain data on MY 1999-2001 soybean plantings or base and MY 2002 peanut plantings or base by farms holding upland cotton base but not producing upland cotton, no correction is possible that would cover these crops. Therefore, both soybeans (for MY 1999-2001) and peanuts (for MY 2002) needed to be excluded from the calculations under Brazil's Methodology or the value-based allocation calculations under the Modified Annex IV Methodology, as discussed below. In addition, no update of the US-Proposed Annex IV Methodology using the US 3 March 2004 summary data was possible.

[6] The United States obviously has no basis to complain about Brazil's use of this yield proxy given its failure to provide yield information on 3 March 2004 or to provide the farm-specific data.

United States notes that MY 1999-2000 soybean market loss assistance payments and MY 2002 peanut direct and counter-cyclical payments were not "farm-based" but "producer-based".[7] Therefore, payments were received by (historic) producers, rather than farms (or their owners). While the United States produced data on soybean and peanut planted acreage on upland cotton farms[8], the United States did not produce any information that would allow the calculation of "producer-based" soybean market loss assistance and peanut direct and counter-cyclical payments received by producers operating upland cotton farms.[9] Yet, these payments should be considered under any allocation exercise (except the "Cotton-To-Cotton" Methodology). The absence of this information prevents Brazil from including these payments in its allocation calculations and, thus, biases Brazil's calculations downward, as discussed below. Any distortions resulting from this shortcoming of the 3 March 2004 us summary data are a consequence of the US failure to produce data on these soybean and peanut payments.

9. With respect to part (a) of the Panel's 3 February 2004 Request pursuant to DSU Article 13, the US 3 March 2004 response provided – after four weeks of what the United States characterizes as an analysis "involving much time and effort"[10] – a file ("NotClose.xls") containing farm-specific data on 28 farms for MY 2002 that would not be covered by the US Privacy Act. At the same time, the United States indicated that, in MY 2002, 197,084 farms produced upland cotton and/or received upland cotton direct and counter-cyclical payments. It is obvious that the farm-specific data covering these 28 farms cannot provide information relevant to this dispute.[11]

10. Brazil reiterates that it does not consider farm-specific planting information to be covered by the US Privacy Act.[12] (Certainly, Brazil's summary calculations in Sections III and IV below, based on the 3 March 2004 US summary data, could not possibly be considered confidential.) But even if the farm-specific planting information were confidential under US law, DSU Article 13 would oblige the United States to produce the information for the Panel and Brazil.[13] Brazil also emphasizes that it remains of the view that farm-specific data would permit the most precise calculation of the amount of contract payments that constitute support to upland cotton, under whichever allocation methodology the Panel deems appropriate.[14]

---

7 US 3 March 2004 Response to the 3 February 2004 Request by the Panel, paras. 10-21.

8 The United States produced for MY 1999, 2000 and 2002 two sets of data, one treating soybeans and peanuts as a contract payment crop and categorizing farms accordingly and one treating the soybeans and peanuts as a non-contract payment crop and categorizing farms accordingly. (*See* US 3 March 2004 Response to the 3 February 2004 Request by the Panel, paras. 17, 21, 31-38).

9 As discussed above, no payment units are provided with the US 3 March 2004 summary data.

10 US 3 March 2004 Response to the Panel's 3 February 2004 Request.

11 *See* Brazil's 13 February 2004 Letter to the Panel, p. 2.

12 Brazil's 18 February 2004 Comments, comments regarding answers 259(a)-(c), paras. 1-21. *See* also Brazil's 28 January 2004 Data Comments, Section 4.

13 *See* Brazil's 28 January 2004 Data Comments, Section 5.

14 While Brazil stated at page 5 of its 13 February 2004 Letter to the Panel that "by producing the complete aggregated information, there would no longer be a need to draw adverse inferences", Brazil notes that the data produced by the United States is not complete, as discussed above. Should the

III. CALCULATION OF SUPPORT TO UPLAND COTTON UNDER VARIOUS ALLOCATION METHODOLOGIES

11. In this Section, Brazil presents the results of applying the four allocation methodologies discussed in Section 5 of Brazil's 18 February 2004 Data Comments. That is, Brazil has applied two acreage-based allocation methodologies ("'Cotton-To-Cotton' Methodology" and "Brazil's Methodology") and two value-based methodologies ("Modified Annex IV Methodology" and "US Annex IV Methodology") to the 3 March 2004 US summary data.[15] The results under Brazil's Methodology replace the estimated amount of support to upland cotton under Brazil's so-called "14/16th" methodology.

Cotton-To-Cotton Methodology[16]

12. First, Brazil has applied the "Cotton-To-Cotton" Methodology to the 3 March 2004 US summary data.[17] This methodology is not affected by the Category A "over-inclusiveness" problem.[18] The "Cotton-To-Cotton" Methodology allocates for each planted acre of upland cotton payments associated with one upland cotton base acre – if available for that category of farms. For Category A farms this means that for each acre planted to upland cotton, payments associated with one upland cotton base acre are allocated.[19] For Category B1 to B3 farms this means that for each acre planted to upland cotton, payments associated with one upland cotton base acre are allocated – up to the amount of upland cotton

United States argue or the Panel believe that Brazil ought to have provided more accurate data on contract payments that constitute support to upland cotton, Brazil requests the Panel to rely nevertheless on the calculations provided by Brazil in this submission. Any shortcoming in these results stems from the refusal of the United States to produce the farm-specific data requested numerous times by the Panel and Brazil. Further, the United States' refusal (1) to produce the farm-specific data or (2) to produce proper data on Category A farms by excluding all farms that do not produce upland cotton, as well as complete contract payment yield or payment unit information would permit the Panel to draw the adverse inferences that this information – if produced – would have shown even higher payments being allocated to upland cotton (*see* Brazil's 28 January 2004 Data Comments, Section 6).

[15] While Brazil uses these results for purposes of the comparison required under Article 13(b)(ii) of the Agreement on Agriculture, the Panel could also use these results to determine the amount of subsidies provided to upland cotton for purposes of Brazil's actionable subsidy claims, should the Panel deem a finding on the amount of subsidies necessary.

[16] *See* Brazil's 18 February 2004 Data Comments, paras. 46-48 and Annex A.1.

[17] For the reasons discussed below in the context of "Brazil's Methodology," Brazil has relied on the categorization treating soybeans in MY 1999-2000 and peanuts in MY 2002 as a non-contract payment crop. That is, Brazil has used the following files: 'PFC1999W.xls', 'PFC2000W.xls', 'PFC 2001W.xls' and 'DCP2002W.xls' as provided by the United States on 3 March 2004. While the "Category A" problem does not affect this methodology, to ensure comparability between the payment allocations for each category of farms, Brazil has used the same categorization as for the calculations under Brazil's Methodology.

[18] Since Category A consists of farms that have more upland cotton base acres than upland cotton planted acres, for each planted acre of upland cotton payments associated with one upland cotton base acre are allocated. All remaining upland cotton and other crop base payments are ignored.

[19] Brazil recalls that these farms are defined as farms that plant less acres of upland cotton than they hold base acres.

base acres held by these farms.[20] For category C farms this means that no allocations are made.[21]

13. Since the 3 March 2004 US summary data did not include information on contract payment yields or payment units by farm category, Brazil used the contract payment yield figures provided or implied in the 28 January 2004 US summary data to calculate payment amounts.[22] After correcting for and eliminating the non-upland cotton producing farms in Category A, Categories A, B1, B2 and B3 consist of farms that previously were included in Category 1 under the US 18/19 December 2003 and 28 January 2004 summary data, as farms planting upland cotton and holding upland cotton base.[23] Accordingly, Brazil applied the contract payment yield for Category 1 farms from the 28 January 2004 US summary data to these four categories of farms in the 3 March 2004 US summary

[20] Brazil recalls that these farms are defined as farms that plant more acres of upland cotton than they hold base acres. Thus, there are not enough upland cotton base acres to allocate payments associated with one upland cotton base acre to each acre planted to upland cotton. No additional allocations are applied under this methodology and, therefore, some upland cotton planted acres are not allocated contract payments at all.

[21] Brazil recalls that these farms are defied as farms that plant upland cotton but do not hold upland cotton base acres. Therefore, no upland cotton contract payments are available for allocation and no non-upland cotton contract payments are allocated under this methodology.

[22] The file 'rPFCsum.xls' contains payment units and base acres per category of farms (1, 2, and 3 referring to farms that (1) hold upland cotton base and plant upland cotton, (2) hold upland cotton base and do not plant upland cotton, and (3) do not hold upland cotton base but plant upland cotton). Since payment units are defined as 85 per cent of the product of base acres and contract yields, payment units and base acres can be used to calculate the required contract yield (payment units / (base acres * 0.85)). The file 'rDCPsum.xls' contains contract yields for all three categories of farms (see above).

[23] To avoid any confusion, Brazil presents the following table detailing the nomenclature of the farm categories in the various US summary data submissions:

Farm Definitions	**3 March 2004 Data**	**18/19 December 2003** **28 January 2004**
Farms Planting Less Cotton Than Their Cotton Base	Category A (erroneously also includes farms that produce no cotton – all formerly Category 2 farms)	Included in Category 1
Farms Planting Cotton And Holding Cotton Base (contract payment crop planting equals crop base)	Category B1	Included in Category 1
Farms Planting Cotton And Holding Cotton Base (contract payment crop planting falls short of crop base)	Category B2	Included in Category 1
Farms Planting Cotton And Holding Cotton Base (contract payment crop planting exceeds crop base)	Category B3	Included in Category 1
Farms Planting Cotton But Not Holding Cotton Base	Category C	Category 3
Farms Not Planting Cotton But Holding Cotton Base	not requested, but erroneously included in Category A	Category 2

data.[24] The contract payment yield for Category C farms under the 3 March 2004 US summary data corresponds to that of Category 3 farms under the 28 January 2004 US categorization.

14. Next, Brazil calculated the payment units by category of farms[25] and multiplied them by the payment rate.[26] The details of Brazil's calculations are presented (by farm category) in electronic form as Exhibit Bra-433 ('Calculations Acreage Based Methodologies.xls').

15. The following table shows the amount of contract payments allocated as support to upland cotton under the "Cotton-To-Cotton" Methodology.

Cotton-to-Cotton Methodology[27]				
MY	PFC Payments	MLA Payments[28]	Direct Payments	CCP Payments
1999	434,945,069	$432,826,830	-	-
2000	411,776,128	$438,349,261	-	-
2001	329,593,231	$452,369,304	-	-
2002	-	-	$391,846,198	$864,980,104

Brazil's Methodology[29]

16. In applying Brazil's Methodology to the new 3 March 2004 US summary data, Brazil again corrected for the over-inclusiveness of farms in Category A[30] and applied the contract yields, as provided by the 28 January 2004 summary data[31], and the payment rates[32] to calculate the amount of contract payments by category of farms.[33] Brazil recalls that its methodology allocates for each acre

[24] Any possible distortion stemming from slightly higher or lower contract yields in Categories A, B1, B2 and B3 than the average contract yield that was reported for category 1 farms in the 28 January 2004 summary data is due to the failure of the United States to provide more specific information.

[25] 85 per cent of the product of base acres and contract yields (using the applicable contract yields).

[26] Exhibit Bra-394 (Agricultural Outlook Tables, USDA, November 2003, Table 17).

[27] For details of the calculations, see Exhibit Bra-433 ('Calculations Acreage Based Methodologies.xls').

[28] As in previous calculations (*see* Brazil's 28 January 2004 Data Comments, Section 9 and 10; Brazil's 18 February 2004 Data Comments, Annex A), market loss assistance payments have been calculated by adjusting the PFC payment according to the ratio of total upland cotton market loss assistance payments to total upland cotton PFC payments (Exhibit Bra-4 ("Fact Sheet: Upland Cotton," USDA, January 2003, p. 6). The United States has never criticized this approach and, in fact, confirmed its accuracy in paragraphs 8-9 of its 3 March 2004 response to the 3 February 2004 Request by the Panel.

[29] *See* Brazil's 20 January 2004 Answers to Questions, paras. 43-55; Brazil's 28 January 2004 Data Comments, Section 9 and Brazil's 18 February 2004 Data Comments, paras. 50-51, Section 6 and Annex A.2.

[30] For instance, Brazil has deducted the amount of upland cotton base held by farms that hold upland cotton base but do not produce upland cotton (as provided by the United States on 28 January 2004) from the amount of upland cotton base held by Category A farms (as provided by the United States in 3 March 2004). A similar deduction has been applied to base and planted acres for each crop for which such data was available in the 28 January 2004 US summary data.

[31] *See* above discussion in the context of the "Cotton-To-Cotton" Methodology and Section II.

[32] Exhibit Bra-394 (Agricultural Outlook Tables, USDA, November 2003, Table 17).

[33] Brazil has used the following files: 'PFC1999W.xls', 'PFC2000W.xls', 'PFC 2001W.xls' and 'DCP2002W.xls' as provided by the United States on 3 March 2004.

planted to a contract payment crop payments associated with one base acre of that crop – as available. All further contract payments not allocated to their respective contract payment crop are pooled and allocated proportionally to the planted acres of contract payment crops to which no contract payments have been assigned under the first step.[34]

17. For the purposes of Brazil's methodology, Brazil treats soybeans as a non-contract payment crop for purposes of MY 1999 and 2000 market loss assistance payments[35] and peanuts as a non-contract payment crop for purposes of MY 2002 direct and counter-cyclical payments. This treatment follows from Brazil's inability to correct the Category A data concerning soybean and peanut plantings, discussed above.[36] In addition and as discussed above, Brazil has not been able to allocate any MY 1999-2000 soybean market loss assistance payments or MY 2002 peanut direct and counter-cyclical payments because no data on these payments has been provided. Accordingly, soybeans and peanuts neither receive contract payment allocations, nor are soybean and peanut contract payments allocated for the relevant marketing years.

18. The details of Brazil's calculations are presented (by farm category) in electronic form as Exhibit Bra-433 ('Calculations Acreage Based Methodologies.xls'). Brazil applied the very same calculation methodology as in its 28 January 2004 Data Comments and in its 18 February 2004 Data Comments.[37] This methodology is not entirely identical to Brazil's 20 January 2004 discussion of its methodology, which anticipated the use of farm-specific data that was never produced by the United States.[38] Thus, certain adjustments, documented in Brazil's 28 January 2004 Data Comments, were necessary.[39]

19. The table below shows the results of Brazil's calculations.

[34] Brazil's 20 January 2004 Answers to Additional Questions, paras. 43-55.

[35] Brazil recalls that the United States has informed Brazil and the Panel that there were no such soybean payments in MY 2001. *See* US 3 March 2004 Response to the 3 February 2004 Request by the Panel, para. 10.

[36] *See* also the more detailed discussed in the context of the Modified Annex IV Methodology, below.

[37] Brazil's 28 January 2004 Data Comments, Section 9 and Brazil's 18 February 2004 Data Comments, paras. 50-51, Section 6 and Annex A.2.

[38] Brazil's 20 January 2004 Answers to Additional Questions, paras. 43-55.

[39] *See* Brazil's 28 January 2004 Data Comments, Section 9.

Brazil's Methodology[40]				
MY	PFC Payments	MLA Payments[41]	Direct Payments	CCP Payments
1999	$501,450,663	$499,008,534	-	-
2000	$478,926,663	$509,833,219	-	-
2001	$385,723,950	$529,409,157	-	-
2002	-	-	$421,367,874	$869,470,827

20. The differences between results of the "Cotton-To-Cotton" Methodology and Brazil's Methodology result from the fact that under Brazil's Methodology a limited amount of non-upland cotton contract payments is allocated as "support to upland cotton." However, the great majority of upland cotton is planted on farms holding upland cotton base acres and their amount of upland cotton base acres closely tracks their amount of upland cotton planted acres. Thus, upland cotton contract payments account for the great majority of contract payments allocated even under Brazil's methodology. The following table presents, by marketing year, the amount of upland cotton planted acres for which there exists a corresponding upland cotton base acre farm category.

Marketing Year[42] Category[43]	**MY 1999**	**MY 2000**	**MY 2001**	**MY 2002**
	- acres -			
A	4,548,886	4,386,073	4,146,352	5,997,438
B1	87,034	94,377	78,075	166,619
B2	2,412,580	2,389,053	2,173,819	2,035,335
B3	3,570,724	3,906,688	4,125,899	3,220,762
C	0	0	0	0
Total	10,619,224	10,776,191	10,524,145	11,420,154
Total Planted Acres	14,572,963	15,388,028	15,463,934	13,541,506
Percentage	72.87 per cent	70.03 per cent	68.06 per cent	84.33 per cent

[40] For details of the calculations, see Exhibit Bra-433 ('Calculations Acreage Based Methodologies.xls').

[41] As in previous calculations (*see* Brazil's 28 January 2004 Data Comments, Section 9 and 10; Brazil's 18 February 2004 Data Comments, Annex A), market loss assistance payments have been calculated by adjusting the PFC payment according to the ratio of total upland cotton market loss assistance payments to total upland cotton PFC payments (Exhibit Bra-4 ("Fact Sheet: Upland Cotton", USDA, January 2003, p. 6). The United States has never criticized this approach and, in fact, confirmed its accuracy in paragraphs 8-9 of its 3 March 2004 response to the 3 February 2004 Request by the Panel.

[42] Brazil has used the following files: 'PFC1999W.xls', 'PFC2000W.xls', 'PFC 2001W.xls' and 'DCP2002W.xls' as provided by the United States on 3 March 2004.

[43] For Category A farms, Brazil has used the amount of upland cotton planted acres, since on those farms upland cotton base acres exceed upland cotton base acres. For the three Categories B1, B2 and B3, Brazil has used upland cotton base acres since for those farms upland cotton planted acres exceed upland cotton base acres. Finally, for Category C farms, Brazil has used "0," since those farms have no upland cotton base acres.

Modified US Annex IV Methodology[44]

21. In applying the first value-based methodology, the Modified Annex IV Methodology, to the new 3 March 2004 US summary data, Brazil again corrected for the over-inclusiveness of Category A and applied contract payment yields, as provided by the 28 January 2004 summary data, and the contract payment rates to calculate the total amount of contract payments by category of farms.[45]

22. Brazil was required to exclude soybeans[46] and peanuts from the allocation calculations under this methodology[47] (as well as under Brazil's Methodology) for the following reasons: First, since the United States did not provide data on soybean and peanut plantings with its 28 January 2004 summary data, Brazil is unable to correct these data items in the US 3 March 2004 Category A summary data.[48] There were three theoretical options available to Brazil to address this problem. First, Brazil could have left in Category A all farms which were included by the United States, but which do not produce upland cotton. This approach would have resulted in distortions because considerable amounts of extra contract payments received by farms not producing upland cotton as well as unknown amounts of extra contract payment crop value generated by these non-upland cotton producing farms would be included in the calculations. Or, second, Brazil could have corrected the over-inclusiveness of Category A for all data items that it could correct leaving the additional soybean and peanut acreage from non-upland cotton producing farms in the pool. This approach would have resulted in distortions because unknown amounts of extra value of soybean and peanut production from non-upland cotton producing farms would be included in the calculations. To avoid these distortions, Brazil has selected the third option – to exclude soybeans and peanuts from the allocation. This choice enables Brazil to correct the Category A data for the inclusion of farms not producing upland cotton, in the manner described above[49], and to proceed with its calculations.

23. Second, Brazil notes that the United States distinguishes the soybean market loss assistance and peanut direct and counter-cyclical payments in MY 1999, 2000 and 2002 as being producer-based rather than farm-based payments. But, the United States never provided information on the amount of these payments. However, payments received by producers of these crops that also owned upland cotton producing farms (to which all other contract payments were made)

---

44 Brazil has discussed this methodology in paragraphs 50-51 and in Annex A.3 of its 18 February 2004 Data Comments.

45 *See* above discussion in the context of the "Cotton-To-Cotton" Methodology and in Section II.

46 This exclusion of soybeans does not apply to MY 2002, for which complete summary data is available.

47 Consequently, Brazil has used to following files as the basis for its calculations: 'PFC1999W.xls', 'PFC2000W.xls', 'PFC 2001W.xls' and 'DCP2002W.xls' as provided by the United States on 3 March 2004.

48 This correction of course concerns the amount of soybean and peanut acreage planted by farms that do not produce upland cotton.

49 *See* Section II above.

would need to be considered for any allocations methodology (except the "Cotton-To-Cotton" Methodology).

24. No doubt Brazil's choice not to include soybean and peanut planted acreage and soybean market loss assistance and peanut direct and counter-cyclical payments leads to distortions. These are unavoidable given the incorrect US reading of the definition of Category A farms. However, Brazil believes that these distortions are relatively minor. Brazil has excluded payments stemming from soybean market loss assistance and peanut direct and counter-cyclical payments[50] as well as the crop value of soybean (for MY 1999-2001) and peanut (for MY 2002) production.[51] Thus, soybeans and peanuts do not contribute contract payments to the pool of payments allocated over the value of the entire contract payment crop production of upland cotton producing farms. But, there are also no contract payments being allocated to soybeans and peanuts for these years. This minimizes distortions by roughly cancelling out over and under-counting effects from their exclusion from the calculation. Brazil notes that, for other crops, the amount of crop plantings and crop payment base is fairly proportionate.[52] Soybeans and peanuts in all likelihood follow a similar pattern. In excluding these crops entirely from the calculations, Brazil minimizes the distortions resulting from the shortcomings of the 3 March 2004 US summary data, based on the assumption that these crops would contribute an equal (or very similar) amount of contract payments to the pool, as they would be allocated based on their share of the total value of contract payment crop production.

25. As in its 18 February 2004 calculations, Brazil calculated, by category of farm, the value of each contract payment crop produced on farms that make up the category. Brazil multiplied the amount of planted acreage times the yield[53] and times the per unit price of the particular crop.[54] Total contract payments for each category of farm were then allocated to upland cotton according to the share of the upland cotton crop value of the total value of contract payment crop production on the farms of that category. The details of Brazil's calculations are presented (by farm category) in electronic form as Exhibit Bra-434 ('Calculations Value Based Methodologies.xls').

26. The table below shows the resulting support to upland cotton under this methodology.

---

[50] For which the United States has not provided any payment information.

[51] For which Brazil is not able to correct the Category A data given the respective data items missing in the 28 January 2004 US summary data.

[52] Compare crop base and crop plantings as reported by the US 3 March 2004 summary data ('PFC1999W.xls', 'PFC2000W.xls', 'PFC 2001W.xls' and 'DCP2002W.xls').

[53] Brazil notes that similar to its 18 February 2004 calculations it has used yields on planted acres for upland cotton and yields on harvested acres for all other contract payment crops, thereby overstating the latter's value and leading to understated allocations of contract payments to upland cotton. *See* Brazil's 18 February 2004 Data Comments, para. 73 and Annex A.3, notes to Tables 3.5-3.8 for further explanation and references to the data.

[54] Exhibit Bra-420 (Agricultural Outlook Tables, USDA, November 2003, Table 17). Brazil notes that the cover page of this exhibit appears to be wrong. The table is, however, correct.

Modified Annex IV Methodology[55]				
MY	PFC Payments	MLA Payments[56]	Direct Payments	CCP Payments
1999	$562,922,665	$560,181,159	-	-
2000	$540,877,974	$575,782,432	-	-
2001	$394,791,930	$541,855,031	-	-
2002	-	-	$462,037,836	$771,636,204

Brazil notes that these allocations are conservative. Absent data on yields per planted acre for any non-upland cotton crop, Brazil applied yields on harvested acres to calculate the amount of crop produced from all planted acres, thereby ignoring abandonment. This calculation leads to overstating the value of non-upland cotton crop production by overstating the amount of such production. By contrast, the value of the upland cotton crop has been calculated by using yields on planted acres, providing an accurate estimate.[57] Thus, Brazil's calculations overstate the value of non-upland cotton contract payment crops produced in each of the farm categories, resulting in lower allocations to upland cotton.

US Annex IV Methodology

27. Brazil could not perform any updated calculations under this methodology based on the 3 March 2004 US summary data. The reason is that Brazil could not exclude from Category A data those farms that do not produce upland cotton.[58] The US Annex IV Methodology would necessitate adjusting Category A data, *inter alia*, concerning planted soybeans acreage in MY 1999-2001 and peanut acreage in MY 2002. However, no such planted acreage data is available in the 28 January 2004 US summary data and, therefore, no such adjustment to Category A can be performed.

---

55 For details of the calculations, see Exhibit Bra-434 ('Calculations Value Based Methodologies.xls').

56 As in previous calculations (*see* Brazil's 28 January 2004 Data Comments, Section 9 and 10; Brazil's 18 February 2004 Data Comments, Annex A), market loss assistance payments have been calculated by adjusting the PFC payment according to the ratio of total upland cotton market loss assistance payments to total upland cotton PFC payments (Exhibit Bra-4 ("Fact Sheet: Upland Cotton," USDA, January 2003, p. 6). The United States has never criticized this approach and, in fact, confirmed its accuracy in paragraphs 8-9 of its 3 March 2004 response to the 3 February 2004 Request by the Panel.

57 *See* Brazil's 18 February 2004 Data Comments, para. 73 and Annex A.3, notes to Tables 3.5-3.8 for further explanation and references to the data.

58 As long as only data concerning contract payment crops was relevant (excluding soybeans and peanuts under the Modified Annex IV Methodology), such an exclusion could be performed based on the 28 January 2004 US summary data, that provided congruous base and planted acreage summary information for these contract payment crops on farms that are now erroneously included in Category A. This allowed for deducting the base and planted acreage summary data for contract payment crops on farms that hold upland cotton base but do not produce upland cotton from the identical summary data items in Category A of the 3 March 2004 US summary data. For instance, Brazil has deducted the amount of upland cotton base held by farms that hold upland cotton base but do not produce upland cotton (as provided by the United States on 28 January 2004) from the amount of upland cotton base held by Category A farms (as provided by the United States in 3 March 2004). A similar deduction has been applied to base and planted acres for each crop for which such data was available in the 28 January 2004 US summary data.

28. Further, for MY 2002, the 3 March 2004 US summary data provides more specific data items, including acreage data for fruits and vegetables, ELS cotton, tobacco and peanuts for all categories of farms. However, because these data items were also not provided in the 28 January 2004 US summary data, Brazil cannot correct the over-inclusiveness of Category A for these data items. In addition, the United States appears to have included more acreage in its "All Other Use Acres" than simply cropland. The sum of all non-contract payment crop acres in the 3 March 2004 US summary data exceeds the additional cropland as reported in the 28 January 2004 US summary data. This again precludes an adjustment of this data item in Category A for its over-inclusiveness, since the 28 January 2004 and the 3 March 2004 sets of summary data do not appear to be congruous.

29. Once more, the inability to exclude the non-upland cotton producing farms from Category A is important, because including a large number of farms that do not produce upland cotton in the allocation calculations would add a large potential for distortions given the significant amounts of plantings and contract payment crop base by these farms.

30. Further, while the 28 January 2004 US summary data provided information on the amount of non-contract payment crop acreage for MY 1999-2001, the 3 March 2004 US summary data fails to do so. Thus, for those marketing years and for purposes of the US Annex IV Methodology, Brazil could not rely on the 3 March 2004 US summary data and categorization of upland cotton farms at all, since the 3 March 2004 US summary data does not contain any information on the plantings of non-contract payment crops on these farms. For purposes of the US Annex IV Methodology, Brazil, however, needs to rely on planting data for non-contract payment crops to estimate the value of their production on upland cotton producing farms – data such as that provided by the United States in its 18/19 December 2003 and 28 January 2004 data submissions. Thus, Brazil's 18 February 2004 US Annex IV Methodology results based on the 28 January 2004 US summary data are more accurate than any calculations that could be performed based on the 3 March 2004 US summary data or some adjusted version thereof. Therefore, Brazil reproduces below its 18 February 2004 results applying the US Annex IV methodology to the 28 January 2004 US summary data.

Annex A.4 Table 4.8[59]

US Annex IV Methodology				
MY	PFC Payments	MLA Payments	Direct Payments	CCP Payments
1999	$440,061,035.8	$437,917,881.4	-	-
2000	$432,996,788.7	$460,939,354.1	-	-
2001	$304,243,319.2	$420,222,029.1	-	-
2002	-	-	$383,057,256.1	$640,389,168.2

Brazil notes that these allocations are conservative for two reasons: (1) the calculations overstate the value of non-upland cotton contract payment crops, as dis-

[59] *See* Annex A.4 of Brazil's 18 February 2004 Data Comments.

cussed in the context of the Modified Annex V Methodology; and (2) the calculations do not account for soybean market loss assistance payments in MY 1999-2000 and peanut direct and counter-cyclical payments in MY 2002.[60]

IV. THE UNITED STATES MY 1999-2002 SUPPORT TO UPLAND COTTON EXCEEDS THE MY 1992 SUPPORT TO UPLAND COTTON UNDER ANY METHODOLOGY

31. In the previous Section, Brazil has updated its 18 February 2004 calculations of the support to upland cotton applying various acreage- and value-based allocation methodologies. In this Section, Brazil combines its results with data on the amount of support to upland cotton from the other support programmes, and provides the Panel with summary tables for each of the 1999-2002 marketing years comparing the support to upland cotton in those marketing years with the MY 1992 level of support to upland cotton.

32. As Brazil discussed in its 18 February 2004 Data Comments, Article 13(b)(ii) of the Agreement on Agriculture endorses no particular methodology. Thus, the Panel needs to choose a reasonable methodology for allocating contract payments as support to upland cotton.[61] Brazil favours its methodology, based on an allocation pursuant to the acreage planted to contract payment crops, but also provides results under the Cotton-To-Cotton Methodology (similarly based on an acreage comparison), as well as two value-based methodologies.

33. However, Brazil strongly urges the Panel to apply an acreage-based methodology – preferably Brazil's Methodology. A particular flaw in a value-based methodology is that allocating counter-cyclical payments over the value of crop production means that allocations for a crop will decrease if prices for that crop fall.[62] Thus, at the time when counter-cyclical payments are "critically

---

60 Brazil's 18 February 2004 Data Comments, para. 52 and note 75 thereto as well as Annex A.4, para. 40. While the missing soybean and peanut contract payments could be corrected for by excluding these crops from any allocations under the previous three methodologies, soybeans and peanuts are a firm part of the allocation calculations under the US Annex IV Methodology because they are part of the overall farm's revenue. They were included in Brazil's 18 February 2004 calculations based on the US 28 January 2004 summary data. Thus, it is only the payment data that remains missing from these calculations resulting in understating the amount of contract payments allocated to upland cotton.

61 Brazil's 18 February 2004 Data Comments, paras. 33-42.

62 Suppose that a farm produces in two consecutive years the same amount of upland cotton and rice. The value of both crops is 50 in the first year leading to an allocation of half of the contract payments received by that farm. In the second year, prices for upland cotton fall to half their pervious level, while rice prices remain the same. Thus, the same amount of upland cotton is only worth 25 in the second year with the value of the rice crop remaining at 50. It follows that upland cotton receives a third of the contract payments allocations (its value is 25 out of a total crop value of 75) and rice receives two thirds of the contract payment allocations. The same principle would apply if rice prices had fallen by half with upland cotton remaining constant. In this case rice would receive an allocation of a third of the contract payments while upland cotton would receive two thirds of the contract payments allocations. In both cases the crop whose price is falling receives a smaller share of the support, contrary to the counter-cyclical (not pro-cyclical) approach of the payments involved.

needed"[63] to offset low prices for a crop, a value-based methodology would allocate these counter-cyclical payments increasingly as support to other crops, whose prices have not fallen. Using a value-based allocation methodology shifts the share of counter-cyclical payments that are allocated to the crop with falling prices away from that crop and to crops with increasing or constant prices. By contrast, allocating contract payments over the acreage planted to contract payment crops – as done by the "Cotton-To-Cotton" Methodology and by Brazil's Methodology – provides an allocation approach that reflects the economic reality and intention behind the counter-cyclical payment support.

34. But Brazil emphasizes that, on the facts of this case, and using whichever methodology the Panel may ultimately choose, the US MY 1999-2002 support to upland cotton exceeds the MY 1992 level in each year and under each methodology (with the exception of the "Cotton-To-Cotton" and the US Annex IV Methodology in MY 2000).[64]

35. The following four tables present the peace clause comparisons for MY 1999-2002. The table below presents Brazil's peace clause comparison for MY 2002.

[63] Exhibit Bra 111, ("The Six Year World Outlook for Cotton and Peanuts: Implications for Production and Prices," Bob McLendon, National Cotton Council, p.1).

[64] Brazil recalls that given the manner in which the United States presented its 3 March 2004 summary data, Brazil was prevented to provide an updated US Annex IV Methodology calculation based on the 3 March 2004 US summary data. *See* Section III, above. Further, neither of the two methodologies captures all support to upland cotton with the "Cotton-To-Cotton" Methodology not capturing any non-upland cotton contract payments that constitute support to upland cotton and the US-Proposed Annex IV Methodology suffering from various data problems, including the non-availability of data on soybean market loss assistance payments for that year.

Budgetary Outlays For Upland Cotton MY 1992 and MY 2002[65]

Programme / Year	1992	2002 (1)	2002 (2)	2002 (3)	2002 (4)
	- $ million -				
Deficiency Payments	1017.4	none	none	none	none
Direct Payments	none	391.8	421.4	462.0	383.1
CCP Payments	none	865.0	869.5	771.6	640.4
Marketing Loan Gains and LDP Payments[66]	866	898	898	898	898
Step 2 Payment	207	415	415	415	415
Crop Insurance	26.6	194.1	194.1	194.1	194.1
Cottonseed Payments	none	50	50	50	50
Total	2,117.0	2,813.9	2,848.0	2,790.7	2,580.6

(1) Cotton-To-Cotton Methodology
(2) Brazil's Methodology
(3) Modified Annex IV Methodology
(4) US Annex IV Methodology (based on 28 January 2004 US summary data)

36. The table below presents Brazil's peace clause comparison for MY 2001.

Budgetary Outlays For Upland Cotton MY 1992 and MY 2001[67]

Programme / Year	1992	2001 (1)	2001 (2)	2001 (3)	2001 (4)
	- $ million -				
Deficiency Payments	1017.4	none	none	none	none
PFC Payments	none	329.6	385.7	394.8	304.2
MLA Payments	none	425.4	529.4	541.9	420.2
Marketing Loan Gains and LDP Payments[68]	866	2,609	2,609	2,609	2,609
Step 2 Payment	207	196	196	196	196
Crop Insurance	26.6	262.9	262.9	262.9	262.9
Cottonseed Payments	none	none	none	none	none
Total	2,117.0	3,849.9	3,983.0	4,004.6	3,792.3

(1) Cotton-To-Cotton Methodology
(2) Brazil's Methodology
(3) Modified Annex IV Methodology
(4) US Annex IV Methodology (based on 28 January 2004 US summary data)[69]

[65] The table below includes the updated contract payment allocations to upland cotton and otherwise reproduces the table at paragraph 73 of Brazil's 22 August 2003 Rebuttal Submission as updated by paragraph 8 of Brazil's 22 December 2003 Answers to Questions and paragraphs 12-14 of the US 22 December 2004 Answers to Questions. Step 2 and marketing loan payments have been updated in light of the US answer to Question 196. *See* US 22 December 2004 Answers to Questions, para. 12.

[66] "Other Payments" have been included in the marketing loan figures.

[67] The table below includes the updated contract payment allocations to upland cotton and otherwise reproduces the table at paragraph 73 of Brazil's 22 August 2003 Rebuttal Submission.

[68] "Other Payments" have been included in the marketing loan figures.

[69] *See* Brazil's 18 February 2004 Data Comments, Annex A.4 Table

37. The table below presents Brazil's peace clause comparison for MY 2000.

Budgetary Outlays For Upland Cotton MY 1992 and MY 2000[70]

Year	1992	2000 (1)	2000 (2)	2000 (3)	2000 (4)
Programme	- $ million -				
Deficiency Payments	1017.4	none	none	none	none
PFC Payments	none	411.8	478.9	540.9	433.0
MLA Payments	none	438.3	509.8	575.8	460.9
Marketing Loan Gains and LDP Payments[71]	866	636	636	636	636
Step 2 Payment	207	236	236	236	236
Crop Insurance	26.6	161.7	161.7	161.7	161.7
Cottonseed Payments	none	185	185	185	185
Total	2,117.0	2,068.8	2,207.4	2,335.4	2,112.6

(1) Cotton-To-Cotton Methodology
(2) Brazil's Methodology
(3) Modified Annex IV Methodology
(4) US Annex IV Methodology (based on 28 January 2004 US summary data)

38. The table below presents Brazil's peace clause comparison for MY 1999.

Budgetary Outlays For Upland Cotton MY 1992 and MY 1999[72]

Year	1992	1999 (1)	1999 (2)	1999 (3)	1999 (4)
Programme	- $ million -				
Deficiency Payments	1017.4	none	none	none	none
PFC Payments	none	434.9	501.5	562.9	440.1
MLA Payments	none	432.8	499.0	560.2	437.9
Marketing Loan Gains and LDP Payments[73]	866	1,761	1,761	1,761	1,761
Step 2 Payment	207	422	422	422	422
Crop Insurance	26.6	169.6	169.6	169.6	169.6
Cottonseed Payments	none	79	79	79	79
Total	2,117.0	3,299.3	3,432.1	3,554.7	3,309.6

(1) Cotton-To-Cotton Methodology
(2) Brazil's Methodology
(3) Modified Annex IV Methodology
(4) US Annex IV Methodology (based on 28 January 2004 US summary data)

70 The table below includes the updated contract payment allocations to upland cotton and otherwise reproduces the table at paragraph 73 of Brazil's 22 August 2003 Rebuttal.

71 "Other Payments" have been included in the marketing loan figures.

72 The table below includes the updated contract payment allocations to upland cotton and otherwise reproduces the table at paragraph 73 of Brazil's 22 August 2003 Rebuttal Submission.

73 "Other Payments" have been included in the marketing loan figures.

39. In sum, the contract payment data provided by the United States on 3 March 2004 (as well as the data provided on 28 January 2004) demonstrates that the United States' support to upland cotton in MY 1999-2002 exceeds the support to upland cotton decided by the United States in MY 1992, within the meaning of Article 13(b)(ii) of the Agreement on Agriculture. The results using any allocation methodology applying any set of US summary data[74] demonstrates their robustness.

[74] *See* Brazil's results in its 28 January 2004 and 18 February 2004 Data Comments.

ANNEX I-27

BRAZIL'S COMMENTS ON US 3 MARCH 2004 ANSWER TO QUESTION 264(B)

10 March 2004

264. (b) Does the US agree with the statement in paragraph 135 of Brazil's 28 January 2004 comments on US responses to questions that the difference between the $1,148 billion in the chart at para. 165 of Brazil's 11 August answers to questions and the $666 million amount in Exhibit US-128 ($1.75 billion) closely corresponds to the total "Claims rescheduled" figure reported by the US in Exhibit US-128 (column F)?

Brazil's Comment:

1. The United States acknowledges, in paragraph 3 of its 3 March 2004 response, that the difference referred to in the Panel's question arises because the United States treats the principal amounts of rescheduled defaults as an immediate, 100 per cent recovery that is passed through as a dollar-on-dollar reduction from the amount of claims outstanding in the year the terms of the rescheduling are agreed.[1]

2. In paragraph 1 of its response, the United States argues that the Brazilian conclusion included in the Panel's question results from Brazil's comparison of *fiscal year* data provided by Brazil with *cohort-specific* data provided by the United States. In fact, as explained at paragraph 34 of Brazil's 18 February 2004 Comments and illustrated in Exhibit Bra-431, Brazil reaches the same conclusion with a comparison of 1993-2002 *fiscal year* data provided by Brazil with 1993-2002 *fiscal year* data provided by the United States.[2]

3. In paragraph 2 of its response, the United States asserts, citing undocumented "[a]ccounting research within the US Government," that "a significant portion" of principal collected on reschedulings "has not been reflected" in US budget line 88.40, tracked in column 2(a) of Exhibit Bra-431, despite the United

---

1 For Brazil's views on this aspect of the US cash-basis accounting methodology for making an assessment under item (j), *see* Brazil's 18 February 2004 Comments, paras. 34-40; Brazil's 28 January 2004 Comments, paras. 134-137; Brazil's 11 August 2003 Answers, para. 162; Brazil's 22 July 2003 Oral Statement, para. 122.

2 Exhibit US-147 also lists (undocumented) data for fiscal years 1992, 2003 and 2004. Including the additional revenue and expense figures for these years does not change the fact that revenue for the CCC export credit guarantee programmes fails to cover the costs and losses of the programs. Exhibit US-147 alleges additional revenue of $38.5 million for 1992, $185.6 million for 2003, and $35.4 million for 2004; and additional costs and losses of $3 million for 1992, $130.1 million for 2003, and $22.8 million for 2004. Accounting for this data (($38.5 + $185.6 + $35.4) – ($3 + $130.1 + $22.8) = $103.6 million) would bring the total net costs and losses down from $1.083 billion, arrived at in Exhibit Bra-431, to $979.4 million.

States' acknowledgement that "[a]s a theoretical matter such 'recovered principal' should be reflected in budget linc 88.40". As the party asserting this fact, the United States bears the burden of proving it (particularly here, where it is addressing a line item from its own budget).[3]

4. Each and every figure used in Brazil's cash-basis accounting methodology for making an assessment under item (j) represents actual (as opposed to estimated) data from official US documents that Brazil has provided to the Panel.[4] The United States has not even *cited* to any documentary support for the figures it has provided in Exhibit US-147 or US-148, let alone *provided* those documents for the Panel's review.

5. Thus, it is impossible for Brazil or the Panel to verify, for example, whether the CCC has, as the United States asserts at paragraph 2, recovered $205 million of the principal on its reschedulings. Moreover, this figure conflicts with other data provided by the United States. In column F of Exhibit US-147, the United States asserts that $1.64 billion of defaulted CCC guarantees have been rescheduled over the period 1992-2003; in Exhibit US-153, the United States asserts that the principal outstanding on these reschedulings amounts to $1.58 billion. Rather than recovering $205 million of the principal on its reschedulings, this data shows that the CCC has recovered only $60 million.

6. In any event, even if the Panel accepts the United States' unsupported assertion that the CCC has recovered $205 million of the principal on its reschedulings, this would not mean that premiums collected for the CCC export credit guarantee programmes meet the operating costs and losses of the programmes. Even if the entire $205 million figure is added to the "claims recovered" column of Brazil's cash-basis accounting calculation (column 2(a) of Exhibit Bra-341) – which by its own admission would be over-crediting the United States for recoveries of the principle on its reschedulings[5] – the result is still that long-term operating costs and losses for the CCC export credit guarantee programmes outpace revenue (not just premiums collected, but all revenue) by $878 million.[6]

---

3 *See e.g.* Appellate Body Report, *Japan – Apples*, WT/DS245/AB/R, para. 157 ("It is important to distinguish, on the one hand, the principle that the complainant must establish a *prima facie* case of inconsistency with a provision of a covered agreement from, on the other hand, the principle that the party that asserts a fact is responsible for providing proof thereof."). Moreover, Brazil again notes that the United States bears the burden, under Article 10.3 of the Agreement on Agriculture, of proving that quantities exported in excess of its reduction commitments have not benefited from export subsidies.

4 *See* chart included in paragraph 165 of Brazil's 11 August 2003 Answers (reproduced in paragraph 129 of Brazil's 28 January 2004 Comments).

5 In paragraph 2 of its response, the United States asserts that "a significant portion of" the principal recovered on its reschedulings is not included in line item 88.40 and column 2(a) of Exhibit Bra-341 – not that *none* of the principal recovered is included in that column.

6 Exhibit Bra-431 shows that the operating costs and losses outpace revenue by $1.083 billion. Deducting the $205 million cited by the United States yields a loss of $878 million by the CCC export credit guarantee programmes.

ANNEX I-28

COMMENTS OF THE UNITED STATES ON THE 10 MARCH 2004 COMMENTS OF BRAZIL ON THE US DATA SUBMITTED ON 3 MARCH 2004

(15 March 2004)

Introduction

1. The United States thanks the Panel for this opportunity to respond to the 10 March comments filed by Brazil[1] relating to the data submitted by the United States on 3 March 2004, in response to the Panel's supplemental request for information. Brazil's 10 March comments consist primarily of a series of calculations using the US 3 March data in each of the methodologies previously explained by Brazil in its 18 February comments. The United States has previously explained, in filings on 11 February[2] and 3 March[3], that none of these methodologies is pertinent for purposes of the Peace Clause.[4] Therefore, we will not repeat much of that analysis in these comments but rather will refer the Panel, as appropriate, to those previous comments by the United States.

2. Brazil states that, because the US 3 March data "is the best information available before the Panel," Brazil "no longer considers that relying on its '14/16th methodology would be appropriate.'"[5] This means that, by Brazil's own statement, the only methodology that Brazil had brought forward from August 2003 until January 2004 to allegedly demonstrate a breach of the Peace Clause is irrelevant to this dispute. Moreover, it is difficult to reconcile Brazil's concession with its view that the Panel need only apply a "reasonable" methodology to calculate the support to upland cotton since Brazil alleges that the 14/16th methodology produces results that are similar to those under its other (flawed) methodologies.

3. Brazil's disavowal of its 14/16th methodology, however, does highlight the shifting nature of Brazil's Peace Clause arguments on decoupled payments. It may be of use to set out just how and how many times Brazil's theories have changed in this dispute.

4. *First*, Brazil argued that all payments for upland cotton base acres were "support to upland cotton." For example, in response to Question 41 from the Panel following the first session of the first substantive meeting, Brazil wrote:

---

1 Brazil's Comments on US 3 March 2004 Data (10 March 2004) ("Brazil's 10 March Comments").

2 Comments of the United States of America on the Comments of Brazil to US Data Submitted on 18 and 19 December 2003 (11 February 2004) ("US 11 February Comments").

3 Comments of the United States of America on the 18 February 2004, Comments of Brazil (3 March 2004) ("US 3 March Comments").

4 *Agreement on Agriculture*, Article 13 ("Agreement on Agriculture").

5 Brazil's 10 March Comments, paras. 2-3.

> "The only US domestic support measures that Brazil is aware of that would meet the test of being 'support to upland cotton' are *those that it listed* for purposes of calculating the level of support in its First Written Submission. *In the view of Brazil, these non-green box domestic support measures are the measures that constitute 'support to' upland cotton* for the purpose of Article 13(b)."[6]

The decoupled measures listed in Brazil's first written submission (paragraphs 144, 148, and 149) were all production flexibility contract payments, market loss assistance payments, direct payments, and counter-cyclical payments *for upland cotton base acres only*. Thus, "in the view of Brazil" as of the first session of the first substantive meeting, only these payments were within the Panel's terms of reference.[7]

5. *Second*, in response to US criticisms, Brazil realized that, on its own terms, the theory that all payments for upland cotton base acres were "support to upland cotton" was not tenable. Brazil's theory ignored the fact that there were fewer acres planted to upland cotton than there were upland cotton base acres, suggesting that payment recipients utilized planting flexibility to plant other crops or nothing at all.

> Thus, following the first session of the first panel meeting, Brazil introduced the so-called 14/16th methodology, which adjusted total expenditures for upland cotton base acres "by the ratio of upland cotton base acres actually planted." In Brazil's words, "only the portion of upland cotton [base] payments that actually benefits acres planted to upland cotton can be considered support to upland cotton."[8]

That is, Brazil amended its theory, arguing that all upland cotton was planted "on" upland cotton base acres.

6. *Third*, under Brazil's fallacious argument that receipt of decoupled payments was necessary for upland cotton producers to cover their costs, Brazil acknowledged that it was not "necessary" that upland cotton be planted on upland cotton base acres – that is, rice and peanuts base acreage also received payments that would allow these alleged costs to be covered. However, Brazil argued that the facts did not support the notion that upland cotton was "planted on" rice or peanuts base acreage.[9] Rather, through the second session of the Panel's first substantive meeting (that is, after the Peace Clause phase of the dispute had concluded), Brazil continued to insist that "at a minimum a significant majority of upland cotton farmers in MY 2002 were farming on upland cotton base acres."[10]

7. *Fourth*, however, even Brazil's own evidence indicated that not all upland cotton was planted "on" upland cotton base acres. For example, as a result of pest

---

6 Brazil's Answer to Question 41 from the Panel, para. 58 (footnote omitted; italics added).

7 *See* US Comment on Brazil's Answer to Question 204 from the Panel, paras. 36-39 (providing additional citations) (28 January 2004).

8 Brazil's Answer to Question 67 from the Panel, para. 130 (table fn. 2-5) (11 August 2003).

9 *See, e.g.*, Brazil's Rebuttal Submission, para. 32, 38 (22 August 2003).

10 Brazil's Further Submission, para. 335; *see also id.*, para. 331.

eradication and adoption of biotechnology, significant acres in the US Southeast previously planted to peanuts, corn, and other crops were newly being planted to upland cotton.[11] Thus, Brazil altered its theory again and argued that "Brazil's methodology assumes that US producers of upland cotton grew upland cotton on upland cotton base acreage," which is "a reasonable proxy, because there will be some upland cotton that is grown on rice (and peanut) base receiving higher payments, and some upland cotton that is grown on, *e.g.,* corn base receiving somewhat lower payments. On average, Brazil's approach would roughly cancel out the over-counting of rice and peanut payments and the under-counting of corn and any other lower-paying programme crop payments."[12]

8. *Fifth*, Brazil suggested in its further rebuttal submission of 18 November 2003, that "the United States has refused to generate information regarding how much and which of the contract payment base acreage was planted to upland cotton."[13] However, Brazil nowhere explained how such an analysis of "how much and which of the contract payment base acreage was planted to upland cotton" could be done. In fact, Brazil suggested that the Panel should request the United States to produce information and that "Brazil would be pleased *to provide the Panel with a precise list of parameters and questions that should be answered* in any such analysis."[14]

9. Brazil, however, did not provide any such "precise list of parameters and questions" until the second panel meeting in December 2003. While Brazil requested certain information through its request in Exhibit BRA-369, Brazil did *not* explain to the Panel or the United States how it proposed to determine the amount of upland cotton acreage "planted on" base acreage for any particular commodity. Indeed, the Panel was compelled on 12 January 2004, to ask Brazil to "submit a detailed explanation of the method by which one could calculate total expenditures to producers of upland cotton under the four relevant programmes on the basis of the data which it seeks."[15]

10. *Sixth*, Brazil put forward on 20 January 2004, *for the first time* its allocation methodology – that is, after further rebuttal submissions had been filed and as the "serious prejudice" phase (and indeed the dispute settlement proceeding) was concluding. Here, Brazil set out its notion of under- and over-planting of programme crop base acreage, which the United States has criticized and rebutted in a series of filings over the last month.

11. *Seventh*, however, Brazil did not stop there. On 28 January 2004, in its comments on the US 18 and 19 December 2003, data (the comments that were to have been filed on 20 January), Brazil set forth yet another in-the-alternative

---

[11] *See* Brazil's Answer to Question 125(7), para. 38 (27 October 2003) ("Testimony from NCC representatives indicated that a number of producers in the south-eastern part of the United States grew upland cotton on corn base acreage during MY1999-2001.") (footnote omitted).

[12] Brazil's Answer to Question 125(8), para. 40 (27 October 2003).

[13] Brazil's Further Rebuttal Submission, para. 50.

[14] Brazil's Further Rebuttal Submission, para. 48 (italics added).

[15] Panel Communication of January 12, 2004 (Question 258).

methodology, a purported application of that December data to the Subsidies Agreement Annex IV methodology.[16]

12. *Eighth*, Brazil put forward on 18 February 2004 – that is, in its last substantive filing in this dispute – *two more* in-the-alternative methodologies to calculate the alleged support to upland cotton from decoupled payments. First, it explained a cotton-to-cotton methodology[17] under which only decoupled payments for upland cotton base acres would be deemed support to upland cotton. Second, it introduced a "modified (programme crop only) annex IV methodology"[18] under which decoupled payments would be allocated only to programme crops in the proportions to which they contributed to the value of programme crop production on a farm.

13. Given this never-ending stream of theories of how and to what extent decoupled income support payments could be support to upland cotton, it would appear that Brazil has made any argument that suited its immediate needs to maximize the purported support to upland cotton. There can be no question that Brazil's incessant in-the-alternative argumentation has prejudiced the United States by significantly increasing the burden in evaluating and responding to Brazil's theories.

14. Brazil has argued that "[w]ithout farm-specific data, there [was] no basis to develop, let alone apply, Brazil's methodology. Brazil could only develop a methodology to apply to actual data when it received the EWG data in mid-November, and when it then sought farm-specific data from the United States."[19] In this statement, however, Brazil concedes that it had not developed – because, allegedly, "there [was] no basis to develop" – its methodology until, at the earliest, mid-November 2003.

- It is simply incredible to read that a complaining party should have chosen to challenge payments which, on their face, are not product-specific support to upland cotton, yet not have developed a methodology to determine the amount of the payments it would consider "support to [that] specific commodity" until at least 6 months into the dispute.
- That is, it is rather startling that Brazil, as the complaining party, began this dispute without the evidence, *or even the legal theory*, necessary to sustain its assertions.

Further, we note that, even if Brazil *had* developed its methodology in mid-November, it did not choose to put this methodology forward until 20 January 2004 (eight months into this dispute), in response to the Panel's Question 258.

---

16 The United States has elsewhere explained that Brazil has not brought forward evidence and arguments to allow the Annex IV methodology to be applied for purposes of its subsidies claims. *See, e.g.*, US 3 March Comments, paras. 29-35, 45-56.

17 Brazil's 18 February Comments, para. 46 ("Brazil first presents the results of using a slight variation of Brazil's methodology.").

18 Brazil's 18 February Comments, para. 50 ("Brazil also applied the revised US summary data to a modified 'Annex IV' methodology allocating total contract payments to farms producing upland cotton over the value of *contract payment* crops produced on these farms.").

19 Brazil's 18 February Comments, para. 84.

15. It is precisely this long delay in developing its Peace Clause arguments that led Brazil first to focus solely on payments for upland cotton base acres, and then only six months or more into the dispute to seek to bring in payments for non-upland cotton base acres. As the United States has argued, Brazil did not identify these payments that are not within the Panel's terms of reference[20] and which, if included in this dispute, would prejudice US rights of defence.[21] Furthermore, that Brazil had not crafted its methodology for Peace Clause purposes until six or eight months into this dispute undermines Brazil's Peace Clause interpretation: that is, Brazil has cast and recast its Peace Clause theories in order to find a theory that would result in US support exceeding the 1992 level. As the United States has demonstrated, however, non-product-specific support (whether green box or not) cannot be allocated as "support to a specific commodity" within the ordinary meaning of that phrase and as defined in Article 1(a) of the Agreement on Agriculture.[22] Thus, there is no basis to allocated decoupled income support payments to upland cotton for purposes of Peace Clause. Brazil various theories also rely on a "budgetary outlays" approach, which, for all the reasons the United States has explained previously, is not found in the Peace Clause text and is the wrong approach for Peace Clause purposes.

Brazil's Attempt to Resurrect a Basis for the Use of Adverse Inferences Is Unsustainable

16. After stating that the US 3 March data "is the best information available before the Panel" and that "the United States appears to have provided *complete summary base and complete summary planted data covering all crops for which data was requested by the Panel and all farms covered by the Panel's request*,"[23] Brazil nonetheless faults the United States for "certain problems" with the data and argues, in the alternative, that the alleged US "refusal" to provide certain data "would permit the Panel to draw the adverse inferences that this data – if produced – would have shown even higher payments being allocated to upland cotton."[24] Brazil's effort to resuscitate its request for "adverse inferences" to be drawn is misguided. First, in its 13 February letter, Brazil stated that "by producing the complete aggregated information, there would no longer be a need to draw adverse inferences."[25] As noted, Brazil has in its 10 March comments stated that the United States has produced "complete summary base and complete summary planted data covering all crops for which data was requested by the Panel and all farms covered by the Panel's request." Therefore, Brazil has implicitly conceded that there is no basis to draw adverse inferences, and its suggestion otherwise is yet another in-the-alternative argument that only serves to add needlessly to the complexity of this dispute.

---

20 US 11 February Comments, paras. 47-50.

21 *See* US Comments on Brazil's Answer to Question 204 from the Panel, paras. 34-42 (28 January 2004).

22 *See, e.g.,* US 3 March Comments, paras. 3-16.

23 Brazil's 10 March Comments, paras. 3-4 (italics added).

24 Brazil's 10 March Comments, para. 10 fn. 14.

25 Brazil 13 February 2004, Letter to the Panel, at 5.

17. This conclusion is confirmed by examining the data that the United States allegedly "refused" to provide. First, Brazil faults the United States for providing data with respect to farms that had upland cotton base acres but planted no upland cotton within Category A.[26] We note that the Panel's supplementary request for information asked for information on farms with "fewer upland cotton planted acres than upland cotton base acres, or equal numbers of each,"[27] which does not exclude farms with no planted acres from its ambit. Indeed, as Brazil points out, on 28 January 2004, and on 19 December 2003, the United States had provided planted and base acreage information relating to (1) farms that both planted upland cotton and had upland cotton base acres and (2) farms that did not plant upland cotton and had upland cotton base acres.[28] It is not apparent from the text of item (b) of the Panel's supplementary request for information that the Panel was seeking the same information that had previously been provided. Because the United States provided the information requested under item (b) with respect to Category A farms, there is no basis for any adverse inference to be drawn.

18. Second, Brazil argues that the US 3 March data "does not provide contract payment yield or payment[] units." However, Brazil itself immediately concedes that "the Panel's 3 February 2004 Request does not ask for this information."[29] Thus, as the payment yield information was not requested by the Panel, the United States could not have refused to provide it, and there is no basis for any adverse inference to be drawn.[30]

19. Third, Brazil states that "the United States did not produce any information that would allow the calculation of 'producer-based' soybean market loss assistance [that is, "oilseed payments" for soybean producers[31]] and peanut direct and counter-cyclical payments received by producers operating upland cotton farms."[32] However, Brazil does not contest that these payments were made to producers and that there were no base acres for these payments on any farms for the relevant years (soybeans in 1999 and 2000, peanuts in 2002). The United States recalls that the Panel's supplementary request for information related to "farms" with upland cotton base acres and/or upland cotton planted acres.[33]

---

26 Given Brazil's repeated complaints in this dispute, it is ironic that Brazil now, in effect, complains that the United States has provided too much information.

27 Panel's Supplementary Request for Information, item (b) (3 February 2004).

28 Brazil's 10 March Comments, para. 6 & fn. 5.

29 Brazil's 10 March Comments, para. 7.

30 Brazil's comment that the United States should have provided information on payment units in "good faith" as it did in its data submissions of 18 and 19 December 2004, and 28 January 2004, fails to mention that Brazil's request for data specifically asked for contract yields to be provided. Exhibit BRA-369 (second paragraph, fourth bullet: requesting "payment yield for each programme crop") (3 December 2003). The United States has responded to all requests for data in this dispute in "good faith" by providing all the data (within the limits of US law) requested.

31 *See, e.g.,* Response of the United States of America to the Panel's 3 February 2004, Data Request, As Clarified on 16 February 2004, paras. 10-13.

32 Brazil's 10 March Comments, para. 8.

33 *See* Panel's Supplementary Request for Information, item (b) (first solid bullet: "How many farms had fewer upland cotton planted acres than upland cotton base acres, or equal numbers of each? We refer to these as 'Category A' farms."; second solid bullet: "How many farms had more

Thus, the Panel's request did not ask for "payments received by producers operating upland cotton farms," and there is no basis to draw an adverse inference from an alleged "failure" to provide information not requested.

20. In sum, Brazil's in-the-alternative renewed request concerning adverse inferences has no basis in fact; either the Panel's supplementary request for information did not request the information or the United States properly responded to the request as drafted. Furthermore, to the extent that Brazil argues that the contract payment yield data or soybeans or peanuts payments received by producers operating upland cotton farms were "necessary" for its Peace Clause analysis, this would demonstrate not that any adverse inference should be drawn but rather that Brazil, as the complaining party bearing the burden of proof, has failed to bring forth evidence to make a *prima facie* case.

Brazil's Allocation Methodologies Are Irrelevant for Peace Clause Purposes and, in any event, Continue to Suffer from Conceptual and Methodological Flaws

21. The United States has set forth in other comments the reasons that no allocation methodology may be employed for purposes of a Peace Clause analysis since the only relevant support is "support to a specific commodity" – that is, "assistance" or "backing" "specially pertaining to a particular" "agricultural crop" (in the ordinary meaning of the terms) or "support ... provided for a basic agricultural product in favour of the producers of the basic agricultural product" (read in the context of the definition of product-specific support in Article 1(a) of the Agreement on Agriculture).[34]

22. Further, we have explained that for purposes of Brazil's serious prejudice claims, the Annex IV methodology[35] would be necessary to identify the subsidy benefit and subsidized product for each of the challenged decoupled income support measures – and Brazil has not brought forward evidence and arguments to allow the Annex IV methodology to be used.[36]

23. Finally, we have previously presented comments on each of Brazil's allocation methodologies.[37] As the calculations in Brazil's 10 March Comments are substantially similar to those it set out earlier, our comments on Brazil's new calculations are limited but also substantially similar to those we have previously provided. In particular, we note that Brazil has simply ignored the US criticisms of its pseudo-"Annex IV" methodology and excluded any sales from fruits and vegetables production, non-crop on-farm activities, and all other off-farm economic activity.

---

upland cotton planted acres than upland cotton base acres? We refer to these as 'Category B' farms."; third solid bullet: "How many farms had upland cotton planted acres but no upland cotton base acres? We refer to these as 'Category C' farms.") (3 February 2004).

[34] *See* US 3 March Comments, paras. 3-16; US 11 February Comments, paras. 7-14.

[35] *Agreement on Subsidies and Countervailing Measures*, Annex IV, paras. 2-3 ("Subsidies Agreement").

[36] *See, e.g.*, US 3 March Comments, paras. 29-35; US 11 February Comments, paras. 18-21.

[37] *See, e.g.*, US 3 March Comments, paras. 36-56; US 11 February Comments, paras. 35-60.

Cotton-to-Cotton Methodology

24. The United States has previously set out its criticism of this methodology, under which decoupled payments for upland cotton base acres on a farm that are equal to or less than the number of upland cotton planted acres are deemed to be support to upland cotton. Indeed, Brazil has never responded to the US explanation that "there are no physical 'base acres' on a farm. Crop base acres are an accounting fiction that do not represent any particular acres on a farm."[38] Thus, the very notion that base acres are "planted to" any particular crop (or, conversely, that a crop is "planted on" any particular base acre) is illusory.

25. We do note that the application of this erroneous methodology to the 3 March data does result in significant downwards revisions in the calculations Brazil previously presented, ranging from $58 million (MY2001 PFC) to $122 million (MY2002 CCP).[39]

Brazil's Methodology

26. Again, the United States has previously set out at length its criticisms of Brazil's methodology. The inconsistencies and logical flaws in this methodology are striking and demonstrate the *post hoc* nature of Brazil's attempt to force an allocation methodology onto decoupled payments. For example:

- There is no physical or economic basis to consider that decoupled payments for base acres of a crop are support to current production of that crop or to other (underplanted) programme crops. Base acres are not physical acres and are not "planted to" anything. A decoupled income support recipient may produce no, one, or multiple products; since money is fungible, those payments in economic terms (but not for purposes of Peace Clause) may be attributed to all (if any) of the recipient's sales.
- Brazil has never examined whether decoupled payments for non-upland cotton base acres "support or maintain" the production of those non-upland cotton programme crops – and thus has demonstrated no basis (on its own theory) for allocating such payments to those crops first.
- Brazil argues that base acres are "planted to" a particular commodity, one-for-one, but has no explanation for how an upland cotton planted acre can also be deemed to be "planted on" multiple base acres at once, as occurs when "underplanted" base acres are totalled and allocated proportionally to all "excess" planted acres (including cotton).[40]

---

[38] *See, e.g.*, US 3 March Comments, paras. 37-38.

[39] *Compare* Brazil's 10 March Comments, para. 15 *with* Brazil's 18 February Comments, para. 47.

[40] For example, in Exhibit BRA-433, Brazil presents calculations for allocating payments under its methodology for the different categories of farms set out in the Panel's supplementary request for information. For marketing year 2002, Category B2 farms planted 2,703,663 acres of cotton and had 2,035,335 base acres of cotton. Thus, Brazil calculates that there were 668,329 overplanted cotton acres eligible for allocated payments. Base acreage for other programme crops for Category B2 farms

- Brazil has never provided any logical explanation for why decoupled income support payments would be attributed to programme crops but not to other crops or other on-farm or off-farm economic activities (as economics and the Annex IV methodology would suggest is necessary).
- Neither has Brazil attempted to apply its own rationale that decoupled payments are "support to a specific commodity" when such payments "cover (or contribute to) the costs of production" of that commodity[41] to any other product produced by payment recipients, thus invalidating its own methodology, under which payments for base acreage is first support to the crop to which the acreage corresponds and then to other programme crops. Using Brazil's own "cost of production" principle, there is no basis to assert that order of analysis since Brazil has presented no evidence that such payments "cover (or contribute to) the costs of production" of those commodities but not others.

The United States has explored at some length these and other logical inconsistencies in Brazil's purported methodology for allocating decoupled payments to particular commodities. Although there is no basis in the Peace Clause to allocate non-product-specific support as support to a specific commodity, we nonetheless invite the Panel to consider these reasons why Brazil's methodology cannot serve as a neutral means to allocate decoupled payments.[42]

27. We also pause to recall that one of Brazil's primary responses to the US criticism that its methodology would result in different subsidization rates for upland cotton on a single farm and would result in the allocation of multiple non-upland cotton base acres per cotton planted acre was that "both of these alleged problems ... do not exist from MY 2002. This is because Brazil's methodology allocates for each planted acre[] of upland cotton only one upland cotton base acre." Brazil then went on to suggest that because in MY 2002 greater than 99 per cent of direct and counter-cyclical payments received by upland cotton producers were for upland cotton base acres and because upland cotton base exceeded upland cotton planted acreage, "the two main US criticisms affect ... at most, 0.9 per cent of the payments at issue for MY 2002."[43]

28. However, Brazil's 10 March comments tell quite a different story. There, Brazil calculates "the amount of upland cotton planted acres for which there exists a corresponding upland cotton base acre [by] farm category."[44] The percentage of upland cotton planted acreage for which an upland cotton base acre exists

exceeded planted acreage for those crops by 1,197,785 acres, and no other programme crop was planted in excess of its base acreage. Thus, Brazil allocated the total payments "free to be allocated" ($21,290,090) from the non-upland cotton base acreage entirely to upland cotton. This means that the 668,329 overplanted cotton acres were "planted on" 1,197,785 "excess" base acres for other programme crops, or each "excess" acre of cotton was "planted on" 1.79 non-upland cotton base acres.

41 Brazil's 18 February Comments, para. 3.

42 *See* US 3 March Comments, paras. 37-44; US 11 February Comments, paras. 35-43; US Comments to Brazil's Answer to Question 258 from the Panel, paras. 207-29 (28 January 2004).

43 Brazil's 18 February Comments, para. 60.

44 Brazil's 10 March Comments, para. 20.

is 72.87 per cent in marketing year 1999, 70.03 per cent in marketing year 2000, 68.06 per cent in marketing year 2001, and 84.33 per cent in marketing year 2002.

- That is, in any given year, approximately 15 to 22 per cent of upland cotton planted acres – between 2.1 million and 4.9 million acres – were allocated payments for non-upland cotton base acres and would be subject to the US criticisms dismissed by Brazil as *de minimis*. Brazil simply ignores this issue in its 10 March comments.

Furthermore, we recall that Brazil stated that "[a]s for some of the US criticisms that might affect the results (except for MY2002), Brazil will control for these effects once the United States provides aggregate data in the manner requested by the Panel."[45] The United States is not aware of any explicit recognition by Brazil of "US criticisms that might affect the results" nor any effort by Brazil in its 10 March comments to "control for these effects."

29. Finally, we note that the application of Brazil's erroneous methodology to the 3 March data again results in significant downwards revisions in the calculations Brazil previously presented, ranging from approximately $43 million (MY2001 PFC) to $120 million (MY2002 CCP).[46]

Modified US Annex IV methodology

30. Brazil presents largely unchanged "modified Annex IV" calculations, for example, excluding both soybeans (marketing years 1999 and 2000) and peanuts (marketing year 2002) as a programme crop.[47] Under this "modified Annex IV" methodology, Brazil allocated total contract payments to upland cotton "according to the share of upland cotton crop value of the total value of contract payment crop production."[48] Thus, the US view of this "modified" methodology remains unchanged: Brazil's approach is fundamentally inconsistent with Annex IV, paragraph 2, under which the subsidy is allocated over "the total value of the recipient firm's sales." Furthermore, there is no plausible basis to maintain that decoupled income support payments are support only to contract payment crops. Brazil also improperly includes the total value of contract payments in its calcu-

---

45 Brazil's 18 February Comments, para. 67.

46 *Compare* Brazil's 10 March Comments, para. 19 *with* Brazil's 18 February Comments, para. 49.

47 We note that the rice prices used by Brazil in its calculations in Exhibit BRA-434 are incorrect. Brazil has mistakenly divided the average rice farm price, reported in dollars per hundredweight (i.e., 100 pounds), by 220.46 instead of by 100 to obtain a price expressed in dollars per pound.

	Brazil 1/	WASDE 2/
MY1999	$0.027	$0.0593
MY2000	$0.025	$0.0561
MY2001	$0.019	$0.0425
MY2002	$0.019	$0.0449

1/ Exhibit BRA-434

2/ *World Agricultural Supply and Demand Estimates*, available at: http://www.usda.gov/agency/oce/waob/wasde/wasde.htm.

48 Brazil's 10 March Comments, para. 24.

lation when only payments for upland cotton base acres are within the scope of this dispute.

"US Annex IV Methodology"

31. Brazil offers no new analysis in its 10 March comments but just repeats the calculations presented in its 18 February filing. Thus, Brazil's "US Annex IV methodology" does not reflect the "US" interpretation of Annex IV, which is based on the text of Annex IV. That text establishes that, if a payment is not "tied to the production or sale of a given product," the subsidized product is all of the recipient firm's sales, and the subsidy for any one product is that product's share of "the total value of the recipient firm's sales."[49] Brazil does not use "the total value of the recipient firm's sales" in its "US Annex IV calculation" and does not even attempt to calculate total sales of upland cotton producers.

32. Because Brazil reiterates its 18 February calculations, Brazil's 10 March calculations are similarly flawed. First, Brazil errs by omitting the value of fruits and vegetables in calculating the total value of non-programme crop production. As the US 3 3 March data shows, in marketing year 2002 alone, 1.2 million acres were planted to fruits and vegetables on farms that reported cotton base acreage.[50] As pointed out in the US comments of 11 February,[51] excluding fruits and vegetables biases significantly downward the value of non-programme crop acreage. For example, the United States estimated the per-acre value of non-programme crops *including* fruits and vegetables was estimated at $281[52] for 2002 – that is, 138 per cent higher than the $118 per acre Brazil calculated when fruits and vegetables are excluded.[53]

33. Brazil suggests that it was not able to make any adjustment to its calculations because of its inability to separate those farms with no planted acres of cotton from Category A. However, Brazil does not explain why it was unable to use the actual planted acreage data, including that for fruits and vegetables, for Category B farms.[54] Nor does Brazil explain why it was unable to use the state-by-state information on plantings to make any adjustment to its use of "the average per-acre value of production of non-programme crops in that marketing year *in the entire United States*."[55]

34. Further, Brazil has not taken any account of the value of on-farm production other than crops, and has presented no data that would allow that calculation to be made. Again, the 1997 ARMS cotton costs of production survey suggested that, had Brazil taken into account the value of non-crop on-farm production, the share of cotton as a per cent of total farm sales would be lower still. For 1997,

---

49 Subsidies Agreement, Annex IV, paras. 2-3.

50 *See* file "DCP02-2W.xls" ("Grand Total (Farms A - C)" row).

51 *See* US 11 February Comments, para. 54.

52 See Exhibit US-154.

53 Brazil's 18 February Comments, Annex A, Table 4.5.

54 Category C farms had no upland cotton base acres and thus received no decoupled payments within the scope of this dispute. To the extent Brazil disagrees, however, the same criticism of Brazil's failure to use the actual planted acreage data applies.

55 Brazil's 28 January Data Comments, para. 90 (italics added).

when the value of cotton was high, the 1997 ARMS cotton costs of production survey reported that cotton accounted for only 44.5 per cent of the total value of agricultural production on cotton farms.[56]

35. Brazil also fails to include off-farm economic activity, which can be substantial, in its calculation. Annex IV, paragraph 2, establishes that the non-tied subsidy is allocated over "the *total value* of the recipient firm's sales," not merely its *farm* sales. As we have previously noted, cotton operations earn almost 30 per cent of income from off-farm sources.[57]

36. Finally, Brazil continues not to make any adjustment for the fact that landowners capture the subsidy benefit of payments on rented acres. As the United States has noted, Brazil has previously conceded that, as of marketing year 1997, 34 to 41 cents per dollar of production flexibility contract payments were capitalized into land rent.[58] Furthermore, certain missing pages from Exhibit BRA-276 report that, during 1998-2000, the capture by landowners through increased rent of production flexibility contract payments increased to an estimated average of 81 to 83 per cent.[59] Thus, Brazil's own evidence does not support its decision not to adjust the subsidy benefit to upland cotton producers downwards to reflect the two-thirds of cotton acres that are rented by producers, not owned.

Conclusion: Brazil Can Only Prevail on the Peace Clause Under an Incorrect Interpretation of the Peace Clause

37. The United States has demonstrated that Brazil's reading of the Peace Clause is not tenable; instead, Brazil invents the concept that non-product-specific support must be allocated to specific commodities. This concept runs directly contrary to the ordinary meaning of the Peace Clause text and directly contrary to its context, including the fundamental separation of product-specific and non-product-specific support in the Agreement on Agriculture.

38. The United States has also demonstrated that Brazil's approach to its "serious prejudice" claims is misguided. As mentioned previously, Brazil's notion that "the effect of the subsidy" may be analyzed without knowing the amount of the challenged subsidy is akin to saying that "the effect of eating" may be determined without knowing how much is being eaten.[60] Of course, to determine "the effect of eating" one must also determine "what" is being eaten (in addition to "how much"); similarly, "the effect of the subsidy" will depend on the nature of the challenged subsidy.[61] Thus, the United States believes that Brazil has failed to make a *prima facie* case with respect to decoupled income support payments

56 US 3 March Comments, para. 50; US 11 February Comments, para. 55.

57 *See* US 3 March Comments, para. 51.

58 Brazil's Answer to Question 179 from the Panel, para. 165 (27 October 2003); Brazil's Opening Statement at the Second Panel Meeting, para. 57.

59 US 3 March Comments, paras. 52-54; Exhibit US-155, at 106.

60 US 3 March Comments, para. 30 fn. 59.

61 *See* Subsidies Agreement, Article 7.2 (request for consultations under Article 7.1 "shall include a statement of available evidence with regard to (a) the existence *and nature* of the subsidy in question") (italics added).

(direct and counter-cyclical payments)[62] under its serious prejudice claims because it has not identified either the subsidy benefit or the subsidized product(s) using the Annex IV methodology. In addition, Brazil has failed to establish that the *effect* of these challenged payments is "serious prejudice"; to the contrary, the United States has demonstrated that the effect of these decoupled measures is no more than minimal.[63]

39. Finally, the United States has demonstrated that using any measurement that reflects the support "decided" by the United States – rather than factors (such as market prices) beyond the United States' control – US support to upland cotton in marketing years 1999-2002 has not exceeded the 1992 marketing year level.[64] Brazil's proposed approach suffers from the key flaws (among others) that it relies on the argument that:

(1) budgetary outlays must be used, despite the fact that the United States never "decided" an expenditure level (a point confirmed by Brazil's own reliance on the marketing loan rate and counter-cyclical target price for purposes of its *per se* and threat of serious prejudice claims[65]); and

(2) decoupled income support measures – the green box direct payments and the non-product-specific counter-cyclical payments[66] – can and must be allocated as "support to a specific commodity," despite the ordinary meaning of those terms in their context in the Agreement on Agriculture.

40. That both of these conditions must be met is evident if one examines the four tables setting out Brazil's Peace Clause comparisons.[67]

- For example, even using budgetary outlays, if decoupled income support payments are removed from Brazil's Peace Clause comparisons, *US measures did not breach the Peace Clause in marketing years 2002 and 2000.* The 1992 support would be $2,117.0

[62] Only direct and counter-cyclical payments were measures in existence at the time the Panel was established during marketing year 2002. Both production flexibility contract payments and market loss assistance payments were recurring subsidies paid with respect to past production that had terminated by the time of the panel request and panel establishment.

[63] *See, e.g.,* US Comments on Brazil's Comments on US Comments Concerning Brazil's Econometric Model, paras. 4-9 (28 January 2004).

[64] *See, e.g.,* US 11 February Comments, paras. 15-17.

[65] *See* Brazil's Further Submission, para. 432 ("The existence of the 72.4 cents per pound support price under the 2002 FSRI Act alone causes production-enhancing and price-suppressing effects. The single fact that these programmes exist ensures a guaranteed revenue amount from the production of upland cotton. This revenue floor is a guaranteed entitlement. That guaranteed revenue floor has the effect of removing any uncertainty and risk about the revenue farmers will receive for the crop. It means that regardless of the actual price development during the marketing year, a farmer knows that he or she will receive at the very least the loan rate for their product, plus price-triggered revenue support granted by the CCP programme.").

[66] Were the Panel to examine the terminated payments prior to the 2002 Farm Act, production flexibility contract payments would be green box, and the market loss assistance payments would be non-product-specific, as notified to the WTO.

[67] Brazil's 10 March Comments, paras. 35-38.

million, and the 2002 and 2000 levels would be $1,557.1 million and $1,218.7 million, respectively.[68]

- On the other hand, even if decoupled income support measures were allocated according to any of Brazil's four erroneous methodologies, *US measures did not breach the Peace Clause in marketing year 2001* if a price-gap calculation is used in place of outlays for marketing loan payments. A price-gap calculation eliminates the effect of market prices on the support provided.[69] US measures conform to the Peace Clause in marketing year 2001 under two different Brazilian allocation methodologies if a price-gap calculation is used.[70]
- Indeed, even without making any changes to Brazil's data, under two of its current "reasonable" methodologies, US measures did not breach the Peace Clause in 2000, the year with the highest market prices and therefore the lowest marketing loan payments.[71]

41. The United States believes that a proper interpretation and application of the Peace Clause must reflect the way in which the United States "decided" support in marketing years 1992 and 2002[72] – and, in the case of US measures, the support to upland cotton as "decided" was a rate of support. However, the United States has demonstrated that even an AMS calculation that reflects the support decided by the United States rather than market prices beyond our control would also demonstrate that US measures conform to the Peace Clause. Brazil's revised budgetary outlay calculations also support this view.

- If neither condition set out above is met – that is, decoupled income support measures are properly excluded from the Peace Clause analysis and price-based marketing loan payments are cal-

68 *See* Brazil's 10 March Comments, paras. 35, 37. This calculation ignores the inappropriate inclusion of crop insurance payments (non-product-specific), cottonseed payments (not in existence at time of panel establishment), and "other payments" (not identified in Panel request). We also note that the marketing year 1999 budgetary outlay level would be $2,431.6 million if decoupled support is excluded. Brazil has alleged that some portion of Step 2 payments are prohibited export subsidies, rather than domestic support, and the United States has argued that "other payments" are not within the Panel's terms of reference. The Panel's view of these issues could result in the 1999 budgetary outlay level too being below the 1992 level.

69 *See* US Rebuttal Submission, paras. 114-17. By holding the external reference price fixed, support measured using a price-gap calculation shows the effect of changes in the level of support (the applied administered price) decided by the United States, rather than changes in outlays that may result from forces beyond our control, such as market prices.

70 For marketing year 2001, support measured using a price-gap calculation for price-based measures and budgetary expenditures for other payments results in $1,251 million. For methodologies (1) ("cotton-to-cotton") and (4) ("US Annex IV methodology"), support was $1,240.9 million and $1,183.8 million. Again, these calculations do not remove crop insurance payments (non-product-specific), any portion of "Step 2" payments, or "other payments" (not within the scope of the dispute).

71 Brazil's 10 March Comments, para. 37 (1992 budgetary outlays were $2,117.0 million; 2000 outlays under the cotton-to-cotton methodology were $2,068.8 million; 2000 outlays under the "US Annex IV Methodology" were $2,112.6 million).

72 The measures (subsidies) provided with respect to marketing years 1999-2001 were no longer in existence at the time of Brazil's panel request and panel establishment. To the extent the Panel were to examine these measures, however, the same analysis would apply.

culated using a price-gap methodology – *US measures did not breach the Peace Clause in any marketing year between 1999 and 2002.*

- Support in marketing year 1992 would be $1,384 million,[73] well above the revised support levels are $659.1 million for marketing year 2002, $458.9 million for marketing year 2001, $582.7 million for marketing year 2000, and $670.6 million for marketing year 1999.[74]
- Again, these lower levels of support "decided" in recent years reflects the United States' decision after the Uruguay Round to move away from the product-specific deficiency payments with high target prices and instead to supplement producer income with a mix of decoupled income supports that are green box (direct payments) or non-product-specific (counter-cyclical payments).

42. Were the Panel to reach the question of serious prejudice or threat thereof, the United States has demonstrated that Brazil has not made a *prima facie* case that the challenged US measures have had that effect. However, the Panel should not even reach that question as the facts demonstrate that the United States has disciplined itself to grant support not in excess of that decided during the 1992 marketing year. Brazil must argue that non-product-specific support can be allocated as support to a specific commodity and must argue that support "decided" means budgetary outlays because without those conditions, it cannot demonstrate a Peace Clause breach. The United States has demonstrated, however, that Brazil's approach is legally unsound and internally inconsistent. It would, moreover, provide no certainty for Members who seek to conform to their WTO obligations. Brazil's constantly shifting methodologies reflect its desire to find an approach to maximize the dollars it could argue are support to upland cotton but do not reflect the legal texts, structure, and concepts found in the Agreement on Agriculture and the Subsidies Agreement.

---

[73] This figure uses the same $1,017.4 expenditure amount that Brazil used for deficiency payments. This figure is not markedly different from the $1,009 price-gap figure calculated by the United States using eligible acreage, but even if actual payment acreage were used, the price-gap payment total would be $867 million. US Comments on New Material in Brazil's Rebuttal Filings, para. 8 (27 August 2003). Thus, the 1992 level of support would still be higher than in marketing years 1999-2002.

[74] These revised figures exclude decoupled payments and use the price-gap calculation for marketing loan payments, which results in a zero level of support since the marketing loan rate was below the fixed reference price. *See* US Rebuttal Submission, para. 117 & fn. 148 (22 August 2003). However, these revised figures do not even remove crop insurance payments (non-product-specific), any portion of "Step 2" payments (which Brazil alleges are, in part, prohibited export subsidies), or "other payments" (not within the scope of the dispute).